THE ASSOMMOIR

ÉMILE ZOLA was born in Paris in 1840, the son of a Venetian engineer and his French wife. He grew up in Aix-en-Provence where he made friends with Paul Cézanne. After an undistinguished school career and a brief period of dire poverty in Paris, Zola joined the newly founded publishing firm of Hachette which he left in 1866 to live by his pen. He had already published a novel and his first collection of short stories. Other novels and stories followed until in 1871 Zola published the first volume of his Rougon-Macquart series with the subtitle *Histoire naturelle et sociale d'une famille sous le Second Empire*, in which he sets out to illustrate the influence of heredity and environment on a wide range of characters and milieus. However, it was not until 1877 that his novel *L'Assommoir*, a study of alcoholism in the working classes, brought him wealth and fame. The last of the Rougon-Macquart series appeared in 1893 and his subsequent writing was far less successful, although he achieved fame of a different sort in his vigorous and influential intervention in the Dreyfus case. His marriage in 1870 had remained childless but his extremely happy liaison in later life with Jeanne Rozerot, initially one of his domestic servants, gave him a son and a daughter. He died in 1902.

BRIAN NELSON is Emeritus Professor of French at Monash University, Melbourne, and a Fellow of the Australian Academy of the Humanities. His publications include *Émile Zola: A Very Short Introduction*, *The Cambridge Companion to Zola*, *The Cambridge Introduction to French Literature*, and *Zola and the Bourgeoisie*; and translations of *The Fortune of the Rougons*, *The Belly of Paris*, *The Kill*, *Pot Luck*, *The Ladies' Paradise*, *His Excellency Eugène Rougon*, and *Earth* (with Julie Rose) for Oxford World's Classics.

ROBERT LETHBRIDGE is a Fellow of Fitzwilliam College, Cambridge, Emeritus Professor of French Language and Literature in the University of London, and Honorary Professor in the School of Modern Languages at the University of St Andrews.

T0055158

OXFORD WORLD'S CLASSICS

___

ÉMILE ZOLA

The Assommoir

___

Translated by
BRIAN NELSON

With an Introduction and Notes by
ROBERT LETHBRIDGE

OXFORD
UNIVERSITY PRESS

OXFORD

UNIVERSITY PRESS

Great Clarendon Street, Oxford, OX2 6DP,
United Kingdom

Oxford University Press is a department of the University of Oxford.
It furthers the University's objective of excellence in research, scholarship,
and education by publishing worldwide. Oxford is a registered trade mark of
Oxford University Press in the UK and in certain other countries

Published in the United States of America by Oxford University Press
198 Madison Avenue, New York, NY 10016, United States of America

British Library Cataloguing in Publication Data

Data available

Library of Congress Control Number: 2021945503

ISBN 978-0-19-882856-3

Printed and bound in Great Britain by
Clays Ltd, Elcograf S.p.A.

CONTENTS

INTRODUCTION

It requires an imaginative leap of a substantial kind to appreciate fully the impact of *L'Assommoir* (translated for this edition as *The Assommoir*)[1] on its nineteenth-century reading public. At first sight, it may not seem inevitable that this story of a woman's struggle for happiness in a working-class district of Paris should have provoked so disproportionate a reaction. Yet both its subject and its treatment guaranteed the novel a *succès de scandale*. Its commercial success, indeed, persuaded Zola's generous publisher to offer the writer the revised contract ultimately responsible for his considerable wealth. More significant is the fact that the novel's appearance constituted a literary event in its own right.[2] It initiated a long and passionate debate about the legitimate scope and formal procedures of modern literature. Only in this context can Zola's Preface, dated 1 January 1877, be understood. For rather than being a mere editorial gesture, this statement (see pp. 3–4) is just one of the very great number of similar declarations he was forced to make in response to attacks (made during the prior serialization of the novel in the press) which tell us a great deal about the cultural and political climate in which he was working. From within that same polemical context, Zola would elaborate the theoretical principles of Naturalism, as a direct consequence of *L'Assommoir*'s reception. Its notoriety encouraged readers to unearth Zola's earlier work. And its qualities, as well as its far-flung reverberations, marked the beginning of his reputation as the most important European writer of his generation. That such contemporary concerns now seem to us like a distant echo is as unsurprising as *L'Assommoir*'s recent designation as a 'landmark of world literature'.[3] Its 'classic' status, however, depends less on the wisdom of hindsight than on a recognition, sustained and enriched by more than a century of critical interpretation, that it is *because* it is the most finely crafted of all Zola's novels that *L'Assommoir* retains its ability to shock,

---

[1] See below, p. xi, on the meaning and connotations of the original French title.

[2] See, in a series significantly entitled 'Les Grands Evénements littéraires', Léon Deffoux, *La Publication de 'L'Assommoir'* (Paris: Malfère, 1931).

[3] Through its inclusion in the series of that name; see David Baguley, *Émile Zola: 'L'Assommoir'* (Cambridge: Cambridge University Press, 1992).

through its unsettling affective tenor and its capacity to move us in powerful and contradictory ways.

As part of the strategy designed to refute charges that he had compromised his aesthetic integrity, Zola's Preface to *L'Assommoir* draws attention to its place within a larger artistic project. Although his Rougon-Macquart cycle was only subsequently increased to the twenty novels mentioned here, it is perfectly true that a study of Parisian working-class life does figure in the outline of the series he submitted to a prospective publisher in 1869. From the start, this series was conceived as a historical panorama of the Second Empire (1852–70), not merely complementing what Balzac had done for the Restoration and the July Monarchy, but also asserting (beyond such a chronological distinction) an originality of its own. A set of private notes headed 'Differences between Balzac and myself' simply confirms, it could be argued, Zola's acute awareness of working in the shadow of *La Comédie humaine*. But in sketching the future *L'Assommoir* at so early a date, the ambitious young novelist was thereby marking out as his own a terrain barely touched by his predecessors.

His prefatory claim that *L'Assommoir* was 'the first novel about the common people that does not lie' (p. 3) was not calculated to gain the unqualified assent of writers like the Goncourt brothers. Their *Germinie Lacerteux* (1864), much admired by Zola, sought (as its authors put it) to give to the 'lower classes' their rightful place in the domain of the novel. But their focus on the physiological destiny of a maidservant remains angled through the barely concealed revulsion of the character's aristocratic mistress. And, not unlike some of Balzac's incidental evocations of the urban poor, the portraits and settings of *Germinie Lacerteux* anticipate only in superficial ways the working-class milieu into which the reader of *L'Assommoir* is plunged.

The 'differences' between Zola and the writers who precede him are by no means limited, in any case, to the appropriation of fictional subjects. He was at pains to point out that it was his approach to his material which differentiated his work from other representations of the social world. That approach is inscribed in the subtitle he gave to his series: 'A Natural and Social History of a Family under the Second Empire'. Zola was thereby making explicit the seminal influence of Hippolyte Taine (1828–93), whose 'humble disciple' he admitted to being. In particular, his project is indebted to the Positivist philosopher's isolation of three principal determinants on human behaviour: heredity, environment, and the historical moment. By tracing the destiny of a single family and its descendants, Zola felt he could give due weight to biological imperatives, lent added intellectual credibility in France by the 1865 translation of Darwin's *On the Origin of Species*. That is to suggest neither that Zola uncritically subscribed to theories of heredity being popularized at the time, nor that these are systematically illustrated in his Rougon-Macquart novels. Preliminary notes for the series as a whole, drawn up in 1868–9, make it clear that he considered heredity a conveniently scientific substitute for the outmoded concept of Fate. Above all, it was intended that the twin focus on the Rougon and Macquart branches of the family would endow Zola's fictional world with an internal coherence. This would be afforded not only by blood ties and comparative experiences, but also by reappearing characters less arbitrarily related than in Balzac's exploitation of the same technique.

Consistent with such aims, all the Rougon-Macquart novels contain cross-references which serve, or seek, to enhance the illusion of overlapping books and lives. *L'Assommoir* is no exception to this rule. We are alerted, for example, to its heroine's provincial origins (p. 27) and to her courtship with Lantier prior to their arrival in Paris (p. 17), which are described in the opening novel of the series, *La Fortune des Rougon* (1871). Her two children by him, Étienne and Claude, are given apprenticeships (pp. 219, 87) which prepare them, above all, for central roles in *Germinal* (1885) and *L'Œuvre* (1886) respectively. That Claude had already appeared as a young artist in *Le Ventre de Paris* (1873), the third novel of the series (whereas *L'Assommoir* is the seventh), is confusing only for a reader who works systematically through *Les Rougon-Macquart* on the mistaken assumption that it is organized as an unfolding family saga. That its members inhabit spheres more clearly delineated than the exactitudes of chronology is confirmed by the failure of Gervaise's sister (also one of the principal characters of *Le Ventre de Paris*, and thus living barely a mile away in the proximity of Les Halles) to attend any of the ceremonial occasions of *L'Assommoir* (see p. 67). This also underlines the general rule, throughout *Les Rougon-Macquart*, whereby characters have such nominal relationships that the juxtaposition of separate biographical 'chapters' is not mutually enriching, as these remain subordinate to the requirements of autonomous texts. On the other hand, the second half of *L'Assommoir* does more than simply announce what is in effect its sequel; for the chapters devoted to Gervaise's daughter's introduction to prostitution lead directly to *Nana* (1880), the novel which bears her name.

This is not the only feature of *L'Assommoir* which encourages a degree of caution before applying to the novel the generalizations frequently encountered in summary accounts of the underlying principles *of Les Rougon-Macquart*. In few other novels of the series, it has to be said, are references to heredity so prevalent. Authorial scepticism notwithstanding, a tainted genetic inheritance is repeatedly invoked as a factor loading the dice against the characters' efforts to avoid a virtually preordained degeneration. To descend from Antoine Macquart (see p. 35) is to repeat an alcoholic destiny which has the force of an ancestral curse. But Coupeau too replays a parental scenario (p. 386), even to the extent of falling off a roof as his father had done before him. Only Goujet seems able to resist this pattern (p. 97), while remaining as vulnerable as the others to the workings of historical circumstance and social milieu.

Certainly in no other Zola novel is the influence of the latter so insistently foregrounded. *L'Assommoir* is not just *set* in a *quartier*; it is the story *of* a *quartier*, with its human figures subject to its utterly material determinants and collective moral horizons. Whereas, in Balzac, habitat and inhabitant are mutually reflective, Zola takes this one stage further by detailing how the environment in which characters live fashions their personality traits and leaves its mark on their bodies. And this includes the less tangible but even more insidious texture of communal values which shapes the individual's life. When the Preface to *L'Assommoir* refers to the 'filth of promiscuity' (p. 3), the associative move between literal and figurative dirt catches that double shaping of a 'downfall' which Zola speaks of as 'inexorable'. The novel is not uniformly melancholic; its ribald strain and comic moments have enchanted many a reader. But if *L'Assommoir is* often held up as evidence of Zola's pessimistic vision, it is because of the sheer weight of his deterministic equations in this book; for these seem to nullify every effort to escape fatalities located not in the edicts of vengeful gods but in the very substance of the stage on which characters progressively decline, 'ultimately to degradation and death' (p. 3). This sombre certainty is even encoded in the title of the

novel. Colombe's bar, the Assommoir, is taken from one of the same
name in Belleville (a working-class area in north-eastern Paris); it was
so well known that an *assommoir* came to be used generically for any
such cheap establishment in which (in keeping with the literal
meaning of the verb *assommer*) one was 'smashed' or 'bludgeoned'
by drink.[4] But, as Brian Nelson's Translator's Note (p. xlvi) underlines, Zola also extends its metaphorical sense, beyond the effects of
alcohol, to embrace everything which serves to 'crush' the human
spirit, starting with contextual forces. This more general variant is
exemplified by his own use of the term 'un coup d'assommoir', referring to Gervaise's awareness of the deleterious impact of mixing with
the wrong sort of people: 'it was like being bashed on the head, it
cracked your skull open and knocked you flat in no time, if you were
a woman' (p. 43).

The properly historical coordinates, on the other hand, are perhaps less precisely aligned in *L'Assommoir* than in some of the other
Rougon-Macquart novels. This is partly as a result of the impression
(or perhaps the illusion) we have that it takes place in a self-enclosed
world, not just in an outlying area of the city but also far removed
from political dates and officially recorded events. There are in fact
a sufficient number of discreet reference points to allow us to recon-
struct the novel's chronology. The wedding in Chapter III, for example, supposedly takes place on 29 July 1850; by the *coup d'état* of
December 1851 (p. 98) Nana has been born and baptized; by this
reckoning Chapter IV extends from 1851 to 1854, and Chapter V
from 1855 to 1858; Chapters VI and VII both take place in 1858;
Chapter VIII takes us up to 1860; Chapter IX covers the period
December 1860 to the beginning of 1862; Chapters X and XI can be
dated 1863–5 and 1866–8 respectively; and it is possible to calculate
that the text closes in 1869, at the very end of the Second Empire. In
this respect, however, the subtitle of the series applies only loosely to
L'Assommoir, and its reception, indeed, confirms that its picture of
the working class was neither exclusively modelled on, nor limited by,
conditions prevailing during the imperial regime of Napoleon III.
Here again, Zola's Preface is instructive, for his highlighting of 'the
poisonous atmosphere of our city slums' (p. 3) has a topical rather

---

[4] On the semantic history of Zola's title, see Fernand Marty, 'Les "Assommoirs"',
Cahiers naturalistes, 86 (2012), 149–73.

than a narrowly historical resonance. Such a lack of precision, of course, serves only to enlarge the target of the novel's concerns. For it deals with one of the major consequences of the Industrial Revolution in France, namely, as Zola indicates here, the teeming slums which grew up around the great cities, populated by labourers newly arrived from the provinces in search of work and by those displaced from renovated urban centres. In that sense, the characters of *L'Assommoir* are the products of an era, as well as of a milieu more specifically described, giving substance to his notion of a 'social history' beyond the 'brackets' of the Second Empire alone.

Yet what the reception of the novel also reminds us of is that to study such a sociological phenomenon, whether in fiction or in a treatise, was to open up what was known as 'the question of the working class', a nineteenth-century topic so fraught with ideological tensions that a declared neutrality or objectivity of stance was seldom taken at face value. Before *L'Assommoir* Zola had already gained a certain notoriety as a writer unwilling to disguise physiological realities with conventional euphemisms. It is not by chance that it was this particular novel which radically changed both the tenor and the stakes of the critical debate at the heart of French cultural life for at least the next decade. For it was to accusations of the gross exaggerations of *L'Assommoir* that Zola mounted a defence based on the argument that the veracity of his descriptions was supported by published sources and his own empirical observations of the social worlds represented in his novels. Polemical pressures so vitiated Zola's accounts of his own achievement (with the strategic analogy of the novelist and natural scientist hardening into a militant Naturalism) that by 1880, in his best-known theoretical work, *Le Roman expérimental*, he was going so far as to claim that the documents assembled by Naturalist writers like himself were entirely responsible for the structure and content of their work: they both preceded the elaboration of character and plot, and were transposed so directly that the creative imagination was virtually redundant. Scholars with access to the preparatory notes for his novels have since shown the more dogmatic statements to be highly misleading, and intelligible only in a climate in which Zola was violently attacked for his depiction of unaesthetic physical appetites and social conditions. *L'Assommoir* was the test case, and as his opponents insisted that obscenity and bias resulted from a perverse and politically motivated representation of reality, so Zola found himself denying that any such distortion had taken place; quasi-scientific evidence, he asserted, was the cornerstone of his objective realism.

As far as the documentation of *L'Assommoir* is concerned, we know (from the preparatory dossier of the novel preserved in the Bibliothèque nationale de France) that Zola had recourse to a number of books which provided him with specialist information. He consulted medical texts describing the pathology of chronic alcoholism; he copied out long lists of working-class slang, culled mainly from Alfred Delvau's *Dictionnaire de la langue verte* (1866); and he carefully annotated Denis Poulot's *La Question sociale: Le Sublime, ou Le Travailleur comme il est en 1870 et ce qu'il peut être* (1870). From this he drew details of the habits and leisure activities of the working class as well as a range of proletarian types. And, notebook in hand, Zola visited the future setting of the novel, returning with vivid sketches of streets, shops, dance halls, and taverns. Yet such research merely supplemented a personal experience which considerably predates the preparation of *L'Assommoir*. For when he himself had first arrived in Paris from Aix-en-Provence in 1859, he had lived in some of the poorest streets of the Latin Quarter, and over the next ten years had moved to a succession of less than salubrious addresses. In 1869 he had conceived his novel about the working class as 'the novel in the Batignolles', the very district (on the edge of the present-day seventeenth *arrondissement*) in which he was then living. Only when he set to work on *L'Assommoir* in August 1875 did he decide to set it somewhat further east, in an area of the city in which not even impoverished artists set up home. In addition to a familiarity with such neighbourhoods, Zola's career as a journalist since the early 1860s had also brought him into contact with the burning issues of the day, amongst which were figuring with increasing prominence the unattended problems posed by urban poverty. A number of his own articles in the opposition press after 1868 forcefully evoke the dehumanizing squalor of parts of the capital, and his bourgeois readers' implied ignorance of such unpalatable realities anticipates the deliberately eye-opening perspectives informing *L'Assommoir*. What might be termed this 'prehistory' of the novel explains both its inclusion in his 1869 prospectus for the Rougon-Macquart series and why he was able to imagine its outline well before embarking on his documentation. From the earliest stages of his planning, the disintegration of a family is built into its narrative direction; and notes dating from

1871–2 already contain in embryo many of the novel's major scenes, framed by the intention to dramatize the humble pleasures and intolerable suffering of working men and women. To restore Zola's documentation to its secondary position in the genesis of *L'Assommoir* is to underline further his creative achievement. For whether we compare it with other texts on the same theme, with his annotations, or even with the most meticulous of his chapter plans, there remains a remarkable imaginative distance between preliminary draft and finished novel.

On 13 April 1876, barely eight months after Zola had started work on *L'Assommoir*, its serialization began in *Le Bien public*, only to come to an abrupt halt at the beginning of June. The last seven chapters appeared not in this daily newspaper, but in a weekly literary review, *La République des lettres*, between 9 July 1876 and 7 January 1877. The reason for this extraordinary transfer in mid-publication was, as Zola himself explained, that the novel had revealed itself to be too disappointingly uncommitted for the left-wing *Bien public*, founded by the radical politician Yves Guyot (1843–1928). *La République des lettres*, on the other hand, was a highbrow journal (directed by the writer Catulle Mendès (1841–1909)) amongst whose contributors were to be found the avant-garde of contemporary novelists and poets. The curious circumstances of *L'Assommoir*'s publication are thus properly symptomatic, uneasily positioned as it has often been seen to be between political equivocation and artistic self-sufficiency.

In 1876–7 the novel was thought to be so ambiguous that, while conservative critics were divided over whether Zola was a dangerous socialist or providing them with evidence that uneducated workers were unfit to vote, their left-wing opponents lamented the fact that *L'Assommoir* painted the working class in so unflattering a light. Marxist critics of the 1930s simply accused its author of a dereliction of intellectual duty in failing to insert appalling social conditions within the dynamic of class conflict. Even today it is not uncommon to find analyses of the novel which criticize Zola not just for a paternalist discourse characteristic of the 'respectable bourgeois' (p. 4) he professed to be, but also, and perhaps above all, for leaving politics *per se* out of *L'Assommoir* altogether. For this apparent omission is often cited as being consistent with the ideologically suspect position of explaining proletarian suffering in the language of environment and heredity rather than in terms of the causal mechanisms of polit-ical systems.

The reader cannot help noticing, indeed, that political realities in the novel seldom *seem* more than a distorted echo in the shape of apocryphal stories (p. 217), unseen riots (p. 98), unconfirmed sight-ings of the Emperor (p. 337), and reports of vacuously radical meet-ings attended by Lantier offstage (p. 220). This is partly a consequence of the pedagogic divisions of Zola's series, organized as 'studies' of different strata of society. More problematic is a note of 1872 in which he envisages within his novel-cycle, to go alongside *L'Assommoir*, 'a second novel about the working class of a particularly political nature', thus signalling the postponement of the latter until the writing of *Germinal*. It is implicitly repeated in the work-notes for *L'Assommoir* when he refers to the fact that 'the novel about Gervaise is not the political novel, but the novel of working-class manners'. That such a distinction is not clear-cut, however, is suggested by the last (and rarely cited) part of this interior monologue when Zola admits to himself that 'there will necessarily be a political dimension, but in the background and to a limited extent'.

It can be argued, in fact, that as well as reflecting that afterthought, *L'Assommoir* is a highly coded text, whose political dimension is sup-pressed and repressed, and yet which is nowhere more visible, para-doxically, than where it seems to be representationally out of sight. That argument is less opaque if we move back from its appearance in volume form in January 1877, and think of it rather as a text of 1875, by the end of which its first three chapters had been completed. Only in the light of that factual readjustment is it possible to consider *L'Assommoir* as a book determined by the very specific prevailing con-ditions of its writing, themselves identifiable in its textual fabric: in its thematized and disguised allusions, and in its ironic devaluations and telling silences.

For it is worth remembering that at this time, and certainly in 1875, writing was a highly problematic activity. If the Commune of 1871 had convinced Zola that working-class politics would have to figure in his series at some stage, this revolution also provided the founders of the Third Republic with the most authoritarian of mandates to impose law and order. During what is thus known as the 'Ordre moral' (translated by Marshal MacMahon (1808–93) into its most severe phase after May 1873), all writers were viewed as potentially subversive, and scriptural repression was taken to obsessive lengths. At the ludicrous end of the spectrum, Casanova's *Memoirs* were judged to be 'politically incorrect' and even La Fontaine's *Fables* were banned; at the other, proscription, exile, and censorship were the order of the day. It is hardly necessary to fill in the details of emblematic constructions like the Sacré Cœur (its white façade symbolically overpainting the 'red' Montmartre where the Commune had started), or the continuing state of emergency which justified the deportation of yet another shipload of Communards to New Caledonia as late as February 1876. The pertinence of the systematic constraints placed on writing at this time is that these are inseparable from the strategic forms adopted by intellectual expression from within a culture for which Stendhal's famous warning (of politics in a novel being like a pistol shot in the middle of a concert) seemed to have a renewed topicality. An understanding of that informing context suggests that structural imperatives alone are insufficient to explain Zola's decision not to give politics a central place in *L'Assommoir*. As he wrote many years later: 'it was only at the time of *L'Assommoir* that, being *unable* to include in that book the political and, above all, the social role of the worker, that I resolved to leave that subject for another novel'.[5] To underline the impotence of 'being unable' is also to focus on the pragmatism which marks the novel's elaboration.

What characterizes the response of writers to such forbidden territory is what might be called a strategy of displacement—literally, of course, to or from London or Geneva, and especially Belgium (where the editor of *La République des lettres* had it in mind to publish several instalments of *L'Assommoir* of a transgressive kind), but also, more interestingly, a displacement to the domain of the historian. This is simply because the historian has the prestige of his work enhanced—spuriously or not—by a scientific apparatus which allows the recounting of acceptable revisionist versions of an archival past. Thus an authorized text of 1873 is *Les Crimes politiques de Napoléon III* (by J. F. G. de Vezzani); a grander example is Taine's *Origines de la France contemporaine*, the first volume of which appeared in 1875–6. While the subtitle of Zola's series registers genuine historical

---

[5] In a letter to Jacques van Santen Kolff of 6 October 1889 (my emphasis); see Zola's *Correspondance*, ed. B. H. Bakker, 10 vols (Montreal: Les Presses de L'Université de Montréal; Paris: Éditions du CNRS 1978–95), vi. 422–3.

ambitions, at least one sharp-eyed reviewer of the early *Rougon-Macquart* quickly grasped that it also cleverly testified to apparently objective credentials. If the Second Empire's demise had deflated the polemical thrust of *La Fortune des Rougon* (which recalled the criminal beginnings of that regime), that novel's 1871 preface was careful to guarantee that both text and series would deal with 'a dead reign'. Four years later, Zola could get away with his study of imperial politics, *Son Excellence Eugène Rougon*, for the same reason, its satirical intentions being overlaid with the official anxiety which had allowed its author to publicize *La Fortune des Rougon* in the press as 'virtually a topical work, at this time of Bonapartist conspiracy'. It is exactly in this kind of superimposition of time frames which effects an allegorization of history that the displacement of political reflection can both assert and deny its interdiction.

Zola's work-notes for *L'Assommoir* reveal that he originally thought of giving his characters rather more defined political attitudes than they are left with in the novel we now read. They also alert us to unsuspected aspects of the text. Monsieur Poisson is not merely the representative of imperial authority; he is also the figure representing the Emperor himself in caricatural form, as the cartoonist André Gill (1840–85) recognized in his own caricatural duplication of this particular 'Badinguet' (p. 217) for the illustrated edition of *L'Assommoir* in 1878. From the character's physical features (which are remarkably similar to those in Zola's other portraits of Napoleon III in *Les Rougon-Macquart*), to his unthinking respect for the printed word (p. 218), to the apocryphal inversion of the Emperor as *sergent de ville* (i.e. a policeman) in London (p. 217) and Poisson's status as Bonapartist spokesman and defender, such substitutions appear to secure within a satirical perspective a politics of the past. They are underscored by images of imperial debauchery and Lantier's prediction of its central protagonist's imminent demise: 'I haven't told you, Badingue,' he called out, 'I saw your boss yesterday in the Rue de Rivoli. He looks an absolute wreck. I wouldn't give him more than six months' (p. 337). So too, in Zola's notes at least, there is an attempt to integrate political chronology and family destinies: Coupeau's decline is charted from 1850 to 1869, and 'the downfall of a working-class family' (p. 3; and using, in the original French, the historically specific term *débâcle*) is calibrated with critical dates such as 1866, when Nana symbolically rejects domestic authority: 'I want to situate her

episode in 1866, when the downfall began. And it will be at that
moment that the important parts of the book will take place.'

On the one hand, therefore, *L'Assommoir* is a self-censoring text.
Zola ultimately leaves out his early reminder to himself to include
'a photograph of a man killed on the barricades in 'forty-eight, sus-
taining the family's revolutionary hatred'. There is no mention of the
fact that in 1848 barricades had been erected in the Rue de la Goutte-
d'Or itself, less than two years before the novel begins. Instead it
transposes and relegates to the margins its overt 'political dimension'.
And wisely so, it should be stressed, given Zola's reputation as a dan-
gerously radical neo-Communard, and the radically dangerous subject he intended to treat. On the other hand, the very imprecision
of the novel's historical references may well have contributed to
L'Assommoir's reception, not least because the period 1871–5 bore an
uncanny resemblance, in the collective imagination, to the post-1848
political history it was now officially free to reject.

One way to negotiate this provocative terrain—which is the jour-
nalistic equivalent of historical allegorization—was to adopt the indir-
ections of what the proscribed writer Jules Vallès (1822–85) called the
'allusionists'. This was a practice in which Zola himself had served an
invaluable apprenticeship on the staff of opposition newspapers surviving on the precarious line between self-regulation and the Censor's
terminal displeasure. Such an art of allusion is, of necessity, equivo-
cal, both recuperable to the safety of historical distance and yet con-
notative for the present. And in *L'Assommoir* it takes a number of
inventive forms. A passing mention of Eugène Sue's election to the
Assembly in 1850 (p. 7), for example, refers to a 'red scare' panic of
such a long time ago, all but forgotten were it not for Victor Hugo's
analogous re-entry on to the democratic stage on 30 January 1876.
This is also true of other dates in the text, like the *coup d'état* (p. 98).
At one level, these function as chronological markers; but they are
resonant ones, nevertheless, within the contemporary questioning of
political freedom and the power of the State. The novel's anticlerical
mockery ('those jokers spewing out their Latin' (p. 275)) lies in the
shadow of the law of 12 July 1875 reinforcing the status of the Church.
So too, in the interpolated socio-political comments mouthed by
the characters, there is the possibility of slippage. This applies to
Legitimist pretensions (p. 98) and more disguised hopes for the
restoration of the Monarchy up until 1877, or Coupeau's castigation

of every kind of regime: 'They can have what they like, a king, an emperor, or nothin' at all, it won't stop me earnin' me five francs . . . No, it's all bullshit' (p. 79). And there is slippage too between the figurative (Lantier and Virginie 'as if they were sitting together on a throne' (p. 335) as they watch Gervaise scrubbing) and the burlesque (Coupeau 'sitting on the throne' (p. 303) in the asylum), with royalism as the target of both. The public meetings to which only Zola's notes refer become the dispersed locations of Lantier's absences; but they are also reassembled in the novel's recurrent *fêtes*, the metaphor of February 1848, and especially, of course, of the initially joyous disorder of the Commune. Linked to this aspect of *L'Assommoir* are its songs, many of which are not only highly coded and subversive refrains, but also often drawn from a repertoire banned both during the Second Empire and the period 1872–6. Singing, at this time, was not an innocent activity; for the Commune itself was sufficient to remind the authorities of the dangers of collective grievances being articulated in harmony. Even the Vendôme column scaled by Gervaise and her friends (p. 73) seems like a less than innocuous tourist destination, as Bec-Salé's later swagger ('he could have flattened the Vendôme column in no time!' (p. 150)) makes clear; readers of *L'Assommoir* were unlikely to have forgotten that its destruction on 16 May 1871 was one of the most ritualized moments of the very revolution the 'Ordre moral' was designed to erase from public consciousness.[6] And if that is preceded by an equally memorable fictional visit to the Louvre, we should not make the mistake of thinking of the characters' outing from the slums as simply an excursion to a splendid art gallery. For the scene represents a visit to the historic and political heart of France as it was; and in a highly political space, both before and after 1870, the wedding party confronts that most politicized of paintings, Géricault's *The Raft of the Medusa*, whose subject and compositional structure make of it a mirror of *L'Assommoir* itself.

That particular episode is brought to an end by powerful voices (p. 72), by the forces of law and order, in a text in which disorder is only just kept in check. Monsieur Poisson's is far from being the sole

---

[6] One of the most penetrating of recent studies of the novel argues that its third chapter is saturated with coded markers of the events of the Commune; see Colette Wilson, 'City Spaces and the Politics of Carnival in Zola's *L'Assommoir*', *French Studies*, 58 (2004), 343–56.

authoritarian profile. Such agents are discreetly spaced across the book as a whole, variegated through museum guards, bailiffs (p. 259), and institutional officials who speak to Gervaise 'rather brusquely', with even a doctor likened to a 'policeman' (p. 386). They are the representatives of the official order, reflected in a 'tall engraving' on the Coupeaus' walls 'of a field marshal prancing on horseback, baton in hand, between a cannon and a pile of cannonballs' (p. 89). Under *Marshal* MacMahon's 'Ordre moral', that seems at least as double-edged as Lorilleux's grotesque championing of law and order. As far as the police themselves are concerned, at a deceptively anecdotal level Zola shows them upholding the moral codes of the street (p. 283) and keeping the pavement clear (p. 284); they are the guardians of property (p. 333), picking up shoplifters (p. 270) and the 'trash' of society (p. 336), closing down shady cafés (p. 366), functioning as the last line of defence against incest (p. 247) and domestic violence (p. 171). Their presence in *L'Assommoir* is so pervasive that the 'all-seeing eye' becomes a forceful image in its own right. Even in quite different contexts, the gaze and features of other characters— themselves collectively 'afraid of the law' (p. 244)—are compared to those of policemen. It seems hardly a coincidence that two policemen should appear at the end of Gervaise's feast. But it is also interesting that they do not negate the disorder they police. The feast remains a moment in the experience of the working-class characters beyond political control: 'Paris belonged to you. . . . Right then, for instance, could they give a damn for the Emperor?' (p. 193). And this could well be juxtaposed to the question asked of *L'Assommoir* by Albert Millaud, one of Zola's most vituperative critics: 'What would M. Zola say if a dramatist paraded . . . every form of human infamy for four acts, leaving it to the fifth to fill the stage with policemen? It's highly probable that the audience would have walked out without waiting for the expiatory conclusion.'[7] It may well be significant that Zola leaves the reader of this novel with the prediction that 'the policeman was on the point of losing his job' (p. 389).

Nor does it seem by chance that *L'Assommoir* should parody censorship itself, just after Zola had published an article on the subject in *Le Sémaphore de Marseille* (July 1875). It is, after all, the overarching

---

[7] *Le Figaro*, 1 September 1876; part of polemic cited in *Correspondance*, ed. Bakker, ii. 485–9.

allusion of all the 'allusionists' sidestepping the Censor. The censoring activities of the aptly named Madame Lerat are thus precisely those of the official arbiters Zola would often accuse of 'a preoccupation with filth verging on the sadistic'. She warns against moral dangers with as little effect as she defends Nana's virtue, and both represents and imposes a linguistic propriety at odds with her prurience: 'as long as you didn't use rude words you could say anything' (p. 321). Anticipating his own language's reception while performatively challenging such hypocrisy, here again Zola offers his readers the most unreassuring of reassurances.

L'Assommoir also has to be considered within that more far-reaching strategy which seeks to protect the freedom of contemporary artistic expression by maintaining the distinction between politics and literature. Even when proposing his novel-series to his publisher in 1868–9, Zola had been careful to spell out his intention to be 'merely an observer and artist rather than a socialist'. Thus all his attempts to offer reassurance about a study of the working class—from the bourgeois self-portrait in the novel's Preface to its stress on philological experimentation—invoke exclusively artistic criteria. He insists that 'my political opinions are not at issue', that the terrible suffering depicted needed no further commentary, that 'I am just the clerk of the court refusing to draw any conclusions from the evidence recorded'. While this last statement is addressed to the radical Guyot, it echoes the defence mounted against the conservative Millaud in September 1876: 'My novels refuse to come to any conclusions because I believe that it's not the business of the artist to do so.'

But to isolate that formula within repeated denials of *parti pris* is to be reminded of one other crucial influence on the author of *L'Assommoir* in the autumn of 1875, namely Zola's rereading of Flaubert's *L'Éducation sentimentale* (1869). In the major study of it which he composed that November, Zola refers to his discovery of 'a new poetics', based on what he calls Flaubert's 'apparent disinterestedness'; as he puts it: 'you will search in vain for any conclusion or moral lesson drawn from the facts'. Between *L'Éducation sentimentale* and *L'Assommoir* there are a number of suggestive parallels. The most obvious is to be found in the final meeting between Goujet and Gervaise, where Zola's work-notes ('her hair is white. Too late') direct us to the corresponding encounter between Frédéric and Mme Arnoux; nor should we forget Flaubert's own ever-present *sergents de ville* who are known as 'les assommeurs'. For *L'Éducation sentimentale* functions, above all, as a model of writing about politics, with its cynical opportunists and political agitators, its revolutionary dreamers and its own proletarian euphoria embraced by an authorial irony which highlights different political points of view while overtly subscribing to none.

What is less certain is whether, in Zola's case too, an aesthetic of impersonality could be construed as an attitude of genuine indifference. The contemporary divorce between politics and culture begs the sort of questions which later persuaded a writer as committed as Vallès that Zola, by contrast, was a man of letters. Indeed, in an 1879 review of the former's *Jacques Vingtras*, Zola expresses the view that Vallès himself should have left 'politics to those who are failed artists', on the comprehensively Flaubertian grounds that 'politics, in these disturbing times, is the preserve of the impotent and the mediocre'. In *L'Assommoir*, Zola's analogous reductio ad absurdum of every political voice in the spectrum has often been criticized, even when qualified by the recognition that he thereby underlines the working-class political apathy registered by his principal historical sources. To insist upon that apathy in a novel about alcoholism is nevertheless to refuse to subscribe to the premise of the *commissions d'enquêtes* (into the causes of the Commune) investigating the links between literal and political intoxication.[8] And it should also be noted that the antithetical distribution of political attitudes among his fictional characters provides Zola with a remarkable freedom. For if it undercuts Lantier's self-serving radicalist claptrap, it simultaneously devalues his allowable derision at the expense of 'useless . . . Republicans [in the Chamber], those lazy buggers on the Left' (p. 236). The effect of these self-cancelling ironies is to delineate an authorial silence. That may be thought of as a ludic detachment; but it is certainly a refusal to play with the profoundly meaningless political labels of the time. 'Politics is just a big joke!' (p. 79). Coupeau's unthinking phrase is also, perhaps, Zola's own considered view.

The very intensity of the political outrage provoked by *L'Assommoir* is testimony to the unease created by these kinds of strategies. It was a hostility not moderated by the self-imposed editorial cuts the

---

[8] See Susanna Barrows, 'After the Commune: Alcoholism, Temperance and Literature in the Early Third Republic', in John M. Merriman (ed.), *Consciousness and Class Experience in Nineteenth-Century Europe* (New York: Holmes and Meier, 1979), 205–18.

serial-contract allowed, Zola's supplementary prefatory reassurances, delays in the publication of the novel in volume-form as a result of the Censor's misgivings, or its sale being prohibited in station bookstalls. It should also be said that the polemical fury which promoted Zola to the rank of 'leader of the literary Commune' (according to one review of *L'Assommoir*) has had massive consequences for the way in which he is still read, notably in the separation of the mythico-poetic from the socio-political (a separation consecrated by the reception of *Germinal*)—which is to read his novels reassuringly out of context. In the particular case of *L'Assommoir*, published at that decisive turning-point of 1876–7, immediately prior to the resumption of political debate, it does seem inappropriate to condemn Zola for leaving politics in the margins.

We might ask instead to what extent his strategies are in fact the only way of writing about politics in a period in which political discourse is still impossible; impossible not only because of official constraints on the freedom of expression, but also because of the paradox that while (as Zola protests in a newspaper article at the time) 'politics is invading every aspect of daily life', with Republican factions opposing each other in the name of the Republic, at the same time the floating political labels of the moment conspire to create an absence of substantive differentiation. And the kind of stance which perfectly corresponds to that crisis of definition may well be the authorial silence or indeterminacy we find in *L'Assommoir*. The most eloquent response to the proscribed celebration of the Fourteenth of July is the analogous silence exploited by Léon Gambetta (1838–82), refusing to publish his *République française* on that very day. That is not to suggest that, in Zola's case, this is a fully thought-out position; nor is it to deny that there are residual tensions and contradictions in the 'writing-in' and the 'writing-out' of the political margins of *L'Assommoir*. But discernible here, in the confrontation between his consciously non-political novel and the political context it refuses to take seriously, is a conjunction of discursive registers; and it seems to have been one, moreover, intuitively recognized by outraged critics of every party as being less a reflection of politics than the politics of a reflection.

At almost 150 years' distance from the 'sound and fury' of *L'Assommoir*'s reception, today's reader of Zola's novel is more likely to be wholly engrossed in the vicissitudes of its heroine's personal story. And, indeed, no other volume in *Les Rougon-Macquart* is so deliberately organized as a fictional biography, as is suggested by the fact that its original title was *The Simple Life of Gervaise Macquart*. Yet that should not cause us to lose sight of the fact that *L'Assommoir* has a historical interest of another kind, not least as one of the nineteenth century's greatest novels about Paris itself. It provides us with a remarkable record, not just of the way of life of the urban poor (so detailed as to constitute a document of exceptional anthropological value), but also of a city now virtually transformed beyond recognition. The very processes of that transformation are alluded to within the novel. By its end, the encroaching geometry of Baron Haussmann's rebuilding of the capital is changing Gervaise's familiar territory, 'becoming so splendid that it made her feel out of place', 'a huge crossroads' (p. 365) of luxurious boulevards driven outwards through the city walls giving Paris its modern shape and leaving both the character and the reader with a sense of a world that has been lost.

The Rue de la Goutte-d'Or still exists, of course, though the Rue Neuve which runs into it had its name changed to the Rue des Islettes in 1877. The appellation 'la goutte d'or' (or 'drop of gold') derives from the fifteenth-century hamlet on the same site, reputed for its golden white wine; and it is quite possible that Zola was aware of the tradition in his choice of these particular streets as the location for his study of a family turning to drink. The area in which the novel takes place corresponds to the south-eastern quarter of today's eighteenth *arrondissement*, hemmed in by the Gare du Nord and the edges of Montmartre, and bounded by the thoroughfares of the Rue Polonceau, the Boulevard de la Chapelle, and the Boulevard Barbès, thus forming an enclave as it did during the Second Empire. It remains a bustling neighbourhood of the underprivileged, but now populated by North African immigrants. In newspaper reports on crime in the French capital, it is often singled out as being infested by drug-dealers; it is certainly not an area where readers of this translation will be made to feel welcome if they venture into it with camera in hand. The probable model for the Hôtel Boncœur is next door to 'Le Maghreb' and the site of Père Colombe's Assommoir was most recently occupied by a Tati department store.

The more fundamental difference is that, at the time the novel takes place, the district lay outside the city boundary constituted by the octroi wall. Between the latter and the military fortifications (p. 65), beyond which lay the Saint-Denis plain, there was a heterogeneous zone of urban construction, cheap housing crammed along uncobbled streets, workshops and small factories, waste ground, places of popular entertainment, cemeteries and allotments, and even vestiges of countryside separating the sprawling suburbs from a Montmartre still rural enough to be considered a village. In the opening paragraphs of *L'Assommoir*, Gervaise looks out over the intersection of Paris proper and these outlying suburbs, and might be thought to be dominating the scene were it not for her apprehension of the city's 'heart of darkness'. Her disorientation at the end not only testifies to a modified topography but also brings to a close her attempts to resist a fearful presence. Only once does she venture inwards, when she visits the Louvre after her wedding, and as this is signposted by 'monstrous beasts' (p. 61), so the ensuing labyrinthine experience is integral to a novel cast as an epic struggle between Gervaise and a devouring Parisian monster with its 'gaping jaws' (p. 7). At the point, in Chapter XII, at which she registers her defeat, she nostalgically recalls outings within her own community's legitimate space, reminding the reader too of an urban reality only otherwise captured in sepia photographs or in Renoir's *Le Moulin de la Galette*. If that particular open-air dance hall is mentioned in *L'Assommoir* (p. 230), so are countless others now forgotten, along with once well-known cafés, restaurants, taverns, theatres, wine merchants, toll-houses, prisons, hospitals, slaughterhouses, the very markers of a mid-nineteenth-century experience lived at an irremediable remove from the Paris we think we know.

Zola's achievement is to have constructed from this patently verifiable experience a work of art. His first biographer and devoted friend, Paul Alexis (1847–1901), recounts a discussion with him on the beach at Saint-Aubin during the planning of *L'Assommoir* in the summer of 1875. 'You see that,' Zola remarked pointing to the gentle curve of the horizon; 'I need something like that . . . something utterly simple, a clear straight line'. He never lost sight of that ambition. It was in the interests of such clarity too, it could be argued, that the political dimension of the novel was much reduced. For the same reason he ultimately abandoned the ending he had first imagined, namely a wildly melodramatic duel between Lantier and Goujet immediately following on from Gervaise's throwing vitriol at the former while

Virginie, his mistress, lay dying in the courtyard. Instead he kept before him the reminder to himself to chart the *progressive* downfall of Gervaise Macquart, plotted and foretold in an inherently credible pattern of gradation. The reader pressed up close to her hopes and fears, to the prosaic details of the unbearable suffering she endures, may be only intermittently aware of *L'Assommoir*'s formal qualities. And yet it is precisely the novel's artistry, its thematic structuring and calculated symmetries, which makes its human drama so compelling. For what Zola has done is to shape the unadulterated realities of nine-teenth-century working-class existence into a work characterized by an exceptional unity of design.

Amongst those realities, for example, few are more vividly con-veyed than the filth and stench of the milieu Gervaise inhabits. This is a world of open sewers and overflowing drains, its streets turned to mud by the rain, its workshops filled with choking dust, its bars thick with rancid smoke. Nor is Zola's claim that *L'Assommoir* is the first novel which has 'the authentic smell of the people' (p. 3) an empty one. For it is pervaded by fetid odours: of unwashed bodies, vomit, bad breath, alcohol, the discharges of slaughterhouse and corpses. That this is the breeding ground of respiratory diseases is as self-evident as the proximity of the Lariboisière hospital, its halls reeking of illness and feverish secretions. It is in every way appropriate, there-fore, that Zola should have chosen a laundress as his protagonist. For a quest for human dignity is thus enacted at the level of a desired cleanliness. It has also been shown, however, that the laundry itself occupies a double-edged place in the contemporary hygienist dis-course which Zola's text so faithfully replicates in its detailing of a 'poisonous atmosphere'.[9] If recourse to it is morally positive, it is nevertheless singled out, in medical treatises on occupational haz-ards, as the particularly dangerous site of bacterial infection and nox-ious vapours. From such facts, as dreadful as they are banal, the novelist makes of Gervaise's shop the symbolic location of equally contradictory forces, a paradise of cleanliness regained as surely as the very conditions of that ideal imply its ultimate loss.

[9] See Mary Donaldson-Evans's detailed study of this theme, in 'Miasmatic Effusions: *L'Assommoir* and the Discourse of Hygiene', in her *Medical Examinations: Dissecting the Doctor in French Narrative Prose, 1857–1894* (Lincoln, NE: University of Nebraska Press, 2000), 74–92.

Gervaise's quest, however, is not limited to this doomed attempt to overcome the material squalor of her working-class environment. For it is inseparable from a larger dream, oft-repeated during the novel and ironically recalled at the point it can no longer be sustained: 'to work, have something to eat, have a little place of her own, bring up her kids, not get knocked about, die in her own bed' (p. 123). The central element of this, translating as it does the French 'avoir un trou un peu propre pour dormir', overlays an escape from filth with the multiple connotations of a womb-like refuge, a beatitudinous state invulnerable to the pressures of the outside world. This is an unconscious obsession on the character's part, to the extent that when a sanctuary is threatened (as when the laundry is invaded by the neighbourhood (p. 168), or the intimacy of her feast in Chapter VII is opened up to the street (p. 206)), Gervaise seeks another, finding in Goujet's smithy 'her only refuge' (p. 169). But it is also the preoccupation which governs the narrative itself. It makes of *L'Assommoir* the novel of Gervaise's successive abodes, from her room in the Hôtel Boncœur (Chapters I–III), her home in the Rue Neuve (Chapter IV), her laundry (Chapters V–IX), the sixth-floor flat to which the Coupeaus have to move when they lose the shop (Chapters X–XIII), all the way to Père Bru's 'little niche' (p. 395) where she ends her days. These are the variations on the snug enclosure equated with Gervaise's happiness, ephemerally realized in the heavenly hues of a shop 'all blue like the sky' (p. 118) only to be cruelly travestied in a den under the stairs.

Such displacements chart a rise and fall symmetrically consistent with what one of Zola's contemporaries, his fellow novelist George Moore (1852–1933), recognized as *L'Assommoir*'s 'pyramid size'. And one of the finest modern studies of it has shown that its triangular shape (built around the apex of the seventh of its thirteen chapters) is enhanced by a thematic structure which provides a more subtle graph of Gervaise's struggle.[10] For if her ideal articulates an antithetical symbolic code (work, cleanliness, and self-control on the one hand; idleness, filth, and indulgence on the other), the novel not only moves from positive to negative values corresponding with the character's decline, but also inserts within the first half of the book the telling signs of a demise of which Gervaise herself is blissfully unaware.

---

[10] See David Baguley, 'Event and Structure: The Plot of Zola's *L'Assommoir*', *PMLA* 90 (1975), 823–33.

In that sense, *L'Assommoir* is shadowed by a tragic irony which reminds the reader, even in the midst of apparent triumphs, of its uncompromising title.

This can be more readily grasped if the other characters are also viewed as properly structural features of the work. Lantier, for example, is the epitome of the anti-values of the novel, with his laziness, his voracious appetites, and his trunk with its 'smell of a slovenly man' (p. 217). By contrast, Goujet is a model of abstinence and hard work, living in a home marvelled at by Gervaise, 'amazed how clean it was' (p. 96). Zola's dispensing with his original idea of a duel between these two rivals for her affections leaves intact their function as the conflicting paths of Gervaise's destiny, while allowing the reader to measure the development of the Coupeau family against the opposing poles they represent. Thus Coupeau himself falls, not just from a roof, but also from an exemplary industriousness to drunken idleness, anticipating Gervaise's own metaphorical descent from the values she once held dear. The minor characters too serve to reflect the curve of her life. The destitute house-painter, Père Bru, whose occupation ('whitewashing ceilings' (p. 168)) is clearly analogous to Gervaise's, becomes the mirror of her misfortune. And if Lalie Bijard also spends her brutalized life trying to keep things clean, her suffering and martyrdom similarly prefigure Gervaise's fate. Bazouge, the undertaker, the very incarnation of filth, with his invitations to renounce her quest in the enforced idleness of death, is a figure who both attracts and repulses her. Less obviously, perhaps, the lazy Virginie Poisson is Gervaise's double, taking over her lover and laundry (and letting it go to ruin for the same reasons), so that the fight between the two women in the wash-house at the beginning of the novel can be seen as symbolic of an inner struggle, with Gervaise's initial victory preparing us for the inevitability of the revenge which awaits her.

Inserted within the rising and falling movement of the novel as a whole, there is a thematic interplay of details no less foreboding. In the depths of her despair, towards the end of Chapter XII, Gervaise takes 'her last walk, from the bloody yards where the slaughtering had taken place to the dimly lit wards where death laid the stiffened corpses in communal shrouds' (p. 372). Yet that space that 'had bounded her entire life' is the object of her gaze in the novel's opening pages, with the landmarks of hospital and slaughterhouse as unambiguously ominous as the stream of dirty water in the alleyway or the stain left by Lantier in the washbasin (p. 29). Even as she starts her new life with Coupeau in Chapter III, a less idyllic future is prefigured, and not just in the storm which threatens to spoil her wedding-day (pp. 64-5), or her first encounter with Bazouge and his ominous predictions (p. 86). For the visit to the Louvre, in the same chapter, provides us with a particularly suggestive example of the ways in which even episodes apparently removed from the claustrophobic darkness of the Rue de la Goutte-d'Or reinforce the novel's overall design.

Indeed, one could go rather further and argue that the Louvre scene mirrors the texture of *L'Assommoir* as a whole. Superficially there is a blatant opposition between the official history and the daily grind: between monumental cleanliness and faubourg squalor, domestic constriction and public space; between 'clear and shiny' parquet floors (p. 69) and the encrusted boards Gervaise scrubs humiliatingly on her hands and knees; between the 'place full of gold' (p. 50) *not* found in the Rue de la Goutte-d'Or and the lavish display of 'gilding' (p. 69) in the Louvre. But the wedding party's itinerary is also reduplicative. Their destination, reached down the same alimentary canal which swallows up the workers, and traversed back and forth along its East–West axis, merely magnifies Gervaise's intersections (p. 121) of work and leisure in her own *quartier.* The enormous building she inhabits there, with its entrails likened to 'the very heart of a city' (p. 41), has its own 'stark and grim' walls (p. 40) and a 'dingy courtyard with its uneven cobbles like a public square' (p. 114). This microcosm of the city, 'the size of a small town, with its streets of stairs and corridors that went stretching on and criss-crossing for ever' (p. 114), thus reflects the Louvre topography the characters are unable to negotiate. That disorientation is precisely anticipated by Gervaise's guided visit to the Lorilleux 'down the endless spiral' of 'echoing corridors': 'this wall going round and round and these glimpses into one little dwelling after another were making her head spin' (p. 48). Monsieur Madinier's charges in the Louvre hurry past as many rooms and images barely sighted until overcome by 'a great jumble of people and things in such a busy riot of colours that everyone was beginning to get a nasty headache' (p. 70). Unifying thematic patterns, working across the spatially alternating warp of street and interior which structures *L'Assommoir*, are thereby woven from a common fund of metaphor.

The Louvre episode, however, is privileged by its position at the end of the novel's exposition, and it echoes with the noise of a stampeding 'herd' (p. 70) with which the text opens ('a herd of cattle', p. 6) and draws to a close ('the trampling of the herd', p. 366). The scene looks both forward and back, generated by passages just written and itself obliquely evoked in retrospect, as Gervaise repeats her labyrinthine wanderings in the midst of discoloured posters, 'turned a dirty yellow by the soot from the trains' which catch her eye (p. 369). It stands between complementary ceremonies of a wedding and a funeral, equally mistimed, gaped at, marked by a misunderstanding of protocol and the incomprehension of a dead language, leaving their participants summarily dismissed, out on the street. It was to an unpromising tomb in Père-Lachaise that the wedding party had also thought of going (p. 66), and the bride-to-be is likened to a neighbour recently deceased (p. 54). The clocks of mortality which chime through *L'Assommoir* strike four o'clock at the Louvre to signal only the first of those expulsions threatened by Monsieur Marescot (p. 290) and, more terminally, by Bazouge. If the episode's pivotal status is underscored by the comparison between the Salon Carré and a church (p. 69), it is fitting that Coupeau should rail against his enforced immobility as being 'stuck there, like an Egyptian mummy' (p. 109). For there are telling shudders (pp. 68, 71) in the presence of archaeological relics and lifeless creatures with 'death masks'. Related to such dissolution, the most striking note introduced by the visit to the Louvre remains the unmaking of people and things. The episode is later replayed with astonishing precision, even in its tempo, in the spectacle of Nana and her friends 'creating havoc' (pp. 138), racing helter-skelter and 'zigzagging their way through groups' (p. 316) as the wedding party had flown on through the Tuileries Garden. Their progress is charted in the fragmentation of physical unity and collective purpose, and in a dismemberment which corresponds to their own metonymic focus on bodily parts in the paintings they see. In the references to corporeal mutilation (pp. 172, 226) and broken statues (p. 217), and in the disintegration of conviviality (p. 83), dirty laundry (p. 220), and Gervaise herself (p. 253), the accelerating disorder unleashed here ripples outwards through the novel.

What is more, many of *L'Assommoir*'s principal motifs are encoded in the artistic works foregrounded by the text, notably in the triptych formed by Géricault's *Raft of the Medusa*, Veronese's *Wedding at Cana*, and Rubens's *Kermesse*. These are aligned into an ambiguous spectrum ranging from voracity to transcendence, and interrelated by the eating which marks the successive phases of Gervaise's destiny. This interpretation only makes sense if we view the great feast of Chapter VII as an occasion when Gervaise herself is figuratively consumed; and it depends crucially on the *Raft of the Medusa* being associated with cannibalism, the most shocking feature of the 1816 event on which it is based, but one eliminated, as was common knowledge, from the final version of the painting. What is certain is that the Géricault confirms the predictive malevolence, in the shape of sphinxes and funereal gloom, which immediately precedes it. In an enduring image of human despair marginalizing a remote glimpse of hope, this painting points not only to a bleak future but also to the illusory 'escape' to the Louvre during which it is seen. As far as the Veronese is concerned, however appropriate it may seem in the context of a wedding, it only assumes its importance in contradistinction to the Rubens. The latter's celebration of carnality and inebriation, irrecuperable to moral judgement, social forms, and temporal constraints, will be concretized in the banquets of *L'Assommoir*, both on the day of the wedding and (especially) in Chapter VII. But the *Kermesse* refers us to other textual moments too. Also well known under its alternative title of *The Village Feast*, it speaks of Gervaise's ideal of pastoral liberation, grotesquely mimed in her courtship with Goujet on the 'last remaining strip of green' behind Montmartre (p. 225). Amongst the 'spicy details' spotted by Boche, 'somebody puking' (p. 71) looks forward to Coupeau's fateful vomiting, as the 'flushed faces' jumping about (p. 207) at the end of the novel's central chapter seem to step out of Rubens's frenzied dance. The two textual segments are linked by the scandalized reaction to Clémence's 'showing everything she'd got' (p. 207) and the sarcastic 'Well, what a fine lot we've got here!' which greets the double 'voiding' of the *Kermesse*. Approached in their 'funny carnival costumes' (p. 68), the Louvre opens up the carnivalesque dimension of *L'Assommoir* noted by the most stimulating of its commentators, inspired by Bakhtin.[11] If the characters remain bewildered by masterpieces perceived only at

---

[11] See David Baguley, 'Rite et tragédie dans *L'Assommoir*', *Cahiers naturalistes*, 52 (1978), 80–96.

the level of overt subject, the reader is alerted to their significance by the narrative sequence of the guided tour. For we are taken from the upright configurations of the sacred in the *Wedding at Cana* to the circular dynamic of the *Kermesse*. It is the rhythm internal to both orgies of gluttony and characteristic of the degradation between and beyond them. Whether or not Gervaise's miraculous six extra bottles (p. 194) catches the biblical allusion,[12] the progressive desacralization ensures that the thirteen at dinner (twelve went to the museum) replace Christ with a goose as the object of reverence, and that her final meal with Goujet is a travesty of the Last Supper. As they go rollicking through the Louvre 'clump[ing] their heels on the noisy floors' (p. 70), it is the rhythm of the visitors' disrespect and the rising cadence of Zola's own description.

Such textual reverberations, most consciously declared through ironic recall, serve to bind together disparate narrative segments. Their prefigurative weight makes it decidedly and, through accretion, increasingly unlikely that Gervaise's ideal will be realized. That is not to deny that the chapters elaborating her fresh start in life (in the appropriately named Rue *Neuve*) have an almost lyrical energy. '[F]our years of hard work' (p. 87) are filled with laughter, friendship, and solidarity, the purposeful enjoyment of uncomplicated times. Yet long before the culmination of this joyous mood in Chapter VII, there is no mistaking the presages of doom. The fragility of Gervaise's hopes is brought into dramatic relief by Coupeau's accident; and, above all, it is her own willing exposure to the anaesthetizing effects of that other *assommoir* which her laundry itself becomes which signals future reversals. Nowhere does Zola underline this more explicitly than when she weakly submits to her husband's drunken attentions:

She stopped struggling, feeling quite dizzy because of the mountain of washing and not in the least put off by Coupeau's alcoholic breath. And the smacking kiss they gave each other full on the mouth, in the middle of all the dirty washing, was like a first step in the slow downward spiral of their life. (p. 129)

Though we may feel that such authorial didacticism is redundant, the tragic force of *L'Assommoir* depends on this 'fatal flaw' in its heroine to complement her status as the passive victim of external circumstances.

[12] See John 2:1–10, on 'the six stone water jars . . . turned into wine!'.

The tension between these agents in her downfall is most clearly visible in her saint's-day feast. For if preparations for the high point of her fortunes are overshadowed by threats of imminent disruption, Lantier's fortuitous return is less insidious than the self-respect forfeited by allowing Coupeau to bring him in, turning a customer away, resorting to the pawnshop in order to purchase more wine, and surrendering to both a physical and moral torpor induced by uninhibited indulgence. Thrift, propriety, and willpower are corroded, not by envy or malice, but by the very good-heartedness which makes Gervaise so sympathetic a character. This is thus another chapter which perfectly synthesizes *L'Assommoir*'s extended design, moving from a precarious harmony to the abdication of all semblance of control.

The second half of the novel takes this movement to its logical conclusion. It is punctuated by more discontinuous reassertions of Gervaise's original ambitions, but these now form the benchmark of her decline. When she is drawn to Lantier's bed, for example, it is bitterly ironic that it is Coupeau lying in his vomit across her own which revives her quest for cleanliness (p. 241). So too attempts to exert parental discipline on Nana, by reference to the family values Gervaise had championed, are gradually overtaken by indifference. More consistently, but equally integrative in terms of the novel's organic unity, each and every element of her ideal is inverted. She wallows in filth ('The dirt itself was like a cosy nest she loved to snuggle into' (p. 253)) and idleness; she goes into debt and lets both her person and her surroundings fall apart; she starts to drink inside Colombe's Assommoir, where previously she had remained outside on the pavement; sleeping with Lantier precisely contradicts her earlier disapproval of infidelity (p. 45); she is beaten often; she becomes the object of communal derision where once she had held her head up high.

Nor can the reader fail to notice how even the weather takes a turn for the worse. Earlier gay and sunlit scenes give way to grey skies and rain-drenched streets, as surely as the Coupeaus' dingy room is a sad reminder of their bright apartment. Seen from the distance of critical analysis, such novelistic techniques and repetitions may seem as artificial as they are heavy with symbolic import. Such is our involvement in Gervaise's plight, however, not least as a result of a narrative perspective increasingly angled through her own point of view, that the sombre colours seem utterly in keeping with *L'Assommoir*'s development. For this traces a decomposition more pervasive than the heroine's progressive loss of human dignity. If the stages of Coupeau's alcoholism, interspersed by remissions which merely postpone his death throes, prefigure Gervaise's animalization, this drama is contextualized by others: the deaths of Maman Coupeau, Lalie Bijard, Père Bru, and Madame Goujet; the definitive departures of Lantier and Nana; the breakup of a family and a community. The book becomes an unremitting catalogue of misery, starvation, and pain, recounted in the most distressingly minute detail. While Gervaise's attempts to prostitute herself are the pathetic counterpoint to Nana's rising star, the supreme humiliation is to be found in her death. But even here, it should be noted, Zola takes care to bring full circle his novel's dominant themes. As the grotesque obverse of her quest, Gervaise consumes filth and becomes a rotting object (p. 395), while her soliciting Bazouge to carry her off makes of her original ideal of a clean place in which to sleep a death wish ultimately realized. She ends her days in suffering utterly disproportionate to the causes of her personal failure. The tragic dimension of *L'Assommoir* is inseparable from our sense of a preordained design taken to such a conclusion and the paradoxical 'satisfaction' generated by the text's inner necessity.

One of the many reasons why *L'Assommoir* is so fiendishly difficult to translate is Zola's extensive use of working-class slang. French editions of the novel invariably include a glossary to assist the modern reader in this respect. But this is not a problem which simply reflects a historical distance from a language which was once familiar. For contemporaries too were so unprepared for this that several reviewers suggested that the novel was accessible only to a working-class audience. Zola's admission, in his Preface, that 'People have taken exception to the words' (p. 3) is something of an understatement. Critics denounced not only unintelligible colloquialisms, but also verbal obscenities and sexual puns equally unprecedented in a nineteenth-century novel. Masked behind the hysteria of this reception there was, indeed, a discernible anxiety, crystallized in Edmond de Goncourt's recognition of Zola's 'deliberate refusal to write in a literary style'. And the latter's denial, in terms of *L'Assommoir*'s philological appeal to 'linguistic researchers' (p. 3), is undoubtedly less eloquent than the now-famous inscription in the copy of the novel he sent to Flaubert: 'en haine du goût' points to the book itself as nothing less than 'a challenge to good taste'. It remains to be asked whether in fact *L'Assommoir* is as radical, in cultural terms, as this might suggest.

To put this question in another way (reformulating it within the novel's own terms of reference), where does *L'Assommoir* situate itself in relation to the artistic tradition exemplified by the works in the Louvre? For if, as has already been suggested, its representation functions as a matrix of thematic and symbolic codes, it is also an emblematic space in which *L'Assommoir* defines its own originality. And central to this is its potential destabilization of our own vantage-point. While the language of the novel is the most visible question mark over the cultural certainties from which we read, other popular forms assert their validity. There is an alternative pictorial tradition, for example, in the contemplation of images on the street (pp. 319, 367). The walls of Goujet's room are those of a different kind of gallery: 'all over the walls were pictures, cut-out figures, coloured prints secured with four nails, and portraits of all kinds of people taken from the illustrated papers' (p. 96); and he cuts some out for Gervaise, as the youngest Bijard children do for themselves (pp. 358–61). The 'poorly executed painting' (p. 97) of Goujet's father is morally instructive. Others are merely decorative: on wall-paper, cardboard boxes, and shop fronts. They allow the characters to visualize, even in the most rudimentary form, their dreams and experiences. Exemplified by Lantier's engravings (p. 218), they are as authoritative as books but less demanding than reading: 'in the evenings he [Goujet] was too tired to read, so he amused himself looking at his pictures' (p. 96). What it is important to notice is that these offset the imagistic complex in the Louvre. The contrast, however, is one of register rather than representation, a substitution of one set of portraits, busts (p. 217), and rustic icons (p. 121) for another. Between the Pascal and the Béranger on the one hand, and the Géricault and the Rubens on the other, there is a symmetry ('the one serious, the other smiling' (p. 89)) not confined to the top of Gervaise's cupboard.

Our implied superiority is, at best, insecure. From a world apart, Gervaise and her friends stumble through a totally unintelligible script, symbolically announced to us by the 'Phoenician characters' (p. 69) they cannot decipher. They are mocked, it can be argued, from the point of view of the regular visitor with whom the reader is complicitous. Our enjoyment of the episode is certainly enhanced if we inhabit a cultural frame of reference wide enough to embrace Monsieur Madinier's incompetence within Zola's elliptical, ironic structure. But our unambiguous mirth at his expense does depend on knowing that Titian's *Young Woman at Her Toilet* (with Venetian auburn rather than yellow hair) is not *La Belle Ferronnière* (by Leonardo), and that the lady in question was reputed to be the mistress not of Henri IV (p. 70) but, at best, of François I and, more probably, of Ludovico Sforza. Without those cultural keys the reader of *L'Assommoir* may be left unsure whether he or she stands above or within this 'comic' scene.

On the other hand, those keys pale into insignificance beside the glossaries designed to allow us to decode a language which invades the point of view of the 'literate' as problematically as the hilarity which enters the Louvre. For two cultural frames are not merely juxtaposed in an implicit hierarchy. As many critics have noted, their interpenetration ultimately contests the narrative voice, eroding the distinction between free indirect speech and authorial stance. In the light of the redirected laughter in the Louvre which transforms incomprehending spectators into amusing spectacle, the 'No, it wasn't possible, nobody could ever have read scribble like that' (p. 69) is as doubly ironic as Augustine 'laughing at jokes she had no business understanding!' (p. 132). For are we not ourselves implicated in the text's punning possibilities? To deny *that*, from a standpoint analogous to the Louvre's guardians of decorum, is to belittle the 'extraordinary innuendoes' invented by Madame Lerat's charges who 'twisted the remark to make it sound suggestive' (p. 323) at her expense, and to refuse to admit that we would like to know the answer to her question about Lantier's chance meeting with Nana: 'In what sense did you see her?' (p. 349). And we might well ask where Zola himself stands in relation to Lantier's self-indulgence, in the midst of the laundresses, 'revelling in their vulgar talk, egging them on while taking care that his own language remained quite refined' (p. 220). Amidst *L'Assommoir*'s rising tide of uncertainly attributable linguistic crudities, Gervaise poses (for the reader too) a different question: 'When he started to talk dirty she never knew if he was joking or not' (p. 284). As the labels on whirling images in the Louvre destabilize the visitors from the Rue de la Goutte-d'Or, so to enter their private linguistic space is to be confronted by proliferating nicknames (of people, shops, bars, and dance halls), exuberant semantic slippage, and a concatenation of song titles. To read the 'tableaux' of *L'Assommoir* from the perspective of the Louvre, in other words, is to stumble through a text parading its signs, self-consciously overdetermined on the one hand (starting with its title) and sense-defying on the other.

Further examples of meanings declared would include onomastic underlinings. In a novel in which eating is a major preoccupation, Mademoiselle Remanjou's name plays with the verb *manger*; just as obviously, Madame Lerat is as vicious as any rodent, and it is all the more ironic, therefore, that she should live on the monastic Rue des Moines. At the other extreme, there is a provocative authorial delight in a working-class slang so arcane in the original French that only an impenetrable translation would do it justice. Or, at the very least, it requires editorial amplification to capture the knowing play (in the case of Monsieur Poisson, for instance) on *poisson* as both drink and pimp, according to Delvau's *Dictionnaire de la langue verte*, recurring as it does in 'Un poisson d'quatr' sous' (translated here as 'Four sous' worth of beer' (p. 206)), in the exuberantly sung 'Qué cochon d'enfant!' (translated here as 'Disgusting Little Beast!' (p. 206)).

The songs of *L'Assommoir*, either alluded to or partially cited, serve to bring this critical problem into sharper relief, occupying as they do a place in the novel more consciously devised than illustrative purposes (of the immemorial habits of labouring men and women) would have warranted. At one level, they allow Zola to engage in indirect commentary. Gervaise's 'old washerwoman's song', for example, ironically refers to her own 'Misery black as coal' (p. 28) at the very moment of 'ferocious glee' which leaves Virginie's rump so black and blue. Many of the songs thus function as an accompaniment to the narrative itself, not least the wickedly appropriate 'My nose is where it tickles me' (p. 240) which takes Lantier back to Gervaise's bed as she is overcome by an insidious sensuality at odds with moral rectitude. The entire singing episode of Chapter VII is deliberately organized in counterpoint, as news of approaching temptation, in the shape of Lantier's return, is interpolated between songs of seduction ('The Volcano of Love, or The Irresistible Trooper' (p. 198)) and resistance ('Pirate Ship Ahoy!' (p. 199)). A similar alternation contrasts the sobriety of 'Abd-el-Kader's Farewell' (p. 200) and the intoxication of 'The Wines of France' (pp. 199–200). We should not forget, however, that these are but the sanctioned pauses in the accelerating rhythm of a transgressive repertoire. For between the serious and the salacious, on the one hand, and respectful silence and a deafening roar, on the other, the chapter as a whole charts the progression of an unbridled laughter. And its disruptive potential is already asserted in the telling disturbance of those muslin curtains between room and street (pp. 198, 205) which separate the private and the public.

Within the domestic space of 'The Simple Life of Gervaise Macquart', the correlation of performer and performance ensures that the songs are angled as mirrors in which characters either locate themselves or are reflected for the reader in individuated echoes. The strains of exotic Spain or Arabia (p. 200) open up 'golden vistas' which had remained encased with 'the little Oriental gods' (p. 71) in the Louvre; and they anticipate the more prosaic flight to Belgium in Goujet's proposal to Gervaise of an elopement 'like the sort of thing that happens in novels' (p. 227). The informing desire of a rural idyll is a recurrent motif: in Coupeau's 'Hey, ho! The baby lambs!' (p. 101) and 'Oh, I do love pickin' strawberries!' (p. 103), and, especially, in the mawkish 'Make Your Nest': 'it reminded them of the country-side, tiny little birds, nectar-laden flowers, dancing under the trees' (p. 200). Of these inconsequential negations of an urban destiny, none is more grotesquely redolent than the title of the last. For it picks up, of course, Gervaise's lifelong dream of 'a cosy nest' (p. 253) so precariously placed between the literal and the figurative. Nor is it by chance that Nana should sing of a limping beast of burden (p. 266). There will be no dignified surrender such as that exemplified by Abd-el-Kader's submission to colonial power (p. 200). Gervaise's 'Oh! Let me sleep' (p. 199) looks forward to a wish finally granted by Bazouge as the novel closes ('Time to go bye-byes, my beauty!'); but not before she was upset by his song, 'There were three pretty girls' (p. 295) which had made her the victim of 'The Volcano of Love'. Her appeals to God go unheard; bereft of familial structures, 'alone and abandoned' (p. 365), she had earlier listened to 'The Child of the Lord' with justified trepidation: 'she felt as if the song was about her own torment, that she was the abandoned child whom the Lord was going to take into his care' (p. 202).

It is only when such private concerns spill over on to the street, however, that recourse to this idiom represents a different kind of threat. The songs of *L'Assommoir* speak of its characters' dislocated experience and may be partially comprehensible to us only in the fragments not distorted by colloquial expression. But for the diverse inhabitants of the Rue de la Goutte d'Or 'who all knew the song, joined in the chorus' (p. 198), to be transmitted from one working-class generation to the next, the singing is a declaration of coherence (in every sense). The banquet is thus contrasted with the wedding-feast which had broken up in rancour because of the absence of a chorus-leader. In a novel apparently so far removed from the political stage, it is here that the authorities' fear of the café-concert is related to the spectre of the barricade. For the most coded songs, voicing unregulated inebriation and sexuality, establish a community invulnerable to political control. The raucous invasion of the muted high culture of the Louvre had been brought to an end by the powerful voices of the guards. Within the characters' own linguistic space, however, patriotic intonations are drowned out; and historical reality and symbolic significance coincide in the aborted appearance of the policemen, 'thinking there must be a riot' (p. 206).

The assault on the parameters of 'taste' is not limited, of course, to the novel's songs. Nor are they the only moment within it where *L'Assommoir* seems to anticipate the official suspicion with which it would be greeted. In a number of ways, however, they both capture its own preoccupations and mirror our reading of the novel as a whole. Thematically resonant, they are also spaced in alternating registers and moods, overlaying the ribald and the pathetic. But the internal arrangement of the songs at the banquet, itself so structurally significant, reflects a textual progression rather than a biographical curve, moving from moral commentary and identifiable narrative tableaux to an increasingly unintelligible script.

This reaches its climax in the sense-defying, disarticulated grammar of Coupeau in the Sainte-Anne asylum. His babble remains only intermittently comprehensible to us, separated as we are from his inchoate laughter and eccentric imaginative world. But the rising cadence of the novel's central chapter is stopped short of that verbal delirium which it also prefigures. It is sectioned off by 'a knowing little nod' (p. 206), exchanged by the representatives of law and order; but also (it could be said) between policing author and readers in search of ordered meanings. In both cases the gesture serves to restore an ironic complicity. From the same vantage-point as that from which the story as a whole will be brought to a close, our sense of an ending survives inherently redundant refrains continuing into the night.

But to move past the songs as permissive spectators of a colourful linguistic episode is to 'overlook', precisely, their activating power. For Zola's juxtapositions are seldom more problematic than when the subversive orthography and lexical arbitrariness of 'Qué cochon d'enfant!' (see note to p. 205) assume an autonomous cultural legitimacy; sung not to, but for and by, the community, and simultaneously excluding those outside it. The hostility engendered by *L'Assommoir* cannot be understood without reference to this perceived threat to the hierarchy between orality and the institutionally inscribed (or uncontrollable laughter and 'common' sense); but also, of course, to the distinction separating their class-related audiences.

There were few more acute observers of the symptoms of such cultural crisis than the poet Stéphane Mallarmé (1842–98). His reaction to *L'Assommoir* focuses on contemporary anxieties about readership. 'Those who accuse you of not having written for the common people', he wrote to Zola on 3 February 1877, 'are in a sense quite wrong, but no more so than those who regret that you have abandoned an established ideal.'[13] This is not to adumbrate a fallacious history of the leisure habits of the proletariat. It is to locate the novel's modernity in its troubling admixture of codification: 'your admirable linguistic experiment, thanks to which the often inept expressions forged by poor devils assume the value of the most beautiful literary formulations.' More inevitably perhaps, given the perspective of a 'man of letters' (as Mallarmé puts it), the recuperative tribute, 'You have contributed to literature something absolutely new', leaves an enlarged category intact. It can be suggested, however, that *L'Assommoir* does more than just accommodate 'beauty in popular form'. If it is 'worthy of its age', it is also because the novel encodes the dissolving boundaries of the popular and Art.

It seems inconceivable that Zola himself was not acutely aware, during the writing of the novel, of what he was doing in this respect. If Madame Lerat's linguistic concerns are specific, the Louvre signals more general preoccupations. For an artist to confront directly, within his work, the norms of the pantheon of art, is an open invitation to the reader to measure *L'Assommoir* against traditional criteria. Less overtly perhaps, the scenes at Sainte-Anne are complementary in so

---

[13] The letter is cited in full in Henri Mitterand's Pléiade edition of *L'Assommoir* (Paris: Gallimard, 1961–7), ii. 1566–7. Mallarmé's remarks are also to be found in introductions to most paperback editions of the novel.

far as it is here that the visit to the Louvre finds itself reflected in another mode: 'It was another huge building, with dismal courtyards, endless corridors' (p. 303). In an epilogue which structurally corresponds to the end of *L'Assommoir*'s exposition, Sainte-Anne remains the only other 'escape' developed beyond a passing reference, and getting there is as tortuous an expedition as the wedding party's excursion. It is as regulated as the Salon Carré, with its own institutional guards and officials. Within it, Coupeau confirms the fate which awaits Gervaise as one of those dehumanized beasts in the Assyrian Gallery described as 'monstrous beasts, half-cat, half-woman' (p. 69).

Over and above this kind of thematic recall, however, these pages allow Zola to return to the problem of representation posed by his copyists in the Louvre, 'with their easels set up in the middle of the crowd, calmly painting away' (p. 70). The foregrounded detail ('what interested them the most') is enlarged beyond the anecdotal by the contemporary debate on artistic originality, and the untroubled copying contrasts with *L'Assommoir*'s self-conscious dimension. The curiosity of the seated observer at Sainte-Anne, with notebook in hand, reflects both the 'curious onlookers' (p. 70) who draw up their chairs to watch the wedding party pass by and Zola's 'literary curiosity to gather together the language of the common people and present it in a carefully fashioned mould' (p. 3). Gervaise engages in a similar mimetic activity, reproducing in a *tableau* (translated here as 'her imitation' (pp. 386, 389, 395)), and for assembled spectators of her own, her husband's terrifying 'performance' (p. 382); as opposed to dance-hall comics imitating what Coupeau was doing ('but they don't do it very well' (p. 382)), Gervaise 'imitated Coupeau to perfection' (p. 389). *L'Assommoir* too was to be, according to Zola's notes, a 'terrifying tableau', and its reception is anticipated in this startling moment of textual introspection: 'they'd accused her of overdoing her imitation' (p. 386), even more precisely echoed in the French term *exagérer*. Alongside all those representations contemplated by the characters, the novel's Preface asserts the power of its 'imagery'. Between the Louvre and Sainte-Anne, it can be argued, Zola explores the hall of mirrors in which such images of experience imagined are threatened by the insertion of a museum wall between art and life. The writer and critic Paul Bourget (1852–1935) caught the structure of *L'Assommoir* exactly: 'it's as if the paintings of life were aligned in a gallery'; but also the paradox: 'Don't you think', he asked Zola, 'that you provoke in us a sense of curiosity which militates against the naturalness of the story[?]'[14] On the one hand, the novel subverts what Zola saw as the desire of a writer like Théophile Gautier (1811–72) to 'immobilize language in a hieratical stasis'; on the other, Bourget puts in a more polite form the charges, expressed by contemporary socialists such as Arthur Ranc (1831–1908), of 'art for art's sake'. If Zola's distaste for the sculptured shapes in the Louvre (with 'their stiff hieratical poses' (p. 69)) is self-evident, the writer's 'carefully fashioned mould' remains double-edged.

The same ambivalence can be detected in the process whereby art and experience seem to parody each other in *L'Assommoir*. Coupeau's zinc-cutting is that of an 'artist'; Goujet's toil produces 'a real jeweller's job' as he fashions rivets 'so beautifully made it'd be worth putting them in a museum' (p. 150); Maman Coupeau fits into her coffin so perfectly that she is 'just like a picture in a frame' (p. 274). Such comparisons operate from both ends of the cultural divide. The songs of the novel may articulate a poetry of common experience, but are themselves cast in the ambiguities of Zola's metaphorical configurations. He uses the term *chanson* for gossip (p. 44), the 'old song' (p. 361) of Gervaise's empty stomach, and Coupeau's 'carnival cry' (p. 382). To the extent that idiom is concretized, we may be left unsure of the differentiated status of the 'poetry' and the 'experience'. Nowhere is this more evident than in the extended references to music. The background instrumentation of moral degeneracy (pp. 46, 81, 367) is used in precisely the same way as Zola exploits the texts of the songs as commentary. Cornets and fiddles seem to be mocked by Veronese's cultural heroes listening to the foregrounded players in *The Wedding at Cana*. But a 'minuet' of long ago and the vulgarity of a 'sleazy music hall' (p. 151) gradually create a complementary rhythm of their own within this oppositional framework. A superimposition is effected in the obscenities sung by drunks 'looking just like choristers at their stalls' (p. 369). Sacred modulations become 'the belly's vespers' (p. 255) as the church organ is reproduced in 'the music of misery' (p. 290). There are the sonorities of running water (p. 56), drumming fingers (p. 383), and a workshop with its own refrain (p. 42). *L'Assommoir* puts us in touch with the 'music' of Coupeau's

---

[14] In a letter of 2 February 1877, cited by Deffoux, *La Publication de 'L'Assommoir'*, 111–12.

comic snoring (p. 262); but also, in the other mode equally character-istic of its songs, with that of crying children (p. 10), heartless grave-diggers (p. 275), and diseased chests (p. 301).

To the extent that such conflations are parodic, Zola seems to register an awareness that revelations of the undisclosed may be transformed into another spectacle of scissored images: as unrespon-sive to suffering as the children's cutting; as inward-looking as Poisson's arabesques; as proliferating as those on Goujet's walls are increasingly obscured; as hallucinatory as the verbiage at Sainte-Anne which dissolves the boundaries of significance and sense. The confidence of Poisson's 'It was printed in a book, so how could he deny it?' (p. 218), in other words, is not one to which Zola unequivo-cally subscribes. *L'Assommoir* nevertheless overcomes those hesita-tions. Delineated structures and the stabilizing reference points of thematic patterns ensure that we can both understand and share the writer's compassion for Gervaise's plight. As she looks at the insub-stantial image of herself, in a savage Paris veiled by driving snow, many readers will feel that art and life have come together. If a texture of garbled utterances accommodates a point of view excluded from our own, the extremes of Coupeau's self-reflecting 'musique nou-velle' (translated here as 'retuned . . . vocal cords', p. 347) are held in check by Zola's orchestration of his fiction. That still leaves the novel at odds with the 'classical' movements and rhythmic precision of Goujet's 'clear melody' (p. 152). But it is in its confrontation with such problems of definition, less in its subject than its enactment, that *L'Assommoir* retains its distinctive hybrid resonance.

TRANSLATOR'S NOTE

THE act of translation is an empathetic act in the sense that it allows translators to become the authors they admire, to recreate through language the narratives they love. This is doubly true in the case of *L'Assommoir*, insofar as the central effect of the novel itself is empathy: that is to say, the reader is invited to enter the characters' world, to see and *feel* the world as they do. This effect is created partly by the phenomenological quality of Zola's writing: the sensory immediacy that informs his characters' relationship with their environment. The effect is greatly heightened, however, by Zola's astonishing invention of a narrative voice that absorbs into itself the thoughts and feelings of the characters. It is as if the characters themselves take on a narrative function, telling their own story. This brings the reader into more direct and sympathetic contact with them and with their culture than would have been the case with conventional narrative. As Zola noted in his preface to the novel, contemporary bourgeois critics were disoriented and shocked, not so much by the novel's subject matter (a simple washerwoman who becomes a tragic heroine) as by its style. One of the challenges for the translator is to ensure that perspective is aligned with the colloquial style; that there is an appropriately close relationship between 'Who is seeing?' and 'Who is speaking?'. The translator, in his or her attempts to capture Zola's own stylistic ventriloquism, must make crucial and consistent choices in terms of register and voice, especially of course in direct speech. Above all, the translator must avoid translating 'up': rendering in elevated or euphemistic language words and phrases belonging to a robustly colloquial register.

The novel contains a great deal of nineteenth-century Parisian *argot* or slang. Zola himself, in his effort to create an authentic representation of working-class language, compiled a lexicon on the basis mainly of the *Dictionnaire de la langue verte* (1866) by Alfred Delvau, and *La Question sociale: Le Sublime, ou Le Travailleur comme il est en 1870 et ce qu'il peut être* (1870) by Denis Poulot (though these served as supplements to the first-hand knowledge he gained after moving to the impoverished parts of Paris in 1859). Any translator of *L'Assommoir* will find it useful to consult Delvau's dictionary (now available via the online website Gallica) in order to gain the best possible understanding of the meaning and nuances of particular words. For example, the sentence: 'On appelait les camarades qui avaient l'air bon zig.' As the Coupeaus' great feast progresses in Chapter VII, the doors and windows are opened and the whole neighbourhood, including passers-by, is invited to join in. The term *zig* evokes the mindset of the workers who frequent the local bars—men fond of a good laugh and who tend, for obvious reasons, to walk in zigzags. Delvau defines *zig* as 'Homme joyeux, bon ami de cabaret et de débauche' (a jolly sort who loves drinking and carousing). The register and implications of the phrase quoted above are best rendered by something simple and direct, like 'they called out to mates who looked ready for a drop', as opposed to: '...pals who looked alright' (Leonard Tancock, Penguin Books, 1970), '...any acquaintance who looked like a decent sort' (Robin Buss, Penguin Books, 2000), or '...mates who seemed like nice chaps' (Margaret Mauldon, Oxford World's Classics, 1995).

How is slang, generally, best handled? The problem is that it is a type of language that is highly specific to time, place, and culture. This means that it is very difficult to translate *argot* for *argot*. It is imperative to maintain the cultural specificity of the text. Slang is also highly mutable and quickly becomes out of date. It is important, therefore, to avoid language that is anachronistic: the translator is writing for a contemporary audience. The translator of *L'Assommoir* must aim, I think, to use vigorously colloquial contemporary language in order to convey to the reader as much as possible of the general colour, and tone, of the nineteenth-century Goutte-d'Or.

Finally, there is the question of the title. The French word *assommoir* is an archaic slang term for a bar or drinking place, but it has other connotations that relate to the novel's themes and narrative structure. The verb *assommer* means to kill by a blow on the head, to knock senseless, or, figuratively, to stun or affect deeply—thus signalling, not just the effects of alcohol but, more generally, the stultifying, destructive, and violent social forces that afflict the urban poor. I conjured with various alternatives to the original title, *L'Assommoir*, but they either stressed too much the place ('The Drinking Den'? 'The Bar'?) without evoking its deadly effects, or referred to the drinking machine ('The Deadly Still'?, 'The Fatal Booze-Machine'?) rather than Père Colombe's bar itself, or concentrated narrowly on the idea of drunkenness and alcoholism ('Hammered!'); and none had a slangy quality. I thought—following in the footsteps of René Clément and his 1956 film of the novel—of calling it simply 'Gervaise', after the central character. But I concluded eventually that keeping the original title was the best option, even though 'L'Assommoir' would mean nothing to English speakers unfamiliar with the novel or with French. At a late stage, however, Judith Luna suggested that the novel be called 'The Assommoir'. This tells non-French readers that it is a thing or place rather than a concept, while the use of the English article is both consistent with the policy in the translation and slightly lessens the pure 'foreignness' of 'L'Assommoir' (compare 'The Moulin Rouge').

My thanks go to Judith Luna, not only for her suggestion but also for a number of other helpful comments. My thanks, too, to Jan Owen for her help in translating the songs, and to Valerie Minogue, for her encouragement and support. I also wish to express my gratitude to the Brown Foundation in Houston, Texas, for a Fellowship that enabled me to spend a richly rewarding month at the Dora Maar House in Ménerbes.

B.N.

SELECT BIBLIOGRAPHY

THE most authoritative French edition of *l'Assommoir* appears in vol. ii of *Les Rougon-Macquart* in the Bibliothèque de la Pléiade (Paris: Gallimard, 1961–7; but regularly updated); the scholarly apparatus, by Henri Mitterand, includes a synopsis of the novel's genesis and composition, a useful glossary, notes on the text, and successive amendments from the manuscript to the final version of *L'Assommoir* in volume form. The complete work-notes for the novel can be found in vol. ii of *La Fabrique des Rougon-Macquart*, edited by Colette Becker (Paris: Honoré Champion, 2005). Good paperback editions of the original French text include those by Jacques Dubois (Paris: Le Livre de poche classique, 1996) and Chantal Pierre-Gnassounou (Paris: Flammarion, 2008). The fullest study of the semantic history of Zola's title, both before and after the publication of the novel, is Fernand Marty 'Les "Assommoirs"', *Cahiers naturalistes*, 86 (2012), 149–73. On the problems of translating *L'Assommoir*, see David Baguley's article in a special issue of the *Cahiers de traductologie* (no. 5): 'Après babil: L'Intraduisible dans *L'Assommoir*', in Arlette Thomas and Jacques Flamand (eds), *La Traduction: L'Universitaire et le praticien* (Ottawa: Éditions de l'Université d'Ottawa, 1984), 181–90, and Brian Nelson, 'Traduire Zola: Une question de voix', in Bruna Donatelli and Sophie Guermès (eds), *Traduire Zola, du XIXe siècle à nos jours* (Rome: Roma Tre Press, 2018), 39–48. As far as the novel's setting is concerned, an indispensable work of reference is Marc Breitman and Maurice Culot (eds), *La Goutte d'Or, faubourg de Paris* (Paris: Hazan, 1988) which includes a first-rate study by Philippe Hamon on the sites of *L'Assommoir*. Alain Pagès and Owen Morgan (eds), *Guide Émile Zola* (Paris: Ellipses, 2002) is an invaluable compendium of facts about the writer's life and work. The definitive biography is Henri Mitterand's 3-volume *Zola* (Paris: Fayard, 1999–2003).

Studies of Zola and Naturalism in English

Baguley, David, *Naturalist Fiction: The Entropic Vision* (Cambridge: Cambridge University Press, 1990; reissued 2006).

Harrow, Susan, *The Body Modern: Pressures and Prospects of Representation* (Oxford: Legenda, 2010).

Hemmings, F. W. J., *Émile Zola* (2nd edn, Oxford: Clarendon Press, 1966; reissued, with corrections, as an Oxford University Press Paperback, 1970); notwithstanding its age, this remains the best general study of Zola's life and work.

Lethbridge, Robert, and Keefe, Terry (eds), *Zola and the Craft of Fiction* (Leicester: Leicester University Press, 1990; reissued in paperback, 1993).

Nelson, Brian (ed.), *The Cambridge Companion to Zola* (Cambridge: Cambridge University Press, 2007).

Nelson, Brian, *Émile Zola: A Very Short Introduction* (Oxford: Oxford University Press, 2020).

Walker, Philip, *Zola* (London: Routledge & Kegan Paul, 1985).

Studies in English on L'Assommoir

Baguley, David, 'Event and Structure: The Plot of Zola's *L'Assommoir*', *PMLA* 90 (1975), 823–33; a stimulating essay, at once essential and accessible.

Baguley, David, *Émile Zola: 'L'Assommoir'* (Cambridge: Cambridge University Press, 1992); this includes a 'Guide to Further Reading' (pp. 111–16) which constitutes the most comprehensive survey of secondary work on the novel prior to 1992, both signalling the level at which such work is pitched and detailing bibliographical references in English and French.

Clark, Roger, *Zola: L'Assommoir* (Glasgow: University of Glasgow French and German Publications, 1990).

Dineen, R. M., 'A Journey through the Labyrinth: Variations on the Theme in *L'Assommoir*', *New Zealand Journal of French Studies*, 20/2 (1999), 5–16.

Donaldson-Evans, Mary, 'Miasmatic Effusions: *L'Assommoir* and the Discourse of Hygiene', in her *Medical Examinations: Dissecting the Doctor in French Narrative Prose, 1857–1894* (Lincoln, NE: University of Nebraska Press, 2000), 74–92.

Furst, Lilian, *L'Assommoir: A Working Woman's Life* (Boston: Twayne, 1990).

Gaitet, Pascale, 'Zola's *L'Assommoir*', in her *Political Stylistics: Popular Language as Literary Artifact* (London: Routledge, 1992), 44–100.

George, Ken, 'The Language of Alcohol in *L'Assommoir*', *French Studies*, 52 (1998), 437–49.

Harrow, Susan, 'Dressed/Undressed: Objects of Visual Fascination in Zola's *L'Assommoir*', in M. Cardy, G. Evans, and G. Jacobs (eds), *Narrative Voices in Modern French Fiction: Studies in Honour of Valerie Minogue* (Cardiff: University of Wales Press, 1997), 143–63.

Lethbridge, Robert, 'Reading the Songs of *L'Assommoir*', *French Studies*, 45 (1991), 435–47.

Lethbridge, Robert, 'A Visit to the Louvre: *L'Assommoir* Revisited', *Modern Language Review*, 87 (1992), 41–55.

Lethbridge, Robert, 'Reflections in the Margin: Politics in Zola's *L'Assommoir*', *Australian Journal of French Studies*, 30 (1993), 222–32.

Minogue, Valerie, *Zola: 'L'Assommoir'* (London: Grant and Cutler, 1991).

Place, David, 'Zola and the Working Class: The Meaning of *L'Assommoir*', *French Studies*, 28 (1974), 39–49.

White, Nicholas (ed.), *L'Assommoir* (London, Everyman, 1995); based on Arthur Symons's 1894 translation, this edition has a good introduction and an interesting appendix on the novel's critical reception (pp. 415–33).

Wilson, Colette, 'City Spaces and the Politics of Carnival in Zola's *L'Assommoir*', *French Studies*, 58 (2004), 343–56; the thrust of this excellent study is included in her *Paris and the Commune, 1871–1878: The Politics of Forgetting* (Manchester: Manchester University Press, 2007), 144–57.

Further Reading in Oxford World's Classics

Zola, Émile, *The Belly of Paris*, ed. and trans. Brian Nelson.

Zola, Émile, *La Bête humaine*, ed. and trans. Roger Pearson.

Zola, Émile, *The Bright Side of Life*, ed. and trans. Andrew Rothwell.

Zola, Émile, *The Conquest of Plassans*, trans. Helen Constantine, ed. Patrick McGuinness.

Zola, Émile, *La Débâcle*, trans. Elinor Dorday, ed. Robert Lethbridge.

Zola, Émile, *Doctor Pascal*, trans. Julie Rose, ed. Brian Nelson.

Zola, Émile, *The Dream*, ed. and trans. Paul Gibbard.

Zola, Émile, *Earth*, ed. and trans. Brian Nelson and Julie Rose.

Zola, Émile, *The Fortune of the Rougons*, ed. and trans. Brian Nelson.

Zola, Émile, *Germinal*, trans. and ed. Peter Collier, introd. Robert Lethbridge.

Zola, Émile, *His Excellency Eugène Rougon*, ed. and trans. Brian Nelson.

Zola, Émile, *The Kill*, ed. and trans. Brian Nelson.

Zola, Émile, *The Ladies' Paradise*, ed. and trans. Brian Nelson.

Zola, Émile, *A Love Story*, trans. Helen Constantine, ed. Brian Nelson.

Zola, Émile, *The Masterpiece*, trans. Thomas Walton, rev. and ed. Roger Pearson.

Zola, Émile, *Money*, ed. and trans. Valerie Minogue.

Zola, Émile, *Nana*, trans. Helen Constantine, ed. Brian Nelson.

Zola, Émile, *Pot Luck (Pot-Bouille)*, ed. and trans. Brian Nelson.

Zola, Émile, *The Sin of Abbé Mouret*, ed. and trans. Valerie Minogue.

A CHRONOLOGY OF ÉMILE ZOLA

1840   (2 April) Born in Paris, the only child of Francesco Zola (b. 1795), an Italian engineer, and Émilie, née Aubert (b. 1819), the daughter of a glazier. The naturalist novelist was later proud that 'zolla' in Italian means 'clod of earth'

1843   Family moves to Aix-en-Provence

1847   (27 March) Death of father from pneumonia following a chill caught while supervising work on his scheme to supply Aix-en-Provence with drinking water

1852–8 Boarder at the Collège Bourbon at Aix. Friendship with Baptistin Baille and Paul Cézanne. Zola, not Cézanne, wins the school prize for drawing

1858   (February) Leaves Aix to settle in Paris with his mother (who had preceded him in December). Offered a place and bursary at the Lycée Saint-Louis. (November) Falls ill with 'brain fever' (typhoid) and convalescence is slow

1859   Fails his *baccalauréat* twice

1860   (Spring) Is found employment as a copy-clerk but abandons it after two months, preferring to eke out an existence as an impecunious writer in the Latin Quarter of Paris

1861   Cézanne follows Zola to Paris, where he meets Camille Pissarro, fails the entrance examination to the École des Beaux-Arts, and returns to Aix in September

1862   (February) Taken on by Hachette, the well-known publishing house, at first in the dispatch office and subsequently as head of the publicity department. (31 October) Naturalized as a French citizen. Cézanne returns to Paris and stays with Zola

1863   (31 January) First literary article published. (1 May) Manet's *Déjeuner sur l'herbe* exhibited at the Salon des Refusés, which Zola visits with Cézanne

1864   (October) *Tales for Ninon*

1865   *Claude's Confession.* A *succès de scandale* thanks to its bedroom scenes. Meets future wife Alexandrine-Gabrielle Meley (b. 1839), the illegitimate daughter of teenage parents who soon separated; Alexandrine's mother died in September 1849

1866 Resigns his position at Hachette (salary: 200 francs a month) and becomes a literary critic on the recently launched daily *L'Événement* (salary: 500 francs a month). Self-styled 'humble disciple' of Hippolyte Taine. Writes a series of provocative articles condemning the official Salon Selection Committee, expressing reservations about Courbet, and praising Manet and Monet. Begins to frequent the Café Guerbois in the Batignolles quarter of Paris, the meeting-place of the future Impressionists. Antoine Guillemet takes Zola to meet Manet. Summer months spent with Cézanne at Bennecourt on the Seine. (15 November) *L'Événement* suppressed by the authorities

1867 (November) *Thérèse Raquin*

1868 (April) Preface to second edition of *Thérèse Raquin*. (May) Manet's portrait of Zola exhibited at the Salon. (December) *Madeleine Férat*. Begins to plan for the Rougon-Macquart series of novels

1868–70 Working as journalist for a number of different newspapers

1870 (31 May) Marries Alexandrine in a registry office. (September) Moves temporarily to Marseilles because of the Franco-Prussian War

1871 Political reporter for *La Cloche* (in Paris) and *Le Sémaphore de Marseille*. (March) Returns to Paris. (October) Publishes *The Fortune of the Rougons*, the first of the twenty novels making up the Rougon-Macquart series

1872 *The Kill*

1873 (April) *The Belly of Paris*

1874 (May) *The Conquest of Plassans*. First independent Impressionist exhibition. (November) *Further Tales for Ninon*

1875 Begins to contribute articles to the Russian newspaper *Vestnik Evropy* (*European Herald*). (April) *The Sin of Abbé Mouret*

1876 (February) *His Excellency Eugène Rougon*. Second Impressionist exhibition

1877 (February) *L'Assommoir*

1878 Buys a house at Médan on the Seine, 40 kilometres west of Paris. (June) *A Love Story* (*Une page d'amour*)

1880 (March) *Nana*. (May) *Les Soirées de Médan* (an anthology of short stories by Zola and some of his naturalist 'disciples', including Maupassant). (8 May) Death of Flaubert. (September) First of a series of articles for *Le Figaro*. (17 October) Death of his mother. (December) *The Experimental Novel*

1882 (April) *Pot Luck* (*Pot-Bouille*). (3 September) Death of Turgenev

1883 (13 February) Death of Wagner. (March) *The Ladies' Paradise* (*Au Bonheur des Dames*). (30 April) Death of Manet

1884 (March) *The Bright Side of Life* (*La Joie de vivre*). Preface to catalogue of Manet exhibition

1885 (March) *Germinal*. (12 May) Begins writing *The Masterpiece* (*L'Œuvre*). (22 May) Death of Victor Hugo. (23 December) First instalment of *The Masterpiece* appears in *Le Gil Blas*

1886 (27 March) Final instalment of *The Masterpiece*, which is published in book form in April

1887 (18 August) Denounced as an onanistic pornographer in the *Manifesto of the Five* in *Le Figaro*. (November) *Earth*

1888 (October) *The Dream*. Jeanne Rozerot becomes his mistress

1889 (20 September) Birth of Denise, daughter of Zola and Jeanne

1890 (March) *La Bête humaine*

1891 (March) *Money*. (April) Elected President of the Société des Gens de Lettres. (25 September) Birth of Jacques, son of Zola and Jeanne

1892 (June) *La Débâcle*

1893 (July) *Doctor Pascal*, the last of the Rougon-Macquart novels. Fêted on visit to London

1894 (August) *Lourdes*, the first novel of the trilogy *Three Cities*. (22 December) Dreyfus found guilty by a court martial

1896 (May) *Rome*

1898 (13 January) 'J'accuse', his article in defence of Dreyfus, published in *L'Aurore*. (21 February) Found guilty of libelling the Minister of War and given the maximum sentence of one year's imprisonment and a fine of 3,000 francs. Appeal for retrial granted on a technicality. (March) *Paris*. (23 May) Retrial delayed. (18 July) Leaves for England instead of attending court

1899 (4 June) Returns to France. (October) *Fecundity*, the first of his *Four Gospels*

1901 (May) *Toil*, the second 'Gospel'

1902 (29 September) Dies of fumes from his bedroom fire, the chimney having been capped either by accident or anti-Dreyfusard design. Wife survives. (5 October) Public funeral

1903 (March) *Truth*, the third 'Gospel', published posthumously. *Justice* was to be the fourth

1908 (4 June) Remains transferred to the Panthéon

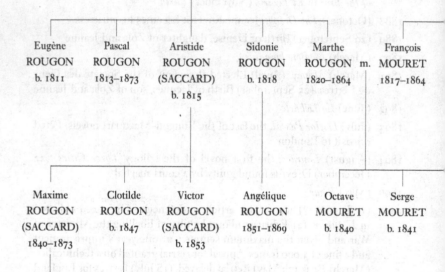

Adélaïde FOUQUE
(Tante DIDE)
1768–1873
m. ROUGON   Lover of MACQUART

Pierre ROUGON
1787–1870
m. Félicité PUECH

| Eugène ROUGON b. 1811 | Pascal ROUGON 1813–1873 | Aristide ROUGON (SACCARD) b. 1815 | Sidonie ROUGON b. 1818 | Marthe ROUGON 1820–1864 m. | François MOURET 1817–1864 |

| Maxime ROUGON (SACCARD) 1840–1873 | Clotilde ROUGON b. 1847 | Victor ROUGON (SACCARD) b. 1853 | Angélique ROUGON 1851–1869 | Octave MOURET b. 1840 | Serge MOURET b. 1841 |

Charles ROUGON (SACCARD) 1857–1873

Child born in 1874 to Clotilde and Pascal ROUGON

FAMILY TREE OF THE ROUGON–MACQUART

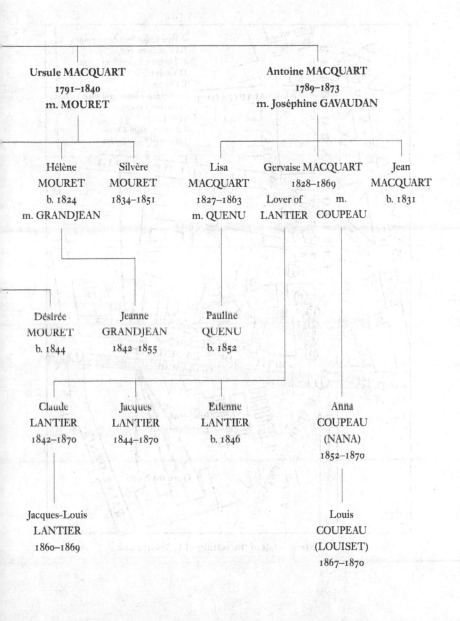

Ursule MACQUART
1791–1840
m. MOURET

Antoine MACQUART
1789–1873
m. Joséphine GAVAUDAN

Hélène
MOURET
b. 1824
m. GRANDJEAN

Silvère
MOURET
1834–1851

Lisa
MACQUART
1827–1863
m. QUENU

Gervaise MACQUART
1828–1869
Lover of   m.
LANTIER COUPEAU

Jean
MACQUART
b. 1831

Désirée
MOURET
b. 1844

Jeanne
GRANDJEAN
1842–1855

Pauline
QUENU
b. 1852

Claude
LANTIER
1842–1870

Jacques
LANTIER
1844–1870

Etienne
LANTIER
b. 1846

Anna
COUPEAU
(NANA)
1852–1870

Jacques-Louis
LANTIER
1860–1869

Louis
COUPEAU
(LOUISET)
1867–1870

MAPS

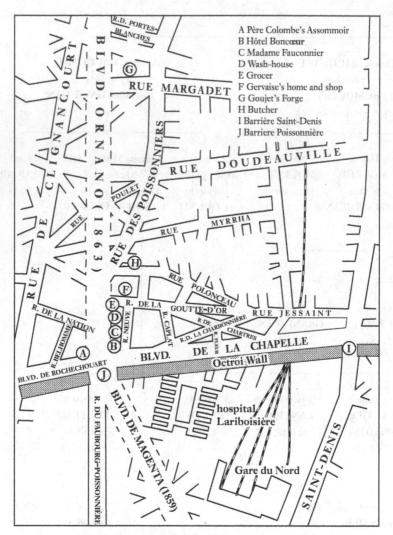

A Père Colombe's Assommoir
B Hôtel Boncœur
C Madame Fauconnier
D Wash-house
E Grocer
F Gervaise's home and shop
G Goujet's Forge
H Butcher
I Barrière Saint-Denis
J Barrière Poissonnière

Street-plan of the setting of L'Assommoir

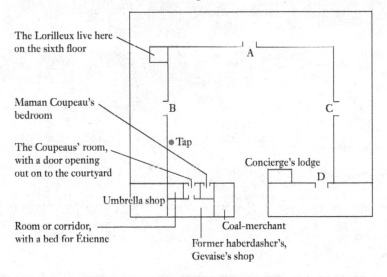

The Lorilleux live here
on the sixth floor

Maman Coupeau's
bedroom

The Coupeaus' room,
with a door opening
out on to the courtyard

Umbrella shop

Room or corridor,
with a bed for Étienne

Tap

A

B

C

Concierge's lodge

D

Coal-merchant

Former haberdasher's,
Gevaise's shop

Zola's plan for the building in the Rue de la Goutte-d'Or

THE ASSOMMOIR

PREFACE

THE Rougon-Macquart series will be made up of twenty novels. The overall plan was settled in 1869, and I am following it with the utmost rigour. *The Assommoir* has come at its appointed time, and I have written it, as I shall write the remaining novels, without deviating in the slightest from my course. Therein lies my strength. I have a goal before me.

When *The Assommoir* was serialized in a newspaper, it was attacked with unprecedented ferocity, denounced, and charged with all manner of crimes. Do I really need to explain here, in these few lines, what my authorial intentions were? I wanted to depict the inexorable downfall of a working-class family in the poisonous atmosphere of our city slums. Alcoholism and idleness lead to a weakening of family ties, to the filth of promiscuity, to the progressive loss of decent feelings, and ultimately to degradation and death. It is simply morality in action.

The Assommoir is without doubt the most moral of my books. I have often had occasion to write about far more horrifying social sores. It is the novel's form that has shocked people. People have taken exception to the words. My crime is to have had the literary curiosity to gather together the language of the common people and present it in a carefully fashioned mould. Yes indeed, the novel's form—there lies my great crime! Yet there are dictionaries of this language, scholars study it and savour its richness and its powerful, striking imagery. It is a treasure-house for linguistic researchers. But even so, no one has understood that my aim was to engage in a purely philological exercise, which I believe to be of great historical and social interest.

In any case I am not defending myself. My novel will be my defence. It is a work of truth, the first novel about the common people that does not lie and that has the authentic smell of the people. And readers should not conclude that the people as a whole are bad, for my characters are not bad, but only ignorant and brought low by the conditions of sweated toil and poverty in which they live. All I ask is that my novels be read, understood, and seen clearly in their context, before they are subjected to the ready-made, grotesque, and odious judgements that are circulating about me and my works. If only people knew how my friends laugh at the incredible stories about me that are fed to the masses! If only they knew that the fearsome, blood-thirsty novelist is in fact a respectable bourgeois, devoted to learning and art, living in quiet seclusion, and whose sole ambition is to leave behind as great and as vital a body of work as he can! I will deny none of the stories about me, I will simply go on writing, trusting that time and the good faith of the public will finally disinter me from all the rubbish that has been heaped upon me.

Émile Zola

Paris, 1 January 1877

CHAPTER I

GERVAISE had waited up for Lantier until two in the morning. Then, shivering all over from sitting half undressed in the cold air from the window, she'd slumped across the bed, feeling feverish, her cheeks wet with tears. For a week now, when they came out of the Veau à Deux Têtes,* where they had their meals, he'd sent her home to bed with the children and not come in himself until the early hours, saying he'd been looking for a job. That particular evening, as she was looking out for him, she thought she saw him go into the Grand-Balcon* dance hall, whose ten blazing windows lit up the black expanse of the outer boulevards* with a sheet of flame, and she'd caught sight of little Adèle, a metal polisher who ate at their restaurant, five or six paces behind him, her hands dangling as if she'd just let go of his arm so they wouldn't be seen together in the glaring lights of the doorway.

When Gervaise woke up at about five o'clock, stiff and aching, she began to sob. Lantier hadn't come back. It was the first time he'd stayed out all night. She sat on the edge of the bed, under the faded strip of chintz hanging from a rod tied to the ceiling with string. And slowly, her eyes misty with tears, she looked round the wretched furnished room, at the walnut chest with one drawer missing, at the three wicker chairs and the grease-stained little table which had a chipped water jug standing on it. An iron bedstead, brought in for the children, blocked the chest and took up two-thirds of the room. Gervaise and Lantier's trunk lay wide open in a corner, completely empty except for an old hat of his right at the bottom, under a pile of dirty shirts and socks; while hanging over the furniture against the walls were a tattered shawl and a muddy pair of trousers, their last remaining things that even the old-clothes dealers wouldn't touch. In the middle of the mantelpiece, between two zinc candlesticks that didn't match, was a bundle of pale pink pawn tickets. It was the best room in the hotel, on the first floor at the front, looking out over the boulevard.

Meanwhile, the two children remained fast asleep, side by side on the same pillow. Claude, who was eight, was breathing gently, his hands on top of the blanket, while Étienne,* who was only four, lay smiling, one arm round his brother's neck. When their mother's

tear-filled eyes fell on them, she began to cry again and pressed
a handkerchief to her mouth to stifle her sobs. Barefoot, without
thinking of putting her slippers on, she went back to the window and
resumed her vigil, leaning on the sill and looking down the road into
the distance.

The hotel stood on the Boulevard de la Chapelle, to the left of the
Barrière Poissonnière.* It was a ramshackle two-storey building,
painted reddish purple up to the second floor, its shutters rotted by
the rain. Above a lantern with cracked glass you could just make out,
between the two windows, the inscription *Hôtel Boncœur,** *prop.*
Marsoullier, in big yellow letters, bits of which had crumbled away
with the damp plaster. The lantern restricted Gervaise's view, so she
straightened up, still holding the handkerchief to her lips. She looked
to the right, towards the Boulevard de Rochechouart, where butchers
in bloodstained aprons were standing about in groups in front of the
slaughterhouses, and from time to time, on the cool breeze, a foul
smell wafted up, the acrid stench of slaughtered animals. To the left
her eyes followed a long stretch of avenue and came to rest almost
opposite, at the white mass of the Lariboisière hospital,* then still
being built. Slowly, from one end of the horizon to the other, her gaze
followed the boundary wall,* behind which, at night, she sometimes
heard the screams of people being murdered; and she stared into its
secluded recesses and dark corners, black with damp and filth, afraid
she would suddenly see Lantier's body lying there, his belly gaping
open with knife wounds. When she looked up, beyond the endless
grey wall that encircled the city, with its strip of wasteland, she saw
a great glow, the golden dust of sunlight already filled with the early-
morning sounds of the city. But her gaze kept returning to the Barrière
Poissonnière, and she craned her neck, becoming slightly dizzy as she
watched an endless stream of men, horses, and carts flowing down
from the heights of Montmartre and La Chapelle* through the two
squat tollbooths. It was like the trampling of a herd of cattle, this mob
that spread out across the roadway whenever there was a sudden stop-
page, this constant procession of men on their way to work, their tool-
bags on their backs and their loaves under their arms, a throng that
poured past and was swallowed up by the city. Thinking she recognized Lantier in the crowd, Gervaise leaned further out, at the risk of
falling; then she pressed her handkerchief harder against her lips, as
if to hold back her pain.

A cheerful young voice made her come away from the window.
'The boss not 'ere, Madame Lantier?'

'No, Monsieur Coupeau, he isn't,' she replied, trying to smile.

He was a roofer who had a little ten-franc room on the top floor.
His toolbag was slung over his shoulder. Seeing the key in the door,
he'd come in to say hello.

'I'm working over at the hospital now, you know,' he went on. 'Nice
May weather we're 'avin'! A bit nippy this mornin', though.'

He looked at Gervaise's red, tear-stained face. When he saw that
the bed hadn't been slept in he gently shook his head; then he went
over to where the boys, with their pink, cherubic faces, lay sleeping,
and said softly:

'Well, well, so the boss is misbehavin', is he? Never mind, don't get
too upset, Madame Lantier. He's really into politics; the other day,
when they all voted for Eugène Sue*—a good bloke, so they say—he
nearly went crazy. It's more than likely he's spent the night with some
mates pullin' that bastard Bonaparte* to pieces.'

'No, no,' she forced herself to murmur. 'It's not what you think.
I know where he is... We've got our problems, like everyone else, for
goodness' sake.'

Coupeau winked, to show he wasn't taken in by this lie, and he left,
offering to fetch her milk if she didn't want to go out; she was a lovely
woman, a fine woman, and she could count on him if she was ever in
trouble. As soon as he'd gone, Gervaise went back to the window.

The herd was still trampling past the barrier in the chilly morning
air. The locksmiths could be recognized by their blue smocks, the
bricklayers by their white overalls, the house-painters by their coats,
with their long smocks showing underneath. From a distance the
crowd was a chalky blur, a neutral shade, made up mainly of faded
blue and dingy grey. Now and then a workman would stop and relight
his pipe, while around him the others walked on, with never a smile,
never a word to a mate, their cheeks sallow, their faces straining
towards Paris, which swallowed them up, one by one, through the
gaping jaws of the Faubourg-Poissonnière.* All the same, some of
them did slow down at both corners of the Rue des Poissonniers, in
front of two bars where the shutters were being taken down; but,
before going in, they stood around for a while on the pavement, casting sidelong glances in the direction of the city, their arms dangling
by their sides, succumbing already to the idea of taking a day off work.

Inside, at the counters, groups were already buying each other rounds, milling about, filling up the bars, spitting, coughing, rinsing their throats with tots of spirits.

Gervaise was keeping an eye on Père Colombe's bar, on the left side of the street, where she thought she'd spotted Lantier, when a fat woman in an apron, without a hat, called up to her from the middle of the road.

'Hey, Madame Lantier! You're up early!'

Gervaise leaned out.

'Oh, it's you, Madame Boche! Yes, I've got a lot to do today!'

'I know, I know. The work doesn't do itself, does it?'

A conversation started up between window and pavement. Madame Boche was concierge of the building in which the Veau à Deux Têtes restaurant occupied the ground floor. Several times Gervaise had waited for Lantier in her lodge, so as not to have to sit at a table alone with all those men having their dinner around her. The concierge said she was just popping over to the Rue de la Charbonnière, to catch a certain tailor before he got up—because her husband couldn't get him to mend the frock coat he'd left with him. Then she went on about one of her tenants who'd brought a woman back with him the night before and kept everybody awake until three in the morning. As she chatted, she stared at Gervaise with intense curiosity; and she gave the impression that she'd come and stationed herself there, under the window, with the sole purpose of finding something out.

'Is Monsieur Lantier still in bed, then?' she suddenly asked.

'Yes, he's asleep,' Gervaise replied, but she couldn't help blushing.

Madame Boche saw the tears welling up again in Gervaise's eyes and, satisfied no doubt, was going on her way, saying what lazy sods men were, when she turned round and shouted:

'It's your morning for the washing, isn't it? I've got some stuff to wash too. I'll keep a place for you, so we can have a chat.'

Then, as if suddenly feeling sorry for Gervaise, she added:

'You poor thing, you shouldn't stay there like that, you'll catch your death… You're blue with cold!'

But Gervaise stayed glued to the window for two more deadly hours, until eight o'clock. The shops had opened. The stream of smocks coming down from the heights had dried up, and only a few latecomers were now striding past the barrier. The same men were still standing in the bars, drinking, coughing, spitting. The workmen had been followed by the girls—metal polishers, milliners, florists—shivering in their flimsy dresses as they trotted along the outer boulevards; they came in groups of three or four, chattering gaily, giggling, and casting bright-eyed glances around them; now and then there would be one by herself, thin, pale, and serious-looking, keeping close to the boundary wall so as to avoid the streams of muck. Next came the office workers, blowing on their fingers and eating their little rolls as they walked: skinny young men, in clothes they'd outgrown, with rings round their bleary eyes, or else little old men tottering along, their faces pale and worn from long hours at their desks, checking their watches so as to time their arrival to the second. Eventually the boulevards resumed their morning calm: the well-to-do men in the neighbourhood strolled about in the sun; mothers, hatless and in dirty skirts, rocked their babies in their arms or changed their nappies on the benches; and a swarm of scruffy, snotty-nosed kids played about, fighting and rolling on the ground, squealing, laughing, or crying. Gervaise felt she was suffocating, fainting with anxiety, all hope gone; it seemed to her that it was all over, this was the end, Lantier would never come back. Her vacant gaze wandered from the old slaughterhouses, black and stinking of blood, to the pale new hospital where, through the gaping holes soon to be rows of windows, she could see empty wards where death would come to claim its victims. She was dazzled by the brilliance of the sky opposite, behind the boundary wall, as the sun rose higher and higher over the vast awakening of Paris.

She was sitting on a chair, her hands on her lap, no longer crying, when Lantier calmly walked through the door.

'You're back!' she cried, trying to throw her arms round him.

'Yes, I'm back. What about it?' he replied. 'You're not going to make a silly fuss again, are you?'

He pushed her aside and, in a gesture of annoyance, tossed his black felt hat on to the chest of drawers. He was twenty-six, short, very dark and good-looking, with a little moustache which he had a habit of constantly twirling. He was wearing a workman's overall and a shabby old frock coat taken in at the waist, and he spoke with a strong Provençal accent.*

Gervaise slumped back on to her chair and began to complain gently, in disjointed little phrases:

'I couldn't sleep a wink. I thought something must have happened to you. Where were you? Where did you spend the night? For God's sake, don't do that again, I'll go mad... Auguste, tell me where you were.'

'I was busy, bugger it!' he said, shrugging his shoulders. 'It was eight when I got to that friend of mine at La Glacière,* the bloke who's going to set up a hat factory. I was there for quite a while, so I thought I'd better stay over... But I don't like all this nosey-parkering, just leave me alone!'

She began to cry again. Lantier's raised voice and violent gestures, knocking over the chairs, woke up the boys. They sat up, half naked, pushing their hair back with their little hands; hearing their mother crying, they began to howl, crying like Gervaise even though they had hardly opened their eyes.

'Ah, the concert's starting!' Lantier shouted furiously. 'I'm warning you, I'll clear out, and this time it'll be for good. Just shut up! Right, that's it. I'm going back where I came from.'

He'd already picked up his hat from the chest of drawers. But Gervaise sprang forward, stammering:

'No, no!'

She managed to quieten the boys, stroking their tears away. She kissed their hair and reassured them with a few loving words. They calmed down at once and started to play around on their pillow, pinching each other and giggling. In the meantime their father had flung himself on the bed without even taking his boots off; he looked dead-beat, his face blotchy from a sleepless night. But instead of falling asleep, he lay there with his eyes wide open, gazing round the room.

'What a dump!' he muttered.

Then, after looking at Gervaise for a moment, he added nastily:

'So you've stopped washin' yourself, 'ave you?'

Gervaise was only twenty-two. She was tall and slim, with delicate features, but already looked quite drawn because of her stressful life. With her hair uncombed, her feet in slippers, and shivering in her white shift marked with dust and grime from the furniture, she looked ten years older, thanks to the hours she'd spent in anguish and tears. Lantier's remark jolted her out of her state of timorous resignation.

'That's not fair,' she said, with some spirit. 'You know very well I do my best. It's not my fault we've ended up here. I'd like to see how you'd manage in one room, with the two kids to look after, without even a stove so we can have hot water. When we got to Paris, instead of frittering your money away, you should have fixed us up some-where straight away, like you promised.'

'I like that!' he shouted. 'You did your bit to get through the dosh, same as me; it's a bit rich to start complaining 'cos we had a good time together!'

But she went on, as if she hadn't heard him:

'Anyway, if we stick at it, we might still be able to get on top of things. I went to see Madame Fauconnier last night, the woman who's got the laundry in the Rue Neuve; she's taking me on from Monday. If you go in with your friend at La Glacière, we'll be back on our feet in six months, then we can get some decent clothes and rent some sort of place we can call home. But we'll have to work hard, really hard...'

Lantier turned his face to the wall, with a bored expression. This infuriated Gervaise.

'Yeah, that's right, everybody knows you'll never die of hard work. You've got big ideas, you'd like to be got up like a gentleman and parade about with tarts in silk skirts. That's right, isn't it? You don't think I look good enough, now you've made me pawn all my dresses. Listen, Auguste, I didn't want to talk about it, I would've waited a bit, but I know where you were last night: I saw you go into the Grand-Balcon with that bitch Adèle. You bloody well know how to choose them! She's a right one, she is! No wonder she shows off... She's slept with the whole restaurant.'

Lantier leapt up from the bed. His eyes were as black as ink in his pale face. He was not a big man, but he had a huge temper.

'Yes, yes, the whole restaurant!' Gervaise repeated. 'Madame Boche is going to kick 'em both out, her and her beanpole sister, because there's always a queue of men on the stairs.'

Lantier raised his fist; then, resisting the urge to hit her, he grabbed her by the arm and shook her violently, making her fall on the boys' bed. They started bawling afresh. And he lay down again, muttering darkly like a man who had finally made up his mind about something:

'You don't know what you've just done, Gervaise. You've made a big mistake. You'll see.'

The boys went on crying for a minute or two. Their mother, still bent over the bed, held them both in her arms, saying over and over in a monotonous voice:

'You poor little things, if it wasn't for you, if it wasn't for you, if it wasn't for you!...'

Lantier lay quietly, no longer listening, his gaze fixed on the strip of faded chintz above his head, lost in his thoughts. Although his eyelids were heavy with tiredness, he stayed like that for nearly an hour without falling asleep. When he turned over and propped himself on his elbow, with a hard, determined look on his face, Gervaise had nearly finished tidying the room. She was making the boys' bed after getting them up and dressing them. He watched her sweep the floor and dust the furniture; the room still looked dark and depressing, with its smoke-blackened ceiling, its wallpaper peeling off with damp, its three rickety chairs and chest of drawers on which her duster only caked and spread the grime. Then, while she was having a good wash, after pinning up her hair in front of the little round mirror that hung from the window catch and which he used for shaving, he seemed to be studying her bare arms and neck, and all the other bare parts of her he could see, as if making mental comparisons. He curled his lip in distaste. Gervaise limped with the right leg, but it could hardly be noticed except when she was tired and her hips ached. That morning, completely exhausted after the night she'd had, she was dragging her leg and leaning against the walls for support.

Silence reigned; not a word more had been spoken. He seemed to be waiting for something, while she, utterly miserable, bustled about trying to look unconcerned. As she was making a bundle of some dirty clothes which had been thrown into a corner behind the trunk, he opened his mouth at last and asked:

'What are you doing? Where are you going?'

At first she didn't reply. Then, when he angrily repeated the question, she replied:

'You can see full well, can't you? I'm going to wash all this. The kids can't live in a pigsty.'

He let her pick up two or three handkerchiefs, and then, after another silence, went on:

'Have you got any money?'

This made her straighten up and look him in the face, still holding the boys' dirty shirts.

'Money? Where on earth do you think I might've pinched some? You know very well I got three francs the day before yesterday on my black skirt. We've had two meals out of that, and it doesn't go very far at the butcher's. Of course I haven't got any money. I've got four sous* for the wash-house. I don't earn money the way some women do.'

He took no notice of this pointed remark, but got off the bed and inspected the few miserable rags hanging round the room. He took down the trousers and the shawl, opened the drawers, and added a nightdress and two women's chemises to the pile, then tossed the whole lot into Gervaise's arms.

'There you are, you can pawn those.'

'Do you want me to pawn the kids as well?' she asked. 'If they'd give us somethin' for the kids, that'd be a big load off our backs, wouldn't it!'

All the same, she did go to the pawnshop. When she came back, half an hour later, she put five francs on the mantelpiece and added the pawn ticket to the others, between the two candlesticks.

'That's all they'd give me,' she said. 'I asked for six, but there was no way. They'll never run out of money, that's for sure. And there's always a crowd there!'

Lantier didn't take the five-franc piece right away. He would have liked there to be some change, so he could leave her something. But when he saw the remains of some ham wrapped in paper and a scrap of bread on the chest of drawers, he made up his mind and slipped the coin into his waistcoat pocket.

'I didn't go for the milk, because we owe them a week,' Gervaise added. 'But I'll be back soon, and while I'm gone you can fetch some bread and some cooked chops and we'll have lunch. Get a bottle of wine as well.'

He didn't say no. Peace seemed restored. Gervaise finished making up the bundle of dirty clothes. But when she was about to take Lantier's shirts and socks from the bottom of the trunk, he shouted at her to leave them alone.

'Don't touch my stuff! I don't want 'em to go!'

'What d'you mean, you don't want 'em to go!' she exclaimed, straightening up. 'Surely you're not thinking of putting these filthy things on again? They need washin'.'

She stared at him anxiously and saw the same hard look on the young man's handsome face, as if nothing would ever soften it again. Losing his temper, he snatched the clothes out of her hands and threw them back into the trunk.

'Do as I say for once, damn it! I said I don't want 'em to go.'

'But why?' She turned pale as a dreadful suspicion began to dawn on her. 'You don't need your shirts right now, you're not going anywhere. So why can't I take 'em?'

He hesitated for a moment, put out by the blazing look in her eyes.

'Why? Why? Because—bloody hell!—you'll go around telling people you look after me, that you do all my washin' and mendin'. Well, I can't stand that. You look after your things, I'll look after mine. Washerwomen expect to be paid, anyway.'

She begged him, protesting she'd never complained, but he slammed the trunk shut and sat on it, shouting 'No!' in her face. He could do what he liked with his own clothes, couldn't he? Then, to avoid her gaze, he went back to the bed and lay down, saying he was sleepy and she should stop bothering him. This time he really did seem to fall asleep.

For a moment Gervaise hesitated. She felt tempted to kick the bundle of washing out of the way and sit down and sew. But Lantier's steady breathing reassured her. She picked up the bluing ball* and the piece of soap left from her last wash, went over to the boys, who were playing quietly by the window with some old corks, kissed them, and whispered:

'Be very good now, and don't make any noise. Papa's asleep.'

As she left, the only sound breaking the deep silence beneath the blackened ceiling was the gentle laughter of Claude and Étienne. It was ten o'clock. A ray of sunlight was coming in through the half-open window.

On the boulevard Gervaise turned left and went down the Rue Neuve de la Goutte-d'Or. She nodded to Madame Fauconnier as she passed her shop. The wash-house was about halfway along, at the point where the street began to go uphill. On top of a flat-roofed building were three huge water tanks, cylinders of grey, galvanized metal studded with rivets, while behind them rose the drying-room, a lofty second storey enclosed on all sides by narrow-slatted shutters for the air to blow through, and behind which items of clothing could be seen drying on brass wires. To the right of the tanks, the narrow pipe from the boiler puffed out white steam in noisy, regular jets. Without hitching up her skirts—for she was used to puddles— Gervaise went in through a doorway cluttered with big jars of bleach. She already knew the manageress, a frail-looking woman with sore eyes who sat in a glass booth with ledgers in front of her, bars of soap on shelves behind her, together with bluing balls in bottles and pound packets of bicarbonate of soda. As she went past, Gervaise asked for her wooden beater and scrubbing brush, which she'd left there after her last wash. Then she took her number and went in.

The wash-house was an immense shed with a flat roof, exposed beams resting on cast-iron pillars, and big clear-glass windows. Pale daylight filtered through the hot steam hanging in the air like a milky fog. Clouds of vapour rose up here and there and spread out, their bluish haze blotting out the far distance. Everywhere there was a clinging dampness, like fine rain, heavy with the smell of soap, a stale, dank, persistent smell sharpened at times by a whiff of bleach. Standing at the washboards along each side of the central aisle were rows of women, their sleeves rolled right up to their shoulders, their necks bare, their skirts hitched up, showing their coloured stockings and heavy laced boots. They were beating away like mad, laughing, leaning back to yell something above the din, then bending forward again over their tubs, a foul-mouthed, rough, ungainly lot, soaked through as if they'd been caught in a downpour, their skin red and steaming. All round and under them water was slopping about, hot water from buckets carried over and tipped out in one go, cold water from taps left on and pissing away, splashes from beaters, drips from washing already rinsed, and the puddles they were standing in trickling away in rivulets over the uneven stone floor. And, amid the shouting, the rhythmic thumping, the soft patter of rain—this storm of noise muffled by the wet ceiling—the boiler, over to the right, covered with a fine dew, completely white, panted and snorted continuously, as if the frenzied vibration of its fly-wheel was regulating the whole monstrous uproar.

Gervaise made her way slowly down the aisle, glancing to left and right. Her bundle of washing, slung over one arm, made one hip higher than the other, so that her limp was more pronounced than usual as she wended her way through the throng of women as they rushed around, jostling her as they did so.

'Come over 'ere, love!' bellowed Madame Boche.

When Gervaise had joined her at the far end on the left, the concierge, who was furiously rubbing a sock, began talking in snatches without stopping what she was doing.

'Get in 'ere, I've kept a place for you. This won't take long. Boche hardly dirties his things. What about you? You won't be too long

either, will you? You haven't got much there. We'll be done by twelve
and then we can go and get a bite to eat... I used to take my stuff to
a laundress in the Rue Poulet, but she ruined everything with all her
bleaching and scrubbing. So now I do it meself. And it saves money.
I only 'ave to pay for the soap... You should 'ave put those shirts to
soak, you know. Those kids of yours are little terrors, they must've sat
in some soot.'

Gervaise was undoing her bundle and spreading out the boys'
shirts; and when Madame Boche advised her to get a bucket of soda
she replied:

'No, hot water will do. I know a thing or two about washin' clothes.'

She'd sorted out the washing and put the few coloured things to
one side. After filling her tub with four buckets of cold water from the
tap behind her, she threw in all the white things; then, hitching up her
skirt and tucking it between her thighs, she got into a sort of upright
box which came up to her waist.

'So you know about washin', eh?' echoed Madame Boche. 'You
were a laundress back 'ome, weren't you, love?'

Gervaise had rolled up her sleeves, revealing her lovely fair-skinned
arms, which were still the arms of a young woman, hardly reddened
at the elbows. She set about getting the dirt out of her things. She
spread a shirt out on the narrow washboard, which had become worn
and whitened by the constant action of the water; she soaped it,
turned it, then rubbed it on the other side.

Before answering, she grabbed her beater and started banging
away, so that her words came out as shouts, punctuated by heavy,
rhythmic blows.

'Yes, that's right, laundress... Since I was ten... Twelve years ago...
We'd go down to the river... It smelt better than it does 'ere...
You should've seen it, a spot under the trees... With clear running
water... You know, in Plassans*... Don't you know Plassans?... Near
Marseilles?'

'You don't 'alf go at it!' exclaimed Madame Boche, amazed at the
energy Gervaise was putting into her beating. 'Bloody hell! I bet you
could straighten an iron bar with those ladylike arms of yours!'

They went on talking at the top of their voices. From time to time
the concierge had to lean over to hear what Gervaise was saying. Soon
all the whites had been beaten out completely. Gervaise plunged the
clothes back into the tub, then took them out one by one for a second

soaping and scrubbing. With one hand she held a garment on the washboard, while with the other she used a short scrubbing brush, which produced dirty froth that fell to the ground in long dribbles. Then, as the scrubbing made less noise, they moved closer together and began to talk more intimately.

'No, we're not married,' Gervaise said. 'I don't make a secret of it. Lantier's not such a nice bloke that you'd want to be married to 'im. If it wasn't for the kids... I was fourteen and he was eighteen when we 'ad the first one. The other one came along four years later... The usual story, you know 'ow it is. I wasn't happy at 'ome, and Macquart, my dad, would give me a kick up the backside as soon as look at me. When it's like that, you look around for a bit of fun, don't you? We might've got married, but for some reason our parents weren't keen.'

She shook her hands, which were getting red in the white suds.

'This Paris water is so 'ard.'

By now, Madame Boche was washing half-heartedly. She kept stopping, taking her time over the soaping so she could stay and listen to the whole story, which she'd been dying to hear for the past two weeks. Her mouth hung half open in her fat, round face; her goggle eyes shone with curiosity. Pleased at having guessed right, she was thinking:

'Yes, I was right, she can't help talkin': they've had a row.'

Then she said out loud:

'So he's not very nice to you?'

'Don't talk to me about it!' replied Gervaise. 'Back 'ome he was all right, but since we've been in Paris I don't know what's got into 'im... The thing is, his mother died last year and left 'im some money, about seventeen hundred francs. After that he wanted to go to Paris. So, seein' as old Macquart was still knocking me about whenever he felt like it, I agreed to go with 'im; so we came up with the two kiddies. He was goin' to set me up as a laundress and work at his own trade as a hatter. We'd 'ave been all right that way. But, you see, Lantier has got big ideas, he can't 'elp spendin' money, all he thinks about is 'avin' a good time. That's all he's good for!... The first place we went to was the Hôtel Montmartre, in the Rue Montmartre;* there were dinners and cabs and visits to the theatre, a watch for 'im and a silk dress for me, because he's not a bad sort when he's in the money. He really went to town, and after two months we were cleaned out. That's when we moved to the Hôtel Boncœur and this rotten life began...'

She suddenly stopped short, with a lump in her throat, fighting back her tears. She'd finished scrubbing her things.

'I've got to get me hot water,' she muttered.

But Madame Boche, much put out by this interruption in the flow of confidences, called out to the laundry boy, who was just passing.

'Charles, sweetie, be a dear and fetch this lady a bucket of hot water. She's in a hurry.'

The boy took the bucket and brought it back full. Gervaise paid him—it was one sou a bucket. She poured the hot water into the tub and soaped the washing one last time with her hands, bending over the washboard in a cloud of steam that clung in grey threads to her golden hair.

'Put some crystals in, I've got some 'ere,' said the concierge obligingly, and she emptied the remains of a bag of soda, which she'd brought with her, into Gervaise's tub. She also offered her some bleach, but Gervaise refused, saying it was only good for grease spots and wine stains.

'I bet he's a bit of a ladies' man,' Madame Boche went on, returning to the subject of Lantier without mentioning him by name.

Gervaise, bent double, her clenched hands deep in the washing, merely shook her head.

'Oh yes,' the concierge persisted. 'I've noticed several little things...'

But when Gervaise, white in the face, suddenly straightened up and stared at her, she corrected herself:

'Oh, I don't really know anythin'. He likes a laugh, I think, that's all... Those two girls in our building, Adèle and Virginie, you know the ones, he likes to 'ave a joke with them, but that's all there is to it, I'm sure.'

Gervaise stood looking at her, her face covered in sweat and her arms dripping wet; her gaze didn't waver. The concierge, annoyed, thumped her chest and gave her word of honour.

'I don't know a thing, I swear!'

Then, calming down, she added in soothing tones, as if speaking to someone who just wants to be humoured:

'If you ask me, I think he's got an 'onest look about him. He'll marry you, love, I'm sure he will!'

Gervaise wiped her forehead with her wet hand. Then she took another piece of washing out of the tub, shaking her head again. For a moment, both were silent. Around them, the wash-house had gone quiet. It was striking eleven. Half the women were perched on the edge of their tubs, an open bottle of wine at their feet, eating sausage in chunks of bread. Only the housewives who'd come to do the family smalls were busy working, with one eye on the clock hanging above the office. Now and again there was the thump of a beater, amid the slightly hushed laughing and chatting muffled by the greedy chomping of jaws, while the shaking and snorting of the boiler went on and on, without rest or pause, and became louder and louder until it seemed to fill the whole vast shed. But not one of the women noticed it; it was, so to speak, the respiratory system of the wash-house, its hot breath collecting under the rafters in an eternal floating mist. The heat was becoming unbearable; through the high windows on the left, rays of sunlight streamed in, lighting up the steamy vapour with opalescent streaks of soft greyish pinks and blues. People were beginning to complain, so the boy Charles went from window to window and pulled down the thick canvas blinds, then crossed to the other side, the shady side, and opened some fan-lights. This was greeted by cheering and a round of applause. A great wave of merriment went round the place. Soon, however, even the last few beaters stopped. The women, their mouths full, were still, except to make an occasional movement with the open knives they were holding. The silence was so complete that you could hear, at the far end, the regular scraping of the stoker's shovel as he scooped up the coal and threw it into the big stove that fed the boiler.

Meanwhile Gervaise was washing her coloured things in the hot soapy water she'd saved. When she'd finished she drew up a trestle and threw all the clothes over it; they made bluish puddles on the ground. Then she began to wring them out. Behind her the cold-water tap ran into a huge tub fixed to the floor, with two wooden bars across it for the clothes. High above the tub were two other bars where things could be left to finish dripping.

'We're nearly done, thank goodness,' said Madame Boche. 'I'll stay and give you a hand with the wringing.'

'Oh, don't bother, thanks,' Gervaise replied as she dipped the coloured things in the clean water and squeezed them. If I 'ad some sheets, though, I wouldn't say no.'

But all the same she had to accept the concierge's help. Together, each holding one end, they were wringing out a skirt, a badly dyed brown wool thing, from which came a stream of yellowish water, when Madame Boche exclaimed:

'Well, look who's here! It's that beanpole Virginie. What's she up to, comin' 'ere with her piddlin' bits of washing done up in a hanky?'

Gervaise looked up quickly. Virginie and she were the same age but Virginie was taller, dark and pretty despite being a bit long in the face. She was wearing an old black dress with flounces, and a red ribbon round her neck; and her hair was carefully done in a bun in a blue chenille net. She paused for a moment in the middle of the central aisle, screwing up her eyes as if looking for somebody; then, seeing Gervaise, she passed close by with an insolent look in her eyes, her nose in the air and swaying her hips, and took up a position in the same row, five tubs away.

'What on earth has got into her!' Madame Boche went on, lowering her voice. 'She's never even washed a pair of cuffs. She's a lazy one, I can tell you! A seamstress who can't so much as sew a button on! And her sister's just the same—the metal polisher, that slut Adèle, who skips work two days out of three. They've got no mother or father as anyone knows about, and what they live on's a mystery, though I could tell you a thing or two... What's she rubbing away at over there? A petticoat? It looks filthy. I bet it could tell a few stories!'

It was clear Madame Boche was trying to be agreeable to Gervaise. The truth was that she often had coffee with Adèle and Virginie, when the girls had a bit of money. Gervaise said nothing, but hurried on, her hands working feverishly. She'd just prepared her bluing in a little three-legged tub. Now she was soaking her whites, stirring them round in the tinted water, which had taken on an almost crimson sheen in the reflections of the light; then, wringing them gently, she hung them over the wooden bars above. All the time she was doing this, she made a point of keeping her back to Virginie. But she could hear her tittering and sensed her sidelong glances. Virginie seemed to have come just to annoy her. When Gervaise happened to turn round for a moment, they both stared at one another.

'Don't take any notice of her,' muttered Madame Boche. 'You're not going to start pullin' each other's hair out, I hope? There's nothing goin' on, I tell you! She's not the one!'

At that moment, as Gervaise was hanging up the last piece of clothing, the sound of laughter came from the entrance to the wash-house.

'There's two kids 'ere askin' for their mum,' shouted Charles.

All the women turned to look. Gervaise saw it was Claude and Étienne. The moment they caught sight of her they ran through the puddles towards her, their shoes untied and their heels clattering on the flagstones. Claude, the elder one, was holding his little brother by the hand. As they went past, the women uttered little cries of affection, touched to see them looking rather scared but smiling all the same. They stopped in front of their mother, still holding each other by the hand, and lifted their little blond heads.

'Did Papa send you?' asked Gervaise.

But as she bent down to tie Étienne's shoelaces, she saw their room key with its brass tag swinging from Claude's finger.

'What's this? You've brought the key!' she exclaimed, very surprised. 'What for?'

The child glanced down, as if remembering the key, which he seemed to have forgotten, and said in a loud, clear voice:

'Papa's gone.'

'Has he gone out to buy somethin' to eat, and told you to come and get me?'

Claude looked at his brother and hesitated, not knowing what to say. Then he went on, all in one breath:

'Papa's gone. He jumped out of bed, put all his things in the trunk, and took the trunk down to a cab. He's gone.'

Gervaise, who was crouching down, stood up slowly, very white, and pressed her hands to her cheeks and temples as if she could feel her head exploding. All she could find to say, over and over, was:

'Oh, my God!... Oh, my God!... Oh, my God!'

Madame Boche, meanwhile, delighted to find herself mixed up in this affair, was questioning the child in her turn:

'Come on, darlin', tell us all about it. He shut the door and told you to bring the key, did he?'

Then she whispered in Claude's ear:

'Was there a lady in the cab?'

The child looked confused again. Then, triumphantly, he repeated his story from the beginning:

'Papa's gone. He jumped out of bed, put all his things in the trunk, and took the trunk down to a cab. He's gone.'

At this, Madame Boche gave up, whereupon he dragged his brother to the tap and they started to play with it, turning it on and off.

Gervaise was beyond tears. Gasping, she leaned against her tub with her face in her hands. She kept giving little shudders and now and again heaved a deep sigh, pressing her fists harder against her eyes, as if she wanted to plunge deeper into the darkness of her abandonment. She felt she was falling into a huge, black pit.

'Come on, duckie, what the hell!' murmured Madame Boche.

'If you only knew! If you only knew!' she said at last in a whisper. 'He sent me to the pawnshop this morning with my shawl and chemises, so he could pay for that cab...'

She began to cry. The thought of her trip to the pawnshop released the tears she'd been holding back. That trip was an abomination, the thing that hurt most. The tears ran down her chin, already wet from her hands, but she never thought of using her handkerchief.

'Come on, hush, pull yourself together, they're all lookin',' said Madame Boche, fussing round her. 'How can you get so upset over a man? Are you still in love with 'im, you poor thing? A minute ago you were really mad at 'im, and now look at you, cryin' your eyes out over 'im! My God, what fools we women are!'

Then she became all maternal.

'A pretty little thing like you, if I may say so!... I can tell you everything now, can't I? You remember how I came past your window earlier? Well, I had my suspicions then. Because, last night, when Adèle came in, I heard a man's footsteps too. I wanted to know who it was, so I looked up the stairs. Whoever it was was already on the second floor, but it was definitely Monsieur Lantier's coat I saw. This morning Boche kept a lookout and saw him come down as cool as a cucumber. He'd been with Adèle, you understand. Virginie's got a gentleman friend now, who she goes to see twice a week. Still, it's not decent—they've only got the one room and an alcove, so I can't imagine where Virginie could've slept.'

She paused for a moment and looked round, then went on in her coarse, husky voice:

'Look at that nasty bitch over there, she's laughin' because you're cryin'. I bet you anythin' that washin' of hers is just an excuse. She packed the other two off and came here so she can tell 'em how you're takin' it.'

Gervaise took her hands away from her face and looked. When she saw Virginie with three or four women round her, whispering and staring in her direction, she went mad with rage. Trembling all over, she turned and reached down, groping on the ground, until she found a full bucket of water, grabbed it with both hands, and hurled the contents at Virginie.

'You bitch!' cried Virginie, jumping back, so that only her shoes were splashed. By now the whole wash-house, all agog since Gervaise had started crying, had crowded round to see the fight. Some, still munching their bread, climbed up on to the tubs, while others came running with their hands covered in soapsuds. A circle formed.

'The bitch!' repeated Virginie. 'What's got into her? She's gone nuts!'

Gervaise stood still, her chin thrust out and her face contorted. She said nothing, not having learned how to deal in insults like a Parisian. Virginie went on:

'Look at her. She's tired of bein' screwed in the country... the soldiers used her as a mattress before she was twelve... she left a leg down there... it just rotted away...'

There was a burst of laughter. Virginie, emboldened, advanced two steps, drew herself up to her full height, and yelled even louder:

'Yeah! Come a bit closer so I can deal with you! We don't want you comin' 'ere and makin' trouble... I don't even know the bloody cow! If she'd caught me just now I'd 'ave given 'er backside a good tannin', I can tell you that. She should tell us what I've done to 'er. C'mon, you bloody tart, tell me what I've done to you!'

'Shut up!' Gervaise stammered. 'You know all right. Where was my 'usband last night? You can shut your mouth or I'll damn well shut it for you.'

'Her 'usband! That's a good one! The lady's 'usband! As if she could catch an 'usband with a leg like that! It's not my fault if he's dumped you. I 'aven't stolen 'im, 'ave I? You can search me if you want. If you must know, he was sick of you, the poor bugger. He's too good for you. I 'ope he's got his collar on at least! Has anybody seen this lady's 'usband? There's a reward out...'

There was another burst of laughter. Gervaise could only go on muttering, almost in a whisper:

'You know all right. You know all right. It's your sister, I'll strangle that sister of yours...'

'Go and 'ave it out with my sister, then,' sneered Virginie. 'It's my sister, is it? Could be! My sister's got a lot more class than you. But what's it got to do with me? Can't people do their washin' in peace these days? Leave me alone! I've 'ad enough of your crap!'

But she it was who started up again, after five or six thumps with the beater, carried away by her own insults. Three times she began, stopped, then began again.

'Well, if you want to know, yes, it was my sister. Are you 'appy now? They're really gone on each other. You should see 'em kissin' and cuddlin'. So he's left you with your bastard kids! Lovely kids they are, with their scabby faces! A gendarme gave you one of 'em, didn't he? And you got rid of three others, so as not to come 'ere with all that extra baggage. Your Lantier told us all about it. Oh, he's told us a lot. He was sick to death of you!'

'Bitch, bitch, bitch!' screamed Gervaise, beside herself, again shaking all over.

She turned round and groped on the floor again; finding only the little tub, she grabbed it by its legs and hurled the bluing water into Virginie's face.

'Bloody cow! She's ruined my dress!' Virginie shrieked. One shoulder was soaked and her left shoulder covered in blue dye. 'Just wait, you bitch!'

She grabbed a bucket in her turn and emptied it over Gervaise. Whereupon a battle royal began. They both ran along the rows of tubs, picking up full buckets and running back to throw them at one another. Each drenching was accompanied by a volley of abuse. Gervaise was now shooting back with her own insults.

'Take that, you cow! Got you! That'll cool you down!'

'Fuckin' bitch! This'll give you a good wash for once!'

'Yeah, yeah, I'll teach you a thing or two, you bloody tart.'

'Here's another one! Wash your mouth out and get cleaned up for tonight, when you do your shift on the Rue Belhomme.'*

In the end they had to fill the buckets up again at the taps. They went on hurling insults while they waited. To begin with their aim was bad and they were hardly touched by the first bucketfuls. But they soon got their eye in. Virginie was the first to get one full in the face; the water got her in the neck and ran down her back and chest, finally running out from under her dress. She was still recovering when a second bucketful caught her from the side, slapping her hard on the left ear and soaking her bun, which came undone like a ball of string. Gervaise was hit first on the legs; and a bucketful filled her shoes and splashed her up to her thighs, then two more drenched her round the waist. Soon it was impossible to keep a tally of the score. Both were streaming with water from head to foot, their bodices sticking to their backs, their skirts glued to their buttocks; they seemed to have shrunk and grown stiff, as they stood there shivering, dripping all over like umbrellas in pouring rain.

'God, they look funny!' croaked one of the onlookers.

The wash-house was having a grand time. The spectators had moved back to avoid being splashed. Applause and jokes mingled with the sluicing of water as the buckets were emptied one after the other. Big puddles formed on the ground and the two women were soon paddling up to their ankles. Then Virginie decided to play dirty; she suddenly grabbed a bucket of boiling soda, which one of her neighbours had asked for, and threw it at Gervaise.

There was a scream. They all thought Gervaise had been scalded. The boiling soda, however, had barely caught her left foot. Maddened by the pain, she hurled a bucket, without filling it this time, at Virginie's legs, making her fall over.

The washerwomen all spoke at once.

'She's gone and broken her leg!'

'Well, the other one wanted to boil 'er alive!'

'The blonde one's in the right, ain't she, if they've pinched 'er bloke!'

Madame Boche kept exclaiming and raising her arms in the air. She'd taken up a position at a safe distance between two tubs, while Claude and Étienne, crying and gasping in terror, clung to her skirts, wailing over and over: 'Maman! Maman!' When she saw Virginie on the ground, she ran over to Gervaise and tugged at her skirt.

'Come on, that's enough! Let's go. This has given me such a turn! I never saw such a set-to!'

But she had to step back and retreat to the safety of the tubs, with the children. Virginie had jumped up and was squeezing Gervaise's throat, trying to strangle her. Gervaise jerked free and grabbed hold of Virginie's hair, hanging on to it as if trying to pull her head off. Once more battle was joined, but silently, without screams or insults. They made no attempt to wrestle, but went for each other's faces with their hands, clawing and scratching at whatever they could reach. The tall brunette's red ribbon and blue chenille net were ripped off; her bodice had split at the neck, showing her bare flesh and most of one shoulder, while the blonde Gervaise, her clothes in disarray—one sleeve of her white bodice torn off somehow—had a split in her chemise that revealed the cleavage of her bare bosom. Bits of clothing were flying in all directions. Virginie was the first to draw blood, leaving three long scratches on Gervaise's face from her mouth to below her chin; Gervaise took care to protect her eyes, closing them at each attack, for fear of being blinded. Virginie was not bleeding yet. Gervaise had been trying to get hold of her ears, furious at her lack of success, but eventually she managed to grab one of her earrings, a yellow glass pear-drop; she pulled it, the ear split, and blood flowed.

'They're killin' each other! Pull 'em apart!' several voices cried.

The women had closed in. They were forming into two camps, some urging the two on as if they were a couple of dogs fighting, while the others turned away, shaking, saying they'd had enough, they couldn't stand it any more. The fight nearly turned into a general brawl. Women were yelling abuse at each other—nasty bitch! useless cow!—and bare arms were raised. Three loud slaps were heard.

Meanwhile, Madame Boche was looking for the laundry boy.

'Charles! Charles!... Where's he got to?'

She found him in the front row, watching with his arms folded. He was a strapping lad with a bull neck. He was laughing, enjoying the sight of the bare flesh on display. The little blonde was nice and round. Wouldn't it be fun if her blouse split open!

'Look!' he murmured, with a wink. 'She's got a birthmark under her arm.'

'So that's where you are!' shouted Madame Boche when she caught sight of him. 'Come on, help us get them apart! You can do that!'

'No thanks! Not by meself!' he said calmly. 'And get me eye scratched like the other day? Not likely! That's not my job, I've got other things to do. Don't worry, there's no need to get too concerned. A bit of bloodlettin' won't hurt 'em. It'll soften 'em up.'

The concierge said something about fetching the police, but the manageress, the pale young woman with the sore eyes, wouldn't hear of it. She repeated several times:

'No, no, I can't 'ave that. It gives the place a bad name.'

The two women were still fighting, on the ground now. Suddenly Virginie got to her knees. She'd just picked up a beater and was waving it in the air. Her voice had turned into a terrible snarl.

'You're goin' to get it now! 'Ave you got all your dirty stuff ready?'

Gervaise also stretched out her hand, grabbed a beater, and held it up like a club. Her voice too had become very shrill.

'So you want a good drubbin', do you? C'mon, show me that filthy skin of yours, and I'll make ribbons of it!'

For a moment they made no move, glowering at each other. With their hair hanging over their eyes, breasts heaving, all muddy, and covered in bruises, they waited for their chance. Gervaise struck the first blow, her beater glancing off Virginie's shoulder. Then she threw herself sideways to avoid the other's beater, which caught her lightly on the hip. Now, having started, they went at it like women beating their washing, rhythmically, with all their might. When a blow struck home, it sounded muffled, as if it had landed in a tub of water.

Around them, the women were no longer laughing. Several had left, saying it made them feel sick, but the ones who'd stayed were craning their necks, and had a cruel glint in their eyes, impressed by how gutsy the two girls were. Madame Boche had taken Claude and Étienne away; their crying could be heard in the distance, mingling with the thuds of the beaters.

Suddenly, Gervaise let out a yell. Virginie had landed a tremendous blow on her arm, above the elbow; a red mark appeared and there was an immediate swelling. At this, she hurled herself at Virginie. They all thought she was going to beat her senseless.

'That's enough!' they shouted.

But the look on Gervaise's face was so frightening that no one dared go near. With extraordinary strength she seized Virginie round the waist and bent her over so that her face was flattened against the stone floor and her bottom was in the air; despite her struggles, Gervaise pulled her skirts all the way up. Finding her knickers underneath, she thrust her hand into the opening and ripped them off, exposing Virginie's thighs and buttocks. Then she raised her beater and began to beat, just as she used to beat in Plassans, on the banks of the Viorne,* when the woman she worked for did the washing for the garrison. The wood sank into the flesh with a dull thud. With each blow, a red weal appeared on the white skin.

'Blimey!' muttered young Charles, wide-eyed with amazement.

At first there was more laughter. But soon the cry 'That's enough!' began again. Gervaise, tireless, deaf to the cries, carried on, bending over her work, concerned not to miss a single spot. She wanted to beat every inch of that skin until it was scarlet with shame. She began to talk to herself, full of ferocious glee as an old washerwoman's song came back to her:

> 'Thwack! Thwack! Margot at the wash...
> Thwack! Thwack! Swings her beater—slosh...
> Thwack! Thwack! Washing from her soul...
> Thwack! Thwack! Misery black as coal...'

She went on: 'This one's for you, this one's for your sister, and this one's for Lantier... Make sure they get theirs when you see 'em. Now, let's do it again. This one's for Lantier, this one's for your sister, this one's for you...

> 'Thwack! Thwack! Margot at the wash...
> Thwack! Thwack! Swings her beater—slosh...'

They had to drag Virginie away. Weeping and extremely red in the face, the lanky brunette grabbed her washing and fled, well and truly defeated. Meanwhile, Gervaise slipped her arm back into the sleeve of her bodice and fastened her skirt. Her arm hurt and she asked Madame Boche to help her carry her washing. The concierge couldn't stop talking about the fight and how she had felt while it was happening; and she said she'd have a look at Gervaise, to see if she was all right.

'Something might be broken... I 'eard a crack...'

But Gervaise wanted to leave. She said nothing in response to the commiserations or garrulous congratulations of the women standing round her in their long aprons. When she had her bundle she made for the door, where her kids were waiting.

'Two hours, that's two sous,' said the manageress, stopping her from the booth where she was already reinstalled.

Two sous? What for? She didn't realize she was being charged for using the wash-house. But she handed over the two sous. Limping badly under the weight of the wet clothes slung over her shoulder, dripping wet herself, her elbow bruised and her cheek bleeding, she went on her way, dragging Claude and Étienne, who trotted along beside her, still upset, their faces tear-stained.

Behind her a tremendous sluice-like noise again filled the wash-house. The women had finished their bread and drunk their wine and, their faces flushed, were pounding away harder than ever, excited by the scrap between Gervaise and Virginie. Along the rows of tubs, once again, you could see a frenzy of arms, sharply outlined figures moving violently backwards and forwards like marionettes on hinges, bending at the waist and twisting at the shoulders. There was much chattering from one end of the shed to the other. The sound of voices, laughter, and crude jokes mingled with a great gurgling of water. Taps spurted, buckets spilled over, a river ran under the tubs. This was the busiest part of the afternoon, when the women battered their washing for all they were worth. In the vast shed, the steam took on a reddish hue, except where round beams of sunlight, shining through holes in the blinds, formed golden circles. The air was thick with a stifling, soap-smelling warmth. Suddenly the shed was filled with a white vapour; the huge lid of the copper in which the washing was boiled rose automatically along a central ratchet, and the gaping mouth of the copper, set inside a brick casing, discharged clouds of steam which had the sickly smell of potash. Meanwhile, alongside, the wringers were working away; in cast-iron cylinders bundles of washing were being drained of water with a turn of the fly-wheel; as the machine turned, panting and blowing, it made the whole wash-house vibrate with the ceaseless working of its steel arms.

When Gervaise began to walk up the path to the Hôtel Boncœur, she began to cry again. It was a dark, narrow side street with a gutter running along the side for slops; the familiar stench made her think back on the fortnight she'd spent with Lantier, a fortnight of misery and squabbling which now filled her with bitter regret. She began to feel completely alone.

Upstairs, the room was bare and filled with sunlight from the open window. The light, with its sheet of golden, dancing dust, showed up the wretchedness of the black ceiling and peeling wallpaper. The only thing left was a woman's little neckerchief, twisted like a piece of string, hanging from a nail over the mantelpiece. The children's bed had been pulled into the middle of the room, away from the chest, whose drawers were now all open and empty. Lantier had washed and finished off the pomade, two sous' worth in a folded playing card; the bowl he had used was still full of greasy water. He'd left nothing behind, and the corner where the trunk used to be now seemed to Gervaise like a gaping hole. Even the little round mirror hanging from the window catch had gone. Then, fearing the worst, she looked at the mantelpiece: Lantier had taken the pawn tickets. The pale pink bundle was no longer there, between the two zinc candlesticks that didn't match.

She hung her washing over the back of a chair and stood looking round, staring at the furniture, too numb even to cry. She had one sou

left of the four she'd saved for the wash-house. Then, hearing Étienne
and Claude laughing by the window, already happy again, she went
over and put her arms round them, lost in thought for a moment as
she looked out at the grey road where that morning she'd seen the
workers emerge from their sleep, and the mighty labours of Paris
begin. By now the day's work made the very cobblestones give off
a burning haze, which hung over the city behind the boundary wall. It
was on to this street, into this blazing heat, that she was being cast out
alone, with her little ones; and she looked along the outer boulevards,
to right and left, her eyes focusing on each end, filled with a nameless
dread, as if, from now on, her life would be lived out within this space,
between a slaughterhouse and a hospital.

CHAPTER II

THREE weeks later, at about half past eleven on a bright sunny morning, Gervaise and Coupeau the roofer were having a brandied plum together in Père Colombe's bar, the Assommoir.* Coupeau had been smoking a cigarette outside on the pavement when Gervaise crossed the street after delivering some laundry, and insisted that she join him. Her big square laundry basket lay beside her on the floor, behind the little zinc table.

Père Colombe's Assommoir stood at the corner of the Rue des Poissonniers and the Boulevard de Rochechouart. The sign outside bore a single word, in tall blue lettering right across: *Spirits*. At the door, planted in two half-casks, were some dusty oleanders. The huge counter with its rows of glasses, its water fountain, and its pewter measuring cups, ran along to the left as you came in, and the large room was decorated all round with huge casks painted light yellow and highly varnished, with hoops and spigots of shining copper. Higher up were shelves displaying bottles of liqueur, jars of brandied fruit, and neatly arranged flasks of all kinds; they concealed the walls, and their bright splashes of apple green, pale gold, and soft reddish-brown were reflected in the mirror behind the counter. But the most striking feature of the place, in a glassed-in yard at the back, behind an oak balustrade, was the distilling apparatus, which the customers could see working away, with its long-necked retorts and tubes coiling down into the ground—a devil's kitchen where half-sozzled workmen would come and lose themselves in alcoholic reveries.

At lunchtime on this particular day the Assommoir was empty. Père Colombe, a stocky man of forty in a sleeved waistcoat, was serving a little girl of about ten who wanted four sous' worth of spirits in a cup. A broad beam of sunlight was streaming in through the door, warming the wooden floor which was permanently wet with the spittle of smokers. And from the counter, from the casks, from the whole room, a smell of spirits rose up, an alcoholic vapour that seemed to bloat and intoxicate even the dust-motes dancing in the sun.

Meanwhile, Coupeau was rolling a fresh cigarette. He looked very spruce in his smock and little blue cloth cap, and each time he laughed he showed a fine set of white teeth. With his protruding lower jaw, slightly flat nose, and fine brown eyes, he looked like a nice friendly dog. His thick curly hair stood up on end. At twenty-six, his skin was still soft. Opposite him, Gervaise, in a black cloth jacket, her head bare, was finishing her plum, holding it by the stem between her fingers. They were sitting close to the street, at the first of the four tables lined up alongside the casks, in front of the counter.

When the roofer had lit his cigarette, he put his elbows on the table and, leaning forward, gazed at Gervaise for a few moments in silence. That morning her pretty face had the milky transparency of fine porcelain. Then, referring to something that was private between them, something they'd already discussed, he asked simply, keeping his voice down:

'So it's no? You're sayin' no?'

'Of course I'm sayin' no, Monsieur Coupeau,' Gervaise replied calmly, with a smile. Surely you're not goin' to start on that again. You promised you'd behave... If I'd known, I wouldn't have agreed to come and 'ave a drink.'

He said nothing, but went on looking at her, very close, with a gaze of unashamed, pleading tenderness, enchanted especially by her lips, pale pink and slightly moist, revealing the bright red of her mouth when she smiled. She didn't draw back, but sat looking placidly at ease and perfectly friendly. After a pause, she went on:

'You can't be serious. I'm an old woman, I've got a big boy of eight... What would we do together?'

'Oh, come on,' murmured Coupeau, with a wink. 'Same as everybody.'

She made a gesture of irritation.

'Ha! Do you think it's all about havin' fun? I can see you've never 'ad to run a home! No, Monsieur Coupeau, I've got important things to consider. Just havin' fun doesn't get you anywhere, you know! I've got two mouths to feed, and they're good eaters, I can tell you! How do you think I'd be able to bring up those kiddies if I didn't take life seriously? And, I must say, my bad luck has really taught me a lesson. You know, men just aren't for me any more. It'll be a long time before I get caught again.'

She put all this to him very calmly, without anger, as if she was discussing some laundry matter, like why she wouldn't starch a shawl. It was clear she'd made up her mind, after long and careful thought.

Coupeau, quite moved, repeated several times:

'You're upsettin' me, really upsettin' me...'

'Yes, I can see that, Monsieur Coupeau,' she replied, 'and I'm very sorry. You mustn't take it to 'eart. If I wanted to have fun, I'd rather have it with you than anybody else. You seem a good sort, you're nice. We could give it a go, and see how long it'd last. I'm not turning my nose up at the idea, and I'm not sayin' it wouldn't work... But what'd be the point if I'm not interested? I've been workin' at Madame Fauconnier's for two weeks now. The kids are goin' to school, I've got a job, I'm 'appy... Best to leave things as they are, I reckon.'

She bent down to pick up her basket.

'But you're keepin' me talkin', they'll be wonderin' where I've got to... You'll find somebody else, Monsieur Coupeau, I'm sure you will, someone prettier than me and without two kids in tow.'

He looked at the clock set in the mirror, and made her sit down again.

'Wait a minute! It's only twenty-five to twelve. I've got another twenty-five minutes... You needn't think I'll try anythin' on, we've got the table between us... Do you hate me so much that you won't even stop for a little chat?'

She put her basket down again, not wanting to seem rude, and they began to talk like old friends. She'd had something to eat before going out with her washing, and he'd bolted his soup and beef so he could keep a lookout for her. While talking to him quite amiably, Gervaise kept gazing out of the windows, between the jars of brandied fruit, at everything that was going on in the street, where the lunch hour had brought out an extraordinary throng of people. Along both pavements, in the narrow space between the houses, there was an endless flow of scurrying feet, swinging arms, and jabbing elbows. The latecomers, held back at work, came racing along with giant strides, looking grim and hungry, and disappeared into the baker's opposite, emerging with a pound loaf under their arm before going into the Veau à Deux Têtes, three doors further along, for the set meal at six sous. Next to the baker was a greengrocer who also sold fried potatoes with mussels and parsley, and a continuous stream of female workers in long aprons came out clutching bags of chips and cups of mussels; other girls— pretty, bareheaded, more dainty-looking—bought bunches of radishes. Leaning forward, Gervaise could see another shop, a charcuterie, full of people, with children coming out holding, in greaseproof paper, a breaded chop, a sausage, or a piece of hot black pudding. Meanwhile, along the road, which even in fine weather was slimy with black mud because of the trampling throng, some workmen were already coming out of the eating houses and strolling along in twos and threes, slapping their thighs, heavy with food, slow and placid amid the jostling crowd.

A group had gathered just outside the Assommoir.

'Come on, Bibi-la-Grillade,'* one of them croaked, 'what about a round of rotgut?'

Five workmen came in and stood at the bar.

'Ha! Look at that crook Colombe!' continued the voice. 'We want the real stuff, and in proper glasses, not thimbles!'

Père Colombe served them, unruffled. Another group of three arrived. Gradually a crowd of overalls formed at the corner of the street, stopped there briefly, then pushed past the dust-grey oleanders into the bar.

'Don't be silly!' Gervaise was saying to Coupeau. 'Sex is all you think about! Of course I loved him... But after the awful way he walked out...'

They were talking about Lantier. Gervaise hadn't seen him again. She thought he was living with Virginie's sister, at La Glacière, at the friend's who was supposed to be setting up a hat factory. Not that she had any intention of running after him. At first she'd been terribly upset and had even wanted to throw herself in the river, but then she'd thought it all over and concluded it was all for the best. If Lantier had stayed she might never have been able to bring up her kids, he got through money so fast. He could come and see Claude and Étienne, she wouldn't kick him out. But as far as she was concerned, she would rather be hacked to pieces than let him touch her again. She said all this in a way that showed her mind was made up, like a woman who had mapped out her life, while Coupeau, still in the grip of his desire for her, carried on making jokes and suggestive remarks in response to everything she said, asking her the crudest questions about Lantier, but in such a light-hearted way, flashing his lovely white teeth, that she was quite unable to take offence.

'I bet you knocked 'im about a bit,' he said finally. 'You're terrible, you are! You beat everybody up.'

She cut him short with a peal of laughter. Yes, it was true, she'd given a good hiding to that hulking great Virginie. That day, she'd have been only too glad to strangle somebody. And she laughed even more when Coupeau told her that Virginie was so mortified at having shown people everything she'd got that she'd left the neighbourhood. Gervaise's face, however, still kept its childlike sweetness, and she held out her chubby hands, saying several times that she wouldn't hurt a fly: she knew about hard knocks only because she'd had a lot of them herself. This set her off talking about her girlhood in Plassans. She'd never been one for running after boys, she wasn't interested, but when Lantier had taken her at fourteen she thought it was nice because he said he was her husband and it was like playing mothers and fathers. Her only weakness, she assured him, was being very soft-hearted, liking everybody, and getting very attached to people who often caused her endless misery. So, when she loved a man, she wasn't interested in fooling about with him, she dreamed only of their living always together and being happy. When Coupeau sniggered and mentioned her two kids, whom she certainly hadn't hatched under her pillow, she rapped him on the knuckles and added that of course she was made the same way as other women, but it was wrong to think that women were always mad keen on that alone; women thought about the home, they worked their fingers to the bone with their housework, and went to bed at night too worn out not to fall asleep straight away. Besides, she was like her mother, a tireless worker who'd died in harness after working like a slave for old Macquart for over twenty years. She was still very slim, whereas her mother had had shoulders broad enough to break down doors, but all the same she took after her in the way she became extremely attached to people. And even her little limp she'd got from her poor mother, whom old Macquart was forever beating half to death.* Scores of times, her mother had told her about the nights when her father had come home drunk and made love to her so violently that he nearly broke her bones; and it must have been on one of those nights that she'd been conceived, with her gammy leg.

'Oh, it's nothin', you 'ardly notice,' said Coupeau, trying to be nice.

She shook her head, for she knew full well that it showed; she'd be bent double by the time she was forty. Then with a little laugh she added gently:

'You're a funny one, fancyin' a cripple.'

At this, with his elbows still on the table, he leaned even closer and started paying her quite bold compliments, as if trying to make her drunk with words. But she went on shaking her head, not letting

herself be tempted, though she found his wheedling tone very pleasant. As she listened, her gaze was fixed on the street, as if interested
once more in the ever-growing crowd. Now, in the empty shops, they
were sweeping up; the greengrocer was taking the last pan of fried
potatoes off the stove and the charcutier* was clearing up the dirty
plates spread across his counter. Groups of workmen were emerging
from all the eating houses; fellows with beards were pushing each other
and playing about like kids, their hobnailed boots making a scraping
noise as they went sliding over the cobbles; others, their hands thrust
deep into their pockets, stood having a quiet smoke, blinking in the
sunlight. They poured on to the pavement, the roadway, and the gutters, streaming out of open shop doors like a slow-moving tide, eddy-
ing round passing carts, and forming a long trail of workmen's smocks
and overalls and old coats all faded and colourless in the golden light
that was spreading down the street. Factory bells could be heard in
the distance, but the workmen were in no hurry, stopping to relight
their pipes; then, after calling to each other from bar to bar, they
finally made up their minds to go back to work, and slouched off.
Gervaise was amused by three workmen, one tall and two short, who
stopped to look back every few paces and eventually came back down
the street and walked straight over to Père Colombe's Assommoir.

'Well,' she murmured, 'those three must be really lazy.'

'Hey,' said Coupeau, 'I know the tall one, it's Mes-Bottes,* he's
a mate of mine.'

The Assommoir had filled up. Everybody was talking very loudly,
sometimes shouting to cut through the din. From time to time a fist
would bang down on the counter and make the glasses clink. The
drinkers were standing in little knots, all packed together, their hands
folded over their bellies or clasped behind their backs; some of them,
over by the casks, had to wait a quarter of an hour before they could
order their drinks from Père Colombe.

'Well, well, if it ain't that swanky old Cadet-Cassis!'* shouted Mes-
Bottes, giving Coupeau a great slap on the shoulder. 'A real gent, who
smokes cigarettes and wears fancy shirts! Tryin' to impress his lady
friend, givin' her a nice little treat.'

'Bugger off!' replied Coupeau, very put out.

But Mes-Bottes just laughed.

'Don't come that! You're no better than the rest of us, mate… Once
a slob always a slob!'

He gave Gervaise a horrible leer and turned his back. She shrank away, quite alarmed. The pipe smoke and the strong smell of all these men, mingled with the alcohol fumes, was making her choke, and she began to cough.

'Drink is such a terrible thing,' she said under her breath.

And she told him that years ago, in Plassans, she used to drink anisette with her mother, but one day it had nearly killed her, and that had put her off it completely, so that now she couldn't stand the sight of liquor.

'Look,' she said, holding up her glass, 'I ate my plum, but I'm leavin' the syrup because it would make me ill.'

Coupeau couldn't understand either how people could swallow spirits by the glassful. A plum now and again, that was all right, but as for rotgut, absinthe,* and that sort of muck, no thanks, they could keep it! His mates could tease him as much as they liked, he stayed outside when those tosspots piled into the boozer. His old man, a roofer like himself, had cracked his head open on the pavement when he fell off the roof at No. 25 Rue Coquenard,* one day when he'd had a skinful; and that memory had kept the whole family off the grog. Every time he went down the Rue Coquenard and saw the spot, he thought to himself that he'd rather drink out of the gutter than have a drink in a cheap bar, even if it was free. And he concluded by saying:

'In our line of business, you've got to 'ave steady legs.'

Gervaise had picked up her basket. However, she didn't stand up, but held it on her lap with a dreamy, far-away look on her face as if the young workman's words had stirred in her vague thoughts about life. And she went on slowly, with no apparent link to what Coupeau had said:

'I don't want anythin' special, you know, I don't ask for much... My ideal would be to get on with me work in peace, always have somethin' to eat and somewhere decent to sleep... You know, just a bed, a table, and a couple of chairs, that's all... Oh, and I'd like, if I could, to bring up me kids and make sure they're good, decent people... And there's one other thing I'd like, if I ever lived with somebody again, it's not to get knocked about; no, I really don't want to be knocked about... That's all I want, really.'

For a while she carried on wondering if there was anything else she'd like, but she could think of nothing else that mattered to her. Nevertheless, she went on, after some hesitation:

'Yes, I suppose I'd like to die in me own bed... After slaving away all me life, it'd be nice to die at home, in me own bed.'

This time she stood up. Coupeau, who'd nodded in approval at each thing she'd said, was already on his feet, worried about the time. But they didn't leave immediately; she was curious and wanted to go and have a look at the big copper distilling apparatus, which was working away under the clear-glass roof of the little courtyard at the back, behind the oak balustrade. Coupeau, who'd followed her, explained how it worked, pointing out the different parts of the machine and showing her the huge retort from which trickled a little stream of pure alcohol. The still, with its strangely shaped containers and endless coils of piping, had a forbidding look; there was no steam coming out of it, but you could just hear a kind of breathing inside, like a subterranean rumbling. It was as if some mysterious midnight task was being carried out in broad daylight by a strong, grim, silent worker. Meanwhile, Mes-Bottes, with his two mates, had come over and was leaning on the oak balustrade, while they waited for a free spot at the counter. He laughed like a pulley that needed oiling as he gazed fondly at the booze-machine. Christ! Wasn't she lovely! There was enough in that big copper belly of hers to keep your whistle wetted for a whole week! He'd have liked it, he really would, if they'd solder the end of the tube between his teeth, so he could feel the stuff, still warm, filling him up like a little river, flowing right down to his feet, never stopping. Hell, yes! That'd suit him perfectly, it'd be a damn sight better than the thimbles they got from that mean old bugger Colombe! His pals all laughed and declared that he was a character and couldn't half talk. The still worked on, silently, with no flame nor any cheerful play of light on its dull copper surface, sweating out its alcohol like a slow but inexhaustible spring which would eventually spill out into the bar-room, spread over the outer boulevards, and engulf the whole, vast expanse of the city. Gervaise shuddered and stepped back; trying to smile, she muttered:

'I know it's silly, but that machine gives me the creeps. Drink always does that to me.'

Then, coming back to her vision of perfect happiness:

'So, don't you think I'm right? It'd be much better to work, eat, have a little place of your own, bring up your kids, and die in your bed...'

'And not get knocked about,' added Coupeau, trying to be funny. 'But I'd never hit you, I really wouldn't, if you'd say yes, Madame

Gervaise. There's no need to be afraid of that, I never drink, and anyway I love you too much. Come on, what about it, tonight? We can keep each other's feet warm.'

He'd lowered his voice and was whispering in her ear as she made her way through the crowd, holding her basket in front of her. But she still said no, shaking her head several times. However, she did turn round to smile at him, and seemed pleased to know he didn't drink. She'd certainly have said yes if she hadn't promised herself never to take up with a man again. At last they reached the door and went out, leaving behind them the crowded bar, which seemed to breathe out into the street the raucous sound of voices and the strong, sweet smell of liquor. Mes-Bottes could be heard calling Père Colombe a crook and accusing him of only half filling his glass. He, Mes-Bottes, was as true as they come, a hell of a guy; he wouldn't take any crap from anybody. His boss could go and fuck himself, he wasn't going back to that dump of his, he was sick of it. And he suggested to his two friends that they should go to the Petit Bonhomme qui Tousse,* a boozer near the Barrière Saint-Denis,* where they had some really good stuff.

'Ah, we can breathe again!' said Gervaise when they were out on the pavement. 'Well, goodbye, and thank you, Monsieur Coupeau. I must get back straight away.'

She was about to set off down the boulevard, but he took her hand and wouldn't let go, saying:

'Why not come with me, round by the Rue de la Goutte-d'Or, it's hardly out of your way. I've got to call in at me sister's before going back to work. We can keep each other company.'

After a while she agreed and they walked slowly up the Rue des Poissonniers, side by side, but not arm in arm. He told her about his family. His mother, Maman Coupeau, used to make waistcoats, but her eyes were going, so now she did some cleaning. She'd turned sixty-two on the third of the previous month. He was the youngest. One of his sisters, Madame Lerat, a widow of thirty-six, was a flower-maker and lived in the Rue des Moines, in Batignolles.* The other sister, who was thirty, had married a chain-maker, a sour bugger by the name of Lorilleux. It was this sister he was going to see, in the Rue de la Goutte-d'Or. She lived in the big tenement building on the left. He usually had his evening meal at the Lorilleux'; it was cheaper that way for all of them. In fact, he was on his way there now to tell them not to expect him that evening, because he'd been invited to a friend's.

Gervaise had been listening, but suddenly broke in and asked with a smile:

'So you're called Cadet-Cassis, are you, Monsieur Coupeau?'

'Oh,' he replied, 'that's a nickname me mates gave me 'cos I usually 'ave a cassis when they drag me into a bar. Might as well be called Cadet-Cassis as Mes-Bottes, don't you reckon?'

'Oh yes, Cadet-Cassis isn't at all bad,' she declared.

Then she asked him about his work. He was still working at the same place, the new hospital, behind the boundary wall. Oh, there was plenty to do; he'd certainly be there for the rest of the year. There were loads of gutters to do!

'You know,' he said, 'I can see the Hôtel Boncœur from up there. You were standin' at the window yesterday and I gave you a wave, but you didn't see me.'

They'd already walked a hundred metres along the Rue de la Goutte-d'Or when he stopped, looked up, and said:

'This is it. I was born a bit further along, at No. 22... This is a bloody big building, though. It's like a barracks inside!'

Gervaise looked up and studied the front of the building. On the street side it had five floors, each with fifteen windows in a line, the black shutters of which, with their broken slats, gave the vast expanse of wall a look of utter desolation. Below, on the ground floor, there were four shops: to the right of the doorway a huge, greasy eating-house, to the left a coal merchant's, a draper's, and an umbrella shop. The building looked all the more colossal because it stood between two rickety little shacks, pressed against it on either side; square-shaped, like a roughly cast block of cement, crumbling and flaking in the rain, this enormous, crude cube rose right up into the pale sky, high above the surrounding rooftops, its mud-coloured sides, unplastered and as stark and grim as prison walls, showing rows of toothing-stones, like decaying jaws gaping in the void. But what especially interested Gervaise was the door, an enormous arched door reaching up to the second floor and opening on to a deep covered entryway, beyond which could be seen the dim light of a large courtyard. Down the middle of the entrance, which was cobbled like the street, ran a gutter flowing with very pale pink water.

'Come on in,' said Coupeau. 'Nobody's goin' to eat you.'

Gervaise preferred to wait in the street, but she couldn't resist stepping through the doorway as far as the concierge's lodge on the right. There, on the threshold, she looked up once more. Inside, each of the four identical walls stretched up six storeys, enclosing the huge square courtyard. The walls were grey, eaten away in leprous yellow patches and streaked with water from the roof; they rose straight from the cobbles to the roof slates, without any moulding, broken only by the drainpipes, with bends at each floor, where the gaping drain-heads had made rusty iron stains. The shutterless windows revealed bare panes of greenish glass, the colour of muddy water. Some were open, with blue check mattresses hanging out to air; others had clothes-lines strung across, with things drying—a whole household's wash, the man's shirts, the woman's camisoles, the kids' pants; there was one on the third floor where a baby's nappy was stretched out, caked with filth. From the top floor to the bottom, the cramped tene-ments were bursting at the seams, scraps of their poverty spilling out through every chink. On each side, at ground level, a tall, narrow doorway, without a frame, cut out of the plaster, led into a cracked hallway at the end of which was a spiral staircase with grimy steps and an iron rail; there were four of these staircases, indicated by the first four letters of the alphabet painted on the wall. The ground floors had been turned into huge workshops, their windows black with grime: a locksmith's forge could be seen blazing away; further on, a carpen-ter's plane could be heard, while near the concierge's lodge a dye-works was discharging the pale pink stream that ran through the archway. The courtyard, dirty with puddles of dye, wood-shavings, and clinkers, had grass growing round its edges and between the uneven cobbles; half of it was filled with a garish light, as if it had been cut in two by the light where the sun ended. On the shaded side, round a dripping tap which kept one spot permanently wet, three lit-tle hens with muddy feet were pecking at the ground, looking for worms. Gervaise let her eyes travel slowly down from the sixth floor to the bottom and up again, astonished at the sheer size of the place, feeling as though she were in the middle of some living organism, in the very heart of a city, fascinated by the building as if she were in the presence of a gigantic human being.

'Is Madame looking for somebody?' called the concierge inquisi-tively, appearing at the door of her lodge.

Gervaise explained that she was waiting for someone. She turned back towards the street, but as Coupeau was taking his time she went into the yard again to take another look, as if drawn to the building

despite herself. It didn't strike her as ugly. Among the odds and ends
at the windows there were some cheerful little touches: a wallflower in
a pot, some canaries tweeting in a cage, shaving mirrors shining like
bright stars in the darkness. Down below a carpenter was singing,
accompanied by the regular whistling noise of his plane, while in
the locksmith's workshop hammers beating rhythmically produced
a loud silvery sound. Then, at nearly every open window, against the
background of the poverty just visible behind, children showed their
laughing, grubby faces, or women could be seen sewing, their calm
profiles bent over their work. They were resuming their tasks after the
midday meal, the men had gone back to their jobs, the building had
returned to its customary tranquillity, broken only by sounds from
the workshops, a sort of lullaby that went on for hours, always the
same. The courtyard really was a bit damp, and Gervaise thought that
if she lived there she'd like to be at the back, on the sunny side. She'd
taken a few steps into the yard, breathing in the musty smell typical of
places where the poor live, a mixture of age-old dust and rotting rubbish; but since the acrid smell of the dye-water predominated, she
thought it wasn't nearly as bad as at the Hôtel Boncœur. She was
already choosing the window she'd like, over in the left-hand corner,
where there was a little window-box planted with scarlet runners,
whose slender stems were beginning to wind round a cat's cradle
of string.

'I've kept you waiting, 'aven't I?' said Coupeau all of a sudden,
coming up behind her. 'They always make a fuss when I don't eat
with 'em, and especially today 'cos my sister bought some veal.'

As she had given a little start of surprise, he in his turn gazed up at
the building, saying:

'You were lookin' at this place. It's always let, from top to bottom.
There are three hundred tenants, I think. If I'd had any furniture, I'd
'ave kept an eye open for a little room 'ere meself. It'd be all right,
don't you think?'

'Yes, it'd be all right,' murmured Gervaise. 'In our street in Plassans
it wasn't as crowded as this. Look, isn't it nice, that window on the
fifth floor, with the scarlet runners?'

Then, persistent as ever, he asked her again if she'd say yes. As
soon as they had a bed they'd rent something here. But she hurried
out through the archway, begging him not to start that nonsense
again. The building could fall down first before she'd ever share a bed

with him there. All the same, when Coupeau left her in front of
Madame Fauconnier's shop, she let him hold her hand for a moment,
out of friendship.

For a month Gervaise and the roofer remained on the best of terms.
He thought she was really gutsy, slaving away at work, looking after
her kids, and still managing to find time in the evening for all kinds of
sewing jobs. Some women were just no good, all they thought about
was having a good time and stuffing themselves, but, bloody hell, she
wasn't a bit like them, she took life seriously! When he said that, she'd
laugh and protest modestly. She hadn't always been so good, worse
luck. She'd remind him that she'd got pregnant at fourteen, and
recalled the litres of anisette she and her mother put away in the old
days. Experience had taught her a few things, that was all. It was
a mistake to think she was strong-willed; on the contrary, she was very
weak, she let herself be pushed around, because she hated causing
people any trouble. Her dream was to live with nice people, because if
you're in bad company, she said, it was like being bashed on the head,
it cracked your skull open and knocked you flat in no time, if you were
a woman. She dreaded thinking about the future and said she was like
a coin tossed up and landing heads or tails, depending on how it hit
the pavement. Everything she'd seen so far, all the bad examples
she'd had round her as a child, had taught her a big lesson. But
Coupeau would make fun of her for having such gloomy thoughts and
would tell her to keep her chin up, while at the same time trying to
pinch her bottom. She'd push him away and give him a slap on the
hand, while he yelped and laughed and declared that for a weak little
woman she wasn't exactly a pushover. As for him, he was easy-going
and didn't think too much about the future. He just took things as
they came. You could always find a bed and a bit of grub somewhere.
The neighbourhood seemed all right, except for a good few drunks
who ought to be cleared out of the gutters. He wasn't a bad sort, some
of what he said was very sensible, and he was even a bit of a dandy,
parting his hair carefully on one side and wearing nice ties and patent
leather shoes on Sundays. Added to that he was as quick and cheeky
as a monkey, with the Parisian working man's love of banter and a gift
of the gab that went well with his boyish looks.

As time went by they did all sorts of good turns for each other at
the Hôtel Boncœur. Coupeau would fetch her milk, run errands, and
deliver her bundles of washing; and in the evening, as he was the first

to arrive home from work, he often took the kids for a walk along the outer boulevard. In return Gervaise would climb up to the little attic room where he slept and go through his clothes, sewing buttons on his overalls and mending his canvas jackets. They grew closer and closer. She was never bored when he was there, he entertained her with the stories he came back with, and the endless wisecracking of the Paris streets, which was still quite new to her. But this continual brushing against Gervaise's skirts aroused Coupeau more and more. He was hooked, no doubt about it! It began to get him down. He carried on with his tomfoolery, but inside he felt in such a state, his stomach in such a knot, that he no longer found anything funny. But he didn't stop his nonsense, blurting out every time he saw her: 'So when's it gonna be?' She knew what he meant, and promised it would be on the twelfth of never. Then he would tease her, turning up in her room holding his slippers, as if he was about to move in. She took it all in good part and carried on as normal without being embarrassed, despite his continual suggestive remarks. So long as he didn't get rough she didn't mind what he did. The only time she became angry was when he pulled out some of her hair trying to make her kiss him.

Towards the end of June Coupeau lost his high spirits. He became very moody. Gervaise, worried by the look in his eye, barricaded herself in at night. Then, after a sulk that lasted from Sunday to Tuesday, he suddenly came and knocked on her door at about eleven o'clock on the Tuesday night. She didn't want to let him in, but his voice was so soft and shaky that in the end she pushed aside the chest of drawers she'd put against the door.

When he came in she thought he must be ill, he seemed so pale, with his red eyes and blotchy face. He stood there, stammering and shaking his head. No, no, he wasn't ill. He'd been crying for the last two hours, up there in his room, crying like a child and biting his pillow so that the neighbours wouldn't hear. He hadn't slept for three days. It couldn't go on like this.

'Listen, Madame Gervaise,' he said, almost choking, on the point of breaking down again. 'This has got to stop, hasn't it? We'll get married. It's what I want, I've made my mind up.'

Gervaise looked most surprised. She became very serious.

'Oh, Monsieur Coupeau,' she murmured, 'whatever put that into your head? You know full well I've never asked that of you. I've never wanted that. No, no, I mean it. Think it over, please.'

But he went on shaking his head, with an air of obstinate determination. He'd thought it all through. He'd come down now because he had to have a good night's sleep. Surely she wasn't going to let him go back upstairs and start crying again! She just had to say yes and he wouldn't bother her any more, she could go to bed in peace. All he wanted was to hear her say yes. They could talk it over in the morning.

'But I'm not goin' to say yes just like that,' replied Gervaise. 'I don't want you to blame me, later on, for makin' you do somethin' silly. Look, Monsieur Coupeau, you shouldn't be so dead set on the idea. You don't know in your own mind how you feel about me. If you went a week without seein' me, you'd get over it, I bet. Men often get married just for one night, the first, but then there are all the other nights, and the days too, a whole lifetime, and they get really tired of it all... Now just sit down, I'd like to talk it over right now.'

And so, until one o'clock in the morning, in that dark room lit by a single smoky candle they forgot to trim, they discussed the project of marriage, keeping their voices low so as not to wake the two children, Claude and Étienne, who lay with their heads on the same pillow, breathing softly. Gervaise kept coming back to the children, pointing to them: she'd be bringing him a funny kind of dowry, she really couldn't saddle him with two kids. Besides, she felt ashamed on his account. What would the neighbours say? They all knew about her lover and what had happened; it wouldn't look nice to go and get married barely two months later. All these reasonable points Coupeau answered with a simple shrug. He couldn't care less what the neighbours thought! He didn't stick his nose into other people's business— he'd be afraid of getting it dirty, for one thing! True, she'd had Lantier before him. But so what? She wasn't some kind of loose woman, she didn't bring men home, as so many women did, even posh women. As for the kids, well, damn it all, they'd grow up, and they'd bring 'em up proper, wouldn't they? He'd never find a woman as gutsy, as kind, and with as many good qualities. Anyway, that wasn't the point. She could've walked the streets, been ugly, lazy, and horrible, and had a whole pack of snotty kids, it wouldn't have made any difference: she was the one he wanted.

'Yes, I want you,' he kept saying, thumping his knee with his fist. 'You're the one I want, right? That's all there is to it.'

Little by little Gervaise began to soften. She felt herself giving in to her heart and senses, overcome by his urgent, all-enveloping desire.

Now she was venturing only timid objections, her hands lying limply on her lap, her face full of emotion. From outside, through the half-open window, the lovely June night breathed in little gusts of warm air, which made the candle gutter and its long, reddish wick smoke. The only sounds to break the deep silence of the sleeping neighbourhood were the childlike sobs of a drunk lying on his back in the middle of the boulevard and, a long way off, a fiddle playing a popular dance-tune for a late-night party in some restaurant, a crystal-clear little melody, as clear and sharp as the sound of a harmonica. Coupeau, seeing Gervaise silent and vaguely smiling, at a loss for further arguments, seized her hands and pulled her towards him. She was in one of those unguarded moods she was so afraid of, when her defences were down and she felt too stirred emotionally to resist or to hurt anyone's feelings. But Coupeau didn't realize that she was surrendering. All he did, to take possession of her, was to go on holding her by the wrists, squeezing them so hard that it felt he was crushing them; the slight pain made each of them give a sigh, as if it relieved their feelings a little.

'Is it yes, then?' he asked.

'What a terrible nuisance you are,' she murmured. 'You really want me to say yes? All right, then, yes... But, my God, we might be making a big mistake.'

He stood up, threw his arms round her, and gave her a rough, clumsy kiss on the face. Then, as the kiss made a loud smacking noise, he was the first to look anxiously towards Claude and Étienne, tiptoeing up to them and lowering his voice:

'Shh! We must be careful,' he said. 'We mustn't wake the kids up... See you tomorrow.'

And he went back up to his room. Gervaise, trembling all over, remained sitting for nearly an hour on the edge of her bed, not even thinking of getting undressed. She was very touched, and thought Coupeau had behaved like a gentleman, for she'd thought at one moment that it was all over, and he was going to spend the night there. Down below, in the street, the drunk was making a raucous sound, like a lost animal. In the distance, the fiddle stopped playing its jolly little tune.

In the days that followed, Coupeau tried to persuade Gervaise to go with him one evening to his sister's in the Rue de la Goutte-d'Or. But she was very shy and seemed terrified at the prospect of this visit to the Lorilleux. She hadn't failed to notice that Coupeau was secretly afraid of the couple. Of course, he wasn't dependent on his sister, who wasn't even the eldest. Maman Coupeau would give her consent straight away, for she never went against her son. However, the fact was that, in the Coupeau family, the Lorilleux were thought to be earning as much as ten francs a day, and that gave them real power. Coupeau wouldn't have dared to get married without their prior approval of his wife.

'I've told 'em about you, so they know about our plans,' he explained to Gervaise. 'Blimey, you're a real baby! Come along tonight. Remember, I warned you, you'll find my sister a bit hard goin', and Lorilleux ain't always very friendly either. The thing is, they're very cheesed off, because if I get married I won't be eatin' with 'em any more and that'll mean they won't be able to save as much money. But don't worry about that, they won't throw you out... Do it for me, it's got to be done.'

These words frightened Gervaise even more. One Saturday evening, however, she did agree to go. Coupeau called for her at half past eight. She'd got all dressed up in a black dress, a cashmere shawl patterned with yellow palm leaves, and a white bonnet trimmed with a narrow band of lace. During the six weeks since she'd started work, she'd saved the seven francs for the shawl and the two francs fifty for the bonnet. The dress was an old one that she'd cleaned and done up.

'They're expectin' you,' said Coupeau, as they were going round by the Rue des Poissonniers. 'They're beginnin' to get used to the idea of me bein' married. They seem in a very good mood tonight. And if you've never seen gold chains bein' made, you can enjoy watchin'. It so 'appens they've got a rush order to get done by Monday.'

'Have they got gold there?' asked Gervaise.

'Damn me, yes—on the walls, on the floor, everywhere.'

By now they'd gone through the archway and across the courtyard. The Lorilleux lived on the sixth floor, staircase B. Coupeau laughed as he told her to hold on tight to the banister and not let go. She looked up and blinked, seeing the towering void of the stairwell, lit by three gas burners, one on every other floor. The last one, right at the top, looked like a star twinkling in a black sky, while the other two cast long, strangely shaped beams of light up and down the endless spiral steps.

'Blimey!' exclaimed the roofer as they reached the first landing, 'it don't 'alf smell of onion soup! Someone's been havin' onion soup, that's for sure.'

Staircase B, dirty and dingy, with its greasy steps and banisters, and its flaking walls showing the plaster underneath, did indeed still reek of cooking. On each landing, noisy echoing corridors led off, with yellow-painted doors blackened around the locks by dirty hands; while at the level of the window the drain-heads gave off a damp, fetid stench that mingled with the pungent smell of cooked onions. From the ground floor to the sixth you could hear the clatter of dishes, the rinsing of pans, and pots being scraped with spoons. On the first landing Gervaise glimpsed, through a half-open door on which the word *Draughtsman* was written in big letters, two men sitting at an oilcloth-covered table from which the dishes had been cleared, chattering away in a cloud of pipe smoke. The second and third landings were quieter; the only sounds coming through the cracks in the woodwork were the rocking of a cradle, the muffled crying of a child, and a rough female voice that went on and on like water from a tap, with no words clearly distinguishable; and she could see cards nailed to the doors, with names on them: *Madame Gaudron, wool carder*, and further on: *Monsieur Madinier, cardboard boxes*. On the fourth floor a fight was going on: a stamping of feet that made the floor shake, furniture being knocked over amid a dreadful racket of blows and curses, but which didn't prevent the neighbours opposite from playing cards with the door open to let in some air. But when she reached the fifth floor Gervaise had to stop to catch her breath; she wasn't used to climbing so many stairs, and this wall going round and round and these glimpses into one little dwelling after another were making her head spin. And now there was a whole family blocking the landing; the father was washing plates on a small earthenware stove near the sink, while the mother, sitting with her back against the banisters, was cleaning up their baby before putting it to bed. But Coupeau kept urging her on. They were almost there. And when at last he reached the sixth floor, he turned round and gave her a smile of encouragement. She was looking up, trying to make out where a piping voice she'd been hearing all the way up the stairs was coming from, shrill and clear, and rising above all the other noises. It was a little old woman who lived up there in an attic room and sang while she dressed thirteen-sou dolls. Then, as a tall girl carrying a bucket of water went into one of the rooms, Gervaise caught a glimpse of an unmade bed with a man in shirtsleeves sprawled on it, waiting and staring into space; when the door closed she saw a handwritten card which announced: *Mademoiselle Clémence, ironing*. At last, at the very top, breathless, her legs aching, curiosity made her look down over the banisters; now it was the gas burners on the ground floor that looked like a star, shining at the bottom of the narrow, six-storey well; and all the smells, all the teeming, rumbling life of the building rose up in a single breath, a blast of hot air that hit her in the face as she leaned forward, as if on the edge of an abyss.

'We're not there yet,' said Coupeau. 'Oh, it's quite an expedition!'

He'd turned into a long corridor on the left. He turned twice more, again to the left, then to the right. The corridor went on and on, branching into others, narrower each time, the walls cracked and peeling, and lit at rare intervals by a dim gas burner; and the doors, all identical and evenly spaced as in a prison or convent, were nearly all wide open, revealing yet more scenes of poverty and toil, suffused with a reddish glow by the warm June evening. At last they arrived at a short little passage that was in complete darkness.

'Here we are,' said Coupeau. 'Be careful! Keep close to the wall; there are three steps.'

Gervaise took about ten more paces, very cautiously, in the dark. She stumbled, then counted the three steps. Meanwhile, at the end of the corridor, Coupeau pushed open a door, without knocking. A bright light fanned out across the floor. They went in.

The room was very narrow, a sort of tunnel, which seemed like an extension of the corridor. A faded woollen curtain, tied back for the time being with some string, divided the tunnel in two. The first section of the room contained a bed pushed into a corner where the attic ceiling sloped down, a cast-iron stove still warm from the evening meal, two chairs, a table, and a cupboard with part of its cornice sawn off to make it fit between the bed and the door. The second section was set up as the workshop: at the back, a small forge with bellows; on the right, a vice fixed to the wall, under a shelf strewn with bits of old iron; and on the left, by the window, a tiny workbench cluttered with pliers, shears, and miniature saws, all very dirty and oily.

'We're 'ere!' yelled Coupeau, going up to the woollen curtain.

But at first there was no reply. Gervaise, feeling very nervous, and particularly excited at the thought that she was about to enter a place full of gold, stood behind Coupeau, stammering and giving little nods by way of greeting. The bright light, which came from a lamp burning on the bench and coals blazing in the forge, made her even more disorientated. After a while, however, she was able to make out Madame Lorilleux, short, red-haired, and rather stout, who, with all the strength of her stubby arms, was using a large pair of pliers to pull at some black wire she had passed through the holes of a draw-plate fixed to the vice. At the bench sat Lorilleux, equally short but slighter of build. Sprightly as a monkey, he was working with tweezers on something so minute that it couldn't be seen between his gnarled fingers. It was he who glanced up first. He was nearly bald, and he had a long, sickly looking face, pale yellow like old wax.

'Ah, it's you. Good, good,' he murmured. 'We 'aven't got much time, you know... Don't come into the workshop, you'd be in the way. Stay in the bedroom.'

He went on with his microscopic work, his face again tinged by the greenish glow of a water globe* through which the lamp cast a bright circle of light on to his work.

'Sit down!' cried Madame Lorilleux in her turn. 'So this is the lady? Good, good.'

She'd finished winding the wire and now took it over to the forge where she revived the fire with a big wooden fan, then made it heat up again before passing it through the last holes in the draw-plate.

Coupeau pulled up the chairs and made Gervaise sit down next to the curtain. The room was so narrow that he was unable to sit beside her. He put his chair behind hers and leaned over her shoulder to explain what Lorilleux was doing. Gervaise, taken aback by the odd reception the Lorilleux had given her, and disconcerted by their sidelong glances, had a buzzing in her ears that prevented her from hearing what he said. She thought the woman looked very old for her thirty years, surly and slovenly, with her hair hanging in a pigtail over her unbuttoned blouse. Her husband, who was only a year older, seemed to Gervaise like an old man, with his mean, hard mouth, as he sat there in his shirtsleeves, his bare feet in down-at-heel slippers. But what took her aback most was the smallness of the workshop, the dirty walls, the rusty iron tools, everything grimy and messy, like a scrap-iron yard. The heat was intense. Beads of sweat formed on Lorilleux's sickly face, while his wife decided to take off her blouse, working away with bare arms, her chemise clinging to her sagging breasts.

'Where's the gold?' Gervaise asked in a whisper.

She peered eagerly into every corner, searching in all the filth for the splendour she'd dreamed of.

Coupeau burst out laughing.

'The gold?' he said. 'Look, there's some there, and there, and some more there, just where you're standing.'

He pointed first to the drawn wire his sister was working on, and then to another bundle hanging on the wall near the vice and looking just like a coil of ordinary wire; then, getting down on all fours and reaching underneath the slatting that covered the workshop floor, he picked up a bit of scrap, a tiny fragment like the point of a needle. Gervaise exclaimed that it couldn't be gold, that nasty black stuff, as ugly as iron! He had to bite the metal and show her the shiny dent left by his teeth. And he went on explaining: the employers supplied the gold wire, already alloyed, and the workers began by passing it through the draw-plate to get it to the right thickness, taking care to reheat it five or six times during the process so it wouldn't break. Of course, you needed a strong grip and lots of practice! His sister wouldn't let her husband touch the draw-plates because of his cough. She had wonderfully strong arms, he'd seen her draw gold as fine as a hair.

Meanwhile, Lorilleux was doubled up on his stool with a coughing fit. In between spasms he said, half choking and still without looking at Gervaise, as if his statement was for his benefit alone:

'I make column chain.'

Coupeau made Gervaise stand up. She should go nearer, to see better. The chain-maker grunted his consent. He was winding the wire prepared by his wife round a mandrel, a very thin steel rod. Next, with a saw, he gently cut along the length of the mandrel so that each turn of the wire made a link. Then he soldered them. The links were placed on a big piece of charcoal. He moistened each one with a drop of borax from the bottom of a broken glass by his side before quickly heating them, until they glowed red, with the horizontal flame of a blowpipe. Then, when he had about a hundred links, he went back to his close work, leaning on the edge of his *cheville*, a piece of board which had been rubbed smooth by the action of his hands. He twisted each link with his pliers, gripping one side as he pushed it into the link above, which was already in place, then reopened it with an awl; this was all done with such unbroken regularity, one link following another so quickly, that the chain gradually grew longer before Gervaise's eyes without her being able to understand exactly how it was done.

'This is column chain,' Coupeau said. 'There's also small-link, heavy-link, curb, and rope. But this is column. It's the only sort Lorilleux makes.'

The chain-maker gave a snigger of satisfaction. Continuing to squeeze together his links, which were invisible between his black finger nails, he shouted:

'Do you know something, Cadet-Cassis? I worked it out this morning. I began when I was twelve, didn't I? Well, d'you know how much column I must've made up to now?'

He raised his pale face, blinking his red eyelids.

'Eight thousand metres! What about that! A piece of chain eight kilometres long! Enough to go round the neck of every woman in the neighbourhood. And it's getting longer all the time, y'know. I reckon I'll soon be able to get from Paris to Versailles.'*

Gervaise had gone to sit down again, quite disappointed. It all seemed so ugly. She smiled to please the Lorilleux. What bothered her most was the fact that they'd said nothing about the marriage, a subject of the greatest importance to her and the only reason she'd come. The Lorilleux continued to treat her as if she was some nosy intruder Coupeau had brought along. When at last a conversation got started, it revolved solely round the other tenants in the building. Madame Lorilleux asked her brother if, on the way up, he'd heard the people on the fourth landing fighting. Those Bénards were at each other's throats every day: the husband always came home blind drunk, and his wife wasn't up to much either, forever shouting the filthiest things. Then they talked about the draughtsman on the first floor, that great beanpole Baudequin, who fancied himself but was always in debt; he smoked non-stop and was always shouting his head off with his friends. Monsieur Madinier's cardboard business was on its last legs; he'd sacked two more girls the day before, and it would serve him right if he did go bust, because he frittered all his money away on drink and let his kids go about with their arses showing through their pants. Madame Gaudron had been up to her tricks again: she was expecting once more, which at her age was hardly decent. The landlord had just given notice to the Coquets, on the fifth floor; they owed three quarters' rent, added to which they insisted on lighting their stove out on the landing, and only the previous Saturday Mademoiselle Remanjou, the old girl on the sixth floor, going down with her dolls, arrived just in time to prevent the Linguerlot kid from being badly burned. As for Mademoiselle Clémence, who took in ironing, she got up to all sorts of things, but you couldn't dislike her, she loved animals and had a heart of gold. What a shame, though, that a lovely girl like that went with all those men! One of these nights they'd find her walking the streets, for sure.

'Here, this one's done,' said Lorilleux to his wife, handing her the piece of chain he'd been working on since lunchtime. 'You can finish it off.'

And he added, with the persistence of a man who can't let go of a joke: 'That's another metre... I'm gettin' closer to Versailles.'

Madame Lorilleux heated the chain once more, then passed it through the final draw-plate for adjustment. Next, she dropped it into a little copper pot with a long handle, full of caustic soda, which she warmed up on the flame of the forge. Coupeau pushed Gervaise forward again so that she could watch this final process. When the chain had been descaled, it turned a dull red colour. It was finished, ready for delivery.

'It's delivered in the rough,' Coupeau explained. 'The polishers rub it up with a cloth.'

But Gervaise felt she couldn't take any more. The room was getting hotter and hotter, she could hardly breathe. They kept the door shut because the slightest draft gave Lorilleux a cold. So, as there was still no mention of the marriage, she wanted to go, and gave Coupeau's coat a little tug. He understood. In any case, he too was beginning to feel embarrassed and irritated by this deliberate show of silence.

''We'll be off, then,' he said, 'so you can get on with your work.'

He waited a few moments, shuffling his feet, hoping for some word, some allusion to the marriage. In the end, he decided to broach the matter himself.

'By the way, Lorilleux, you'll be my wife's witness, won't you? We're countin' on it.'

Pretending to be surprised, the chain-maker looked up and sniggered, while his wife put down the draw-plates and went to stand in the middle of the workshop.

'You really mean it, then?' he muttered. 'You never know, with old Cadet-Cassis, whether he's havin' you on or not.'

'Ah, yes! So this is the lady,' his wife said, staring at Gervaise. 'Well, it's not for us to say anything. It's a funny idea to go and get married, though. But if that's what you both want. If it doesn't work, you'll only 'ave yourselves to blame, that's all that can be said. And it doesn't work very often, not often at all...'

Lingering over these last words, she shook her head, her gaze travelling from Gervaise's face to her hands, then her feet, as if she would have liked to undress her and examine every pore of her skin. Evidently, she found her better-looking than she'd expected.

'My brother's a free agent,' she went on in her sharp little voice. 'Of course, the family might have preferred... We all 'ave different ideas. But things can turn out in such funny ways. It's not something I want to argue about, though. Even if he'd brought us the lowest of the low, I'd 'ave said: "Go on, marry her, and leave me out of it." And yet, you know, he wasn't doin' too badly here, with us. He's not exactly thin, you can see he's 'ad plenty to eat. Always a hot meal, right on the dot... By the way, Lorilleux, don't you think the lady's a bit like Thérèse, you know, the woman opposite, who died of consumption?'

'Yes, she does look a bit like 'er,' replied the chain-maker.

'And you've got two kids, 'aven't you? Well, as far as that's concerned, I said to my brother: "I can't understand how you can marry a woman with two kids." You shouldn't take it the wrong way, if I look at it from his side, it's only natural... And, apart from that, you don't look very strong. Don't you agree, Lorilleux, she doesn't look very strong?'

'No, she doesn't, not at all.'

They didn't mention her leg. But Gervaise understood, from their sidelong glances and pursed lips, that that was what they were referring to. She stood before them, wrapped in her thin shawl with its yellow palm leaves, answering in monosyllables as if she was being tried in front of a pair of judges. Coupeau, seeing she was upset, intervened.

'That's enough! It doesn't make any difference what you say. The wedding's gonna be on Saturday the twenty-ninth of July. I've worked it out on the almanac. All right? Does that suit you?'

'Oh yes, it suits us,' said his sister. 'There was no need to ask. I won't stop Lorilleux from bein' a witness. We don't want any argy-bargy.'

Gervaise hung her head, and for the sake of something to do, poked her toe into one of the gaps in the wooden slatting that covered the workshop floor; then, fearing she might have displaced something when she took it out, she bent down and felt around with her hand. Lorilleux jumped over with the lamp and inspected her fingers suspiciously.

'You've got to be careful,' he said. 'Little bits of gold can stick to the bottom of your shoes and you can carry them away without realizin'.'

The Lorilleux made a terrible fuss. The employers didn't allow for a milligram of waste. Lorilleux showed her the rabbit's foot he used to brush up specks of gold on the board he worked on, and the leather apron he spread over his knees to catch the droppings. The workshop was swept carefully twice a week; they kept the sweepings and burnt them, then sifted the ashes, and every month they would recover as much as twenty-five or thirty francs' worth of gold.

Madame Lorilleux kept her eyes fixed on Gervaise's shoes.

'We don't mean no offence,' she murmured with an ingratiating smile, 'but perhaps Madame could have a look at the soles of her shoes.'

Gervaise, blushing to the roots of her hair, sat down again and lifted her feet to show there was nothing there. Coupeau had already opened the door, with a curt 'Goodnight!' and called to her from the corridor. She followed him out, stammering some polite phrase to the effect that she hoped they'd see each other again and get on well together. But the Lorilleux had already gone back to their work at the back of their burrow of a workshop, where the little forge was glowing like a last remaining piece of coal burning white-hot in the intense heat of a furnace. The wife, her chemise slipping down off one shoulder, her skin reddened in the glare of the fire, was pulling away at another wire, her neck swelling with each tug, the muscles standing out like pieces of cord. The husband, bending over in the green light cast by the water globe, was starting on a new length of chain, twisting the link with his pliers, gripping it on one side, inserting it into the link above, and reopening it with the awl, on and on like a machine, never wasting a second to wipe the sweat from his face.

When Gervaise emerged from the corridor onto the sixth-floor landing, she couldn't help saying, with tears in her eyes:

'That didn't look very promising!'

Coupeau shook his head angrily. He'd get his own back on Lorilleux for the way he'd treated them that evening. Did you ever see such a mean bugger! As if they'd try to snaffle three grains of his gold dust! All the nonsense they talked just showed how miserly they were. Perhaps his sister had imagined he'd never get married, so she could carry on saving four sous on his dinner? Anyway, it was going to be the twenty-ninth of July all the same. They could go to hell!

But Gervaise still felt quite downcast as she went down the stairs, tormented by a strange kind of panic that made her peer anxiously into the long shadows cast by the banisters. By now the stairwell was deserted and asleep, lit only by the gas burner on the second floor, its tiny flame flickering like a night light in that murky pit. You could almost hear, behind the closed doors, the heavy silence, the dead sleep of workers who'd gone to bed straight from the supper table. However, stifled laughter came from the room of the girl who took in ironing, and a thin shaft of light shone through Mademoiselle Remanjou's keyhole: they could just hear her snipping away with her scissors, still cutting out gauze dresses for her thirteen-sou dolls. Further down, in Madame Gaudron's, a child was still crying. And the stench from the drain-heads was stronger than ever in the dark, heavy silence.

Then, in the courtyard, as Coupeau called in a sing-song voice for the concierge to open the door, Gervaise turned round to look at the building one last time. It seemed to have grown bigger under the moonless sky. The grey walls, as though cleansed of their leprous patches and smeared with shadows, stretched upwards, looking even barer now that their flat expanse was stripped of the rags hung out during the day to dry in the sun. The shuttered windows slept. A few here and there, brightly lit, were like eyes, making it seem that some odd corners of the building were squinting. Above each entrance, lined up from bottom to top, the windows of the six landings rose like slender towers of pale, glimmering light. A beam from a lamp in the cardboard box workshop on the second floor made a splash of yellow across the courtyard cobbles, piercing the dark shadows that enveloped the ground-floor workshops. And from the depths of this darkness, in the damp corner of the yard, came the sound of the dripping tap, each drop echoing loud and clear in the silence. It seemed to Gervaise that the house was on top of her, crushing her under its weight, icy on her shoulders. It was that stupid fear again, a childish fancy that she'd smile about later.

'Look out!' shouted Coupeau.

To get out, she had to jump over a big puddle that had trickled from the dye-works. That day the puddle was blue, a deep blue like a summer sky, twinkling with stars reflected from the concierge's little night-lamp.

CHAPTER III

GERVAISE didn't want to do anything special for the wedding. Why spend the money? Besides, she still felt a bit shy about it: she didn't see any point in advertising the marriage to the whole neighbourhood. But Coupeau protested that you couldn't get married just like that, without some sort of meal. He couldn't care less about the neighbours! They'd do something quite simple, a little outing in the afternoon, then a spot of dinner in the first eating house they came to. And no music afterwards, for sure, nothing to get the ladies to wiggle their bums about. Just a few little drinks, then everybody back home and off to bye-byes.

The roofer laughed and joked, and finally got Gervaise to give in when he swore there'd be no larking about. He'd keep an eye on the drinks and make sure nobody got pissed. So he arranged for a simple meal at five francs a head, at Auguste's Moulin d'Argent* on the Boulevard de la Chapelle. It was a little wine bar where the prices were reasonable, with an area for dancing in the yard at the back, under three acacia trees. They'd be fine in a room on the first floor. Over the next ten days he mustered guests from his sister's building in the Rue de la Goutte-d'Or: Monsieur Madinier, Mademoiselle Remanjou, Madame Gaudron and her husband. He even persuaded Gervaise to let him invite two of his mates, Bibi-la-Grillade and Mes-Bottes; it was true Mes-Bottes always had a bit of a thirst, but he also had such a hilariously big appetite that he was always invited on outings so they could all enjoy the look on the landlord's face when he saw how much would disappear into that gaping mouth of his.

Gervaise, for her part, promised to bring her boss, Madame Fauconnier, and the Boches, who were fine people. That would make fifteen round the table, which was quite enough. When there are too many of you, it always ends in a row.

Coupeau, however, had no money. Though he didn't want to show off, he did want to do things properly. He borrowed fifty francs from his boss, out of which he first bought the ring, a twelve-franc gold ring, which Lorilleux managed to get wholesale for nine. Then he ordered a frock coat, trousers, and a waistcoat from a tailor in the Rue Myrrha, to whom he gave only twenty-five francs as a down payment;

his patent leather shoes and bolivar hat* were still serviceable. When he'd put aside the ten francs needed to pay for his meal and Gervaise's (the children's would be on the house), he had exactly six francs left, the cost of a pauper's Mass. Personally he had no use for Holy Joes, and it broke his heart to hand over his six francs to those greedy layabouts who didn't need his money to keep their whistles wet. But you had to admit, a wedding without a Mass just wasn't a wedding. He went to the church himself to haggle, and for an hour was caught up with a little old priest in a dirty cassock, who was as grasping as a market stallholder. He had a good mind to give him a slap across the face. In the end, as a joke, he asked him if he had a cut-price Mass tucked away somewhere, not too shop-soiled, that would be just the job for a nice young couple. The little old priest, grumbling that God would take no pleasure in blessing their union, finally agreed to let him have his Mass for five francs. So at least he'd saved a franc.

Gervaise, too, wanted to do things properly. As soon as the marriage had been decided on, she arranged to work extra hours in the evening and managed to put aside thirty francs. She'd set her heart on a little silk cape marked at thirteen francs in the Rue du Faubourg-Poissonnière. She treated herself to that and then, for ten francs, bought from the husband of one of Madame Fauconnier's laundry-women, who'd died, a dark blue woollen dress which she altered completely to fit her own figure. With the remaining seven francs she bought a pair of cotton gloves, a rose for her bonnet, and shoes for her elder boy Claude. Fortunately the kids' smocks were presentable. She spent four nights cleaning everything and darning the tiniest holes in her stockings and chemise.

Finally, on the Friday evening, the eve of the big day, when Gervaise and Coupeau came home from work, they had to slave away until eleven o'clock. Then, before going to their own beds to sleep, they spent an hour together in Gervaise's room, very thankful that all the fuss would soon be over. Despite their determination not to go to any great lengths for the neighbours, they had ended up taking the whole thing very seriously and tiring themselves out. By the time they said goodnight they were ready to drop. All the same, they heaved a great sigh of relief. Now it was all settled. Coupeau's witnesses were Monsieur Madinier and Bibi-la-Grillade, while Gervaise had Lorilleux and Boche. They were to go quietly to the town hall and the church, the six of them, without dragging a whole lot of others along.

The bridegroom's two sisters had even declared they'd stay at home, since their presence wasn't required. Maman Coupeau, on the other hand, had begun to cry, saying she'd go on ahead and hide in a corner; so they promised to take her with them. As for the rest of the party, they'd all meet up at one o'clock at the Moulin d'Argent. From there they'd go out to Saint-Denis* to work up an appetite; they'd go by train and come back on foot, along the main road. The party was shaping up quite nicely, not some great spree, just a bit of fun, a nice quiet little outing.

On the Saturday morning, as he was dressing, Coupeau felt a pang of anxiety as his gaze fell upon his one-franc piece. It had just occurred to him that it would only be polite to stand the witnesses a glass of wine and a slice of ham to tide them over until dinner. And there might be unexpected expenses, too. One franc wouldn't be enough, that was clear. So, after taking Claude and Étienne along to Madame Boche, who was to bring them to the dinner in the evening, he rushed round to the Rue de la Goutte-d'Or and boldly asked Lorilleux to lend him ten francs. Not that it didn't pain him to ask, because he could already see the face his brother-in-law would pull. Lorilleux grumbled and gave a nasty sneer, before finally coughing up the two five-franc pieces. But Coupeau heard his sister mutter that this was 'a good start'.

The ceremony at the town hall was to be at ten-thirty. It was a beautiful day, with the streets baking hot under a blistering sun. So as not to attract attention, the bridal pair, Maman Coupeau, and the four witnesses divided into two groups. Gervaise led the way on Lorilleux's arm, followed by Monsieur Madinier with Maman Coupeau; on the other side of the street, twenty paces behind, came Coupeau, Boche, and Bibi-la-Grillade. These three, in black frock coats, walked along with their shoulders hunched and their arms dangling; Boche was wearing yellow trousers; Bibi-la-Grillade, with no waistcoat, was buttoned up to the neck, and showed just a tiny bit of a stringy tie. Only Monsieur Madinier wore a dress coat, with square-cut tails, and passers-by stopped and stared at this elegant gentleman escorting fat Maman Coupeau, in her green shawl and black bonnet with red ribbons. Gervaise, in her dark blue dress, with a narrow little cape round her shoulders, looked very sweet and cheery as she listened patiently to the snide little comments of Lorilleux, who was buried in a huge overcoat in spite of the heat; from time to time, as they rounded a corner, she would turn her head slightly and smile back at Coupeau, who looked ill at ease in his new clothes, all shiny in the sunlight.

Even though they walked very slowly they arrived at the town hall a good half-hour too early, and as the mayor was late their turn didn't come until eleven. They sat down and waited in a corner of the room, staring at the high ceiling and the bare walls, keeping their voices down and pushing their chairs back with exaggerated politeness every time an office boy went past. But under their breath they called the mayor a lazy bugger; no doubt he was with his fancy woman, having a massage for his gout, or perhaps he'd had one too many and swallowed his official sash. However, when the mayor did appear, they stood up respectfully. They were told to sit down again, and had to sit through three weddings, quite big and posh affairs, with brides in white, little girls in ringlets, bridesmaids with pink sashes, and endless processions of gentlemen and ladies done up to the nines and all looking very swish. Then, when they were called, they almost couldn't be married at all, because Bibi-la-Grillade had disappeared. Boche found him down in the square, smoking his pipe. And what a snooty lot they were in this place, turning their noses up at you because you didn't have white gloves to wave at them! And the formalities—the reading of the Code,* the questions they were asked, the signing of the documents—were got through so fast that they were left staring at each other, wondering if they hadn't been diddled out of at least half the ceremony. Gervaise, feeling dazed and on the verge of tears, pressed her handkerchief to her lips. Maman Coupeau cried buckets. They all took great care over the signing of the register, writing their names in big ungainly letters, except the bridegroom, who put a cross, as he was unable to write. They each gave four sous for the poor. When the office boy handed Coupeau the marriage certificate, at a nudge from Gervaise he forked out another five sous.

It was a fair hike from the town hall to the church.* On the way the men had a beer and Maman Coupeau and Gervaise cassis and water. They had to tramp down a long street on which the sun was beating straight down, without the tiniest bit of shade. The beadle was waiting for them in the middle of the empty church; he hustled them over to a little side chapel, asking angrily if they were trying to make fun of religion by being so late. A priest came striding over with a surly expression on his face, looking pale with hunger, a server in a dirty surplice trotting before him. He rushed through the Mass, mumbling the Latin phrases, turning round, bowing, spreading his arms, all at top speed, while casting sidelong glances at the bride and groom and their witnesses. The bridal couple, quite disconcerted, stood before the altar, not knowing when they were supposed to kneel, stand up, or sit down, and waited for signals from the server. The witnesses remained respectfully on their feet the whole time, while Maman Coupeau, overcome once more, sobbed into the missal she'd borrowed from a neighbour. By now it had struck twelve, the last Mass had been said, and the church was filled with the sound of sacristans shuffling about and noisily putting chairs back in place. The high altar, it appeared, was being made ready for some saint's day, for there was a banging of hammers as workmen put up hangings. And at the back of the side chapel, amid a cloud of dust from the beadle's broom as he swept the floor, the surly-looking priest quickly passed his desiccated hands over the bowed heads of Gervaise and Coupeau, as though consecrating their union in the middle of a sort of house-moving, while the Good Lord was taking a break between two proper Masses. When the members of the wedding party had once more signed a register in the vestry and found themselves back outside in the bright sunshine of the porch, they stood there for a few moments, dazed and breathless from having been rushed along at such speed.

'So that's that!' said Coupeau, with an embarrassed laugh. He was shifting uneasily from one foot to the other, for he didn't find it at all funny. Nevertheless he added: 'Well, they don't hang about. All over in a jiffy… It's just like goin' to the dentist: before you can say "ouch!" you're spliced, and you 'aven't felt a thing.'

'Yes, yes, very neatly done,' Lorilleux sniggered. 'They hitch you up in five minutes, and that's it for the rest of your life. Poor old Cadet-Cassis!'

The roofer took it all in good part as the four witnesses slapped him on the back. Meanwhile Gervaise, smiling through her tears, was hugging Maman Coupeau and saying something in answer to the old lady's stuttering remarks:

'Don't you worry. I'll do my best. If it doesn't work out, it won't be my fault. No, that's for sure, 'cos I really want to be happy… Anyway, it's done now, isn't it? It's up to the two of us to get along and make a go of it.'

Then they went directly to the Moulin d'Argent. Coupeau had taken his wife's arm. They walked fast, laughing, as if carried away by excitement, some two hundred metres in front of the others, oblivious to the houses, the passers-by, and the traffic. The deafening noises of the street rang in their ears. When they reached the Moulin d'Argent, Coupeau immediately ordered two litres of wine, some bread, and some sliced ham in the little glass-partitioned room on the ground floor—no plates or tablecloth, just a snack. Then, seeing that Boche and Bibi-la-Grillade were working up a serious appetite, he ordered another litre of wine and a piece of Brie. Maman Coupeau wasn't happy, she was too overcome with emotion to eat. Gervaise was dying of thirst and drank several glasses of water barely tinged with wine.

'This is on me,' said Coupeau, going straight over to the counter, where he paid four francs and five sous.

By now it was one o'clock and the guests were arriving. Madame Fauconnier, a portly lady but still attractive, was the first to appear; she was wearing a cream-coloured dress with a floral pattern, a pink scarf, and a bonnet smothered in flowers. Next came Mademoiselle Remanjou, thin as a wraith in her eternal black dress, which people imagined she wore even in bed. She arrived with the Gaudrons: the husband, as big as a house, seemed on the point of bursting out of his brown jacket every time he moved, while his pregnant wife's enormous belly was accentuated even more by a bright purple skirt. Coupeau explained that there was no need to wait for Mes-Bottes, who would be meeting up with them on the road to Saint-Denis.

'Well, well!' exclaimed Madame Lerat as she came in, 'we're in for a soaking! That'll be fun!'

She called them all over to the door to look at the sky. Inky-black storm clouds were building up to the south of the city. Madame Lerat, the eldest of the Coupeaus, was a tall, gaunt, masculine-looking woman with a nasal voice; she was got up in an ill-fitting puce dress with long fringes, which made her look like a skinny poodle emerging from the water. She was waving her parasol about like a stick. She kissed Gervaise and went on:

'The heat out there is incredible. It's like stepping into a furnace.'

Everyone now declared they'd felt a storm coming for quite a while. When they'd left the church, Monsieur Madinier had had no doubts about what was brewing. Lorilleux said his corns had kept him awake from three o'clock that morning. Anyway, it was bound to come, it had been much too hot for three days now.

'Yes, it's likely to pour,' agreed Coupeau, standing in the doorway and anxiously studying the sky. 'There's only my sister to come, then we can get going.'

Madame Lorilleux was indeed late. Madame Lerat had gone round to pick her up, but she'd found her only just putting on her stays and they'd had words. 'So,' the lanky widow whispered in her brother's ear, 'I left her to it. She's in a foul mood! You'll see when she gets 'ere.'

They had to hang around for another quarter of an hour, cooling their heels in the bar, pushed and jostled by the men coming in for a quick one at the counter. Every so often Boche, Madame Fauconnier, or Bibi-la-Grillade would go outside to the edge of the pavement and gaze up at the sky. There was no rain at all, but it kept getting darker, and gusts of wind, blowing along the ground, were raising little eddies of white dust. At the first clap of thunder Mademoiselle Remanjou crossed herself. All eyes turned to the clock over the mirror: it was already twenty to two.

'Here it comes!' cried Coupeau. 'The angels are weepin'.'

A squall of rain swept across the street, and women ran for cover holding their skirts with both hands. It was in the middle of this first downpour that Madame Lorilleux arrived, breathless and furious as she struggled in the doorway with her umbrella, which wouldn't close.

'Did you ever see anything like it!' she spluttered. 'I got caught in it just as I left. I had half a mind to go back in and change. It's a damn shame I didn't... A great wedding this is! I told you! I said you should put it off till next Saturday. And now of course it's raining, because nobody would listen to me! All right, then, let it pour!'

Coupeau tried to calm her down, but she told him to shut up. He wouldn't be the one to fork out for her dress if it was ruined. It was a black silk dress that hardly allowed her to breathe. The bodice was too small, so it pulled at the buttons and strained at the shoulders, while the sheathe-like skirt hugged her thighs so tightly that she had to walk with tiny little steps. But all the same the other women were looking her up and down with pursed lips, impressed by the way she was turned out. She seemed not to have noticed Gervaise, who was sitting next to Maman Coupeau. She called Lorilleux over and asked for his handkerchief, then retired to a corner of the bar and, one by one, carefully wiped the raindrops from the silk.

Meanwhile the downpour had suddenly stopped, but it was getting even darker, almost like night, a livid night shot through with great sheets of lightning. Bibi-la-Grillade kept saying with a laugh that it was going to piss cats and dogs, for sure. Whereupon the storm broke with tremendous force. For half an hour it bucketed down and the thunder growled and roared continuously. The men, standing in the doorway, gazed at the grey curtain of rain, the overflowing gutters, and the spray which flew up from the puddles forming on the pavement. The women had all sat down, quite afraid, and were holding their hands over their eyes. They were now too tense to talk. When Boche ventured a joke about the thunder, saying St Peter was sneezing up there, no one reacted. But, as soon as the thunderclaps became less frequent and died away in the distance, they began to get impatient again and vented their frustration on the storm, swearing and shaking their fists at the clouds. The sky was now an ashen grey and a fine drizzle was falling as if it would never stop.

'It's gone two,' cried Madame Lorilleux. 'We can't spend the night 'ere, can we?'

When Mademoiselle Remanjou suggested setting off for the country just the same, even if they got no further than the moat round the fortifications,* there was a cry of protest: the roads would be in a fine mess, and they wouldn't even be able to sit on the grass; and besides, it didn't look as if it was over, there might be another deluge on the way. Coupeau, who was watching a workman walking calmly along in the rain, dripping wet, muttered: 'If that old sod Mes-Bottes is waitin' for us on the Saint-Denis road, there's not much chance he'll get sunstroke!'

That made them laugh. Nevertheless, their mood was going from bad to worse. It was past a joke. They'd have to decide what to do. They surely couldn't hang about gawping at each other until dinner! So for the next fifteen minutes, as the rain fell showing no sign of abating, they sat racking their brains. Bibi-la-Grillade suggested a game of cards; Boche, who was sly and given to anything smutty, said he knew a really funny little game called 'Confessions'; Madame Gaudron talked of going to have some onion tart in the Chaussée de Clignancourt; Madame Lerat would have liked them to tell each other stories; Gaudron wasn't bothered, he was happy to stay put, but thought they should start eating right away. Each suggestion was met with objections and bickering: this was a silly idea, that would bore them all to death, they'd be taken for a bunch of kids. Lorilleux, determined to put his oar in, proposed simply walking along the outer boulevards to Père-Lachaise,* where they could have a look at the tomb of Héloïse and Abélard* if there was time. At this, Madame Lorilleux, unable to contain herself any longer, blew up. She was off—that's what *she* was going to do! Was this their idea of a joke? She'd got all dressed up, she'd got soaked to the skin, just to hang about forever in a bar! No, no, she'd had enough of a wedding party like this. She'd be better off in her own home!

'Get out of my way! I'm going!'

When her husband had managed to calm her down, Coupeau went up to Gervaise, who was still sitting in a corner chatting quietly with her mother-in-law and Madame Fauconnier.

'You haven't suggested anything, have you?' he said, not yet daring to address her by the familiar *tu*.*

'Oh, I'll go along with anything,' she replied with a laugh. 'I'm not fussy. We can leave, or stay here, I don't mind. I'm very happy as I am.'

And indeed her face seemed aglow with quiet contentment. Since the guests had arrived she'd chatted with each in turn, her voice soft and slightly tremulous with emotion, but she looked perfectly self-controlled, and didn't get involved in any of the arguments. Throughout the storm she'd sat gazing at the sky, as if in the sudden flashes of lightning she could see important events far off in the future.

Monsieur Madinier had not yet suggested anything. He was leaning against the counter with his coat-tails spread wide, conscious of his status as an employer. He spat, with great deliberation, rolled his big eyes, and said:

'Of course, we could go to the museum…'*

He stroked his chin, narrowed his eyes, and looked round.

'There are antiquities, drawings, paintings, loads of things. It's very educational… You've never been, perhaps? It's definitely worth going, at least once.'

They all looked at each other quizzically. No, Gervaise had never been, nor had Madame Fauconnier, nor Boche, nor any of the others. Coupeau thought he'd been one Sunday, but he couldn't remember much about it. They were still hesitating when Madame Lorilleux, who was greatly impressed by Monsieur Madinier's air of import-ance, said she thought his suggestion was very appropriate, very nice. Since they'd lost a day's work anyway, and were all dressed up, they might as well go somewhere where they could learn something. Everyone agreed. As it was still raining a little, they borrowed some umbrellas from the proprietor, old umbrellas left behind by customers, blue, green, and brown, and set off for the museum.

The party turned right and went back into Paris down the Faubourg Saint-Denis. Once again Gervaise and Coupeau led the way, hurrying along ahead of the others. Monsieur Madinier now had Madame Lorilleux on his arm, as Maman Coupeau had stayed in the bar because of her legs. Next came Lorilleux and Madame Lerat, Boche and Madame Fauconnier, Bibi-la-Grillade and Mademoiselle Remanjou, with the Gaudrons bringing up the rear. There were twelve of them, again making quite a procession along the pavement.

'Oh, it's got nothing to do with us, nothing at all,' Madame Lorilleux was explaining to Monsieur Madinier. 'We don't know where he picked her up, or rather we know only too well; but it's not for us to say anything, is it? My husband had to buy the ring. And this mornin' we were no sooner out of bed than we had to lend 'em ten francs, otherwise there'd 'ave been no weddin' at all... A bride who doesn't bring a single relative to 'er weddin'! She says she's got a sister in Paris, married to a butcher. So why wasn't she invited?'

She broke off to point to Gervaise, who was limping badly because of the sloping pavement.

'Look at 'er! I ask you!... Gimpy!'*

The nickname 'Gimpy' ran through the group like wildfire. Lorilleux sniggered and said that was what they should call her. But Madame Fauconnier leapt to Gervaise's defence: they shouldn't make fun of her, she was neat as a pin and could get through work like nobody's business when she had to. Madame Lerat, never short of a suggestive remark, called Gervaise's leg a 'love pin', adding that lots of men liked that sort of thing, though she refused to explain further.

The wedding party emerged from the Rue Saint-Denis and crossed the boulevard.* They waited a moment because of the stream of carriages, then ventured on to the road, which the storm had turned into a river of mud. It was starting to rain again, so they opened their umbrellas, and under these sorry-looking objects, held over them by the men, the ladies walked along holding their skirts up. The procession straggled out over the mud, from one side of the street to the other. As they picked their way across, a couple of urchins yelled 'Hey, the circus is in town!' Passers-by came running to have a look and grinning shopkeepers stood watching from behind their windows. Against the grey, wet background of the boulevard and the milling crowds, the procession of couples stood out like splashes of colour: the dark blue dress of Gervaise, Madame Fauconnier's cream floral dress, Boche's canary yellow trousers. The stiffness of people wearing their Sunday best really did make Coupeau's shiny frock coat and Monsieur Madinier's square-cut tails look like funny carnival costumes, while Madame Lerat's tatty skirt made for an odd mixture of styles, as they trailed along in the reach-me-down finery of the poor. But what caused the greatest hilarity was the men's hats, ancient hats long preserved, their sheen having disappeared in dark cupboards, their shapes quite comical, tall, bell-shaped, or pointed, with amazing brims, curled or flat, too wide or too narrow. The smiles grew even broader when, at the very end, to bring the spectacle to a close, Madame Gaudron the wool-carder came sailing along in her bright purple dress, her huge pregnant belly well to the fore. Not that the party was in any hurry, for they took it all good-naturedly, enjoying the attention and laughing at the jokes.

'Look! Here comes the bride!' cried one of the urchins, pointing at Madame Gaudron. 'Oh dear, she's got a bun in the oven already!'

The whole group shrieked with laughter. Bibi-la-Grillade turned round and said the kid certainly had a point. The carder laughed the loudest, and started to preen herself; there was nothing to be ashamed of, was there? On the contrary, plenty of the women who stared at her as they went past would've been glad to be in her condition.

By now they were in the Rue de Cléry. Then they took the Rue du Mail. When they arrived at the Place des Victoires, they came to a halt. The bride's left shoelace had come undone, and while she was retying it at the foot of the statue of Louis XIV,* the couples gathered closely round her, joking about the bit of calf she was showing as they waited. At last, after going down the Rue Croix-des-Petits-Champs, they reached the Louvre.

Monsieur Madinier politely asked if he could lead the way. It was a very big place and you could easily get lost; besides, he knew the best things to see, because he'd often come here with an artist friend, a very clever young fellow whose drawings were bought by a large packaging firm for putting on their boxes. When they entered the Assyrian Gallery,* on the lower level, they all gave a little shiver. My word, it was a bit on the cool side! The room would have made a great wine cellar. Slowly, tilting their heads back and blinking, the couples walked along between the giant stone statues, the black marble gods silent in their stiff hieratical poses, and the monstrous beasts, half cat, half woman, whose shrunken noses and swollen lips made their faces look like death masks. They thought they were very ugly. People could carve stone a damn sight better these days. An inscription in Phoenician characters stopped them in their tracks. No, it wasn't possible, nobody could ever have read scribble like that. But Monsieur Madinier, who'd already reached the first landing with Madame Lorilleux, was calling to them, his voice echoing under the vaulted ceiling:

'Come on! Don't waste your time on that stuff... What you want to see is up here, on the first floor!'

The starkness of the staircase intimidated them, and their awe was increased by a magnificent usher in a red waistcoat and gold-braided livery who seemed to be waiting for them on the landing. Respectfully, walking as quietly as they could, they entered the French Gallery.

Then, without pausing, dazzled by the gold of the frames, they sped through the string of small galleries, seeing the pictures go past, too many to look at properly. You'd have had to spend an hour in front of each one to understand them. Blimey, what a lot of paintings! They went on forever! They must be worth a fortune. Then, at the end, Monsieur Madinier suddenly stopped them in front of the *Raft of the Medusa** and explained what it was about. They all stood silent, transfixed. When they set off again, Boche summed up the general feeling: it was really good.

In the Apollo Gallery,* what amazed everyone the most was the parquet floor, which was clear and shiny like a mirror, and reflected the legs of the benches. Madame Remanjou closed her eyes, feeling as if she was walking on water. They shouted to Madame Gaudron to be careful to set her feet down flat, because of her condition. Monsieur Madinier wanted to show them the gilding and painting on the ceiling, but looking up gave them a crick in the neck and they couldn't make anything out. Then, before going into the Salon Carré,* he pointed to a window and said:

'That's the balcony from which Charles IX* fired on the people!'

He looked around to see if there were any stragglers, then raised his hand to call a halt in the middle of the Salon Carré. In hushed tones, as though in church, he said that everything in this room was a masterpiece. They went round the Salon. Gervaise asked what the

Wedding at Cana* was about; it was silly not to write the subjects on the frames. Coupeau stopped in front of the *Mona Lisa*, saying she reminded him of one of his aunts. Boche and Bibi-la-Grillade sniggered as with sidelong glances they drew each other's attention to the naked women. Antiope's thighs* gave them a special thrill. And, right at the back, the Gaudrons, the husband open-mouthed, the wife with her hands on her belly, stood gaping in sentimental wonder at Murillo's *Virgin*.*

Having completed the tour of the Salon, Monsieur Madinier was all for going round again: it was well worth it. He was very attentive to Madame Lorilleux, on account of her silk dress, and each time she asked him a question he answered gravely, with tremendous self-assurance. As she showed an interest in Titian's mistress,* whose yellow hair she thought quite like her own, he told her it was La Belle Ferronnière,* a mistress of Henri IV, about whom there had been a play at the Ambigu.*

Next the party set off down the long gallery that houses paintings of the Italian and Flemish schools. More pictures, and still more pictures, of saints, of men and women whose faces meant nothing to them, landscapes all black, animals gone all yellow, a great jumble of people and things in such a riot of colours that everyone was beginning to get a nasty headache. Monsieur Madinier had fallen silent and was now walking slowly along at the head of the procession, which trailed behind him, the couples in the same order, necks craning and heads uplifted. Centuries of art passed before their stunned incomprehension: the subtle plainness of the primitives, the splendour of the Venetians, the rich, radiant life of the Dutch. But what interested them the most was the copyists, with their easels set up in the middle of the crowd, calmly painting away; an old lady perched on a tall ladder, using a whitewash brush to paint a pale blue sky on an enormous canvas, impressed them especially. Meanwhile, word must gradually have spread that a wedding party was visiting the Louvre; painters came running up with broad grins on their faces, curious onlookers sat down on benches to watch the procession in comfort, while the attendants bit their lips so as not to make ribald remarks. And the wedding party, weary now and feeling less intimidated, dragged their hobnailed boots and clumped their heels on the noisy floors, like a trampling herd running amock in the austere, tranquil orderliness of the galleries.

Monsieur Madinier still said nothing: he was waiting to spring a surprise on them. He strode up to Rubens's *Kermesse.** There, still saying nothing, he simply rolled his eyes salaciously in the direction of the picture. The ladies, when they'd got up close, let out little shrieks and turned away, blushing furiously. The men, sniggering, held them back and studied the canvas for the spicy details.

'Have a look at this!' Boche kept saying. 'This picture's worth the money. Here's somebody puking. And there's somebody watering the dandelions. And that one, just look at what he's up to! Well, what a fine lot we've got here!'

'Let's move on,' said Monsieur Madinier, delighted with his success, 'there's nothing more to see around here.'

So the party retraced its steps, through the Salon Carré and the Apollo Gallery. Madame Lerat and Mademoiselle Remanjou complained that their legs were killing them. But the cardboard-box maker wanted to show Lorilleux the antique jewellery. It wasn't far, at the back of a little room he could find with his eyes closed. Nevertheless he went the wrong way and dragged the party through seven or eight cold, deserted galleries, with nothing in them except plain glass cases displaying endless rows of broken pots and hideous little figurines. They were all beginning to shiver and were bored to death. Then, looking for a way out, they found themselves surrounded by drawings. There ensued another long trudge; the drawings seemed never to end, one room after another, and none of them in the least interesting, just scrawled-on pieces of paper in glass cases against the walls. Monsieur Madinier, in a panic but not wanting to admit he was lost, headed for some stairs and took the party up to the next floor. This time they found themselves in the Maritime Gallery, surrounded by models of instruments and cannons, relief maps and ships the size of toys. Finally, after walking for a quarter of an hour, they came to another staircase and went down it, only to find themselves back among the drawings. At this point, in total despair, they wandered through the galleries at random, still in pairs, still trailing behind Monsieur Madinier, who kept mopping his forehead, beside himself with rage at the management, whom he accused of having altered the position of the doors. The attendants and visitors watched in wonder as they went past. In less than twenty minutes they were sighted once more in the Salon Carré, in the French Gallery, and going past the glass cases where the little Oriental gods lay slumbering. Never would they get out. With their feet killing them, and all hope abandoned, they made a tremendous din as they clattered along, leaving Madame Gaudron and her big belly far behind.

'Closing time! Closing time!' shouted the attendants in thunderous voices.

They were very nearly locked in. One of the attendants had to take them in hand and show them to an exit. Then, in the courtyard, after fetching their umbrellas from the cloakroom, they began to breathe again. Monsieur Madinier recovered his composure: he should have turned left; he remembered now that the jewels were to the left. In any case, the whole party affected to be glad to have seen so much.

It was striking four. There were still two hours to fill before dinner. They decided to go for a little walk to pass the time. The ladies were worn out and would have preferred to sit down, but since nobody was offering to buy drinks they set off along the embankment. Then the rain came down again, so hard that the ladies' outfits got spoilt, in spite of their umbrellas. Madame Lorilleux, her heart sinking at every drop that fell on her dress, suggested they should shelter under the Pont-Royal,* and declared that if they didn't come with her she'd go down on her own. So the party climbed down under the bridge. It was really nice there. In fact, you could say it was a grand idea. The ladies spread their handkerchiefs on the cobbles and sat down with their knees apart, pulling with both hands at the blades of grass growing between the stones and watching the black water flow past, as though they were in the country. The men amused themselves shouting very loudly to get an echo back from the arch in front of them. Boche and Bibi-la-Grillade took turns hurling insults into space, yelling 'You dirty swine!' and laughing their heads off when the echo came back; then, when they got hoarse, they picked up some flat stones and played ducks and drakes. The rain had stopped but they were having such a good time that they all forgot about moving on. The Seine bore along patches of oil, old corks, vegetable peelings, rubbish of all sorts which would swirl round for a moment, held back by an eddy in the turbulent waters, made darker still by the shadow of the arch; while overhead on the bridge the buses and cabs rumbled on, amid all the tumult of the city, of which they could see nothing but rooftops, as if they were at the end of a tunnel. Mademoiselle Remanjou sighed and said that if there'd been some greenery it would have reminded her of a spot on the Marne* where she used to go, in 1817 or thereabouts, with a young man she was mourning still.

Monsieur Madinier, however, gave the signal for them to leave. They crossed the Tuileries Garden, where their orderly progress in pairs was upset by a throng of children playing with hoops and balls. Then, at the Place Vendôme, as they were all looking up at the column,* Monsieur Madinier had an idea which he thought would please the ladies: he proposed that they should go up and see the view of Paris. They thought this would be great fun. Yes, yes, they must go up, they'd have something to laugh about for ages. Besides, it would be very interesting for people like them who'd always kept their feet solidly on the ground.

'I can't see Gimpy daring to go up, with that leg of hers,' muttered Madame Lorilleux.

'I'll go up!' said Madame Lerat. 'But not if there's a man behind me.'

And up they went. All twelve of them climbed the narrow spiral staircase in single file, stumbling on the worn steps and holding on to the walls. Then, when it became pitch dark, they burst out laughing. The ladies made little squeals as the men tickled them and pinched their legs. But better not to say anything—just pretend it was mice! Anyway, it didn't go too far: the men knew where to stop, to keep things decent. Then Boche thought of something funny which got everybody going. They called out to Madame Gaudron, as if she'd been left behind, asking her whether she could get her belly through. Imagine! If she'd become stuck, unable to move up or down, she'd have blocked the way, and no one would ever be able to get out. And they laughed at the idea of the pregnant woman's belly with such a great gust of hilarity that the column began to shake. At this point Boche, now well away, declared that they'd grow old in this chimney stack: would it go on forever, right up to heaven? Then he tried to scare the ladies by shouting that the column was swaying. Meanwhile, Coupeau said nothing; he was just behind Gervaise, holding her round the waist, and he could feel her relaxing in his arms. When they suddenly emerged into the light, he was kissing her on the neck.

'You're a fine pair! Don't mind us!' exclaimed Madame Lorilleux, trying to sound shocked.

Bibi-la-Grillade, looking furious, muttered through clenched teeth:

'You made such a noise I couldn't even count the steps.'

But Monsieur Madinier was already on the platform, pointing out the famous landmarks. Madame Fauconnier and Mademoiselle Remanjou refused to come out from the stairway: the very thought of the pavement down below made their blood run cold; the most they would do was take a few quick peeps through the little door. Madame Lerat was bolder and walked right round the narrow platform, keeping close to the bronze dome. But it really was pretty scary, when you thought that all it would take was one false step. Bloody hell, what a fall that would be! The men paled a little as they looked down at the square. It was like being suspended in mid-air, cut off from everything. No, seriously, it really turned your stomach! Monsieur Madinier advised them all to look up, straight ahead into the far distance, that would stop them from getting dizzy. And he carried on, pointing out the Invalides, the Panthéon, Notre-Dame, the Tour Saint-Jacques,* and Montmartre. Then it occurred to Madame Lorilleux to ask whether it was possible to see the Moulin d'Argent on the Boulevard de la Chapelle, where they were going to have their dinner. Whereupon they spent ten minutes searching for it, even starting to quarrel, each of them placing it in a different spot. Around them stretched the vast greyness of Paris, with its deep valleys and billowing rooftops stretching away to the bluish horizon. The whole of the Right Bank lay in shadow, beneath a great ragged sheet of copper-coloured cloud; a broad ray of sunlight, streaming out from the cloud's gold-fringed edge, lit up the myriad windows of the Left Bank, making them sparkle, and highlighting that part of the city so that it stood out against a perfectly clear sky, washed clean by the storm.

'There wasn't much point coming up here just to have a row,' said Boche angrily, starting to go down the stairs.

The party went down in sullen silence, broken only by the clatter of shoes on the steps. At the bottom, Monsieur Madinier offered to pay, but Coupeau wouldn't hear of it, and thrust twenty-five sous—two sous each—into the attendant's hand. It was nearly half past five; they had just enough time to get back. They set off along the boulevards and the Faubourg Poissonnière. But Coupeau felt the outing couldn't end like that, and bundled them all into a bar for a glass of vermouth.

The meal had been ordered for six o'clock. They'd been waiting at the Moulin d'Argent for twenty minutes by the time the party arrived.

Madame Boche had arranged for her lodge to be looked after by a lady who lived in the building, and was chatting with Maman Coupeau in the first-floor room where the table was laid. She'd brought the two boys, Claude and Étienne, who were chasing each other under the table, sending the chairs in all directions. When Gervaise came in and saw the boys, whom she hadn't seen all day, she sat them on her knee, hugging them and giving them big kisses.

'Have they been good?' she asked Madame Boche. 'They haven't been driving you potty, I hope?'

And while Madame Boche was telling her about the hilarious things the little scallywags had said during the afternoon, Gervaise picked them up again and held them tight, in a sudden rush of affection.

'It must be funny for Coupeau, though,' Madame Lorilleux was saying to the other ladies, at the far end of the room.

Gervaise had managed to keep her calm good humour of the morning. Since coming back from the outing, however, she'd begun to feel quite sad, as she sat looking at her husband and the Lorilleux in her quiet, thoughtful way. She felt that Coupeau was a little afraid of his sister. Only the night before he had shouted and sworn that he'd put them in their place if they let him down with their poisonous tongues. But face to face—it was now quite clear to her—he was almost servile, hanging on their every word, and becoming very worried if they seemed annoyed. And this made her uneasy about the future.

Now they were only waiting for Mes-Bottes, who hadn't yet shown up.

'Oh, damn it!' Coupeau exclaimed. 'Let's get started. He'll roll up, you'll see; he's got a nose like a bloodhound, he can smell good food from miles away... He must be havin' fun if he's still hangin' about on the road to Saint-Denis!'

So, in very high spirits, the party sat down with a great scraping of chairs. Gervaise was between Lorilleux and Monsieur Madinier, and Coupeau between Madame Fauconnier and Madame Lorilleux. The other guests sat wherever they liked, because it always led to grumbling and arguments if the seating was arranged beforehand. Boche slipped in between Mademoiselle Remanjou and Madame Gaudron. As for Madame Boche and Maman Coupeau, at the far end, they had agreed to look after the boys, cutting their meat and giving them something to drink (but not too much wine!).

'Isn't anyone going to say grace?' asked Boche while the ladies were arranging their skirts under the table, for fear of stains.

But Madame Lorilleux didn't care for that kind of joke. The noodle soup, almost cold, was lapped up in no time, to a great sucking noise of lips on spoons. They were served by two waiters wearing greasy short jackets and none-too-white aprons. Sunlight streamed in through the four windows opening on to the acacias in the courtyard; after the stormy day the evening was clear and balmy. The reflections from the trees in this damp little corner cast a greenish light over the smoke-filled room and made the shadows of the leaves flicker across the tablecloth, which smelled slightly of mildew. At each end of the room hung a fly-blown mirror, which made the table seem to stretch on forever; it was laden with thick yellowing crockery blackened by knife-scratches full of grease from dirty washing-up water. Each time a waiter came up from the kitchen the door at the far end swung open and a strong smell of burnt fat blew in.

'Don't all talk at once,' said Boche, as they bent silently over their plates.

They were having their first glass of wine and eyeing two meat pies being served by the waiters, when Mes-Bottes came in.

'You're a nice lot, I must say!' he shouted. 'I waited around on the road for three bloody hours! A gendarme even came up and asked to see my papers. What a dirty trick to play on a friend! You could at least 'ave sent a cab to pick me up. Really, jokin' apart, it's a bit much. And it rained that 'ard I got water in me pockets. I bet I've still got some fish swimmin' around in 'em, enough for a good fry-up.'

They were all killing themselves laughing. Old Mes-Bottes was quite sozzled; he'd put away a couple of bottles, if only to protect himself from all that frog-piss that had come down on him.

'Well, if it isn't His Excellency 'imself!' said Coupeau. 'Sit yourself down over there, next to Madame Gaudron. You see, we've been waiting for you.'

Oh, they needn't have bothered, he'd soon catch up with them. He called three times for more soup, great platefuls into which he cut enormous chunks of bread; then, when the pies came, they were all astounded. What a guzzler! The astonished waiters formed a relay to pass him bread—thin slices which he swallowed in one mouthful. In the end he got annoyed and asked for a whole loaf to be put next to him. The landlord, quite alarmed, peered for a moment round the door. The party had been expecting this, and it sent them all into fresh fits of laughter. That'd give the bugger something to think about! He was such a devil, that old Mes-Bottes! Hadn't he once eaten twelve hard-boiled eggs and drunk twelve glasses of wine while the clock was striking twelve? It wasn't every day you came across someone who could do that. Mademoiselle Remanjou, quite touched, gazed at him as he chewed, while Monsieur Madinier, trying to find the right word to express his almost reverent admiration, declared that such capacity was extraordinary.

Silence fell. A waiter had just placed on the table a fricassee of rabbit, in a huge dish as deep as a salad bowl. Coupeau, always ready with a quip, came out with a good one:

'Hey, waiter, I reckon you caught this rabbit on the roof, it's still miaowing.'

And indeed a faint miaowing, perfectly imitated, seemed to be coming from the dish. It was Coupeau, doing it in his throat without moving his lips; it was a party trick of his that never failed, so that whenever he ate out he always ordered a fricassee of rabbit. Then he purred. The ladies, unable to stop laughing, kept dabbing their faces with their napkins.

Madame Fauconnier asked for the head; she liked only the head. Mademoiselle Remanjou adored the bacon. And when Mes-Bottes said he preferred the little onions, when they were nicely browned, Madame Lerat pursed her lips and muttered: 'I know what he means.'

She was a dry old stick, and led a cloistered life, working away day after day; no man had so much as set foot in her home since her husband's death, but she was forever coming out with smutty remarks—an absolute mania for double entendres and suggestive allusions so obscure that no one else could understand them. When Boche leaned over and, in a whisper, asked her to explain, she simply said:

'Little onions... Enough said, I think.'

But the conversation was getting serious. They were all talking about their work. Monsieur Madinier was waxing lyrical about cardboard boxes: there were some real artists in that line of business, and he mentioned special gift-boxes—he'd seen the models—which were absolute marvels of luxury. But Lorilleux sneered; he was very proud of working in gold, it was as if he could see it shining from his fingers and his entire person. In fact, as he never tired of saying, in the olden days jewellers used to wear swords; and he cited the example of Bernard Palissy,* not knowing who he was. As for Coupeau, he told them about a weathercock one of his mates had made, quite a masterpiece; it consisted first of a column, then a shaft of corn, then a basket of fruit, then a flag, all wonderfully lifelike and made entirely of pieces of zinc cut out and soldered together. Madame Lerat was showing Bibi-la-Grillade how to make a rose stem, turning the handle of her knife over and over between her long fingers. The voices grew louder as they all began to speak at once; above the din could be heard the shrill voice of Madame Fauconnier, complaining about her girls, saying that only the day before a slut of an apprentice had burnt a pair of sheets.

'You can say what you like,' yelled Lorilleux, thumping on the table. 'Gold is gold!'

This truism silenced everyone except Mademoiselle Remanjou, who declared in her piping voice:

'Then I pull their skirts up and sew them underneath. I stick a pin in their heads to keep the bonnet in place, and that's it—they sell for thirteen sous.'

She was telling Mes-Bottes about her dolls, as his jaws ground slowly on like millstones. He kept nodding, but he wasn't listening. He was keeping an eye on the waiters in case they took away a dish before he'd scraped it clean. They'd eaten a veal stew with green beans. Now the roast was being brought in, two scraggy chickens lying on a bed of cress which the heat of the oven had faded and dried up. Outside, the last rays of the setting sun were touching the upper branches of the acacias. The greenish light in the room was thick with the steam rising from the table, stained now with wine and gravy and littered with crockery and cutlery, while all along the wall dirty plates and empty bottles, dumped there by the waiters, looked like so much rubbish tipped off the table. It was very hot. The men took off their coats and went on eating in their shirtsleeves.

'Madame Boche, please don't stuff them like that,' said Gervaise, who wasn't saying much but was keeping an eye on Claude and Étienne from a distance.

She got up and went round behind their chairs to chat with them for a minute. Kids had no sense, they'd eat all day without ever saying no; and she herself served them some chicken, just a little off the breast. But Maman Coupeau said that, for once, they should be allowed to give themselves a tummy ache. Madame Boche, under her breath, accused her husband of pinching Madame Lerat's knees. Oh yes, he was a sly one, he couldn't help himself. She'd seen his hand disappear under the table. If he did that again, Jesus Christ, she'd bash him on the head with a carafe.

There was a lull in the conversation and Monsieur Madinier could be heard talking politics.

'Their law of the thirty-first of May* is an absolute disgrace! Now you have to have two years' residence. Three million citizens struck off the roll! They say Bonaparte is really upset about it, because he loves the people,* as we all know.'

He was a Republican himself, but he admired the prince because of his uncle, the likes of whom they'd never see again. At this Bibi-la-Grillade flared up: he'd worked at the Élysée* and he'd seen Bonaparte up close, just as he could see Mes-Bottes sitting there on the other side of the table! Well, that bastard president looked exactly like a police nark, he really did. They said he was going to do a tour down Lyons* way; it would be a bloody good riddance if he fell into a ditch and broke his neck. As the discussion was turning nasty, Coupeau had to intervene.

'You're a load of mugs to get worked up about politics! Politics is just a big joke! What difference does it make to the likes of us? They can have what they like, a king, an emperor, or nothin' at all, it won't stop me earnin' me five francs, and eatin' and sleepin', will it? No, it's all bullshit!'

Lorilleux shook his head. He'd been born on the same day as the Comte de Chambord,* the twenty-ninth of September. This coincidence seemed very significant to him, engendering in him a fantasy whereby the king's possible return to France was connected with his own personal fortunes. He never said precisely what he hoped for, but gave people to understand that something most wonderful would then come his way. So, whenever he wanted something that was beyond his reach, he'd put it off until later, 'when the king comes back'.

'As a matter of fact,' he said, 'I saw the Comte de Chambord one evening...'

All heads turned towards him.

'Oh yes, indeed. A big man, in an overcoat; he looked a nice bloke. I was at my mate Péquignot's, he sells furniture in the Grande-Rue de la Chapelle. The Comte had left his umbrella there the day before. So in he came and said: "Would you be so kind as to give me my umbrella." Very simply, just like that. Oh yes, it was 'im alright, Péquignot swore it was.'

Not one of the guests expressed the slightest doubt. They'd reached the dessert. The waiters were clearing the table with a great clattering of plates when Madame Lorilleux, who until then had been very proper and ladylike, let out a 'Damn the bugger!', because one of the waiters, as he was removing a dish, had let something wet drip on to her neck. Her silk dress would be stained for sure. Monsieur Madinier had to inspect her back, but he swore there was nothing to be seen. Meanwhile, in the middle of the table, the waiters had set a salad bowl containing some floating islands, flanked by two plates of cheese and two of fruit. The floating islands, with the overcooked egg whites crumbling into the custard, were greeted by a reverent silence; it hadn't been expected, and was thought quite classy. Mes-Bottes was still eating. He'd demanded another loaf. He polished off the two cheeses and, as there was still some custard left, he got them to pass him the bowl and wiped it clean with big chunks of bread, as if it was soup.

'That gentleman is amazing,' said Monsieur Madinier, once again lost in admiration.

Then the men stood up to fetch their pipes, pausing for a moment behind Mes-Bottes to slap him on the back and ask if he felt better now. Bibi-la-Grillade lifted him up in his chair, but, Christ Almighty, the bugger now weighed twice what he did before! Coupeau joked that their friend had only just got started, and he'd carry on scoffing bread like that all night. The waiters fled in terror.

Boche had gone downstairs for a moment, and came back to tell them how the landlord was sitting behind his counter, deathly pale, while his good lady, all in a tizz, had just sent out to see if the bakers were still open. Even the cat looked a bit down in the mouth. What a scream! It was well worth the price of the dinner; they must never have a meal out without that great guzzler Mes-Bottes. The men, smoking their pipes, gazed at him enviously: a bloke must have the constitution of an ox to be able to put it away like that!

'I'm glad I don't have to feed you,' said Madame Gaudron. 'No, thank you!'

'Come off it, Mum,' said Mes-Bottes, giving a sideways glance at his neighbour's belly. 'You've 'ad more than wot I 'ave.'

There was applause and cries of 'Well said!' You couldn't beat that! By now it was quite dark, and three gas burners had been lit, casting big patches of flickering light amid the pipe smoke. The waiters, after serving coffee and cognac, had taken away the last piles of dirty plates. Down below under the three acacias, the dancing was starting. A little band, a cornet and two violins, was playing very loudly, mingling with shrill female laughter in the warm night air.

'Now, what about a burnt brandy!' bellowed Mes-Bottes. 'Two litres of firewater, plenty of lemon, not too much sugar!'

But Coupeau, seeing Gervaise's anxious face across the table, stood up and said they wouldn't have any more to drink. They'd got through twenty-five bottles—one and a half per person, counting the kids as grown-ups, and that was more than enough. They'd had a bite to eat, nice and friendly-like, without any to-do, because they all liked one another and wanted to celebrate a family occasion together. It had gone off well and they were having a good time, and it wouldn't do if they now went and got pissed, not if they wanted to show respect for the ladies. In a word (and this was his point) they'd come together to drink the health of the newly-weds, not to drink themselves under the table. This little speech, delivered with conviction by the roofer, who put his hand on his heart at the end of every sentence, was greeted with warm approval by Lorilleux and Monsieur Madinier, but the other men, Boche, Gaudron, Bibi-la-Grillade, and especially Mes-Bottes, all four of them quite drunk, sniggered and declared in husky voices that they were bloody parched and needed to do something about it.

'Them as are thirsty are thirsty, and them as aren't aren't,' pronounced Mes-Bottes. 'So, we'll order the burnt brandy. We're not twisting any arms. The nobs can ask for some sugared water.'

And as the roofer was starting to deliver another little speech, he slapped himself on the backside and bawled:

'You can kiss that! Waiter, two litres of brandy!'

Thereupon Coupeau said that was all very well, but they'd better settle up for the meal straight away. That way there'd be no arguments. There was no reason why decent folk should pay for boozers. It turned out that Mes-Bottes, after a lot of searching through his pockets, could only produce three francs and seven sous. Well, why had they let him hang about on the road to Saint-Denis? He couldn't just stand there and get completely soaked, so he'd broken into his five-franc piece. It was all their fault! In the end he handed over three francs, keeping the seven sous for the next day's tobacco. Coupeau was furious, and would have clocked him one if Gervaise, alarmed, hadn't begged him not to, pulling him back by the coat. He decided to borrow two francs from Lorilleux, who refused but then slipped him the money in secret, for his wife would certainly never have allowed it.

Meanwhile, Monsieur Madinier was going round with a plate. The unaccompanied ladies, Madame Lerat, Madame Fauconnier, and Mademoiselle Remanjou, were the first to place their five-franc pieces on it, very discreetly. Then the men went into a huddle at the far end of the room to work things out. There were fifteen of them, which made seventy-five francs. When the seventy-five francs were on the plate, each man added five sous for the waiters. It took a quarter of an hour of laborious calculations before it was all sorted out to everybody's satisfaction.

But when Monsieur Madinier, who wanted to do the paying himself, asked for the proprietor to come up, they were all dumbfounded to hear him say with a smile that that didn't cover the bill at all. There were extras. And when the word 'extras' was greeted with furious protests, he went into details: twenty-five litres of wine instead of twenty, the number agreed on originally; the floating islands, which he'd added when he saw that the dessert looked a bit skimpy; and finally, a small carafe of rum, which had been served with the coffee, in case anyone fancied a drop. At this, a terrible row broke out. Coupeau, seeing himself held responsible, tried to defend himself: he'd never said anything about twenty litres, and as for the floating islands, they were part of the dessert—too bad if the proprietor had thrown them in off his own bat; and the carafe of rum, that was a swizz, just an excuse for padding the bill by slipping on to the table drinks people would barely notice.

'It was on the coffee tray,' Coupeau shouted; 'so, it should count as part of the coffee. Now bugger off! Take your money, an' I'll be damned if we ever set foot in this dump again!'

'Another six francs,' insisted the proprietor. 'I want my six francs. And I'm not even counting the three loaves that gentleman had!'

They all crowded round him, yapping and gesticulating angrily. The ladies in particular cast aside their customary reserve and flatly refused to add another centime. A nice wedding meal, this was! Thank you very much! Mademoiselle Remanjou swore she'd never be seen dead, ever again, at a dinner like this one! Madame Fauconnier hadn't liked the food at all; at home, for forty sous, she could have made a tasty little dish. Madame Gaudron complained bitterly that she'd been shoved down to the worst end of the table, next to Mes-Bottes, who hadn't paid the slightest attention to her. In short, functions like these always ended badly. When you wanted people to come to your wedding, you should damn well invite them as proper guests! Gervaise, who had taken refuge with Maman Coupeau at one of the windows, said nothing. She felt ashamed, for she had the impression that all these recriminations were being laid at her door.

In the end Monsieur Madinier disappeared with the proprietor. They could be heard arguing down below. Half an hour later he came back up, saying he'd settled the matter by handing over three francs. But the wedding party was still annoyed, and kept returning indignantly to the question of the extras. And the hubbub increased when Madame Boche suddenly turned violent. She'd been keeping an eye on her husband, and now saw him in a corner with his arm round Madame Lerat. Thereupon she hurled a carafe at him with all her might, smashing it against the wall.

'It's easy to see your husband's a tailor, Madame,' said the tall widow, pursing her lips suggestively. 'He's a dab hand with skirts. All the same, I gave him a few good kicks under the table.'

The evening was spoiled. The general mood was going from bad to worse. Monsieur Madinier suggested a sing-song, but Bibi-la-Grillade, who had a fine voice, was nowhere to be found; after a while, however, Mademoiselle Remanjou, leaning on a window sill, spotted him cavorting under the acacias with a buxom, bare-headed girl. The cornet and the two fiddles were now playing 'Le Marchand de moutarde',* a quadrille with a lot of hand-clapping in country-dance style. This started a stampede: Mes-Bottes and the Gaudrons went down and even Boche slipped away. From the windows the couples could be seen jigging about between the leaves, which had been turned a crude, artificial green by the lanterns hanging from the trees. The night was breathlessly still, as if exhausted from the intense heat. In the dining room a serious conversation had started up between Lorilleux and Monsieur Madinier, while the ladies, still seething with resentment, inspected their dresses for stains.

Madame Lerat's fringes must have dipped into the coffee. Madame Fauconnier's cream dress was covered in gravy. Maman Coupeau's green shawl had fallen off a chair, and had turned up in a corner all crumpled and trodden on. But it was Madame Lorilleux who was

really fuming. There was a stain on the back of her dress, and there
was no use their saying there wasn't, because she could feel it. Finally,
by twisting about in front of the mirror, she managed to see it.

'There! What did I tell you!' she yelled. 'It's chicken gravy. The
waiter will have to pay for the dress. I'll take him to court. It's the last
straw. I should have stayed in bed... I'm off. I've had it up to here
with this lousy wedding!'

She flounced out, making the staircase shake as she stomped downstairs. Lorilleux ran after her, but the best he could do was get her to
wait five minutes on the pavement in case they decided to go home
together. She should have gone home after the storm, as she'd wanted.
She'd get her own back on Coupeau for this terrible day. When her
brother heard how upset she was, he seemed quite dismayed, and
Gervaise, to spare him any more trouble, agreed to leave straight
away. So, without further ado, they all exchanged goodnight kisses,
and Monsieur Madinier undertook to see Maman Coupeau home.
Madame Boche was to have Claude and Étienne for the first night;
their mother needn't worry, the little ones were already fast asleep on
their chairs, their bellies weighed down by the floating islands. The
newly-weds were finally setting off with Lorilleux, leaving the rest of
the group in the dining room, when a fight broke out down below on
the dance floor, between some of their party and another lot; Boche
and Mes-Bottes, who'd started kissing a young lady, didn't want to
give her back to a couple of soldiers she was with, and were threatening to clean up the whole caboodle, to the excited accompaniment of
the cornet and the two fiddles playing the polka from *The Pearl Fishers*.*

It wasn't yet quite eleven. On the Boulevard de la Chapelle and
throughout the whole of the Goutte-d'Or district, the fortnightly
payday, which happened to fall on that Saturday, was being celebrated
with a huge, drunken din. Madame Lorilleux was waiting under a gas
lamp, twenty metres from the Moulin d'Argent. She took Lorilleux's
arm and marched ahead without looking back, at such a pace that
Gervaise and Coupeau got quite out of breath trying to keep up. From
time to time they had to step into the road to avoid a drunk lying
sprawled on the pavement. Lorilleux turned round, wanting to patch
things up:

'We'll see you to your door,' he said.

But Madame Lorilleux said in a loud voice that she thought it
funny that they were spending their wedding night in a dump like the

Hôtel Boncœur. Shouldn't they have put the wedding off and saved a bit of money, so as to buy some furniture and spend the first night in a place of their own? They'd be ever so comfortable, wouldn't they, jammed together in a ten-franc garret where they could hardly breathe.

'I've given notice, we're not going to be up there,' Coupeau replied timidly. 'We're keepin' Gervaise's room, it's bigger.'

Madame Lorilleux swung round, quite taken aback.

'Well, that beats everything!' she cried. 'You're sleepin' in Gimpy's room!'

Gervaise turned quite pale. The nickname, used to her face for the first time, was like a blow on the head. What's more, she knew very well what her sister-in-law meant: it meant the room where she'd lived for a month with Lantier, the room where bits and pieces of her former life were still lying about. Coupeau didn't see that; he was just hurt by the nickname.

'You shouldn't call other people names like that,' he snapped. 'P'raps you don't know everybody round 'ere calls you Cow Brush,* because of your hair. You don't like that, do you? Anyway, why shouldn't we keep the first-floor room? The kids won't be there tonight; we'll be fine.'

Madame Lorilleux, terribly offended at being called Cow Brush, said no more, trying to stand on her dignity. To comfort Gervaise, Coupeau gave her arm a little squeeze, and even managed to make her laugh by whispering in her ear that they were setting up house with precisely seven sous, three big coins and a little one, which he jingled with his hand in his trouser pocket. When they reached the Hôtel Boncœur they said goodnight rather frostily. Then, just as Coupeau was pushing the two women together for a kiss, telling them not to be silly, a drunk who had seemed to be about to pass them on the right, suddenly lurched to the left and came between them.

'Look who it is! It's Père Bazouge!' said Lorilleux. 'He's had a skinful!'

Quite alarmed, Gervaise flattened herself against the door of the hotel. Père Bazouge was an undertaker's assistant of about fifty. His black trousers were splashed with mud, his black coat was slung over his shoulder, and his black leather hat had been bashed in by a fall he must have had.

'Don't be scared, he won't hurt you,' Lorilleux went on. 'He's a neighbour of ours, third room along the corridor, before our place. He'd be in trouble if his boss saw him like this!'

Meanwhile Père Bazouge had taken offence at Gervaise's reaction.

'C'mon!' he stammered, 'we don't eat people in our line of business. C'mon, darlin', I'm as good as the next man... True enough, I've 'ad a few! When there's work on, you've got to keep oilin' the wheels. None of you lot could 'ave carried a bloke that weighs ninety kilos down from the fourth floor to the street—just the two of us, and without droppin' 'im. Me, I like to see people 'appy and cheerful.'

But Gervaise was retreating further into the doorway, overcome by a desire to burst into tears, feeling as if her little day of happiness had been spoiled. Forgetting all about kissing her sister-in-law, she begged Coupeau to make the drunk go away. Thereupon Bazouge, very unsteady on his feet, expressed his philosophical disdain.

'That won't stop you from goin' the same way, darlin'. P'raps you'll be 'appy to go, one day. Yes, I know a few women who'd say thank you if I came for 'em.'

And as the Lorilleux were trying to drag him away, he turned round and mumbled a final remark, between two hiccups:

'When you're dead—mark me words—when you're dead, you're dead for a very long time!'

CHAPTER IV

THERE followed four years of hard work. In the neighbourhood Gervaise and Coupeau were thought of as a steady couple who kept to themselves, didn't fight, and took a regular Sunday walk over Saint-Ouen* way. Gervaise put in twelve-hour days at Madame Fauconnier's, and still managed to keep her home as clean as a new pin and get a meal ready for her family morning and night. Coupeau never drank too much, brought his fortnightly pay straight home, and smoked a pipe at the open window before turning in, to get a bit of fresh air. They were held up as an example because they were so pleasant and likeable. And, as they earned nearly nine francs a day between them, people thought they must be putting by quite a tidy amount.

But, especially in the early days, they had to work like hell to make ends meet. Their wedding had saddled them with a debt of two hundred francs. And they hated the Hôtel Boncœur, which they thought was a horrible place, full of nasty people; they dreamed of having a home of their own, with their own furniture which they could take pride in. At least a score of times, they worked out how much they'd need: in round figures, it came to three hundred and fifty francs, if they didn't want to skimp and would have a saucepan or frying pan to lay their hands on whenever they needed one. They'd given up hope of saving such a large sum in under two years, when they had a stroke of luck: an old gentleman in Plassans asked them to send Claude, the older boy, so he could put him in boarding school. It was the generous whim of an eccentric art lover who'd been most impressed by some sketches of people the lad had done. Claude was already costing them an arm and a leg. With only the younger boy, Étienne, to support, they managed to put aside the three hundred and fifty francs in seven and a half months. On the day they bought their furniture, from a second-hand dealer in the Rue Belhomme, they went for a walk along the outer boulevards before going home, their hearts bursting with joy. There was a bed, a bedside table, a marble-topped chest of drawers, a cupboard, a round table covered in oilcloth and six chairs, all in old mahogany, as well as the bedding, linen, and kitchen utensils as good as new. For them this was like a serious, decisive start in life, something that, by making them householders, gave them a certain standing among the well-established people of the neighbourhood.

For two months they'd been busy trying to decide where to live. What they wanted more than anything was to rent a place in the big building in the Rue de la Goutte-d'Or. But there wasn't a single room to let there, so they had to abandon their long-cherished dream. To tell the truth, Gervaise didn't really mind; the idea of living just a few doors away from the Lorilleux really scared her. So they looked elsewhere. Coupeau, very sensibly, was keen not to be too far away from Madame Fauconnier's, so that Gervaise could pop home any time she liked. And after a while they made a lucky find, a big room, with a little one off it and a kitchen, in the Rue Neuve de la Goutte-d'Or, almost opposite the laundry. It was in a small two-storey house with a very steep staircase leading up to just two apartments, one on the right, the other on the left; the ground floor was occupied by a man who hired out carriages which he kept in sheds round a huge yard next to the street. Gervaise was delighted: it was like being back in the country, with no neighbours and no tittle-tattle to worry about, a nice quiet spot that reminded her of a lane in Plassans behind the ramparts; and, as the final stroke of luck, she could see her own window from the laundry, without even putting down her iron, by just leaning forward a little.

They moved in in April on the quarterly rent day. Gervaise was now eight months pregnant. But she was very gutsy, and would say jokingly that the child gave her a hand when she was working; she could feel its little fists pushing inside her, giving her strength. And she got very cross with Coupeau when he tried to make her lie down and take it easy! She'd lie down when the contractions started. That'd be soon enough, because now, with another mouth to feed, they'd have to work even harder! She was the one who cleaned the place, helping her husband to put back the furniture afterwards. She worshipped those pieces of furniture, she wiped them lovingly, and was heartbroken when she saw the slightest scratch. If she banged into them when she was sweeping she'd stop dead, almost as if she'd given herself a knock. The chest of drawers was especially dear to her: it looked so fine and solid, a thing of real distinction. Her secret dream, which she didn't dare mention to Coupeau, was to have a clock which she'd stand right in the middle of the marble top—the effect would be magnificent. If there hadn't been a baby on the way she might have risked buying her clock. But, with a sigh, she put it off till later.

The couple were enchanted with their new abode. They put Étienne's bed in the little room, where there was still space for another child's cot. The kitchen was the size of a pocket handkerchief and pitch dark, but if the door was left open they could see well enough, and in any case it wasn't as if Gervaise had to cook for thirty people, all she needed was room to make her stew. As for the larger room, it was their pride and joy. First thing in the morning they'd close the white calico curtains round the bed recess and the bedroom was immediately transformed into a living room, with the table in the middle and the cupboard and chest of drawers facing each other. Because the fireplace burned up to fifteen sous' worth of coal a day, they'd blocked it up; a little cast iron stove that stood on the marble slab kept them warm for seven sous when it was really cold. And then Coupeau had decorated the walls as best he could, promising himself that he'd make further embellishments later on. A tall engraving of a field marshal prancing on horseback, baton in hand, between a cannon and a pile of cannonballs, took the place of a mirror; on the chest of drawers two rows of family photographs stood on either side of a gilt-edged china bowl that had once been a holy water stoup but in which they now kept matches; on top of the cupboard a bust of Pascal* faced a bust of Béranger*—the one serious, the other smiling, they seemed to be listening to the cuckoo clock next to them. It really was a lovely room.

'Guess how much we pay here?' Gervaise would ask everyone who came to see them.

And when people guessed their rent to be higher than it was, she'd cry exultantly, delighted to have such a nice place for so little money:
'A hundred and fifty francs, that's all! It's next to nothing!'

The Rue Neuve de la Goutte-d'Or itself had a lot to do with their contentment. Gervaise practically lived in it, constantly going back and forth from her place to Madame Fauconnier's. And in the evenings Coupeau was now in the habit of going down and smoking his pipe on the doorstep. The rough cobbled street, which had no pavement, went steeply uphill. At the top, on the Rue de la Goutte-d'Or side, there were some dingy shops with dirty windows—cobblers, coopers, a doubtful-looking grocery store, and a wineshop that had gone bust and whose shutters had been closed for weeks and were covered with posters. At the other end, in the direction of Paris, some four-storey houses blocked out the sky; their ground floors were occupied by laundries, a whole row of them clustered together; the only bright note in the general gloom was a barber's shop of the sort you find in country towns, its front painted green, its window full of delicately coloured bottles, its polished sign gleaming. But the most cheerful part of the street was the middle, where the buildings, not so tall and more spaced out, let in air and sunlight. The sheds belonging to the man who hired out carriages, the soda-water factory next door, and the wash-house opposite created a big open space, very quiet, in which the muffled voices of the washerwomen and the regular breathing of the boiler only seemed to reinforce the stillness. Patches of waste ground stretching back from the street and little pathways disappearing between black walls gave it a village-like feel. Coupeau, who liked to watch the few passers-by stepping over the constant stream of soapy water, said it reminded him of a place one of his uncles had taken him to, when he was five. Gervaise took particular delight in a tree in a courtyard to the left of her window, an acacia with a single branch stretching out, whose few leaves were enough to lend a certain charm to the whole street.

Gervaise had her baby on the last day of April. The contractions started in the afternoon, at about four o'clock, while she was ironing a pair of curtains at Madame Fauconnier's. She didn't want to go home straight away, but sat twisting and turning on a chair and doing a bit of ironing when the pain subsided for a moment. The curtains were urgent and she was determined to finish them; besides, it might just be tummy ache, and you shouldn't make a fuss about that. But just as she was talking about starting on some men's shirts she suddenly turned white. She had to leave the laundry and cross the street, bent double and holding on to the walls. One of the other washerwomen offered to go with her. She wouldn't hear of it, but asked her to fetch the midwife from the Rue de la Charbonnière, round the corner. There surely wasn't any urgency. She probably had the whole night ahead of her. It wasn't going to prevent her from getting Coupeau's supper ready when she got home; then she'd see about lying on the bed for a few minutes without getting undressed. But on the stairs she was taken so bad that she had to sit down right there, on one of the steps; and she held her fists tight against her mouth to stop herself from crying out, because she couldn't bear the idea of some man coming up and finding her there. After a while the pain went and she managed to open the door, very relieved, sure it must have been a false alarm. That evening she was planning to make a stew with some bits of mutton chop. All seemed well as she peeled the potatoes. She was browning the meat in a pan when the sweating and contractions started again. She stirred the gravy, shifting from one foot to the other, blinded by tears. Even if she was having a baby that wasn't a reason to let Coupeau go without his supper. At last she had her stew simmering over a banked fire. She went back into the living room, thinking she had time to lay one end of the table. But she had to put the bottle of wine down again very quickly; unable to get as far as the bed, she collapsed on to a mat, and gave birth to her baby. When the midwife arrived, a quarter of an hour later, it was there that she delivered the afterbirth.

Coupeau was still working on the new hospital. Gervaise didn't want him to be disturbed on the job. When he got home at seven he found her in bed, well wrapped up and very pale against the pillow. The baby was crying, swaddled in a shawl at her feet.

'Oh, you poor thing!' said Coupeau, kissing her. 'An' there I was, less than an 'our ago, laughin' an' jokin' with me mates, while you were yellin' your 'ead off! Well you don't 'ang about, do you? It's all over before you know it.'

She smiled faintly and murmured:

'It's a girl.'

'Of course!' the roofer said jokingly, to cheer her up. 'I ordered a girl! And a girl it is! You can do anythin' I ask, can't you?'

Picking up the baby, he went on:

'Let's 'ave a look at you, you little devil! You've got a dark little mug. But don't worry, it'll brighten up. You must be a good girl and not misbehave; grow up sensible, like Papa and Maman.'

Gervaise gazed at her daughter, very serious, her wide-open eyes clouding over with a touch of sadness. She shook her head; she would have liked a boy, because boys could always get by and didn't run so many risks in a place like Paris. The midwife had to take the little creature out of Coupeau's hands. And she told Gervaise not to talk; it was bad enough having so much noise going on around her. Then the roofer said he'd have to go and let Maman Coupeau and the Lorilleux know; but he was starving and wanted to have his supper first. Gervaise was very upset to see him serving himself, running into the kitchen to get the stew, eating it out of a soup plate, not being able to find the bread. In spite of the midwife's orders, she couldn't help fretting, twisting about between the sheets. It was so silly she hadn't managed to lay the table, but the pains had laid her out as if she'd been hit on the head with a club. Her poor husband wouldn't like it if she lay there taking it easy while he had such a poor supper. At any rate, she hoped the potatoes were properly done. She couldn't remember now whether she'd salted them.

'That's enough talkin'!' said the midwife.

'That'll be the day, when you can stop her gettin' all worried,' said Coupeau, with his mouth full. 'If you weren't 'ere I bet she'd get out of bed to cut me some bread... Stay there on your back, you silly old thing! You've got to take care of yourself, or it'll be two weeks before you're on your feet again... It's very good, this stew you made. Madame's goin' to 'ave some too, aren't you, Madame?'

The midwife declined, but said she wouldn't say no to a glass of wine, because it had given her such a turn to find the poor woman on the mat with her baby. Coupeau finally took himself off to announce the news to the family. He came back half an hour later with the whole lot of them, Maman Coupeau, the Lorilleux, and Madame Lerat, who happened to have called in on them. The Lorilleux, faced with how well the young couple were doing, had become as friendly as could be, praising Gervaise to the skies, but hinting with certain gestures—little nods and winks—at reservations, as if they were deferring their final verdict. After all, they knew what they knew; but they didn't want to go against the opinion of the whole neighbourhood.

'I've brought the whole tribe,' cried Coupeau. 'I couldn't stop them, they wanted to see you. You're not allowed to say a word. They'll just stay a while and look at you, without any fuss, right? I'm goin' to make them some coffee, the very best!'

He disappeared into the kitchen. Maman Coupeau, after kissing Gervaise, went into raptures at the size of the baby. The other two women also planted smacking kisses on Gervaise's cheeks. And all three stood by the bed, exclaiming a lot as they told stories of various childbirths, strange cases some of them, but said it was usually no worse than having a tooth out. Madame Lerat examined the baby all over and declared it well formed, adding pointedly that *this* one would grow up into a proper woman; though, as she found the head rather pointed, she gently kneaded it, in spite of the child's cries, to make it round. Madame Lorilleux angrily snatched the baby from her: there was no telling what harm you might do to a creature, playing about with it like that when its skull was so soft. Then she tried to tell who the baby took after. This nearly caused a row. Lorilleux, peering past the women, kept saying the baby didn't look at all like Coupeau; the nose a little bit maybe, but even then! She was the spitting image of her mother, except for her eyes; those eyes definitely didn't come from *their* family.

Meanwhile Coupeau was still in the kitchen. They could hear him struggling with the stove and the coffee pot. Gervaise was getting worked up again: it wasn't a man's job to make coffee; and she shouted instructions to him, in spite of the fierce shushings of the midwife.

'Tell that silly bugger to shut up!' said Coupeau, coming in with the coffee pot. 'She's a right pain, going on like that!... We'll have this in glasses, if you don't mind—the cups are still at the shop.'

They sat down round the table and the roofer insisted on pouring the coffee himself. It smelt nice and strong, it wasn't any old rubbish. When the midwife had sipped her glass, she left: everything was going well enough and they didn't need her any more; if Gervaise had a bad night, they could send for her in the morning. She hadn't even got down the stairs before Madame Lorilleux was calling her an old soak and a lazy so-and-so. She put four lumps of sugar in her coffee and took fifteen francs off people just so they could have a baby on their own! But Coupeau stood up for her. He'd be happy to hand over the fifteen francs; after all, those women spent their youth studying, they were right to charge a lot. Then Lorilleux got into an argument with Madame Lorilleux; he claimed that if you wanted a boy you had to turn the head of your bed towards the north, whereas she, shrugging her shoulders, said that was a load of nonsense, and invoked another method that consisted of hiding under the mattress a bunch of fresh nettles picked in the full sun, without letting your wife know. They'd pushed the table close to the bed. Until ten o'clock Gervaise lay there, smiling vacantly, her head turned sideways on the pillow, sinking slowly into a state of complete exhaustion. She could see, she could hear, but she didn't have the strength to venture a single word or gesture; she felt as if she was dead, but it was an easy death, in which she enjoyed watching the others living around her. Every now and then a little cry would come from the baby, amid the loud voices going on and on about some murder the day before in the Rue du Bon-Puits, at the end of La Chapelle.

Then, when they were getting ready to go, there was talk of the christening. The Lorilleux had agreed to be godparents. They grumbled about it, but if they hadn't been asked they would have carried on something shocking. Coupeau didn't see why the baby had to be christened at all. It wouldn't give her ten thousand a year, would it? But it might give her a cold. The less you had to do with priests the better. Maman Coupeau called him a heathen; while the Lorilleux, though they didn't go to church to take communion, prided themselves on being religious.

'We can go on Sunday, if you want,' said the chainmaker.

Gervaise nodded and everybody kissed her goodbye and told her to look after herself. They also said goodbye to the baby. Each of them in turn leaned over the poor little quivering creature with smiles and fond words, as if it could understand. They called it Nana, the baby name for Anna, her godmother's name.

'Goodnight, Nana... Be a good girl, Nana...'

When they'd finally gone, Coupeau pulled his chair up next to the bed and finished his pipe, holding Gervaise's hand in his. He smoked slowly, dropping a remark or two between puffs, deeply moved.

'So, old girl, did they get on your nerves? I couldn't stop 'em comin', you know. After all, it shows how they all mean well. But it's nicer to be on your own, isn't it? I wanted to 'ave you all to meself for a bit. I thought they'd never go!... You poor old thing, it must really 'ave 'urt! Those little mites, when they come into the world, they've got no idea the trouble they cause! It must feel as if your belly's bein' split open. Where does it 'urt? I'll kiss it better.'

He gently slipped one of his big hands under her back and drew her towards him, kissing her belly through the sheet, with a simple working man's tenderness towards his wife, who was still suffering from the birth. He kept asking if he was hurting her, and said he would like to ease her pain by blowing on her. Gervaise was very happy. She swore she wasn't in any pain at all now. All she could think of was to get back on her feet as soon as possible, because from now on there'd be no time for taking it easy. But he told her not to worry. Wasn't it his job to provide for the little one? He'd be a rotten bugger if he ever left her saddled with the kid to take care of. There wasn't anything very clever about making a baby, was there? What counted was bringing it up properly.

That night Coupeau hardly slept. He'd covered the fire in the stove, and every hour he had to get up to give the baby a few spoonfuls of warm sugared water. Nevertheless, he went off to work in the morning as usual. He even used his lunch-break to go to the town hall to register the birth. Meanwhile Madame Boche had heard the news and came over to spend the day with Gervaise. But Gervaise, after sleeping soundly for ten hours, was beginning to fret, saying she was feeling stiff all over from staying in bed so long. She'd fall ill if they didn't let her get up. When Coupeau came home in the evening she told him what she'd had to put up with: of course she trusted Madame Boche, but it drove her mad to see a stranger making herself at home in her room, opening the drawers and fiddling with her things. The next day, when the concierge came back after running an errand, she found her up and dressed, sweeping the floor and getting her husband's dinner ready. There was no way she'd go back to bed. What sort of woman did they take her for! Rich ladies could act as if they were tired out if they wanted. When you're not rich, there's no time for that sort of thing.

Three days after having her baby she was back ironing petticoats at Madame Fauconnier's, banging away with her irons and dripping with sweat from the heat of the stove.

On the Saturday evening Madame Lorilleux, as godmother, brought over her christening presents: a thirty-five-sou bonnet and a pleated christening robe trimmed with lace, which she'd got for six francs because it was shop soiled. The following day Lorilleux, as godfather, presented the new mother with six pounds of sugar. They knew how things should be done. What's more, that evening they didn't turn up empty-handed to the meal given by the Coupeaus. The husband arrived with a bottle of vintage wine under each arm, while the wife came carrying a large custard tart she'd bought at a well-known cakeshop in the Chaussée de Clignancourt. The only thing was, they went round telling everybody in the neighbourhood about their generosity; they'd spent close to twenty francs. When Gervaise heard about the way they'd been blabbing she was furious, and stopped giving them credit for their generosity.

It was at the christening party that the Coupeaus first got to know their neighbours across the landing. The other apartment in the little house was occupied by two people, a mother and son, by the name of Goujet. Until then they'd just exchanged greetings on the stairs or in the street, nothing more; in fact these neighbours seemed a bit stand-offish. But the mother had brought up a bucket of water for Gervaise the day after the birth, and Gervaise thought it would only be right to invite them to the meal, especially as they seemed very nice. And so, naturally, they got to know each other.

The Goujets came from the Nord.* The mother repaired lace; the son, a blacksmith by trade, worked in a factory that made bolts. They'd been living in the apartment across the landing for five years. Their quiet, regular life concealed a tragic past: one day in Lille the father, in a drunken rage, had killed a workmate with an iron bar, and had then hanged himself in his prison cell with his handkerchief. After this calamity the widow and her son had moved to Paris, but still felt the tragedy hanging over them; they were seeking redemption by leading extremely respectable, inoffensive, hard-working lives. There was even a hint of pride involved, for they had begun to see themselves as better than other people. Madame Goujet, always in black and with her forehead framed by a sort of nun's coif, had a placid, white, matronly face, as if the whiteness of the lace and the delicate work of her fingers had endowed her with an air of serenity. Goujet was a colossus of twenty-three, superbly built, with a rosy face, blue eyes, and the strength of Hercules. His mates at the factory called him Gueule-d'Or* on account of his magnificent golden beard.

Gervaise took to these people straight away. The first time she went into their home she was amazed how clean it was. No doubt about it, you could blow anywhere, you wouldn't raise a speck of dust. And the floor shone like a mirror. Madame Goujet took her into her son's room to have a look. It was as pretty and bright as a girl's room, with a little iron bedstead with muslin curtains, a table, a washstand, and a little bookshelf on the wall; and all over the walls were pictures, cut-out figures, coloured prints secured with four nails, and portraits of all kinds of people taken from the illustrated papers. Madame Goujet said with a smile that her son was a big baby; in the evenings he was too tired to read, so he amused himself looking at his pictures. Gervaise forgot about the time and spent an hour with her neighbour, who had gone back to lacework by the window. She was fascinated by the hundreds of pins holding the lace, happy just to be there, breathing in the good clean smell of Madame Goujet's home, in which this delicate handiwork created an atmosphere of silent contemplation.

The Goujets seemed even nicer the better you got to know them. They worked very long hours and put more than a quarter of their earnings into a savings account.* In the neighbourhood they were treated with respect and people talked about their thrift. There was never a hole in Goujet's clothes, and he always went off to work in spotless overalls. He was very polite, even rather shy, despite his broad shoulders. The washerwomen at the end of the street laughed at the way he averted his eyes as he walked past. He didn't like their coarse language and thought it was disgusting that women should use so many foul words. One day, however, he'd come home slightly drunk. Madame Goujet's only reproach was to show him a portrait of his father, a poorly executed painting they had dutifully kept, hidden away in the chest of drawers. Since then Goujet drank no more than was good for him, though he had nothing against wine, because a workman needs wine. On Sundays he'd go out with his mother on his arm; usually they went over towards Vincennes,* but sometimes he'd take her to the theatre. He was quite devoted to her, and spoke to her as if he was still a little boy. With his square head and overdeveloped muscles, because of his heavy work with the hammer, he was like some great farm animal: slow-witted but very good-natured.

In the early days Gervaise's presence made Goujet feel embarrassed. Then, after a few weeks, he got used to her. He'd watch out for her so as to carry up her shopping or laundry, treating her with down-to-earth familiarity, like a sister, cutting pictures out of the newspaper specially for her. But one morning he opened her door without knocking and surprised her only half dressed, washing her neck; for a week after that he couldn't look her in the face, so that in the end he made her blush as well.

Cadet-Cassis, with his quick Parisian banter, found Goujet a bit of a dummy. It was all very well not to get sozzled and not chat up girls in the street, but damn it, a man should be a man, otherwise he should simply wear a skirt. He teased Goujet in front of Gervaise, accusing him of making eyes at all the women in the neighbourhood, an accusation which the giant smith hotly denied. But that didn't prevent the two workmen from being friends.

They'd call for one another in the morning and set off together, and sometimes they'd have a glass of beer before coming home. Since the christening party they'd used the familiar *tu*, because saying *vous* all the time is so long-winded. That was the extent of their friendship when Gueule-d'Or did Cadet-Cassis a tremendous favour, one of those favours you remember for the rest of your life. It was on the second of December.* The roofer, just for a lark, had the bright idea of going down into the city to watch the rioting. Not that he gave a toss about the Republic, Bonaparte, and all that lot; but he loved the smell of gunpowder and thought the shooting great fun. He got stuck behind a barricade and could easily have been nabbed as a rioter if the smith hadn't turned up at just the right moment, thrown his huge frame in the way, and helped him to get away. As they went back up the Rue du Faubourg-Poissonnière, Goujet walked fast and looked very serious. He took an interest in politics and was a Republican, but a moderate one, believing in justice and the common good. But he had taken no part in the fighting, and gave his reasons: the workers were tired of being the pawns of the bourgeoisie and having nothing to show for it. February and June* had been huge lessons for them, so from now on the workers were going to let the bourgeois do as they thought best. When he reached the top of the Rue des Poissonniers, he turned and looked back over Paris; there was some pretty bad stuff going on down there, and one day the workers might be sorry they'd stood by and done nothing. But Coupeau just laughed and said those silly buggers were mad to risk their hide just so that those lazy sods in the Chamber could keep drawing their twenty-five francs.* That evening the Coupeaus invited the Goujets to supper, and during dessert Cadet-Cassis and Gueule-d'Or solemnly kissed each other on both cheeks. Now they were friends for life.

For three years the lives of the two families on either side of the landing went on without incident. Gervaise brought up her baby girl without ever missing more than two days' work, a week at most. She'd become increasingly skilled at working with fine linen, and earned up to three francs a day. So she decided to put Étienne, who was now nearly eight, in a little school in the Rue de Chartres for five francs a week. Despite still having two children to care for, the couple put aside twenty or thirty francs each month in the savings bank. When they had put away six hundred francs Gervaise could hardly sleep for dreaming of the future: her great ambition was to set up on her own, rent a little shop, and employ her own laundry girls. She had it all worked out. After twenty years, if the business went well, they'd be able to buy an annuity and live on it somewhere in the country. But she was afraid to take the risk. She said she was looking around for a shop, to give herself time to think it over. The money was safe enough in their savings account; in fact, it was slowly growing. In these last three years she'd satisfied only one of her desires: she'd bought herself a clock; and even this clock, in rosewood, with twisted columns and a brass pendulum, had to be paid for over a year in twenty-sou instalments every Monday. It annoyed her when Coupeau said he'd wind it up; no, she was the only one allowed to take off the glass globe and reverently wipe the columns, as if the marble top of the chest of drawers had been transformed into a chapel. Under the glass globe, behind the clock, she hid the savings book. And often, when she was dreaming about her shop, she'd stand there, transfixed, staring at the moving hands as if she was waiting for a particular, very special moment to make up her mind.

The Coupeaus went out almost every Sunday with the Goujets. They were nice little outings: fried fish at Saint-Ouen, or rabbit at Vincennes, nothing fancy, under the trees at some open-air restaurant. The men only drank to satisfy their thirst and came home as sober as could be, with the ladies on their arms. Before they went to bed the two families would tot up the cost and divide it between them, and there was never any argument about the odd sou. The Lorilleux were jealous of the Goujets. It seemed funny, they said, that Cadet-Cassis and Gimpy should always go out with strangers when they had a family of their own. Oh no, they didn't care two hoots now about their family! Now they had a bit of money put aside, they didn't half give themselves airs! Madame Lorilleux, very annoyed at losing her hold over her brother, began bad-mouthing Gervaise again. But Madame Lerat stood up for her, defending her with some extraordinary stories of attempts on her virtue on the boulevard at night, from which Gervaise emerged like the heroine of some play, beating off her assailants with a few clips round the ear. As for Maman Coupeau, she tried to make them all get on with each other, and to stay on good terms with all her children; her eyesight was getting worse, she'd only one cleaning job left now and was grateful when one or the other of them slipped her the odd five francs.

On Nana's third birthday Coupeau came home in the evening to find Gervaise in a very agitated state. There was nothing the matter, she said. But, as she was setting the table the wrong way round and kept standing still with the plates in her hand, lost in thought, her husband insisted on being told.

'Well, it's this,' she admitted at last, 'that little draper's shop in the Rue de la Goutte-d'Or is up for rent. I saw the notice an hour ago when I went to get some bread. It gave me quite a shock.'

It was a well-kept shop in the very building where they had originally dreamed of living. There was the shop, a room behind, and two other rooms, one on either side. In short, it was just right for them; the rooms were rather small, but well laid out. The only trouble was, she thought it was too dear; the owner was talking about five hundred francs.

'So you went in to 'ave a look an' ask how much, did you?' said Coupeau.

'Oh, you know, just out of curiosity!' she replied, feigning indifference. 'I'm looking around, I go in wherever there's a board up, it doesn't commit you to anything... But it's definitely too dear. And perhaps it would be a mistake to set up on me own.'

But after supper she came back to the subject of the draper's shop. She drew a plan of the place on a bit of newspaper. And, gradually, she talked it through, calculating the size of different areas and arranging the rooms as if she had to move her furniture in the next day. Then Coupeau, seeing how keen she was, encouraged her to go ahead and rent it; she'd never find anything decent for less than five hundred francs, and anyway they might be able to get the rent knocked down a bit. The only snag was going to live in the same building as the Lorilleux, whom she couldn't stand. But this made her cross: she didn't hate anybody; carried away by her desire for the shop, she even defended the Lorilleux—they weren't really that bad, they'd get along all right. When they'd gone to bed and Coupeau was fast asleep, she was still thinking how to arrange the rooms, though she hadn't definitely made up her mind to go ahead and rent the place.

The next day, when she was alone, she couldn't resist the urge to take the glass globe off the clock to look at the savings book. To think that her shop was in there, in those pages covered with ugly scribbles! Before setting off for work she consulted Madame Goujet, who was all in favour of her setting up on her own; with a husband like hers, a decent sort who didn't drink, she was bound to do well and not lose any money. At lunchtime she even went up to see the Lorilleux to ask their opinion; she didn't want to give the impression she was hiding anything from the family. Madame Lorilleux was quite taken aback.

What! Gimpy was going to have her own shop now! Though cut to the quick, she muttered something in an effort to seem pleased: the shop was just right, Gervaise should definitely take it. However, when she got over the shock, she and her husband both mentioned the dampness in the courtyard and how dark the ground-floor rooms were. Oh, it was just the sort of place that gave you rheumatism! Still, if she'd made up her mind to go ahead and take it, nothing they said would stop her, would it?

That evening Gervaise laughingly admitted that it would have made her ill if anyone had stopped her from taking the shop. Nevertheless, before signing up, she wanted to take Coupeau to see it and try to get something knocked off the rent.

'All right, tomorrow if you like,' said her husband. 'Come an' fetch me around six at the house where I'm workin' in the Rue de la Nation, an' we'll go round by the Rue de la Goutte-d'Or on the way home.'

Coupeau was just finishing the roof of a new three-storey house. That very day, in fact, he was due to lay the last sheet of zinc. As the roof was almost flat, he'd set up his workbench there, a large plank of wood on two trestles. A beautiful May sunset was turning the chimney-tops gold. And, high up against the clear sky, the workman was calmly cutting the zinc with his shears, leaning over his bench like a tailor cutting out a pair of trousers in his shop. Against the wall of the neighbouring house his assistant, a slim, fair-haired lad of seventeen, was keeping up the fire in the brazier with an enormous pair of bellows, each puff from which sent up a cloud of sparks.

'Hey, Zidore! Put the irons in!' shouted Coupeau.

The assistant shoved the soldering irons into the middle of the glowing coals, which looked pale pink in the bright sunlight. Then he began working his bellows again. Coupeau was holding the last sheet of zinc. It had to be fixed on the edge of the roof, near the guttering; here, the roof suddenly sloped away, with a yawning drop to the street below. The roofer, wearing cloth slippers and appearing quite at home, shuffled forward, whistling the tune of 'Hey, Ho! The Baby Lambs!'. When he reached the steep bit he let himself slide down, then braced himself with one knee against a chimney-stack, hanging halfway out over the street, one leg dangling. Each time he leaned back to shout to the bone-idle Zidore, he'd catch hold of a corner of the brickwork because of the pavement down below.

'C'mon, slowcoach! Gimme those irons! Stop starin' into space! The work won't do itself!'

But Zidore was in no hurry. He was interested in some nearby roofs and in a thick column of smoke rising up in the distance, over by Grenelle;* it could be a fire. However, he did crawl on his belly until his head appeared over the edge of the steep part, and passed the irons to Coupeau, who began soldering the sheet of zinc. He crouched down or stretched forward, always managing to keep his balance, squatting on one haunch, perching on one toe, or hanging on by one finger. He had incredible nerve, infinite confidence. He defied all danger. It was like an old friend. It was the street that was afraid of him. He never stopped smoking his pipe, and turned round from time to time and calmly spat into the street.

'Look, it's Madame Boche!' he shouted suddenly. 'Hallo, Madame Boche!'

He'd just noticed the concierge crossing the street. She raised her head and recognized him. A conversation started between roof and pavement. She stood looking up, her hands tucked under her apron. He was now standing, his left arm round a flue pipe, leaning forward.

'You 'aven't seen my wife, 'ave you?'

'No, not at all,' replied the concierge. 'Is she round 'ere somewhere?'

'She's supposed to be comin' to get me... Is the family well?'

'Yes, thanks. I'm the invalid, and look at me!... I'm just on my way to the Chaussée de Clignancourt to get a leg of mutton. The butcher near the Moulin Rouge* only charges sixteen sous.'

They had to raise their voices because a cab was passing along the broad, deserted roadway. Their words, shouted at the top of their voices, brought a little old lady to her window, where she settled, with her elbows on the sill, thrilled at the sight of a man on the roof opposite, as if she hoped to see him fall at any moment.

'Cheerio, then!' yelled Madame Boche. 'I don't want to keep you.'

Coupeau turned round and took the iron Zidore was holding out. But just as the concierge was moving off, she saw Gervaise on the opposite side of the street, holding Nana by the hand. She was already looking up to tell Coupeau when Gervaise made a quick gesture to stop her, and in a low voice, so as not to be heard up above, she explained what she was afraid of: she was concerned that if she appeared all of a sudden it might give her husband a shock and he'd fall. In four years she'd only fetched him once from work. Today was the second time. She couldn't bear watching him, her blood ran cold when she saw her man up there between heaven and earth, in places where even the sparrows wouldn't dare to perch.

'It can't be very nice,' said Madame Boche. 'My 'usband's a tailor, so I don't 'ave that sort of worry.'

'If you only knew...', Gervaise went on. 'At the beginning I'd be in a panic all day. I kept imagining 'im on a stretcher with 'is 'ead bashed in. I don't think about it as much now. You get used to it. And you've got to earn a livin' somehow. But it's a hard way to do it, riskin' your life more than most.'

She fell silent, hiding Nana in her skirts, afraid the child might call out. In spite of herself she couldn't help watching; she went quite pale. Just then Coupeau was soldering the far edge of the sheet, near the gutter; he slid down as far as possible, but still couldn't quite reach the far end. So, moving slowly as workmen do, calmly and deliberately, he ventured a little further. For a moment he was right over the pavement, no longer holding on, getting on quietly with his work; and from below you could see the tiny white flame sputtering under the soldering iron as he carefully moved it along. Gervaise said not a word; choking with terror, she raised her clasped hands in an involuntary gesture of supplication. Then she let out her breath, noisily: Coupeau had just climbed back up the roof, without hurrying, taking the time to spit one last time into the street.

'So you're spying on me, are you?' he called out cheerfully as he caught sight of her. 'Isn't she silly, Madame Boche? She didn't want to shout up to me. Hang on, I'll be finished in ten minutes.'

All he had left to do was put a cowl on a chimney, a simple little job. The laundress and the concierge stayed where they were on the pavement, chatting about the neighbourhood and keeping an eye on Nana to make sure she didn't get her feet wet in the gutter, where she was looking for minnows; they kept glancing up at the roof, smiling and nodding, as if to show they weren't in a hurry. Across the road the old woman was still at her window, watching the man and waiting.

'What's that old cow staring at?' said Madame Boche. 'I don't like the look of 'er!'

Up above they could hear the roofer's strong voice singing 'Oh, I do love pickin' strawberries!'.* Now, bending over his workbench, he was cutting the zinc like an artist. He'd traced an arc with a pair of compasses and was cutting out a big fan-shaped piece with a pair of curved shears; then, with his hammer, he gently beat this fan into a pointed mushroom shape. Zidore was using the bellows again on the coals in the brazier. The sun was going down behind the house, in a great burst of pink light that slowly grew paler, turning a soft lilac. And, up in the sky, at this quiet moment of the day, the silhouettes of the two workers stood out starkly, enormously enlarged, along with the dark outline of the workbench and the strange shape of the bellows.

When he had cut out the cowl he shouted across:

'Zidore! Pass me the irons!'

But Zidore had vanished. Cursing, Coupeau looked round for him, calling his name through the open attic skylight. After a while he spotted him on a neighbouring roof, two houses away. The young lad had gone off to have a look round; his skimpy blond hair blew in the breeze as he stood blinking at the vastness of Paris.

'Hey, you lazy sod! Do you think you're in the country or something!' said Coupeau angrily. 'P'raps you're like Monsieur Béranger— writin' poetry? Gimme those irons! 'Avin' a little stroll on the roof-tops! Did you ever hear anythin' like it! Perhaps you'd like to go an' fetch your girlfriend and give 'er a serenade? Now gimme the bloody irons, you daft bugger!'

He finished the soldering and shouted down to Gervaise:

'That's it, I'm comin' down!'

The chimney to which he had to fit the cowl was in the middle of the roof. Gervaise, quite relaxed now, went on smiling as she watched him moving about. Nana, very pleased to suddenly catch sight of her father, clapped her little hands. She sat down on the pavement, so she could get a better view of what he was doing up there.

'Papa! Papa!' she yelled at the top of her voice. 'Papa, look at me!'

The roofer tried to lean forward, but his foot slipped. Then suddenly, stupidly, like a cat falling over its own paws, he slid down the gentle slope of the roof, unable to stop himself.

'Damn!' he said in a strangled voice.

And he fell. His body described a slight arc, turning over twice before he landed in the middle of the street with the dull thud of a bundle of washing thrown from a great height.

Gervaise gave a terrible scream. She stood there, unable to move, her arms raised. Passers-by ran up and a crowd gathered. Madame Boche, shocked, her legs almost giving way beneath her, took Nana in her arms to cover her face and stop her from seeing. Meanwhile, across the street, the little old woman calmly shut her window, as if satisfied.

Eventually four men carried Coupeau to a chemist's on the corner of the Rue des Poissonniers; he lay there for nearly an hour, on a blanket in the middle of the shop, while somebody went to get a stretcher from the Lariboisière hospital. He was still breathing, but the chemist kept shaking his head. Gervaise, kneeling beside him, couldn't stop sobbing, her face smeared with tears, blinded, in a daze. Automatically, she reached out and, very gently, felt her husband's limbs. Then she drew back, catching sight of the chemist who had told her not to touch him; but a few seconds later she began again, unable to stop herself from making sure Coupeau was still warm, thinking that somehow she was helping him. When the stretcher finally arrived, and there was talk of taking him to the hospital, she got to her feet and said fiercely:

'No, no, not the hospital!... We live on the Rue Neuve de la Goutte-d'Or.'

They tried to explain that it would cost a lot of money to keep her husband at home, but it was no use. She repeated stubbornly:

'Rue Neuve de la Goutte-d'Or. I'll show you which door... What difference does it make to you? I've got money. He's my husband, isn't he? I insist.'

So they had to carry Coupeau home. As the stretcher made its way through the dense crowd in front of the chemist's shop, the local women were talking excitedly about Gervaise: the lass might have a limp, but she wasn't lacking in spirit! She'd see her husband through, whereas at the hospital the doctors just let you peg out if they thought you were really sick, to save themselves the trouble of making you better. Madame Boche, after taking Nana home with her, had come back and, still shaking, was telling the story of the accident in endless detail.

'I was just going to get a leg of mutton, I was right there, I saw 'im fall,' she said, over and over again. 'It was because of 'is little kid, he wanted to lean over and see her, and then—bang! I 'ope to God I never see anyone fall like that again! Anyway, I'd better go and get my leg of mutton.'

For a week it was touch and go. The family, the neighbours, everybody, expected him to give up the ghost at any moment. The doctor, a very expensive doctor who charged five francs a visit, was afraid there might be internal injuries; this term caused great alarm, and the neighbours went around saying the roofer's heart had been dislodged by the fall. But Gervaise, pale from lack of sleep, serious, determined, just shrugged her shoulders. Her husband's right leg was broken, they all knew that; it would get mended, they needn't worry. As for the rest, the dislodged heart, she'd put it back in the right place. She knew how to deal with hearts—with care, cleanliness, and constant support. She showed tremendous faith, convinced she could help him through simply by staying close and caressing him gently when he had a temperature. She never had a moment's doubt. For a whole week she was constantly on her feet, hardly speaking, completely taken up by her determination to save him, forgetting the children, the street, the whole city. On the evening of the ninth day, when the doctor finally declared the patient out of danger, she sank on to a chair, her legs like jelly, exhausted, sobbing uncontrollably. That night she allowed herself a couple of hours' sleep, her head resting on the end of the bed.

Coupeau's accident had upset the family's normal routines. Maman Coupeau spent the nights with Gervaise, but by nine o'clock she'd fall asleep on her chair. Every evening, on her way home from work, Madame Lerat took the long way round to call in and hear the latest. At first the Lorilleux had come two or three times a day, offering to sit up with Gervaise and even bringing an armchair for her. But disagreements soon arose about how to look after sick folk. Madame Lorilleux claimed she'd saved enough people in her time to know how you should set about it. She also accused Gervaise of pushing her aside, of keeping her away from her brother's bed. Of course it was natural that Gimpy should want to take care of Coupeau because, after all, if she hadn't gone and bothered him in the Rue de la Nation, he wouldn't have fallen. The only thing was, the way she was looking after him, she was bound to finish him off.

When she saw Coupeau out of danger, Gervaise stopped guarding his bedside so jealously. Now they could no longer kill him, she was no longer wary of letting people come near him. The family made themselves at home round the sickroom. The convalescence was going to be a very long one; the doctor had spoken of four months. Now, during the long hours when Coupeau slept, the Lorilleux told Gervaise how stupid she was. A lot of good it had done to keep her husband at home! In the hospital he'd have been back on his feet in half the time. Lorilleux said he'd have liked to fall ill, with some minor ailment, to show her he'd go into Lariboisière without a moment's hesitation. Madame Lorilleux knew a woman who'd just come out; well, she'd had chicken twice a day. And they both worked out, for the twentieth time, how much the four months of convalescence would cost: first, all the days off work, then the doctor and the medicines, and later on the good wine and fresh meat. If the Coupeaus managed only to use up their savings, they should count themselves damned lucky. But it was likely they'd run into debt. That was their business, of course. As long as they weren't counting on the family, which didn't have the means to keep an invalid at home. It was just Gimpy's bad luck; she could have done like everybody else and let her husband be taken to the hospital. But no: it all went to show how stuck up she was.

One evening Madame Lorilleux was malicious enough to ask all of a sudden:

'So, what about your shop? When are you going to rent it?'

'Yes,' sniggered Lorilleux, 'the concierge is still expecting you.'

Gervaise was completely taken aback. She'd forgotten all about the shop. But she could see their malicious glee at the thought that her dream was in ruins. Indeed, from that evening onwards they never missed a chance to needle her about it. If someone mentioned an unrealizable wish, they'd say it would come true when Gervaise had a shop of her own with a fine frontage giving out on to the street. And they laughed at her behind her back. She tried not to think too badly of them, but it really seemed they were pleased about Coupeau's accident, seeing that it had prevented her from setting up her laundry in the Rue de la Goutte-d'Or.

So then she herself tried to turn it all into a joke and show them how gladly she parted with her money to get him well again. Each time she took the savings book from under the glass dome of the clock, she'd say cheerily, if they were there:

'I'm going out now, to rent my shop.'

She hadn't wanted to take all the money out at once. She asked for it a hundred francs at a time, so as not to keep a lot of cash in the chest of drawers; besides, she was vaguely hoping for some miracle, a sudden recovery that would make it possible not to withdraw the whole amount. Each time she came back from the bank she'd work out on a scrap of paper how much they had left—just to know where they stood. Although the hole in their nest-egg got bigger and bigger, she'd smile calmly and in her sensible way continued to keep account of the disaster. After all, wasn't it a consolation that the money was being put to good use, and was there to draw on just when they needed it? And so, without any regret, she'd carefully put the book back under the dome, behind the clock.

The Goujets were very kind to Gervaise during Coupeau's illness. Madame Goujet was always ready to help; she never went out without asking if she needed any sugar or butter or salt; and the evenings when she made a stew she always took her the first of the broth; and if she saw that Gervaise had too much to do she'd even help her with the cooking or give her a hand with the dishes. Every morning Goujet would take her buckets and fill them at the fountain in the Rue des Poissonniers: that saved her two sous. Then, after dinner, if the room was not overrun by the Coupeau family, the Goujets would come and sit with her. For two hours, until ten o'clock, the smith would smoke his pipe and watch Gervaise busying herself round the invalid. He'd never utter more than ten words the whole evening. He'd sit there with his big blond head sunk between his giant shoulders, touched by the sight of her pouring herbal tea into a cup and stirring the sugar without making any noise with the spoon. When she tucked in the bedclothes and made encouraging noises to Coupeau in her gentle voice, he was quite overcome. He'd never come across such a fine woman. Even her limp became a quality, bringing all the more credit to her, seeing how she was on the go all day tending her husband. She never sat down for more than a quarter of an hour, barely long enough to have a bite to eat, and that was the honest truth. She was constantly running over to the chemist's, taking care of all the dirty jobs, and working like a slave to keep the room, in which they did everything, in good order; and never a word of complaint, always pleasant, even in the evening, when she was so tired that she could hardly keep her eyes open. And in this atmosphere of devotion, surrounded by medicine bottles, the smith began to feel deep affection for Gervaise as he watched her caring for her husband with all her heart and soul.

'So, mate, you're patched up again,' he said one day to Coupeau. 'I never thought you wouldn't be: your wife is like God Almighty!'

He himself was on the point of getting married. At least, his mother had found a very suitable girl, a lacemaker like herself, whom she was keen for him to marry. To please her he'd said yes; and the wedding date had even been fixed for the beginning of September. The money for setting up house had been sitting in the savings bank for ages. But when Gervaise asked him about the wedding he'd shake his head and mumble in his slow, deliberate way:

'Not all women are like you, Madame Coupeau. If all women were like you a man would marry a dozen of them.'

Meanwhile, after two months, Coupeau was able to start getting up. He couldn't get far, just from the bed to the window, and even then Gervaise had to support him. There he'd sit in the Lorilleux' armchair, with his right leg stretched out on a stool. This joker, who had always laughed about people who broke their legs when there was ice about, was most aggrieved by his own accident. He couldn't be philosophical about it. He'd spent two months in bed cursing and driving everybody mad. What sort of existence was it, lying on your back with one leg strung up like a piece of salami sausage! Oh yes, he'd got to know the ceiling pretty well; there was a crack in the corner over the bed he could draw with his eyes closed. Then, when he settled in the armchair, it was another tale of woe. How long would he be stuck there, like an Egyptian mummy? There wasn't much to look at in the street, no one ever went past, and it stank of bleach all day long. No really, he was getting like an old man, he would have given ten years of his life to be able to go and see how the fortifications were doing. And he always ended up railing against fate. His accident wasn't fair, it shouldn't have happened to him; he was a good worker, not an idler or a boozer. If it had been somebody else, he might have understood.

'My old Dad', he'd say, 'broke 'is neck one day when he was pissed. I'm not sayin' he deserved it, but at least you can understand how it happened. But there I was, dead sober, all calm and collected, not a drop of booze in me body, an' I go and fall just because I wanted to turn round to give Nana a wave. Don't you think it's a bit much? If there's a God up there, he's got a funny way of doin' things. I'll never be able to swallow it.'

And even when he'd regained the use of his legs, he continued to harbour a grudge against his job. What a lousy job it was, having to spend your days up in the guttering like a cat. They knew what they were doing, those bourgeois! They sent you to your death, while they hadn't got the guts even to venture up a ladder, they just sat snugly by their fires and didn't give a damn what happened to the poor. He even got to the point of saying that everyone should do their own roofing. Hell! If there was any justice in the world, that was how it should be: if people didn't want to get wet, they should be the ones to make sure they were under cover. He was sorry he hadn't learnt a different trade, something more pleasant and less dangerous: carpentry, for example. That was his old man's fault too: fathers had the stupid habit of shoving their kids into their own line of work, regardless.

For another two months Coupeau had to walk on crutches. At first he managed to get downstairs and smoke a pipe at the doorstep. Then he was able to go as far as the outer boulevard, dragging himself along in the sunshine and sitting for hours on a bench. During these long outings his good humour and devilish wit began to return. And along with the pleasure of being alive, he enjoyed doing nothing, letting his body relax and his muscles slacken into a delicious state of lethargy; it was as if he was being slowly taken over by sloth, which was using his convalescence to get inside his skin and permeate his body with a titillating languor. He'd come home feeling in fine fettle, saying jokingly that this was the life and why couldn't it last forever. When he was able to do without crutches he went on longer excursions, calling in at building sites to see his old mates. He would stand in front of houses under construction, arms folded, sniggering and shaking his head; he'd make fun of the workmen as they toiled away, sticking out his leg to show them where all that sweating and slaving got you. The time he spent jeering at the labour of others satisfied his grudge against work. Of course he'd go back to it, he'd have to; but he'd put it off for as long as he could. He had good reason not to be too keen. And, anyway, it was so nice to take it easy for a while.

When Coupeau felt a bit bored in the afternoons he'd go up and see the Lorilleux. They were full of sympathy for him and ingratiated themselves with all sorts of little attentions. In the first years of his marriage, thanks to Gervaise, he'd escaped from their clutches. But now they were winning him back, teasing him about being afraid of his wife. Wasn't he a real man, then? However, the Lorilleux were extremely careful, going out of their way to praise Gervaise to the skies. Coupeau, though not yet trying to turn it into an argument, would swear to Gervaise that his sister adored her, and asked her not to be so nasty to her. The couple's first quarrel, one evening, was over Étienne. The roofer had spent the afternoon with the Lorilleux.

When he came home, as supper wasn't ready and the kids kept saying they were hungry, he suddenly lost his temper and gave Étienne a clip round the ear. And he carried on grousing for at least an hour: the brat wasn't his, he didn't know why he put up with him in the house; one of these days he'd chuck him out. Until then he'd accepted the boy without any fuss. The next day he was talking about wanting more respect, and three days later he was kicking Étienne up the backside morning and evening, so that when the lad heard Coupeau coming up the stairs he'd run across to the Goujets', where the old lacemaker kept a corner of the table for him to do his homework.

Gervaise had been back at work for some time. She no longer had the bother of taking off and putting back the glass dome of the clock; their savings had all gone, and she now had to work like a Trojan, work for four, for there were four mouths to feed. And she had to feed the lot of them. When she heard people say they felt sorry for her, she would leap to Coupeau's defence. Just imagine what he'd been through! It wasn't surprising he now had a bit of a chip on his shoulder. He'd be all right, though, once he'd fully recovered. And if it was suggested that Coupeau seemed quite well and could surely go back to work, she'd protest. No, no, not yet! She didn't want to have him in bed again. She'd heard what the doctor had said, hadn't she? She was the one who stopped him from going back to work, telling him every morning to take his time and not push himself. She even slipped the odd franc into his waistcoat pocket. Coupeau accepted this as quite natural, and complained of all sorts of aches and pains so he'd be coddled; six months later he was still convalescing. Now, on the days when he went to watch others working, he'd be happy to go and have a glass of wine with his mates. It was nice in the bar, after all; you could have a laugh and just stay for a few minutes. No harm in that. Only hypocrites pretended to drink because they were dying of thirst. They'd been quite right to make fun of him in the past—a glass of wine had never killed anybody. But he thumped his chest and said it was a point of honour for him never to drink anything but wine, always wine, never spirits; wine made you live longer, didn't make you feel ill, and didn't make you drunk. Several times, however, after a day spent loafing about, wandering from one building site to another, and from bar to bar, he came home the worse for wear. On those days Gervaise shut the apartment door, saying she had a bad headache, so that the Goujets wouldn't hear Coupeau's drivel.

But gradually she became depressed. Every morning and evening she'd go along to the Rue de la Goutte-d'Or to look at the shop, which was still for rent; but she did this furtively, as if it was something childish, unworthy of a grown woman. The shop was beginning to obsess her again: at night, when the light was out, she lay awake with her eyes closed, dreaming about it, as if enjoying some forbidden pleasure. Once again she did her sums: two hundred and fifty francs for the rent, one hundred and fifty for fitting the place out, and a hundred francs as a float to get her through the first two weeks: in all, five hundred francs at least. If she didn't talk about it all the time, it was because she was afraid it might seem she was sorry that their savings had all been swallowed up by Coupeau's illness. She often went quite pale because she'd nearly let her dream slip out, and she'd stop in mid-sentence, as embarrassed as if she'd been about to say something indecent. Now it would take four or five years of work before she could save such a large sum. What distressed her most was not being able to set herself up straight away; then she'd have been able to support the family without any help from Coupeau, giving him a few more months to get used to the idea of going back to work; this would have put her mind at rest, because she'd be sure of the future and free of the secret little panic attacks that seized her sometimes when he came home very merry, singing and telling her about some nonsense old Mes-Bottes had got up to after he'd bought him a bottle.

One evening when Gervaise was alone in the apartment, Goujet dropped in but didn't rush off almost immediately as he normally did. He sat smoking his pipe and looking at her. He clearly had something important to say, and was mulling it over without being able to decide just how to put it into words. Finally, after a pregnant silence, he made up his mind, took his pipe out of his mouth, and blurted:

'Madame Gervaise, would you let me lend you some money?'

She was bending over the chest of drawers, looking for some dusters. She straightened up, very red in the face. So he must have seen her that morning, standing in a trance in front of the shop for nearly ten minutes. He was smiling awkwardly, as if she might be offended by his suggestion. But she firmly refused: she'd never accept money without knowing when she'd be able to pay it back. Besides, the amount was really too much. When, dismayed by her refusal, he kept urging her to accept his offer, she finally cried:

'But what about your wedding? I can't take money you've saved for your wedding, can I?'

'Oh, don't worry about that,' he replied, blushing in his turn. 'I'm not going to get married. It was just an idea. I'd much rather lend you the money, I really would.'

At that they both lowered their eyes. There was something very tender between them which they couldn't express in words. She accepted. Goujet had already told his mother. They crossed the landing and went to see her straight away. She was looking serious, even a little sad, with her calm face bent over her embroidery frame. She didn't want to go against her son, but she didn't approve of his plan and said why not, very frankly: Coupeau was going to the bad, he would fritter away all the money from the shop. In particular, she couldn't forgive the roofer for having refused to learn to read, during his convalescence; her son had offered to teach him, but Coupeau had told him to mind his own business, saying that book-learning never helped to put food on the table. This had nearly caused a falling-out between the two men; from then on each went his own way. But now Madame Goujet, seeing the pleading look on her big boy's face, was very nice to Gervaise. It was agreed that they'd lend their neighbours five hundred francs; the loan would be repaid in twenty-franc instalments every month until it was all paid off.

'Ha! That smith's obviously got his eye on you,' laughed Coupeau when he heard the news. 'It doesn't worry me, he's such a dummy. He'll get his money back. But I must say, if he was dealing with crooks he'd really be taken for a ride.'

The Coupeaus rented the shop the following morning. All day long Gervaise ran backwards and forwards between the Rue Neuve and the Rue de la Goutte-d'Or. Seeing her tripping along so lightly, so excited that she no longer limped, people said she must have had an operation.

CHAPTER V

As it happened, the Boches had moved out of the Rue des Poissonniers at the end of the April quarter and taken over the concierge's lodge in the big tenement building in the Rue de la Goutte-d'Or. Funny how things turn out! One of Gervaise's worries, after living so peacefully without a concierge in her little place in the Rue Neuve, was that she'd be back in the power of some nasty creature who'd make a fuss about a drop of water she might spill or a door she might close too loudly in the evening. Concierges are such a vile breed! But with the Boches it should be pleasant enough. They knew one another and always got on. They'd be like family.

On the day when the Coupeaus went to sign the lease, Gervaise had a lump in her throat as she walked under the big archway. So she was really going to live in this huge building, the size of a small town, with its streets of stairs and corridors that went stretching on and criss-crossing for ever. The grey walls with the bits of washing drying in the sun at the windows, the dingy courtyard with its uneven cobbles like a public square, the rumble of work coming through the walls, all filled her with very mixed feelings: joy at finally being on the point of realizing her ambition, and fear that she might not succeed and would be crushed in the great struggle against starvation which she could feel around her. The locksmith's hammers and the carpenter's planes banged and hissed in the ground-floor workshops, and she felt she was doing something very daring, that she was throwing herself into the middle of a machine in motion. The water from the dye-works running under the archway that day was a very soft apple-green. She smiled as she stepped over it; she thought the colour was a good omen.

The appointment with the landlord was in the Boches' lodge. Monsieur Marescot, who had a big cutlery business in the Rue de la Paix,* had once worked as a knife-grinder on the streets. It was said that now he was worth several millions. Aged fifty-five, he was a big man with a bony frame, and sported a decoration in his buttonhole. He liked to show off his huge working man's hands, and loved taking away his tenants' knives and scissors to sharpen them himself, just for the pleasure of it. There was nothing stuck-up about him, people thought, because he'd spend hours with the concierges, in the gloomy recesses of their lodges, going through the accounts. That was where he did all his business. The Coupeaus found him sitting at Madame Boche's greasy table, hearing how the seamstress on the second floor, staircase A, had refused to pay and had used foul language to boot. Then, when they'd signed the lease, Monsieur Marescot shook the roofer by the hand. He liked working people, he said. There was a time when he'd had to struggle himself. But hard work would always see you through. After counting the two hundred and fifty francs for the first two quarters, which he stowed away in his deep pocket, he told them the story of his life and showed them his decoration.

Gervaise was a bit taken aback by the attitude of the Boches. They acted as if they didn't know her. They fussed round the landlord, bowing and scraping, hanging on his every word and constantly nodding in approval. Suddenly Madame Boche rushed out and chased away a gang of kids who were paddling about in front of the communal water tap, which had been left running and was flooding the courtyard. As she walked back, stern and erect in her flowing skirts, she looked up and studied all the windows, as if to make sure that everything in the building was in order, her pursed lips expressing the authority vested in her now that she had three hundred tenants in her charge. Boche was again talking about the seamstress on the second floor: in his opinion she should be thrown out; he worked out how much rent she owed, with the self-importance of an administrator whose management of affairs was in danger of being compromised. Monsieur Marescot approved of the idea of turning her out, but he wanted to wait until the half-quarter. It was hard to throw people out into the street, and besides it didn't put a single sou in the landlord's pocket. Gervaise gave a little shiver, wondering whether she too would be thrown into the street one day if some stroke of bad luck prevented her from paying. The smoke-filled lodge, full of dark furniture, was as damp and dismal as a cellar; under the window, what light there was fell on the tailor's worktable, where an old coat lay waiting to be turned; meanwhile, Pauline, the Boches' little girl, a redheaded four-year-old, sat quietly on the floor, watching a piece of veal simmering on the stove, enraptured by the rich aroma rising from the pan.

Monsieur Marescot was again holding out his hand to the roofer when Coupeau raised the subject of redecorating, reminding Marescot of an earlier conversation when he'd promised to discuss the matter. But this irritated the landlord: he hadn't promised anything, and anyway redecorating was never done in the case of shops. Nevertheless he agreed to go and have a look at the place, followed by the Coupeaus and Boche. The draper had taken with him all his fittings of shelves and counters; the shop was completely bare, revealing its black ceiling and cracked walls from which some old yellow paper was hanging loose. There, in the empty, echoing rooms, a furious argument broke out. Monsieur Marescot shouted that it was up to shopkeepers to decorate their own shops, because after all a tradesman might want to do his place up all in gold, and he, the landlord, couldn't put gold everywhere; then he described how he'd set up his own shop in the Rue de la Paix, he'd spent more than twenty thousand francs on it. Gervaise, with a woman's obstinacy, kept repeating what seemed to her an irrefutable argument: if it was an apartment, he'd stick up some wallpaper, wouldn't he? So, why not do the same for the shop? All she was asking for was for the ceiling to be whitewashed, and some new wallpaper.

Boche, meanwhile, remained aloof and inscrutable; he looked round, gazing at the ceiling, saying not a word. Coupeau gave him meaningful looks, but he seemed unwilling to take advantage of his great influence over the landlord. Eventually, however, he did betray a slight change of expression, a thin little smile accompanied by a nod. Thereupon Monsieur Marescot, exasperated and looking very unhappy, and spreading out his fingers in spasms like a miser clutching the gold someone is trying to snatch from him, gave in to Gervaise and promised to do the ceiling and the papering, on condition that she'd pay half the cost of the paper. Then he hurried away, not wanting to hear another word.

Then, when Boche was alone with the Coupeaus, he slapped them heartily on the back. What about that! He'd pulled that off very nicely. If it hadn't been for him they'd never have got their wallpaper and their ceiling. Had they noticed how Marescot had glanced at him for his opinion and agreed as soon as he'd seen him smile? Then he told them in confidence that he was the real power in the building: he decided who should be given notice, he let to people he liked, he collected the rents, which he kept for up to a fortnight in a drawer. That evening, as a polite way of saying thank you, the Coupeaus sent the Boches two bottles of wine. The present was worth it.

The following Monday work was started on the shop. Buying the wallpaper proved quite a business. Gervaise wanted grey paper with blue flowers, to make the walls bright and cheerful. Boche offered to go with her, to help her choose. But he had strict orders from the landlord not to spend more than fifteen sous a roll. They stayed in the shop for an hour, and Gervaise kept coming back to a very pretty chintz at eighteen sous a roll; she became quite desperate, finding all the others horrible. Eventually the concierge gave in; he'd take care of it, he'd count in an extra roll if need be. On the way home Gervaise bought some cakes for Pauline. She didn't want to seem ungrateful; she was always keen to show her appreciation to anyone who did her a good turn.

The shop was supposed to be ready in four days. The work went on for three weeks. At first they'd talked only of washing down the paint-work. But this paintwork, originally a kind of maroon, was so dirty and dingy that Gervaise let herself be persuaded to have the whole frontage done in light blue, picked out with yellow. The redecorating seemed to go on forever. Coupeau, who was still not working, would turn up early in the morning to see how it was going. Boche would put down the coat and trousers whose buttonholes he was mending and come over to 'supervise his men'. They would stand there all day staring at the painters, their hands behind their backs, smoking and spitting and commenting on every brush-stroke. The removal of a nail would engender endless discussion and profound reflection. The painters, two big jolly fellows, were constantly coming down from their ladders and planting themselves in the middle of the shop, where they'd stand for hours nodding and joining in the discussion while gazing at the job they'd only just started. It didn't take long to whitewash the ceiling. It was the painting that seemed as if it might never get finished. It simply refused to dry. At about nine o'clock the men would turn up with their pots of paint, put them down in a corner, have a quick look round, then disappear; they wouldn't be seen again that day. They'd gone to have some lunch, or else they had a little job to finish round the corner in the Rue Myrrha. At other times, Coupeau would take the whole gang off for a drink: Boche, the painters, and any mate of theirs who happened to be passing. So bang would go another afternoon! Gervaise was quite beside herself. Then suddenly, in a couple of days, it was all finished, the paintwork varnished, the paper hung, the rubbish carted away. The workmen had

rushed through the job, treating it as a game, whistling on their ladders and singing fit to deafen the entire neighbourhood.

They moved in at once. During the first few days Gervaise was as
excited as a child with a new toy when she crossed the road after some
errand. She'd begin to dawdle, smiling at the sight of her home. From
a distance, in the middle of the black row of the other shopfronts, her
shop seemed to her full of light, so cheerful and new, with its pale
blue sign on which the words *Laundry: Quality Work* were painted in
large yellow letters. In the window, which was closed in at the back
with little muslin curtains and papered in blue to set off the whiteness
of the linen, men's shirts were laid out and women's bonnets hung up,
their ribbons tied to brass wires. She thought her shop looked very
pretty, all blue like the sky. It was blue inside as well; the wallpaper, an
imitation of Pompadour* chintz, represented a trellis with morning-
glories running up it; the huge worktable, taking up two-thirds of the
room, was covered with a thick ironing blanket and draped with
a piece of cretonne printed with large blue sprigs, to hide the trestles.
Gervaise would sit on a stool, very happy with her beautiful establishment, sighing with contentment, and gazing fondly at her brand-new
equipment. But her eyes were always drawn first to the cast-iron stove
on which ten irons could be heated at once, arranged round the grate
on sloping stands. She'd go and kneel in front of it, examining it,
always afraid that her silly little apprentice would wreck the stove by
stuffing it with too much coke.

The living quarters behind the shop suited them well enough. The
Coupeaus slept in the first room, where they also cooked and had
their meals; a door at the back opened on to a courtyard. Nana's bed
was in the room on the right, a sort of large broom cupboard lit by
a round skylight near the ceiling. As for Étienne, he shared the room
on the left with the dirty washing, which lay on the floor in great piles.
There was, however, one drawback, which at first the Coupeaus didn't
want to admit: the walls streamed with water because of the damp,
with the result that they could hardly see properly after three in the
afternoon.

The new shop caused a sensation in the neighbourhood. People
said the Coupeaus had rushed into things and were bound to get into
trouble. And indeed they had spent all the Goujets' five hundred
francs on setting up the shop, without even keeping something to live
on for the first fortnight, as they'd intended. On the morning when

Gervaise threw back her shutters for the first time, she had just six francs in her purse. But she wasn't worried: customers had started to come in and it all looked very promising. A week later, on the Saturday, before going to bed, she sat up for two hours working everything out on a scrap of paper and then woke Coupeau to tell him, beaming with joy, that they'd be able to make pots of money—provided they were careful.

'Would you believe it!' Madame Lorilleux proclaimed up and down the street, 'That daft brother of mine will put up with anything! Gimpy's living in style now. That's her all over!'

The Lorilleux and Gervaise were now at daggers drawn. At first, while the shop was being done up, they'd nearly died of jealousy; the mere sight of the painters from a distance made them cross over to the other side of the street, and they'd go home gnashing their teeth. That useless creature with a blue shop, it was enough to make decent folk give up! So, on the second day, when the apprentice threw out a bowl of starch just as Madame Lorilleux was leaving the building, she'd stormed about accusing her sister-in-law of getting her girls to insult her. All relations were severed and whenever they met they just stared at each other.

'Oh yes, they're leading a fine life!' Madame Lorilleux kept saying. 'We all know where she got the money for her bloody shop! From the blacksmith, that's how she earned it. And those people aren't very nice either! Didn't the father slit his throat to save the guillotine the trouble? Anyway, there was something nasty like that!'

She accused Gervaise quite openly of sleeping with Goujet. She lied, claiming she'd caught them together one evening on a bench on the outer boulevard. The thought of this friendship, and the pleasures her sister-in-law must be enjoying, exasperated her still more; she had an ugly woman's regard for propriety. Every day her resentment rose to her lips:

'What's that cripple got that makes people go after her like that? Nobody shows any interest in me!'

Then she started spreading endless tittle-tattle among the neighbours. She had a whole story to tell. On the wedding day, she'd had a funny feeling! She had a sure instinct, and she knew already how it was bound to turn out. Of course, later on, Gimpy had soft-soaped them so much that, for Coupeau's sake, she and her husband had agreed to be godparents to Nana, even though it had cost an absolute packet, a christening like that. But now, you know, even if Gimpy was at death's door and asking for a glass of water, she wouldn't be the one to give it to her. She couldn't stand women who were brazen, shameless sluts. Nana, of course, would always be welcome if she came to see her godparents; you can't blame the kid for the way her mother carried on, can you? Coupeau shouldn't need to be told what to do. Any other man, in his place, would have stuck his wife's arse in a tub of cold water and given her a good hiding; but that was his business, all they asked of him was to insist on respect for his family. Good God! If Lorilleux had caught her, Madame Lorilleux, in the act, she'd have known about it! He'd have stabbed her with his scissors.

The Boches, however, who frowned on any quarrelling in the building, thought the Lorilleux were in the wrong. True enough, the Lorilleux were quiet, respectable people who worked the whole live-long day and paid their rent on the dot. But in this matter, frankly, jealousy was driving them potty. What's more, they were real skin-flints, absolute misers, the sort of people who hid their bottle of wine when you went up to see them, so they wouldn't have to offer you a glass; in short, they weren't at all nice. One day Gervaise had just given the Boches some cassis and soda water, and they were drinking it in their lodge, when Madame Lorilleux stalked past and pretended to spit in front of their door. After that, every Saturday, when Madame Boche swept the stairs and passages, she'd leave a pile of rubbish outside the Lorilleux' door.

'My God!' cried Madame Lorilleux, 'Gimpy's always giving those swine something to guzzle! Birds of a feather! They'd better not give me any trouble, or I'll complain to the landlord. You know, only yesterday I saw that sly bugger Boche getting up real close to Madame Gaudron. Fancy going after a woman of her age, with half a dozen kids! It's disgusting! If I see them carrying on again, I'll tell Madame Boche, so she can give 'er bloke a good clip round the ear. That'd be a laugh!'

Maman Coupeau still saw both households; she agreed with every-body and even managed to get herself invited to dinner more often than usual, by listening sympathetically to her daughter one evening and to her daughter-in-law the next. For the time being Madame Lerat wasn't going near the Coupeaus because she'd fallen out with Gimpy about a Zouave* who'd slashed his mistress's nose with a razor; she'd defended the Zouave because she thought the razor-slash a very

loving gesture, though she hadn't explained why. Then she'd managed to infuriate Madame Lorilleux even more by telling her that
Gimpy, in conversation, in front of fifteen or twenty people, hadn't
thought twice about referring to her as Cow Brush—just like that!
Yes, the Boches and all the neighbours called her Cow Brush now.

While all this backbiting was going on Gervaise remained calm and
cheerful, often standing at the door of her shop, greeting her friends
as they passed with a nod and a smile. She liked to put down her iron
for a minute or two and come out to enjoy looking at the street, her
heart swelling with the pride of a shopkeeper who has her own little
bit of pavement. The Rue de la Goutte-d'Or belonged to her, and so
did the streets nearby, and so did the whole neighbourhood. When
she stood there, in her white bodice, her arms bare and her blonde
hair dishevelled by the work, she'd crane her neck slightly and look to
the left and then to the right, to both ends of the street, and take in the
scene: the passers-by, the houses, the road, the sky. To the left the Rue
de la Goutte-d'Or, peaceful and deserted, stretched out as if into the
country, with women chatting quietly on their doorsteps. To the right,
a few metres away, was the Rue des Poissonniers, noisy with traffic
and the continuous tramp of people swirling back and forth, making
that end of the street the hub of a whole working-class world. Gervaise
loved the street, the jolting of the wagons over the potholes between
the big cobbles and the milling crowds whose flow along the narrow
pavements was broken here and there by steep pebbly slopes. The
three metres of gutter in front of her shop took on immense importance for her, becoming a wide river she liked to imagine as very clean,
a strange, living river, its waters tinted by the building's dye-works in
the most delicate of shades amid the surrounding black mud. And she
became intrigued by other shops: a huge grocer's with a display of
dried fruits held in place by finely meshed netting, a workers' draper
and outfitter, selling smocks and overalls with arms and legs spread
wide, swaying with the slightest breeze. In the fruiterer's and the
tripe shop she'd catch glimpses of the ends of counters, on which
splendid-looking cats lay purring serenely. Her neighbour, Madame
Vigouroux, the coal merchant, would return her greeting; a plump
little woman with a swarthy face and bright eyes, she'd fritter the day
away laughing with the men, leaning against her shopfront that she'd
had painted in a complicated design of logs on a maroon background,
to make it look like a country cottage. Her neighbours on the other

side, the Cudorge ladies—mother and daughter—who owned the
umbrella shop, never showed their faces; their shop window was dark
and their door, decorated with two little zinc parasols painted bright
red, was always shut. But before she went back inside, Gervaise would
glance across the road at a high blank wall, all white, with a single vast
gateway, through which could be seen a blacksmith's forge blazing in
a courtyard cluttered with carts and wagons with their shafts in the
air. On the wall the word *Farrier* was inscribed in big letters surrounded by a fan of horseshoes. All day long the hammers rang out
on the anvil, while showers of sparks lit up the gloomy yard. And at
the bottom of the wall, in a hole no bigger than a cupboard, between
a scrap-iron merchant and a roast-potato vendor, there was a watchmaker, a distinguished-looking gentleman in a frock coat, who was
constantly poking into watches with tiny little tools as he sat at a worktable covered with delicate objects reposing under glass bells, while
behind him the pendulums of two or three dozen miniature cuckoo
clocks all swung in unison, amid the dirt and squalor of the street and
the rhythmic hammering from the farrier's yard.

The neighbours all thought Gervaise was very nice. Of course
there was plenty of gossip about her, but everybody agreed that she
had lovely big eyes and a sweet little mouth with fine white teeth. In
short, she was a pretty blonde, and if it hadn't been for the misfortune
of her leg she would have been regarded as truly beautiful. She was
now twenty-eight, and had filled out a bit. Her delicate features had
taken on a certain chubbiness and her movements had become slower
and more deliberate. Nowadays she would sometimes sit dreaming on
the edge of a chair as she waited for her iron to heat, and a smile of
contentment would spread over her round face. She had grown very
fond of her food, they all agreed; but it was no sin, quite the opposite.
When you earn enough to treat yourself to little luxuries you'd be silly
to live on potato peelings, wouldn't you? Besides, she always worked
hard, going to endless trouble for her customers, staying up all night
with the shutters closed if there was an urgent job to finish. As
they said in the neighbourhood, she was born under a lucky star:
everything she turned her hand to was a success. She did the washing
for the building—Monsieur Madinier, Mademoiselle Remanjou, the
Boches—and even took some customers away from her former
employer, Madame Fauconnier, some city ladies who lived in the Rue
du Faubourg-Poissonnière. By the second fortnight she'd had to take

on two assistants, Madame Putois and Clémence, the lanky girl who used to live on the sixth floor; that meant she now had three staff, including the cross-eyed little apprentice, Augustine, who was as ugly as they come. Some people might well have had their heads turned by such luck. You could understand if she indulged herself with a nice dish or two on a Monday, after slaving away all week long. In any case she needed to; she would have turned into a complete lazybones and expected the sheets to iron themselves if she hadn't sunk her teeth into something really delicious, something that made her mouth water just to think about it.

Never had Gervaise been so amiable to everybody. She was as sweet and gentle as a lamb; she seemed to have a heart of gold. Apart from Madame Lorilleux, whom she called Cow Brush to get her own back, there was no one she disliked; she tried to see the best in everybody. When she was feeling relaxed after a good lunch followed by coffee, she'd sink into a mood of indulgence towards the whole world. She'd say: 'We must be nice to each other, mustn't we, if we don't want to live like savages.' When people said how kind she was, she just laughed. A fine thing it would be if she'd been unkind! It was no credit to her if she was kind! Hadn't all her dreams come true? What was left for her to wish for? She recalled her ideal of long ago, when she was down and out: to work, have something to eat, have a little place of her own, bring up her kids, not get knocked about, die in her own bed. Her ideal had been more than realized; she now had everything she'd wished for, and more. As for dying in her own bed, she'd add jokingly, she was counting on that, but as late as possible, of course.

Gervaise was especially nice to Coupeau. Never a cross word, never a complaint behind his back. The roofer had finally gone back to work, and as the place where he was working was on the other side of Paris, she'd give him forty sous every morning for his lunch, his little nip, and his tobacco. The only thing was that two days out of six he'd stop on the way, drink the forty sous with a pal, and come back at lunch with some cock-and-bull story. On one occasion he hadn't even gone very far, but treated himself, along with Mes-Bottes and three others, to a slap-up meal, with snails, a roast, and a bottle of fine wine, at the Capucin* over by the Barrière de la Chapelle; then, as his forty sous weren't enough, he'd got a waiter to take the bill to his wife and tell her he was in hock. Gervaise laughed and shrugged her shoulders.

What was the harm if her bloke was having a bit of fun? You had to give men a bit of rope if you wanted things to be peaceful at home. Otherwise, there'd be arguments and it would soon come to blows. After all, you had to make allowances: Coupeau's leg was still bothering him, and the others led him on, so he had to go along with them so as not to seem a clod. Anyway, it didn't matter; if he came home a bit tiddly he went to bed, and two hours later he'd be all right again.

Meanwhile, the hot weather had arrived. One Saturday afternoon in June, when there was a lot of urgent work to be done, Gervaise herself had filled the stove with coke—there were ten irons heating round the roaring flue-pipe. At that time of day the sun was shining straight into the shop window and the hot pavement sent shimmering patterns up on to the ceiling; and this blaze, tinged with blue because of the paper on the shelves and in the window, threw a blinding light across the worktable, like sunlight filtered through fine linen. The temperature inside was unbearable. The street door had been left open, but not a breath of air came in; the garments drying on the brass wires steamed and became stiff as boards in less than three-quarters of an hour. In the sweltering heat a deep silence had reigned for a few minutes, broken only by the dull thud of irons on the thick calico-trimmed blanket.

'Oh, Lord!' said Gervaise. 'We're goin' to melt! It's enough to make you want to take your chemise off!'

She was squatting on the floor in front of an earthenware pot, busy starching some linen. In her white petticoat, with her sleeves rolled up and her bodice slipping off her shoulders, her arms and neck bare, she was all rosy, and sweating so much that loose wisps of her tousled blonde hair were sticking to her skin. She was carefully dipping bonnets, men's shirt fronts, whole petticoats, and the lace edging of women's knickers into the milky water. Then she rolled them up and laid them in a square basket, after dipping her hand into a bucket and sprinkling water over the parts of the shirts and knickers that hadn't been starched.

'This basket's for you, Madame Putois,' she said. 'Can you get a move on? It's drying straight away, in an hour we'd have to do it all over again.'

Madame Putois, a small woman of forty-five, showed no sign of sweating as she ironed away, buttoned up in an old brown jacket. She hadn't even taken off her bonnet, a black bonnet with green ribbons that were turning yellow. She was standing up straight in front of the worktable, which was too high for her, her elbows raised, pushing her iron with jerky, puppet-like movements. Suddenly she exclaimed:

'No, please, Mademoiselle Clémence, put your bodice back on! You know I can't abide indecency. While you're about it, you might as well show us everything. There are three men across the street already.'

Clémence muttered under her breath that Madame Putois was a stupid old cow. She was suffocating, so why not make herself comfortable? Not everybody had dried-up skin! And could anybody really see anything? At this point she raised her arms, so that her majestic breasts nearly burst out of her bodice and her shoulders strained against her short sleeves. Clémence was so hell-bent on always having a good time that she'd be worn out by the time she was thirty; after a night on the tiles she didn't know which side was up, she'd fall asleep over her work, feeling as if her head and her belly were stuffed with rags. But Gervaise kept her on nevertheless because no other girl could iron a shirt as well as she could. She had a special knack with men's shirts.

'They're all mine, ain't they?' she declared at last, slapping her bosom. 'And they don't bite, they don't do nobody no 'arm.'

'Clémence, put your bodice back on,' said Gervaise. 'Madame Putois is right, it's not decent. People might start thinkin' my shop is somethin' else altogether.'

So Clémence got dressed again, grumbling as she did so. What a fuss about nothing! As if passers-by had never seen a pair of tits before! And she took her annoyance out on the apprentice, squinty Augustine, who was standing next to her ironing easy stuff like stockings and hankies; she pushed her and knocked her with her elbow. But Augustine, with the sly bitchiness of an ugly duckling always being picked on, got her own back by spitting on her dress from behind, without anyone seeing.

Meanwhile Gervaise had just started on a bonnet belonging to Madame Boche that she wanted to do extra carefully. She'd prepared some hot-water starch so as to make it look as good as new, and was gently ironing the inside with a *polonais*, a little iron rounded at both ends, when a woman walked in, a bony creature with a blotchy face and soaking wet skirts. It was one of the head washerwomen, with three girls under her, at the Goutte-d'Or wash-house.

'You're too early, Madame Bijard!' Gervaise shouted. 'I said this evening... It's very awkward just now!'

But the washerwoman began to protest, saying she was afraid she wouldn't have time to get everything hung up to dry that day, and Gervaise agreed to let her have the dirty washing straight away. They went to fetch the bundles of washing from the room on the left where Étienne slept, and came back with huge armfuls which they dropped on the floor at the back of the shop. The sorting took a good half-hour. Gervaise made separate piles all round her, throwing all the men's shirts together, then all the women's chemises, the handkerchiefs, the socks, the dishcloths. When she came across something belonging to a new customer, she'd mark it with a cross in red thread, so she'd recognize it. A stale stench rose in the warm air as they sorted through all this dirty laundry.

'What a pong!' said Clémence, holding her nose.

'Ha! If it was clean, they wouldn't be givin' it to us, would they?' Gervaise remarked calmly. 'Of course it smells!... We said fourteen chemises, didn't we, Madame Bijard? Fifteen, sixteen, seventeen...'

She went on counting out loud. She was used to filth, and didn't find it in the least disgusting; she thrust her bare pink arms into the piles of chemises yellow with dirt, dishcloths stiff with grease from washing-up water, socks eaten away by sweat. Yet, despite the strong smell that hit her in the face as she bent down, a kind of dreamy contentment came over her. Perched on a stool, bent double, reaching out to right and left, slowly, smiling vaguely, her eyes misty, she seemed intoxicated by this human stench. It was as though her laziness began at this moment, that it came from the asphyxiating reek of these dirty clothes poisoning the air around her.

Just as she was shaking out a nappy so soaked in piss that she couldn't tell what it was, Coupeau walked in.

'Bloody 'ell!' he mumbled, 'What a scorcher! Enough to split your 'ead open.'

He had to steady himself against the worktable to prevent himself from falling over. It was the first time he'd got so completely sozzled. Until then he'd come home a bit tipsy, nothing more. But this time he had a black eye, the result of an accidental knock in some brawl. His curly hair, which was already showing a few white strands, must have brushed against a wall in some low dive, because he had a cobweb hanging over the back of his neck. However, he was his usual jolly self, and though he looked a bit older, his features were tightly drawn, and his lower jaw stuck out more, he was still, he said, as cheerful and good-natured as they come, and had a complexion that would be the envy of a duchess.

'I'll tell you what 'appened,' he went on, turning to Gervaise. 'It was Pied-de-Céleri,* you know the one, the bloke with the wooden leg. Well, he's goin' back 'ome and he wanted to buy us all a drink. We would 'ave been all right if it 'adn't been for the bloody sun. Out there in the street they're all feelin' real wobbly. Honest! They can 'ardly walk straight.'

Clémence started laughing at the idea of Coupeau finding the whole street drunk, and this set him laughing too, so much so that he nearly choked. He kept shouting:

'They're all soused, the lot of 'em! What a scream! But it ain't their fault, it's the sun...'

The whole shop was laughing now, even Madame Putois, who disapproved of drunks. Squinty Augustine was cackling like a hen, openmouthed, nearly choking. Gervaise had a feeling that Coupeau had not come straight home, but had spent an hour with the Lorilleux, who put all sorts of nasty thoughts into his head. When he swore he hadn't, she joined in the laughter, full of indulgence, and didn't even take him to task for missing another day's work.

'The things he comes out with!' she murmured. 'Did you ever 'ear such nonsense!'

Then, in a motherly tone, she added:

'Why don't you go and lie down? You can see we're busy, and you're in the way... That makes thirty-two handkerchiefs, Madame Bijard; plus two, makes thirty-four...'

But Coupeau didn't feel sleepy, so there he stood, swaying back and forth like a pendulum and grinning in a defiant, provocative way. Anxious to get rid of Madame Bijard, Gervaise called Clémence over and got her to count the laundry items while she made the list. As she picked up each piece, the cheeky devil made some crude remark, commenting on their customers' wretched poverty, or their bedroom secrets, making a washerwoman's special jokes about every hole and every stain she came across. Augustine pretended not to understand, but kept her ears wide open, dirty little thing that she was. Madame Putois pursed her lips, thinking it was bad to talk like that in front of Coupeau; a man has no business looking at dirty washing; people who were nice kept it out of sight. As for Gervaise, concerned to get the job done, she seemed not to hear. As she made the list, she looked carefully at each item, to see who it belonged to, and not once did she make a mistake, but put a name to each piece, recognizing it by its smell or its colour. Those napkins belonged to the Goujets, obviously: you could see they'd never been used to wipe the bottom of any saucepan. That pillowcase certainly came from the Boches, because of the pomade Madame Boche left all over her linen. And you didn't have to stick your nose into Monsieur Madinier's flannel vests to know they were his: the wool was always discoloured, his skin was so greasy. She knew other details too, the secrets of each person's personal cleanliness, the undies of neighbours who swanned around in silk dresses, the number of stockings, handkerchiefs, and shirts certain people got dirty in a week, the way other people tore certain things, always in the same place. There were loads of little stories she could tell. Madame Remanjou's chemises, for example, were the subject of endless comment: they became worn round the top, which meant that the old girl had pointed shoulders; and they were never dirty, even if she wore them for a fortnight, which proved that at that age you're like a plank of wood it'd be hard to get the tiniest drop of anything out of. In this way, every time they sorted the washing, they undressed the entire Goutte-d'Or neighbourhood.

'This one's really yummy!' cried Clémence, opening another bundle.

Gervaise recoiled in a sudden fit of revulsion.

'That's Madame Gaudron's lot,' she said. 'I don't want to do hers any more, I'm looking for an excuse. I'm no fussier than the next person, I've 'ad to deal with some really disgusting washin' in me time; but honestly, that stuff, I just can't. It's enough to make me throw up. What does the woman do, to get 'er clothes into such a state!'

She begged Clémence to get a move on, but the girl carried on with her commentary, sticking her fingers into holes and remarking on the items concerned, which she waved about like banners of filth triumphant. Meanwhile the piles surrounding Gervaise had grown bigger. Still perched on the edge of her stool, she'd almost disappeared behind the shirts and petticoats; before her lay sheets, knickers, and tablecloths, like a great mass of foulness; and there, in the middle of this rising tide, her arms and neck still bare, with little wisps of her blonde hair sticking to her temples, she looked rosier and more languid than ever. She'd forgotten about Madame Gaudron's washing and its smell, and regained her composure, smiling her nice professional smile as she poked about in the piles to make sure everything was in order. Squinty Augustine, who loved throwing shovelfuls of coke into the stove, had just filled it so full that its cast-iron plates glowed red. The shop seemed ablaze as the slanting sun beat on the window. Then Coupeau, made even more sozzled by the heat, suddenly became quite emotional. He walked towards Gervaise with his arms outstretched.

'You're a good li'l woman,' he mumbled. 'Let's 'ave a kiss.'

But he got tangled up in the petticoats lying in his way, and nearly fell over.

'You're such a nuisance,' said Gervaise, not really annoyed.

But no, he wanted a kiss, he had to have a kiss because he loved her so much. Mumbling away, he went round the pile of petticoats and tripped over the pile of shirts; then, determined to get to Gervaise, he got his feet caught and fell flat on his face, among the dishcloths. Gervaise was beginning to lose patience and pushed him away, shouting that he'd get everything mixed up. But Clémence, and even Madame Putois, thought she shouldn't be so hard on him. After all, he was being nice. Surely she could let him kiss her.

'You don't know how lucky you are, Madame Coupeau,' said Madame Bijard, whose drunkard of a husband, a locksmith, gave her a battering every evening when he came home. 'If mine was like that when he's 'ad too much, I'd be very pleased!'

Gervaise had already calmed down, sorry she'd been so sharp. She helped Coupeau to get back on his feet and offered him her cheek with a smile. But the roofer, unconcerned by the presence of the others, grabbed hold of her breasts.

'Don't mind me sayin' it,' he mumbled, 'but your washin' smells somethin' awful! But I still love you, y'know.'

'Let go, you're ticklin' me,' she cried, laughing still louder. 'You silly thing! How can anybody be so daft?'

But he held her in his arms and wouldn't let go. She stopped struggling, feeling quite dizzy because of the mountain of washing and not in the least put off by Coupeau's alcoholic breath. And the smacking kiss they gave each other full on the mouth, in the middle of all the dirty washing, was like a first step in the slow downward spiral of their life.

Meanwhile, Madame Bijard was tying the clothes up in bundles, while chatting about her little girl, two-year-old Eulalie, who already had the maturity of a grown woman. She could be left on her own; she never cried or played with matches. Eventually Madame Bijard took the bundles away one by one, her tall frame bent double under the weight, purple blotches appearing on her face.

'This is unbearable, we're roasting,' said Gervaise, wiping her face before starting again on Madame Boche's bonnet.

Then, noticing that the stove was red-hot, they threatened to give Augustine a good hiding. The irons were getting red as well. You never knew what she was going to do next! You couldn't turn your back without her doing something stupid. Now they'd have to wait a quarter of an hour before they could use the irons. Gervaise damped down the fire with two shovelfuls of ash. She also had the idea of hanging a pair of sheets over the wires under the ceiling, like blinds, to block out the sun. That made it quite pleasant in the shop. It was still pretty warm, but it was like being in an alcove full of white light, shut away from the world in a little home of your own, even though, through the sheets, footsteps could be heard along the pavement; and it left you free to make yourself comfortable. Clémence took off her bodice. As Coupeau refused to go and lie down he was allowed to stay, but he had to promise to sit quietly in a corner, because now they absolutely had to get down to work.

'What's that useless creature done with the *polonais* this time?' grumbled Gervaise, referring to Augustine.

They were always having to hunt for the little iron, which they'd find in the oddest places, where the apprentice, they maintained, hid it out of spite. Gervaise finally finished the lining of Madame Boche's bonnet. She'd started by doing the lace roughly, stretching it by hand, then perking it up with a few strokes of the iron. It was a bonnet with a very elaborate brim made up of ruffles alternating with embroidered lace insertions; so she had to concentrate, working carefully in silence, ironing the ruffles and insertions with a 'cock', an egg-shaped iron fixed to a wooden handle.

Silence reigned. For a moment all you could hear was dull thuds on the ironing blanket. On both sides of the huge square table Gervaise, her two assistants, and the apprentice stood bent over their work, their shoulders rounded, their arms constantly moving back and forth. Each had her 'square' to her right, a piece of flat brick covered with scorchmarks from over-hot irons. In the middle of the table, on the edge of a dish filled with cold water, were a moist rag and a little brush. In a jar that had once contained brandied cherries was a bunch of lilies in full bloom, its cluster of big snowy petals making the room look like a corner of some royal garden. Madame Putois had started on the big basket of washing Gervaise had got ready, table napkins, women's knickers, bodices, and pairs of sleeves. Augustine was dawdling over her stockings and dishcloths, her nose in the air, watching a huge fly buzzing overhead. As for Clémence, she had got up to her thirty-fifth shirt of the morning.

'Wine! Never spirits!' proclaimed the roofer all of a sudden, apparently feeling he had to make this declaration. 'Spirits aren't good for me, mustn't 'ave none!'

Clémence took an iron off the stove with her metal and leather holder and held it to her cheek to see if it was hot enough. She rubbed it on her 'square', wiped it on a cloth hanging from her belt, and set to work on her thirty-fifth shirt, beginning with the front and the two sleeves.

'Oh, Monsieur Coupeau,' she said after a minute, 'a drop of brandy don't do no 'arm. Makes me feel really frisky, if you know what I mean. And anyway, the sooner you kick the bucket the better. I don't kid meself, I know I won't make old bones.'

'You're such a misery, always goin' on about dyin'!' interrupted Madame Putois, who didn't like morbid talk.

Coupeau had got to his feet in annoyance, thinking he was being accused of drinking brandy. He swore on his own head and on those of his wife and child that there wasn't a drop of brandy in his body, and he went up to Clémence and breathed in her face so she could smell. Then, when he was right up against her bare shoulders, he began to snigger. He wanted to have a look. Clémence had folded the back of the shirt and run the iron across each side, and had now moved on to the sleeves and collar. But as he kept pushing up against her, she made a crease and had to take the brush from the dish and smooth out the starched cloth.

'Madame!' she cried, 'Keep 'im off me, please!'

'Leave 'er alone and be'ave yourself,' said Gervaise, quite unruffled. 'Can't you see we're busy?'

Well, so what if they were busy? It wasn't his fault. He wasn't doing anything wrong. He wasn't touching, he was just looking. Wasn't he allowed to look any more at the lovely things the Lord had made? She had a great pair of tits, that tart Clémence! She could put 'em on show and let blokes 'ave a feel at two sous a go, nobody'd want their money back. By now the girl had stopped complaining and was laughing at these crude drunken compliments. She even began to trade jokes with him. He was teasing her about the men's shirts. So, she was a specialist in men's shirts, was she? Oh yes, in fact she lived in 'em. Heavens above, she knew everything there was to know about them and how they were made. Plenty of 'em had passed through her hands, hundreds and hundreds of 'em! Fair-haired or dark, all the blokes in the neighbourhood went about with her handiwork on their backs. But through all this banter she went on with her work, her shoulders shaking with laughter; she'd made five wide pleats down the back by inserting the iron through the front, then she folded the front part down again and ironed it into broad pleats as well.

'This is the tail!' she said, laughing even more.

Squinty Augustine exploded, thinking this joke hilarious. They promptly told her off. What an idea, a kid like her laughing at jokes she had no business understanding! Clémence handed her her iron; the apprentice used the irons on her dishcloths and stockings when they weren't hot enough for the starched things. But she took hold of this one so clumsily that she gave herself a 'cuff'—a long burn on the wrist. Bursting into tears, she accused Clémence of deliberately making her do it. The assistant, who'd gone to get a very hot iron for a shirt front, shut her up by threatening to iron both her ears if she carried on like that. In the meantime she'd slipped a woollen cloth under the shirt front and was slowly applying her iron to it so as to give the starch time to come out and dry. The front was becoming as stiff and shiny as glossy cardboard.

'God damn it!' swore Coupeau, who was shuffling about behind her with a drunkard's persistence.

He stood on tiptoe, cackling like a badly oiled pulley. Clémence was leaning heavily on the worktable, her wrists turned inwards, her elbows held high and wide apart, her head bent under the effort she was making; and all her bare flesh seemed to swell, her shoulders rising and falling as the muscles contracted under her delicate skin, while her breasts, damp with sweat, swelled in the rosy shadow of her gaping bodice. He put his hands out, wanting to touch her.

'Madame! Madame!' shouted Clémence, 'Tell 'im to give over, for God's sake! I'll 'ave to leave if this goes on. I won't be treated like this.'

Gervaise had just placed Madame Boche's bonnet on a hat stand covered with a cloth and was goffering the lace very carefully with the little iron. She looked up just as the roofer was reaching out again, groping inside Clémence's bodice.

'Coupeau, you just can't be'ave,' she said in a tired voice, as if scolding a child who keeps wanting to have jam without any bread. 'You'd better go to bed.'

'Yes, go and lie down, Monsieur Coupeau, that'd be best,' declared Madame Putois.

'Well,' he stammered, still sniggering, 'you're a miserable lot! Can't people 'ave a bit of fun any more? I've always got on well with women, an' I've never got any of 'em into trouble. I give 'em a pinch or two, but I don't go no further. It's just a way of showin' me appreciation. An' anyway, when you show your goods off, it's so a bloke can 'ave a proper look, innit? Why's that big blonde showin' off everythin' she's got, then? No, it ain't right!'

And turning to Clémence:

'You know, love, there's no need to get on your 'igh 'orse. If it's 'cos there are other people 'ere...'

But he wasn't able to carry on. Gervaise took hold of him, quite gently, with one hand and put the other hand over his mouth. He pretended to resist, just in fun, as she pushed him towards the back of the shop to the bedroom. Getting his mouth free, he said he didn't mind going to bed so long as the big blonde came too, to keep his tootsies warm. Then they heard Gervaise taking off his boots. She undressed him, rough-handling him a bit, but in a motherly way. When she pulled his trousers down, he roared with laughter, letting her get on with it, sprawling on his back in the middle of the bed; but then he began to wriggle about, saying she was tickling him. Eventually she managed to tuck him in, very carefully, like a child. Was he comfy now? He didn't answer, but called out to Clémence:

'C'mon, love, I'm waitin' for you.'

Just as Gervaise came back into the shop, squinty Augustine got a tremendous wallop from Clémence. It was because of a dirty iron Madame Putois had picked up from the stove; quite unsuspecting, she'd dirtied a whole bodice with it; and because Clémence, accused of not cleaning her iron, had tried to deflect the blame on to Augustine, swearing to high heaven that the iron wasn't hers, despite the layer of burnt starch on the bottom, the apprentice, incensed by such injustice, had deliberately spat on the front of her dress. The result was a well-aimed blow. The girl held back her tears and cleaned the iron with a piece of candle, but each time she had to go behind Clémence, she saved up some saliva and spat on her skirt, laughing inwardly as it trickled down.

Gervaise went back to goffering the lace on the bonnet. In the sudden quiet that followed, they could hear Coupeau's slurred voice in the back room. He was still in a jovial mood, giggling away to himself and muttering odd phrases:

'Me wife, daft thing! Daft, puttin' me to bed! Daft as anythin', in the middle o' the day, when you don't feel sleepy!'

Then, all of a sudden, he began to snore. Gervaise heaved a sigh of relief, pleased that at last he was resting, sleeping off his boozing on two good mattresses. And in the silence she began to speak in a slow, steady voice, without taking her eyes off the little goffering-iron she was moving briskly back and forth.

'What do you expect? He doesn't know what he's doing, so there's no point gettin' cross with 'im. If I did, it wouldn't do no good. I prefer to just go along with what he says, and get 'im off to bed; that way, at least, it's all done with and I can relax. He's not a bad man, and he's very fond of me. You saw 'ow much he wanted to gimme a kiss. That's a really nice thing about 'im, because there's lots of men, when they've been drinkin', who go off to a brothel. But he always comes straight back 'ere. He likes to joke with the girls, but that's all. So really, Clémence, there's no need to get upset. You know what men are like when they're pissed, they'd kill their mum and dad and not remember a thing. So I forgive 'im, with all me 'eart. He's no different from the rest!'

She said all this in a flat, dispassionate tone, already quite used to Coupeau's binges. She felt she had to justify her tolerance but already saw no harm in his pinching the girls' bottoms in her own house. When she stopped speaking silence returned and remained unbroken. Madame Putois, each time she took a garment, pulled the basket out from under the cretonne table-cover; then, when the garment had been ironed, she reached up with her short arms and put it on a shelf. Clémence was just finishing the pleats of her thirty-fifth man's shirt.

There was still loads of work to get through: they'd calculated that they'd have to stay up till eleven o'clock, if they hurried. Now that there was nothing to distract them, they were all slogging away, ironing for all they were worth. Their bare arms moved back and forth, patches of pink that brought out the whiteness of the linen. The stove had been filled up again with coke, and as the sun, shining between the sheets, fell directly onto it, the intense heat could be seen rising up in the shaft of sunlight, like an invisible flame making the air quiver. It was so stifling under the skirts and tablecloths hanging from the ceiling to dry that Augustine ran out of saliva and let the tip of her tongue stick out between her lips. The place smelled of overheated metal, of starch-water gone sour, of scorched irons, a stale bathtub smell to which the four women, their bare arms working away, added the more pungent smell of their sweat-drenched necks and hair, while the bunch of lilies, in the green water of the jar, gave off a scent that was very pure and very strong. And every now and then, amid the sounds of the ironing and the scraping of the poker in the stove, Coupeau's snoring could be heard, like the regular ticking of a great clock keeping time with the tremendous labours of the laundry.

The mornings after his binges the roofer would have a terrible hangover that meant his hair would lose its curls, his mouth would taste foul, and his mush would be all puffy and crooked for the rest of the day. He'd get up late, not stirring till about eight; then he'd hang around in the shop, unable to make up his mind to go to work. Another day lost. Throughout the morning he'd complain that his pins felt like cotton wool, and said it was mad to go on the piss like that, it buggered up your whole system. What's more, you ran into a lot of bad types who wouldn't leave you alone; you'd get dragged from one bar to the next, without wanting to; you got into all sorts of scrapes and ended up completely plastered. Hell, no! Never again! He'd no intention of dropping dead in some bar, not while he was still in his prime! But after lunch he'd perk up and give his throat a good clearing out to make sure his voice was still in working order. He'd start denying he'd been drunk the night before, just a bit tipsy maybe. They didn't make 'em like him any more, sound as a bell, a grip like iron, able to drink any amount without batting an eyelid. Then he'd spend the whole afternoon mooching round the neighbourhood. When he'd made himself a thorough nuisance to the assistants, Gervaise would give him twenty sous to get him out of the way, and off he'd go, to buy his tobacco at the Petite-Civette,* in the Rue des Poissonniers, where he usually had a brandied plum if he bumped into one of his mates. Then he'd polish off the twenty sous at François's, at the corner of the Rue de la Goutte-d'Or, where they had a pleasant little wine, quite young, that tickled your throat rather nicely. It was a real old-style bar, dark and low-ceilinged, with a smoke-filled room alongside where they served soup. There he'd stay till evening, on a merry-go-round of drinks; he had a tab there, and the landlord had solemnly promised never to send the bill to his old lady. You had to rinse your mouth out a bit, didn't you, to get rid of the foul taste from the day before. And one glass always leads to another. Anyway, he'd always been a decent sort of bloke, he didn't go in for skirt-chasing, though he liked a good laugh of course, and got a bit merry sometimes, but within reason, 'cos he had no time for those disgusting sods who drank all the time and were always pissed. And he'd go home as happy as a lark.

'Has your boyfriend been round?' he'd sometimes ask Gervaise, to tease her. 'We never see 'im these days, I'll 'ave to go an' fetch 'im.'

The boyfriend was Goujet. The smith was careful, indeed, not to come too often, for fear of being in the way and causing gossip. But he seized on any opportunity, he'd bring round the laundry, or pass by on the pavement twenty times a day. There was a corner at the back of the shop where he liked to sit for hours, not moving, smoking his little pipe. Once every ten days or so, after his evening meal, he'd venture in and settle down; he hardly said a word, but sat gazing at Gervaise, only taking his pipe out of his mouth to laugh at everything she said. When they worked late in the shop on Saturdays, he'd seem to forget about the time, apparently finding it more fun there than at the theatre. Sometimes the girls went on ironing until three in the morning. A lamp hung on a wire from the ceiling, its shade casting a big circle of bright light which made the piles of washing look like soft white snow. The apprentice would put up the shutters, but since the July nights were boiling hot they left the street door open. And as the night wore on, the girls would unfasten their bodices to be more comfortable. In the lamplight their delicate skin looked golden, Gervaise's especially, for she was becoming quite plump, and her white shoulders shone like silk, while her neck had a crease like a baby's with a little dimple in it that Goujet could have drawn from memory, he knew it so well. Then, overcome by the intense heat of the stove and the smell of the clothes steaming under the irons, he'd sink into a gentle reverie, his mind wandering and his eyes fixed on the women as they hurried on with their task, their bare arms moving back and forth, working well into the night so that the neighbours could wear their Sunday best. All around the nearby houses were settling down to sleep; the deep silence of slumber slowly descended. Midnight struck, then one, then two. The cabs and the passers-by had all gone. Now, in the dark, deserted street, the doorway of the shop sent forth a solitary beam of light, like a strip of yellow cloth unrolled along the ground. Occasionally a step could be heard in the distance and a man would come into sight; and when he crossed over the strip of light he'd crane his neck, surprised by the sound of ironing, carrying away with him a fleeting vision of half-undressed women in a reddish haze.

Goujet, seeing that Gervaise didn't know what to do with Étienne, and wanting to save him from Coupeau's kicks, had got him taken on at his bolt factory, to work the bellows. The trade of nailsmith, though not attractive in itself, because of the dirtiness of foundries and the tedium of forever hammering away at the same piece of iron, paid reasonably well, ten or twelve francs a day. The kid, now twelve, could soon be apprenticed if he liked the work. And so Étienne had become another link between the laundress and the smith, who would bring the boy home and describe how well he was doing. Everyone kept telling Gervaise, jokingly, that he had a crush on her. She was well aware of it, and blushed like a young girl, with a bashful flush that turned her cheeks apple red. Oh, the poor dear boy, there was no harm in it! He'd never said anything, never misbehaved, never made a suggestive remark. There weren't many as decent as him. Without admitting it, she felt a great joy at being loved in this way, like a holy virgin. When she was really upset about something, she'd think of the smith, and that would make her feel better. If they found themselves alone together, they felt no awkwardness; they smiled at each other quite naturally, without needing to put their feelings into words. It was a sensible kind of affection, with no suggestion of anything improper, because it's so much better to keep your peace of mind if you can manage to be happy that way.

Towards the end of the summer, however, Nana began to turn the house upside down. She was now six, and was becoming a little terror. So as not to have her always in the way, her mother took her every morning to a little school in the Rue Polonceau, run by a Mademoiselle

Josse. There she would pin the other girls' dresses together at the back, fill the teacher's snuffbox with ash, and get up to even nastier tricks better left unmentioned. Twice Mademoiselle Josse threw her out, but then took her back so as not to lose the six francs a month. As soon as she got out of school Nana made up for having been shut inside by creating havoc under the archway and in the yard, where the laundry-women, unable to bear the din she made, told her to go and play. There she joined forces with Pauline, the Boches' daughter, and Victor, son of Gervaise's former employer, a great lump of ten who loved running about with very small girls. Madame Fauconnier, who had remained on good terms with the Coupeaus, would send the boy round herself. In any case, the building simply teemed with kids, swarms of them who'd come racing down the four staircases at any hour of the day and scatter across the yard like flocks of noisy, scavenging sparrows. Madame Gaudron alone had nine to let loose, some fair, some dark, unkempt, snotty, with trousers pulled up to their eyes, socks falling round their ankles, and tattered jackets showing patches of white skin under the grime. Another woman, who delivered bread, had seven to unleash from her place on the fifth floor. They poured out of every room. In this horde of pink-nosed vermin, whose faces got washed only when it rained, there were tall kids as skinny as beanpoles, fat ones already pot-bellied like little old men, and tiny tots barely out of the cradle, still unsteady on their feet, who had no idea what was going on and crawled about on all fours when they wanted to get anywhere. Nana reigned supreme over this great gaggle, bending to her will girls twice her size, only deigning to delegate a little of her authority to Pauline and Victor, who ministered to her every wish. The little minx was forever talking about playing mummy, she'd undress the littlest ones and then dress them again, she'd insist on examining the others all over, fondling them and treating them as despotically as an adult with a perverted imagination. Any game they played under her command got them into trouble. The gang would paddle about in the coloured water from the dye-works and end up with their legs dyed blue or red up to the knees, then they'd dash off to the locksmith's where they'd pinch nails and iron filings, and then they'd run over to the carpenter's workshop, where they'd throw themselves on to the great piles of shavings and have fun rolling around with their bums in the air. The yard belonged to them, echoing with the clatter of little boots as they helter-skeltered around, and with their shrieks each time they took off again. Some days even the yard wasn't big enough for them, so they'd dive down into the cellars, then run back up, climb the whole length of a staircase, follow another corridor, on and on for hours, shouting all the time, the giant building shaking as if from a stampede of wild animals.

'Those kids are the bloody limit!' Madame Boche would shout. 'People can't 'ave much else to do to 'ave so many! And then they complain that they 'aven't got enough to eat!'

Boche liked to say that kids sprouted up out of poverty like toad-stools on a dunghill. The concierge screamed at them all day long, threatening them with her broom. After a while, she locked the door to the cellar, having found out from Pauline, when she was giving her a slap, that Nana had taken it into her head to play doctor down there in the dark; the little devil was dispensing 'remedies' with sticks.

Then, one afternoon, there was a terrible drama. It was bound to happen sooner or later. Nana had thought up a very entertaining little game. She'd stolen one of Madame Boche's clogs from outside her lodge, tied a piece of string to it, and started pulling it along like a cart. Then Victor had the idea of filling it with apple peelings. A procession was formed. Nana marched along in front, pulling the clog, with Pauline and Victor to her left and right. Then the entire gaggle of kids followed in order, the bigger ones first, then the little ones, all pushing and shoving; an infant in petticoats, no bigger than a man's boot, with a crumpled bonnet over one ear, brought up the rear. And the procession intoned some sad song, full of 'ohs' and 'ahs'. Nana had told them they were going to play at funerals: the apple peelings were the corpse. When they'd gone round the yard once, they began all over again. They thought it was great fun.

Madame Boche, ever watchful and suspicious, came out of her lodge to have a look. 'What on earth are they doing?' she muttered.

And when she realized what was happening:

'They've got my clog!' she screamed, furious. 'The little buggers!'

She dished out a few clouts to left and right, slapped Nana round the face, and gave Pauline a kick up the backside for being so daft as to let them take her mother's clog. It so happened that, at that moment, Gervaise was filling a bucket of water at the communal tap. When she saw Nana bloody-nosed and sobbing, she nearly set upon the concierge. Did you hit a child as if you were felling an ox? Anyone who did that must be completely heartless, the lowest of the low. Of course, Madame Boche gave as good as she got. When you had such a dreadful creature for a daughter you ought to keep her under lock and key. Eventually Boche himself appeared at the door of the lodge and shouted to his wife to come inside and stop wasting her time arguing with scum like that. The rift between them was total.

Truth to tell, things hadn't been going well between the Boches and the Coupeaus for at least a month. Gervaise, very generous by nature, was always giving them bottles of wine, cups of broth, oranges, pieces of cake. One evening she'd taken the remains of a chicory and beetroot salad over to the lodge, knowing that the concierge would sell her soul for a bit of salad. But the next day she'd turned white on hearing Mademoiselle Remanjou describe how Madame Boche, in front of a group of people, had thrown the salad away with a show of disgust, saying that, thank God, she hadn't yet been reduced to eating other people's leftovers. From that moment there was no question of any presents whatever: no more bottles of wine, no more cups of broth, no more oranges, no more pieces of cake—nothing at all! You should've seen the Boches' faces! For them it was as if the Coupeaus were stealing from them. Gervaise realized her mistake: if she'd never been stupid enough to give them so much, they wouldn't have come to expect it and would have carried on being nice and friendly. But now the concierge never tired of bad-mouthing her. When the October rent day came round, she carried on endlessly to the land-lord, Monsieur Marescot, saying that the laundress, who was a day late with the rent, frittered her money away on all kinds of nice things to eat; the result was that Monsieur Marescot, not exactly over-polite himself, walked into the shop without bothering to take his hat off and demanded his money, which moreover was handed to him on the spot. Naturally the Boches had offered an olive branch to the Lorilleux. Now it was with them that they did their guzzling in the lodge, with effusive displays of friendship and reconciliation. If it hadn't been for that Gimpy they'd never have fallen out at all; she'd stir up trouble anywhere. Oh yes, the Boches knew what she was like, they understood what the Lorilleux had to put up with. And they all made a point of sneering every time she walked under the archway.

One day, however, Gervaise went up to see the Lorilleux. She wanted to talk about Maman Coupeau, who was now sixty-seven. Her eyes had completely gone. And her legs were no good either. She'd had to give up her last cleaning job and was in danger of starving to death unless someone helped her out. Gervaise thought it shameful that a woman of that age, with three children, should be utterly abandoned. And as Coupeau refused to speak to the Lorilleux, telling Gervaise she could go and see them by herself if she wanted to, up she went, barely able to contain herself.

She went in without knocking, like a whirlwind. Nothing had changed since that first evening when the Lorilleux had given her such a sour reception. The same faded woollen curtain divided the living area from the workshop; the tunnel-like place seemed as if it had been designed for an eel. At the far end Lorilleux, bent over his workbench, was squeezing together the links of a piece of column chain one by one, while Madame Lorilleux, standing in front of the vice, was pulling some gold thread through the draw-plate. The little forge shone pink in the bright daylight.

'Yes, it's me!' said Gervaise. 'You're surprised, I suppose, seein' the way things are between us. But, as you can imagine, I've not come on account of me or you. I'm here on account of Maman Coupeau. Yes, I've come to see whether we're going to let her wait for other people's charity before she gets a crust of bread.'

'Well, that's a nice way to come in!' muttered Madame Lorilleux. 'Some people 'ave got a cheek!'

And, turning her back, she went on pulling the gold thread, acting as if her sister-in-law wasn't there. But Lorilleux raised his pale face, and exclaimed:

'What's that you're sayin'?'

Then, as he'd heard perfectly well, he went on:

'She's bin makin' up stories again, 'as she? She's a fine one, that Maman Coupeau, goin' about tellin' everybody 'ow badly off she is! Well, she ate here just the day before yesterday. We do what we can, we do. We're not rollin' in it. If she's tellin' tales in other people's places she can stay there, 'cos we won't 'ave people spyin' on us.'

He picked up his piece of chain again and, turning his back as well, added almost regretfully:

'When everybody puts in five francs a month, we'll do the same.'

Gervaise had calmed down, chilled by the Lorilleux' stony faces. She'd never set foot in their place without feeling uncomfortable. Keeping her eyes fixed on the squares of wood the Lorilleux had put on the floor to catch the flecks of gold, she put her case in a reasoned manner. Maman Coupeau had three children: if they each gave five francs that would only make fifteen, and that really wasn't enough, you couldn't live on that; they'd have to find three times as much. But Lorilleux protested. Where did she expect him to steal fifteen francs a month from? People were funny, they imagined he was rich because he had gold in his place. Then he started running Maman Coupeau down: she wouldn't give up her coffee in the morning, she was fond of her little nip, in fact she was behaving like someone who wasn't short of money. Of course, everybody liked their comforts, but if you hadn't managed to put aside a single sou, you did like other people and tightened your belt. In any case, it wasn't as if Maman Coupeau was too old to work; there was nothing wrong with her eyesight when it came to helping herself to a nice piece of meat at the bottom of a dish; truth be told, she was a crafty old girl who just wanted to spoil herself. Even if he could afford it, he wouldn't think it right to keep someone in idleness.

In spite of all these disingenuous arguments Gervaise remained conciliatory and tried to deal with them calmly. She tried to appeal to their better nature. After a while, however, the husband didn't even bother to reply. The wife was standing in front of the forge now, pickling a length of chain in the little long-handled saucepan full of nitric acid. She still pointedly kept her back turned as if she was miles away. As Gervaise went on talking she watched them stubbornly working away, amid the black dust of the workshop, their bodies twisted, their clothes patched and grease-stained, themselves as hardened and blunted as old tools, in their cramped, mechanical labour. Suddenly, her anger welled up again and she shouted:

'All right, keep your money, I prefer it that way! I'll take her in! I took a stray cat in the other night, I can certainly take your mother in. She won't have to go without, she'll have her coffee and her little nips! My God, what a horrible family!'

At this Madame Lorilleux swung round, brandishing the saucepan as if about to throw the acid in her sister-in-law's face.

'Get out!' she spluttered. 'Clear off, or I won't be responsible! And don't count on those five francs, 'cos I'll give you bugger-all! Five francs! Christ! Maman would be your skivvy and you'd pocket me five francs. If she goes to live with you, tell 'er she can kick the bucket as far as I'm concerned. Now piss off!'

'You bitch!' said Gervaise, slamming the door behind her.

She brought Maman Coupeau to live with them the very next day. She put her bed in the little room where Nana slept, lit by the round skylight near the ceiling. The move didn't take long, as the only furniture Maman Coupeau had was the bed, an old walnut cupboard which they put in the room for dirty washing, a table, and two chairs; they sold the table and had the chairs recaned. And on her very first evening there the old lady did a bit of sweeping and washing up, in short made herself useful, happy that her troubles were over. The Lorilleux were livid, especially as Madame Lerat had made it up with the Coupeaus. One fine day the two sisters, the flower-maker and the chain-maker, actually came to blows over Gervaise: Madame Lerat had the temerity to approve of Gervaise's conduct in regard to their mother; then, seeing Madame Lorilleux's annoyance and unable to resist teasing her, she remarked that the laundress had the most wonderful eyes, eyes you could light candles with. Thereupon, after exchanging a few slaps, they both swore they'd never have anything to do with each other again. Now Madame Lerat spent her evenings in the shop, where she was greatly entertained (though she'd never admit it) by Clémence's smutty talk.

Three years went by. There were several more quarrels and reconciliations. Gervaise couldn't care less about the Lorilleux, the Boches, or anybody else who didn't see eye to eye with her. If there was something they didn't like, they could lump it, couldn't they? She was earning what she wanted, that was the main thing. She had become very well thought of in the neighbourhood because, when it came down to it, there weren't many customers like her, paying on the nail and never haggling or bellyaching. She bought her bread from Madame Coudeloup in the Rue des Poissonniers, her meat from big Charlie, a butcher in the Rue Polonceau, and her groceries from Lehongre in the Rue de la Goutte-d'Or, almost opposite her shop. François, the wine merchant at the corner of the street, delivered her wine in fifty-bottle crates. Her neighbour Vigouroux, whose wife's bottom must have been black and blue from being pinched by all the men, let her have coke at the same rate as the gas company. And it was certainly the case that her suppliers did their best for her, knowing they had everything to gain from keeping on good terms. So when she was out and about, just in her slippers and without a hat, she'd be greeted on all sides; she felt at home, the streets all around were like extensions of her own place, which opened directly on to the pavement. Nowadays, she'd spin out an errand, for she loved being outside surrounded by all the people she knew. On days when she didn't have time to cook, she'd go out and buy something ready-cooked and chat with the cookshop man, whose shop was on the other side of the building, a great barn of a place with big grimy windows through which you could see the dim light of the courtyard beyond. Or else she'd stop to talk, her hands full of plates and bowls, at some ground-floor window, where she'd glimpse a cobbler's room with an unmade bed, the floor strewn with old clothes, two rickety cradles, and a pot of cobbler's wax full of dirty water. But the neighbour she respected most was the watchmaker opposite, the dapper gentleman in the frock coat who was always poking into his watches with his tiny tools. Often she'd go across the road to say hello, laughing with pleasure as she looked into his little workplace, hardly bigger than a cupboard, and saw his merry little cuckoo clocks, their busy pendulums all going at once, but never in time with each other.

CHAPTER VI

ONE autumn afternoon, after delivering some washing to a customer in the Rue des Portes-Blanches,* Gervaise found herself at the bottom of the Rue des Poissonniers just before dusk. It had rained that morning, the air was very mild, and a smell was rising from the damp cobbles. Struggling with her big basket and breathing hard, Gervaise slackened her pace and let her body relax as she walked up the street, feeling a vague sensual craving, made stronger still by her tiredness. She'd have loved something nice to eat. Looking up and seeing the sign of the Rue Marcadet, she suddenly had the idea of dropping in on Goujet at the forge. He'd said many times that she should stop by some day if she felt like seeing how they worked with iron. Of course, in front of the other workmen, she'd ask for Étienne and make it look as if she'd come just to see the boy.

The bolt and rivet factory must be somewhere at this end of the Rue Marcadet, though she wasn't exactly sure where, especially as there were often no numbers on the shacks separated by patches of waste ground. It was a street she wouldn't have lived in for all the gold in the world, a wide, dirty street, black with coal dust from the surrounding factories, with cobblestones all broken and ruts full of stagnant water. On each side was a row of sheds, big workshops with glass roofs, and grey, unfinished-looking constructions showing their brickwork and wooden frames—an untidy mass of ramshackle buildings flanked by dubious-looking lodging houses and sleazy little taverns, with occasional gaps through which you could catch glimpses of the countryside. All she could remember was that the factory was near a rag and scrap-iron merchant's place, a sort of open sewer at ground level where, according to Goujet, stuff worth hundreds of thousands of francs was stashed away. Amid the din of the factories, she tried to get her bearings; narrow pipes on the roofs blew out great clouds of steam, a sawmill made regular screeching noises as if a piece of calico was suddenly being ripped apart, while button factories made the ground shake with the rumbling and click-clack of their machines. As she stood gazing in the direction of Montmartre, not sure whether she should carry on any further, a gust of wind dislodged the soot from a tall chimney and blew it into the street. She had screwed up her eyes and was half choking when she heard the rhythmic sound of hammering: without realizing, she was just opposite the forge, which she then recognized by the yard full of rags and scrap iron next door.

She still hesitated, however, not sure how to get in. There was a gap in a broken fence, through which a pathway seemed to lead to a demolition site full of rubble. As a puddle of muddy water barred the way, someone had thrown down a couple of planks. She decided to venture across the planks, turned left, and found herself lost in a strange forest of carts tipped up with their shafts in the air, and tumble-down hovels with only their wooden frames left standing. Further on, casting a ray of light through the murky darkness, a fire glowed red. The sound of hammers had stopped. She was picking her way gingerly towards the light when a workman passed close by, his face black with coal dust and bristling with a goatee beard. He gave her a sidelong glance with his pale eyes.

'Please Monsieur,' she said, 'is this where a boy called Étienne works? He's my son.'

'Étienne, Étienne,' repeated the workman in a hoarse voice, swaying unsteadily on his feet. 'No, don't know any Étienne.'

When he opened his mouth he gave off the smell you get from old brandy casks when you take out the bung. And as this encounter with a woman in a dark corner was clearly beginning to make him feel he might be able to take liberties, Gervaise stepped back.

'But Monsieur Goujet works here, doesn't he?'

'Ah, Goujet! Yes! I know 'im all right,' said the workman. 'If it's Goujet you're after, go on down to the end.'

And, turning round, he shouted in his cracked tinny voice:

'Hey, Gueule-d'Or, there's a lady 'ere askin' for you!'

But his shout was drowned by renewed hammering. Gervaise went down to the end, came to a door, and peered in. Inside was a huge workshop, and at first she couldn't see anything at all. In a corner the forge fire, nearly out, glimmered faintly, like a pale star—just enough to prevent complete darkness. Great shadows floated about. From time to time black shapes passed in front of the fire, blotting out that last remaining point of light, shapes of men of incredible size, their colossal limbs hard to make out. Afraid to venture any further, Gervaise called out softly from the doorway:

'Monsieur Goujet! Monsieur Goujet!'

Suddenly everything was lit up. The bellows had roared into life and a jet of white flame spurted out. The shed could now be seen quite clearly. It was enclosed by wooden partitions, with holes that had been roughly plastered over and corners reinforced by brickwork. Flying coal dust had given the whole workshop a coat of grey soot. Cobwebs, weighed down by years of accumulated dirt, hung from the beams like rags left there to dry. Round the walls, on shelves, hanging from nails or just lying about in dark corners, were all kinds of old iron implements, bashed-in utensils, and huge tools, whose hard, jagged, lustreless shapes she could just make out. The white flame grew bigger, lighting as if with a dazzling ray of sunshine the beaten earth floor where the polished steel of four anvils, securely set in their blocks, took on a silvery sheen spangled with gold.

Then Gervaise saw Goujet next to the forge, recognizing him by his handsome golden beard. Étienne was working the bellows. Two other men were there as well, but she saw only Goujet. She went over and stood in front of him.

'What's this! It's Madame Gervaise!' he cried, his face lighting up. 'What a nice surprise!'

But, seeing his mates giving him funny looks, he pushed Étienne towards his mother, saying:

'You've come to see the boy. He's a good lad, he's really getting into it.'

'Well,' she said, 'it wasn't easy findin' this place. It's like the end of the earth.'

She described how she'd got there. Then she asked why they didn't know Étienne's name in the workshop. Goujet laughed and explained that they all called the boy Zouzou because he had his hair cropped short, like a Zouave. While they were talking, Étienne stopped working the bellows and the flame died down to a rosy glow, leaving the workshop in semi-darkness again. The smith, touched by Gervaise's visit, gazed at her as she stood there smiling, looking so nice and radiant in the glimmering light. They'd both stopped speaking, but then he seemed to remember something, and broke the silence.

'Excuse me, Madame Gervaise, there's something I've got to finish. But you can stay here, you're not in anybody's way.'

She stayed. Étienne was applying himself to the bellows again and the forge was blazing, sending out showers of sparks, especially as the boy, wanting to show his mother what he could do, was producing an absolute hurricane of blasts. Goujet, tongs in hand, stood watching an iron bar, waiting for it to heat up. The fire threw an intense light on him, without shadow. His sleeves were rolled up and his shirt open at the neck, showing his bare arms, his bare chest, and his pink skin, like a girl's, covered with curly blond hair. With his head bent forward between his muscular shoulders, his face attentive, and his pale eyes fixed on the flame, he looked like a giant at rest, tranquil in his strength. When the iron bar was white-hot he gripped it with the tongs and cut it into even pieces on an anvil, hitting it gently as if he was cutting glass. Then he put the pieces back in the fire, taking them out again one by one, to work them into shape. He was making hexagonal rivets. He put each piece into a heading frame, levelling the top to make the head, flattening the six sides, then tossing each finished rivet, still red-hot, on to the ground, where they stopped glowing. He hammered away without a pause, swinging a five-pound hammer with his right hand, each blow finishing a detail as he turned and worked his iron with such skill that, all the while, he was able to go on talking and looking at people. The anvil gave out a silvery ring. He was completely at ease, not sweating at all, hammering away happily, with as little apparent effort as when he cut out pictures at home in the evening.

'These are little rivets, twenty millimetres,' he said in answer to Gervaise's questions. 'You can do up to three hundred a day. But it takes practice, your arm soon gets tired.'

When she asked whether his wrist didn't get stiff by the end of the day, he laughed. Did she take him for a young lady? His wrist had had a pretty rough time over the last fifteen years; it was now like iron itself, he'd spent so much time working with his tools. But she was right to ask: a gent who'd never made a rivet or a bolt and who wanted to play around with his five-pound hammer would be all aches and pains after a couple of hours. It didn't look like much, but even really tough blokes were often completely worn out after just a few years. Meanwhile the other men were all hammering away at once. Their big shadows danced in the light, the red of the iron as it was taken out of the fire flashed in the darkness, sparks flew under the hammers and shone like suns from the tops of the anvils. And Gervaise, caught up in the rhythms of the workshop, felt happy to be there. She had no desire to leave.

She was making a wide detour, to get closer to Étienne without risking getting her hands burnt, when she saw the dirty, unshaven workman she'd spoken to in the yard come in.

'So you found 'im, Madame?' he said in his bantering drunkard's voice. 'Hey, Gueule-d'Or, I was the one who told the lady where to find you…'

The man's name was Bec-Salé,* alias Boit-sans-Soif, a real character, a champion bolt-maker, who kept himself well oiled along with his tools, with a bottle of rotgut a day. He'd popped out for a quick one, because he didn't feel sufficiently lubricated to wait until six o'clock. When he learned that Zouzou was called Étienne, he thought it was a scream, and burst out laughing, showing his black teeth. Then he realized who Gervaise was. Just the day before, he'd had a drink with Coupeau. She could ask Coupeau about Bec-Salé, he'd tell her straight away what a tremendous character he was! Good old Coupeau! He was a terrific bloke, always ready to stand a round even when it wasn't his turn.

'I'm pleased to know you're 'is wife,' he kept saying. 'He deserves a pretty wife… Hey, Gueule-d'Or, ain't she pretty?'

He was starting to get flirtatious and was pressing against her. She picked up her basket and held it in front of her to keep him at bay. Goujet was annoyed, realizing that his mate was trying to make fun of him because of his friendship with Gervaise.

'Come on, you lazy sod,' he shouted. 'When are we goin' to do the forty-millimetre bolts? Do you feel like it now you're tanked up, you bloody boozer?'

The smith was referring to an order for some large bolts, which needed two of them at the anvil.

'Right now, if you want, you big baby!' replied Bec-Salé. 'Look at you, still suckin' your thumb, and pretendin' you're a man! You may be big, I've seen off plenty like you!'

'All right, straight away! Come on, just us two!'

'Let's go to it, smart-arse!'

Excited by the presence of Gervaise, they were challenging each other. Goujet put the ready-cut pieces of iron into the fire, then fixed a large-gauge heading frame to an anvil. His opponent went over to the wall and fetched two twenty-pound sledgehammers, the two big sisters of the workshop, which the men called Fifine and Dédèle.* And he didn't stop bragging, talking about half a gross of bolts he'd forged for the lighthouse at Dunkirk, real gems, so beautifully made it'd be worth putting them in a museum. Jesus, no, he wasn't afraid of competition! You could turn the city upside down, you wouldn't find anybody to match him. This was going to be fun, they'd soon see what was what.

'The lady can be the judge,' he said, turning towards Gervaise.

'Enough talk!' shouted Goujet. 'Put your back into it, Zouzou! It's not hot enough, lad.'

Then Bec-Salé asked:

'We'll strike together, right?'

'No, mate! We'll each do our own bolts!'

This idea sent a cold shiver down the other man's spine. For all his bluster, his mouth went dry. Forty-millimetre bolts done by one man alone, that was unheard of, especially as the bolts were to be round-headed—something devilishly hard to do, requiring tremendous skill. The three other men in the place had dropped their work to watch, and a tall, gaunt fellow bet a bottle of wine that Goujet would lose. Meanwhile, the two smiths chose their hammers with their eyes closed because Fifine weighed half a pound more than Dédèle. Bec-Salé was lucky enough to put his hands on Dédèle, leaving Goujet with Fifine. And, while the iron was heating, Bec-Salé, his cocky self again, struck poses next to the anvil, making eyes at Gervaise as he stood there tapping his foot like a man about to fight a duel, already making as if he was swinging Dédèle through the air. Yes, he was all set: he could have flattened the Vendôme column in no time!

'Right, get on with it!' said Goujet, putting one of the pieces of iron, as thick as a girl's wrist, into the heading-frame.

Bec-Salé leaned back and swung Dédèle with both hands. Small and wiry, with a goatee beard and wolfish eyes gleaming beneath his untidy mop of hair, he put every ounce of himself into each blow of the hammer, leaping off the ground as though lifted into the air by his own momentum. He was like a wild animal setting upon the iron as if enraged to find it so hard; he even gave a little grunt of satisfaction when he thought he'd landed an especially telling blow. Perhaps it was true that for other men the grog weakened their muscles, but he needed booze, not blood, in his veins; the drop he'd just had was warming his body like a boiler, he felt he had the power of a bloody steam-engine. That evening it was the iron that was afraid of *him*; his pounding was making it softer than a plug of tobacco. And didn't

Dédèle dance! She did the *grand entrechat*, her feet in the air and showing off her underwear, like a good-time girl at the Élysée-Montmartre;* because you can't hang about, iron is such a crafty devil, it cools down very fast, just to let the hammer know what it thinks of it. In thirty strokes Bec-Salé had shaped the head of his bolt. But he was panting, his eyes were popping out of their sockets, and he was in a fury at the sound of his joints cracking. So, carried away, leaping about and yelling, he unleashed two more blows, just out of spite at his own discomfort. When he removed the bolt from the frame, it was misshapen, its head to one side like a hunchback's.

'There, ain't that a beauty?' he said nevertheless, as cocky as ever, presenting his work to Gervaise.

'Oh, I'm afraid I'm no expert, Monsieur,' she replied diplomatically.

But she could clearly see on the bolt the marks of the last two strokes—Dédèle's last two kicks—and she was delighted, screwing up her mouth so as not to laugh, because now Goujet had every chance of winning.

Now it was Gueule-d'Or's turn. Before he began he gave the laundress a look full of confidence and affection. Then, without hurrying, he stood back and brought the hammer down with great regular swings. His technique was classical: precise, balanced, and flowing. In his hands Fifine didn't dance like a showgirl in some sleazy music hall, kicking her legs up over her head, but, in perfect time, raised her head and then bowed, like a noble lady of old gravely leading a minuet.

Fifine's heels beat the measure and sank with studied artistry into the red-hot iron on the head of the bolt, first flattening the metal in the centre, then shaping it with a series of rhythmically precise blows. Of course, it wasn't brandy that Gueule-d'Or had in his veins, but blood, pure blood that pulsed down into his hammer and regulated his task. What a magnificent sight when you saw him at work! The leaping flames of the forge shone directly on him. His short hair curling down over his low forehead and his fine golden beard falling in ringlets caught the light, illuminating his whole face, so you could truly say he had a face of gold. What's more, he had a neck like a marble pillar, as white as a child's, a huge chest broad enough for a woman to lie on, and sculptured shoulders and arms that might have been modelled on those of a giant statue in a museum. When he braced himself to strike you could see his muscles swell like mountains of flesh rippling and hardening under the skin; his shoulders, his chest, and his neck expanded; he seemed to spread a glowing light all around him; he was beautiful and mighty, like a benevolent god. Twenty times already he'd brought Fifine down, his eyes fixed on the iron, drawing in his breath at each stroke, with just two big beads of sweat running down his temples. He counted: twenty-one, twenty-two, twenty-three. Fifine calmly went on with her curtseys, like the noble lady she was.

'Bloody show-off!' sneered Bec-Salé.

But Gervaise, standing opposite Gueule-d'Or, was watching him with an affectionate smile. What fools men were! These two were hammering away just to impress her, weren't they? She knew all right what was going on: they were fighting over her with their hammer-blows like two big cockerels strutting about in front of a little white hen. Did you ever hear of anything so funny? The heart sometimes has the strangest ways of declaring itself. Yes, it was all for her benefit, this great clanking of Dédèle and Fifine on the anvil; it was for her, all this pounding of iron; it was for her, this blazing forge with its roaring fire and showers of bright sparks. They were forging their love for her, vying with each other to see who could do it best. And, yes, it did give her pleasure, deep down, for women like compliments. The blows of Gueule-d'Or's hammer, especially, found an echo in her heart; they rang there, as on the anvil, in a clear melody that seemed to match the excited pulsing of her blood. It sounds silly, but she felt something was being thrust inside her, something solid, like bolt-iron. Before coming into the forge, as she walked along the damp pavement at dusk, she'd felt a vague longing, a desire for something nice to eat; and now she felt satisfied, as if Gueule-d'Or's hammer-blows had nourished her. She had no doubt he would win! He was the one she'd belong to. Bec-Salé was too ugly, in his dirty smock and overalls, jumping up and down like a monkey who'd escaped from a zoo. She waited, very flushed but enjoying the tremendous heat and delighting in being shaken from head to foot by Fifine's final blows.

Goujet was still counting.

'And that makes twenty-eight!' he cried, putting down the hammer. 'Finished! You can have a look.'

The head of the bolt was smooth and clean, without a single burr, a real jeweller's job, as round as a moulded billiard ball. The workmen looked and nodded: there was no denying it, it was perfect! Bec-Salé tried to laugh it off, but words failed him and he went back to his anvil with his tail between his legs. Gervaise, meanwhile, had moved close to Goujet as if to get a better look. Étienne had put down the bellows, the workshop was again filling with shadows, and the fire, like a red sunset, suddenly gave way to complete darkness. The smith and the laundress found it extremely pleasant to feel the darkness enveloping them, in this shed black with soot and filings, and smelling of old iron; they couldn't have been more alone if they had arranged to meet in some thicket in the Bois de Vincennes.* He took her hand as if he'd won her.

Then, outside, they exchanged not a word. He could find nothing to say except that she could have taken Étienne home had there not been another half-hour of work to do. She was about to leave when he called her back, wanting to keep her a few minutes longer.

'You haven't seen everything, let me show you. It's really interesting.'

He led her to the right, into another shed where the boss was installing a whole lot of machinery. She hesitated before going in, overcome by an instinctive fear. The huge room was shaking with the vibration of the machines; great shadows floated about, streaked fiery red. But he smiled reassuringly, telling her there was nothing to be afraid of, though she should be careful not to let her skirts trail too close to the gear wheels. He walked in front and she followed, surrounded by a deafening din made up of all kinds of hissing and rumbling noises, among clouds of smoke peopled with weird shapes, black figures rushing about, machines waving their arms, she couldn't make out which was which. The walkways in between were very narrow; you had to step over obstacles, avoid holes, stand aside to get out of the way of trolleys. You couldn't hear yourself speak. She still couldn't see anything, everything was dancing about. Then, feeling a sensation like a great beating of wings above her head, she glanced up and stopped to look at the driving-belts, long ribbons that hung across the ceiling like a gigantic spider's web, its threads spreading in all directions. The steam-engine was in a corner, behind a low brick wall; the belts seemed to run of their own accord, drawing their momentum from the depths of the shadows, gliding by with a gentle, regular, continuous motion, like the flight of some nightbird. But then she nearly fell when she stumbled against one of the ventilator pipes that branched out across the beaten earth floor delivering their breaths of cold air to the little forges next to the machines. And that was what he showed her first: he opened the air vent to one of the furnaces, making big flames flare up on all four sides in the shape of a fan, a dazzling, serrated collar faintly tinged with red; the light was so bright that the workmen's little lamps seemed like spots of shade in sunlight. Then, raising his voice to explain things to her, he moved on to the machines: the mechanical shears that ate through iron bars, biting off a piece each time they snapped shut and spitting them out behind, one at a time; the bolt and rivet machines, tall and complicated, forging heads with a single turn of their screws; the trimming machines with cast-iron fly-wheels and a ball, also in cast-iron, that beat the air furiously each time the machines trimmed a piece; the thread-cutters, worked by women, cutting threads on the bolts and their nuts, their steel gear-wheels shining with oil as they clicked round. In this way she was able to follow every stage of the work, from the iron bars propped against the walls to the finished bolts and rivets, piled up higgledy-piggledy in boxes in every corner. She understood it all now, and smiled and nodded; but she was a little nervous all the same, uneasy at being so small and vulnerable in the midst of these big, powerful metalworking machines, and from time to time she'd turn round, startled by the dull thud of a trimmer. She was getting used to the dark, and when a furnace suddenly threw out a blaze of light with its collar of flames, she was able to make out the recesses where men stood motionless, watching over the jigging fly-wheels. In spite of herself, she kept looking up at the ceiling, her gaze returning to the lifeblood of the machines, the belts above her, a huge, silent force gliding through the formless shadows beneath the roof.

Meanwhile, Goujet had come to a halt in front of one of the rivet machines, and was standing there, staring, deep in thought, his head bowed. The machine was turning out forty-millimetre rivets with the tranquil ease of a giant. And in truth nothing could be simpler. The stoker took the piece of iron from the furnace; the striker placed it in the heading frame, which was kept under a constant stream of water to ensure that the steel would remain tempered; and that was that—the screw came down and the bolt fell to the ground, its head as round as if it had been cast in a mould. In twelve hours this blasted contraption turned out hundreds of kilos of them. Goujet was not a vindictive man, but there were times when he would gladly have picked up Fifine and smashed up all this metal, in sheer anger at the fact that its arms were stronger than his. It upset him, even though he told himself that human flesh couldn't fight against iron. The day would come, of course, when the machines would kill off the manual worker; already their daily wage had dropped from twelve francs to nine, and there was talk of more cuts to come; when it came down to it, there was nothing attractive about these great brutes that turned out rivets and bolts as if they were making sausages. For a good three minutes he gazed at this one in silence, his brow furrowed, his handsome golden beard bristling fiercely. Then, slowly, his features softened into a look of gentle resignation. He turned to Gervaise, who was pressed against him, and said with a sad smile:

'Well, we can't compete with that! But perhaps one day it'll be for the general good.'

Gervaise didn't give a damn for the general good. The machine-made bolts seemed to her badly made.

'What I mean', she cried, getting quite worked up, 'is that they're too perfect. I like yours better. You can see in yours the hand of an artist.'

He was very happy to hear her say this, because for a minute he'd been afraid she might look down on him after seeing the machines. He might well be stronger than Bec-Salé, but the machines were stronger than him. When at last he said goodbye to her in the yard, he was so happy that when he took her hands in his he nearly crushed them.

Every Saturday the laundress went to the Goujets' to deliver their washing. They still lived in the little house in the Rue Neuve de la Goutte-d'Or. During the first year she'd regularly repaid them twenty francs a month out of the five hundred she owed; so as not to muddle things up, they did their sums at the end of each month, and she'd add what was necessary to make up the twenty francs, because the Goujets' laundry would rarely amount to more than seven or eight francs a month. She'd paid off about half the sum when, one quarterly rent-day, because some customers had failed to settle up and she couldn't think what to do, she'd had to run round to the Goujets' and borrow the money for her rent. On two other occasions she'd asked them for help so she could pay her workers, with the result that the debt had gone back up to four hundred and twenty-five francs. Now she wasn't giving them any cash at all and was working off the debt with free washing alone. It wasn't that she was working less or that business was bad. Quite the contrary. But she was often short, the money seemed to melt away and she was happy when she just made ends meet. After all, if you can get by there's not much to complain about, is there? She was putting on weight and giving in to all the little self-indulgences that go with a bigger stomach; she no longer seemed able to think about the future. Never mind, the money would keep coming in, and putting it aside would only make it go rusty. But despite this Madame Goujet behaved like a mother towards Gervaise. Sometimes she'd lecture her gently, not because of the money she was owed but because she was fond of her and afraid she might come to grief. She never even mentioned the money. On that subject she was the soul of tact.

It so happened that the day after Gervaise's visit to the forge was the last Saturday of the month. When she arrived at the Goujets', where she always insisted on going herself, her basket had weighed so heavily on her arms that it took her a good two minutes to catch her breath. No one knows how heavy washing is, especially when there are sheets.

'Are you sure it's all there?' asked Madame Goujet.

She was very strict on this point. She liked to get her laundry back without a single piece missing: to keep everything in order, she said. Another thing she insisted on was that the laundress should come on the precise day they'd agreed, and always at the same time; that way, nobody's time was wasted.

'Oh yes, it's all here,' said Gervaise with a smile. 'You know I never leave anything behind.'

'True,' agreed Madame Goujet. 'You're slipping in some ways, but not yet in that.'

While Gervaise emptied her basket and put the linen on the bed, the old lady sang her praises: she never scorched things or tore them like so many others, or pulled buttons off with the iron; the only thing was that she used too much blue and starched shirt fronts too much.

'Look, this is like cardboard,' she went on, making a shirt-front crack. 'My son doesn't complain, but it cuts into his neck. Tomorrow his neck'll be all red by the time we get back from Vincennes.'

'Oh, don't say that!' exclaimed Gervaise, quite upset. 'Dress shirts 'ave got to be a bit stiff, unless you want them to flop about. That's how gentlemen 'ave them. I do all your things meself. The girls never touch them, and I'm really careful, believe me. I'd do something ten times over if I 'ad to, because it's for you.'

She blushed as she said these last words, for she was afraid of giving away the pleasure she took in ironing Goujet's shirts herself. Of course, there was nothing wrong about this, but even so she felt slightly embarrassed.

'Oh, I'm not criticizing your work,' said Madame Goujet. 'You do it really well. This bonnet, for example, it's perfect. Nobody else can make the embroidery stand out like that. And the goffering's so even! I can tell it's your handiwork straight away. If you give even a dishcloth to one of your girls, you can see the difference. All I'm sayin' is that you should use a bit less starch. Goujet doesn't want to look like a gentleman.'

While she was talking, she'd picked up the book and was ticking off the items. Everything was indeed there. When they went over the account, she saw that Gervaise was charging six sous for a bonnet; she expressed her surprise at this, but had to agree it wasn't really a lot as things went: no, men's shirts five sous, women's knickers four, pillow-cases one and a half, aprons one, it wasn't dear when you considered that many laundries charged anything up to a sou more for all these things. Then, when Gervaise had called out the items of dirty washing while the old lady wrote them down, she shoved them into her basket; but she still didn't leave, but stood there awkwardly, as if she had a request that made her feel awkward.

'Madame Goujet,' she said at last, 'if you don't mind, I'd be glad to take the money for the laundry this month.'

As it happened, that month the cost was quite high, the sum they'd just worked out together came to ten francs seven sous. Madame Goujet looked at her thoughtfully for a moment. Then she said:

'If that's what you want, my dear. I don't want to keep the money from you if you need it. But it's not the way to pay off debts. I'm only sayin' this for your own good. You really should be careful.'

Gervaise hung her head at this admonishment, and mumbled that the ten francs would make up the money for a promissory note she'd signed for her coke merchant. But Madame Goujet became sterner still when she heard mention of a promissory note. She cited her own case as an example: she was cutting down on expenses now that Goujet's daily wage had gone from twelve francs to nine. If you weren't careful when you were young you'd starve when you were old. However, she held back from telling Gervaise she gave her her washing just so she could pay off her debt; in the past she'd done all her own washing, and she'd go back to doing her own washing if the laundry was going to keep making her fork out to this extent. When Gervaise had the ten francs seven sous, she thanked Madame Goujet and hurried off. Once out on the landing she breathed easily again and could have danced for joy, for she was already getting used to the hassle and unpleasantness of money troubles, and the only thing she remembered about them afterwards was the satisfaction of getting out of them, until the next time.

It was that very Saturday that Gervaise had the strangest encounter as she was going down the stairs from the Goujets'. She had to stand to one side against the banister with her basket to make room for a tall bareheaded woman who was carrying a mackerel on a piece of paper, very fresh and still bleeding at the gills. She recognized Virginie, of all people, the girl whose skirt she'd pulled up in the wash-house. They stared at each other. Gervaise closed her eyes, thinking for a moment that she'd get the mackerel full in the face. But no, Virginie gave her a faint smile. So the laundress, whose basket was blocking the stairs, made an effort to be civil.

'Sorry,' she said.

'That's all right,' replied the tall brunette.

They stood there in the middle of the staircase, chatting, instantly reconciled, without making a single allusion to the past. Virginie, now twenty-nine, had turned into a fine-looking woman, well built, with an oval face set off by two coils of jet-black hair. She told her story right away to make clear she'd gone up in the world: she was now married, since that spring, to a former carpenter who'd done his military service and was now trying to get a job in the police, because a government job is more secure and respectable. She'd just been out to get him a mackerel.

'He loves mackerel,' she said. 'You've got to spoil the devils, haven't you? But why don't you come up? I'll show you our place. There's a bit of a draught here.'

When Gervaise, in her turn, told her about her own marriage and that she'd lived in those very rooms and had even had her baby girl there, Virginie urged her still more eagerly to come up. It's always a pleasure to revisit places where you've been happy. She'd lived for five years across the river in Gros-Caillou.* That's where she'd met her husband, when he was in the army. But she'd got fed up there and dreamed of coming back to the Goutte-d'Or neighbourhood where she knew everybody. She'd been living for a fortnight now in the room opposite the Goujets. Of course everything was still in a mess, but it'd sort itself out after a while.

Then, on the landing, they finally told each other their names.

'Madame Coupeau.'

'Madame Poisson.'

And from then on they called each other by their full names, Madame Coupeau and Madame Poisson, just for the pleasure of being proper married ladies now, after having known each other in less orthodox circumstances. Even so, deep down Gervaise still felt a little mistrustful. Maybe the tall brunette was patching things up so she could get her revenge more easily for the drubbing she'd had in the wash-house and was cooking up some diabolical two-faced scheme. Gervaise resolved to stay on her guard. For the moment Virginie was being so nice that she had to be nice too.

Upstairs in their room, Poisson, the husband, a pasty-faced individual of thirty-five with a red moustache and a tuft of beard under his chin, was sitting at a table near the window. He was making little boxes. His only tools were a penknife, a saw no bigger than a nail file, and a pot of glue. The wood he was using came from old cigar-boxes, then strips of unpolished mahogany on which he carved fretwork and patterns of extraordinary delicacy. All day long, from one year's end to the next, he made the selfsame box, eight centimetres by six. But then he'd inlay it, or think up a new kind of lid, or put in compartments. He did it for his own amusement, as a way of killing time until his appointment as a policeman came through. The only thing he retained from his old trade as a carpenter was this passion for little boxes. He didn't sell his work, he gave it away as presents to people he knew.

Poisson stood up and politely greeted Gervaise, whom Virginie introduced as an old friend. But he was no talker and promptly picked up his little saw again. Every now and then, however, he'd cast a glance at the mackerel, which was lying on the chest of drawers. Gervaise was very pleased to see her old home again; she described how her furniture had been arranged, and pointed to the spot on the floor where she'd given birth. What a small world it was! When they'd lost all contact, so long ago, they'd never have dreamed they'd meet again like this, living one after the other in the same room. Virginie told her a bit more about herself and her husband: he'd inherited a small legacy from an aunt, and in due course he'd set her up in business, but for the time being she was carrying on with her sewing, running up dresses on demand. Finally, after a good half-hour,

Gervaise got up to go. Poisson hardly turned round. Virginie saw her out and promised to return her visit; and of course, she'd send her her laundry, that went without saying. And as she kept her talking on the landing, it occurred to Gervaise that she wanted to tell her about Lantier and her sister Adèle the metal polisher. The idea churned her up inside. But not a word was spoken about that unpleasant subject, and they bade each other farewell in a most friendly manner.

'Bye for now, Madame Coupeau.'

'See you soon, Madame Poisson.'

This was the beginning of a great friendship. A week later Virginie couldn't walk past the laundry without calling in, and she'd stay there for two or three hours chatting away, until the silent, stone-faced Poisson, worried she might have been run over, came looking for her. Gervaise, seeing the seamstress coming in every day, soon became fixated on a strange idea: she couldn't hear her start a sentence without thinking she was about to say something about Lantier; and she couldn't help thinking about Lantier the whole time Virginie was there. It was all quite silly, because she couldn't care less about Lantier and Adèle and what had become of them. She never asked about them, nor did she have any desire for news of them. No, it was something beyond her control. They were lodged in her head the way you get some irritating tune on the brain and can't get rid of it. In any case, she didn't bear any grudge against Virginie; none of it was her fault, was it? She enjoyed her company a great deal, and would call her back a dozen times before letting her go home.

Meanwhile winter had arrived, the fourth winter the Coupeaus had spent in the Rue de la Goutte-d'Or. December and January were exceptionally severe that year. It froze unbelievably hard. After New Year's Day the snow lay in the street for three days without melting. It didn't stop them working, quite the opposite: winter is the nicest season for laundry workers. It was lovely and cosy in the shop. You never saw icicles on the windows, as you did on the grocer's and the milliner's across the road. The stove, stuffed full of coke, kept the place as hot as a Turkish bath; the washing steamed away as if it was midsummer; and it was so cosy with the doors shut and everywhere warm, so warm you could have dozed off with your eyes open. Gervaise would say with a laugh that it felt like being in the country. And indeed the carriages no longer made a sound as they rolled along on the snow, and you could hardly hear the footsteps of the passers-by.

The only noise to be heard in the great, chilly silence was the voices of children, the shouts of a gang of them who'd made a big slide along the gutter outside the blacksmith's. Now and again she'd go over to the door, wipe the condensation off one of the panes with her hand, and look out to see what the locals were up to in this icy weather; but there was no sign of life in any of the nearby shops; the neighbourhood, blanketed by snow, seemed to have battened down the hatches, and she'd only exchange a nod with the coal lady next door, who'd been walking about bareheaded and grinning from car to ear ever since the frost had set in.

What was really nice, in this awful weather, was to have a good hot coffee in the middle of the day. The assistants couldn't grumble, because Gervaise made it very strong with hardly any chicory in it—unlike Madame Fauconnier's coffee, which was absolute dishwater. The only trouble was when Maman Coupeau was the one to pour the water over the grounds; then it took forever because she'd doze off in front of the kettle. On these occasions the girls would do a bit more ironing after their lunch until the coffee was ready.

And indeed, the day after Twelfth Night, half past twelve had struck and the coffee still wasn't ready. That day it just wouldn't go through. Maman Coupeau kept tapping the filter with a spoon, but you could hear the drops falling one by one, no faster than before.

'Just leave it,' said Clémence. 'It makes it muddy if you do that. We'll have plenty to eat and drink today.'

She was arranging a man's shirt, separating the pleats with her nail. She had a dreadful cold, her eyes were puffy and her throat was racked by fits of coughing that made her double up over the worktable. And yet she wasn't even wearing a scarf round her neck, and was shivering in a cheap woollen dress. Next to her Madame Putois, swathed in flannel and wrapped up to her ears, was ironing a petticoat, turning it over on the dress board, the narrow end of which was resting on the back of a chair; they'd spread a sheet underneath so it wouldn't get dirty if it brushed the floor. Gervaise took up half the table herself with some embroidered muslin curtains she was ironing, moving the iron straight up and down with outstretched arms so as to avoid making creases. All of a sudden the coffee began to run through noisily, and she looked up. Squinty Augustine had made a hole in the coffee grounds by sticking a spoon into the filter.

'Stop that!' shouted Gervaise. 'What's got into you? We'll be drinking mud now.'

Maman Coupeau had laid out five glasses in a row on a free corner
of the table. The girls stopped work. Gervaise always poured the coffee herself, after putting two lumps of sugar in each glass. This was
the moment of the day they always looked forward to. On this particular day, as each of them was taking her glass and squatting down
on a little stool in front of the stove, the street door opened and in
came Virginie, shivering all over.

'Bloody hell,' she said, 'it cuts right through you! I can't feel me
ears any more! This cold's a real bastard.'

'Ah, it's Madame Poisson!' cried Gervaise. 'You've come just at the
right time... You can 'ave some coffee with us.'

'Well, I won't say no. It chills you to the bone just crossin' the
street.'

There was still some coffee, fortunately. Maman Coupeau fetched
a sixth glass and, out of politeness, Gervaise let Virginie help herself
to sugar. The girls moved along to make room for her near the stove.
She shivered for a little while, her nose red, clasping her glass to warm
her numbed fingers. She'd just come from the grocer's, where you
froze to death just waiting for a little bit of cheese. And she said how
wonderfully warm it was in the shop; honestly, it was like walking into
an oven, enough to wake the dead; it gave you such a nice tingling
feeling. Then, as she warmed up, she stretched out her long legs. And
all six of them slowly sipped their coffee in this little break from their
work, in the stuffy moist atmosphere of drying washing. Only Maman
Coupeau and Virginie were sitting on chairs; the others, on their
stools, seemed to be sitting on the floor; in fact squinty Augustine had
pulled out a corner of the sheet from under the petticoat and was
lying on it. For a while nobody spoke; they just sat with their noses in
their glasses, enjoying the coffee.

'It really is good,' declared Clémence.

But a coughing fit nearly made her choke. She leaned her head
against the wall so she could cough harder.

'That's a very nasty cough,' said Virginie. 'Where did you pick
that up?'

'Who knows?' replied Clémence, wiping her face with her sleeve.
'It must've been the other night. There were two girls 'avin' a fight
just outside the Grand-Balcon. I wanted to watch, so I stayed there in

the snow. What a punch-up! I nearly died laughing. One of 'em had her nose split open, the blood was pourin' out. When the other one—a great beanpole like me—saw the blood, she cleared off in a flash... Anyway, durin' the night I started coughin'. And I must say men are 'opeless when they sleep with a woman: they take all the bed-clothes an' leave you completely uncovered...'

'All very nice, I'm sure,' muttered Madame Putois. 'You're killin' yourself, my girl.'

'So what if I am! As if life's much fun anyway. You slave away all bloody day for fifty-five sous, you swelter in front of the stove from mornin' till night, no, honestly, I'm sick of it! Anyway, this cold won't do me the favour of gettin' me out of it, it'll go away the same way it came.'

There was a silence. That devil Clémence liked cavorting about in dance halls, shrieking her head off, but when she was at work she'd get them all down with her talk about pegging out. Gervaise knew what she was like and just said:

'You're a miserable bugger after a night on the tiles, aren't you?'

The fact was that Gervaise would rather not hear any talk about catfights. Because of the set-to in the wash-house, it made her feel awkward when Virginie was there and somebody started talking about kicks on the shins or slaps across the chops. And indeed, Virginie was looking at her at that moment and smiling.

'Oh,' she murmured, 'I saw two of them pulling each other's hair out yesterday. Goin' at it 'ammer and tongs, they were.'

'Who was it?' asked Madame Putois.

'The midwife down at the end of the street and the girl who works for her, you know, the little blonde one. She's a real bitch, that girl! She was yelling at the midwife: "Yes, yes, you got rid of that baby for the fruiterer's wife, and I'll go and tell the police if you don't give me my money." You should've heard the way she carried on! So then the midwife fetched 'er one, bam! Right on 'er conk! Then the bloody little bitch went for her mistress's eyes, and scratched her and pulled her hair out, oh yes, by the roots! The butcher 'ad to drag 'er away.'

The girls laughed dutifully. Then they all took a greedy little swallow of coffee.

'Do you really think she did that, got rid of a baby?' said Clémence.

'How the hell do I know?' replied Virginie. 'That's what everybody said! But I wasn't there, was I? It goes with the job, though. They all get rid of 'em.'

'That's right,' said Madame Putois. 'How can anybody trust 'em? Get maimed for life? No thanks! There's one thing that always works, though. Drink a glass of holy water every night and make the sign of the cross three times on your belly with your thumb. It's just like passin' wind.'

Maman Coupeau, who they all thought was asleep, shook her head. No, she knew another method, which never failed. You had to eat a hard-boiled egg every two hours and put spinach leaves on your loins. The four women listened, very serious. But squinty Augustine, who would often burst out laughing without anybody knowing why, let out one of the hen-cackles that was her usual way of laughing. They'd forgotten she was there. Gervaise lifted up the petticoat and saw her on the sheet, rolling about like a little pig with her legs in the air. She pulled her out and gave her a slap to make her stand up. What was she laughing about, the silly goose? What business did she have listening to what the grown-ups were saying? For a start she could deliver the washing for a friend of Madame Lerat's, in Batignolles. As she said this, Gervaise slipped the basket under her arm and pushed the girl towards the door. Snivelling and complaining, Augustine set off, dragging her feet in the snow.

Meanwhile, Maman Coupeau, Madame Putois, and Clémence were debating the efficacy of hard-boiled eggs and spinach leaves. Then Virginie, who'd been lost in thought, her coffee glass in her hand, said quietly:

'The Lord knows, you fight and then you make up, it all comes right in the end if your 'eart's in the right place.'

Leaning towards Gervaise, she said with a smile:

'No, I don't hold it against you. That business in the wash-house, remember?'

The laundress was very embarrassed. This was what she'd been afraid of. Now, she guessed, the subject of Lantier and Adèle was bound to come up. The stove was roaring away, its red-hot flue giving out more and more heat. In this drowsy atmosphere the girls, lingering over their coffee to put off getting back to work as long as possible, were gazing out at the snow in the street, with expressions of languid enjoyment on their faces. They'd reached the stage of exchanging confidences, telling each other what they'd have done if they'd had ten thousand francs a year; they wouldn't have done anything at all, they'd have spent whole afternoons like this, keeping warm and letting the work go to hell. Virginie had moved closer to Gervaise so the others wouldn't be able to hear. And Gervaise felt quite helpless, no doubt because of the heat, so weak and helpless that she didn't have the strength to change the subject; she was even waiting for what Virginie was going to say, enjoying the feeling of anticipation that took hold of her, though she wouldn't have admitted it.

'I 'ope I'm not upsettin' you, am I?' the seamstress went on. 'It's bin on the tip of me tongue many times. Anyway, now we're on the subject... It's somethin' we can talk about, isn't it?... But, really, I've got no 'ard feelins about what 'appened. It's the 'onest truth! No 'ard feelins at all.'

She shook what was left of her coffee so as to get all the sugar, then took three sips, making little sucking noises. Gervaise, her heart in her mouth, still said nothing, wondering whether Virginie really had forgiven her for her drubbing, for she could see little yellow glints in her black eyes. The great she-devil must just have covered her resentment up.

'You had an excuse,' she went on. 'You'd just had a nasty trick played on you, a really filthy trick. Fair's fair, after all! If it 'ad bin me, I'd 'ave taken a knife to 'im.'

She took three more sips, sucking the edge of the glass. Her slow drawl had gone now, and she added quickly, without a pause:

'Not that it brought them any luck. God, no! They went to live in some dump over by La Glacière, in a nasty street where you're always knee-deep in mud. A couple of days later I went over in the mornin' to 'ave a bite to eat with 'em; a hell of a bus ride, I can tell you! Well, my dear, I found 'em already 'avin a row. Yes, when I got there they were thumpin' each other. A fine pair of lovebirds! Adèle's not worth the rope to 'ang 'er with, you know. She may be my sister, but that don't mean I can't say she's a real bitch. She's done the dirty on me lots of times; it'd take too long to tell you, and anyway it's just between me an' 'er. As for Lantier, well you know 'im, he's not much cop either. Such a nice fella, ain't he? He'll knock you about as soon as look at you, and he uses his fists too... So they were bashin' each other like anythin'. You could 'ear 'em at it as you went up the stairs. The police came one day. Lantier wanted some olive-oil soup—'orrible stuff they 'ave down south—and as Adèle said it was disgustin', they threw everythin' at each other, the bottle of oil, the saucepan, the soup tureen, the lot. The neighbours couldn't stop talkin' about it.'

She told Gervaise about other fights and went on and on about the couple. She knew things about them that would make your hair stand on end. Gervaise listened to it all without saying a word, her face pale, a nervous twitch like a little smile at the corners of her mouth. It was nearly seven years since she'd had any word of Lantier. She'd never have thought that his name, whispered in her ear like this, would have given her such a strange burning sensation in the pit of her stomach. No, she'd had no idea she'd be so keen to know what had become of that wretch, who'd treated her so badly. It was impossible to be jealous of Adèle now, but all the same she laughed to herself when she thought of them bashing each other. She imagined Adèle's body covered in bruises, it amused her and made her feel avenged. She could have stayed there all night listening to Virginie's stories.

She didn't ask any questions because she didn't want to seem particularly interested. But it was as though a gap in her life was suddenly being filled; her past, now, ran directly into her present.

Virginie, meanwhile, had stuck her nose back into her glass and was sucking at the sugar, her eyes half closed. Realizing she ought to say something, Gervaise tried to look indifferent and asked:

'Are they still living at La Glacière?'

'Oh no!' answered Virginie. 'Didn't I tell you? They split up a week ago. One morning Adèle packed up her things and took off, and Lantier didn't run after her, I can tell you.'

Gervaise let out a little cry and repeated:

'They've split up!'

'Who's split up?' asked Clémence, breaking off her conversation with Maman Coupeau and Madame Putois.

'Nobody,' said Virginie. 'People you don't know.'

She was studying Gervaise and saw she was very agitated. She moved even closer, seeming to take a malicious delight in going on with her story. Suddenly, she asked Gervaise what she'd do if Lantier came prowling round; because men are so funny, Lantier was quite capable of returning to his first love. Gervaise drew herself up straight and became very proper and dignified. She was a married woman, she'd show him the door, and that'd be that. There could never be anything between them again, not even a handshake. Really, she'd have to be completely spineless if she ever looked at that man again.

'Of course,' she said, ''he's Étienne's father, and that's a bond I can't break. If Lantier wants to see Étienne I'll send the boy to him, because you can't stop a father lovin' his child. But as far as I'm concerned, Madame Poisson, I can tell you I'd sooner be chopped into little pieces than let 'im touch me with the tip of 'is finger. It's all over.'

As she said these last words she made the sign of the cross, as if to seal her vow for ever. And wanting to end the conversation, she made as if she was waking up with a start, and shouted to the girls:

'C'mon, you lot! D'you think the clothes are goin' to iron themselves? You're gettin' lazy! Hop to it!'

The girls were in no hurry; drowsy and listless, they sat with their arms hanging limply, an empty glass with a few coffee grounds still clasped in one hand. They carried on chatting.

'It was that little Célestine,' Clémence was saying. 'I knew her. She had a thing about cat fur. You know, she could see cat fur everywhere, an' she was always rollin' 'er tongue round like this, 'cos she thought 'er mouth was full of it.'

'Well,' said Madame Putois, 'I 'ad a friend who 'ad a tapeworm. Fussy creatures they are! It'd twist 'er stomach in knots when she didn't give it chicken. Just imagine, 'er 'usband only earned seven francs a day, and most of it went on treats for the worm…'

'I could 'ave cured 'er in no time,' said Maman Coupeau. 'You just 'ave to swallow a grilled mouse. It poisons the worm straight away.'

Gervaise herself had slipped back into a pleasant state of idleness. But she shook herself and stood up. A whole afternoon spent doing nothing! That was no way to fill your purse! She was the first to get back to her curtains, but she found they were stained with coffee, and she had to rub the stain off with a damp cloth before she could carry on with the ironing. The girls had a good stretch in front of the stove and hunted grumpily for their iron-holders.

As soon as Clémence moved she had another coughing fit, so bad she seemed she was coughing up her lungs; but then she finished her shirt and pinned the sleeves and collar. Madame Putois had gone back to her petticoat.

'Well, see you later,' said Virginie. 'I came out to buy a piece of cheese. Poisson will think I got frozen on the way.'

But she'd only gone three steps along the pavement when she opened the door again to shout that she could see Augustine at the end of the street, sliding about on the ice with some boys. The little devil had been gone a good two hours. She ran in red-faced and out of breath, her basket on her arm, her hair stuck together with a snowball, and took her scolding with a shifty look, saying the ice made it hard to walk. Some kid must have stuffed bits of ice into her pockets as a joke, because half an hour later her pockets began spraying water all over the shop.

Every afternoon was like this now. The shop became the refuge of everyone in the neighbourhood who wanted to escape from the cold. The whole of the Rue de la Goutte-d'Or knew it was nice and warm there. There was always a little gaggle of women chatting away as they warmed themselves by the stove, their skirts pulled up to their knees. Gervaise was proud of this cosy warmth and encouraged people to come in—she held court, as the Lorilleux and the Boches nastily put it. The truth was that she was always kind and helpful, so much so that she got poor folk to come in if she saw them shivering outside. She took a particular liking to an old man of seventy, a former house-painter who lived in the big building, in a hole under one of the staircases, where he was slowly dying of cold and hunger. He'd lost his three sons in the Crimea* and, for the past two years, now that he could no longer hold a paintbrush, had been living on whatever came his way. As soon as Gervaise saw Père Bru stamping his feet in the snow to get warm she'd call him in and find a place for him by the stove, and often she'd even insist that he eat a piece of bread and cheese. Père Bru, with his bent back, white beard, and face wrinkled like an old apple, would sit for hours without saying a word, listening to the crackling of the coke. Perhaps he was dreaming about his fifty years of work up ladders, half a century spent painting doors and whitewashing ceilings all over Paris.

'So, Père Bru,' the laundress would sometimes ask, 'what are you thinking about?'

'Everythin' and nothin',' he'd answer, as if in a daze.

The girls teased him, saying he must be in love. But he didn't hear them and would slip back into his sombre, dreamy silence.

From that time on, Virginie often talked to Gervaise about Lantier. She seemed to enjoy making Gervaise think about her former lover, for the pleasure of embarrassing her with all sorts of conjectures. One day she said she'd bumped into him; and when the laundress didn't react, she said no more, and not until the following day did she give her to understand that he'd talked about her at some length, and very affectionately. Gervaise was very troubled by these whispered conversations in a corner of the shop. Lantier's name still gave her a burning sensation in the pit of her stomach, as if the man had left there something of himself, under her skin. Of course she had no doubts about herself, she wanted to live like a virtuous woman, because virtue is halfway to happiness. And so she never thought of Coupeau in this regard, for as far as her husband was concerned she had nothing to reproach herself with, not even in thought. It was the smith she was thinking about, with a faltering and uneasy heart. It seemed to her that the return of Lantier into her consciousness, slowly taking possession of her in this way, was making her unfaithful to Goujet, to their unspoken love, with its sweet companionship. There were days when she was sad, believing she was wronging her dear friend. She'd have liked to feel affection for no one but him, apart from her family. All this engaged the finest part of her being, far above the base thoughts Virginie was waiting to read on her face.

When spring came, Gervaise sought refuge in the company of Goujet. She was unable now to sit down and think about anything without her mind turning immediately to her first lover; she pictured him leaving Adèle, putting his clothes back into their old trunk, and going back to her with the trunk on the roof of the cab. When she went out she'd be seized all of a sudden by silly little panic attacks, right there in the street; she thought she could hear Lantier's step behind her, was afraid to turn round, began to tremble, imagined she could feel his hands taking hold of her round the waist. He was bound to be spying on her; one afternoon he'd pounce on her; and the thought brought her out in a cold sweat, because he'd surely kiss her on the ear as he used to do, to tease her. It was this kiss she dreaded; it made her deaf just to think about it, filling her head with a kind of buzzing that blotted out everything but the beating of her heart. So, when these fears came over her, the forge was her only refuge; there she became calm and smiling again, under the protection of Goujet, whose thunderous hammer drove away her bad dreams.

What a happy spring it was! The laundress took special care of her customers in the Rue des Portes-Blanches, always delivering the washing personally because the errand, every Friday, was a perfect excuse to go down the Rue Marcadet and call in at the forge. As soon as she turned the corner she'd feel as carefree and light-hearted as if she was going on a picnic. The strips of waste ground bordered by grey factories, the roadway black with coal dust, and the plumes of steam over the roofs delighted her as much as a mossy path in a wood,

winding its way between great clumps of greenery; and she loved the
dim skyline, streaked by the tall factory chimneys, and the heights of
Montmartre blocking off the sky with their chalky houses dotted with
evenly spaced windows. Then, as she drew near, she'd slow down,
jumping over the puddles and taking pleasure in picking her way
through the deserted mess of the demolition site. In the distance she
could see the glow of the forge, even though it was midday. Her heart
would leap to the rhythm of the hammers. By the time she went in
she'd be very flushed, the little blonde curls at the back of her neck
flying about, as if she were a woman coming to meet her lover. Goujet
would be waiting for her, bare-armed and bare-chested, and on those
days he'd hammer more loudly on the anvil so as to be heard from
further away. He'd sense her arrival and greet her with a broad silent
grin through his golden beard. But she didn't want to interrupt him
in his work, she'd beg him to pick up his hammer again because she
liked him all the more when he swung it with his big muscular arms.
She'd walk over and give Étienne a little pat on the cheek as he worked
the bellows, and she'd stay there for an hour watching the bolts being
made. They never exchanged more than a few words, but they
couldn't have expressed their affection better had they been alone
together in a bedroom with the door double-locked. The sniggering
of Bec-Salé didn't bother them at all, because they didn't hear him.
After a quarter of an hour she'd begin to feel a bit stifled; the heat, the
strong smell, the smoke rising up made her dizzy, while the dull thud-
ding shook her from head to foot. There was nothing more she
desired, her pleasure was complete. If Goujet had taken her in his
arms it wouldn't have moved her more deeply. She'd move closer to
him to feel the wind from his hammer on her cheek, to be part of the
blow he was striking. When sparks pricked her soft hands she didn't
draw them back but, on the contrary, delighted in this rain of fire that
stung her skin. He, of course, sensed how happy she was there; he'd
save his difficult jobs for Fridays, so as to woo her with all his strength
and all his skill; he threw himself into his work, almost breaking the
anvil in two, panting, his body vibrating with the joy he was giving
her. All through that spring their courtship filled the workshop with
the sound of thunder. It was an idyll in a Titan's forge, amid blazing
fires, the great shed shaking, its soot-blackened frame almost cracking
under the strain. Each piece of the iron he pounded, moulding it like
red sealing-wax, bore the rough imprint of their love. Each Friday

when Gervaise left Gueule-d'Or she'd walk slowly back up the Rue des Poissonniers, contented, weary, at peace in mind and body.

Little by little her fear of Lantier subsided and she became herself again. At that time she would still have been very happy had it not been for Coupeau, who was definitely going to the bad. One day, as she was coming back from the forge, she thought she saw Coupeau in Père Colombe's Assommoir drinking with Mes-Bottes, Bibi-la-Grillade, and Bec-Salé. She walked past quickly so she wouldn't seem to be spying on them. But then she turned round: yes, it was Coupeau, knocking back his little glass of brandy as if to the manner born. So he'd been lying, he was on spirits now! She went home in despair; all her old horror of spirits came back. She could forgive him wine, because wine does the workman good; spirits, on the other hand, were dreadful things, poisons that took away a man's appetite for food. The government ought to stop people from making the vile stuff!

When she arrived at the Rue de la Goutte-d'Or she found the whole place in a commotion. The girls had left the worktable and were in the yard, looking upwards. She asked Clémence what was going on.

'It's Bijard,' she said. 'He's beatin' 'is wife up. He was waitin' for 'er under the archway, pissed as a newt. He kept punchin' 'er all the way up the stairs and he's still at it up there, in their room. Listen, can't you 'ear 'er screamin'?'

Gervaise ran up the stairs. She liked her washerwoman, Madame Bijard, who was a very plucky woman. She hoped she'd be able to make Bijard stop it. Upstairs, on the sixth floor, the door to the room was wide open and several of the other tenants were on the landing, shouting, while Madame Boche was standing in the doorway screaming:

'Stop that! We're goin' to fetch the police!'

Nobody dared venture into the room because Bijard could get really violent when he was drunk. In fact he was never really sober. On the rare days when he worked he'd set a bottle of brandy next to his locksmith's vice and take a swig every half-hour. It was the only thing he lived on now. He'd have gone up in flames if you'd lifted a match to his mouth.

'We can't let 'im kill 'er!' said Gervaise, shaking all over.

She went in. The attic room was very clean, but cold and stark, stripped bare by Bijard's boozing; he would take the very sheets off the bed to pay for drink. In the fight the table had got pushed up against the window and the two chairs were upside down, their legs in the air. Madame Bijard was lying on the floor, in the middle of the room; her skirts, still wet from the wash-house, clung to her thighs, clumps of her hair had been pulled out, she was bleeding, and each time Bijard kicked her she let out a series of groans. To begin with he'd knocked her down with his fists, now he was stamping on her.

'You bitch! You bitch! You bitch!' he kept growling, grunting the word each time he gave her a kick, madly repeating it, kicking harder as his voice grew hoarser.

Then his voice failed him altogether, but he went on kicking silently, insanely, standing stiffly in his tattered smock and overalls, his face purple under his filthy beard, his bald pate covered in big red blotches. On the landing the neighbours were saying he was beating her because she'd refused to give him a franc that morning. Boche's voice could be heard at the bottom of the stairs, calling to his wife:

'Come down, let 'em kill each other, it'll be good riddance!'

Meanwhile Père Bru had followed Gervaise into the room. The two of them tried to reason with the locksmith and edge him towards the door. But he kept turning back, saying nothing, foaming at the mouth, a murderous expression shining in his pale, alcohol-inflamed eyes. The laundress had her wrist twisted and the old man was thrown against the table. On the floor Madame Bijard was breathing more heavily than ever, her mouth wide open and her eyes closed. Bijard's kicks were missing her now, but he kept on trying, blind with rage, even hitting himself with his wild blows. And throughout this scene Gervaise could see, in a corner of the room, little Lalie, now four years old, watching her father as he battered her mother. In her arms, as if to protect herself, she was holding her baby sister Henriette, only just weaned. She stood there, her head wrapped in a piece of printed calico, very pale and solemn-looking. Her big black eyes were staring intently, with never a tear.

Eventually Bijard tripped over a chair and fell flat on the floor, where they left him to snore. Père Bru helped Gervaise lift up Madame Bijard, who was now sobbing violently; Lalie, who'd moved closer, watched her mother cry, already used to such events, and resigned to them. As the laundress went downstairs again through the now quiet building she could still see the girl's eyes, the eyes of a child of four, as serious and unafraid as the eyes of a grown woman.

'Monsieur Coupeau's on the pavement opposite,' shouted Clémence as soon as she saw her. 'He looks completely sloshed.'

Coupeau was just crossing the street. He nearly smashed a pane of glass as he staggered through the door. He was dead drunk, his teeth clenched, his nose pinched. Gervaise could see at once the poison from Père Colombe's Assommoir in the polluted blood that discoloured his skin. She wanted to laugh it off and put him to bed, as she always did when he was lit up by wine. But he pushed her aside without opening his mouth and raised his fist as he brushed past and dropped on to the bed. He was just like the other one, the drunkard snoring upstairs, worn out with beating his wife. A chill came over Gervaise as, with a sinking heart, she thought about the men in her life, about her husband and Goujet and Lantier, and despaired of ever being happy.

CHAPTER VII

GERVAISE'S saint's day was the nineteenth of June. On these occasions the Coupeaus put on a real spread, the sort of binge you'd come away from as round as a barrel, your belly full for the rest of the week. All their spare cash was scraped together. As soon as the couple had a few sous, they blew them on food. They added imaginary saint's days to the calendar just as an excuse for a good feed. Virginie was all in favour of Gervaise stuffing herself with tasty little treats. When you've got a man who drinks it all away, it's only fair, isn't it, not to let the whole caboodle go down his throat, but to fill your own stomach first? Since the money was going to disappear anyway, it might as well go to the butcher as well as the wine merchant. Gervaise, her love of food increasing, was only too happy to use this excuse. Too bad! If they couldn't save a single bloody sou it was Coupeau's fault. Meanwhile, she'd put on more weight and her limp was worse, because her leg seemed to be getting shorter as it grew fatter.

That year they started talking about the party a month in advance, thinking about what dishes to prepare and licking their lips in anticipation. The whole shop was dying for a binge. It had to be an absolute knock-out, something tremendous and extraordinary, because—damn it all!—it's not every day you get to have a good time! The laundress's big problem was deciding who to invite; she wanted twelve at table, no more, no less. Gervaise herself, her husband, Maman Coupeau, and Madame Lerat, that already made four from the family. She'd have the Goujets and the Poissons as well. At first she thought she'd definitely not ask her assistants, Madame Putois and Clémence, so as not to make them too familiar, but as the party was always being discussed in front of them and they looked so long in the face, she ended up saying they could come. Four and four's eight, and two's ten. Then, since she was determined to make up the full number, she made it up with the Lorilleux, who'd been hovering round her for some time; at least, it was agreed that they'd come down for the meal and make peace over a drink. After all, family quarrels can't go on for ever. Besides, the idea of the party softened everybody's heart. The opportunity was too good to refuse. Only, when the Boches heard about the planned reconciliation, they immediately started to make up to

Gervaise, all politeness and smiles; so they had to be invited too. There! That would make fourteen, not counting the children. Never had she given such a dinner; it made her feel quite scared, but flushed with pride.

The anniversary happened to fall on a Monday. This was a stroke of luck, for Gervaise could count on the Sunday afternoon to start the cooking. On the Saturday, as the assssistants were rushing through their work, there was a long debate in the shop to settle once and for all what they were going to eat. Only one dish had been decided on, three weeks before: a fat roast goose. Their mouths watered when they talked about it. The goose had even been bought already, and Maman Coupeau fetched it out so that Clémence and Madame Putois could feel its weight. They exclaimed at how huge it looked, its rough skin swollen with yellow fat.

'How about *pot-au-feu* to begin with?' said Gervaise. 'Soup and a bit of stew, that's always good... Then we should have something with a sauce.'

Clémence suggested rabbit, but they had that all the time, everybody was sick to death of it. Gervaise hankered after something classier. When Madame Putois mentioned *blanquette de veau** they all looked at each other with broadening smiles. That was a great idea, nothing could be as impressive as *blanquette de veau.*

'After that,' Gervaise went on, 'we'd still need something else with a sauce.'

Maman Coupeau thought of fish, but the others made a face and banged their irons down harder. No one liked fish, it didn't sit well in the stomach and there were all those bones. Squinty Augustine dared to mention she liked skate, but Clémence gave her a thump to shut her up. Finally, when Gervaise had hit on *épinée de cochon*,* which made them all smile again, Virginie burst in, her face aglow.

'You've come just at the right time!' cried Gervaise. 'Maman Coupeau, show 'er the bird.'

Maman Coupeau fetched the bird again, and Virginie had to weigh it in her hands. She gasped. Bloody hell, it was heavy! But she quickly put it down on the edge of the worktable, between a petticoat and a pile of shirts. Her mind was on something else, and she led Gervaise into the back room.

'Listen, love,' she whispered, 'I wanted to warn you... You'll never guess who I bumped into down the street. Lantier, my dear! He's hanging about out there, sniffing around. So I came 'ere as fast as I could. It gave me quite a turn. I was thinkin' of you, of course.'

The laundress went as white as a sheet. What could that wretched man want with her? And he'd turned up right in the middle of the preparations for the party! That was just her luck, she couldn't even enjoy herself for a little while in peace. But Virginie said she shouldn't get worked up about it. Heavens above, if Lantier took it into his head to follow her about, she could tell the police and have him locked up. Since her husband had got his appointment as a policeman a month before, Virginie had got very high and mighty and kept talking about arresting everybody, declaring loudly that she wished someone would pinch her bottom in the street, just so she could haul the cheeky devil to the station and hand him over to Poisson herself. Gervaise gestured to her to be quiet because the girls were listening. She led the way back into the shop and, trying to sound very calm, said:

'Now, what about veggies?'

'How about *petits pois au lard*?'* said Virginie. 'I'd be happy just with that.'

'Yes, yes, *pois au lard*,' agreed all the others, while Augustine, getting excited, kept ramming the poker into the stove.

At three o'clock the next day, Sunday, Maman Coupeau lit the two cooking stoves as well as a third, earthenware one borrowed from the Boches. At half past three the stew was bubbling away in a big pot lent by the restaurant next door, their own pot being considered too small. They'd decided to cook the veal and the pork the day before, because those dishes are better heated up; only they wouldn't thicken the cream sauce for the veal until they were ready to sit down at the table. There'd still be quite enough to do on Monday: the soup, the *pois au lard*, the goose. The back room was all lit up by the fires in the three stoves; browning for the sauces was sputtering in the pans, giving off a strong smell of burnt flour, while the big pot puffed out jets of steam like a boiler, its sides shaking with deep and solemn gurgling noises. Maman Coupeau and Gervaise, each wearing a white apron, bustled round the room, cleaning the parsley, hunting for the pepper and salt, and turning the meat with a wooden spoon. They'd sent Coupeau off somewhere to get him out of their way, but they still had people breathing down their necks all afternoon. The cooking smells in the kitchen smelled so good throughout the whole building that the neighbours came down one after another, inventing different excuses to drop in simply to find out what was being cooked, and they hung around waiting until Gervaise had to take the lids off the pans. Then, at about five, Virginie appeared. She'd seen Lantier again; honestly, you couldn't set foot in the street without bumping into him. Madame Boche had also just seen him, down at the corner, nosing about in a very shifty way. On hearing this, Gervaise, who'd been on the point of slipping out to buy a sou's worth of fried onions for the stew, came over all of a tremble and didn't dare leave, especially as the concierge and the seamstress were scaring her to death with terrible stories about men lying in wait for women with knives and pistols hidden under their frock coats. And it was true! You could read about it in the papers every day; when one of those buggers gets into a fury at finding an old flame happy with somebody else, there's no telling what he might do. Virginie obligingly offered to go and get the onions. Women should stick together, and she couldn't let the poor girl have her throat slit. When she came back she said Lantier had disappeared; he must have realized he'd been spotted, and taken off. Despite that he was all they could talk about over the pots and pans for the rest of the afternoon. When Madame Boche said she thought she should tell Coupeau, Gervaise became very agitated and begged her not to say a word. A fine thing that would be! Her husband must have suspected something was going on, because, the last few days, when he went to bed, he'd sworn and banged on the wall with his fists. Her hands trembled at the thought of two men fighting over her; she knew what Coupeau was like, he was jealous enough to go for Lantier with his shears. And while the four of them became absorbed in this drama the sauces simmered gently on the banked stoves. When Maman Coupeau took the lids off the pots, the veal and pork made discreet little bubbling sounds, while the stew went on snoring like a happy cantor asleep in the sun. In the end they each took a cup and had a drop of broth with bread, to see what it tasted like.

Monday finally came. Now that Gervaise was going to have fourteen to dinner, she was afraid she might not be able to fit them all in. She decided to lay the table in the shop but, even so, first thing in the morning she was using a tape measure to work out which way to put the table. Then they had to move all the washing out and dismantle the worktable: this table, on different trestles, was to serve as a dining table. And then, in the middle of all this shifting about, a customer turned up and made a scene, complaining she'd been waiting for her washing since Friday; they obviously didn't give a damn about her, but she wanted her washing right away. Gervaise apologized and lied through her teeth: it wasn't her fault, she was cleaning the shop, and the girls wouldn't be back till the next day. She managed to calm the customer down and sent her on her way, promising to see to her washing at the first opportunity. But as soon as she'd gone Gervaise exploded. Really! If you listened to your customers, you wouldn't have time to eat! You'd slave away all your life for their precious sakes! You couldn't be ordered about constantly, could you? No, even if the Grand Turk walked in with a collar to be done, and offered her a hundred thousand francs, she wouldn't do a stroke of ironing that Monday, because it really was time she enjoyed herself a bit.

The whole morning was spent finishing the shopping. Three times Gervaise went out and came back laden like a mule. But when she was about to set off again to order the wine, she realized she didn't have enough money left. She could have got the wine on credit, but the household couldn't be left without any money at all, because of the hundreds of little expenses you don't think of. In the back room she and Maman Coupeau were in despair, having worked out that they needed an extra twenty francs at least. Wherever could they lay their hands on those four five-franc pieces? Maman Coupeau, who'd once done the cleaning for a minor actress at the Théâtre des Batignolles, was the first to suggest the pawn shop. Gervaise laughed with relief. What a fool she was! She hadn't thought of that. She quickly folded her black silk dress, put it in a towel, and pinned it up. Then she slipped it under Maman Coupeau's apron, telling her to hold it flat against her stomach, on account of the neighbours— there was no need for them to know anything. She went to the door to make sure nobody was following the old lady. But Maman Coupeau hadn't got as far as the coal merchant's when Gervaise called after her.

'Maman! Maman!'

She made her come back inside the shop and, taking her wedding ring off, said:

'Here, take this as well. We'll get more.'

When Maman Coupeau brought back twenty-five francs Gervaise jumped for joy. Now she could order six more bottles of quality wine to have with the goose. That'd be one in the eye for the Lorilleux.

For the last two weeks that had been the Coupeaus' dream: to put the Lorilleux in their place. What a lovely pair they were, the two of them. The sly devils shut themselves in, didn't they, when they had something special to eat, just as if they'd pinched it. Yes, they'd cover the window with a blanket to hide the light and make everybody think they were sleeping. Naturally, that kept people from going up there; and, all by themselves, they tucked in for all they were worth, wolfing down their food as fast as they could and keeping their voices low. And even the next day, they took care not to throw the bones on the dust-heap, because then everybody would know what they'd had; instead, Madame Lorilleux would go to the end of the street and throw them into a drain; one morning, Gervaise had caught her emptying a basketful of oyster shells down there. No, those tight-fisted buggers were as mean as hell, and all their little dodges came from their mania for seeming poor. Well, she'd teach them a lesson, she'd show them other people weren't stingy. If she could, she'd have set up her table in the middle of the street so as to invite any passers-by to join her. Money's not meant to grow mouldy, is it? It looks pretty when it gleams, all new, in the sunlight. She was so different from the Lorilleux now that when she had five francs she managed to give people the impression she had ten.

Maman Coupeau and Gervaise talked about the Lorilleux as they laid the table, at about three. They'd hung some big curtains over the shop window, but as it was hot they'd left the door open, so that the whole street was able to inspect the table. The two women didn't lay down a single carafe, bottle, or salt cellar without trying to do it in a way that would annoy the Lorilleux. They had set the places so they'd have a good view of how splendidly it was arrayed, and the best crockery had been reserved for them, for Gervaise and Maman Coupeau knew full well that real china plates would give them a terrible shock.

'No, no, Maman, don't give them those napkins! I've got two damask ones.'

'Good,' muttered the old girl, 'that'll push them over the brink.'

They smiled at each other, standing on either side of the big white table whose fourteen neatly aligned place settings made them swell with pride. It was like a shrine in the middle of the shop.

'Anyway,' Gervaise went on, 'why are they such misers? You know, last month, they were lying when she told everybody she'd lost a piece of chain while she was deliverin' it. Honestly! As if that woman ever loses anything! It was just so they could plead poverty, and not give you your five francs.'

'I've only seen my five francs twice, so far,' said Madame Coupeau.

'I bet they'll invent some other story next month. That's why they cover up their window when they've got rabbit for dinner. You'd have every right to say to them, wouldn't you, "If you can eat rabbit, you can easily afford to give your mother five francs." They just look after themselves! What would've 'appened to you, if I 'adn't taken you in with us?'

Maman Coupeau nodded. That day she was dead set against the Lorilleux because of the grand meal the Coupeaus were giving. She loved cooking, gossiping over the pots and pans, and turning the home upside down to get ready for a party. In any case she got on pretty well with Gervaise most of the time. When they did have cross words, as happens occasionally in every family, the old girl would grumble and say how horribly unlucky she was to be at her daughter-in-law's mercy. Deep down, though, she must have felt some affection for Madame Lorilleux; she was her daughter, after all.

'It's true, isn't it?' said Gervaise. 'You wouldn't be so well fed with them, would you? No coffee, no snuff, no treats! D'you think they'd 'ave put two mattresses on your bed?'

'No, of course not,' replied Maman Coupeau. 'When they arrive I'll stand right opposite the door to see the look on their faces.'

Just thinking about the look on the Lorilleux' faces gave them no end of fun. But it wouldn't do just to stand there staring at the table. The Coupeaus had had lunch very late, at about one, on cold cuts because the three ovens were already being used and they didn't want to dirty the crockery they'd washed for the evening. By four o'clock the two women were in the full throes of cooking. The goose was sizzling away in a roasting pan they'd put on the floor against the wall, next to the open window; the bird was so huge that they'd had to jam it in by force. Squinty Augustine, sitting on a little stool in the full glare reflected from the roasting pan, was solemnly basting the goose with a long-handled spoon. Gervaise was busy with the *pois au lard*, Maman Coupeau, in a tizz because of all the different dishes, was whirling about waiting for the moment to heat up the pork and the veal. At about five the guests began to arrive. First came the two laundry assistants, Clémence and Madame Putois, wearing their Sunday

best, the former in blue, the latter in black. Clémence was carrying
a geranium, Madame Putois a heliotrope; and Gervaise, whose hands
were all white with flour, had to give each of them two big kisses with
her hands behind her back. Then, hard on their heels, came Virginie,
got up like a real lady, in a printed muslin dress, with a hat and scarf,
even though she only had to walk across the street. She had a pot of
red carnations. She took the laundress in her arms and gave her a big
hug. Finally, in came Boche with a pot of pansies, Madame Boche
with a pot of mignonette, and Madame Lerat with a citronella, the
soil of which had dirtied her purple merino dress. They all embraced,
crowding into the room with its three stoves and the roasting pan, the
heat from which was overpowering. They could hardly hear each
other speak because of the noise of frying. Somebody's dress caught
in the pan, which caused quite a stir. The smell of the roast goose was
so strong that everybody's mouths began to water. Gervaise thanked
each of them very nicely for their flowers, but all the while carried on
thickening the sauce for the *blanquette* in the bottom of a soup bowl.
She'd put all the pots of flowers in the shop, at the end of the table,
without taking off their tall white paper wrapping. A fragrant scent of
flowers mingled with the cooking smells.

'Do you want a hand?' said Virginie. 'To think you've been slaving
away for three days preparing all this food and it'll be gobbled up in
no time!'

'Well, it wouldn't get cooked by itself!' Gervaise replied. 'No, don't
get your hands dirty. Look, it's all ready. There's just the soup to do.'

They all made themselves at home. The ladies put their shawls and
bonnets on the bed, and pinned up their skirts so they wouldn't get
dirty. Boche, who'd sent his wife back to keep an eye on the lodge
until it was time to eat, was already pushing Clémence into the corner
by the stove and asking her if she was ticklish; Clémence gasped and
squirmed, her shoulders hunched up and her bosom nearly bursting
out of her bodice, for the mere idea of being tickled sent shivers all
over her. The other ladies, so as not to be in the cooks' way, had also
gone into the shop where they stood against the walls, facing the table;
but they carried on talking through the open door and kept returning
to the back room, filling it with loud bursts of chatter and crowding
round Gervaise, who, a steaming spoon in her hand, forgot what she
was doing so that she could join in the talk. They were all laughing
and cracking broad jokes. When Virginie said she hadn't eaten for two

days to make room for the meal, that disgusting Clémence went one
better by saying she'd made room that morning by having an enema,
as the English do. Thereupon Boche told of a way to digest very
quickly, which was to squeeze yourself in a door after each course;
this was another thing the English did, and it allowed you to eat for
twelve hours at a stretch without upsetting your stomach. When
you're asked out to dinner, it's only good manners, isn't it, to eat?
People don't put veal, pork, and goose on the table just to be looked
at. Their hostess needn't worry; they'd lick the plates so clean she
wouldn't have to wash them the next day. And they all seemed to be
whetting their appetite by coming to sniff at the pans and the roaster.
The ladies began to behave like little girls, pushing each other and
running from room to room, making the floor shake, spreading the
kitchen smells with their flying skirts, and kicking up a tremendous
racket, the sound of their laughter mingling with the noise of Maman
Coupeau's knife chopping up the bacon.

At that moment, when they were all jumping about and shouting
just for the hell of it, Goujet appeared. He was too timid to come in,
but stood there with a big white rose bush in his arms, a magnificent
plant whose stem reached up to his chin so that his golden beard
seemed adorned with flowers. Gervaise ran up to him, her cheeks
flushed from the heat of the stoves. But he didn't know what to do
with his rose bush; when she took it from him he just stammered
something, not daring to kiss her. So she stood on tiptoe and put her
cheek to his lips; but he was in such a nervous state that he kissed her
on the eye, so roughly that he could have blinded her. They both
stood there, trembling.

'Oh, Monsieur Goujet, it's so beautiful!' she said, putting the rose
bush next to the other plants, where its crown of foliage towered above
the rest.

'Not at all, not at all,' he said, not knowing what else to say.

He heaved a great sigh, composed himself somewhat, and announced
that they shouldn't expect his mother, who was having one of her
attacks of sciatica. Gervaise was very sorry and said she'd keep a bit of
goose, because she was determined that Madame Goujet should eat
some of the bird. Everybody had arrived now. Coupeau must be wandering about somewhere in the neighbourhood with Poisson, whom
he'd gone to pick up after lunch; they'd turn up soon, they'd promised to be back by six on the dot. So, as the soup was nearly ready,

Gervaise called Madame Lerat over and said she thought it was time to go up and fetch the Lorilleux. Madame Lerat immediately became very grave, for it was she who'd conducted all the negotiations and arranged with both parties how the reconciliation would be carried out. She put her shawl and bonnet on again and went up, holding herself erect, with an air of great importance. Down below, Gervaise carried on stirring the noodle soup in silence. A sudden hush had fallen. Everyone waited solemnly.

It was Madame Lerat who appeared first. She had been right round via the street so as to bestow more pomp on the ceremony of reconciliation. She held the shop door wide open, while Madame Lorilleux, in a silk dress, stood on the threshold. All the guests had stood up and Gervaise stepped forward, kissed her sister-in-law according to plan, and said:

'Come in. It's all behind us, isn't it? We'll both be nice to each other now.' And Madame Lorilleux replied:

'Let's keep it that way. I'd like nothin' more.'

When she'd come in Lorilleux also stopped on the threshold and waited to be kissed before entering the shop. Neither of them had brought flowers; they'd decided not to, because it would've looked too much like giving in to Gimpy if they'd come bearing flowers the first time. Gervaise called to Augustine to bring out two bottles of wine. Then, at the end of the table, she began to pour and gathered everybody together. They all took a glass and clinked them, drinking to friendship and family. There was a silence as the whole company drank, the ladies lifting their elbows as they drained their glasses to the last drop.

'There's nothing nicer before a good feed,' declared Boche, smacking his lips. 'It's better than a kick up the arse, anyway.'

Maman Coupeau had taken up position opposite the door, to see the look on the Lorilleux' faces. Tugging at Gervaise's skirt, she led her into the back room. Bending over the soup, they talked in rapid whispers.

'What a sourpuss!' said the old woman. 'You couldn't see 'em, but I could! When she saw the table, well, 'er face went all twisted, like this, and the corners of 'er mouth went right up to 'er eyes; and as for 'im, all he could do was cough—he 'alf choked! Just look at 'em over there, completely dumbstruck.'

'It's terrible to see people that jealous,' said Gervaise.

It was true, the Lorilleux did have a funny look about them. Of course, nobody likes to be put in the shade, especially in families; if one lot gets ahead, it rankles with the others, it's natural. But you try to hold it in, don't you? You don't make a show of it. Well, the Lorilleux couldn't hide their feelings. They couldn't help scowling and looking thoroughly put out. After a while it became so obvious that the other guests kept looking at them and asking if they felt all right. Never would they be able to stomach the table with its fourteen place settings, its white cloth and napkins, its bread ready-sliced. It was like being in a posh restaurant on the boulevards. Madame Lorilleux walked round the room, averting her eyes so as not to see the flowers, and surreptitiously felt the big tablecloth, tormented by the idea that it must be new.

'We're ready!' announced Gervaise as she reappeared with a smile, her arms bare and wisps of golden hair floating round her temples.

The guests, looking rather fed up, were crowding round the table. They were all hungry, and kept giving little yawns.

'Once his nibs is back,' the laundress went on, 'we can get started.'

'Hmm. The soup's bound to get cold!' said Madame Lorilleux. 'You can never rely on Coupeau. You shouldn't 'ave let him slope off.'

It was already half past six. Everything was getting burnt now, and the goose would be overdone. Gervaise, quite upset, suggested that someone could go and look round the streets to see if Coupeau was in one of the bars. Then, when Goujet offered to go, she said she'd go with him. Virginie, concerned about her husband, went along as well. The three of them, bareheaded, took up the whole pavement. The blacksmith, in his frock coat, had Gervaise on his left arm and Virginie on his right—like a basket with two handles, as he put it; this struck them as so funny that they had to stop, overcome with laughter. Seeing their reflection in the butcher's window, they laughed even harder. With Goujet dressed all in black, they looked like a pair of dolled-up tarts, the seamstress with her pink-flowered muslin dress, the laundress in a white percale dress with blue polka-dots, her arms bare, a little grey silk scarf knotted round her neck. People turned round to watch them go by, looking so glowing and happy, all dressed up on a normal weekday, making their way through the crowd in the Rue des Poissonniers on that warm June evening. But it was no laughing matter. They went up to the door of every bar and poked their heads in, looking along the counter at the customers. Had that devil

Coupeau gone all the way to the Arc de Triomphe for his tipple? They'd already scoured the upper part of the street, looking in all the likely places: the Petite-Civette, famous for its brandied plums; Mère Baquet's, where you could get Orléans wine for eight sous; the Papillon,* haunt of coachmen, always a difficult lot to please. No sign of Coupeau. Then, as they were walking down towards the boulevards, as they were passing François's bar on the corner, Gervaise let out a little scream.

'What's the matter?' Goujet asked.

The laundress wasn't laughing any more. She was deathly pale, and so overcome that she nearly fell. Virginie understood in a flash when she saw Lantier calmly having his dinner at a table inside the bar. The two women hurried the blacksmith on.

'I twisted my ankle,' said Gervaise, as soon as she was able to speak.

Finally, at the bottom of the street, they found Coupeau and Poisson in Père Colombe's Assommoir, standing in the middle of a group of men. Coupeau, in a grey smock, was shouting, gesticulating furiously, and banging his fist on the counter; Poisson, off duty that day, was wearing a tightly buttoned old brown coat; he was listening to him with a morose expression on his face, not saying a word, his red beard and moustache bristling. Goujet left the women on the pavement, went in, and put his hand on the roofer's shoulder. But when Coupeau caught sight of Gervaise and Virginie outside, he flew into a rage. What the hell did these bitches want? The skirts were chasing him now! Well, he wasn't going to budge; they could eat their shitty dinner all by themselves. Just to calm him down, Goujet had to join in a round of drinks, and even then the roofer was mean enough to drag it out for five minutes. When he finally emerged, he said to his wife:

'I'm not 'avin' this. I'm stayin' put. It's my business where I want to go!'

She didn't say anything. She was trembling all over. She must have been talking with Virginie about Lantier, because Virginie pushed her husband and Goujet ahead, telling them to walk in front. Then the two women took up position on either side of Coupeau, to distract him and prevent him from seeing Lantier. He wasn't really the worse for wear, more stupefied by yelling than by drink. Out of pure devilment, just because they seemed to want to keep to the left-hand pavement, he gave them a shove and crossed over to the right. They ran after him in alarm and tried to block his view into François's bar. But he must have known Lantier was there. Gervaise was stunned to hear him growl:

'Yes, luv, there's a bloke in there we know, ain't there? D'you take me for an idiot? Just let me catch you at it again, gallivantin' an' makin' eyes!'

He started swearing and cursing. It wasn't him she was looking for, with her arms bare and her mug all powdered, it was that old pimp of hers. Then, suddenly, he started to rant and rave about Lantier. The bastard! The shit! One of them would have to end up on the floor, with his guts hanging out. Lantier seemed oblivious to what was happening and went on slowly eating his *veau à l'oseille.** A crowd began to gather. Finally Virginie dragged Coupeau away and, as soon as they got round the corner, he calmed down. Even so, they returned to the shop in a less cheerful mood than when they'd left it.

The guests were waiting round the table with long faces. Coupeau shook hands with everybody, playing up a bit to the ladies. Gervaise, feeling on edge, was quietly telling them where to sit when she suddenly realized that, as Madame Goujet hadn't come, one place would be empty, the one next to Madame Lorilleux.

'There's thirteen of us!' she said, shaken by this further sign of the bad luck she'd felt hanging over her for some time.

The ladies had already sat down, but stood up again looking worried and annoyed. Madame Putois offered to leave because, in her opinion, you should take things seriously; in any case, she wouldn't have anything, the rich food wouldn't be good for her. Boche, for his part, just grinned: better to be thirteen than fourteen, they'd all get a bit more to eat, that was all.

'Wait a minute!' Gervaise said. 'I know what I can do!'

She stepped outside and called to Père Bru, who just happened to be crossing the street. The old boy came in, bent and stiff, saying not a word.

'Sit yourself down,' said Gervaise. 'You'd like to have dinner with us, wouldn't you?'

He just nodded: he didn't mind if he did, it was all the same to him.

'Might as well be 'im as somebody else, eh?' she went on, lowering her voice. 'He doesn't have a decent meal very often. At least he'll have one today! Now we needn't feel guilty stuffing ourselves.'

Goujet had tears in his eyes, he was so touched. The others were touched too, and thought it a very nice idea, adding that it would bring them all good luck. Madame Lorilleux, however, didn't seem too pleased to be next to the old man; she moved away, casting looks of disgust at his rough hands and his patched and faded smock. He sat with bowed head, clearly having no idea what to do with the napkin on the plate before him. In the end he picked it up and put it carefully on the edge of the table; it didn't occur to him to lay it across his knees.

Gervaise was at last serving the noodle soup when Virginie pointed out that Coupeau had disappeared again: perhaps he'd gone back to Père Colombe's bar. This didn't go down at all well. It was too bad: no one was going to go running after him this time, he could stay out in the street if he wasn't hungry. However, as the spoons were scraping the bottom of the bowls, Coupeau reappeared with two flowerpots, one under each arm: a pot of wallflowers and a pot of balsam. The whole table clapped. He gallantly placed them on each side of Gervaise's glass; then he bent down and kissed her, saying:

'I'd forgotten you, ducky. But we still love each other, don't we, especially on a day like today.'

'Coupeau's in a good mood tonight,' Clémence whispered to Boche. 'He's had just the right amount to make him pleasant.'

Coupeau's nice behaviour restored the festive spirit that for a moment had seemed in danger. Gervaise relaxed and was all smiles again. The guests were finishing the soup. Then the bottles went round the table and they drank the first glass of wine, just a few drops, undiluted, to help the noodles down. In the next room the children could be heard quarrelling: Étienne, Nana, Pauline, and little Victor Fauconnier. It had been decided that the four of them should have their own table and they'd been told to be very good. Squinty Augustine, who was minding the stoves, had to eat off her knees.

'Maman! Maman!' Nana suddenly cried. 'Augustine's dipping her bread in the roaster!'

Gervaise rushed in and caught Augustine just as she was burning her mouth trying to bolt down a slice of bread soaked in boiling goose fat. She gave her a slap because the blasted girl was yelling that she was doing nothing of the sort.

After the beef, when the *blanquette* appeared, in a salad bowl because they didn't have a dish big enough, a gale of laughter went round the table.

'Things are really starting to get serious,' declared Poisson, who rarely said much.

It was half past seven. They'd closed the shop door so as not to be spied on by the neighbours, especially the little watchmaker across the street, who'd been staring at them with eyes like saucers, watching every mouthful so greedily that he'd begun to put them off eating altogether. The curtains draped over the windows let in a strong, white, even light which cast no shadow and fell on the table, with its symmetrically arranged place settings and its pots of flowers in their tall paper collars; the pale glow of the lingering twilight made the guests appear quite distinguished. Virginie found the right word: she looked round the room, all closed in and hung with muslin, and declared it was 'really cosy'. When a cart passed by in the street, the glasses jumped around on the tablecloth and the ladies had to shout as loud as the men. But there wasn't much conversation; they were on their best behaviour and being awfully polite to each other. Coupeau was the only one wearing a smock, because, he said, you don't need to put yourself out if you're among friends, and anyway the smock is the working man's garment of honour.

The ladies, their bodices tightly laced, had their hair so plastered down with pomade that it reflected the light, while the men sat well back from the table, puffing out their chests and sticking out their elbows for fear of spilling something on their coats.

My God! What a dent they made in the *blanquette*! Although there wasn't much talking, there was a mighty lot of chewing. The salad bowl was emptying fast; a spoon stood straight up in the thick sauce, a rich yellow sauce that quivered like jelly. They fished about in it for pieces of veal; there were still some left, and as the bowl was passed from hand to hand, faces peered into it, hunting for mushrooms. The big loaves of bread standing against the wall behind the guests seemed to be melting away. Between mouthfuls you could hear the thump of glasses being put down on the table. The sauce was a bit on the salty side and it took four bottles to wash down that bloody *blanquette*, which slipped down like cream, then set your insides on fire. And they hardly had time to draw breath before the *épinée de cochon* arrived, steaming on a deep platter and flanked by big round potatoes. There were gasps. Blimey! This was inspired! Everybody loved pork and spuds. Now they really were going to get up an appetite, and they all cast sidelong glances at the dish as it went round, wiping their knives on their bread in readiness. Then, when they'd got their helping, they dug each other in the ribs and chatted away with their mouths full. Wasn't it divine, this pork! Tender but firm. You could feel it sliding down inside you, all the way to your toes! And the spuds were stunning. This time it wasn't at all salty, but because of the spuds you needed to rinse your mouth every minute or so. Four more bottles were polished off. Their plates were wiped so clean that they didn't need to be changed for the *pois au lard*. Oh, vegetables hardly counted. You could put them away by the spoonful and hardly notice. Delicate food, stuff for the ladies, so to speak. The best thing about the peas was the bits of bacon, fried to perfection so that they smelt like a horse's hoof. Two bottles were enough for the peas.

'Maman! Maman!' Nana cried suddenly. 'Augustine's taking things from my plate!'

'Stop bothering me! Give her a slap!' answered Gervaise, her mouth full of peas.

In the next room, at the children's table, Nana was playing the lady of the house. She was sitting next to Victor and had put Étienne next to little Pauline; that way, they could play at being two married couples at a dinner party. At first Nana had served her guests very nicely, with all the airs and graces of a grown-up; but then she'd given in to her passion for bacon and had kept it all for herself. Squinty Augustine, who'd been prowling round the table, had taken advantage of the situation and grabbed a handful of the bacon, under the pretext of sharing it equally. Nana was furious and bit her on the wrist.

'You know what,' muttered Augustine, 'I'm going to tell your mother that after the *blanquette* you made Victor give you a kiss.'

But order was restored when Gervaise and Maman Coupeau came in to take the goose off the spit. At the big table, they were leaning back in their chairs, taking a breather. The men were unbuttoning their waistcoats, the ladies were dabbing their faces with their napkins. There was a kind of lull in the meal, though one or two of them, their jaws still working away, kept swallowing large mouthfuls of bread, without even being aware of it. They waited, letting their food settle. Night had gradually fallen, and a dull, ashen greyness was deepening behind the curtains. When Augustine placed two lighted lamps on the table, one at each end, the bright light revealed the mess: the greasy plates and knives, the wine-stained tablecloth covered with crumbs. A stifling smell rose all round, but their noses turned towards the kitchen, drawn by certain warm odours wafting from it.

'Can we give you a hand?' asked Virginie.

She got up and went into the next room. One by one, all the women followed her. They stood round the roaster, watching with keen interest as Gervaise and Maman Coupeau tugged at the goose. Then cries went up in which could be heard the children's squeals of excitement and the noise they made jumping for joy. There was a triumphal re-entry into the other room, with Gervaise carrying the goose with arms outstretched, her sweaty face lit up by a great silent laugh; the women walked behind, laughing like her; while Nana, bringing up the rear, stood on tiptoe to get a better look, her eyes popping out of her head. When the goose was on the table, huge, golden, dripping with fat, they didn't attack it right away. Amazement and respectful surprise had struck them all dumb. They were reduced to winks and nods to indicate their approval. What an absolute beauty! What legs! What a breast!

'It didn't get that fat by just lickin' the walls, that's for sure!' said Boche.

Then they started going into details about it. Gervaise gave the facts: it was the best bird she could find at the poulterer's in the Faubourg Poissonnière; it had weighed twelve and a half pounds on the coal merchant's scales; they'd used a whole bushel of coal roasting it; and she'd got three basins of dripping out of it. Virginie chipped in to boast that she'd seen the bird before it was cooked: you could have eaten it just as it was, she said, the flesh was so soft and white, with skin like a blonde! The men all chuckled mischievously, and smacked their lips. Except for Lorilleux and his wife, who sniffed, most put out to see a goose like that on Gimpy's table.

'So, come on,' said the laundress at last, 'we can't eat it whole. Who's going to carve? Not me! It's too big, I'm quite scared of it.'

Coupeau volunteered. Dammit, it was simple enough, you just had to get hold of the legs and pull; the pieces were just as good that way. But there was a chorus of protest and the carving knife was forcibly taken from him; no, when he carved, he turned the whole thing into an absolute battlefield. There was a brief pause as they looked round for another volunteer. Finally, Madame Lerat said very sweetly:

'Well, I think Monsieur Poisson should do it. Yes, Monsieur Poisson, obviously.'

And since the rest of them didn't seem to understand what she meant, she added, in an even more cajoling tone:

'Of course it should be Monsieur Poisson, he knows all about weapons.'

She gave the policeman the knife she was holding, and the whole table laughed with approval and relief.

Poisson gave a stiff soldierly nod and placed the goose in front of him. His neighbours, Gervaise and Madame Boche, moved away to give him elbow room. He took his time, carving with great sweeping movements, his eyes fixed on the bird as if to nail it to the dish. When he thrust the knife into the carcass, which made a cracking noise, Lorilleux emitted a patriotic cry:

'Oh, if only it was a Cossack!'*

'Did you ever fight any Cossacks, Monsieur Poisson?' asked Madame Boche.

'No, only Bedouins,'* the policeman replied, detaching a wing. 'There aren't any Cossacks left.'

Complete silence fell. Every neck was craned, all eyes followed the movements of the knife. Poisson had a surprise in store. Suddenly, with a final stroke of the knife, the hind part of the bird came away and stood straight up, rump in the air, showing the parson's nose. There were cries of admiration. There was nothing like an old soldier to enliven a party. Meanwhile the goose had discharged a stream of juice from the gaping hole in its rear, which sent Boche into a fit of giggling.

'I'm game,' he whispered, 'if anybody wants to pee in my mouth like that.'

'You dirty thing!' cried the ladies. 'How can anybody be so dirty!'

'He's the most disgustin' man I've known!' said Madame Boche, especially annoyed. 'Just shut up! You'd make any trooper blush. He's just doin' it so he can 'ave it all for 'imself!'

At this point Clémence could be heard repeating, above the din:

'Monsieur Poisson! Keep the parson's nose for me, Monsieur Poisson!'

'My dear, the parson's nose is yours by right,' said Madame Lerat in her discreetly suggestive way.

By now the goose was all carved up. The policeman, after giving them a little while to admire the parson's nose, had separated the pieces and arranged them round the dish so they could help themselves. The ladies, complaining of the heat, were beginning to undo their dresses. Coupeau shouted that this was his place and he didn't give a damn about the neighbours, and threw the street door wide open. The party thus continued amid the rumbling of cabs and the tramping of feet on the pavements. Then, with their jaws rested and fresh room in their stomachs, they began eating again, falling on the goose with furious energy. Just having to wait and watch the goose being carved, as that joker Boche put it, had made the veal and the pork sink right down to his ankles.

My God, they really put it away! No one could remember having such a good excuse for indigestion. Gervaise looked enormous as she sat leaning forward on her elbows eating big pieces of white meat, not saying a word for fear of missing a mouthful. She was a little ashamed, however, to let Goujet see her like that, greedy as a pig; but, seeing her all pink in the face from food, he was eating too much himself, and even in her greed she was so nice and kind! She didn't say anything, but every other minute she broke off to look after Père Bru and put something nice on his plate. It was quite touching to see her, loving food as she did, take a bit of wing she'd been about to put in her mouth and give it to Père Bru, who had no real idea what he was eating and gobbled everything, his head bent over his plate, stupefied by so much food, having long forgotten what even bread tasted like. The Lorilleux were working their rage off on the goose, grabbing enough to last them three days; they would have gobbled the dish, the table, and the whole shop if they could have brought Gimpy to grief that way. All the ladies had wanted some of the carcass—the carcass is the ladies' part. Madame Lerat, Madame Boche, and Madame Putois were gnawing the bones, while Maman Coupeau, who adored the neck, was tearing the meat off it with her two remaining teeth. As for Viginie, she liked the skin when it was nice and crispy, and the men all gallantly handed her their skin until Poisson glared at her and told her to stop because she'd had enough; on a previous occasion, when she'd eaten too much goose, she'd had to stay in bed for two weeks with an upset stomach. But this annoyed Coupeau, who passed Virginie a nice piece of leg, shouting that, damn it all, if she couldn't polish that off then what sort of woman was she! When had goose ever done anybody any harm? On the contrary, it was a remedy for diseases of the spleen. You could even eat it on its own, without bread, like a dessert. As far as he was concerned, he could go on eating it all night without any ill effects at all, whereupon, just to show them, he shoved a whole drum-stick into his mouth. Meanwhile, Clémence was finishing her par-son's nose, smacking her lips as she sucked at it, wriggling about on her chair with laughter at the dirty jokes Boche was whispering in her ear.

God, yes, they really stuffed themselves! If you're goin' to do it, you might as well do it properly, eh? And if you only have a real binge once in a blue moon, you'd be bloody mad not to fill yourself up to the eyeballs. You could see their bellies gettin' bigger by the minute, you honestly could! The women looked pregnant. Every one of 'em fit to burst, the greedy pigs! Their mouths wide open, grease all over their chins, their faces were just like backsides, and so red you'd swear they were rich people's backsides, with money pouring out of them.

And the wine, my friends! The wine flowed round the table like the water flowing in the Seine, or like a stream when it's rained and the earth is parched. When Coupeau poured he held the bottle high, to see the red jet foam in the glass; and when a bottle was empty he made a joke of turning it upside down and pretending to squeeze its neck the way a woman milks a cow. Another dead soldier! In a corner of the shop the pile of dead soldiers was getting bigger, a cemetery of bottles where they threw the scraps from the tablecloth. When Madame Putois asked for some water, Coupeau stood up indignantly and removed all the carafes from the table. Since when did decent folk drink water? Did she want to have frogs in her stomach, then? Glasses were being emptied in one go: the liquid streaming down their throats sounded like rainwater gushing down drainpipes during a storm. It was raining wine! Cheap wine that tasted at first of the cask, but which you soon got used to, so that after a while it had a kind of nutty bou-quet. Damn it all, the Jesuits could say what they liked, the fruit of the vine was a bloody good invention! They all laughed in approval; after all, a working man couldn't get along without wine: old Noah must have planted the vine for roofers, tailors, and blacksmiths. Wine cleaned you up and made you relax after work, it got you going when you were feeling lazy, and when it started playing tricks on you, well, what the hell, then you felt everything was going your way and Paris belonged to you. And anyway, the working man, worn out, stony broke, and treated like shit by the bourgeois, had a fat lot to be happy about, he could hardly be blamed for getting plastered now and again, just to make life seem a bit rosier. Right then, for instance, could they give a damn for the Emperor? Very likely the Emperor was pissed as well, but who cared? He couldn't be more pissed and having a better time than they were. To hell with all those nobs! As far as Coupeau was concerned, everybody could go to hell. He thought the ladies were all right though, and he tapped his pocket, jingling his three sous and laughing as if he was shovelling gold. Even Goujet, normally so sober, was a bit far gone. Boche's eyes had shrivelled up and Lorilleux's had got paler than ever, while Poisson's bronzed ex-soldier's face looked ever more severe. They were already pie-eyed. And the ladies were a bit tiddly as well, just a bit, with their cheeks flushed and a need to loosen their clothes which made them take off their shawls; Clémence was the only one who went a bit too far. But suddenly, Gervaise remembered the six bottles of quality wine she'd forgotten to serve with the goose; she brought them out and refilled the glasses. Whereupon Poisson got to his feet and said, glass in hand:

'To the good health of our hostess.'

With a great scraping of chairs, the whole party stood up and, amid the general hubbub, stretched out their arms and clinked glasses.

'Here's to fifty years from now!' cried Virginie.

'No, no,' replied Gervaise, smiling and very touched. 'I'll be too old then. The time comes, y'know, when you're 'appy to go.'

Meanwhile, through the open door, the whole neighbourhood was watching and enjoying the spectacle. Passers-by stopped in the beam of light that fanned out across the cobbles, and laughed with pleasure at the sight of people tucking in with such gusto. Coachmen, bending forward on their boxes to whip their nags, would glance in and shout some funny remark: 'Can we 'ave some too? Hey, missus, you look as if you need the midwife!' The smell of goose spread delight and good cheer all along the street; the grocer's boys opposite felt they could actually taste it, while the fruiterer and the tripe-shop woman kept appearing at their doors to have a sniff and lick their lips. The street seemed to be getting an attack of indigestion. Madame Cudorge and her daughter, from the umbrella shop next door, and whom nobody ever saw, crossed the road one after the other, looking out of the corners of their eyes, their faces as red as if they'd been making pancakes. The little watchmaker, sitting at his workbench, couldn't carry on working, he was drunk from counting the bottles and sat there excited among his jolly cuckoo clocks. Yes, the neighbours were all worked up, said Coupeau. So why try to hide? They'd really got going now, and no longer felt embarrassed to be seen at table; on the contrary, they were pleased and excited to have all these people gathering round, gaping greedily; they would have liked to break down the shopfront and push the table out into the roadway and have their dessert there, under people's noses, amid the bustle of the street. There was nothing bad about the way they looked, was there? So there was no reason to shut themselves up like a lot of selfish pigs. Coupeau, seeing that the little watchmaker was dying for a drink too, held up a bottle, and when the man nodded, he carried the bottle and glass over to him. They began to establish a true fellowship with the street. They toasted passers-by. They called out to mates who looked ready for a drop. The feast spread from one person to the next, until the whole of the Goutte-d'Or could smell the food, and feel it in their bellies, in one tremendous bacchanal.

Madame Vigouroux, the coal merchant, had been walking up and down in front of the door for several minutes.

'Hey! Madame Vigouroux! Madame Vigouroux!' they all yelled.

In she came, with a silly giggle, looking spruced up and so fat she was almost bursting out of her bodice. Men loved pinching her, because they could pinch her without ever finding a bone. Boche got her to sit next to him and in no time he'd quietly grabbed her knee under the table. But she was used to that kind of thing and calmly drained a glass of wine, telling them the neighbours were watching from their windows and some of the people in the building were starting to get annoyed.

'Oh, we'll take care of that,' said Madame Boche. 'We're the concierges, aren't we? Keeping the noise down is our job. Let them come to us and complain, we'll tell them where to get off.'

In the back room, a furious battle had just been raging between Nana and Augustine over the roaster, which they both wanted to scrape clean. For fifteen minutes the roaster had been bouncing about on the floor, clattering like an old saucepan. Now, Nana was attending to little Victor, who had a goose bone stuck in his throat; she was prodding him under the chin with her fingers and making him swallow big lumps of sugar as a remedy. But that didn't stop her from keeping an eye on the grown-ups' table. Every few minutes she'd run in asking for wine, bread, or meat, for Étienne and Pauline.

'Here, take this, and that's enough!' her mother would say. 'Now stop pestering me!'

The children couldn't swallow another bite, but they carried on eating just the same, banging out a hymn tune with their forks to keep themselves in the mood.

Meanwhile, in the middle of all the din, a conversation had started up between Père Bru and Maman Coupeau. The old man, still deathly pale despite the food and wine, was talking about his sons killed in the Crimea. Oh, if only those boys had lived, he'd have had something to eat every day. But Maman Coupeau, her speech slightly slurred, leaned over and said:

'Children can give you a lot of grief, though! Look at me. I might seem 'appy enough, but I've shed a tear or two. No, don't wish for children.'

Père Bru shook his head.

'Nobody'll give me any work now, anywhere. I'm too old. When I go into a workshop, the young fellas just laugh at me an' ask if I was the one what cleaned Henri IV's boots.* Last year, I could still make thirty sous a day paintin' a bridge; I 'ad to lie on me back with the river runnin' right underneath. Ever since then I've 'ad a bad chest. Now it's nothin' doin', they won't take me on anywhere.'

He looked down at his poor stiff hands and went on:

'You can understand it, 'cos I'm no good for anythin'. They're right, I'd do the same. You see, the trouble is, I'm not dead. Yes, it's me own fault. When you can't work no more, you should just lie down an' die.'

'Well, to be honest,' said Lorilleux, who'd been listening, 'I can't understand why the government doesn't do anythin' to 'elp people what can't work 'cos they get ill or disabled. I was readin' about it the other day in a newspaper...'

Poisson thought he had to defend the government.

'Workers aren't soldiers,' he declared. 'The Invalides,* that's for soldiers... You can't expect the impossible.'

Dessert was served. In the middle of the table stood a sponge cake in the shape of a temple with a dome made of slices of melon; and on top of the dome was an artificial rose with a butterfly, made out of silver paper, hovering alongside it on the end of a wire. In the heart of the flower two drops of gum represented dewdrops. To the left of the cake was a piece of cream cheese swimming in a dish, while to the right another dish was piled high with big bruised strawberries, running with juice. However, there was still some salad left, big leaves of cos lettuce drenched in oil.

'Go on, Madame Boche,' Gervaise urged, ''ave a bit more salad. I know you love it.'

'No, thanks! I'm really full,' replied the concierge.

Gervaise turned to Virginie, who'd stuck her finger down her throat, as if she was trying to push down the food she'd eaten.

'No, I'm full too,' she said. 'There's no more room. I couldn't eat another mouthful.'

'Come on, force yourself,' Gervaise went on, smiling. 'There's always a bit of room left. You don't 'ave to be 'ungry to eat salad. You can't let this lettuce go to waste, surely.'

'You can 'ave it tomorrow,' said Madame Lerat. 'It's better after it's soaked up the oil.'

The ladies, breathing hard, gazed wistfully at the salad bowl. Clémence told how she'd once eaten three bunches of cress for lunch. Madame Putois could beat that, she was able to eat whole heads of cos lettuce as they were, without trimming them, just with a sprinkling of salt. They could all live on salad, they could eat it by the bucketful. Helped along by their conversation, they proceeded to finish the salad.

'I could go on all fours in a field,' said Madame Boche, her mouth full.

The idea of dessert was a joke. A dessert didn't count. It had appeared a bit late, but that didn't matter: they'd nibble at it all the same. When you were ready to explode like a bomb, you couldn't let yourself be beaten by a few strawberries and a bit of cake. In any case, there was no hurry, they had plenty of time, the whole night if they wanted. So they stacked their plates with strawberries and cream cheese. The men lit their pipes, and as the better wine was all gone, they went back to the ordinary stuff, drinking as they smoked. But they wanted Gervaise to cut the cake straight away. Poisson, in his most gallant manner, stood up and, taking the rose, presented it to the hostess amid general applause. She had to attach it with a pin on her left breast, near her heart. Every time she moved, the butterfly gave a flutter.

'But of course!' exclaimed Lorilleux, just making a discovery, 'it's your worktable we're eating on! Well, I'd be surprised if so much work has been done on it before!'

This nasty crack went down very well. A stream of witticisms followed. Clémence couldn't swallow a spoonful of strawberries without saying she was touching them up with the iron; Madame Lerat made out that the cream cheese tasted of starch; while Madame Lorilleux kept muttering through clenched teeth that it was a fine thing to gobble your money so fast on the very table where you'd had such a job earning it. A storm of shouts and laughter erupted.

But suddenly a powerful voice made them all fall silent. It was Boche, who had risen to his feet and, with a wicked twinkle in his eye, had started singing 'The Volcano of Love, or The Irresistible Trooper'.

                 'It's me, Blavin, wowin' all the girls...'

The first verse was greeted with thunderous applause. Yes, yes, they'd have a sing-song, and everybody should have a turn! There was nothing like a good sing-song! They put their elbows on the table or leaned back in their chairs, nodding at the best bits and taking a drink during the choruses. That devil Boche specialized in comic songs. It was enough to send the wine bottles into fits, the way he played the soldier boy saluting with his fingers spread wide and his hat on the back of his head. After 'The Volcano of Love' he went straight into 'The Baroness of Follebiche',* one of his star turns. When he came to the third verse he turned to Clémence and crooned in a slow, seductive voice:

> 'Milady was entertainin' late,
> Her sisters four, likewise:
> One blonde and three brunettes with eight
> Irresistible eyes.'

Quite carried away, the whole company joined in the chorus, the men beating time with their feet, the ladies clinking their knives on their glasses. They all bawled:

> 'Good God! Who's gonna cop the bill
> For all the grog this lot can swill!
> Good God! Who's gonna cop the bill
> For what they swill and swill and swill!'

The shop windows rattled and the singers' powerful breathing made the muslin curtains flutter. Meanwhile, Virginie had disappeared twice already, and each time she came back she'd bent down and whispered something in Gervaise's ear. When she came back a third time, she said, amid the general din:

'He's still at François's, my dear, pretending to read the paper. I'm sure he's up to something.'

She was talking about Lantier. She'd been keeping an eye on him. With each fresh report Gervaise looked more worried.

'Is he drunk?' she asked Virginie.

'No,' she replied. 'He seems quite sober. That's what I don't like. What's he hanging about a bar for if he's not drinking? Dear me, I hope nothing bad's going to happen!'

The laundress, very worried now, begged her not to say anything. All of a sudden complete silence had fallen. Madame Putois had risen to her feet and was about to sing 'Pirate Ship Ahoy!'. The guests, silent and attentive, were all gazing at her; even Poisson had put his pipe on the table to listen more attentively. Tiny and impassioned, she stood rigidly erect, her face white under her black bonnet; she kept thrusting her left fist forward with fierce conviction as she boomed out, in a voice much bigger than herself:

> 'With a tail wind, in full sail,
> Freebooters on our trail,
> We curse the pirate scum!
> To the cannons, boys—the scrum
> deserves a round of rum!
> They're bound for kingdom come,
> Those scurvy pirate crowds!
> We'll string 'em from our shrouds!'

This was powerful stuff. Hell, it made you feel you were there! Poisson, who'd once been on a sea voyage, slowly nodded his head, to show his approval of each detail. It was obvious, as well, that the song meant something personal to Madame Putois. Coupeau leaned over and told how, one evening in the Rue Poulet, Madame Putois had fought off four men who'd tried to molest her.

Meanwhile, Gervaise, helped by Maman Coupeau, was serving coffee, even though everyone was still eating the cake. They wouldn't let her sit down again, shouting it was her turn to sing. She resisted, looking so pale and ill at ease that they asked her if the goose hadn't agreed with her. So she sang 'Oh! Let me sleep!' in a sweet, gentle voice; and when she came to the chorus, to the wish for a sleep filled with lovely dreams, her eyes started to close as she gazed vaguely out into the darkness of the street. Immediately afterwards, Poisson gave the ladies a stiff little nod and broke into a drinking song, 'The Wines of France', but he sang completely out of tune; only the last verse, the patriotic one, went down well, because when he got to the bit about the Tricolour, he raised his glass very high, waved it about, and finally tipped it down his wide open throat. Then came a succession of romantic ballads; they heard about Venice and gondoliers in a barcarolle by Madame Boche, Seville and Andalusian beauties in a bolero by Madame Lorilleux, while Lorilleux went so far afield as to sing of the perfumes of Araby, apropos of the loves of Fatima the dancing girl. Round the grease-spotted table, in the indigestion-laden air, golden vistas were evoked, wherein could be seen ivory skin and ebony tresses, moonlit kisses to the strumming of guitars, houris showering the ground beneath their feet with pearls and precious jewels. The men sat blissfully smoking their pipes, while the ladies wore unconscious smiles of sensual pleasure, and all of them imagining they were far away, in a land of rich perfumes. When Clémence started warbling 'Make Your Nest' with a tremolo in her voice, that also delighted them, for it reminded them of the countryside, tiny little birds, nectar-laden flowers, dancing under the trees, in fact the things you could see in the Bois de Vincennes when you went there for a picnic. They were soon laughing again when Virginie started on 'My Little Riquiqui',* imitating a *vivandière*,* with one hand on her hip and her elbow out, while twisting her other wrist as though pouring wine into an imaginary glass. This went down so well that they begged Maman Coupeau to sing 'The Mouse'.* The old girl refused, swearing she didn't know that dirty song, but eventually she began it in her thin, quavery voice, her wrinkled face and beady little eyes bringing out all the double entendres as she sang of the terror of Mademoiselle Lise pulling her skirts tight at the sight of the mouse. The whole table rocked with laughter; the ladies couldn't keep their faces straight, and kept flashing glances at the men next to them; it wasn't a dirty song, after all, it didn't have any rude words in it. Boche, meanwhile, was playing at being the mouse running up and down Madame Vigouroux's calves. Things might have got out of hand if Goujet, at a glance from Gervaise, hadn't restored order with 'Abd-el-Kader's Farewell',* which he sang in his deep bass voice. Now there was someone with a good set of lungs! The song came forth from his great golden beard as if from a brass trumpet. When he cried out, 'Oh, my noble companion!'— referring to the warrior's black mare—every heart beat faster and they applauded without waiting for the end, so sonorously had he sung.

'Your turn, Père Bru, your turn!' said Maman Coupeau. 'Sing your song now. The old ones are the best!'

They all turned towards the old man and egged him on. He sat there in a kind of trance, his face a lifeless, leathery mask, staring at them and appearing not to understand. They asked if he knew 'The Five Vowels'. His head sank lower; no, he couldn't remember it, all the songs from the good old days were jumbled up in his poor noddle. Just as they were deciding to leave him in peace, he seemed to remember something, and in a hollow, faltering voice, began:

'Tra la la, tra la la,
Tra la, tra la, tra la la!'

His face lit up, as though this refrain had awakened in him the memory of some happy time long ago which only he could appreciate, and he listened with childlike delight to his own fading voice:

'Tra la la, tra la la,
Tra la, tra la, tra la la!'

'I say, my dear,' Virginie whispered in Gervaise's ear, 'I've just been to 'ave a look again. It was really botherin' me. Lantier's not there any more.'

'You didn't run into 'im outside?' asked Gervaise.

'No, I was walkin' quite fast, it didn't occur to me.'

But as she looked up, she broke off and gasped:

'Oh, my God! He's there, across the street. He's lookin' this way!'

Filled with alarm, Gervaise risked a quick glance. A crowd of people had gathered in the street to listen to the singing. The grocer's boys, the tripe-shop woman, and the little watchmaker had formed a group as if they were spectators at a show. There were soldiers, men in frock coats, and three little girls of five or six who stood holding hands, very serious, looking on in wonderment. And indeed, there was Lantier, right in the front, watching and listening, as calm as could be. He really had a nerve! Gervaise felt a chill spread through her body, and she sat not daring to move as Père Bru went on:

'Tra la la, tra la la,
Tra la, tra la, tra la la!'

'All right, mate, that'll do!' said Coupeau. 'D'you know the rest? You can sing it for us some other time, eh, when we're in the mood.'

Some of them laughed. The old man stopped short, cast his pale eyes round the table, and sank back into his former state of brutish self-absorption. The coffee was finished and Coupeau had asked for more wine. Clémence had started on the strawberries again. For a few minutes the singing stopped, and the conversation turned to a woman who'd been found hanged that morning in the house next door. It was Madame Lerat's turn, but she needed to do various things to prepare. She dipped the corners of her napkin in a glass of water and dabbed it on her temples, because she was too hot. Then she asked for a drop of brandy, drank it, and carefully wiped her lips.

'How about "The Child of the Lord"?' she murmured. 'Yes, "The Child of the Lord"...'

So, the tall, masculine-looking Madame Lerat, with her long nose and her square policeman's shoulders, began:

> 'The child cast from a mother's love
> Finds shelter in a holy place.
> God guards her from his throne above.
> The lost child knows the good Lord's grace.'

Her voice, tremulous at times, lingered meaningfully on certain words; she slanted her eyes towards Heaven, while her right hand hovered over her bosom and from time to time would be pressed to her heart in a gesture full of passionate feeling. Gervaise, finding Lantier's presence unbearable, could not hold back her tears; she felt as if the song was about her own torment, that she was the abandoned child whom the Lord was going to take into his care. Clémence, very drunk, suddenly broke into sobs, put her head on the table, and tried to stifle her hiccups with the tablecloth. There was an emotionally charged silence. The ladies had pulled out their handkerchiefs, and were wiping their eyes, their heads held high, proud that they could show such feeling. The men sat with bowed heads, staring straight ahead and blinking. Poisson, choking and clenching his teeth, twice broke off his pipe, spitting the bits on to the floor without stopping smoking. Boche still had his hand on Madame Vigouroux's knee, but was no longer pinching her, overcome by a vague feeling of remorse and respect, as two large tears ran down his cheeks. They were all as drunk as skunks and as tender-hearted as lambs. It was as if they were weeping wine! When the chorus came round again, even more slowly and mournfully, they all gave in and blubbered into their plates, letting themselves go completely, wallowing in emotion.

But Gervaise and Virginie, despite themselves, couldn't keep their eyes off the pavement across the street. Madame Boche was the next to notice Lantier, and she let out a little cry while still wiping away her tears. Now all three were looking worried as they exchanged involuntary nods. My God, what if Coupeau turned round, what if Coupeau saw him! There'd be hell to pay! There'd be blood! Seeing something was up, Coupeau asked:

'What on earth are you looking at?'

He looked round and saw Lantier.

'Christ! That's too much! The bastard! The fuckin' bastard! No, that's the bloody limit. I'm gonna stop this.'

As he stood up, spluttering terrible threats, Gervaise begged him:

'Listen, please... Put that knife down. Stay here, don't do somethin' silly.'

Virginie grabbed the knife he'd picked up from the table, but she couldn't stop him from going out and walking up to Lantier.

The rest of the company, swept up on a tide of emotion, weeping even louder, were oblivious to what was happening, as Madame Lerat sang on, in heart-rending tones:

'The orphan girl was lost, her pleas
And desperate cries by none were heard
But the rushing wind and the swirling trees.'

The last line trailed away like the mournful howling of a storm. Madame Putois, taking a sip of wine, was so overcome that she spilt some of it on the tablecloth. Meanwhile, Gervaise sat frozen, one hand pressed to her mouth to prevent her from crying out, blinking with terror, and expecting at any moment to see one of the two men out there knock the other to the ground. Virginie and Madame Boche were also watching with great interest. Coupeau, surprised by the fresh air, had nearly ended up in the gutter as he tried to throw himself at Lantier, who'd simply stepped to one side, his hands in his pockets. Now they were both yelling insults at each other. Coupeau, especially, was really letting Lantier have it, calling him a dirty swine and saying he'd have his guts for garters. Their voices were loud and furious, their gestures violent; they swung their arms at each other so fiercely you'd have thought they'd come out of their sockets. Gervaise began to feel faint and closed her eyes, because it seemed to be going on forever and she kept thinking they were going to bite each other's noses off, their faces were that close. But then, as the noise seemed to have stopped, she opened her eyes again and was dumbfounded to see them chatting quietly.

Madame Lerat's voice rose higher, warbling tearfully, as she started a new verse:

> 'The poor mite, overcome by fear,
> Was found the next day, nearly dead...'

'Some women are real bitches, you have to admit!' said Madame Lorilleux, to everyone's approval.

Gervaise exchanged glances with Madame Boche and Virginie. Were Coupeau and Lantier making up then? They were still across the road, talking. They were still exchanging insults, but in a friendly way, calling each other things like 'silly bugger' in tones that sounded almost endearing. People were watching them, so they started walking slowly along the street, side by side, turning back again every ten steps or so. Their conversation was very animated. Suddenly it looked as if Coupeau was getting angry again, because Lantier was refusing to agree to something Coupeau wanted. Then the roofer gave Lantier a push, making him cross the street and come into the shop.

'I meant it! Honestly!' he shouted. 'Come and 'ave a glass of wine. Men are men, right? We're meant to get along...'

Madame Lerat was coming to the end of the last chorus. The ladies all joined in, twisting their handkerchiefs in their hands:

> 'The lost child is the child of God.'

Compliments rained down on the singer as she sat down, pretending to be totally drained. She asked for something to drink—she put too much feeling into that song and was always afraid she'd wreck her nerves. Meanwhile, the whole table was staring at Lantier, who was sitting quietly next to Coupeau, and already eating the last piece of cake, dipping it into a glass of wine. Apart from Virginie and Madame Boche, no one knew who he was. The Lorilleux did suspect that something funny was going on, but they had no idea what exactly, and just sat there with pursed lips. Goujet had noticed that Gervaise was upset about something, and was eyeing the newcomer suspiciously. As an awkward silence had fallen, Coupeau said simply:

'This is a friend of mine.'

Then, turning to his wife:

'Come on, then... Is there any more coffee?'

Gervaise was looking from one to the other, a blank, stupefied expression on her face. At first, when her husband had pushed her old lover into the shop, she'd put her hands to her head with the same instinctive reaction she had in a storm, at each clap of thunder. She couldn't believe what was happening; surely the walls would collapse and fall on top of them. But then, seeing the two men sitting there, and the muslin curtains not even moving, it suddenly all seemed quite normal. The goose hadn't really agreed with her; she'd certainly eaten too much of it, and it was preventing her from thinking clearly. She was overcome with a blissful, numbing state of drowsiness that kept her slumped over the table, wanting only to be left in peace. Why get all worked up, for God's sake, when no one else was, and things seemed to be working out by themselves to everybody's satisfaction? She got up to see if there was any coffee left.

In the back room, the children were fast asleep. Augustine had terrorized them throughout the dessert, pinching their strawberries and scaring them with terrible threats. Now she was feeling very ill, bent double on a little stool, ashen-faced and silent. Fat Pauline had let her head fall on Étienne's shoulder, and he was asleep himself over the table. Nana was sitting on the bedside mat next to Victor, holding him close, with one arm round his neck; half asleep, her eyes shut, she kept repeating in a weak little voice:

'Oh, Maman, I do feel bad... Oh, Maman, I do feel bad...'

'It's no wonder!' muttered Augustine, her head rolling from side to side. 'They're sozzled; and they were singing away just like the grown-ups.'

Seeing Étienne gave Gervaise a fresh jolt. It made her feel almost ill to think that the boy's father was there, eating cake in the next room, and hadn't shown any desire to go and give him a kiss. She nearly woke Étienne to carry him in. But then, once again, she thought it was all right that things were turning out so easily. It wouldn't have done, she felt sure, to spoil the end of the dinner. She went back in with the coffee pot and poured a cup for Lantier, who hardly seemed to notice her.

'Now it's my turn,' said Coupeau, his speech slurring. 'The best for last, eh? All right, then, I'll sing "Disgusting Little Beast!".'*

'Yes, yes! "Disgusting Little Beast!",' they all yelled.

The racket was starting again, Lantier was forgotten. The ladies got their glasses and knives ready, to accompany the chorus. They were already laughing in anticipation as they watched Coupeau swaying about, shifting from one foot to the other, with a roguish glint in his eye. In a croaky voice, like an old woman, he sang:

> 'Mornings, I stagger up, and blimey,
> I come all over queer,
> So I send him down to the Grève* to buy me
> Four sous' worth of beer.*
> Though I told 'im not to take all day
> 'E's an hour at the very least,*
> And 'e's swigged down half of me booze* on the way:
> Disgusting little beast!'

The ladies, tapping on their glasses, took up the chorus with a tremendous show of gaiety:

> 'Disgusting little beast!
> Disgusting little beast!'

The Rue de la Goutte-d'or itself was joining in now; the whole neighbourhood was singing 'Disgusting Little Beast!'. Across the street, the little watchmaker, the grocer's boys, the tripe-shop woman, and the greengrocer, who all knew the song, joined in the chorus, exchanging slaps just for fun. The whole street was getting drunk, it really was; the mere smell of the party at the Coupeaus' was enough to get them staggering about on the pavement. And it must be said that inside the shop they were all well and truly sloshed. They'd been getting there steadily ever since the first glass of undiluted wine, after the soup. Now they were going at it like crazy, all of them bawling their heads off, all of them bursting with food, in the reddish haze of the two guttering lamps. The din from this great jamboree drowned the noise of the last carriages. Two policemen came running, thinking there must be a riot, but when they saw Poisson they gave him a knowing little nod and went slowly on their way, side by side, along the dark street.

Coupeau had reached this verse:

> 'Sundays at la P'tit'-Villette,
> Soon as the day cools down,
> We drop in on my Uncle Tinette,*
> The topnotch cesspit man.

> To get us cherries, fresh,* 'alf-price,
>   Spit the pits and 'ave a feast.
> Then 'e up and rolls into Unc's merchandise:
>   Disgusting little beast!
>   Disgusting little beast!'

At this, they fairly raised the roof, and such a deafening roar went up in the still, warm air of the night that the revellers began applauding themselves, for surely no one could possibly yell any louder.

No one could ever remember quite how the party ended. It must have been very late, that was for sure, because there wasn't a single cat left in the street. It was even possible that they joined hands and danced round the table, but they weren't sure. It was all lost in a golden haze, in which flushed faces bobbed about, grinning from ear to ear. They definitely had some wine with sugar towards the end, but they couldn't remember whether someone had put salt in the glasses instead, for a lark. The children must have got undressed and into bed by themselves. The next day Madame Boche boasted that she'd given her husband a good clout on catching him in a corner, chatting up Madame Vigouroux; but Boche couldn't remember a thing about it and treated it as a joke. What everyone agreed on, though, was the indecent way Clémence had carried on. She was definitely not someone who could be invited anywhere; she'd ended up showing everything she'd got, and had then thrown up all over one of the muslin curtains and completely ruined it. At least the men went outside into the street to do it; Lorilleux and Poisson, when their stomachs started playing up, got as far as the charcutier's. You can always tell when someone's been well brought up. For instance, the ladies, Madame Putois, Madame Lerat, and Virginie, finding the heat too much for them, had simply retired to the back room and taken off their corsets, and Virginie had even had a lie-down on the bed for a moment, to guard against any mishap later on. Then they'd all seemed to melt away, one after another, but all in a body, disappearing into the darkness, but not without creating one final din, with a furious argument between the Lorilleux, and a persistent, mournful 'tra la la, tra la la' from Père Bru. Gervaise was pretty sure Goujet started to cry when he left; Coupeau was still singing; as for Lantier, he must have stayed until the end. At one moment, she felt something like his breath in her hair, but she couldn't say if it was Lantier or just the warm night air.

Madame Lerat refused to walk home to Batignolles at that time of night, so they took a mattress off the bed, pushed the table to one side, and spread it out for her in a corner of the shop. There she slept, among the remains of the dinner. And all night long, as the Coupeaus lay dead to the world, sleeping off the effects of the party, a neighbour's cat, taking advantage of an open window, gnawed at the bones of the goose, finally finishing the bird off to the crunching sound of its tiny teeth.

CHAPTER VIII

THE following Saturday Coupeau didn't come home for dinner, but brought Lantier back with him at about ten o'clock. They'd had a meal of sheep's trotters together at Thomas's restaurant in Montmartre.

'There's no need to be cross, old girl,' said the roofer. 'As you can see, we ain't bin on the piss. There's no risk of that with this bloke, he keeps you on the straight and narrow.'

He described how they'd bumped into each other in the Rue Rochechouart. After dinner, Lantier had refused to have a drink at the Boule-Noire,* saying that when you're married to a nice, decent woman you shouldn't spend your time hanging about in seedy bars. Gervaise listened with a faint smile. No, of course she wasn't going to get cross, she felt too awkward. Ever since the party, she'd been expecting her old lover to turn up again before long, but the sudden arrival of the two men now, just when she was going to bed, had taken her by surprise, and her hands trembled as she tied up her hair, which had fallen loose.

'I tell you what,' Coupeau went on. 'Seein' as he was thoughtful enough to say we shouldn't 'ave a drink when we were out, you can give us one now. It's the least you can do.'

Gervaise's assistants had left hours ago. Maman Coupeau and Nana had just gone to bed. So Gervaise, who'd begun to put up the shutters when they appeared, left the shop open and put some glasses and what was left of a bottle of cognac on a corner of the worktable. Lantier remained standing, and avoided speaking to her directly. But when she was pouring his drink, he said:

'Just a drop for me, Madame, please.'

Coupeau looked at them, and then said bluntly that he hoped they weren't going to act all stupid! Bygones were bygones, weren't they? If you went on bearing grudges after nine or ten years, you'd end up never talking to anybody! No, no, he believed in being completely open about things! To begin with, he knew who he was dealing with, a good woman and a good man, two good friends in fact! He knew he had nothing to be worried about, he knew they could be trusted.

'Of course, of course...,' Gervaise kept repeating, looking down and hardly knowing what she was saying.

'She's like a sister now, just a sister,' murmured Lantier.

'Then shake 'ands, for Christ's sake,' cried Coupeau, 'and let those bloody bourgeois think what they like! When you can think like that, you're better off than a millionaire. For me, friendship is the main thing, 'cos friendship is friendship, there's nothing more important.'

He kept pounding his chest so violently, and seemed so worked up, that they had to calm him down. All three clinked glasses and drank in silence. Now Gervaise could take a proper look at Lantier, for on the night of the party she'd seen him through a haze. He'd put on weight and looked quite chubby; because of his shortness his arms and legs seemed too big. But his features, though puffed out a little because of his life of idleness, were still quite fine; and as he tended his pencil moustache very carefully, he wouldn't have been taken to be older than he was, thirty-five. That evening he was wearing grey trousers and a dark blue coat, and looked quite the gentleman, complete with a round hat; he even had a watch and a silver chain from which a ring was hanging, a keepsake no doubt.

'I'm off,' he said. 'I live miles away.'

He was already outside on the pavement when the roofer called him back and made him promise he'd never come their way without dropping in to say hello. Meanwhile Gervaise, who'd quietly disappeared, came back pushing Étienne in front of her. He was in his nightshirt, already half asleep. He smiled and rubbed his eyes; but when he saw Lantier he became embarrassed and started trembling, darting anxious glances at his mother and Coupeau.

'Don't you recognize this gentleman?' asked Coupeau.

The boy looked down and didn't answer. Then he gave a little nod to show he did.

'Well, then, don't be silly, go and give 'im a kiss.'

Lantier stood waiting, looking calm and serious. When Étienne finally went up to him, he bent down and offered both cheeks, then gave the boy a big kiss on the forehead. At this, the lad plucked up enough courage to look at his father, but suddenly burst into tears and ran off in a panic, his nightshirt flapping, while Coupeau scolded him for being rude.

'He's upset,' said Gervaise, looking pale and upset herself.

'He's usually very nice and polite,' Coupeau said. 'I've brought 'im up all right, you'll see. He'll get used to you. He needs to get to know people. And anyway, if only for 'is sake, we couldn't 'ave stayed enemies forever, could we? For 'is sake we should 'ave made it up ages ago, 'cos, you know, I'd rather put me 'ead on the block than keep a father from seein' 'is own kid.'

Thereupon he suggested they finish off the bottle. The three of them clinked glasses again. Lantier showed no surprise, but took it all in his stride. Before leaving, to show his appreciation to Coupeau, he insisted on helping him to shut up the shop. Then, brushing the dust off his hands, he wished the couple goodnight.

'Sleep well. I'm going to try and catch the omnibus. I'll see you soon. That's a promise.'

From that evening on, Lantier often turned up in the Rue de la Goutte-d'Or. He always came when the roofer was there, asking after him as soon as he crossed the threshold, pretending to have come entirely on his account. Then, sitting with his back to the window, always spruce, freshly shaved, and in his frock coat, he'd chat politely and be quite the well-educated gentleman. In this way the Coupeaus gradually got to know what he'd been doing during the past eight years. At one point he'd managed a hat factory, and when they asked him why he'd given it up, he just mumbled something about a crooked partner, a southerner like himself, a complete wastrel who'd squandered all the firm's money on women. But his former status as a manager was stamped on his personality, like a title of nobility that would remain his forever. He was always saying he was about to pull off a splendid business deal: various hatmakers were going to set him up and entrust him with great responsibilities. In the meantime, he did absolutely nothing, but just strolled about in the sun with his hands in his pockets, like a man of leisure. On the occasions when he complained about his lot, and someone ventured to mention a factory that was taking people on, he'd smile pityingly and declare he had no intention of starving to death while working his guts out for other people. And yet, as Coupeau said, the bloke couldn't just be living on fresh air. Yes, he was a smart one all right, he knew how to look after himself, he must be in on some sort of racket, because he looked pretty well off, and clean shirts and fancy neckties have to be paid for. One morning Coupeau had seen him having his boots shined on the Boulevard Montmartre. The truth of the matter was that Lantier was a great talker when it came to other people, but said nothing or lied about himself. He wouldn't even say where he lived. No, he was staying with a friend somewhere, miles away, just until he got a great position; and he said there was no point in anybody coming to look for him because he was never there.

'For every ten jobs you see going, there's only one good one,' he often said. 'There's no sense in starting somewhere if you're not going to stay more than twenty-four hours. For instance, one Monday I began at Champion's in Montrouge.* That evening, I got into an argument with Champion about politics, we didn't see eye to eye at all. So, on the Tuesday morning, I just left. After all, we're not living in the days of slavery and I've got no intention of selling myself for seven francs a day.'

It was early November. As a gallant gesture, Lantier brought bunches of violets for Gervaise and her two assistants. Gradually his visits became more frequent, until he was coming nearly every day. It seemed as if he was out to charm the household and the entire neighbourhood; and he began by making up to Clémence and Madame Putois, paying them both the most assiduous attentions, regardless of the difference in their ages. After a month of this treatment the two women adored him. The Boches, greatly flattered because he'd called on them at their lodge to pay his respects, went into raptures over his good manners. As for the Lorilleux, when they learned who this gentleman was who had turned up during dessert at the party, they poured endless abuse on Gervaise for having the gall to bring her old fancy man into her home. But one day Lantier went up to see them and made such a good impression by ordering a chain for a lady of his acquaintance that they asked him to sit down and kept him for an hour, quite taken with his conversation, and even wondering how such a distinguished gentleman could ever have lived with Gimpy. In the end, the hatter had succeeded so well in ingratiating himself with everyone in the Rue de la Goutte-d'Or that his visits to the Coupeaus no longer bothered anyone and seemed quite natural. Goujet was the only one who kept out of his way. If he happened to be there when Lantier arrived, he would take himself off so as not to have to make the fellow's acquaintance.

Meanwhile, during the first weeks of Lantier's rampant popularity, Gervaise felt deeply troubled. She had the same burning sensation in the pit of the stomach she'd felt on the day of Virginie's revelations. What she feared most was that she'd be helpless to resist him if he found her alone one evening and tried to kiss her. She thought about him too much, was too wrapped up in him altogether. Gradually, however, she began to relax when she saw how respectful he was, never looking her in the face, never so much as touching her with a fingertip when the others had their backs turned. And then Virginie, who seemed able to read her mind, made her feel ashamed of her nasty thoughts. What was she so afraid of? You couldn't meet a nicer man. Of course there was nothing for her to be afraid of now. And one day she managed to get them together in a corner and to steer the conversation towards the question of their feelings. Lantier, choosing his words carefully, gravely declared that his heart was dead and that all he wanted now was to devote himself to the welfare of his son. He never mentioned Claude, who was still in the Midi. Every evening he'd kiss Étienne on the forehead, but he didn't know what to say to the boy if he stayed in the room; he'd forget all about him and start flirting with Clémence. So Gervaise, her mind at rest, thought the past was all over with. Lantier's actual presence made her memories of Plassans and the Hôtel Boncœur fade. Now that she saw him all the time, she stopped dreaming about him. She even felt a certain disgust at the thought of their former relationship. Yes, it was over now, quite finished! If he ever dared to come after her again, she'd slap his face or, better still, tell her husband. And once again, without the slightest qualm, but with great tenderness, her thoughts turned to her friendship with Goujet.

One morning when she arrived at work, Clémence reported that the previous evening, at about eleven, she'd run into Monsieur Lantier with a woman on his arm. She described the incident in very crude language, and not without a certain malice, curious to see how her boss would react. Yes, Monsieur Lantier was going up the Rue Notre-Dame-de-Lorette;* the woman was blonde, one of those worn-out boulevard tarts with nothing on under their silk skirts. Just for a lark she'd followed them. The tart had gone into a charcuterie to buy some ham and shrimps. Then, in the Rue de la Rochefoucauld,* Monsieur Lantier had hung about on the pavement in front of one of the houses, looking up at the windows, until the tart, who'd gone in alone, gave him the all-clear to join her. Despite Clémence's dirty innuendoes, Gervaise calmly went on ironing a white dress. From time to time the story brought a faint smile to her lips. Those southerners, she said, were all mad about women, they couldn't do without them, even if it meant scooping them up from a dung heap with a shovel. And that evening when Lantier turned up she was amused when Clémence teased him about his blonde. Actually he seemed quite flattered to have been noticed. The woman was an old friend he still saw from time to time, when it didn't put anybody out; she had lots of style, with an apartment done up in rosewood; and he mentioned some of her former lovers: a viscount, a rich dealer in china, and a notary's son. Personally, he liked women who used perfume, and he was just holding up to Clémence's nose a handkerchief his friend had scented for him when Étienne came in. At this, he went all serious and kissed the boy, adding that all that nonsense meant nothing to him and that his heart was dead. Gervaise, bending over her work, nodded in approval. And in the end, once more, Clémence got what she deserved for being so mean, because she'd felt Lantier pinch her bottom a few times on the sly and she was dying of jealousy because she didn't stink of musk like that boulevard tart.

When spring came round again, Lantier, now virtually one of the family, was talking about coming to live in the neighbourhood to be closer to his friends. He wanted a furnished room in a nice, respectable building. Madame Boche and Gervaise herself did their best to find one for him. They scoured all the nearby streets. But he was too fussy, he wanted a large courtyard, a ground-floor room, in fact every imaginable convenience. And every evening now at the Coupeaus' he seemed to be calculating the height of the ceilings and studying the layout of the rooms, as if longing for a place just like theirs. Oh, it would be perfect for him! He'd easily find a little spot for himself in a quiet, cosy corner. And each time he'd conclude his inspection with the words:

'My word, yes! You've got a really nice set-up here!'

One evening when he'd had dinner with them and made his usual pronouncement over dessert, Coupeau, who now addressed him with the familiar *tu*, suddenly cried:

'You must stay here, me old pal, if that's what you'd really like. We'd manage...'

And he explained that the room for the dirty clothes, properly cleaned up, would be lovely. Étienne could sleep in the shop. They'd put a mattress on the floor, that was all.

'No, no,' said Lantier, 'I can't have that. It'd put you out too much. It's very good of you, but I think we'd be too much on top of each other... And in any case, we all want a bit of privacy, don't we? I'd have to go through your bedroom, and that wouldn't always be such fun.'

'Listen to the silly sod!' the roofer replied, choking with laughter and banging on the table to get his voice back, 'He's always going on about that sort of thing!... You brainless bugger, where's your imagination? That room's got two windows, right? Well, one of 'em can be knocked down to the ground an' turned into a door. Then, y'see, you could come in through the yard. We can even block up the connecting door if we want. We could lead our own lives: you'd 'ave your place and we'd 'ave ours.'

There was a silence. The hatter murmured:

'Well, if it was like that, maybe... But no, I'd still get in your way.'

He was careful not to look at Gervaise, but he was obviously waiting for a word from her before accepting. She was quite taken aback by her husband's idea; not that the thought of Lantier living with them upset or worried her particularly, but she couldn't think where she'd put the dirty washing. Meanwhile, the roofer was pointing out the advantages of the arrangement. Their rent, five hundred francs, had always been a bit steep. Well, their mate could give them twenty francs a month for a furnished room; it wouldn't be too much for him, and it would help them on rent day. He added that he'd fix up a box under their bed big enough to hold the dirty washing of the whole neighbourhood. Gervaise still hesitated, and looked at Maman Coupeau as if to make out what she thought; but Lantier had won her over months ago by bringing her lozenges for her catarrh.

'I'm sure you wouldn't be in our way,' she said at last. 'We could work things out...'

'Thanks, but I don't think so,' said the hatter. 'You're too kind, I'd be taking advantage.'

At this Coupeau flew off the handle. How much longer was he going to mess about? They'd said they'd like him to come! He'd be doing them a favour, couldn't he see that? Then he yelled:

'Étienne! Étienne!'

The boy had fallen asleep with his head on the table. He woke up with a start.

'Listen, tell 'im it's what you want... Yes, this man 'ere... Say out loud: "That's what I want!"'

They all began to laugh. But Lantier quickly put on his serious, concerned look. He shook Coupeau's hand across the table and said:

'I accept... In the name of friendship. And for the kid's sake.'

The very next day, when Monsieur Marescot, the landlord, was chatting with the Boches in their lodge, Gervaise spoke to him about their plan. At first he seemed not to like it at all, refusing and getting angry, as if she'd asked him to pull down a whole wing of his building. After a while, however, following a minute inspection of the premises and a look at the upper floors to see whether they'd be affected, he gave them his permission on condition that he would bear none of the expense; and the Coupeaus had to sign a piece of paper, by which they undertook to restore everything to its previous state at the end of their lease. That same evening the roofer brought home some mates of his, a bricklayer, a carpenter, and a painter, good blokes who'd take care of the little job after hours, just to do him a favour. Even so, the fitting of the new door and the cleaning of the room still cost a good hundred francs, not counting several bottles of wine to help the job along. Coupeau said he'd pay them later, with his lodger's first lot of rent. But then there was the furniture. Gervaise left Maman Coupeau's cupboard there and added a table and two chairs from her own room, but she had to buy a washstand and a bed, together with all the bedding, a hundred and thirty francs in all, which she'd have to pay off at ten francs a month. But even though, for the first ten months, Lantier's twenty francs would be swallowed up by the debts, there'd be a nice profit later on.

It was early June when Lantier moved in. Coupeau had offered to go round to pick up his trunk, to save him the thirty sous for the cab. But the hatter seemed embarrassed, saying his trunk was too heavy, as if he wanted to keep the whereabouts of his place a secret right to the last. He arrived in the afternoon at about three o'clock. Coupeau wasn't there. Gervaise, standing at the shop door, turned very pale when she saw the trunk on the cab. It was their old trunk, the one she'd done the journey from Plassans with; but now it was scratched and broken, and held together with rope. She saw it coming back to her as she had often dreamed it would, and she could imagine it was being brought back in the very same cab in which that bitch Adèle had run off with him. Meanwhile Boche was giving Lantier a hand. She followed them in, silent and feeling slightly dazed. When they'd put the trunk down in the middle of the room, she remarked, just for something to say:

'Well, that's a job well done.'

Then, seeing that Lantier was undoing the ropes and not even looking at her, she pulled herself together and added:

'Monsieur Boche, you'll have a drink, won't you?'

She went off to fetch a bottle and some glasses. Just at that moment Poisson, in uniform, was walking past. She gave him a little wave, with a wink and a smile. The policeman understood perfectly. When he was on duty and somebody winked at him, that meant he was being offered a glass of wine. In fact he'd even walk up and down for hours in front of the laundry waiting for Gervaise to give him a wink. Then, so as not to be seen, he'd go in through the yard and have a drink in private.

'Aha!' said Lantier, seeing him come in, 'it's you, Badingue!'*

He called him Badingue as a joke, to make fun of the Emperor. Poisson reacted in his usual stiff way, and you couldn't tell whether it offended him or not. In any case, though they had different political views, the two men had become good friends.

'You know the Emperor was a policeman in London,* don't you?' said Boche. 'It's true! He used to round up drunken women.'

Gervaise had filled the glasses on the table. She didn't want to drink, she felt too churned up. But she stood watching Lantier take off the last pieces of rope, dying to know what was in the trunk. She could remember, in one corner, a pile of socks, two dirty shirts, and an old hat. Were they still there? Was she going to see those relics of the past again? Before lifting the lid of the trunk Lantier picked up his glass and clinked it with the others.

'Your health!'

'And yours!' replied Boche and Poisson.

The laundress refilled the glasses. The three men wiped their lips with their hands. Then, at last, Lantier opened the trunk. It was chock-a-block with a jumble of newspapers, books, old clothes, and bundles of dirty washing. One after the other he took out a saucepan, a pair of boots, a bust of Ledru Rollin* with its nose broken, an embroidered shirt, and a pair of work trousers. As she leaned over, Gervaise caught a smell of tobacco, the smell of a slovenly man who only bothers about the top layer, the part of himself people can see.

No, the old hat wasn't in the corner on the left any more. Instead there was a pincushion she'd never seen before, a present from some woman. She began to calm down, but she felt vaguely sad as she continued to gaze at the objects as they emerged and wondered if they dated from her time or from the time of others.

'Hey, Badingue, have you seen this?' Lantier asked.

He thrust under the policeman's nose a little book printed in Brussels:* *Les Amours de Napoléon III*,* illustrated with engravings. Among other things, it contained the story of how the Emperor had seduced the thirteen-year-old daughter of a cook; and there was a picture of him, bare-legged and wearing nothing but the sash of the Legion of Honour, chasing a young girl who was fleeing from his lechery.

'Splendid!' exclaimed Boche, his furtive sensuality aroused. 'That's the way!'

Poisson was speechless; he couldn't think of anything to say in defence of the Emperor. It was printed in a book, so how could he deny it? But as Lantier kept waving the book under his nose and laughing, he threw his arms wide and cried:

'Well, so what? It's human nature, isn't it?'

This shut Lantier up. He arranged his books and newspapers on a shelf in the cupboard; and as he seemed quite disappointed at not having a little bookshelf hanging on the wall above the table, Gervaise promised to get him one. He had Louis Blanc's *Histoire de dix ans*,* minus the first volume, which he'd never had; Lamartine's *Girondins*,* in two-sou instalments; and Eugène Sue's *Les Mystères de Paris* and *Le Juif errant*,* not to mention a stack of philosophical and humanitarian works he'd picked up in junk shops. But it was his newspapers that he cherished and valued most. He'd been collecting them for years. Every time he read an article in a café that expressed his own views and seemed well written, he bought the paper and kept it. In this way he'd built up a huge collection of newspapers, of different dates and types, stacked together in no particular order. When he took this bundle out of the bottom of the trunk, he gave it a few friendly pats, and said to the two other men:

'See this? It's mine and nobody else can claim to have anything like it. You can't imagine what's in there. I mean, if you put half these ideas into practice, society would be sorted out overnight. Yes, that Emperor of yours and all 'is narks would be bloody well done for...'

But he was cut short by the policeman, whose red moustache and beard seemed to be bristling fiercely in his pale face.

'And the army? What'd you do with the army?'

At this Lantier got completely carried away. He thumped his newspapers furiously, and shouted:

'I want to do away with the military, I want the brotherhood of nations... I want equal wages for all, profit-sharing, and the glorification of the proletariat... Every type of freedom! Every last one! And divorce!'*

'Yes, yes, divorce, for the sake of morality!' Boche chimed in.

Poisson, assuming a majestic air, declared:

'But even though I don't want any of your freedoms, I'm still free!'

'If you don't want them, if you don't want them...', stuttered Lantier, choking with rage. 'No, you're not free! And if you don't want to be free, I'll stick you in Cayenne!* Yes, that's what I'll do! Along with your Emperor and his whole fuckin' gang!'

They had a set-to like this every time they met. Gervaise disliked arguments, and would usually intervene. Rousing herself from the stupor she'd fallen into on seeing the trunk, which carried such bitter-sweet memories, she pointed to the glasses of wine.

'Yes, of course,' said Lantier, taking his glass, suddenly calm again. 'Cheers.'

'Cheers,' responded Boche and Poisson, clinking glasses with him.

Boche, however, was shifting uneasily from one foot to the other, clearly worried about something. Squinting at the policeman, he said quietly:

'This is just between us, isn't it, Monsieur Poisson? We show you things and say things...'

But Poisson didn't let him finish. He put his hand on his heart, as if to indicate that was where it would all stay. Of course, he would never inform on his friends. As Coupeau had now turned up, they drank a second bottle. The policeman then took off through the yard and resumed his beat, walking with steady, stern, solemn tread.

To start with, after Lantier's arrival, everything at the laundry was topsy-turvy. Lantier did indeed have his own room, his own entrance, and his own key, but at the last minute it had been decided not to block up the connecting door, so more often than not he came and went through the shop. The dirty washing was also a big problem for Gervaise, for her husband had done nothing about the box he'd mentioned, and she was forced to stuff the clothes just anywhere, but mostly under her bed, which wasn't very pleasant on summer nights. And it was a terrible nuisance for her to have to make up Étienne's bed every evening in the middle of the shop; when her assistants worked late, the boy would fall asleep on a chair, waiting for them to finish. So when Goujet talked to her about sending Étienne to Lille, where his old boss, an engineer, was looking for apprentices, she was quite taken with the idea, especially as the boy, who wasn't happy at home and wanted to be his own master, begged her to agree. But she was afraid Lantier would flatly refuse. He'd come to live with them solely to be near his son, and he wouldn't want to lose him two weeks after moving in. However, when she broached the matter with him, very fearfully, he warmly approved, saying that young workers need to see a bit of the world. The morning Étienne left, Lantier gave him a little speech about his rights, then embraced him and declared:

'Never forget: a worker who produces is not a slave, but anyone who produces nothing is a parasite.'

After that the household resumed a life of routine, and things calmed down as they settled into new habits. Gervaise had got used to having the dirty washing all over the place, and to Lantier's comings and goings. He still talked about important business deals; sometimes he'd go out wearing a clean shirt and with his hair carefully combed, and would disappear, sometimes staying out all night, pretending on his return that he was worn out, with a splitting headache, as if he'd just spent twenty-four hours discussing matters of the gravest importance. In reality he'd just been taking things easy. There was no danger of him getting calluses on his hands! He usually got up around ten and would take a stroll in the afternoon if he liked the look of the weather; or if it was raining he'd stay in the laundry reading his newspaper. It was the perfect place for him; he loved being surrounded by skirts, worming his way in among the women, revelling in their vulgar talk, egging them on while taking care that his own language remained perfectly decent. This explained why he so enjoyed the company of laundresses, who are not a prudish race. When Clémence treated him to her full repertoire he'd sit there smiling sweetly, playing with the ends of his little moustache. The smells, the sweating bare-armed girls banging their irons down, the whole shop like a bedroom littered with the underwear of all the women in the neighbourhood, seemed to him like the place of his dreams, a long sought-after haven of idleness and pleasure.

In the early days Lantier took his meals at François's, on the corner of the Rue des Poissonniers. But of the seven days in the week he'd have dinner with the Coupeaus three or four times, so that in the end he suggested he should become a proper boarder: he'd give them fifteen francs every Saturday. After that he never left the house, but settled in once and for all. From morning to night he could be seen going from the shop to the room at the back, in his shirtsleeves, shouting orders; he even dealt with the customers, in fact he seemed to be running the place. He got tired of François's wine, and persuaded Gervaise to buy her wine from Vigouroux, the coal merchant next door, and would go and pinch Madame Vigouroux's bottom when he and Boche went round to put in their orders. Then he decided that Coudeloup's bread wasn't baked properly, and started sending Augustine to buy bread at Meyer's, the Viennese bakery in the Faubourg Poissonnière. He also changed the grocer, Lehongre, and only stuck with big Charlie, the butcher in the Rue Polonceau, because of his political views. After a month, he wanted all the cooking done in oil. As Clémence said jokingly, it was impossible to get rid of the oil stains on that bloody Provençal! He'd make the omelettes himself, cooking them on both sides so they were browner than pancakes and as hard as *galettes*.* He kept a close eye on Maman Coupeau, insisting that the steaks be very well done, like shoe leather; he added garlic to everything and got angry if they sprinkled herbs on the salad—they were weeds, he shouted, and there might easily be poison in them. But his great delight was a special soup, vermicelli cooked to a thick consistency, into which he'd empty half a bottle of oil. Only he and Gervaise could eat it, because the others, the Parisians, had been as sick as dogs one day when they'd been bold enough to try it.

Little by little Lantier became involved in the family's affairs. As the Lorilleux always made a fuss about coughing up Maman Coupeau's five francs, he pointed out that they could be taken to court. Who did they think they were! They ought to be giving the old lady ten francs, not five! And he went up to collect the money himself, so determined and yet so suave that Madame Lorilleux didn't dare refuse. Madame Lerat gave ten francs now as well. Maman Coupeau could have kissed Lantier's hand, especially as he now acted as judge and jury in the quarrels between her and Gervaise. When the laundress lost patience with her mother-in-law, and spoke to her roughly, making the old lady take to her bed in tears, he gave them both a lecture, and insisted they kiss and make up, asking if they thought their silly squabbles were nice for other people. It was the same with Nana: in his opinion they were bringing her up very badly. He wasn't wrong on that score, because when her father started walloping her her mother took her side, and when her mother smacked her her father hit the roof. Nana, delighted to see her parents at each other's throats, felt she was forgiven in advance and got away with murder. Her latest craze was to go and play in the blacksmith's yard across the street; she'd spend all day there, swinging on the shafts of the carts, or hiding with a gang of kids at the far end of the dingy yard, lit only by the red glow of the forge; suddenly she'd come racing out, shouting, her hair flying and her face all dirty, followed by a trail of brats, as if a volley of hammering had put the little buggers to flight. Lantier was the only one who could give her a telling-off, but even so she knew very well how to get round him. That little bitch of ten would mince about in front of him like a lady, swinging her hips and fluttering her eyes, eyes that were already full of vice. In the end he'd taken over her education; he was teaching her how to dance and to speak in his Provençal dialect.

A year went by in this way. In the neighbourhood it was thought that Lantier must have independent means, since this was the only possible explanation for the Coupeaus' extravagant lifestyle. Of course Gervaise was still earning, but now that she was keeping two men who were not working, the laundry alone was certainly not bringing in enough, especially as it wasn't doing so well; customers were leaving and the assistants just fooled about all day. The truth was that Lantier wasn't paying anything at all, neither rent nor keep. For the first month or two he'd paid something on account, but after that all he did was talk about a big sum of money coming his way, which would allow him to pay everything off in one go, later on. Gervaise no longer dared ask him even for a centime. She bought the bread, the wine, and the meat on tick. Bills were mounting up on all sides, at the rate of three or four francs a day. She hadn't paid a sou to the furniture dealer, or to Coupeau's three mates, the bricklayer, the carpenter, and the painter. They were all starting to complain and people were less polite to her in the shops. But she seemed almost intoxicated by this plunge into debt; she got carried away, choosing the most expensive things and giving way to her love of food now that she no longer paid for anything. At heart, however, she remained thoroughly honest, dreaming of making hundreds of francs in a day, just how she couldn't say, so she'd be able to dole out fistfuls of money to her creditors. In a word, she was getting deeper and deeper into trouble, and the further she sank the more she talked about expanding her business. However, around midsummer, Clémence left, because there wasn't enough work for two assistants and she'd been waiting for weeks to get paid. And in the midst of this gradual collapse, Coupeau and Lantier were having a grand old time stuffing themselves. These two boon companions, wallowing in food and drink, were gobbling up the laundry, growing fat on what was left of the business; they egged each other on to take double helpings and giggled as they slapped their bellies over dessert, to make the food go down faster.

The great topic of conversation among the neighbours was whether Lantier was back with Gervaise. Opinions were divided. According to the Lorilleux, Gimpy was doing everything she could think of to get the hatter back, but he wasn't having any of it, finding her too moth-eaten; he had much prettier girls in town. The Boches, on the other hand, were sure that the laundress had gone back to her former lover on the very first night, as soon as that ninny Coupeau had started snoring. Either way, it all seemed quite unsavoury; but there are so many disgusting things in life, and much worse ones, that in the end people thought the *ménage à trois* quite natural, even rather nice, because there were no fights and a front of decency was maintained. You could be sure that if you stuck your nose into some other homes in the neighbourhood, you'd smell things that were much worse. At least, at the Coupeaus', it was all very friendly. The three of them ploughed their own little furrow, got sozzled together and hopped into bed together, all nice and cosy-like, without ever keeping the neighbours awake. In any case, everyone was won over by Lantier's good manners. All the gossips were charmed into silence. And when, in the uncertainty about whether there was anything going on between Lantier and Gervaise, the greengrocer said in front of the tripe-shop woman that they weren't lovers, the tripe-shop woman seemed to think it was a real pity because it made the Coupeaus less interesting.

Meanwhile, Gervaise was quite untroubled on this score, never giving a thought to such disgusting ideas. In fact it came to the point where she was accused of being cold-hearted. The family couldn't understand why she bore a grudge against Lantier. Madame Lerat, who never tired of meddling in people's love affairs, now dropped in every evening. Lantier, she declared, was irresistible; even the grandest ladies were bound to fall into his arms. As for Madame Boche, if she'd been ten years younger, she wouldn't have answered for her virtue. A covert conspiracy was growing ever stronger, slowly pushing Gervaise towards him, as if all the women around her had to satisfy their own need by giving her a lover. But Gervaise couldn't understand it; she didn't see what was so attractive about Lantier. He'd certainly changed for the better: nowadays he always wore a frock coat, and he'd picked up a certain education in cafés and political meetings. But she, who knew him so well, could look into his eyes and see right into his soul, and there she saw so much that made her shudder. In any case, if others found him so appealing, why didn't they sample the gentleman for themselves? One day she hinted as much to Virginie, who was the most enthusiastic. Then, to get Gervaise worked up, Madame Lerat and Virginie told her what Lantier had been getting up to with Clémence. No, of course she hadn't noticed a thing, but as soon as she went out on an errand, the hatter would take the girl into his room. They were still sometimes seen together, so he must be going round to her place.

'So what?' Gervaise said, her voice trembling slightly. 'What's that got to do with me?'

And she looked into Virginie's tawny eyes, with their glints of gold, like the eyes of a cat. Was this woman her enemy, and trying to make her jealous? But the seamstress put on an air of dumb innocence and said:

'It's got nothing to do with you, of course... But you should tell him to leave that girl alone, because she'll only cause him trouble.'

The worst of it was that Lantier took encouragement from all this and began to change the way he behaved towards Gervaise. Now, when they shook hands, he held hers in his for a few moments. She was worn down by his stares, by the brazen way he looked at her, in which she could clearly read what he was after. If he passed behind her he'd thrust his knees into her skirt and blow on her neck as if to lull her to sleep. But he still stopped short of any bald declaration. One evening, however, finding himself alone with her, without saying a word he pushed her in front of him up to the wall at the back of the shop, where she stood trembling as he tried to kiss her. By chance, Goujet came in at that very moment. She struggled free and moved away from Lantier. The three of them exchanged a few words as if nothing had happened. Goujet had gone very pale and lowered his eyes, imagining he'd disturbed them and that she'd struggled so as to avoid being kissed in public.

The next day Gervaise was wandering around the laundry, very distressed, unable even to iron a handkerchief. She was desperate to see Goujet and explain how Lantier had forced her up against the wall. But ever since Étienne had gone to Lille, she no longer dared go into the forge, where Bec-Salé would greet her with his ironic snigger. In the afternoon, however, she gave in to her urge and picked up an empty basket, saying she was going to collect some petticoats from her customer in the Rue des Portes-Blanches. Then, when she got to the Rue Marcadet, she walked slowly up and down in front of the bolt factory, hoping she'd be in luck. For his part, Goujet must have been expecting her, for she hadn't been there five minutes before he came out, as if by chance.

'Ah, you've been on an errand,' he said, with a faint smile. 'Are you on the way home?'

He just wanted something to say. In fact, Gervaise was standing with her back to the Rue des Poissonniers. They walked on together towards Montmartre, side by side but without linking arms. They both wanted to get away from the factory, so it wouldn't seem they'd arranged to meet there, in front of the entrance. Heads down, they followed the uneven roadway, amid the rumble of the factories. Then, about two hundred yards further on, quite mechanically, as if they both knew exactly where they were going, they turned to the left, still without saying a word, and came to a piece of waste ground. Situated between a sawmill and a button factory, this last remaining strip of green had yellow patches where the grass was scorched; a goat, tethered to a stake, was going round in circles, bleating, while at the far end a dead tree was rotting away in the sun.

'You know,' murmured Gervaise, 'you'd think we were in the country.'

They went over and sat under the dead tree. The laundress put her basket by her feet. Opposite, the Butte Montmartre rose up in stacks of tall yellow and grey houses interspersed with clumps of sparse greenery; and when they tilted their heads back, they could see the great expanse of sky above the city, its blazing purity broken only to the north by a trail of little white clouds. But the light dazzled them, and they lowered their gaze to the flat horizon, where the outskirts of the city formed a chalky backdrop; their eyes were drawn in particular to the jets of steam coming from the slender chimney of the sawmill, breathing them out in deep sighs which seemed to relieve their heavy hearts.

'Yes,' Gervaise went on, embarrassed by the silence, 'I was on an errand, I came out...'

After desperately wanting to explain, she suddenly found herself unable to say anything. She was overcome by a great feeling of shame. And yet she was well aware that they had come to this place of their own accord, to talk about that one thing; and they actually were talking about it, without having to say a word. What had happened the evening before was there between them like a great, heavy weight.

Then, with a terrible feeling of sadness, her eyes full of tears, she described the last moments of Madame Bijard, her washerwoman, who'd died that morning after much suffering.

'It was because of a kick Bijard gave her,' she said in a soft, expressionless voice. 'Her stomach swelled up. He must have damaged something inside her. My God! She was in agony for three days. There are bastards who've been sent to the galleys for less than what he did. But the law would 'ave too much to do if it bothered about all the women done in by their 'usbands. One more kick's neither 'ere nor there, is it, when you get kicked every day. And what's more, to save 'er 'usband from the scaffold, the poor woman said she'd 'urt her stomach by fallin' on a tub… She screamed all through the night, before she went.'

The blacksmith said nothing, clenching his fists and nervously pulling up clumps of grass.

'It's less than a fortnight', she went on, 'since she weaned her youngest, little Jules; that's one good thing, at least the baby won't suffer… But it leaves that little kid Lalie with two babies to look after. She's not even eight, but she's as steady and responsible as a proper mother. And her father's always knocking her about… Some people are just born to suffer.'

Goujet looked at her and said all of a sudden, his lips trembling:

'You really hurt me yesterday. I can't tell you how much.'

Gervaise turned pale and clasped her hands as he went on:

'I know it was bound to happen. But you should have talked to me and told me what was going on, so I wouldn't be left wondering…'

He couldn't finish what he was saying. She stood up, realizing that Goujet thought she and Lantier were back together, as all the neighbours said. Stretching out her arms, she cried:

'No, no, I swear… He was pushing me, he was going to kiss me, it's true, but his face didn't even touch mine, and it's the first time he's tried… I swear, on my life, on my children's, on everything I hold sacred!'

But he shook his head. He didn't believe her, because women always deny things like that. Then Gervaise became very serious and said slowly:

'You know me, Monsieur Goujet, and you know I'm not a liar. Well, I'm telling you: it's not like that, on my word of honour, and it never will be. Never! If that day ever came, I'd be the lowest of the low, I'd never deserve the friendship of a decent man like you.'

As she spoke, her face was so beautiful in its openness and honesty that he took her hand and made her sit down again. He was breathing freely once more, feeling a surge of happiness within him. It was the first time he'd held her hand like this, squeezing it in his. They were both silent. Above them, the flight of white clouds was gliding slowly across the sky, like swans. In the corner of the field, the goat had turned towards them and was watching them, bleating softly at long, regular intervals. And without letting go of each other's hands, their eyes filled with tenderness, they gazed into the distance, at the grey slope of Montmartre amid the tall forest of factory chimneys on the horizon, in these mean and desolate outskirts of the city where the clumps of greenery round the dingy taverns brought tears to their eyes.

'Your mother's not happy with me, I know,' Gervaise went on quietly. 'Don't say it's not true... We owe you so much money!'

But, to make her be quiet, he became quite rough, shaking her hand until it hurt. He didn't want her to talk about the money. Then, after a pause, he said hesitantly:

'Listen, I've been thinking for a long time about suggesting something... You're not happy. My mother's sure things aren't working out for you...'

He stopped, unable to get the words out.

'Well, we should go away together.'

She stared at him, not quite understanding at first, taken aback by this sudden declaration of a love about which he'd never spoken a word before.

'How do you mean?' she asked.

'Yes,' he went on, looking down, 'we could go away and live somewhere, in Belgium if you like... It's pretty well my country... If we both worked, we'd soon be all right.'

She blushed scarlet. If he'd taken her in his arms and kissed her, she'd have felt less embarrassed. What a funny man he was, to propose eloping, like the sort of thing that happens in novels and high society.

Well, all around her she saw working men chasing after married women, but they didn't even take them to Saint-Denis—they got on with it on the spot, no messing.

'Oh, Monsieur Goujet, Monsieur Goujet...', she murmured, and could think of nothing else to say.

'So, you see, there'd just be the two of us,' he continued. 'Other people bother me, you know. When I care for somebody, I don't want to see them with anybody else.'

By now, however, she'd pulled herself together and was saying no, sounding very sensible:

'It's not possible, Monsieur Goujet. It would be very wrong... I'm married, aren't I? I've got children... I know you're fond of me and I'm hurting you, but we'd both feel guilty, we wouldn't be happy... I'm fond of you, too—too fond to let you do something silly. And it would be silly, it really would... No, it's better to stay as we are. We respect each other, and we feel the same way. That's important, and it has helped me many a time. With people like us, if you do the right thing, it pays off in the end.'

He nodded as he listened. He agreed with her, he couldn't say otherwise. Suddenly, there in broad daylight, he took her in his arms, held her very tight, and gave her a burning kiss on the neck, as if he wanted to eat her. Then he let her go, not asking anything further and saying not another word about their love. She shook herself, not at all angry, feeling they both deserved that little bit of pleasure.

Goujet, meanwhile, trembling violently from head to foot, moved away from her to avoid the temptation of taking her in his arms again; he went down on his knees and, not knowing what to do with his hands, began picking dandelions which he threw from where he was into her basket. Some magnificent golden dandelions were growing there, in the middle of the scorched grass. This little game distracted him and, gradually, calmed him down. With fingers stiffened by constant use of the hammer he gently broke off the flowers and tossed them one by one; his good-natured eyes, the eyes of a faithful dog, shone with pleasure each time a flower landed in the basket. Gervaise was leaning with her back against the dead tree, relaxed and cheerful, raising her voice so as to be heard above the sighing noise of the saw-mill. When they left the waste ground, walking side by side and talking about Étienne and how much he liked Lille, her basket was full of dandelions.

Deep down, where Lantier was concerned, Gervaise didn't feel as
sure of herself as she'd said. Certainly, she was determined not to let
him touch her with so much as a fingertip; but she was afraid, if he
did touch her, of her old weakness, of the easy-going, complaisant
attitude she often gave in to, just to please others. However, Lantier
didn't try anything again. He found himself alone with her several
times and did nothing. He now seemed to be interested in the tripe-
shop woman, who was forty-five and very well preserved. Gervaise
talked about the tripe-shop woman in front of Goujet, to reassure
him. And when Virginie and Madame Lerat sang the hatter's praises,
she told them he could manage very well without their admiration,
since all the women in the neighbourhood had a crush on him.

Coupeau, for his part, was going around proclaiming that Lantier
was a true friend, the truest there was. People could gab about them
as much as they liked, he knew what was what, and didn't give a damn
about the gossip, because he had right on his side. When all three of
them went out on Sundays, he made his wife and Lantier walk in
front, arm in arm, just to thumb his nose at the neighbours; and he
glared at everybody, ready to thump anyone who dared even to snigger. It's true he found Lantier a bit stuck up, accusing him of being
a sissy when it came to hard liquor, and pulled his leg because he
could read and talked like a lawyer. But, apart from that, he declared
that he was a bloody good bloke. In fact you couldn't find two better
blokes in the whole of La Chapelle.* In a word, they understood one
another, they were made for each other. Friendship between men is
stronger than love between a man and a woman.

One thing must be said, and that's that Coupeau and Lantier would
go off together on the most almighty binges. Lantier was now borrowing from Gervaise—ten francs here, twenty francs there—whenever
he could sniff any money in the house. It was always for his great
business ventures. On these occasions, he'd lead Coupeau wildly
astray: taking him off on what he said was an errand, but which would
take hours, he'd settle down with him in a nearby restaurant, where
they'd stuff their faces with dishes you can't get at home, washed
down with fine wines. Coupeau would have preferred to carouse in
a less fancy manner, but he was impressed by the hatter's high-class
tastes, and the way he could pick out on the menu sauces with the
most extraordinary names. You couldn't imagine anyone so finicky
and fussy. It seems they're all like that in the south. For example, he

wouldn't touch anything too hot, he interrogated the waiters as to whether there was anything in stews that wasn't good for him, and sent back meat if he thought it had too much salt or pepper. It was even worse with draughts; he was terrified of them, and would make a hell of a fuss if a door was left open. In addition, he was very tight-fisted, leaving just a couple of sous for the waiter after a seven- or eight-franc meal; but in spite of that, he put the fear of God into them all. He and Coupeau were very well known along the outer boulevards from Batignolles to Belleville.* They'd go to a place in the Grande Rue des Batignolles to eat tripe *à la mode de Caen*,* which was served up on little chafing dishes. In Montmartre, at the bottom of the hill, in the Ville de Bar-le-Duc,* they feasted on the finest oysters in that part of the city. When they ventured up the hill to the Moulin de la Galette,* they'd have sautéed rabbit. In the Rue des Martyrs, the Lilas* specialized in *tête de veau*,* while the Lion d'Or* and the Deux Marronniers* on the Chaussée de Clignancourt served fried kidneys that were simply delicious. But most often they turned left, towards Belleville, where a table was kept for them at the Vendanges de Bourgogne,* the Cadran Bleu,* or the Capucin, all reputable places where you could order anything with your eyes shut. These outings all took place on the sly, and they'd talk about them in veiled terms as they nibbled at Gervaise's potatoes. One day Lantier even brought a woman to their table under the trees outside the Moulin de la Galette; Coupeau left him with her when the dessert appeared.

Needless to say, you can't live it up and work at the same time. So, from the moment Lantier moved in, Coupeau, who already did precious little, got to the point where he no longer picked up a tool. When he got tired of just mooning about and did get some work, his mate would track him down, rib him mercilessly for hanging at the end of his knotted rope like a ham being cured, and get him to come down and have a quick one. And that was it: the roofer would walk off his job and go on a binge that would last for days, even weeks. Oh, such wonderful binges: a tour of all the bars in the neighbourhood, the morning's hangover slept off by lunchtime, and the drinking started up again in the evening; round after round of firewater, extending into the night like fairy lights at a party, until the last candle went out with the last glass consumed! But Lantier, the crafty bugger, never stayed to the end. He let Coupeau get lit up, then left him to it and went back home smiling his amiable smile. Though he did get a bit sloshed, he took his drink very well, so that nobody noticed. You could only tell, if you knew him well, by his eyes, which grew smaller, and his behaviour towards women, which grew bolder. The roofer, on the other hand, became quite gross; he couldn't drink now without ending up in a disgusting state.

And so it happened that, early in November, Coupeau went on a binge that ended most unpleasantly both for him and for others. The day before he'd found some work. On this occasion Lantier was full of high-flown sentiments, singing the praises of work, saying that work ennobles man. On the first morning, he actually got up while it was still dark in order, quite seriously, to escort his mate to his work site, to honour him as a labourer truly worthy of the name. But as they arrived at the Petite-Civette, which was just opening, they went in for a brandied plum, one only, intending simply to drink to their firm resolve to change their ways. Across from the counter, sitting on a bench with his back against the wall, was Bibi-la-Grillade, glumly smoking his pipe.

'Hey, look who's takin' it easy!' said Coupeau. 'Don't you feel like workin', you old bugger?'

'No,' replied their mate, stretching. 'It's the fuckin' people you 'ave to work for... I walked out on mine yesterday... They're all bastards, the whole lot of 'em...'

And he accepted a plum. He must have been sitting there on the bench waiting for somebody to buy him a drink. But Lantier stood up for the bosses: they sometimes had a lot to put up with—he knew a thing or two about it, having been in business himself. The workers were pretty bad! Always boozing, not giving a damn about their work, leaving you in the lurch bang in the middle of an order, and only turning up again when the money ran out. For instance, he'd had a little bloke from Picardy with a craze for being driven around in cabs; so, as soon as he got his week's pay, off he'd go in cabs for days on end. Was that the sort of thing a working man should do? Then, suddenly, Lantier started attacking the bosses as well. Oh yes, he could see the whole picture, and he told everybody exactly what he thought. A foul lot they were, exploiting everybody shamelessly, living on other people. He, thank God, could sleep with a clear conscience, for he'd always been a friend to his men, preferring not to make millions out of them as others did.

'Come on, mate, let's get going,' he said to Coupeau. 'We've got to be'ave ourselves, or we'll be late.'

Bibi-la-Grillade came out with them, swinging his arms. Outside, dawn was barely breaking, its dim glow made dimmer still by the reflection of the muddy road; it had rained during the night and the air was very mild. The gaslights had just been turned out; the Rue des Poissonniers, in which patches of darkness still lingered, trapped between the buildings, was filling with the muffled tramp of workmen going down into Paris.

Coupeau, his roofer's bag slung over his shoulder, marched on with the cocky air of a man who for once in his life meant business. He turned round and asked:

'Bibi, d'you want a job? The boss said I was to bring a mate if I could.'

'No way,' said Bibi-la-Grillade. 'You'd better ask Mes-Bottes, he was lookin' around for something yesterday. Hang on, he's bound to be in there.'

And sure enough, as they reached the end of the street they saw Mes-Bottes in Père Colombe's bar. Despite the early hour, the Assommoir was all lit up, with the shutters raised and the gaslights on. Lantier waited at the door, telling Coupeau to be as quick as he could because they only had ten minutes.

'What! You're goin' to work for that Bourguignon* bastard!' cried Mes-Bottes, when Coupeau had talked to him. 'You won't catch me in that dump again! No, I'd rather starve until next year... Believe me, mate, you won't last three days in that place!'

'It's really bad, is it?' asked Coupeau, becoming quite worried.

'Oh, as bad as it gets... You can't do anything without the guy being on your back the whole time. And the way they talk to you! His missus calls you a drunkard, and you aren't allowed to spit! I told 'em where they could put their job the first day I was there, believe you me!'

'Well, it's good to be warned. I won't be stayin' there long if that's what you've got to put up with. I'll give it a go this mornin', but if the boss steps out of line I'll pick 'im up, drop 'im on his missus, and stick 'em together like a pair of kippers!'

Coupeau shook his mate's hand to thank him for his useful advice, and was on his way out when Mes-Bottes exploded. Fuckin' hell! Was that Bourguignon bastard going to stop them having a drink? Were men no longer men, then? Surely the bastard could wait five minutes. So Lantier went in to join them for a round, and the four of them continued standing there at the counter. Mes-Bottes, in his down-at-heel shoes and filthy smock, and his cap squashed down on his head, was now bawling away and glaring round the Assommoir as if he owned it. He'd just been proclaimed Emperor of Piss-Pots and King of Hogs for having eaten a salad of live cockroaches and bitten a piece out of a dead cat.

'Come on, you bloody Borgia!'* he yelled at Père Colombe, 'gimme some o' the yellow stuff, your best donkey-piss.'

When Père Colombe, pale and phlegmatic in his blue jersey, had filled the four glasses, the gents drained them in one go, so as not to let the drink go flat.

'Christ, it bloody well does you good on the way down,' muttered Bibi-la-Grillade.

But old Mes-Bottes was telling a funny story. On Friday he'd been so drunk that his mates had stuck his pipe in his mouth with a handful of plaster. It would've done for anyone else, but he just swaggered about glorying in it.

'Are you gentlemen havin' another?' asked Père Colombe in his oily voice.

'Yes, the same again,' said Lantier. 'It's my round.'

They were talking about women now. The previous Sunday Bibi-la-Grillade had taken his missus to an aunt's in Montrouge. Coupeau asked after Malle des Indes,* a laundress from Chaillot* who was well known in Père Colombe's bar. They were about to down their drinks when Mes-Bottes shouted to Goujet and Lorilleux who were just walking past. They came up to the door but wouldn't come in. The blacksmith didn't feel like drinking anything, while the chain-maker, ashen faced and shivering, thrust the gold chains he was delivering deep into his pocket, coughed, and declined to join in, saying even a tiny drop of spirits made him feel quite ill.

'Bloody hypocrites!' grunted Mes-Bottes. 'I bet they knock it back when nobody's lookin'.'

He sniffed at his glass and then went for Père Colombe.

'You bloody crook! You've changed the bottle!... You can't fool me, y'know!'

Day had broken and a dingy light now filled the Assommoir. The landlord was turning off the gas burners. Coupeau, meanwhile, was making excuses for his brother-in-law: drink just didn't agree with him, and you shouldn't hold that against him as if it was a crime. He even defended Goujet, saying he was lucky if he never had a thirst. And he was talking about going off to work when Lantier, in his best man-of-the-world manner, gave him a little sermon: you paid for your round, at the very least, before sloping off; you couldn't just walk out on your friends like a coward, even if duty called.

'When's he goin' to stop bein' such a pain about his job!' shouted Mes-Bottes.

'It's your round then, is it, mate?' Père Colombe asked Coupeau.

Coupeau paid for his round. But Bibi-la-Grillade, when his turn came, leaned over the bar and whispered something to the landlord, who slowly shook his head. Mes-Bottes understood and sounded off again about Père Colombe, this time for being such a miser. What! A twerp like him thinking he could treat a mate of theirs like that! Every booze-seller would put a drink on the slate! Did you come to a dump like this just to be insulted! The landlord was unperturbed; leaning forward, his big fists on the edge of the counter, he said politely, several times:

'Lend the gentleman some money, that would be simpler.'

'Christ Almighty! Yes, I'll lend 'im some,' shrieked Mes-Bottes. 'Here, Bibi, take this and shove it down 'is fuckin' throat!'

He was now well away. Irritated by the bag Coupeau still had slung over his shoulder, he turned to him and said:

'You look like a nursemaid. Put the baby down. It's turnin' you into a hunchback.'

Coupeau hesitated a moment; then, as if he'd made up his mind after careful reflection, he calmly put his bag on the floor, saying:

'It's too late now. I'll go there after lunch. I'll say the missus 'ad a bellyache... Listen, Colombe, I'll leave me tools under this bench and pick 'em up at twelve.'

Lantier nodded his approval. A man has to work, that goes without saying; but when you happen to be with friends, good manners come first. The idea of a good old binge had gradually tickled the fancy of all four of them, and now, overcome with lethargy, they looked questioningly at one another. Then, realizing that they had five whole hours to play with, they were filled with an intense feeling of joy, slapping each other on the back and bellowing endearments into each other's faces, especially Coupeau, who seemed younger now that a load had been taken off his mind, and kept calling the others 'me old

cock!' They had another round, then went on to La Puce qui Renifle,*
a little dive with a billiard table. Lantier made a face at first because
the place wasn't exactly clean; the hooch cost a franc a litre, or ten
sous for a half, served in two glasses; and the regulars had made such
a mess of the billiard table that the balls stuck to it. But once they
started to play, Lantier, who was a wizard with the cue, recovered his
good grace and good humour as, puffing out his chest, he accompanied each cannon with a wiggle of his hips.

When it was time for lunch, Coupeau had an idea. He stamped his
foot and shouted:

'Let's go an' get Bec-Salé. I know where he's workin'... We can
take 'im with us to 'ave trotters with hollandaise sauce at Mère
Louis's.'

They all noisily approved. Yes, Bec-Salé was bound to be feeling
like some trotters with hollandaise. So off they went. The streets were
a yellowish colour and it was drizzling, but they were too warm inside
to feel this gentle sprinkle on their limbs. Coupeau led the way to the
bolt factory in the Rue Marcadet. As they got there a good half-hour
before it was time to knock off for lunch, the roofer gave a couple of
sous to a kid to go in and tell Bec-Salé his missus had been taken bad
and she wanted him home right away. The blacksmith came strutting
out at once, perfectly relaxed, scenting a good feed.

'Ha! You load of pisspots!' he said, seeing them hiding in a doorway. 'I guessed it was you... So what's on the menu?'

At Mère Louis's, as they sucked on the little bones from the trotters, they returned to the attack on the bosses. Bec-Salé said there was
a rush job on at his place. Oh, the boss wasn't fussed about the odd
quarter of an hour; even if you didn't turn up on time he'd still be all
right, he should count himself lucky you went back at all. In any case,
there was no way any boss would dare sack Bec-Salé, because they just
couldn't find blokes of his calibre any more. After the trotters they
had an omelette. And a bottle of wine each. Mère Louis had her wine
sent up from the Auvergne,* it was the colour of blood and you could
cut it with a knife. They were beginning to have fun, the party was
warming up.

By the time they got to the dessert, Bec-Salé was shouting: 'That
fuckin' boss of mine is such a pain! Can you believe it, he's just
decided to 'ang a bell up in that dump of 'is. A bell! That's the sort of
thing you 'ave for slaves... Well, it can ring as long as it likes today!

There's no way I'm goin' back to that anvil! I've been at it for five days, I can give it a miss... If he kicks up a stink, I'll tell 'im to fuck off.'

'I'm goin' to 'ave to leave you,' said Coupeau, looking very serious. 'I must go and work. I promised me wife... 'Ave fun. I'll be with you boys in spirit, y'know.'

The others fell about laughing, but Coupeau seemed so serious that when he said he was going to fetch his tools from Père Colombe's, they all went with him. He took his bag from under the bench and put it in front of him while they all had a final snifter. At one o'clock they were still standing each other rounds. So Coupeau, with a gesture of annoyance, put the tools back under the bench; they were getting in his way, he couldn't get close to the counter without stubbing his foot against them. It was too silly to go to work now, he'd go the next day. The other four, who were now engaged in an argument about wages, didn't seem surprised when the roofer suggested, without any explanation, that they take a little stroll on the boulevard to stretch their legs. It had stopped raining. The stroll amounted to no more than a couple of hundred yards; strung out in single file with their arms dangling, they walked in silence, rather overcome by the fresh air, unhappy at being outside. Instinctively, without even needing to nudge each other, they wandered slowly back up the Rue des Poissonniers to François's for a glass of the best. They really needed it to lift their spirits. It got you down, being in the street; the mud was so bad you wouldn't even turn a policeman out into it. Lantier steered the others towards the private bar, a poky little room with just one table in it and separated from the public bar by a frosted glass partition. As a general rule he preferred private bars because they were more classy. They were nice and cosy there, weren't they? It was just like being at home, you could even have a nap if you wanted without being bothered. He asked for the newspaper, spread it out on the table, and looked over it with knitted brows. Coupeau and Mes-Bottes had started a game of piquet.* Two bottles and five glasses stood on the table.

'So, what are they on about in the paper?' asked Bibi-la-Grillade.

Lantier didn't reply immediately. Then, without looking up:

'I'm looking at the parliamentary page. What a useless lot those Republicans are, those lazy buggers on the Left. Do the people elect them just to spout a load of syrupy drivel? Here's one who believes in God, and yet he's suckin' up to the bastards in the government. If

I was elected, I'd get up on the rostrum and say "Bollocks!" Just that, 'cos that's what I think!'

'Did you know Badingue got a slap from 'is missus the other day, in front of the whole Court?' said Bec-Salé. 'It's true! And about nothing, just some silly squabble. He was a bit pissed.'

'Give us a rest with your bloody politics!' cried the roofer. 'Read about the murders, they're much more interesting.'

And, going back to his game, he declared three nines and three queens:

'I've got three down the drain and three lovely ladies... Those skirts never leave me alone.'

They emptied their glasses. Lantier began to read aloud:

'A shocking crime has brought terror to the commune of Gaillon* (Seine-et-Marne). A son has murdered his father with a spade, to rob him of thirty sous...'

They all uttered cries of horror. There was one they'd gladly have gone to see having his head removed! No, the guillotine was too good for him, he should have been chopped into little bits. They were equally appalled by a story of infanticide, but Lantier, taking a high moral position, excused the woman and put all the blame on her seducer—because, after all, if some shit of a man hadn't got the poor woman in the family way, she'd never have been able to drown it in a water closet. But what really got them excited were the exploits of the Marquis de T——: coming away from a ball in the Boulevard des Invalides* at two in the morning, he'd seen off three thugs; without even taking his gloves off, he'd dealt with the first two by butting them in the stomach, and had grabbed hold of the third by the ear and marched him off to the police station. What about that! Too bad he was a nobleman.

'Just listen to this,' Lantier went on. 'I've got to the society news. "The Comtesse de Brétigny's eldest daughter is soon to marry the young Baron de Valençay,* aide-de-camp to His Majesty. Among the wedding presents are more than three hundred thousand francs' worth of lace."'

'So bloody what!' interrupted Bibi-la-Grillade. 'We don't want to know what colour her nightdress is. The girl can 'ave as much lace as she wants, she'll still lose 'er cherry the same way they all do.'

As Lantier looked as if he was going to carry on reading, Bec-Salé snatched the paper out of his hands and sat on it, saying:

'Come on, that's enough! I'll keep it nice and warm... That's all paper's good for...'

Mes-Bottes, who had been studying his hand, thumped the table triumphantly. He'd got ninety-three.

'The Revolution!' he cried. 'A flush in clubs makes twenty, right? Then, a diamond straight, twenty-three; three kings, twenty-six; three knaves, twenty-nine; three aces, ninety-two... So when I play Year One of the Republic, ninety-three.'*

'You're done for, mate,' the others cried to Coupeau.

They ordered two more bottles. Their glasses were constantly being refilled and they were getting more and more drunk. By about five it was beginning to get disgusting, and Lantier, who'd gone quiet, was getting ready to slip away; yelling and spilling wine all over wasn't his style. Coupeau stood up at this point to make the boozer's sign of the cross. Tapping his head he pronounced Montpernasse, on his right shoulder Menilmonte, on his left shoulder La Courtille, in the middle of his belly Bagnolet,* and in the pit of the stomach sautéed rabbit, three times. The hatter took advantage of the commotion caused by this little exercise and quietly made off. His mates didn't even notice he'd gone. By now he was pretty tight, but once out in the fresh air he pulled himself together and walked calmly back to the shop, where he told Gervaise that Coupeau had gone off with some friends.

Two days went by. The roofer had still not turned up. He was knocking around in the neighbourhood, no one quite knew where. Some people said they'd seen him at Mère Baquet's, at the Papillon, or at the Petit Bonhomme qui Tousse. But while some were sure he was alone, others said they'd run into him in the company of seven or eight other drunks. Gervaise shrugged her shoulders in resignation. Oh well, she'd just have to get used to it. She didn't run after him; in fact, if she caught sight of him in a bar, she'd make a detour to avoid putting his back up. So she waited for him to come home, listening at night in case she heard him snoring outside the door. He'd fall asleep anywhere—on a pile of rubbish, on a bench, on a patch of waste ground, in the gutter. The next day, having hardly slept off the previous day's drinking, he'd start all over again, banging on the shutters of taverns and careering off once more on a wild reel of tots, big glasses, and bottles, losing his friends and then finding them again, wandering off and stumbling back befuddled, seeing the streets dance before his eyes, seeing night fall and day break, no thought in his head except drinking and sleeping it off wherever he happened to be. When he'd finally slept it all off, it would be over. All the same, on the second day, Gervaise went to Père Colombe's Assommoir, to see what she could find out; he'd been seen there five times, and that was all anyone could tell her. She had to be satisfied with taking home his bag of tools, which was still under the bench.

That evening, seeing she was upset, Lantier offered to take her to the café-concert,* to cheer her up. She declined at first, saying she wasn't in the mood. She wouldn't have said no otherwise, because he made the offer in too straightforward a way for her to suspect anything. He seemed concerned at her situation, and his manner was quite fatherly. Coupeau had never stayed out for two nights running. Despite herself, she kept going to the door every ten minutes, iron in hand, to look up and down the street to see if there was any sign of him. She said she had pins and needles in her legs, and couldn't stand still. Of course, for all she cared, Coupeau could break a leg or fall under a cab and be killed, it would be good riddance; she no longer had the slightest feeling, she declared, for a bastard like that. But all the same it was maddening to be wondering all the time if he'd be coming back or not. So, when the gaslights were lit, and Lantier started talking again about the café-concert, she accepted. After all, she'd be a fool to deny herself a bit of pleasure when her husband had been out on the town for three days straight. Since he was staying out, she'd go out as well. The place could burn to the ground as far as she was concerned. Life was getting her down so much that she was ready to put a match to it herself.

They had a quick bite to eat, she urged Maman Coupeau to go to bed straight away, and at eight o'clock she went off on Lantier's arm. Having closed the shop, she left by the courtyard door and gave the key to Madame Boche, saying that if her pig of a husband turned up, would she kindly see him to bed.

The hatter was waiting for her under the archway; he'd spruced himself up and was whistling a little tune. She was wearing her silk dress. They walked slowly, close together; as they were caught in the shafts of light coming from the shops, they could be seen talking softly and smiling at each other.

The café-concert was in the Boulevard de Rochechouart; once a small café, it had been enlarged by the addition of a wooden structure in the back yard. A string of glass globes outlined the entrance with bright lights. Several tall posters, stuck on wooden boards, stood on the ground next to the gutter.

'Here we are,' said Lantier. 'Tonight, first appearance of Madame Amanda, popular singer.'*

Then he spotted Bibi-la-Grillade, who was also reading the poster. Bibi had a black eye, evidently the result of a fight the night before.

'So, where's Coupeau?' Lantier asked, glancing round. 'You've lost 'im, 'ave you?'

'Oh, ages ago! 'Aven't seen 'im since yesterday,' Bibi replied. 'We got into a punch-up coming out of Mère Baquet's. I don't like it when things get violent. What 'appened was we got into an argument with the waiter at Mère Baquet's about a bottle he tried to make us pay for twice... So I scarpered and went to 'ave a bit of a kip.'

He was still yawning, he'd slept for eighteen hours. But he'd sobered up completely, though he seemed in a daze and his ragged old jacket was covered in fluff; he must have gone to bed fully dressed.

'So you don't know where my 'usband is?' asked Gervaise.

'No, no idea... It was five when we left Mère Baquet's. Yes, that's it!... He may well 'ave gone down the street. Yes, come to think of it, I saw 'im go into the Papillon with a coachman. God, what silly sods we are! No good for anything!'

Lantier and Gervaise had a very nice evening at the café-concert. At eleven, when the place closed, they ambled back, in no particular hurry. The air was quite nippy and people were making their way home in groups; there were some young women laughing loudly, in the shadows under the trees, because their blokes were getting a bit too fresh. Lantier was humming one of Mademoiselle Amanda's songs: 'My nose is where it tickles me.'* Gervaise, getting carried away, as if half drunk, took up the refrain. It had been very hot in there, and what with the two drinks she'd had, together with the pipe smoke and the smell of all those bodies packed together, she was feeling quite queasy. But the strongest impression she carried away with her was of Mademoiselle Amanda. Never would she have dared to appear in public with so little on. But, to give the lady her due, she had the most wonderful skin. And Gervaise listened with sensual curiosity as Lantier went into details about her person, with the air of a man who knew exactly what he was talking about.

'Everybody's asleep,' said Gervaise, after ringing three times before Boche released the door-pull.

The door opened, but the porch was in darkness, and when she knocked on the window of the lodge to ask for her key, Madame Boche said something which at first she couldn't understand. Finally, she understood that the policeman Poisson had brought Coupeau home in a dreadful state, and that the key ought to be in the lock.

'My God!' muttered Lantier when they were inside. 'What's he done? It stinks like hell.'

Indeed it did. Gervaise, who was trying to find some matches, kept stepping in something wet. When she'd managed to light a candle, a pretty sight met their eyes. Coupeau had vomited everywhere: it was all over the room; the bed was covered in it, the carpet too, and even the chest of drawers was splattered. What's more, Coupeau had fallen off the bed where Poisson must have dumped him and was snoring away, in the middle of his own filth. He was sprawled at full length, wallowing like a pig, with one cheek smeared with vomit, breathing foul breath out of his open mouth, his hair, already grey, brushing against the large puddle round his head.

'The dirty pig! The dirty pig!' Gervaise kept repeating, extremely angry. 'He's puked up everywhere. Not even a dog would've done that, a dying dog would be more decent.'

Neither of them dared move, not knowing where to put their feet. He'd never come home so drunk or made such a disgusting mess in the room. The sight of it dealt a severe blow to whatever feelings his wife still had for him. In the past, when he'd come home a bit tipsy or quite pickled, she'd been indulgent rather than feeling repelled. But this was too much, it turned her stomach. She wouldn't have touched him with a bargepole. The mere thought of this slob's skin in contact with hers filled her with horror, like having to lie next to someone who'd died of some foul disease.

'But I must sleep somewhere,' she muttered. 'I can't sleep in the street... Oh well, I'll climb over him somehow.'

She tried to step over Coupeau's prone body but had to catch hold of a corner of the chest of drawers to prevent herself from slipping on the vomit. Coupeau completely blocked off the bed. So Lantier, smiling to himself at the thought that she certainly wouldn't be laying her head on her own pillow that night, took her hand and said in a fervent whisper:

'Gervaise… Listen, Gervaise…'

She understood what he meant and pulled her hand away, so flustered that she said *tu* to him as she used to.

'No, leave me… Please, Auguste, go to your room… I'll manage. I'll climb in from the bottom.'

'Come on, Gervaise, don't be silly,' he kept saying. 'It smells really awful, you can't stay here… Come with me. What are you afraid of? He can't hear us, can he?'

She carried on struggling, furiously shaking her head. In her agitation, as if to show she meant to stay where she was, she began to take off her clothes, throwing her silk dress on to a chair, and stripping until she stood there in her chemise and petticoat, all white, her neck and arms bare. It was her bed, wasn't it? She wanted to sleep in her own bed. Twice more she tried to find a clean spot and get in, but Lantier wouldn't give up, putting his arms round her, saying things that set her blood on fire. What a fix she was in, with a hopeless husband in front of her, preventing her from slipping decently into bed, and a shit of a man behind, whose only thought was to take advantage of her predicament and have her again! As the hatter was beginning to raise his voice, she begged him to be quiet. And she stopped to listen, straining her ears in the direction of the little room where Nana and Maman Coupeau were sleeping. She could hear heavy breathing, so they must be asleep.

'Leave me alone, Auguste, you'll wake them up,' she went on, clasping her hands together. 'Be sensible. Some other day, somewhere else. Not here, where my daughter might see.'

He said nothing, but just smiled, kissing her slowly on the ear, in the teasing way he used to kiss her in the old days, to excite her. A weakness came over her and she felt a great buzzing in her head and a great shudder go through her body. Even so, she took one more step forward, but had to give up. It was no good, her revulsion was too great and the smell was getting so bad that, had she stayed, she would have been sick herself in the bed. Coupeau, dead to the world, with leaden limbs and mouth askew, was sleeping off his bender as if he was lying on a feather mattress. The whole street could have come in and had his wife and he would not have been disturbed in the slightest.

'It's no use,' she mumbled. 'It's his fault, I can't help it… My God, he's turned me out of me own bed… I haven't got a bed of me own any more… No, I can't 'elp it, it's his fault.'

She was trembling, hardly knew what she was doing. And as Lantier guided her into his room, Nana's face appeared behind one of the panes in the glass door of the little room. She had just woken up and had got quietly out of bed in her nightdress, pale with sleep. She looked at her father, lying in his vomit; then, with her face pressed to the glass, she stood there watching intently, very serious, until her mother's petticoat disappeared into the other man's room, opposite. Her staring eyes, the eyes of a perverted child, shone with sensual curiosity.

CHAPTER IX

THAT winter, Maman Coupeau was nearly carried off by a choking fit. Every year, in December, her asthma was sure to keep her flat on her back for two or three weeks. She was getting on, seventy-three come St Anthony's Day.* What's more, she was in a pretty decrepit state, the slightest thing would set her wheezing, even though she was big and plump. The doctor said that one day she'd have one of her attacks and pop off just like that.

When she was laid up in bed, she became as nasty as the mange. Of course, the little room she slept in with Nana was hardly very cheerful. Between the child's bed and hers there was just room for two chairs. The faded grey wallpaper hung down in strips. From the round skylight near the ceiling came a pale, dim light as in a cellar. Being there would make anybody feel old, especially if you couldn't breathe properly. At night when she couldn't sleep she'd listen to the child breathing, at least that helped to pass the time. But during the day, since no one came to see her from morning till night, she moaned, and wept, and kept repeating to herself for hours on end, rolling her head about on the pillow:

'This is misery! This is such misery! They're goin' to leave me 'ere to die in prison, that's what they're goin' to do!'

And when someone did come to see her, Virginie or Madame Boche, to ask how she was, she didn't answer, but launched straight into her lamentations:

'Dear me, yes, it don't 'alf cost a lot, the food I eat 'ere! I wouldn't 'ave nearly as much to put up with if I was with strangers! For instance, I wanted a cup of tisane—well, they brought me a whole jugful, just to make me feel bad about drinkin' too much of it. And then there's Nana. I brought that kid up meself, but now she runs off barefoot first thing in the mornin' and I don't see her again all day. Anyone'd think I smell bad. But at night she's out to the world, she'd never wake up once to see if I'm all right. I'm just a burden to them, they're just waitin' for me to kick the bucket. Well, it won't be long. I 'aven't got a son any more, that laundress bitch took 'im from me. She'd beat me to death if she wasn't afraid of the law.'

It was true Gervaise was a bit rough at times. The place was going to the dogs, they were all on edge and flying off the handle at the slightest provocation. One morning when Coupeau had a hangover he shouted: 'The old girl keeps sayin' she's goin' to die, so what's she waitin' for!' and this had cut Maman Coupeau to the quick. They complained about how much she cost them, and said to her face that if she wasn't there they'd spend a lot less. If truth be told, though, she didn't behave very well either. For example, when she saw her eldest daughter, Madame Lerat, she'd start bellyaching, accusing her son and daughter-in-law of starving her to death, all in order to wheedle twenty sous out of Madame Lerat, which she'd spend on nice titbits to eat. And she told the Lorilleux the most terrible tales about where their ten francs went—on things Gervaise fancied, new bonnets, cakes eaten on the sly, and even worse things she didn't dare mention. Two or three times she nearly brought the family to blows. Sometimes she took one side and sometimes the other. In short, it was a madhouse.

When her asthma was at its worst, one afternoon when Madame Lorilleux and Madame Lerat were both by her bedside, Maman Coupeau blinked her eyes at them as a sign that they should bend down close to her. She could hardly speak. She whispered softly:

'Shockin' goins-on! I heard 'em last night. Yes, yes, Gimpy and the hatter! Goin' at it like anythin'! Coupeau's a fine one. Shockin'!'

In short gasps, coughing and choking, she told them how her son must have come home dead drunk the night before. And, as she couldn't sleep, she'd heard everything—Gimpy's bare feet on the floor, Lantier calling to her in a whisper, the connecting door being opened very gently, and all the rest. It must have gone on until early morning, she couldn't be sure of the time because, try as she might to stay awake, she'd finally dozed off.

'And the worst of it', she went on, 'is that Nana must have heard as well. She was very restless all night, though she usually sleeps like a log. She was tossin' and turnin' as if she had live coals in her bed.'

The two women didn't seem surprised.

'Of course!' murmured Madame Lorilleux. 'It must have started the first day he came! As long as Coupeau doesn't mind, it's none of our business. But still! It doesn't do our family any credit.'

'If I'd been there,' said Madame Lerat, pursing her lips, 'I'd have given her a fright, I'd have shouted somethin', like "I can see you!" or

"Police!" A servant girl who works for a doctor told me that, according to her master, a fright like that at a certain moment can kill a woman stone dead. And if she'd been struck dead there and then, it would've been only right, wouldn't it? She'd have been punished right where she'd sinned.'

Soon the whole neighbourhood knew that Gervaise went to Lantier's room every night. Madame Lorilleux made a great show of indignation in front of the neighbours; she felt sorry for her brother, that silly fool who was being made the biggest cuckold around; and the only reason, she said, why she still set foot in that madhouse was to see her poor mother, who was forced to live in the midst of such vice. With one accord, the neighbours put all the blame on Gervaise. She must have been the one to lead the hatter astray. You could see it in her eyes. Yes, in spite of the nasty rumours, they all continued to have a soft spot for that sly devil Lantier, who went on behaving like a real gent, reading his paper as he strolled down the street, always gallant and attentive to the ladies, never short of sweets and flowers to give them. He was just behaving naturally as cock of the roost, a man's a man after all, you couldn't expect him to say no to women if they threw themselves at him. But there was no excuse for her, she was a disgrace to the Rue de la Goutte-d'Or. And the Lorilleux, who were Nana's godparents, got the kid to go up to their place so they could pump her for details. When they asked her roundabout questions she'd put on her gormless look, lowering her long, soft eyelashes as if to hide the flame in her eyes.

In the midst of all this public indignation, Gervaise went quietly about her business, weary and half asleep. At first she'd felt very guilty and very shameless, and had been disgusted with herself. When she left Lantier's room she'd wash her hands and then, with a wet cloth, rub her shoulders so hard she nearly scraped the skin off, as if to get rid of the filth. If, after that, Coupeau tried to fool around, she'd get annoyed and run off shivering to the back of the shop to get dressed; and she wouldn't let the hatter touch her if her husband had just kissed her. She'd have liked to change her skin when she changed men. But gradually she got used to it. It was too tiring to wash every time. Her lazy habits sapped her will, her need to be happy made her find what pleasure she could in the situation. She was indulgent towards herself and others, just trying to arrange things so that nobody would get upset. As long as her husband and her lover were content, as long as the household chugged along as normal and they all had a nice time from morning to night, well fed, pleased with life, and taking things easy, there was nothing to complain about, was there? After all, she couldn't be doing anything so very wrong, since it was all working out to everybody's satisfaction; you normally get punished when you do wrong. In this way, her shamelessness became a habit. Now it all worked like clockwork; each time Coupeau came home drunk, which happened at least every Monday, Tuesday, and Wednesday, she went across to Lantier's room. She divided her nights between them, and after a while she even took to leaving Coupeau fast asleep, if he was snoring too loudly, and going over to snooze in peace in the hatter's bed. It wasn't that she felt more attached to him. No, it was just that she found him cleaner and she could sleep better in his room; it was like having a bath. In short, she was like a cat who loves curling up for a nap on clean sheets.

Maman Coupeau never dared say anything openly about all this. But when they had a quarrel, and the laundress had shaken her up a bit, the old girl would make some pretty pointed remarks. She'd say she knew some men who were really stupid and some women who were complete sluts; and she'd mutter other things, cruder still, with all the coarseness of expression of someone who'd once worked in the tailoring trade. The first few times, Gervaise had stared at her very hard without saying anything. Later, however, she defended herself in general terms, also without being explicit. If a woman was married to a drunkard, a dirty pig who wallowed in his own filth, she might be forgiven for looking around for someone cleaner. She went further, making the point that Lantier was just as much her husband as Coupeau was, perhaps more so. Hadn't she started going with him when she was fourteen? Hadn't she had two children by him?* Well, since that was the case, it was all excusable and nobody had the right to throw stones. She said she was only doing what was natural. And they'd better not start picking on her, because she'd soon give them a dose of their own medicine. The Rue de la Goutte-d'Or didn't exactly smell of roses! Little Madame Vigouroux was on her back in the coal from morning to night. Madame Lehongre, the grocer's wife, was sleeping with her brother-in-law, a terrible slob she wouldn't touch with a bargepole. That prissy little watchmaker across the street was nearly had up at the Assizes for something dreadful, sleeping with his own daughter, a brazen creature who worked the boulevards.

And with a sweep of her arm she indicated the whole neighbourhood, saying she'd need a good hour to go through all those folks' dirty laundry, all sleeping together like animals, fathers, mothers, kids, jam-packed, rolling about in their own filth. Oh yes, there was so much she could tell, there was filth wherever you looked, everywhere stank of it. Yes, yes, it was a pretty picture in this part of Paris, with men and women living on top of each other because they were so poor! If you put them together in a mortar, and pounded them up, all you'd get out of them would be enough dung to fertilize the cherry trees on the plain of Saint-Denis.

'It'd be better for them not to spit in the air, so it doesn't land on their own faces,' she'd shout when pushed too far. 'They should mind their own business. Live and let live. I don't criticize other people, as long as I'm not dragged through the mud by them as what's up to their necks in it themselves.'

And one day, when Maman Coupeau said something particularly provocative, she'd answered between clenched teeth:

'You're takin' advantage of the fact you're laid up in bed. It's not right, you know very well I'm good to you, I've never said anythin' about your carryings-on. Oh yes, I know all about it, a fine old time you had—two or three men while Père Coupeau was still alive. No, you needn't start coughin', I've had my say. All I'm askin' is that you leave me alone.'

The old lady had almost choked. The next day, when Goujet came to collect her mother's washing, Maman Coupeau called him into her room and kept him sitting by her bed for a long time. She knew how he felt about Gervaise, and she'd noticed he'd been depressed and unhappy for some time, suspecting the awful things that were going on. So, to get her own back for the row of the day before, she bluntly told him the truth, sobbing and moaning as if Gervaise's bad behaviour affected her the most. When Goujet came out of the little room, he was so overcome that he had to lean against the wall. Then, when Gervaise came back, Maman Coupeau shouted that Madame Goujet wanted her to take the washing over straight away, whether it was ironed or not; and she seemed so excited that Gervaise guessed she'd been telling tales and imagined the painful scene and the heartbreak that lay in store.

Very pale, her legs already turning to jelly, she put the washing in a basket and set off. It was years now since she'd repaid a sou of her debt to the Goujets. It still stood at four hundred and twenty-five francs. She took the money for the washing every time, saying she was hard up. It made her feel ashamed, because she seemed to be taking advantage of Goujet's friendship to do him out of his money. Coupeau, less scrupulous now, would snigger, saying that Goujet must have been kissing and cuddling her on the sly and took that as payment. But Gervaise, despite the relationship she'd fallen into with Lantier, was most indignant, and asked her husband if that was what he wanted. Nobody could speak ill of Goujet in front of her; her affection for him was like a remnant of her integrity. And so, each time she delivered the laundry to these good folk, she felt sick at heart as soon as she set foot on their staircase.

'So, you've come at last,' Madame Goujet said curtly as she opened the door. 'When I want to order my coffin, I'll ask you to go and do it for me.'

Gervaise went in feeling so awkward she didn't even dare mumble an excuse. She couldn't be relied on to be punctual any more, never arrived on time, kept some customers waiting a whole week. Little by little, she was letting everything go.

'I've been waiting since last week,' the lacemaker went on. 'And what's more you lie. You send your girl to tell me some story: you're just doing my things, it'll all be brought over that evening, or else there's been an accident, it's fallen into a bucket. And in the meantime I lose a whole day's work, nothing comes and I get quite worried. No, it's not good enough. Well, let's see what you've got in the basket! Let's hope it's all here this time! Have you brought the pair of sheets you've had for the last month, and the shirt you forgot last time?'

'Yes, yes,' Gervaise mumbled. 'I've got the shirt, here it is.'

But Madame Goujet protested that it wasn't theirs, and she wouldn't take it. Now she was being given other people's things! This was too much! Already the previous week she'd had two handkerchiefs that didn't have her mark on them. She certainly didn't like the idea of getting laundry from goodness knows where. And after all, she preferred her own things.

'And the sheets?' she went on. 'You can't find them, can you? Well, my girl, you'll have to look for them, because I must have them by tomorrow morning!'

There was a silence. Gervaise sensed that the door of Goujet's room behind her was ajar, and this made her feel even more upset.

She imagined he was in there; and how awful if he'd overheard all these reproaches, to which she had no reply because they were fully justified! She assumed a meek, submissive air, looking down and putting the washing on the bed as quickly as possible. But things got still worse when Madame Goujet began to inspect the items one by one. She picked each one up, then dropped it, saying:

'You know, you're really losing your touch. I used to be able to compliment you each time, but not now. These days you do things just anyhow, you make a mess of everything. Look at this shirt front, it's got scorch marks on the pleats. And the buttons are all torn off. I don't know how you manage it, but there's never a button left on. And look at this! Here's a petticoat I'm not going to pay for. It's still dirty, all you've done is spread the dirt. No thanks! If the clothes don't even get clean now!...'

She stopped, counted the articles, and cried:

'What! Is this all you've brought? There are two pairs of stockings missing, six towels, a tablecloth, and some dusters! What do you take me for? I said I wanted everything back, ironed or not. If your girl doesn't bring me the rest within the hour, there'll be trouble—I'm warning you.'

At that moment, Goujet coughed in his room. Gervaise gave a start. To think she was being spoken to like this in front of him! She stood there in the middle of the room, feeling very awkward and embarrassed, waiting to be handed the dirty clothes. But after checking everything, Madame Goujet quietly sat down again by the window and carried on darning a lace shawl.

'And the washing?' Gervaise asked timidly.

'No, thank you,' the old lady replied. 'Nothing this week.'

Gervaise turned pale. Madame Goujet was taking away her custom. At this, she felt so upset that she had to sit down on a chair, because her legs were giving way under her. She made no attempt to defend herself, and all she could say was:

'Is Monsieur Goujet ill?'

Yes, he wasn't feeling well, he'd had to come home instead of going to the forge, and he'd just gone to lie down to rest. Madame Goujet's tone was very serious, sitting there in her black dress as usual, her white face framed by her nun-like headdress. The day rate for bolt-makers had been cut again; it had gone down from nine francs to seven, because of the machines that now did all the work. And she explained that they were trying to economize on everything; she was going to start doing her own washing again. Of course, it would have come in very handy if the Coupeaus had paid back the money her son had lent them. But she certainly had no intention of setting the bailiffs on them because they couldn't pay. When she mentioned the debt, Gervaise lowered her eyes and seemed to be following the nimble play of the lacemaker's needle as it picked up the stitches one by one.

'But', continued Madame Goujet, 'if you tried to cut back a bit, you'd be able to pay it off. After all, you eat very well, and spend a lot, I'm sure. If you gave us just ten francs a month…'

She was interrupted by Goujet's voice, calling:

'Maman! Maman!'

She came and sat down again, but changed the subject. Her son had no doubt begged her not to talk about the money. But, in spite of herself, she returned to the subject of the debt five minutes later. Oh yes, she'd foreseen what was happening, the roofer was drinking the shop away, and he'd drag his wife down with him. If her son had listened to her, he'd never have lent the five hundred francs. He'd be married by now, he wouldn't be eating his heart out, with nothing to look forward to in life. She was getting angry, not mincing her words, directly accusing Gervaise of having conspired with Coupeau to take advantage of her poor mugglns of a son. Oh yes, there were some women who played the hypocrite for years, but it all came out in the end.

'Maman! Maman!' Goujet called again, this time quite urgently.

She stood up, and when she came back she said, as she took up her work again:

'Go in, he wants to see you.'

Trembling, Gervaise went in, leaving the door ajar. She was deeply affected because it was as if they were admitting to Madame Goujet their feelings for each other. She looked round once again at the quiet little room, with its walls covered in pictures and its narrow iron bed-stead, like the room of a fifteen-year-old boy. Goujet, his huge body as if drained of strength by what Maman Coupeau had told him, was stretched out on the bed; his eyes were red and his fine blond beard was still wet with tears. In his first moments of rage he must have pounded his pillow with his great fists, for it was torn and feathers were coming out.

'Maman's wrong, you know,' he almost whispered. 'You don't owe me anything. I won't hear another word about it.'

He sat up and looked at her. His eyes filled with tears again.

'Are you ill, Monsieur Goujet?' she asked softly. 'Tell me. what's wrong.'

'It's nothing. I tired myself out yesterday. I'm going to have a nap.'

But then, his feelings gushing out, he cried:

'My God, my God, it should never have happened, never! You gave me your word. And now there it is, there it is! Oh my God, I can't bear it! Please go!'

With a gentle gesture he begged her to leave. She didn't go over to the bed, she went out as he asked, dazed, unable to say anything to comfort him. In the next room she picked up her basket, but still didn't go, trying to find something to say. But Madame Goujet went on with her mending, without looking up. In the end it was she who said:

'Goodnight, then. Send the washing back and we'll settle up later.'

'Yes, all right, goodnight,' mumbled Gervaise.

She closed the door slowly, casting one last look at this clean, well-ordered home where, she felt, she was leaving something of her better self. She made her way back to the shop in the stupid, mechanical way cows wander home, hardly aware of the way they're going. Maman Coupeau, out of bed for the first time, was sitting next to the stove. But Gervaise made no attempt to take her to task; she was too tired, her bones ached as if she'd been beaten. Life, she felt, was just too hard, and short of kicking the bucket straight away there was just no answer to the pain of it all.

From now on, Gervaise didn't give a damn about anything. She'd send people packing with a vague wave of the hand. Each time a fresh problem arose she'd take refuge in her one remaining pleasure, her three meals a day. For all she cared the shop could have crumbled to dust; as long as she wasn't underneath it she'd gladly have walked away in the clothes she was wearing. And indeed the shop was collapsing, not all at once, but bit by bit, every day. One by one the customers were losing patience and taking their washing elsewhere. Monsieur Madinier, Mademoiselle Remanjou, and even the Boches, had gone back to Madame Fauconnier, whom they found more reliable. People eventually got tired of waiting three weeks for a pair of stockings and putting on shirts that still had the previous Sunday's grease-spots on

them. Gervaise, her appetite undiminished, bade them good riddance, telling them it was a good job they were clearing off, she was
bloody glad she wouldn't have to handle their filthy things any more.
All right! The whole neighbourhood could bugger off, she'd be shot
of a whole heap of muck, and she'd have that much less work. The
only customers she kept were those who paid late or not at all, the
tarts, and women like Madame Gaudron, whose stuff smelled so bad
that no other laundry in the Rue Neuve would take it. The shop had
become so run down that she'd had to dismiss her last assistant,
Madame Putois, and was left alone with her apprentice, squinty
Augustine, who was getting more stupid by the day. And even then
there wasn't always any work for them to do and they'd hang about for
whole afternoons, squatting on their stools. In short, complete disaster. You could smell it a mile off.

Naturally, as apathy and poverty took hold, so did squalor. You'd
never have recognized the lovely sky-blue shop that had once been
Gervaise's pride and joy. The woodwork and windowpanes at the
front, which were never cleaned, were constantly spattered all over
with mud from passing carriages. In the window, hanging on the brass
rod, were three grey rags that had belonged to customers who'd died
in hospital. And inside it was even shabbier: the damp from washing
hung up near the ceiling to dry had made the wallpaper come unstuck;
the Pompadour chintz was hanging in shreds like cobwebs heavy with
dust; in a corner, the broken stove, full of holes made by the poker,
looked like a heap of old iron in a junk shop; the worktable seemed as
if it had been used by a whole regiment, stained as it was with wine
and coffee, plastered with jam, and greasy from the Monday feasts.
And along with all that there was a smell of starch gone sour and
a stench made up of mildew, burnt fat, and general dirt. But Gervaise
felt quite at home in the midst of it all. She hadn't noticed the shop
getting dirty; she just went along with it, and became as used to the
shreds of wallpaper and the greasy woodwork as she was to wearing
torn skirts and not washing her ears. The dirt itself was like a cosy
nest she loved to snuggle into. To let things slide, to wait for the dust
to stop up the holes and spread a velvety coat over everything, to feel
the whole place sinking around her in a numbing state of idleness, was
a truly sensual pleasure, a kind of intoxication. To be left in peace was
all that mattered, she didn't care about the rest. Her debts were still
mounting, but she'd stopped worrying about them. She was losing all

scruples: she'd pay or not pay, it was all left vague, and she'd rather not think about it. When one shop would no longer give her credit, she'd open an account at the place next door. She owed money everywhere, every ten yards or so. Just to take the Rue de la Goutte-d'Or, she no longer dared to walk past the coal merchant's, the grocer's, or the fruiterer's, and that meant that to get to the wash-house she had to go round by the Rue des Poissonniers, a good ten minutes' walk. Shopkeepers started accusing her of being a cheat. One evening, the man who'd sold her the furniture for Lantier caused a bit of a stir by yelling that, if she didn't cough up the money she owed, he'd grab hold of her and get paid in kind. Of course, scenes like that left her all of a tremble; but she'd just shake herself like a dog, and that was it, it wouldn't spoil her appetite that evening. Cheeky buggers, bothering her like that! She hadn't got any money, and she couldn't produce it out of thin air, could she! Besides, shopkeepers were a load of sharks, they deserved to wait for their money. And she'd go back to sleep in her little corner, trying not to think about what was sure to happen in the end. She'd go under! But until then, she wouldn't let anybody upset her.

Meanwhile, Maman Coupeau was on her feet again. For another year, the shop scraped by. Of course, during the summer there was a bit more work—the white skirts and cotton dresses of the girls who worked the outer boulevards. But they were going steadily downhill, sinking a little deeper into the mire each week, but still with ups and downs, some evenings when they just stared at the empty larder, others when they stuffed themselves with veal until they nearly burst. Maman Coupeau was always to be seen in the street with parcels tucked under her apron, ambling along as if out for a walk, heading for the pawnshop in the Rue Polonceau. She would hunch her shoulders and wear the unctuous, self-righteous expression of a devout churchgoer on her way to Mass; and she quite enjoyed it, it amused her to dabble in money, and haggling with old clothes dealers titillated her passion for gossip. The assistants in the Rue Polonceau had got well used to her; they called her 'Maman Four Francs', because she always asked for four francs when they offered her three, for bundles no bigger than a knob of butter. Gervaise would have put the house itself in hock; her mania for pawning things was such that she'd have shaved her head if she'd been able to get a loan on her hair. It was all so easy; how could you resist going there for a bit of loose change when you needed a loaf of bread? The whole caboodle went the same way: linen, clothes, even tools and furniture. In the early days, if she had a good week, she'd take the opportunity to redeem her stuff, though back it'd go the following week. But later on she stopped caring and let it all go, and sold her pawn tickets. There was just one thing that broke her heart, and that was to pawn her clock to pay a twenty-franc bill to a bailiff who came to serve a writ. Until then she'd sworn she'd rather starve to death than part with her clock. When Maman Coupeau carried it off in a little hatbox, she slumped on to a chair, with tears in her eyes, as if everything she owned was being taken away from her. But when Maman Coupeau came back with twenty-five francs, this unexpected sum, five francs more than she'd anticipated, consoled her greatly; she sent the old girl out again straight away to buy four sous' worth of grog in a tumbler, just to celebrate the five-franc piece. Often nowadays, when they were on good terms, they had a tipple together on a corner of the worktable, a mixture of brandy and cassis. Maman Coupeau had the knack of bringing the tumbler back in her apron pocket without spilling a drop. No need for the neighbours to know, was there? In fact the neighbours knew perfectly well. The fruiterer, the tripe-shop woman, and the grocer's boys would say: 'Look! The old girl's off to see Uncle' or 'Look! The old girl's got her glass of grog in her apron.' And of course this turned the neighbours even more against Gervaise. She was guzzling everything up, the whole shop would soon disappear down the hatch. Yes, yes, a few more mouthfuls and the place would be as clean as a whistle.

In the midst of this general devastation Coupeau was flourishing. That bloody pisspot was in fine form. He was getting positively fatter on plonk and firewater. He ate a lot and made fun of the weedy Lorilleux, who said booze was a killer; in response, he'd tap his belly whose skin was stretched by fat, like the skin of a drum. He'd play him a tune on it, the belly's vespers, with rolls and thumpings on his great drum such as would've made a fortune for a tooth-puller in a fairground. But Lantier, annoyed at having no belly himself, said it was yellow fat, unhealthy fat. No matter, Coupeau drank on, for his health, he said. His mop of hair, speckled now with grey, was like flaming brandy. His drinker's face, with its ape-like jaw, was seasoned purplish by the alcohol. And he was as cheery as ever, telling his wife to shut up if she tried to talk about her troubles. As if men should concern themselves with such piddling things! If the cupboard was bare, it had nothing to do with him. He had to have his grub morning and evening, and he didn't care where it came from. When he spent weeks without working, he became even more demanding. Meanwhile, he'd still give Lantier a slap on the back, as friendly as ever. Of course, he knew nothing of his wife's misconduct; at least certain people, the Boches, the Poissons, swore to God that he had no idea, and that it would be a disaster if he ever found out. But Madame Lerat, his own sister, would shake her head and say she knew some husbands who didn't mind. One night Gervaise was finding her way back in the dark from Lantier's room when she felt a pat on her behind; she was terror-stricken, but in the end decided she must just have bumped against the bedstead. Surely the situation was too awful to make light of it; her husband couldn't find it funny to play tricks like that on her.

Lantier wasn't wasting away either. He made sure he looked after himself, measuring his waistline by his trouser belt, always afraid he'd have to loosen or tighten it. He liked himself just as he was, he didn't want to put on weight or lose any, out of vanity. That made him fussy about his food, because he judged every dish according to its effect on his waistline. Even when there wasn't a sou in the house, he had to have things that were nourishing but light, like eggs and cutlets. Ever since he'd started sharing the wife with the husband, he'd seen himself as an equal partner in the household: he'd pocket any small change lying about, and kept Gervaise at his beck and call, grumbling and growling and seeming more at home there than Coupeau. In short, it was a house with two masters, and the second master, the cleverer one, pulled the blanket over to his side, managing to get the best of everything: the wife, food, the lot. He was picking them clean! And he no longer cared if people saw what he was doing. Nana remained his favourite, because he liked pretty little girls. He paid less and less attention to Étienne, because boys, he said, should know how to take care of themselves. If someone called to see Coupeau, Lantier was always there in his slippers and shirtsleeves; he'd appear from the back of the shop with the irritated look of a husband who'd been disturbed, and he'd speak for Coupeau, saying it amounted to the same thing.

Life was hardly a barrel of laughs for Gervaise, caught as she was between these two men. She had no complaints about her health, thank God! She was putting on weight, however, like Coupeau. But to be lumbered with two men to look after and please was often more than she could cope with. God only knows, one husband's enough trouble. The worst of it was that the devils got on very well together. They never quarrelled; in the evening, after dinner, they sat grinning at each other, elbows on the table; and all day long they snuggled close to each other like a couple of pleasure-loving cats. And on days when they came home in a bad mood, they took it out on her, egging each other on. Go on, sort the bitch out! She had a broad back, and when they both yelled at her it made them even better pals. And there was no point in her trying to protest! At first, when one of them yelled at her, she'd look imploringly at the other to get him to say something in her defence. But it hardly ever worked. Now she just took it all, hunching her shoulders, realizing that they enjoyed knocking her about because she was so round, round as a ball. Coupeau was very foul-mouthed and called her dreadful names. Lantier, on the other hand, chose his insults with care, saying things no one else said, which hurt her even more. Fortunately you get used to anything; in the end all the abuse and unfairness slid off her smooth skin like water off a duck's back. She even came to prefer them angry, because when they were nice they pestered her more, always asking her to do something, so that she couldn't even iron a bonnet in peace. They'd ask for little snacks, she had to add salt or not add salt, pander to their every whim, coddle one and then swaddle the other. By the end of the week her head would be spinning and her legs aching, she'd be in a complete daze, looking half crazy. It's the sort of life that wears a woman out.

Yes, Coupeau and Lantier were wearing her out, that was it. They were burning her at both ends. Of course, the roofer had had no education, but the hatter had had too much, or rather he'd had an education the way men who don't wash wear a white shirt, to hide the dirt underneath. One night, she dreamt she was standing on the edge of a well; Coupeau was punching her to make her move forward while Lantier was tickling her from behind to make her jump sooner. That's what her life was like! She was in such good hands, it was no wonder her life was falling apart. It was hardly fair of the neighbours to blame her for her slovenly ways, for her troubles were not of her making. Sometimes, when she thought about it, a shudder would run through her, but then she'd think that things could be even worse. It was better to have two men, for instance, than to lose your two arms. Feeling her situation to be natural enough, and not at all unusual, she did her best to get some kind of happiness out of it. What proved how cosy and easy-going the whole thing was becoming was that she didn't hate Coupeau any more than Lantier. In a play at the Gaîté* she'd seen a horrible woman who loathed her husband and poisoned him for the sake of her lover; and this had made Gervaise angry, because her own feelings were not at all like that. Didn't it make more sense for the three of them to live together in peace and harmony? No, none of that nonsense for her; it messed up your life, which was hard enough as it was. So in spite of the debts and the threat of poverty, she'd have told you she'd have been content enough with her existence, if only the roofer and the hatter hadn't worked her so hard and yelled at her so much.

Unfortunately, as autumn approached, things got even worse in the Coupeau household. Lantier made out he was losing weight, and mooched around with a long face which got longer every day. He moaned about everything, and turned his nose up at potato soup, a vile concoction he couldn't eat, he said, without getting a stomach ache. And the slightest little flare-up turned into a full-scale row, each one blaming the others for the dire straits they were in, and it was a hell of a job to patch things up before they all dossed down for a bit of shut-eye. When the bran runs out, donkeys start biting each other, don't they? Lantier could sense disaster looming; it troubled him to realize that the household was already so broke, so cleaned out, that he could see the day when he'd have to put his coat on and look somewhere else for board and lodging. He'd got so used to his little nest and to all the habits he'd fallen into, pampered by everybody; it was a real land of plenty, the like of which he'd never find again. Well, you can't have your cake and eat it! When it came down to it, it was his own belly he was getting angry with, because that's where the business had gone. But that wasn't how he saw things; he was furious with the other two for having let the place go to the dogs in two years. Really, the Coupeaus were just not up to it. And he shouted at Gervaise for frittering the money away. Christ! What was going to happen to him? His friends were leaving him in the lurch just when he was about to pull off something wonderful, a job in a factory that paid six thousand francs, enough to keep them all in luxury.

One evening in December there was nothing whatever for dinner. The cupboard was bare. Lantier became very gloomy. He would go out very early and tramp around in search of some other place, where a nice smell of cooking would smooth away the wrinkles. He'd sit for hours next to the stove, thinking. Then, all of a sudden, he became very friendly with the Poissons. He stopped teasing the policeman by calling him Badingue, and went so far as to agree that the Emperor might be a decent bloke after all. In particular, he seemed to appreciate Virginie, a very capable woman, he said, who had her head screwed on properly. It was obvious he was buttering them up. You might even think he wanted to board with them. But his devious mind was plotting something much more complicated than that. Virginie had told him she'd love to set herself up with a shop of some kind, and he never stopped telling her what a marvellous idea this was. Yes, she was perfectly cut out to run a shop: she was tall and energetic, and she had such a nice manner. There was no limit to the amount of money she could make! Since the capital had been there for some time, a legacy from an aunt, she had every reason to give up the four dresses she cobbled together every season, and set up in business. He pointed out the people who were making their fortunes, like the fruiterer on the corner, and a little woman who sold crockery on the outer boulevard. And the time was just right: you could almost sell the sweepings from under the counter. But Virginie wasn't sure: she was looking for a shop to rent, and didn't want to leave the neighbourhood. At this, Lantier took her off into corners, and had whispered conversations with her for ten minutes at a stretch. He seemed to be urging her into something, and she'd now stopped saying no and was giving him authority to act. It was as if they had a secret; there were winks and hurried words, and even the way they shook hands seemed to betoken some dark plot. From then on the hatter, as he sat eating his dry bread, kept a sharp eye on the Coupeaus; and he'd become very talkative again, driving them half mad with his endless grumbling. All day long Gervaise had her nose rubbed in their poverty, which he obligingly detailed to her. It wasn't on his account—Good Lord no!—that he was saying all this. He'd starve to death with his friends if it came to it. But it was only sensible to take stock of the situation as it really was. They owed at least five hundred francs in the neighbourhood, to the baker, the coal merchant, the grocer, and others. What's more, they were two quarters behind with the rent, so that made another two hundred and fifty. The landlord, Monsieur Marescot, was even talking about evicting them if they didn't pay by the first of

January. Finally, the pawn shop had taken everything, they didn't have three francs' worth of knick-knacks left to pawn, they'd cleaned the place out so thoroughly. The nails were still on the walls, that was all, apart from two books that might fetch three sous.

Gervaise, bewildered by what he said, and stunned by his calculations, would lose her temper and bang on the table, or burst into tears like a baby. One evening she loudly declared:

'I'm clearing out of here tomorrow! I'd sooner put the key under the door and sleep in the street than carry on like this, worried sick about what's going to happen.'

'It'd be better', said Lantier slyly, 'to transfer the lease, if you can find somebody. When you've both decided to give up the shop…'

She interrupted him, yelling even louder:

'Straight away! Straight away! It'd be good riddance!'

At this point Lantier became quite businesslike. By transferring the lease, they'd probably be able to get the new tenant to pay the two overdue quarters. Then he ventured to mention the Poissons, reminding Gervaise that Virginie was on the lookout for a shop; perhaps the laundry would suit her. Now he came to think of it, he'd heard her say she'd like one just like it. But on hearing Virginie's name, Gervaise calmed down. She'd see; when you were in a temper you always talked about chucking things in, but when you stopped to think things didn't seem that simple.

For the next few days, whenever Lantier broached the subject again, Gervaise replied that she'd been in worse pickles and managed to get out of them. How on earth would she be better off, not to have the shop at all? That was no way to put food on the table. No, she'd do just the opposite, take on some more assistants and get new customers. This was how she responded to Lantier's arguments, which pictured her as down-and-out, crushed by debts, without the faintest hope of getting back on her feet. But he was tactless enough to mention Virginie again, and that made her really dig her heels in. No! Never! She'd always had her doubts about the genuineness of Virginie's friendship, and if Virginie wanted the shop, it was to humiliate her. She'd gladly hand it over to the first woman who came in off the street, but not to that great hypocrite who'd obviously been waiting years to see her fall flat on her face. Oh, she could see it all now! Now she knew the reason for the yellow sparks that lit up that creature's cat-eyes. Yes, Virginie had never got over the hiding she'd had in the wash-house, and she'd been nursing her grudge all this time. Well, she'd be well advised to put that grudge on ice if she didn't want another hiding! And pretty soon too, so she'd better get her arse ready. At first, in response to this outburst, Lantier gave Gervaise a similar tongue-lashing, calling her pig-headed, a gossip-monger, and stuck-up, and was so carried away that he called Coupeau a clod, who didn't know how to make his wife treat a friend with respect. Then, realizing that getting angry would put everything at risk, he swore that he'd never get involved in other people's affairs again, because you were never thanked for it; and indeed, from then on he seemed to give up trying to persuade them to transfer the lease, just biding his time until an opportunity arose to bring the matter up again and get Gervaise to agree.

January had arrived, with filthy weather, wet and cold. Maman Coupeau, who'd coughed and wheezed her way through December, had had to take to her bed again after Epiphany. This was no surprise: it came to her every winter like an annuity. But this time everybody said she'd only leave her room feet first; and indeed, though she was a big, well-built woman, her cough had a terrible graveyard rattle to it, one eye was dead already, and one side of her face was all twisted. Of course, her children wouldn't have finished her off, but she'd been hanging on for so long, and was such a burden that, deep down, they hoped she'd die, as a deliverance for everybody. She'd be much better off herself, too, because she'd had her time. And when you've had your time, you've got nothing to regret. The doctor had been sent for once, but hadn't even bothered to come a second time. They gave her herbal teas, they didn't abandon her completely. Every hour they'd look in to see if she was still alive. She could no longer speak, her breathing was so bad, but with her one good eye, which was still bright and clear, she'd stare at them; and that one good eye expressed so much: regret for her lost youth, sadness at seeing her family in such a hurry to be rid of her, and fury at the way that vicious little Nana brazenly went and stood in her nightgown spying through the glass door.

One Monday night Coupeau came home sozzled. Ever since his mother had been at death's door, he'd been in a maudlin state. When he was in bed and snoring his head off, Gervaise stayed up for a while. She usually kept watch over Maman Coupeau for part of the night. Nana was very good too; she still slept next to the old woman and said that if she heard her dying she'd get up and tell everybody. That particular night, as Nana was asleep and the sick woman seemed to be dozing peacefully, Gervaise gave in to Lantier, who was calling her from his room, telling her to come and get some rest. They left one candle alight, on the floor behind the cupboard. But at about three in the morning, Gervaise leapt out of bed, shivering and in a panic. She thought she'd felt a cold breath pass over her body. The candle had burned out, and she groped around feverishly in the dark for her petticoat. She made her way to the little room, bumping into the furniture, and lit a small lamp. The heavy silence of the night was broken only by the two deep notes of Coupeau's snoring. Nana was lying on her back, breathing gently through her full lips. Gervaise lowered the lamp, setting great shadows dancing, and lit up Maman Coupeau's face; it was very white, her head had rolled sideways, and her eyes were open. She was dead.

Quietly, without crying out, and icy cold, Gervaise went back to Lantier's room, moving carefully in the dark. He'd gone back to sleep. She bent down and said softly:

'It's all over, she's dead.'

At first, heavy with sleep and only half awake, he growled:

'Just shut up and lie down. There's nothing we can do if she's dead.'

Then, propping himself up on one elbow, he asked:

'What's the time?'

'Three o'clock.'

'Only three! Get back into bed then. You'll catch cold. We'll deal with it in the morning.'

But she didn't listen, and got fully dressed. He snuggled back under the blanket, his face to the wall, muttering that women always had funny ideas. Why be in a hurry to tell everybody there was a death in the house? It wasn't a very pleasant thing, in the middle of the night, and he was annoyed at having his sleep spoilt by such a gloomy thought. Gervaise took all her things back to her own bedroom, even her hairpins, sat down, and had a good cry, now that there was no danger of being caught with the hatter. Deep down, she was very fond of Maman Coupeau, and although at first she'd felt only fear and annoyance that she'd chosen such an inconvenient time to go, she now felt very sad. She wept all alone, loudly, in the silence, while Coupeau snored on: he was deaf to the world, she'd called him and shaken him, but decided to leave him in peace, thinking that if he woke up it would only be one more bother. When she went back to the body, she found Nana sitting up, rubbing her eyes. The child realized what had happened and, perverted little creature that she was, craned her neck to get a better view of her grandmother; she said nothing, but trembled a little, taken aback and yet pleased at this sight of death, which she'd been looking forward to for two days, like something naughty that children are not allowed to see or know about. Seeing this white mask, so taut and drawn by the last gasp for life, the pupils of her kittenish eyes dilated and she felt her spine tingle as it did when she stood glued to the glass door, spying on things that little brats like her had no business watching.

'Come on, get up,' said her mother quietly. 'I don't want you to stay here.'

She hopped reluctantly out of the bed, keeping her head turned and continuing to stare at the dead woman. Gervaise couldn't think where to put Nana for the rest of the night. She'd decided to make her get dressed when Lantier, in trousers and slippers, walked into the room; he hadn't been able to get back to sleep and was a little ashamed of his behaviour. That solved it.

'She can sleep in my bed,' he said. 'There's plenty of room.'

Nana looked up at her mother and Lantier with her big bright eyes, and put on the silly baby-like expression she assumed on New Year's Day when people gave her chocolates. She needed no encouragement; off she went in her nightie, her bare feet hardly touching the floor; she slid like a snake into the bed, which was still nice and warm, and stretched out, her little body hardly making a bump under the blanket. Each time her mother came in, she saw her lying there, her eyes gleaming, wide awake, very still, very flushed, clearly turning lots of things over in her mind.

Meanwhile, Lantier had been helping Gervaise to dress Maman Coupeau, and it was no small job, because the old lady was a good weight. No one would have thought she was so plump and so white-skinned. They'd put stockings on her, a white petticoat, a bodice, and a cap—in short, her best things. Coupeau was still snoring on his two notes, one deep, which went to the bottom of the scale, the other sharp and high-pitched: it was like church music, the sort they play on Good Friday. So, when the corpse had been dressed and decently laid out, Lantier poured himself a glass of wine, to pick himself up, for he was feeling a bit queasy. Gervaise was rummaging in the chest of drawers for a little copper crucifix she'd brought with her from Plassans, but then she remembered that Maman Coupeau herself must have sold it. They lit the stove and spent the rest of the night dozing on chairs, finishing the bottle of wine Lantier had opened, fretful and sulky with each other, as if they were somehow to blame for the death.

At about seven, before it was light, Coupeau finally woke up. When he was told what had happened, he stayed dry-eyed at first, not sure what to say, thinking it might be some kind of joke. Then he threw himself on the floor next to his mother, kissed her, and cried his eyes out, shedding such great tears that he made the sheet wet by wiping his face with it. Gervaise started sobbing again, very touched by her husband's grief, and feeling quite warm towards him; yes, deep down, he was a better man than she'd thought. Coupeau's distress was mixed in with a dreadful hangover. He kept running his fingers through his hair, he had the foul taste in his mouth he always had the morning after, and he was still a bit tipsy despite his ten hours' sleep. Clenching his fists, he started wailing. God in heaven! His poor mother, whom he loved so much, dead and gone! And his splitting headache was killing him! It was like having a crown of burning coals on his head, and now his heart was being torn out as well! No, fate was too cruel to torment a man so!

'Come on, mate,' said Lantier, helping him to his feet. 'You've got to pull yourself together.'

He poured him a glass of wine, but Coupeau wouldn't have it.

'What's the matter with me? I've got a taste of copper in me throat. It's because of Maman: when I saw 'er, I got this taste of copper. Maman! Oh God! Maman, Maman…'

And he started crying again, like a child. All the same, he did drink a glass of wine, to put out the fire in his chest. Lantier soon made himself scarce, on the pretext of telling the family and registering the death at the town hall. He needed some fresh air. So he didn't hurry, smoked a few cigarettes, and enjoyed the cold morning breeze. When he left Madame Lerat's in Batignolles, he even went into a local café for a hot cup of coffee. And he stayed there a good hour, thinking.

Meanwhile, by nine o'clock, the family had gathered at the laundry, where the shutters were kept closed. Lorilleux didn't shed a tear; in any case, he had an urgent job on, and went back almost immediately to his workshop, after standing about for a couple of minutes with a suitably mournful face. Madame Lorilleux and Madame Lerat had kissed the Coupeaus and were dabbing a few tears from their eyes. But Madame Lorilleux, having cast a quick glance round the little room where the corpse lay, suddenly piped up to say it wasn't the done thing, to put a lighted lamp next to a dead body; you had to have candles. So Nana was sent out to buy a packet of candles, long ones. Bless me! If you happened to die at Gimpy's, she'd lay you out in a pretty odd way! How clueless she was, she didn't even know what to do with a corpse! Hadn't she ever buried anyone before? Madame Lerat had to go up to her neighbours to borrow a crucifix, and the one she came back with was too big, a cross of black wood with a painted cardboard Christ nailed to it, which covered the whole of Maman Coupeau's chest and looked as if it was crushing her with its weight. After that, they looked for some holy water, but nobody had any, and it was Nana again who had to run to the church to fetch some in a bottle. In a trice, the room looked quite different: a candle was burning on a little table, next to a glass of holy water with a sprig of boxwood in it. Now, if anyone called, at least it would look decent. And they arranged the chairs in a circle in the shop, to receive people.

Lantier didn't come back until eleven. He'd made enquiries at the undertaker's.

'The coffin costs twelve francs,' he reported. 'If you want a Mass, it'll cost another ten. Then there's the hearse, and the cost of that varies according to the trappings...'

'Oh, there's no point in that,' muttered Madame Lorilleux, looking up with a surprised and worried expression on her face. 'It wouldn't bring Maman back, would it? We mustn't spend more than we can afford.'

'Of course not,' replied the hatter. 'I only got the figures so you'd know... Tell me what you want, and after lunch I'll go and see to it.'

They talked in hushed tones, in the dim light that filtered in through the shutters. The door of the little room stood wide open, and through the gaping hole came the heavy silence of death. Children's laughter was rising up from the courtyard, where a group of kids was dancing round in the pale winter sunlight. Suddenly, Nana's voice was heard; she'd slipped away from the Boches', where she'd been sent, and was issuing orders in her shrill tones. The kids'

heels beat time on the cobbles, and the words they were singing rose
into the air like a flock of jabbering birds:

> 'Our donkey, silly ass,
> Has gone an' 'urt 'er leg
> So Madame's dolled 'er up
> In a dinky sock, tra la,
> And lilac shoes, tra la la la,
> Lilac shoes, tra la!'

After a pause, Gervaise said:

'We don't have much money, of course, but we do want to do things
properly. Just because Maman Coupeau didn't leave us anything is no
reason to shove her in the ground like a dog. No, we should have
a Mass, and a nice hearse.'

'And who's going to pay for it?' asked Madame Lorilleux fiercely.
'Not us, we lost money last week; and not you either, because you're
stony broke. Perhaps you can see now where it's got you, wanting to
show off all the time!'

When they asked Coupeau what he thought, he mumbled something, made a gesture of indifference, and carried on dozing on his
chair. Madame Lerat, however, said she'd pay her share. She agreed
with Gervaise, they ought to do things properly. So the pair of them
worked out the sum on a bit of paper: altogether, it would come to
about ninety francs, because they decided, after much discussion, on
a hearse with a narrow pall.

'There are three of us,' concluded Gervaise. 'If we each pay thirty
francs, it won't ruin us.'

But Madame Lorilleux replied angrily:

'Well, not me! Not me! It's not because of the thirty francs. I'd give
a hundred thousand if I had them, and if it'd bring Maman Coupeau
back. But I can't abide all this showing off. You've got your shop, and
you want to show off in front of everybody. Well, we won't be part of
it. We don't give ourselves airs. You can do as you like. You can put
plumes on the hearse if that's what takes your fancy.'

'Nobody's asking you for anything,' Gervaise replied after a pause.
'I'd rather sell myself than have anything to reproach myself with.
I kept Maman Coupeau without your help and I can bury her without
your help just as well. I'm telling you straight, as I did before: I take
in stray cats, and that's why I'd never leave your mother in the gutter.'

At this, Madame Lorilleux burst into tears, and Lorilleux had to persuade her not to leave. The quarrel became so noisy that Madame Lerat, who was doing her best to calm them, felt impelled to go over to the little room and have a quick look at the corpse, as if she half expected the old woman to be awake and listening to what was being said about her just a few feet away. At that moment, the little girls in the courtyard started dancing and singing again, with Nana's shrill voice dominating the others:

> 'Our donkey, silly ass,
> Has got a tummy ache
> So Madame's dolled 'er up
> In a dinky tummy band, tra la,
> And lilac shoes, tra la la la,
> Lilac shoes, tra la!'

'My God, those kids don't half get on your nerves with their singing!' Gervaise said to Lantier. She was now very upset, almost crying with frustration and distress. 'Go and shut 'em up, and send Nana back to Madame Boche with a good kick up the you-know-what!'

Madame Lerat and Madame Lorilleux went off to have a bite to eat, promising to come back later. The Coupeaus sat down at table to have some cold meats, but they had no appetite and hardly dared to let their forks make a noise on the plate. They felt very confused and upset at having poor Maman Coupeau lying there like a millstone round their necks; it was as if she filled every room. Their lives had been turned upside down. At first, they wandered about not finding what they were looking for, and they ached in every limb as if they all had a hangover. Lantier went off again to the undertaker's, with Madame Lerat's thirty francs and sixty that Gervaise, her hair flying and looking like a madwoman, had rushed over to borrow from Goujet. In the afternoon, a few visitors came, neighbours dying of curiosity who turned up heaving sighs and rolling their eyes pathetically; they'd go into the little room, stare at the corpse while making the sign of the cross and shaking the sprig of boxwood dipped in the holy water, after which they'd sit in the shop and talk interminably about the dear departed, never tiring of repeating the same phrases for hours on end. Mademoiselle Remanjou had noticed that her right eye was still open; Madame Gaudron kept saying that she had a wonderful complexion for her age; and Madame Fauconnier couldn't get over the fact that she'd seen her having a cup of coffee three days before. Really, you could be here one minute and gone the next, everyone should be ready. By evening the Coupeaus had started to have had enough. It was just too much for a family, to have to keep a body so long. The government should have made a new law about it. There was the evening, a whole night, and all the next morning still to come! It would never end. When you can't cry any more, your sorrow turns to anger, doesn't it, and you might do something you shouldn't. Maman Coupeau, lying stiff and silent in the little room, seemed everywhere present in the house, like a great burden weighing everybody down. In spite of itself, the family fell back into its usual routine, and lost the respect due to death.

'Have a bite to eat with us,' Gervaise said to Madame Lerat and Madame Lorilleux when they reappeared. 'We're all too miserable, we should stay together.'

They laid the supper things on the worktable. The sight of the plates reminded everybody of the great meals they'd had there. Lantier had come back. Lorilleux came down again. A pastry-cook had brought round a pie, because Gervaise didn't feel up to cooking herself. Just as they were sitting down, Boche appeared, saying that Monsieur Marescot was asking if he could pay his respects, and the landlord made his entry, looking very solemn and wearing his decoration on his frock coat. He nodded without saying a word, and went straight to the little room, where he knelt down.

He looked most devout: he prayed with the rapt expression of a priest, then made the sign of the cross in the air while sprinkling holy water on the body with the sprig of boxwood. The whole family had got up from the table and stood watching, deeply impressed. Having finished his devotions, Monsieur Marescot came back into the shop and said to the Coupeaus:

'I've come for the two quarters' rent. Can you settle up?'

'No, Monsieur, not really,' stammered Gervaise, quite put out at having this mentioned in front of the Lorilleux. 'You see, what with all our troubles…'

'Yes, of course, but we all have our troubles,' replied the landlord, spreading out his huge workman's hands. 'I'm very sorry, but I can't wait any longer. If I don't have the money the day after tomorrow, I'll be forced to have you evicted.'

Gervaise, her eyes full of tears, clasped her hands and looked imploringly at the landlord. He shook his big bony head to indicate that supplications were useless. Besides, the respect due to the dead forebade all discussion. He discreetly withdrew.

'My apologies for disturbing you,' he murmured. 'Don't forget, the day after tomorrow.'

And as he passed the little room again on his way out, he paid his last respects to the body with a devout genuflection through the open door.

At first they ate quickly so as not to seem to be enjoying their meal. But they dallied over the dessert, feeling they needed to relax a little. From time to time Gervaise or one of the two sisters, their mouths full and still holding their napkins, would get up and have a quick look in the little room; and when they sat down again, still chewing, the others would look at them for a second to see if everything was all right in there. But as time wore on, they got up less often and Maman Coupeau was forgotten. They'd made a big pot of coffee, very strong, so they could stay awake all night. The Poissons came at eight. They were offered a drink. At that point, Lantier, who'd been studying Gervaise's face, seemed to seize an opportunity he'd been waiting for all day. As they were talking about the awfulness of landlords who came and demanded their money in a house where there'd been a death, Lantier suddenly said:

'That bastard's an absolute Jesuit, acting all religious like that! If I was you, I'd tell 'im what he can do with his shop!'

Gervaise, totally worn out, her nerves all frayed, replied instinctively:

'Yes, you're right, I won't wait for the bailiffs. I'm sick of it all, really sick of it all.'

The Lorilleux, delighted at the thought that Gimpy wouldn't have the shop any more, warmly approved. People had no idea how much a shop costs. Even if she earned only three francs working for somebody else, she wouldn't have any expenses and she wouldn't run the risk of losing a lot of money. They got Coupeau to echo what they said; drinking non-stop, he was still in a very maudlin state, crying all by himself into his plate. As Gervaise seemed to be coming round, Lantier gave the Poissons a wink. Whereupon Virginie took up the theme, saying in her smooth-tongued way:

'You know, we could work something out between us. I could take over the rest of the lease and fix things up with the landlord. That way you wouldn't have anything to worry about any more.'

'No thanks,' replied Gervaise, giving herself a shake as if she felt a chill. 'I know how to get the money, if I want to. I'll work; I've got my two arms, thank God, to get me out of trouble.'

'You can discuss it later,' Lantier hastened to say. 'Now isn't the time. Tomorrow perhaps.'

At that moment Madame Lerat, who'd gone into the little room, uttered a faint cry. She'd had a fright, because she'd found the candle burnt out. They all fussed about until they'd lighted another, shaking their heads and saying that it wasn't a good sign when the light went out beside a corpse.

The wake began. Coupeau had lain down, not to sleep, he said, but to think, and within five minutes he was snoring. Nana cried when they sent her off to the Boches', for she'd been looking forward all day to sleeping in her special friend Lantier's big warm bed. The Poissons stayed until midnight. After a while they made some mulled wine in a salad bowl, because the coffee had made the ladies very edgy. The conversation took a sentimental turn. Virginie talked about the country; she'd like to be buried at the edge of a wood, with wild flowers on her grave. Madame Lerat already had the sheet for her shroud, which she kept in a cupboard and scented with lavender; she wanted something nice to smell while she pushed up the daisies. Then, suddenly changing the subject, the policeman described how he'd arrested a tall, nice-looking girl that morning, for stealing from a pork-butcher's shop; when they'd stripped her at the station, they'd found ten sausages hanging round her body, front and rear. When Madame Lorilleux said disgustedly that she'd never eat any of those sausages, they all had a good chuckle. The wake was livening up, while still observing the proprieties. But just as they were finishing the mulled wine, a strange sound, like gently running water, came from the little room. They all looked at each other.

'It's nothing,' Lantier said calmly, lowering his voice. 'She's empty-ing out.'

They all nodded, reassured by this explanation, and put their glasses down on the table.

Eventually the Poissons left. Lantier went too, saying he'd stay with a friend, so his bed would be free for the ladies to rest on for an hour or so in turns. Lorilleux went up to bed alone, saying this was the first time this had happened since he was married. Then Gervaise and the two sisters, alone with the sleeping Coupeau, settled down round the stove, on which they stood the coffee to keep it hot. There they sat, huddled together, bending forward with their hands under their aprons and their noses close to the fire, speaking very softly in the dead silence of the sleeping neighbourhood. Madame Lorilleux was complaining that she didn't have a black dress and would've preferred not to have to buy one, because they were so hard up; and she asked Gervaise whether Maman Coupeau had kept the black skirt they'd given her for her birthday. Gervaise had to go and find the skirt. Yes, it would do all right, if it was taken in at the waist. But Madame Lorilleux also wanted any old linen, and mentioned the bed, the cupboard, and the two chairs, and looked round for any small items that would have to be shared out. There was nearly a quarrel. Madame Lerat smoothed things over, and she was quite fair-minded, saying that since the Coupeaus had looked after the old lady, they were certainly entitled to have her few bits and pieces. Then the three of them dozed off again over the stove, after lapsing into an endless stream of gossip. Every now and then they shook themselves awake, drank some coffee, and poked their heads round the door of the little room, where the candle, which they were supposed not to trim, was burning with a sad red flame made bigger by the misshapen, sooty wick. Towards morning they began to shiver, despite the heat of the stove. Too much talking had left them tense and exhausted; their mouths were dry and their eyes were sore. Madame Lerat threw herself on Lantier's bed and started snoring like a man, while the other two, their heads drooping and touching their knees, slept by the fire. At dawn they awoke with a start. Maman Coupeau's candle had gone out again. And as the soft trickling sound could be heard once more in the darkness, Madame Lorilleux, as if to reassure herself, repeated the explanation aloud:

'She's emptying out,' she said, lighting another candle.

The funeral was set for ten-thirty. What a nice morning to look forward to, especially on top of the night and the day before! Although Gervaise was flat broke, she'd have given a hundred francs to anybody prepared to come and take Maman Coupeau away three hours earlier. No, however much you love somebody, when they're dead they become a burden; in fact, the more you love them, the quicker you want them out of the way.

Fortunately the morning of a funeral is full of distractions. There are all sorts of preparations to take care of. First, they had breakfast. Then Père Bazouge turned up, the undertaker's assistant from the sixth floor, bringing the coffin and a sack of bran.

'This is for 'ere, right?' he said, and put down the coffin, which made a creaking noise because it was new.

But just as he tossed the sack of bran next to it, he gaped in astonishment on seeing Gervaise standing before him.

'Beg pardon, sorry, I've made a mistake,' he stammered. 'They told me it was for 'ere.'

He'd already picked up the sack again, and Gervaise had to shout at him:

'No, leave it, it *is* for here.'

'Damn and blast it! Why can't they explain things properly!' he went on, slapping his thigh. 'I get it now, it's for the old girl.'

Gervaise had gone as white as a sheet. Père Bazouge had thought the coffin was for her. He was still talking, trying to apologize as nicely as he could.

'Y'see, they told me yesterday someone 'ad popped off, on the ground floor. So of course I thought… Y'know, in our line of business these things go in one ear and out the other. But anyway, let me say good for you! The later the better, eh? Even though life's not always much fun. Not much fun at all.'

As she listened she backed away, afraid he might grab hold of her with his big dirty hands and carry her off in his box. Once before, on her wedding night, he'd told her he knew women who'd thank him if he came to take them away. Well, she hadn't got to that stage yet! The idea sent a cold shiver down her spine. Her life was in a mess, but she didn't want to say goodbye to it just yet; no, she'd rather starve for years than have it all over and done with in a second.

'He's pissed,' she muttered, with a mixture of disgust and fear. 'They should at least not send us pisspots. They charge enough.'

At this, he became all sarcastic and rude.

'All right, love, it'll do for another time. Don't worry, I'll be ready when you are! Just say the word. I'm the ladies' comforter. And there's no need to look down your nose at Père Bazouge, 'cos he's 'eld real posh ladies in 'is arms, much posher than you. They didn't mind 'im takin' care of 'em, they were 'appy to carry on snoozin' in the dark.'

'That's enough, Bazouge!' Lorilleux said sternly, attracted by the sound of voices. 'Jokes like that are uncalled for. If we made a complaint, you'd be sacked. Go on, 'op it—you've got no respect for principles.'

The undertaker's assistant took himself off, but for some time they could hear him muttering to himself in the street:

'Principles? What sort of principles? There's no such thing as principles. There's only respectability.'

At last, it struck ten. The hearse was late. People were already in the shop, friends and neighbours, Monsieur Madinier, Mes-Bottes, Madame Gaudron, Mademoiselle Remanjou; and every few minutes a man or a woman would poke their head out through the open doorway, between the closely shuttered windows, to see if the slow old hearse was coming or not. The family had assembled in the back room and were shaking hands with everyone. There were short silences, punctuated by bursts of whispering—a nervous, feverish wait and brief rustlings of skirts as Madame Lorilleux hunted for her handkerchief or Madame Lerat looked around for a prayer book she could borrow. Each person on arriving could see the open coffin standing in the middle of the little room, in front of the bed; and, despite themselves, they couldn't help looking at it out of the corner of their eye, calculating that fat old Maman Coupeau would never fit into it. They looked at each other, all obviously thinking the same thing without actually putting it into words. But then there was a flurry of activity outside the door. Monsieur Madinier came in and, opening his arms wide, announced in solemn, formal tones:

'They're here!'

It still wasn't the hearse. Four undertaker's assistants filed in briskly, with the red faces and thickened hands of removal men, their filthy black clothes worn thin and shiny from constantly rubbing against coffins. Père Bazouge was in the lead, very drunk but looking very dignified: he always pulled himself together as soon as he was on a job. They said not a word, their heads slightly bent, already weighing Maman Coupeau with their eyes. And they didn't hang about. The poor old girl was packed away in the twinkling of an eye. The shortest of the group, a young man with a squint, had emptied the bran into the coffin and was kneading it as he spread it out, as if making bread. Another, a tall thin one with a face full of mischief, laid the sheet on top of the bran. Then: one, two, three, hup! All four took hold of the body and lifted it, two at the feet and two at the head. It was as quick as tossing a pancake. The onlookers might have thought Maman Coupeau had jumped into the coffin herself. She'd slipped in as if she belonged there, fitting perfectly, so perfectly that they heard her rub against the new wood. She touched all round, just like a picture in a frame. So she did fit after all, which amazed everybody; obviously, she must have shrunk since the day before. Meanwhile, the undertaker's men had stood up and were waiting; the short one with the squint held the lid as an invitation to the family to make its last farewells, while Bazouge put some nails in his mouth and held the hammer at the ready. Then Coupeau, his two sisters, Gervaise, and some of the others knelt down and kissed the departing parent, their hot tears rolling down over the stiff, ice-cold face. The sobbing went on for some time, the lid came down, and Père Bazouge drove in his nails as expertly as a packer in a warehouse, two taps for each, so that they could no longer hear themselves sobbing in the din of this carpentry work. It was over. They were now ready to go.

'Fancy showing off at a time like this!' said Madame Lorilleux to her husband when she saw the hearse in front of the door.

The hearse was the sensation of the neighbourhood. The tripe-shop woman called out to the grocer's boys to look, the little watch-maker came out on to the pavement, the neighbours all leaned out of their windows. And everyone talked about the pall, with its white cotton fringe. The Coupeaus would have done better to pay their debts, wouldn't they? But, as Lorilleux said, when you're proud, it always shows, no matter what.

'It's terrible!' Gervaise was saying about the chain-makers, at the same time. 'To think those skinflints haven't even brought a bunch of violets for their own mother!'

It was true, the Lorilleux had come empty-handed. Madame Lerat had brought a wreath of artificial flowers, and on the coffin there was also a wreath of immortelles and a bouquet which the Coupeaus had purchased. The undertaker's men must have given a mighty heave to lift the coffin and put it on the hearse. The procession took a long time to get organized. It was led by Coupeau and Lorilleux, wearing frock coats and carrying their hats; Coupeau, whose maudlin state had been stoked by two early morning glasses of white wine, was leaning on his brother-in-law's arm, his legs shaky and his head aching. Then came the men, Monsieur Madinier very solemn and all in black; Mes-Bottes, with a coat over his smock; Boche, whose yellow trousers seemed screamingly out of place; Lantier, Gaudron, Bibi-la-Grillade, Poisson, and several others. Then came the ladies: Madame Lorilleux, trailing Maman Coupeau's made-over skirt, and Madame Lerat wearing a shawl to hide her improvised mourning, a blouse trimmed with lilac; and behind them came Virginie, Madame Gaudron, Madame Fauconnier, Mademoiselle Remanjou, and the rest. When the hearse, after an initial shudder, set off slowly down the Rue de la Goutte-d'Or, amid signs of the cross and raising of hats, the four undertaker's men took the lead, two in front and the other two on either side. Gervaise had stayed behind to lock up the shop. She handed Nana over to Madame Boche and ran to join the procession, while the little girl, holding the concierge's hand under the archway, watched with enormous interest as her grandmother disappeared down the street in that fabulous carriage.

Just as Gervaise, quite out of breath, was catching up with the procession, Goujet appeared from the opposite direction. He joined the men, but turned round and greeted her with a little nod, and in such a nice way that she suddenly felt very unhappy and started to cry again. She was no longer weeping for Maman Coupeau, she was weeping for something terrible, she couldn't say exactly what, which she found unbearable. All the way to the church, she held her handkerchief to her eyes. Madame Lorilleux, whose puffy cheeks were dry, kept giving her sidelong glances, as if accusing her of putting on an act.

The ceremony was quickly dealt with, though the Mass dragged on a bit because the priest was very old. Mes-Bottes and Bibi-la-Grillade chose to stay outside, because of the collection. Monsieur Madinier spent the entire ceremony studying the priests, and he communicated his findings to Lantier: those jokers spewing out their Latin had no idea what it was they were gabbling: they did a burial the same way they did a baptism or a wedding, it didn't mean a thing to them. Then Monsieur Madinier criticized all the ceremonial stuff, the candles and the mournful voices, the whole show put on for the families. Really, you lost your loved ones twice, once at home and again in the church. And all the men agreed with him, because yet another painful moment came when, at the end of the Mass, there was a strange mumbling of prayers and the mourners had to file past the body and sprinkle holy water. Fortunately the cemetery* wasn't far away, the little cemetery of La Chapelle, a bit of garden just off the Rue Marcadet. The procession, when it arrived, had more or less broken up; everybody was chatting about their own affairs as they clumped along. The hard ground reverberated, and they would have liked to stamp their feet to keep warm. The gaping hole, beside which the coffin was laid, was already frozen, white and stony as in a chalk quarry; the mourners, grouped round little piles of gravel, were not amused at having to wait in the cold and stare at the hole. Finally a priest in a surplice emerged from a little hut; he was shivering and you could see his breath steaming with every *De profundis* he uttered. After the last sign of the cross he rushed off, clearly not wanting to start over again. The gravedigger picked up his shovel, but the ground was so hard that he could only loosen big heavy clods, which made an impressive sound as they dropped on to the coffin, a regular bombardment, such a cannonade that you'd have thought the wood would crack. However self-centred you might be, it's a sound that breaks your heart. The weeping began again. Even when they'd left and were out of the cemetery, they could still hear the thuds. Mes-Bottes, blowing on his fingers, loudly declared: 'My God, poor old Maman Coupeau isn't going to be very warm!'

'Ladies and gents,' said Coupeau to the little group of friends who were still in the street with the family, 'please let us offer you something...'

And he led the way into A la Descente du Cimetière,* a bar in the Rue Marcadet. Gervaise stayed outside on the pavement and called to Goujet, who was moving off after giving her another nod. Why wouldn't he have a glass of wine? But he was in a hurry to get back to work. They stood looking at each other for a few moments in silence.

'I'm sorry about the sixty francs,' Gervaise said at last. 'I was going half mad, and I thought of you...'

'Oh, that's all right, there's no need to say sorry,' he interrupted. 'You know I'm always ready to help, if you're in trouble. But don't say anything to my mother—she's got her own ideas and I don't want to upset her.'

She went on looking at him; and seeing him so kind and so sad, with his wonderful golden beard, she was on the point of accepting the proposal he'd made long ago, to go away with him so they could be happy together somewhere. Then another wicked thought occurred to her, to borrow the two quarters' rent, at whatever cost. Trembling, she went on in a caressing tone:

'We're still friends, aren't we?'

He nodded and replied:

'Yes, of course, we'll always be friends. But you must understand, it's all over.'

And he strode away, leaving Gervaise stunned, his last words ringing in her ears like the tolling of a church bell. As she went into the bar she could hear, deep inside her: 'It's all over, it's all over; well, I've got nothing left to live for if it's all over.' She sat down, swallowed some bread and cheese, and emptied a full glass somebody had put in front of her.

It was a long, low-ceilinged room on the ground floor, with two large tables. Bottles of wine, hunks of bread, and big wedges of Brie were set out in a row. It was just a snack, without plates or a table-cloth. Further away, near the roaring stove, the four undertaker's men were finishing their lunch.

'Ah well,' declared Monsieur Madinier, 'it comes to us all. The old make way for the young. Your place will seem very empty when you get back.'

'Oh, my brother's giving notice,' Madame Lorilleux cut in. 'That shop costs the earth.'

They'd been working on Coupeau. Everybody was urging him to give up the lease. Even Madame Lerat, who'd been well in with Lantier and Virginie for some time, and was quite tickled by the idea that they must fancy each other, talked about bankruptcy and prison, and assumed a terrified look. Then, suddenly, the roofer got angry, his mawkishness turning to rage under the influence of the wine.

'Listen!' he yelled, shoving his face close to his wife's. 'Bloody well listen to me! You always 'ave things your way. Well, this time we're going to do what I want.'

'Ha!' said Lantier, 'When did you ever get her to agree to anything by just talking to her? You'll need a mallet to bang it into her skull.'

And they both went at her for a while. Not that it prevented everybody's jaws from carrying on working. The Brie was disappearing, the wine was flowing. Meanwhile, Gervaise was weakening under the onslaught. She said nothing, because her mouth was always full as she kept stuffing it with bread and cheese as if she'd been starving. When they started to flag, she looked up and said quietly:

'That's enough. I don't care about the shop any more. I'm sick of it. D'you understand? I don't care! I've finished with it!'

At this, they ordered more bread and cheese, and started to talk business. The Poissons would take over the lease and would also be responsible for the two overdue quarters. Boche, with a self-important air, agreed to the arrangement in the name of the land-lord. He even offered the Coupeaus there and then the lease on a new place: the vacant rooms on the sixth floor, on the same corridor as the Lorilleux. As for Lantier, well, he'd like to keep his room, if that was all right with the Poissons. The policeman nodded: no, he didn't mind at all; friends are friends, whatever their political views. And Lantier, not concerning himself further with the transfer of the lease, now that he'd settled his own little piece of business, took a huge chunk of bread and spread it with Brie; he leaned back and ate it with concentrated pleasure, his face flushed, glowing with sly sat-isfaction as he looked at Gervaise, and then Virginie, through half-closed eyes.

'Hey! Père Bazouge!' called Coupeau, 'come and 'ave a drink. We're not stuck-up, we're all workers.'

The four undertaker's men were on the point of leaving, but came back to share a drink. They didn't mean to complain, but the lady just now did weigh a fair bit and was worth a glass of wine. Père Bru was staring hard at Gervaise, but said not a word out of place. Beginning to feel uncomfortable, she got up and left the men, who were now quite pickled. Coupeau, pissed as a newt, started blubbering again, saying it was because of his grief.

That evening, when Gervaise was back home, she just sat on a chair, in a daze. The rooms seemed huge and empty. Of course it was good to have the place off their backs. But it wasn't just Maman Coupeau she'd left at the bottom of that hole in the little cemetery in the Rue Marcadet. Too many things had gone; what she'd buried that day was part of her own life, her shop, her pride as an employer, and other feelings as well. Yes, the walls were bare, and so was her heart, it was a complete washout, a fall into the gutter. She felt too weary to pick herself up; she'd pull herself together later on, if she could.

When Nana was getting ready for bed at ten o'clock that night she started crying and made a scene. She wanted to sleep in Maman Coupeau's bed. Her mother tried to scare her, but she was too precocious; death merely filled her with intense curiosity. So, to have some peace and quiet, they let her lie down where Maman Coupeau had lain. The kid liked big beds in which she could stretch out and roll around. That night she slept very soundly in the lovely tickly warmth of the feather bed.

CHAPTER X

The Coupeaus' new lodgings were on the sixth floor, staircase B. You went past Mademoiselle Remanjou's and took the corridor on the left. Then you had to turn again. The first door was the Bijards'. Almost opposite, in a stuffy hole under a little staircase that led to the roof, slept Père Bru. Two doors further on you came to Bazouge's. Finally, next to Bazouge, were the Coupeaus, with one room and a box room overlooking the yard. And a bit further on, down the corridor, there were only two more families before you reached the Lorilleux at the far end.

One room and a box room, that was all. That was where the Coupeaus were roosting now. And the larger room was no bigger than your hand. They had to do everything there, sleep, eat, the lot. Nana's bed just fitted into the box room; she had to undress in the main room and they left the door open at night so she wouldn't suffocate. It was so small that Gervaise had left a few things for the Poissons when she gave up the shop, because she couldn't fit everything in. With the bed, table, and four chairs, the place was chock-a-block. Even so, she'd been unable to part with her chest of drawers, and she'd cluttered up the floor space with the lumping great thing, which blocked half the window. One of the shutters was broken and couldn't be opened properly, so that made the place even darker. When she wanted to look out into the yard there wasn't room to lean on the sill with her elbows, for she was getting very fat, and had to bend sideways and twist her neck to see anything.

For the first few days she just sat and cried. It seemed too hard to cope with, not being able to move about in her own home after being used to plenty of space. She couldn't breathe, she sat at the window for hours, squeezed between the wall and the chest of drawers, getting a stiff neck. It was the only place where she could breathe freely. But the yard only made her more miserable. Opposite, on the sunny side, she could see her dream of long ago, the fifth-floor window where, every spring, scarlet runners wound their slender stalks round a cat's cradle of string. Her own room was on the shady side, where a pot of mignonette would be dead within a week. No, her life wasn't turning out so well, this wasn't at all the kind of existence she'd hoped for. Instead of having flowers round her as she grew older, she was sinking into the mire. Leaning out one day, she had a strange sensation: she thought she could see herself down there under the archway, near the concierge's lodge, staring up, examining the building for the first time; and this jump back of thirteen years made her heart miss a beat. The yard looked just the same, the bare walls were hardly blacker or more dilapidated; the same stench was coming up from the drain-heads; washing was still drying on lines strung across the windows, with babies' nappies caked with filth; down below, the uneven paving stones were still messy with the locksmith's clinkers and the carpenter's shavings, and in the damp corner by the tap there was even a puddle from the dye-works of the same pretty pale blue as the blue she'd seen that first time. But she herself, now, felt very different, very worn out. To start with, she was no longer down there looking up towards the sky, happy and confident, making plans for a nice home. She was up in a garret in the most miserable part of the building, the dingiest part, where you never saw a single ray of sunshine. That was why she was crying, she could hardly be happy with the way things had turned out.

And yet, once Gervaise began to get used to it, the Coupeaus' life in the new place seemed quite promising. Winter was almost over and the few francs from the furniture they'd sold to Virginie helped them get settled. Then, when the fine weather arrived, they had a stroke of luck. Coupeau was taken on for a job in the country, at Étampes;* and he was there for nearly three months without drinking, cured for a while by the country air. People don't realize how it quenches a boozer's thirst just to get away from the air of Paris, where the streets are saturated with the smell of wine and spirits. When he came back, he looked as fresh as a daisy, and he brought with him four hundred francs, which they used to pay off the two quarters owing on the shop, for which the Poissons had stood as guarantors, as well as the most pressing of their various small debts in the neighbourhood. Gervaise could once more walk down two or three streets she had been avoiding. Of course, she'd gone back to ironing, by the day. Madame Fauconnier, who was very nice as long as you buttered her up, had been good enough to take her back. She even paid her three francs, the rate for a top-grade worker, out of consideration for her former position as an employer. So it looked as if the household should be able to get along all right. And, if they worked and saved,

Gervaise could even see the day when they'd be able to pay everything off and settle down into a decent sort of life. At least, that was what she imagined when she got all excited about the amount of money her husband had earned. When her excitement subsided, she was ready to take life as it came, and said that good times never last.

What the Coupeaus did find very distressing was seeing the Poissons move into their shop. They certainly weren't jealous by nature, but it got on their nerves to hear people deliberately talk in front of them about the wonderful improvements their successors had made. The Boches, and especially the Lorilleux, never tired of going on about it. To listen to them, you'd think there'd never been a finer shop. And they talked about the filthy state the Poissons had found the place in, saying that the cleaning alone had cost thirty francs. After some thought, Virginie had decided on a high-class grocery shop, selling things like sweets, chocolates, coffee, and tea. Lantier had strongly recommended that sort of business, because according to him there were huge amounts of money to be made out of confectionery. The shop was painted black, picked out with gold lines, two classy colours. Two carpenters worked for a week fitting out racks, glass cases, and a counter with shelves for the jars, such as you find in sweetshops. It must have made quite a dent in the little legacy Poisson had been holding in reserve. But Virginie was exultant, and the Lorilleux, abetted by the Boches, didn't spare Gervaise a single rack, glass case, or jar: they loved seeing her face fall. Even if you're not the jealous type, it's maddening when other people step into your shoes and start trampling all over you.

There was also, underneath all this, the man question. It was reported that Lantier had dropped Gervaise. The neighbourhood considered this a very good thing. After all, it brought a bit of respectability back to the street. And all the credit for the break was given to the crafty hatter, who was still the darling of the ladies. People came up with details, claiming he'd had to give Gervaise a few thumps to make her leave him alone, she was so hung up on him. Of course nobody said what the real situation was, because those who might have known found it too simple and not interesting enough. It could be said that Lantier had dropped Gervaise in the sense that he'd stopped having her at his beck and call night and day; but there was no doubt that he went up to see her on the sixth floor whenever he felt like it, because Mademoiselle Remanjou would run into him coming out of the Coupeaus' at the most ungodly hours. In short, their relationship was still going on in a random, casual sort of way, without either of them finding much pleasure in it; an old habit, a matter of mutual convenience, nothing more. But what complicated the situation was that the neighbours, now, had got Lantier and Virginie sleeping between the same sheets. Here again, they were getting ahead of themselves. There was no doubt that he had his eye on the tall brunette, which was hardly surprising, considering that she was replacing Gervaise in every way in the household. In fact there was a joke going round, according to which he'd gone to fetch Gervaise from his neighbour's bed, and come back with Virginie, keeping her with him until daybreak, not recognizing her in the dark. The story made everybody laugh, but in reality he hadn't got that far, and hardly ventured beyond pinching Virginie's bottom. But that didn't stop the Lorilleux from talking indulgently in front of Gervaise about the love affair between Lantier and Madame Poisson, in the hope of making her jealous. The Boches, too, declared to everyone that they'd never seen a more handsome couple. The funny thing in all this was that the Rue de la Goutte-d'Or didn't seem to mind this new *ménage à trois*; oh no, morality, which had been so severe towards Gervaise, was soft on Virginie. Perhaps the smiling indulgence of the street had something to do with the fact that her husband was a policeman.

Fortunately, Gervaise was not given to jealousy. Lantier's infidelities left her unmoved, because it was a long time since warm feelings came into the relationship. She'd heard foul stories, without ever asking to be told, about the hatter's dealings with girls of all sorts, dolled-up things you could pick up in the street at all hours, and it mattered so little to her that she'd gone on indulging him, for she was never angry enough to break off. However, she wasn't able to accept so easily her lover's new fancy. With Virginie it was different. They'd thought it up between them with the sole aim of having a bit of fun at her expense; and while she didn't care what they got up to in bed, she did expect some consideration. So when Madame Lorilleux or some other spiteful creature made a point of saying in her presence that Poisson was now wearing the horns, she'd go very pale, she felt a tightening across her chest and a burning in the pit of her stomach. But she'd bite her lip and take care not to lose her temper, so as not to give her enemies that pleasure. But she must have given Lantier a piece of her mind, because one afternoon Mademoiselle Remanjou thought she heard the sound of a slap. Anyway, there was definitely a row, because Lantier didn't speak to her for two weeks, but he was the one who went and made it up, and the usual routine got going again as if nothing had happened. Gervaise chose to make the best of things; she didn't want to have another scrap with Virginie and make her life even more difficult. She wasn't twenty any more and these days she didn't care that much for men, at least not to the point of getting into a fight over them and risking being run in. But she put it down on the account, along with the other things.

Coupeau found it all great fun. The complaisant husband, who'd turned a blind eye to his own cuckolding, laughed his head off at Poisson's horns. In his own home it didn't count, but when it happened to somebody else he found it hugely funny, and he was mad keen to spot all cases of misbehaviour, when a neighbour's wife became a bit free with her favours. What a duffer that Poisson was! And to think he wore a sword, and felt he had the right to push people around in the street! Then Coupeau had the nerve to start teasing Gervaise. Well, well, her boyfriend had dumped her good and proper! She never had any luck: first off, she'd got nowhere with blacksmiths, and now the hatters were giving her the flick. Obviously, she hadn't picked the right trades. Why not try a bricklayer, a dependable type, someone used to mixing good, solid plaster? Of course he said all this in fun, but it didn't stop Gervaise from feeling quite sick when he stared at her with his little grey eyes as if he wanted to drill the words right into her. When he started to talk dirty she never knew if he was joking or not. A man who's on the booze from one end of the year to the other loses all sense of things, and there are some husbands who are very jealous at twenty, whom drink makes very complaisant on the question of fidelity by the time they're thirty.

You should have seen Coupeau strutting about in the Rue de la Goutte-d'Or! He referred to Poisson as 'the cuckold'. That'd shut the gossips up! It wasn't him who was the cuckold now. Oh, he knew what he knew. If, in the past, he'd seemed not to hear, obviously it was because he didn't like tittle-tattle. Every man knows what he's about and can scratch himself where it itches. Well, he didn't itch and he wasn't going to scratch himself just to please other people. And what about the policeman, could *he* hear what people were saying? Yet this time there was no doubt; the lovers had been seen together, it wasn't just idle talk. And he became quite indignant: he couldn't understand how a man, a government employee at that, could tolerate such scandalous goings-on in his own home. The policeman must like other men's leavings, that was all you could say. On evenings when Coupeau got bored, sitting all alone with his wife up there under the roof, none of this stopped him from going down and dragging Lantier upstairs to join them. He found the place depressing now that his mate was no longer with them. He'd jolly things up between Lantier and Gervaise if he saw they weren't getting along. Damn it all! Who the hell cares what people think? Is there a law against enjoying yourself in your own way? He'd snigger, and his shifty boozer's eyes would shine with broad-minded ideas, ideas about sharing everything with the hatter, to make life more fun. And it was on those evenings especially that Gervaise wasn't sure whether he was joking or not.

While all this was going on Lantier maintained a dignified, fatherly air. Three times he'd averted major quarrels between the Coupeaus and the Poissons. It was in his own interests, of course, that the two households should get on. Thanks to the kind but firm eye he kept on Gervaise and Virginie, they continued to profess great friendship for one another. He ruled over blonde and brunette alike with the serene assurance of a pasha, enjoying the fruits of his scheming. The sly devil was already devouring the Poissons while still digesting the Coupeaus. It was as easy as pie! He'd swallowed one shop and was starting on a second. It sometimes seems that fortune smiles only on men like him.

It was in June of that year that Nana made her first communion. She was nearly thirteen, she'd shot up like nobody's business, and was as cheeky as they come; the year before, she'd been kicked out of her catechism class for bad behaviour, and the priest had only let her back in for fear she'd never return and he'd be sending another heathen out into the world. Nana danced for joy at the thought of the white dress which the Lorilleux, as her godfather and godmother, had promised her; the couple were talking about their present all over the building. Madame Lerat was to give the veil and bonnet, Virginie the purse, and Lantier the prayer book, so that the Coupeaus were able to look forward to the ceremony without worrying too much. And the Poissons, who'd been planning to have a house-warming party, even chose that very day to do so, no doubt on the suggestion of Lantier. They invited the Coupeaus and the Boches, whose daughter was also making her first communion. In the evening, they'd have a nice dinner, a leg of mutton with a few veggies.

It so happened that the evening before, just as Nana was gazing in wonder at the presents spread out on the chest of drawers, Coupeau came home in a dreadful state. The air of Paris was beginning to have its effect again. He started yelling at his wife and daughter, using a drunkard's logic and language that was quite unbefitting in the circumstances. Though Nana herself, it might be said, was starting to become foul-mouthed because of the dirty talk she constantly heard around her. When there was an argument, she thought nothing of calling her mother a bitch or a cow.

'Where's me grub!' the roofer yelled. 'Gimme me grub, you fuckin' bitches! Look at those bloody females with their fancy clothes! I'll shit on all that stuff if I don't get me grub!'

'What a pain he is when he's pissed!' Gervaise muttered impatiently. Turning towards him, she said:

'It's just heating up, so stop botherin' us.'

Nana was playing at being all modest, because she thought it was the appropriate thing to do that evening. She went on gazing at the presents on the chest of drawers, lowering her eyes and pretending not to understand the vile things her father was saying. But when he'd been on a binge the roofer could be an absolute pest. He got up close to her and went on:

'I'll give you white dresses! I suppose it's so you can make yourself some tits with a pair of paper balls down the front, like last Sunday? Yeah, yeah, I know what's goin' on in your 'ead. I see you wiggling your arse! Those glad rags tickle your fancy, don't they? They give you ideas. Get away from 'em, you little bugger! Keep your paws off! Stick 'em in a drawer before I wipe your face with 'em!'

Nana, her eyes still lowered, said nothing. She'd picked up the little bonnet and asked her mother how much it had cost. As Coupeau reached out to grab it, Gervaise pushed him away, and shouted:

'Leave 'er alone! She's bein' nice, she's not doin' any 'arm.'

At this, he really let fly.

'You bitches! Mother 'n' daughter, what a pair. It's a fine thing goin' and swallowin' God's body while makin' eyes at all the men! Just say it's not true, you little tart! I'll dress you up in a sack, an' we'll see if that tickles as much. Yes, in a sack! That might make you think twice about your bloody priests. Why should I want 'em to teach you all about sin? Bloody 'ell, you two 'ad better listen to me!'

This time Nana swung round in a fury, while Gervaise had to hold her arms out to protect the things Coupeau said he was going to rip up. The girl glared at her father and, forgetting what her confessor had told her about behaving nicely, spat out through clenched teeth: 'Pig!'

As soon as Coupeau had finished his meal he was snoring. Next morning he woke up in an excellent mood. He was still a little hung over from the day before, but only enough to make him pleasant. He watched the girl being made ready and became quite sentimental over the white dress, remarking that it took almost nothing to turn that little terror into a proper young lady. In short, as he said, it was natural for a father to be proud of his daughter on a day like that. And you should have seen how smart Nana looked, smiling like a self-conscious bride in her too-short dress. When they went down and she saw Pauline at the door of the lodge, all dressed up too, she studied her carefully, then smiled sweetly, finding Pauline not as well turned out as herself, but done up like a parcel. The two families left together for the church. Nana and Pauline led the way, prayer books in hand, and holding their veils, which were billowing in the wind; they said nothing, bursting with pride as people came out of shops to watch, and putting on pious expressions when they heard comments about how sweet they looked. Madame Boche and Madame Lorilleux hung back because they were exchanging views about Gimpy—a spendthrift whose daughter would certainly not be taking her first communion if her relations hadn't given her everything, yes, everything, even a new shift out of respect for the holy table. Madame Lorilleux was especially concerned about the dress, which was her present, shouting at Nana and calling her a 'dirty thing' every time she got some dust on her skirt by walking too close to the shops.

In church, Coupeau cried the whole time. It was silly, but he couldn't help it. He was overwhelmed by the way the priest spread his arms and the little girls, like angels, walked with their hands together; the organ music made him feel all funny inside, and the lovely smell of the incense made him sniff, as though someone had shoved a bunch of flowers into his face. In short, he was carried away. There was one hymn in particular, something so sweet, while the kids were taking communion, that seemed to enthral him, sending shivers up and down his spine. And all around him, too, people were dabbing their eyes. Yes, it was a wonderful day, the best day of his life. But when they came out of church and he went to have a drink with Lorilleux, who'd stayed dry-eyed and was teasing him, he turned nasty again and started accusing the black-coats of burning devilish herbs in their churches to deprive men of their strength. Anyway, he wasn't making a secret of it, he'd shed a few tears; it just went to show he didn't have a heart of stone. And he ordered another round.

The house-warming at the Poissons' that evening was very jolly. From the beginning of the meal to the end, nothing happened to mar the reign of friendship. However bad things get, there are always good times now and then, when people who hate each other get on fine. Lantier, with Gervaise on his left and Virginie on his right, was charming to both, paying them every attention like a cock who wants peace in his hen house. Opposite them, Poisson wore his usual policeman's expression, dreamy, calm, and stern, maintaining his habit, from long hours on the beat, of staring vacantly into space, apparently thinking about nothing. But the queens of the party were the two girls, Nana and Pauline, who'd been allowed to keep their dresses on; they sat stiffly, afraid of getting stains on themselves, and each time they took a mouthful they were told to keep their heads up and swallow properly. After a while, Nana got fed up with this and dribbled her wine down the front of her dress. This caused a great to-do; the dress was removed immediately and the bodice was rinsed in a glass of water.

Then, over dessert, they talked seriously about the children's futures. Madame Boche had decided that Pauline would go into a workshop where they did pierced work in gold and silver and you could make five or six francs a day. Gervaise wasn't sure yet; Nana hadn't shown any particular flair. She was a real tearaway, of course; she liked that, but she hadn't shown any interest in doing anything else.

'If I were you,' said Madame Lerat, 'I'd get her to be a flower-maker. It's a nice, clean job.'

'Flower-makers are all slags,' muttered Lorilleux.

'Thanks a lot!' replied the widow, pursing her lips. 'You're very charming, I must say. Let me tell you, I'm no soft touch, I don't lie flat on me back as soon as I hear a whistle!'

They all did their best to shut her up.

'Madame Lerat! Really, Madame Lerat!'

Meaningful glances were cast in the direction of the two first com-
municants, who'd stuck their noses in their glasses to keep from giggling. Until then, even the men had been minding their language, out
of a sense of decency. But Madame Lerat paid no attention. What
she'd just said she'd heard in the best company. In any case, she prided
herself on knowing her own mother-tongue; she was often compli-
mented on the way she could discuss any subject, even in front of
children, without ever offending the rules of propriety.

'There are some very respectable women in the flower trade, I'd
have you know!' she shouted. 'They're made the same as other
women, of course, they're not just skin all over. But they know how to
behave, and when they do decide to stray they show a lot of taste in
the men they choose. Yes, they get that from the flowers, and it's
what's kept me so young.'

'Bless me,' interrupted Gervaise, 'I've got nothing against the
flower trade. It's got to be something Nana likes, that's all. There's no
point in going against what a child wants to do in life. Come on, Nana,
don't just sit there, tell us. Would you like to be a flower-maker?'

Nana was bending over her plate, picking up crumbs with her
moistened finger, which she then sucked. She didn't say anything for
a while, just smiling in the wicked way she had.

'Yes, Maman, I'd like that,' she said at last.

So it was arranged right then. Coupeau agreed to have Madame
Lerat take Nana to her workshop in the Rue du Caire* the very next
day. And everyone talked gravely about life's responsibilities. Boche
said that Nana and Pauline were grown-up women now they'd taken
communion. Poisson added that now they should know how to cook,
darn socks, and run a home. There was even talk of them getting
married and having children one day. The kids just listened and
laughed to themselves, wriggling against each other, excited at the
idea of being women, and blushing self-consciously in their white
dresses. But what excited them most was when Lantier asked them
teasingly whether they didn't already have their little husbands.
And they forced Nana to admit that she was very sweet on Victor
Fauconnier, the son of her mother's employer.

'So that's that!' Madame Lorilleux said to the Boches as they were
leaving. 'She's our goddaughter, but if they get her to be a flower-
maker, we won't want anything more to do with her. She'll be just
another tart on the streets. She'll fly the coop within six months.'

As they went up to bed the Coupeaus agreed that everything had gone off well and the Poissons weren't bad people. Gervaise even thought the shop had been nicely set up. She'd expected to find it painful to spend an evening like that in her old home where others, now, were settling in so well, and she was surprised that she hadn't felt angry even for a moment. Nana, as she was undressing, asked her mother whether the dress of the young lady on the second floor who'd got married the previous month was made of muslin like hers.

But that was the last happy day the family would have. During the next two years things went steadily downhill. The winters were especially hard. They managed to find something to eat during the fine weather, but hunger came with the rain and cold; the cupboard was bare and they had nothing but memories to feed on, in their little Siberia of a home. December was a cruel month. It crept in under the door, bringing every kind of hardship, the closing-down of factories, the numbing idleness of hard frosts, the black misery of wet weather. The first winter, they still had a fire sometimes and huddled round the stove, preferring to keep warm rather than eat; the second winter, the stove was unused, and stood there chilling the room, like some mournful cast-iron monument. But what most got them down, finished them off, was having to pay the rent. Oh, the January quarter— when there wasn't a bean in the place and old Boche handed them the bill! It was even colder then, with a terrible north wind. Monsieur Marescot would turn up the following Saturday, wrapped in a heavy overcoat, his big paws stuffed into woollen gloves, talking as usual about turning them out, while out in the street the snow went on falling as if making a bed for them, a bed with white sheets on the pavement. They would have sold their very flesh to pay the rent. It was rent day that emptied the cupboard and kept the stove cold. A wail of lamentation filled the whole building. There was weeping on every floor, the music of misery echoed along the stairs and corridors. If there'd been a death in every family, it wouldn't have produced so terrible a dirge. A real Last Judgement, the end of days, life unliveable, the poor crushed under foot. The woman on the third floor went on the streets for a week, at the corner of the Rue Belhomme. One workman, the bricklayer on the fifth, robbed his employer.

Of course, the Coupeaus had only themselves to blame. However tough things are, you can always get by if you're thrifty and careful— like the Lorilleux, who always produced their rent on the dot, screwed

up in dirty scraps of paper; but really those two lived so frugally that
it was enough to put you off work altogether. Nana wasn't earning
anything yet with her flowers; in fact, her keep was costing them quite
a bit. By this time, Gervaise was no longer well thought of at Madame
Fauconnier's. She seemed to be losing her touch more and more,
making such a mess of her work that her employer had reduced her
pay to two francs, the rate for unskilled labour. Despite that, she was
very proud and touchy, quick to remind everybody that she'd once
had her own business. She'd miss whole days or else she'd flounce out
in a huff; once, for example, she'd been so cross with Madame
Fauconnier for taking on Madame Putois and making her work side
by side with her own former assistant that she'd stayed away for
two weeks. After performances like that she'd be taken back out of
charity, which made her even more resentful. Naturally, at the end of
the week, her pay packet was pretty small. She'd say sourly that, one
of these Saturdays, it would be she who'd have to pay Madame
Fauconnier. As for Coupeau, perhaps he did have work, but if he did
he was certainly donating his wages to the government, because since
his job at Étampes not once had she seen the colour of his money.
When he came home on payday she no longer looked at his hands.
He'd come sauntering in, his pockets empty, often not so much as
a handkerchief in them—bugger it, yes, he'd even lost his snot-rag, or
else some sod, one of his mates, had pinched it. At first he'd make up
figures, invent some cock-and-bull story about ten francs gone on
a whip-round, twenty francs that must have dropped out of his pocket
through a hole he'd show her, or fifty francs to pay off imaginary
debts. After a while, he stopped bothering. The money just went
somewhere, that's all! It wasn't in his pocket, it was in his belly—
another way of bringing it home to his wife, and not very funny. On
the advice of Madame Boche, Gervaise would sometimes lie in wait
for him when he came out of work so she could nab the money while
it was still warm, but that didn't get her very far because his mates
tipped him off, and the money disappeared into his shoes or some
other hiding-place that was even less clean. Madame Boche was very
artful in this respect, because Boche had a way of doing the vanishing
trick with ten-franc coins, which he tucked away in secret hiding-
places so he could buy treats for certain lady friends. She'd inspect
the minutest corners of his clothes and usually find the missing coin
in the peak of his cap, sewn in between the leather and the cloth. But

the roofer was not one to pad his clothes with gold! He put it inside his body, and Gervaise could hardly take her scissors and cut his belly open.

Yes, they had only themselves to blame if they went from bad to worse each season. But you never admit things like that to yourself, especially when you're in the gutter. They blamed it on bad luck and declared that God had it in for them. Their place had become a complete mess, and they fought all day long. But they hadn't actually come to blows yet, except for the odd slap in the heat of an argument. The saddest part of it all was that now they'd opened the cage door and let affection fly out, other feelings had flown away too, like canaries. The kindly warmth of a family, when father, mother, and children are tightly bound to each other, had gone, leaving them shivering and alone in their separate corners. The three of them, Coupeau, Gervaise, and Nana, were as prickly as could be, jumping down each other's throats at the slightest provocation, their eyes full of hatred; it was as if something had broken the mainspring of the family, the mechanism which, when everyone is happy, makes their hearts beat in unison. Gone were the days when Gervaise would be scared stiff if she saw Coupeau working on the edge of a roof, twelve or fifteen metres above the roadway! She wouldn't have given him a shove herself, but if he'd simply fallen—well, bugger it, it would hardly have been a great loss to the world! On days when they were in the middle of a big argument, she'd scream that she hoped they'd soon bring him back home on a stretcher. That was what she was waiting for, it'd make her day. What use was he, the drunken sod, apart from making her cry, eating her out of house and home, and driving her into bad ways. Well then, with men as useless as that you should shove them in the ground as fast as you could, so you could do a jig on their grave to celebrate your freedom. And when the mother said 'Kill 'im!', the daughter answered 'Bash 'im on the head!' Nana would read the accidents column in the paper and make remarks that were quite unnatural in a daughter. Her father had such luck that he'd been knocked down by an omnibus and it hadn't even sobered him up. When the hell was the bastard going to snuff it?

In the midst of this poverty-racked existence, Gervaise's own suffering was made worse by the agonies of hunger she could feel all around her. That corner of the building was the paupers' corner, where three or four families seemed to have made a pact to go without food some days. Their doors might open, but they hardly ever let out any smell of cooking. All along the corridor there was a deathly silence, and the walls rang hollow, like empty stomachs. Occasionally certain sounds could be heard, the wailing of women, the crying of starving kids, or families setting on each other instead of eating. A general cramp in the jaw seemed to leave all these famished mouths gaping open, while chests grew hollow just from breathing the air in which not even a gnat could have survived for want of food. But what Gervaise found most heart-rending was Père Bru in his hole under the stairs. He'd creep in like a dormouse, curling up in a ball to ward off the cold, and lie there for days at a time, on a pile of straw, without moving. Not even hunger got him to come out, for what would be the point of going out and working up an appetite when nobody had invited him for a meal? When he hadn't been seen for three or four days the neighbours would push open his door and look to see if he was still breathing. Yes, he was still alive, only just; even death had forgotten him! Whenever Gervaise had any bread, she'd throw him a few crusts. Even though she was growing embittered and, on account of her husband, hated men, she could still feel genuinely sorry for animals, and Père Bru, the poor old thing, was like a dog to her, a useless animal that not even the slaughterhouse wanted for the skin or the fat. It preyed on her mind to know he was always there, on the other side of the corridor, abandoned by God and man, feeding solely off himself, reverting to the size of a child, withered and dry like an orange left to shrivel on a mantelpiece.

Gervaise also found it very unpleasant to be so close to Bazouge, the undertaker's assistant. A thin partition was all that separated the two rooms. He couldn't stick his finger in his mouth without her hearing. From the moment he came home in the evening she couldn't help hearing every stage of his little routine: the black leather hat landing on the chest of drawers with a thud like a spadeful of earth, the black coat being hung up and brushing against the wall like the wings of some nightbird, then all his black clothing tossed on the floor, forming a pile of funeral trappings in the middle of the room. She could hear him walking about, and listened nervously to his slightest movement, jumping out of her skin if he bumped into the furniture or made a clatter with the dishes. The wretched old drunkard became a kind of obsession, in which vague fear mingled with morbid curiosity. He was merry enough, always pissed, completely off his head on Sundays, forever coughing, spitting, singing silly songs, shouting obscenities, and fighting with the four walls before managing to find his way to bed. She'd go as white as a sheet, wondering what on earth he was up to in there; she imagined the most appalling things, convincing herself that he must have brought back a dead body and was stowing it under his bed. After all, there was a story in the papers about an undertaker's assistant who'd collected the coffins of little children in his room, to save himself a bit of trouble by only having to make one trip to the cemetery. One thing was certain: when Bazouge came in, you could smell death through the partition. You might have thought you were living next to Père-Lachaise, close to all the graves. There was something terrifying about the creature, the way he was always laughing to himself, as if he found his trade a source of amusement. And even when he'd finished his roistering and was flat on his back, he snored in such an extraordinary way that it often made Gervaise hold her breath. She'd lie there for hours straining her ears, imagining that funeral processions were passing through her neighbour's room.

Yes, and the worst of it was that, even in her terror, she felt a compulsion to put her ear to the partition to get a better idea of what was going on. Bazouge fascinated her the way handsome men fascinate virtuous women: they'd like to touch but don't dare because their upbringing prevents them. If fear hadn't held her back, Gervaise would have liked to touch death to get an idea of what it was like. She behaved so oddly sometimes, holding her breath, listening intently, hoping that some movement of Bazouge's would reveal the key to it all, that Coupeau would ask her with a snigger if she'd become keen on the undertaker's man next door. She'd get cross and talk about moving home, because she so hated living near him; but in spite of herself, as soon as the old boy came home, bringing with him his graveyard smell, she'd fall back into her musings, looking nervous and excited like a wife dreaming of tearing up her marriage vows. Hadn't he twice offered to wrap her up and take her away with him to a place where the joy of sleep is so intense that all your woes are instantly forgotten? Perhaps that place really was wonderful. Gradually, the temptation to put it to the test became stronger. She'd have liked to try it for two weeks or a month. Oh, to sleep for a month, especially in winter, the month when the rent was due, when life's troubles were just too much! But it wasn't possible, you had to go on sleeping for ever if you started sleeping for an hour; and that thought chilled her to the bone, and her infatuation with death would vanish in the face of the implacable, everlasting friendship demanded by the earth.

One evening in January, however, she pounded on the partition with both fists. She'd had a terrible week, pushed about by everybody, with no money left, and no heart for anything. That evening she felt quite ill, was slightly feverish, and saw lights dancing before her eyes. So instead of throwing herself out of the window, as she'd thought of doing for a moment, she started banging and shouting:

'Père Bazouge! Père Bazouge!'

The undertaker's assistant was taking off his shoes and singing 'There were three pretty girls'. He must have had a good day at work, because he seemed even more sozzled than usual.

'Père Bazouge! Père Bazouge!' shouted Gervaise, louder still.

Couldn't he hear? He could come and fetch her straight away, just pick her up and carry her off to wherever he took his other women, rich and poor alike, to give them comfort. She didn't like his song about 'three little girls', because she saw in it the arrogance of a man who has too many lovers.

'What's up? What's up?' stuttered Bazouge. 'Who's been took sick? I'm comin', duckie.'

At the sound of that hoarse voice Gervaise woke up as if from a nightmare. What had she done? She'd banged on the partition, for sure. Then, as if feeling on her backside a whack from a cane, terror made her tighten her buttocks, and she shrank back, imagining she could see Bazouge's huge hands coming through the wall to grab her by the hair. No, no, she didn't want to, she wasn't ready. If she'd knocked it must have been with her elbow, as she was turning over. And a shiver of horror ran through her from her knees up to her shoulders at the thought of being carted away in the old man's arms, all stiff, with a face as white as chalk.

Bazouge's voice came again:

'So there's nobody there now? Just 'ang on. I'm always ready to 'elp a lady out.'

'No, it's nothin',' Gervaise managed to gasp. 'I'm all right, thank you.'

As Bazouge dozed off, grumbling and growling, Gervaise stood there anxiously, listening to him, not daring to move for fear that he might think he'd heard her knock again. She swore to herself that she'd be more careful from now on. Even if she was at death's door she wouldn't ask her neighbour for help. She said this to reassure herself, for there were moments when, despite the panic she'd been in, she felt the same terrified fascination.

Even in her miserable attic, amidst all her troubles and those of her neighbours, Gervaise did find a fine example of courage in the home of the Bijards. Little Lalie, the eight-year-old kid who was no bigger than two sous' worth of butter, kept house as well as any grown-up; and it was no easy job, for there were two younger ones to look after, her brother Jules and her sister Henriette, tots of three and five, whom she had to keep an eye on all day long while also sweeping the floor and washing the dishes. Ever since Bijard had killed his missus with a kick in the belly, Lalie had become the little mother of the family. Without saying a word, all by herself, she'd taken the dead woman's place, to the extent that her brute of a father, no doubt to make the likeness perfect, now beat the daughter as he used to beat the mother. When he came home drunk he just had to have a woman to batter. He didn't even notice how small Lalie was; he hit her as he would hit a grown woman. A single clout would cover her whole face, and her skin was still so soft that the marks left by his five fingers would be visible for two days. The thrashings were shameful; blows rained down for the least little thing—it was like a raging wolf falling on a timid, gentle kitten, pitifully thin, who took it all without complaining, with a look of resignation in her lovely eyes. No, Lalie never rebelled. She might bend her neck a bit to protect her face, but she never cried out, so as not to upset the other people in the building. When her father got tired of knocking her round the room with his shoe, she'd wait until she felt strong enough to stand up, and then get back to work, washing the little ones, getting food ready, not leaving a speck of dust on the furniture. Being beaten was just part of her daily round.

Gervaise had taken a great liking to her little neighbour. She treated her as an equal, as a grown-up woman who knows about life. It must be said that Lalie had a pale, serious face, and an expression like an old maid's. Listening to her talk, you'd have thought she was thirty. She knew all about shopping, mending, and housekeeping, and she talked about the children as though she'd already borne two or three herself. It made you smile, to hear an eight-year-old talk like that, but then you'd feel a lump in your throat and turn away so as not to cry.

Gervaise asked her in as often as she could and gave her whatever she could in the way of food and old clothes. One day, when she was trying an old jacket of Nana's on her, she was shocked to see her back black and blue, her elbow grazed and still bleeding, all her innocent flesh brutalized and sticking to her bones. Père Bazouge could get his box ready, she wouldn't last long at this rate! But the child begged her not to say anything; she didn't want her father to get into trouble because of her. She made excuses for him, saying he wouldn't have been so cruel if he hadn't been drinking. Drinking made him lose control, he no longer knew what he was doing. She forgave him, you have to forgive mad people for everything they do.

From then on Gervaise kept an eye on Lalie and tried to intervene as soon as she heard Bijard coming up the stairs. But most of the time she simply caught a whack herself. During the day, when she went in, she often found Lalie tied to the foot of the iron bedstead. This was an idea of the locksmith's: before leaving he would tie her up by the legs and round the middle with thick ropes, no one knew why; a mad whim that had got into his drunken skull, no doubt as a way of terrorizing the kid even when he wasn't there. Lalie, stiff as a board, with pins and needles in her legs, would stay tied up all day; once she even spent a whole day and night like that, when Bijard forgot to come home. When Gervaise, outraged, said she'd untie her, Lalie begged her not to touch any of the ropes because her father became furious if he didn't find the knots tied just as he'd left them. She was all right really, it gave her a rest; and she'd say this with a smile, her little cherub's legs swollen and numb. What upset her was that she couldn't get on with her work, tied to the bed like that, only able to stare at the mess the place was in. Her father ought to have thought of something else. All the same, she kept charge of the children, making them do as they were told, calling them over to have their noses wiped. As her hands weren't tied she'd knit while waiting to be set free, so her time wouldn't be completely wasted. The most painful part was when Bijard untied her; she'd crawl about on the floor for a good quarter of an hour, unable to stand up because her circulation had gone.

The locksmith had thought up another little game as well. He would heat coins in the stove until they were red-hot and put them on the corner of the mantelpiece. After a short while he'd call Lalie over and tell her to go and buy some bread. The unsuspecting girl would pick up the coins but immediately drop them with a scream, shaking

her burnt little hand. At this, he would fly into a rage. What had he
done to deserve such a terrible little slut! Now she was losing his
money! He threatened to give her a belting if she didn't pick the
money up at once. If she hesitated, she got a first warning, a blow of
such force that it made her see stars. Without a word, her eyes brim-
ming with tears, she picked up the coins and went off, tossing them up
and down in the palm of her hand to get them cool.

No, you'd never believe the fiendish ideas a drunkard can dream
up. For example, one afternoon Lalie was playing with the children
after she'd finished tidying up. As the window was open, there was
a draught from the corridor that kept nudging the door open.

'It's Monsieur Hardi,'* the girl said. 'Do come in, Monsieur Hardi.
Please do come in.'

And she curtsied to the door, greeting the wind. Henriette and
Jules, standing behind her, curtsied and bowed too, thoroughly enjoying the game and giggling as though they were being tickled. She was
pink with pleasure at seeing them so amused, and began really to
enjoy herself—something that happened once in a blue moon.

'Good afternoon, Monsieur Hardi. How are you, Monsieur Hardi?'

But suddenly the door was thrown open and Bijard came in. The
whole scene changed. Henriette and Jules fell back on their bottoms,
against the wall, while Lalie, terrified, stopped short in the middle of
a curtsey. The locksmith was holding a brand new drayman's whip,
with a long whitewood handle and a leather lash ending in a piece of
string. He put the whip down in the corner, by the bed, but didn't give
Lalie the usual kick, though she was already preparing for it by turning her back. He was grinning and showing his black teeth; he was
very drunk, his face all aflame with an idea for a bit of fun.

'So, playin' at bein' a tart are you, you little bitch? I could hear you
dancin' as I came up the stairs. Come over 'ere! Closer, for Christ's
sake! An' turn round, I don't want to smell your arse. What are you
shakin' for? I'm not touchin' you, am I? Take me shoes off.'

Lalie, terrified at not getting her usual thrashing, turned quite pale.
She took off his shoes. He'd sat down on the edge of the bed and now
lay down fully dressed, without shutting his eyes, watching his daughter as she moved round the room. She carried on with her work, but
was so stupefied by his stare that little by little she became rigid with
fear and in the end broke a cup. At this, without getting up, he reached
for the whip and showed it to her.

'Now then, my little chuck, have a look at this: it's a present for you. Yes, that's another fifty sous you've cost me. This toy means I won't have to run about any more, and it won't do you no good tryin' to hide in corners. Wanna have a try?... So, you're breakin' cups now, are you? C'mon, get to it, dance! Make your curtsies to Monsieur Hardi!'

He didn't even sit up, but just lay sprawled there, his head pressed against the pillow, cracking the big whip all round the room with a sound like a postilion whipping up his horses. Then, bringing his arm down, he wrapped the thong around Lalie's middle, winding her and then unwinding her like a top. She fell over and tried to crawl away, but he caught her again and set her back on her feet.

'Gee up!' he yelled. 'It's the donkey race! It's a great idea for a winter mornin'. I can stay in bed, I won't catch a cold, an' I can round up me little flock without scrapin' me chilblains. In the corner there, gotcha! And over there, gotcha again! Oh, and if you crawl under the bed, I'll hit you with the handle! Gee up! Gee up! Clippety-clop!'

A slight froth had formed on his lips and his yellow eyes were nearly starting out of their dark sockets. Lalie, mad and screaming with pain, leapt about all over the room, curled into a ball on the floor, flattened herself against the walls; but the slender thong of the great whip reached her wherever she was, cracking in her ears like gunshot and leaving long weals on her flesh. It was like the capering of an animal being trained to do tricks. The poor thing jumped and jumped—what a sight!—with her heels in the air like kids skipping ever faster. Completely out of breath, bouncing about like a rubber ball, she let herself be hit, blinded and exhausted by the search for a safe spot. Her brute of a father was gleefully calling her a little tart and asking whether she'd had enough and understood now that she hadn't got a hope of getting away from him.

But suddenly Gervaise rushed in, drawn by the child's screams. The sight that greeted her filled her with rage.

'You bastard!' she yelled. 'Leave her alone, you animal! I'm going to report you to the police!'

Bijard growled, and muttered:

'Listen, you fuckin' cripple! Mind your own business. D'you expect me to wear gloves when I give her a hidin'? I'm just givin' her a warnin', can't you see, just to show her how long me arm is.'

A final crack of the whip caught Lalie on the face. Her upper lip was split open and blood began to flow. Gervaise picked up a chair and was about to attack the locksmith. But the child stretched her hands out, begging her to stop, saying it was nothing and was all over now. She wiped away the blood with a corner of her apron and calmed the children, who were howling as if they were the ones who'd been whipped.

When Gervaise thought about Lalie she felt she didn't have too much to complain about after all. She wished she had the courage of that eight-year-old child, who alone endured as much as all the other women on the staircase put together. She'd seen her eating nothing but dry bread for three months, and not even enough of that to satisfy her hunger, so skinny and weak was she that she could hardly walk without holding on to the walls; and when she secretly took her scraps of meat, it broke her heart to see the child, with tears rolling down her cheeks, nibble it in tiny bits because her throat was so shrunken that she could hardly swallow. But despite everything she was always kind and devoted, wise beyond her years, carrying out her duties as a little mother to the point of sacrificing her life to maternal instincts awakened all too soon in someone so innocent and frail. Gervaise watched this dear creature, a model of suffering and forgiveness, trying to learn from her how to bear her own martyrdom in silence. All that remained of Lalie now was the look of resignation in her big dark eyes, in whose depths you could see nothing but endless pain and misery. Never a word, just those big dark eyes, open wide.

As time went by, the poison from Père Colombe's Assommoir began to ravage the Coupeaus' home too. Gervaise could see the time coming when her man would take up a whip, like Bijard, and make her dance. And the trouble she saw ahead naturally made her more sensitive to the trouble the child was in. Yes, Coupeau was in a bad way. Gone were the days when the grog put colour in his cheeks. He could no longer slap his belly and boast that the bloody stuff made him fat, for the ugly yellow fat of the early years had melted away; he was getting thin, his complexion turning livid with a greenish tint, like a corpse rotting in a pond. His appetite had gone, too. Gradually he'd lost his taste for bread and he'd even started to turn his nose up at cooked food. You could put the tastiest stew in front of him, his stomach would have none of it and his rotting teeth refused to chew. To keep going he needed his daily supply of spirits; that was his ration, his food and drink, the only form of nourishment he could digest. In the morning, as soon as he got out of bed, he'd be bent double for a good quarter of an hour, racked with coughing, holding his head and spitting bile, as bitter as aloes, that came up in his throat. It never failed, you could have the chamber pot ready in advance. He didn't feel steady on his feet again until he'd had his first glass of comfort, an effective medicine that cauterized his insides. But as the day wore on, his strength revived. At first he'd had a funny feeling, a kind of tingling, in his hands and feet, and he'd laugh about it, saying somebody was tickling him, the missus must have put itching powder in the bed. Then his legs had become heavy and the tickling turned into terrible cramps that gripped his flesh like a vice. That wasn't so funny. There was nothing to laugh about now. He'd stop short on the pavement, his head swimming, his ears buzzing, stars flickering before his eyes. Everything turned yellow, the buildings moved about, and he'd stagger for a few seconds, afraid he'd fall flat on his back. At other times, even when the sun was hot, he'd start shivering as though icy water was running down his spine. But what bothered him most was the way his hands had begun to shake; his right hand especially must have done something very wicked, it had such nightmares. Christ! Wasn't he a man any more, was he turning into an old woman! He'd tense his muscles furiously and grasp his glass, saying he'd hold it as steady as if it were in the hand of a marble statue, but however hard he tried, the glass still did its little jig, jumping to the right, then to the left, with quick, regular trembling movements. So then he'd empty the glass down his throat in a rage, shouting that what he needed was a few dozen like that and then he'd show everybody how to carry a barrel without a single finger shaking. But Gervaise told him that on the contrary he'd have to stop drinking if he wanted to stop his shakes. So he told her to go to hell and swallowed drink after drink, and then tried again, flying into a rage and blaming the passing omnibuses for his unsteady glass.

One evening in March Coupeau came in soaked to the skin. He'd walked home with Mes-Bottes from Montrouge, where they'd had a good bellyful of eel soup; and they'd been caught in a downpour all the way from the Barrière des Fourneaux to the Barrière Poissonnière, quite a stretch of road. During the night he was taken with a terrible cough; he was very flushed, had a frightful temperature, and his chest was heaving like a pair of worn-out bellows. When the Boches' doctor saw him the next morning and listened to his chest, he shook his head and, drawing Gervaise aside, advised her to have her husband taken to the hospital right away. Coupeau had pneumonia.

This time, of course, Gervaise had no objection. There had been a time when she'd have let herself be chopped into little pieces rather than hand him over to the quacks. At the time of the accident in the Rue de la Nation she'd used up all her savings on nursing him. But such fine feelings don't last when a man turns bad. No, she wasn't going to put herself through all that again. They could take him away for good—she'd thank them heartily for it. And yet, when the stretcher arrived and they loaded Coupeau on to it like a piece of furniture, she went quite pale and bit her lip; and though she still muttered that it was a good job they were taking him, her heart wasn't in it and she wished she had just ten francs in her drawer so as not to have to let him go. She went with him to Lariboisière and watched the male nurses put him to bed at one end of a long ward, where rows of patients with corpse-like faces raised their heads and watched this new one coming to join them. A nice place to die all right, with its suffocating smell of fever and its chorus of consumptive coughs that made you want to cough your own lungs out, not to mention that the ward looked like a miniature Père-Lachaise, with its rows of white beds like an avenue of graves. Then, as he was just lying there flat on his pillow, she left, not having anything to say and unfortunately having nothing in her pocket to comfort him. Outside, opposite the hospital, she turned round and looked at the building. And she thought of the time, so long ago, when Coupeau was on the roof, leaning over the gutters and fitting his lengths of zinc, singing in the sunshine. He didn't drink in those days, and his skin was like a girl's. She would lean out of her window in the Hôtel Boncœur and look for him, and see him up there in the sky; and they'd both wave their handkerchiefs, smiling at each other by telegraph. Yes, Coupeau had worked there, never suspecting he was working for himself. Now, instead of being up on the roof like a cheeky, randy cock sparrow, he was down below, in the little nest he'd made for himself in the hospital, and had come there, dirty and unshaven, to die. My God, how far away those days of courting seemed now!

Two days later, when Gervaise came to see how Coupeau was getting on, she found his bed empty. A sister explained that they'd had to take him to the Sainte-Anne asylum* because during the night he'd suddenly gone off his head. Totally crazy, he was, trying to bash his head in against the wall and howling so that the other patients couldn't sleep. Apparently it was the drink. It had been fermenting in his body and, while he was flat on his back and weak with the pneumonia, had seized its chance to attack his nerves and throw them out of gear. Gervaise went home in a very agitated state. Life was going to be really fun if they let him out. Nana kept yelling that they must keep him in the hospital, otherwise he'd end up doing them both in.

It wasn't until the Sunday that Gervaise was able to go to Sainte-Anne. It was quite a long way. Fortunately the omnibus from the Boulevard Rochechouart to La Glacière stopped quite close to the asylum. She went down the Rue de la Santé* and bought two oranges so as not to turn up empty-handed. It was another huge building, with dismal courtyards, endless corridors, and a smell of stale medicaments—not exactly the sort of place that would lift your spirits. But, when they'd shown her into a cell, she was surprised to find Coupeau almost jolly. He happened to be sitting on the throne, a very clean wooden box, which didn't give out the least smell; and they had a good laugh at her finding him doing his business, with his arse exposed. Well, you know how it is when you're ill. He sat there in state, like the Pope, and started to chatter away just as he used to. Oh, he was much better now, he was regular again.

'And what about the pneumonia?' asked Gervaise.

'All gone! They just whisked it out. I'm still coughing a bit, but I don't 'ave to clear me tubes out no more.'

Then, as he got off the throne to return to bed, he started joking again:

'You've got a tough nose. You don't mind a pinch of snuff, do you?'

And they laughed even more. Deep down, they felt happy. Sharing a good laugh about this indelicate matter was their way of showing each other they felt happy, without actually saying so. Anyone who has had to do with sick people knows how wonderful it is to see them in proper working order again.

When he was back in bed, she gave him the two oranges and he was quite touched. He was becoming his old pleasant self again now he was drinking herbal tea and could no longer leave his better feelings behind in some bar. After a while she plucked up enough courage to ask him about his attack of delirium, and was surprised to hear him talk quite normally, like in the good old days.

'Oh, yes,' he said, making fun of himself. 'I talked a whole load of drivel. I was seein' rats, would you believe, and crawlin' about on all fours tryin' to put salt on their tails. And you were shoutin' to me, because some men were after you. All sorts of bloody nonsense like that, ghosts in broad daylight... I can remember it all very clearly, so me noddle is workin' all right. But it's over now. I dream a bit when I drop off to sleep, and I do 'ave a few nightmares, but everybody 'as nightmares.'

Gervaise stayed with him until evening. When the doctor came round at six o'clock, he made Coupeau hold out his hands. They hardly shook now, just a little bit in his fingertips. But, as night fell, he started to get more and more agitated. Twice he sat up, staring at the floor, in the parts of the room that were in shadow. Suddenly he reached out and seemed to squash some creature against the wall.

'What's the matter?' asked Gervaise, frightened.

'It's the rats!' he muttered.

Then, after a silence, in which he seemed to drift off to sleep, he began to writhe about and talk in strange snatches.

'Bloody hell! They're bitin' me! The buggers! Look out! Pull your skirt tight! Be careful of that bastard behind you! Christ, they've knocked her over! Just look at 'em laughin'! You sods! You bloody devils!'

He was hitting out into space; then, pulling at his blanket, he rolled it into a bundle and held it against his chest as if to protect himself from attack by the bearded men he was seeing. At this, a warder ran in and Gervaise left, horrified by this scene. But when she went back a few days later, she found Coupeau quite better. Even the nightmares had gone, and he slept like a child for ten hours at a stretch without moving. So they let his wife take him home. Before he was discharged, however, the doctor gave him the usual good advice, and cautioned him to consider it well. If he started drinking again he'd go downhill very quickly and it would be the end of him. It was entirely up to him. He'd seen how fit and well he could be when he was off the drink. So, he must carry on at home with the sober life he'd led at Sainte-Anne, and pretend he was still under lock and key and that bars didn't exist.

'He's right, that doctor,' said Gervaise in the omnibus taking them back to the Rue de la Goutte-d'Or.

'Definitely,' replied Coupeau.

Then, after a few moments' thought, he added:

'But, y'know, just a drop now and then won't kill a man. It's good for the digestion.'

And that very evening he put away a lot of grog, for his digestion. For a week, however, he was quite sensible. He was a big coward at heart and didn't fancy ending up in Bicêtre.* But his craving got the better of him—the first shot led inevitably to a second, a third, then a fourth, so that by the end of the second week he'd gone back to his usual ration of half a litre a day. Gervaise was so exasperated she could have clobbered him. To think that, having seen him back to his old self in the asylum, she'd been stupid enough to dream of having a decent life with him again! There went another dream of happiness, and surely it would be the last. Oh well, now that nothing, not even fear of an early death, could make him change, she swore she wouldn't bother any more—their home could go to the dogs, she didn't care—and she declared that she too would find her own pleasure where she could. The hell of their previous existence began again, dragging them even deeper into the mire, without a glimmer of hope for better times. When her father slapped her, Nana would ask furiously why the bastard wasn't still in the hospital. She couldn't wait to start earning some money, she said, so she could buy him more drink and see him snuff it all the sooner. As for Gervaise, one day when Coupeau was saying he should never have married her, she lost her temper. So, she'd brought him other men's leavings, had she? She'd picked him up in the street, had she, tricking him with her sweet, innocent air? What a bloody nerve! Every time he opened his mouth lies came out of it. The truth was she hadn't really wanted him. He'd gone down on his knees to beg her to have him, while she'd told him he should really think about it. And if she could have her time over again, she'd bloody well say no! Yes, she'd already had one man, but if a woman is a good worker, even so, she's worth more than a lazy sod who drags his own and his family's name through the filth of every bar. That day, for the first time at the Coupeaus', they really went for each other, and so fiercely that the broom and an old umbrella got broken.

Gervaise was as good as her word. She became even more slovenly, stayed away from the laundry more often, sat around jawing all day, and went as limp as a rag when it came to doing anything. If she dropped something on the floor, it could just stay there: she couldn't be bothered to bend down and pick it up. She was getting bone lazy.

She had no intention of tiring herself out. So she took things easy and never swept the floor until she was practically falling over the mess. Meanwhile, the Lorilleux made a show of holding their noses when they walked past the Coupeaus' room: a real cesspit, they said. They kept themselves to themselves at the end of the corridor, safe from all the misery wailing through that part of the building, shutting themselves in so they wouldn't have to lend a few sous. Such kind-hearted people! Such obliging neighbours! Pull the other one! You just had to knock and ask for a match, a pinch of salt, or a jug of water, and you'd be sure to have the door slammed in your face. If it was a matter of helping the neighbours, they proclaimed that they never meddled in other people's affairs; but if there was any opportunity for backbiting, they'd get involved straight away. With the bolt shot home and a blanket hung up to block the keyhole and the cracks, they'd treat themselves to an orgy of tittle-tattle, without laying aside their gold wire for a second. Gimpy's downfall in particular kept them purring all day long like cats being stroked. She'd gone down the drain, y'know—not a sou left! They'd watch her going to the shops and snigger at the tiny bit of bread she'd bring back under her apron. They worked out on which days she had nothing to eat. They knew how thick the dust was in her home, how many dirty plates were left lying about, and each further sign of her surrender to poverty and sloth. And her clothes! Disgusting stuff a ragpicker wouldn't bother to pick up! My God, she didn't have any finery now, that once beautiful blonde, that floozie who once upon a time was always wiggling her behind in her fancy blue shop. Look where it got people, being mad on guzzling and feasting. Gervaise, who suspected they were always bad-mouthing her, would take her shoes off and put her ear to their door, but the blanket prevented her from hearing anything. One day, however, she caught them calling her 'Big Boobs', no doubt because she still had quite a bosom, in spite of a diet that was making her lose weight. But in any case, she couldn't care less about them; she went on speaking to them, so that people wouldn't talk, though she expected nothing but insults from those bastards and couldn't even be bothered now to answer back and show them up for the idiots they were. Anyway, what the hell? She'd do as she liked, either stay put and twiddle her thumbs, or get moving if there was any kind of pleasure to be had, but not otherwise.

One Saturday, Coupeau had promised to take her to the circus. Well, to see ladies galloping round on horses and jumping through paper hoops—that really was worth stirring yourself for. Coupeau had just had a fortnight's pay, so he could part with forty sous; and they were even going to have a meal out, because Nana had to stay very late at work that evening to help with an urgent order. But seven o'clock came and there was no Coupeau; at eight still no sign of him. Gervaise was furious. Her pisspot of a husband was no doubt blowing his wages with his mates in the local bars. She'd washed a bonnet and had spent most of the day trying to patch up an old dress so as to make herself presentable. Finally, at about nine, ravenously hungry and purple with rage, she decided to go out and see if she could find Coupeau in the neighbourhood.

'Looking for your 'usband?' cried Madame Boche, when she saw the look on her face. 'He's at Père Colombe's. Boche has just had some brandied cherries with 'im.'

Gervaise thanked her and took off along the pavement, determined to go and wring Coupeau's neck. A drizzly rain was falling, which made the expedition even less pleasant. But when she reached the Assommoir, the thought that she herself might come a cropper if she laid into her man suddenly calmed her down and made her more cautious. The bar was ablaze, its gaslights burning, the mirrors shining like suns, the flasks and jars brightening the walls with their glass of different colours. She stood there for a moment, craning her neck and pressing her face to the window, peering between two of the jars. She spotted Coupeau at the back of the room, sitting with some mates at a little zinc-topped table, all looking blurred and bluish in the haze of pipe smoke. As she couldn't hear what they were bawling at each other, it struck her as funny the way they were waving their arms about and thrusting out their chins, their eyes popping out of their heads. How, for God's sake, could men leave their wives and homes to shut themselves up like that in a hole where they could hardly breathe! The rain was running down the back of her neck; she straightened up and went off along the outer boulevard, turning things over in her mind, not daring to go in. Coupeau would have given her a nice reception, he hated it when she came chasing after him. Apart from which, she didn't think it was a nice place for a respectable woman. But as she walked along under the dripping trees she began to shiver, and it occurred to her that she might be catching a nasty chill. Twice she went back and stood at the window, pressing her face to it once more, annoyed at the sight of those blasted boozers, sitting there nice and dry, shouting and drinking. The light from the Assommoir was reflected in the puddles, which shimmered and bubbled as the rain continued to fall. Each time the door opened and closed with a clatter of its brass strips, she would move back, stepping into the puddles and splashing herself. Finally, deciding it was just too silly to keep doing this, she pushed the door open and walked straight up to Coupeau's table. After all, it was her husband she was coming for, wasn't it? And she had a perfect right to, since he'd promised to take her to the circus that evening. Too bad if he didn't like it! She didn't want to dissolve out there in the street, like a bar of soap.

'Hey! It's you, old girl!' the roofer cried, choking with laughter. 'Blimey, what a turn-up for the books! Ain't she a scream!'

They were all laughing—Mes-Bottes, Bibi-la-Grillade, Bec-Salé. Yes, they thought she was a scream, but they didn't say why. Gervaise stood there, a bit taken aback. Coupeau seemed in a good mood, so she ventured to say:

'We're going out—remember? We'd better get a move on. We'll still be in time to see something.'

'I can't get up. I'm stuck, I really am,' Coupeau replied, still laughing. 'See what you can do. Pull me arm, as 'ard as you can. No, sod it, 'arder than that. Come on, pull!... See? What did I tell you? It's that bugger Colombe, he's screwed me to the bench.'

Gervaise had played along, and when she finally let his arm go they all thought it was so funny they fell about, braying and rubbing shoulders like donkeys being curry-combed. The roofer laughed from ear to ear—a laugh so huge you could see right down his throat.

'Come on, you silly bugger,' he said at last. 'Sit down for a minute, can't you! We're better off 'ere than gettin' pissed on outside... Well, yeah, I didn't come 'ome 'cos I 'ad things to do. And there's no point makin' a face, it won't do you no good... Move up a bit, you lot, and make a bit o' room.'

'Madame might prefer to sit on my knee,' said Mes-Bottes. 'That would be more romantic.'

Not wanting to draw attention to herself, Gervaise took a chair and sat down at a short distance from the table. She looked at what the men were drinking: absinthe. It shone in their glasses like gold. There was a little pool of it on the table, and Bec-Salé was dipping his finger in it as he talked, and writing a woman's name, Eulalie, in big letters. Bibi-la-Grillade, she thought, looked haggard and skinnier than a plucked chicken. Mes-Bottes's nose was in full bloom, a real Burgundy Blue dahlia. All four of them were very dirty, their filthy beards stiff and yellow as chamber-pot brushes, their smocks in tatters, their fingernails funeral black. But at least it was all right to be seen with them, because although they'd been at it since six, they were still well behaved, even if on the brink of becoming completely sozzled. Gervaise could see two other men knocking it back at the counter, so pissed they were tipping their drinks out under their chins and soaking their shirts, thinking they were wetting their whistles. Père Colombe, a big man, was quietly pouring the rounds, displaying his huge arms, which always ensured respect among his customers. It was very warm, and the pipe smoke was rising like a dust cloud in the blinding gaslight, enveloping the drinkers in a slowly thickening fog; and out of this fog came a deafening, confused din, of cracked voices, clinking glasses, curses, and fists banging on tables like the sound of guns going off. Gervaise had adopted an aloof expression, because such a scene isn't very nice for a woman, especially if she isn't used to it; she was choking, her eyes were smarting, and her head was beginning to throb from the alcohol fumes that pervaded the room. Then, suddenly, she felt there was something even more unpleasant going on behind her. She turned round and saw the still, the booze machine, working away in the little glassed-in yard, its devil's kitchen rumbling away deep inside it. At night the copper containers looked duller, lit just by red, star-shaped reflections on their curved surfaces; and the shadow cast by the machine on the wall behind it conjured up obscene shapes, figures with tails, monsters opening their jaws as if to gobble everyone up.

'Hey, misery-guts—don't make that face!' yelled Coupeau. 'I can't stand killjoys. What'll you have?'

'I don't want anything,' replied Gervaise. 'I haven't had anything to eat yet.'

'All the more reason. A little drop of something keeps you goin'.'

As she didn't react, Mes-Bottes turned the charm on again.

'I'm sure Madame would like something sweet,' he said softly.

'I like men who don't get pissed!' she replied sharply. 'I like people to bring home their pay and keep their word when they make promises.'

'So that's what's upsettin' you!' said the roofer, still laughing. 'You want your share. So why not 'ave a drink? It'd be out of me pay. Go on, 'ave one.'

She stared at him, looking very serious, a dark crease appearing on her forehead. Then she said, slowly and deliberately:

'Yes, you're right, that's a good idea. That way, we'll drink the money up together.'

Bibi-la-Grillade stood up to fetch her a glass of anisette. She pulled her chair up to the table. As she was sipping her drink, she suddenly remembered something: she remembered the brandied plum she'd had with Coupeau, long ago, sitting at the table near the door, when he was courting her. In those days she'd eat the plum and leave the brandy. And now here she was drinking neat spirits. Oh, she knew herself all right, she didn't have an ounce of willpower. She just needed a little push from behind to send her tumbling headlong into drink. Actually, she thought the anisette tasted rather nice, though a bit too sweet and sickly perhaps. She drained her glass as she listened to Bec-Salé telling them about his affair with fat Eulalie, the woman who sold fish in the street. Bloody artful she was—she could sniff him in a bar while she was wheeling her barrow along the pavement. It was no good his mates tipping him off and hiding him, she usually nabbed him; as a matter of fact, just the previous day she'd given him a good smack round the chops to teach him not to skip work. Now that was really funny. Bibi-la-Grillade and Mes-Bottes, laughing their socks off, kept slapping Gervaise on the shoulder, and now she was laughing as well, as if they were tickling her and she couldn't help it. They said she should do the same as fat Eulalie—bring her iron and run it over Coupeau's ears on Colombe's counter.

'Thank you very much!' said Coupeau, upending the glass of anisette his wife had just emptied. 'You put that away double-quick! Look at this, boys, she doesn't 'ang about!'

'Would Madame like another one?' asked Bec-Salé.

No, she'd had enough. Even so, she hesitated. The anisette made her feel a bit sick, and she'd rather have had something stiffer to settle her stomach. She kept darting glances at the booze machine behind her. That bloody great pot, as round as the belly of a fat tinker woman, with its twisted snout sticking out, sent shivers down her spine, shivers in which fear was mixed with desire. It was like the metal innards of some monstrous whore, of some sorceress who was distilling, drop by drop, the fire that burned within her. A pretty source of poison, a thing so brazen, so obscene, it should have been buried in a cellar! But, for all that, she would have liked to get close to it, to sniff

the smell and taste the filthy stuff, even if it might burn her tongue
and make it peel like an orange.

'What's that you're drinkin'?' she asked the men slyly, her eyes
lighting up at the lovely golden colour in their glasses.

'That, old girl, is Père Colombe's camphor,' Coupeau replied.
'Come on, we'll give you a drop to try.'

They brought her a glass of it. She made a face at the first sip, and
Coupeau went on, slapping his thigh:

'It gives your throat a good scrape, don't it? You've got to swallow
it in one go. A drink of that every day will keep the doctor away.'

After her second glass, Gervaise no longer felt her gnawing hunger.
And she'd stopped feeling angry with Coupeau because he'd not kept
his promise. They'd go to the circus some other time; anyway, watching a lot of acrobats galloping round on horses wasn't that much fun.
It wasn't raining in Père Colombe's bar, and even if your wages were
melting away in drink, at least it was going into your own belly, clear
and shiny like liquid gold. They could all go to hell! She didn't get
that much pleasure from life, and anyway, it was a consolation to have
her share in blowing the money. She felt good there, didn't she, so
why shouldn't she stay? They could let off a cannon if they wanted,
she wasn't going to budge, not now she was nicely settled. She was
simmering nicely in the warmth, her blouse sticking to her back,
filled with a sense of well-being that made her limbs feel heavy. She
sat chuckling to herself, gazing into space with her elbows on the
table, greatly amused by two men at a nearby table, one a hulking
great brute and the other a midget, both so pissed they were embra-
cing each other most lovingly. Yes, it was fun to be in the Assommoir,
with Père Colombe's great moon face, like a lump of lard, and the
customers smoking their clay pipes, yelling and spitting, and the big
gas burners lighting up the mirrors and the bottles of liquor. The
smell no longer bothered her; on the contrary, she felt a pleasant tickling in her nose, and she thought it smelt nice; her eyelids drooped
and her breathing grew shallow as she abandoned herself to the delicious drowsiness creeping over her. After her third tot, she let her
chin fall on her hands, and saw nothing then but Coupeau and his
mates. She was sitting face to face with them, very close, feeling their
hot breath on her cheeks, staring at their dirty beards as if counting
the bristles. By now they were all pretty far gone. Mes-Bottes was
chewing on his pipe and dribbling, as silent and solemn as a sleepy

bullock. Bibi-la-Grillade was telling a story about how he had once emptied a litre bottle in one go, by holding it bottom-up and pouring it straight down his throat.

Meanwhile, Bec-Salé had fetched the wheel of fortune from the counter and was playing Coupeau for the price of the drinks.

'Two hundred! Lucky bastard! You get the high numbers every time!'

The wheel turned, the pointer squeaked, and the picture of Fortune, a big woman in red placed under glass, whirled round, until it was just a blur in the middle, like a wine stain.

'Three hundred and fifty! You must've kicked it, you bugger! Bloody hell! I'm not playing any more!'

Gervaise was fascinated by the wheel. She was really knocking it back now and calling Mes-Bottes 'sonny boy'. Behind her the booze machine was still working away, making a low rumbling noise like an underground stream; and, feeling she couldn't ever stop it or impede its progress, she was overcome with a cold rage, with an urge to jump on top of the huge still as if it were a living creature, to stamp on it with her heels and split its belly open. Then everything became confused in her head, she could see the machine moving and feel its copper claws clutching hold of her, and the stream now seemed to be flowing through her own body.

The room began dancing round and the gaslights were flying about like shooting stars. Gervaise was quite drunk. She could hear a furious argument going on between Bec-Salé and that twister Colombe. The bloody thief had padded the bill! Did he take himself for a highwayman or something? All of a sudden there was a lot of shouting and the sound of tables being overturned. Père Colombe was throwing everybody out, just like that, with a few heaves of his mighty arms. They called him a rotten swindler—and all sorts of other names— from the other side of the door. It was still raining and a cold wind was blowing. Gervaise lost Coupeau, found him, lost him again. She wanted to get home and groped her way along the shopfronts, surprised by the sudden darkness. At the corner of the Rue des Poissonniers she sat down in the gutter, thinking she must be at the wash-house. All that running water made her head spin; she felt terribly ill. At last she got there and, as she walked quickly past the concierge's lodge, she clearly saw the Lorilleux and the Poissons sitting at table and their looks of disgust when they noticed the state she was in.

She never knew how she got up those six flights of stairs. At the top, just as she was turning into the corridor, little Lalie, hearing her step, came running out, her arms wide open to embrace her, saying with a laugh:

'Madame Gervaise, Papa hasn't come home yet, come in and look at my babies asleep. They look ever so sweet!'

But when she saw the laundress's stupefied expression she drew back, trembling. She knew that smell of spirits, those dull eyes, that twisted mouth. Gervaise staggered past her without a word, leaving the child standing at her door, gazing after her with her dark, serious eyes.

CHAPTER XI

NANA was getting taller and becoming more aware of her charms. At fifteen she'd shot up like a beanstalk and was very fair-skinned and shapely, in fact as chubby as a cherub. Yes, there she was at fifteen, fully developed but no corset yet. A real baby face, all peaches and cream, a cute little nose, rosebud lips, and peepers so sparkling that men wanted to light their pipes at them. Her mass of blonde hair, the colour of ripe oats, seemed to have powdered her forehead with golden freckles, like a band of sunshine. A fine figure of a girl, as the Lorilleux said, a kid who still needed her nose wiping for her, but whose body had the curves and fullness of a mature woman.

Nana didn't have to stuff balls of paper down her dress any more. She had tits of her own, a brand new pair, white as satin. And she wasn't self-conscious about them, she would have liked them even bigger, and dreamt of tits like a wet-nurse, so reckless and greedy are the young. What made her particularly alluring was her wicked habit of poking the tip of her tongue out between her teeth. She'd probably tried it out in front of mirrors and thought she looked nice that way. So, all day long, she stuck out her tongue to make herself look more attractive.

'Hide that lying tongue!' her mother would yell.

And Coupeau would often join in, banging his fist and swearing: 'Put that red rag away!'

Nana had become very particular about her appearance. She didn't always wash her feet, but she bought such narrow boots that she suffered like a martyr, and if anybody asked her why she'd gone purple in the face she'd say she had a stomach ache rather than own up to her vanity. When there was nothing to eat at home it was difficult for her to get dolled up, but at such times she achieved miracles by bringing bits of ribbon back from the workshop and creating something out of shabby old dresses covered with bows and rosettes. Summer was when she came into her own. Every Sunday, dressed in her six-franc percale dress, she filled the whole neighbourhood of the Goutte-d'Or with her golden beauty. She was well known everywhere from the outer boulevards to the fortifications, from the Chaussée de Clignancourt to the Grande-Rue de la Chapelle. They called her the 'little chick' because she really had the tender flesh and fresh look of a young chicken.

There was one dress in particular that suited her to perfection. It was white with pink spots, very simple, with no trimmings. The skirt was rather short and showed her feet, and the loose, wide sleeves revealed her arms up to the elbows; the neckline, which she'd enlarged with pins into a heart shape, working in a dark corner of the stairs to avoid her father's slaps, set off her snowy neck and the golden shadow between her breasts. And that was all, except a pink ribbon tied round her blonde hair, with its ends fluttering at the back of her neck. Done up like this, she was as fresh as a bunch of spring flowers. She gave off the fragrance of youth with her warm body, which was that of a child who was already a woman.

Sunday was the day when she could mingle with the crowd, with all the men who ogled her as they passed. All week long she looked forward to Sunday, pricked by all sorts of little desires, feeling stifled indoors, longing to get out into the fresh air and stroll in the sun through the throng of people all got up in their Sunday best. She'd start dressing early in the morning, and would spend hours in her chemise in front of the bit of mirror that hung above the chest of drawers; and as the whole building could see her through the window, her mother would get annoyed and ask her if she was going to spend much longer walking about half naked. But Nana would calmly go on sticking kiss-curls to her forehead with sugar and water, sewing buttons back on her boots, or putting a stitch in her dress, her legs bare, her chemise slipping off her shoulders, her hair all over the place. She looked stunning like that, Coupeau would say, laughing and teasing her: a regular Mary Magdalene. She could have put herself on show as a wild woman, at two sous a peek. Or he'd yell at her: 'Cover yourself up while I'm eating!' She was lovely, so white and delicate under her mane of blonde hair, and then turning all pink in her fury at him, not daring to answer her father back but breaking the cotton with a snap of her teeth that would send a quiver through her beautiful white body.

As soon as they'd finished the midday meal she'd hurry down into the courtyard. The building seemed to be dozing quietly in the warm Sunday afternoon. The workshops on the ground floor were closed and apartment windows, gaping open, revealed tables already set for the evening meal, waiting for families who were out working up an appetite with a stroll along the fortifications. On the third floor a woman was spending the day cleaning her room, pulling the bed out, shifting the furniture round, and singing the same song over and over again in a soft, sentimental voice. With the workshops all quiet, Nana, Pauline, and some of the other big girls would play shuttlecock in the empty, echoing yard. There were five or six of them who had grown up together and were becoming the queens of the building, sharing between them the admiring glances of the men. Whenever a man crossed the yard, there was a burst of high-pitched laughter and the girls' starched skirts would rustle like a gust of wind. Above them blazed the Sunday sky, sultry and heavy, as though languid from idleness and whitened by the dust of strolling feet.

But the games of shuttlecock were just an excuse for them to get away. Suddenly a great silence would descend on the building. The girls had slipped out into the street for a stroll on the outer boulevards. Linked arm in arm, taking up the whole width of the road, the six of them walked along in their light-coloured dresses, with ribbons tied round their hair. Their bright eyes, darting quick glances to right and left from under their eyelids, saw everything there was to see, and when they laughed they threw back their heads, displaying the soft roundness of their chins. When, during these noisy bursts of gaiety, a hunchback passed by or they came upon an old woman waiting for her dog at a corner, the line would break up, one or two hanging back while the others yanked them forward; and they'd sway their hips, falling on top of each other or flopping about, just to attract attention and make their bodices stretch tightly over their swelling breasts. The street belonged to them; they'd grown up in it lifting their skirts to pee next to the shops; and now they lifted their skirts up to their thighs to adjust their garters. They sped along through the slow-moving, pasty-faced crowd, between the slender boulevard trees, from the Barrière Rochechouart to the Boulevard Saint-Denis, bumping into people, zigzagging their way through groups, and turning round to shout things amid shrieks of laughter. Their fluttering dresses left in their wake an impression of their insolent youth; they displayed themselves there in the open air, in the glaring sunlight, with the crude vulgarity of street urchins, as delicious and desirable as virgins* returning from bathing with their hair still damp.

Nana would walk in the middle, her pink and white dress flashing in the sun. She would give her arm to Pauline, whose dress, yellow flowers on a white background, also shone brightly, flecked with tiny flames. As they were the biggest, the cheekiest, and the most fully developed members of the gang, they were its leaders, basking in the stares and the compliments. The younger ones tagged along, trying to puff themselves up so as to be taken seriously. Nana and Pauline had carefully worked out several stratagems for getting the boys' attention. If they ran until they were out of breath, it was to show off their white stockings and make their hair-ribbons flutter in the wind. And when they stopped, pretending to be gasping for breath, their breasts heaving, if you looked around you'd be sure to see someone they knew, some boy from the neighbourhood; then they'd saunter along, whispering and laughing to each other, but keeping a sharp watch out of the corners of their eyes. They went on their Sunday outings chiefly in quest of these chance encounters in the midst of the jostling crowd. Big lads in their Sunday best, wearing jackets and felt hats, would stop them for a moment on the edge of the pavement, joking and trying to catch hold of them round the waist. Twenty-year-old workmen in grey smocks would stand and chat to them, their arms folded, blowing the smoke from their clay pipes in their faces. It didn't amount to much, since these boys had grown up with them in the streets. Nevertheless the girls were already making their choices from among them. Pauline was always running into one of Madame Gaudron's sons, a carpenter of seventeen who would buy her apples. Nana could spot Victor Fauconnier, the laundress's son, from the other end of the avenue; she would meet him in dark corners for a kiss. But it never went further than that; the girls were wise enough not to do anything silly through ignorance, though they loved to talk dirty.

Then, when the sun went down, their great delight was to stop and watch the street entertainers. Conjurors and strongmen would come along and spread their worn-out carpets on the road. A gaping crowd would gather and form a circle while the performer, in the middle, would flex his muscles in his faded vest. Nana and Pauline would stand for hours in the thick of the crowd. Their pretty clean dresses would get crushed between dirty coats and overalls. Their bare arms and necks and their uncovered hair would feel the hot, foul breath around them, and in this atmosphere of wine and sweat they'd laugh away, enjoying it all without the slightest sense of disgust, their faces rosier than ever, thoroughly at home on their natural dunghill.

Around them they heard all sorts of crude remarks and obscenities, the language of drunkards; but it was their language, they had grown up with it, and so they'd turn round with a smile, unperturbed, without the faintest blush on their pale, delicate cheeks.

The only thing they didn't like was bumping into their fathers, especially when the men had been drinking; and so they watched out for them and gave each other warning:

'Hey, Nana!' Pauline would suddenly cry. 'Your old man's over there!'

'So he is! And he's not 'alf pissed!' Nana would reply, very put out. 'I'm gettin' out of 'ere! I don't want a wallopin'. Oh look, he's tumbled over! If only he'd break his bloody neck!'

At other times, when Coupeau headed straight towards her, and she didn't have time to run away, she'd crouch down, whispering:

'Come on, you lot, hide me! He's lookin' for me, he said he'd give me a kick up the arse if he caught me around 'ere again.'

When he'd walked past, she'd stand up and they'd all follow him, bursting with laughter. Would he see her or wouldn't he? It was a real game of hide-and-seek. One day, however, Boche had come and marched Pauline home by the ear, and Coupeau had driven Nana back with kicks up the backside.

The sun was going down and they took one last turn before walking home in the dim twilight, amid the weary crowd. The air was thick with dust, making the lowering sky duller still. The Rue de la Goutte-d'Or might have been a street in a small country town, with women gossiping on doorsteps and high-pitched voices breaking the silence of a neighbourhood empty of vehicles. The girls would stop for a moment in the courtyard to pick up their rackets, trying to give the impression they'd been there all the time. Then they'd walk up the stairs, thinking up some story, which often they didn't need, finding their parents about to come to blows because the food wasn't cooked properly or wasn't properly salted.

By now Nana had qualified as a flower-maker, getting two francs at Titreville's, the place in the Rue du Caire where she'd served her apprenticeship. The Coupeaus wanted to keep her there, under the watchful eye of Madame Lerat, who'd been forewoman for the last ten years. Each morning her mother would note the time on the cuckoo clock as her daughter set out on her own, looking sweet in an old black dress that was too tight across the shoulders and too short; it was Madame Lerat's responsibility to note the time she arrived, and let Gervaise know. They allowed her twenty minutes to get from the Rue de la Goutte-d'Or to the Rue du Caire, which was enough, because those lasses have legs like deer. Sometimes she arrived dead on time, but so red and out of breath that she must have covered the distance from the barrier in ten minutes, after dilly-dallying on the way. Most often she arrived seven or eight minutes late, and all day long she would fawn over her aunt, giving her imploring looks, trying to gain her sympathy and stop her telling. Madame Lerat, who understood the young, would lie to the Coupeaus, but would give Nana long lectures, stressing her own responsibility and the dangers a girl faced in the streets of Paris. Heavens above! She herself was followed often enough! So she would keep watch over her niece, her eyes gleaming with her prurient obsessions, excited by the thought that she was watching over and protecting the innocence of the poor little dear.

'Listen,' she kept saying, 'you must tell me everything. I'm too good to you. I'd have to throw myself in the Seine if anything bad happened to you. You do understand, dear, don't you, that if a man talks to you, you must tell me exactly what he says, every word. Are you sure no one has spoken to you?'

Nana couldn't help laughing, with a funny curl of the lip. No, men didn't talk to her. She walked too fast. Besides, what would they say? She had nothing to discuss with them, had she? And she'd explain why she was late, looking all innocent: she'd stopped to look at some pictures, or else she'd been with Pauline, who wanted to tell her something. Anyone who didn't believe her could follow her; she always kept to the left-hand pavement, and she sped along as if on wheels, leaving all the other girls behind. One day, in fact, Madame Lerat had caught her hanging about in the Rue du Petit-Carreau* with three other no-good flower-girls, staring up at a window and laughing because a man was shaving there; but Nana had angrily protested that she was simply going to the baker on the corner to buy a one-sou bun.

'Oh, I keep an eye on 'er, don't you worry,' Madame Lerat would say to the Coupeaus. 'You can take my word for it. If some bastard even tried to pinch her, I'd throw myself in between.'

The workshop at Titreville's was a large mezzanine room with a huge trestle table in the middle. Along the four bare walls, where the plaster showed through tears in the dingy grey paper, were shelves laden with old cardboard boxes, parcels, and abandoned flower designs left there to gather dust. The gas burners had given the ceiling a smearing of soot. The two windows were so big that the girls, as they sat at the table, could watch the people going past on the pavement opposite.

To set a good example, Madame Lerat was always the first to arrive. Then for a quarter of an hour the door would swing to and fro as the young flower-makers hurried in one after the other, perspiring and dishevelled. One July morning Nana was the last to arrive, which was hardly unusual.

'Well,' she said, 'I won't be sorry when I've got my own carriage.'

And without even taking off her hat, a black thing she called her 'cap', which she was tired of patching up all the time, she went over to the window and, leaning out, looked up and down the street.

'What are you looking at?' asked Madame Lerat, her suspicions aroused. 'Did your father come with you?'

'Of course not,' Nana replied calmly. 'I'm not looking at anything. I'm just looking to see how hot it is. Honestly, it's enough to make you ill, having to run like that.'

The heat that morning was stifling. The girls had lowered the blinds, but through them could still keep an eye on what was happening in the street; at last they'd settled down to work, in two rows, on each side of the table, with Madame Lerat installed at the top end. There were eight of them, and each had in front of her her pot of glue, her pincers and other tools, and her goffering cushion. The table was littered with bits of wire, cotton reels, wadding, green and brown paper, and leaves and petals cut out of silk, satin, or velvet. In the middle, in the neck of a large carafe, one of the girls had stuck a simple little spray of flowers that had been fading on her blouse since the evening before.

'I must tell you,' said Léonie, a pretty brunette, as she leaned over the cushion on which she was goffering rose petals, 'poor Caroline is very unhappy with that bloke who used to wait for her in the evenings.'

Nana, who was busy cutting little strips of green paper, exclaimed:

'That's no bloody surprise! He's got a different girl for every day of the week!'

Suppressed giggles ran round the table, and Madame Lerat felt she had to give them a ticking-off. Screwing up her nose, she muttered:

'There's no need to talk like that, my girl! You should mind your language. I'll tell your father and we'll see what he thinks.'

Nana puffed out her cheeks, as if holding back a guffaw. Her father? What a joke! What about his language! But suddenly Léonie whispered urgently:

'Look out! Here's the boss!'

Sure enough Madame Titreville, a tall gaunt woman, was just walking in. As a rule she stayed downstairs in the shop. The girls were quite afraid of her, because she was always very serious.

She went slowly round the table, at which all heads were now bent in silent activity. She called one girl a numbskull and made her start a daisy all over again. Then she departed as stiffly as she'd come.

'Oops!' exclaimed Nana, amid general groans.

'Really, young ladies! Really!' said Madame Lerat, trying to look stern. 'I shall be obliged to take steps...'

But they paid no attention, for they were not in the least afraid of her. She was too easy-going, tickled to be surrounded by these young things, whose eyes sparkled with mischief, taking them aside to pump them about their boyfriends and even telling their fortunes if there was room on the table for the cards. She was a terrible old gossip, and her leathery skin and masculine body would quiver with delight whenever she could get them on to her favourite subject. The only thing she didn't like was rude words; as long as you didn't use rude words you could say anything.

There was no doubt about it, the workshop was the perfect place for rounding off Nana's education! Of course, she had a lot of natural talent, but being with a group of girls already tainted with poverty and vice—that provided the finishing touch. They were all on top of each other, going to the bad together like a basket of apples when there are some rotten ones among them. Of course, they behaved themselves in company, so as not to seem too bad or use language that was too disgusting. In a word, they posed as nice young ladies. But when they could get into a corner and whisper in each other's ears, it was all dirty talk. No sooner had two of them got together than they started giggling about something filthy. Then in the evening, on their way home, they'd exchange confidences, stories that would make your hair stand on end; they'd linger on the pavement, talking excitedly amid the bustle of the crowd. On top of that, for girls like Nana who were still virgins, there was also an unhealthy atmosphere in the workshop, a smell of low dance halls and wild nights, brought in by the girls who were forever on the town, with their hastily done-up hair and their skirts so crumpled that they looked as if they'd slept in them. The sluggishness of mornings-after, the rings round the eyes (which Madame Lerat called, accurately enough, the black eyes of love), swaying hips, and hoarse voices—all this created in the workshop an atmosphere of dark perversion, in contrast to the bright colours and fragility of the artificial flowers. Nana would sniff, intoxicated, whenever she sensed next to her a girl who had already tasted the forbidden fruit. For a long time she sat next to big Lisa, who was said to be pregnant; and she'd keep looking at her closely, as if expecting her to swell up and burst at any moment. It was hardly a question of her learning anything new. The little devil knew it all, having learnt everything on the street, in the Rue de la Goutte-d'Or. It was just that in the workshop she could see it going on, and gradually she began to develop both the desire and the nerve to do it herself.

'It's so hot in here,' she muttered, going over to a window as if to lower the blind a bit more. But instead she leaned out, looking again up and down the street. At the same time, Léonie, who was watching a man standing on the pavement opposite, said:

'What's that old bloke doing? He's been spying on us for at least a quarter of an hour.'

'It's some old lecher, no doubt,' said Madame Lerat. 'Nana, come and sit down! I told you not to stand at the window.'

Nana picked up the violet stalks she was rolling and the whole work-shop started talking about the man. He was a well-dressed gentleman of about fifty, wearing an overcoat, sallow-faced, very serious and dignified-looking, with a neatly trimmed grey beard. For a full hour he stood there in front of a herbalist's shop, staring up at the blinds of the workshop. The girls kept bursting into giggles, which were drowned by the noise from the street; they bent busily over their work, but glanced out from time to time so as not to lose sight of the gentleman.

'Look!' said Léonie. 'He's got a monocle. He looks really posh. I bet he's waiting for Augustine.'

But Augustine, a tall, unattractive blonde, replied sourly that she didn't go for old men. Whereupon Madame Lerat, shaking her head, murmured with her thin smile full of innuendo:

'You're making a mistake there, my dear; old men can be very affectionate.'

At this point Léonie's neighbour, a plump little creature, whispered something in her ear; Léonie promptly fell back in her chair, giggling uncontrollably. Twisting round to look at the gentleman, and giggling more than ever, she managed to splutter:

'That's it! Yes, that's it! Oh, you've got such a dirty mind, Sophie!'

'What did she say? What did she say?' they all asked, dying to know.

Léonie, wiping the tears from her eyes, didn't answer. When she'd recovered somewhat she went back to her goffering and declared:

'I can't repeat it.'

They kept asking, but she just shook her head, still laughing. Then Augustine, who was sitting on her left, begged her to whisper it in her ear. Augustine doubled up in her turn. Then she passed on what she'd heard, and it ran round the table from ear to ear to the sound of exclamations and suppressed laughter. When they'd all heard Sophie's dirty joke, they looked at each other and they all exploded at once, though blushing and slightly ashamed. Madame Lerat was the only one in the dark. She was very annoyed.

'Ladies, it's very rude what you're doing. You should never whisper in front of other people. It was something indecent, I suppose. Charming!'

But she didn't dare ask them to repeat what Sophie had said, though she was desperate to know. Nevertheless, while looking down at her work with an air of offended dignity, she revelled in the girls' conversation. Nobody could say anything, even something completely innocent, about her work for instance, without the others immediately seeing some double meaning in it; they twisted the remark to make it sound suggestive, getting extraordinary innuendoes out of simple phrases like: 'my pincers have got a crack in them', or 'who's been poking about in my pot?' And they made everything apply to the gentleman loitering across the street; he was the real focus of every allusion. His ears must have been burning! They ended up saying the silliest things in their desire to be clever. But that didn't stop them finding the game very amusing, their eyes flashing with excitement as they came up with more and more outrageous comments. There was no cause, however, for Madame Lerat to be angry, they weren't saying anything indecent. She herself had them all in fits when she said:

'Madame Lisa, my flame's gone out, can you pass me yours?'

'Madame Lerat's flame's gone out!' they all shrieked.

She started saying:

'When you're my age, ladies...'

But they weren't listening, all talking instead about calling the gentleman up to get Madame Lerat's flame going.

Nana played a very active part in this festival of mirth. You should have seen her! Not a single double meaning escaped her. She even came out with some pretty spicy things herself, sticking out her chin to emphasize them, bursting with delight. She was in her element in this atmosphere of depravity. And while squirming with laughter on her chair, she went on rolling her violet stems. She had an amazing knack, doing them quicker than you can roll a cigarette. She'd just pick up a thin strip of green paper, and in a flash the paper was wrapped round the wire; then, a drop of glue at the top to stick it down, and there it was: a fresh, delicate sprig of greenery, ready to pin to a lady's bosom. The trick lay in her fingers, the tapering fingers of a whore, which looked so supple, soft, and caressing. That was the only part of the job she'd been able to master, and she was given every stalk in the workshop to make, because she did them so well. Meanwhile the gentleman on the pavement opposite had disappeared. The girls were settling down and getting on with their work in the intense heat. When the clock struck noon, time for lunch, they all stood up and moved around. Nana rushed to the window, and then said she was going out and would do any errands they wanted. Léonie asked for two sous' worth of shrimps, Augustine a bag of fried potatoes, Lisa a bunch of radishes, Sophie a sausage. Then, as Nana was going down the stairs, Madame Lerat, who'd been struck by Nana's interest in looking out of the window, went striding after her, saying:

'Wait a minute, I'll come with you, there's something I need to get.'

And who should she see standing there in the alley but the gentleman, as large as life, giving Nana the eye! The girl went very red. Her aunt grabbed her by the arm and marched her along the pavement, with the gentleman close behind. So, the old lecher was after Nana! Well, how nice, at fifteen and a half, to have men trailing after her! Madame Lerat peppered her with questions. Nana said she had no idea who he was. He'd been following her for five days, she couldn't show her face outside without bumping into him. She thought he was in business in some way—yes, a button manufacturer. Madame Lerat was very impressed. She turned round and gave the man a quick glance.

'You can tell he's well off,' she muttered. 'Listen, my dear, you must tell me everything. You've got nothing to be scared of now.'

As they talked they'd been hurrying from one shop to another—the charcuterie, the fruiterer's, the cookshop—until the various orders made quite a pile in their arms. But this didn't bother them, and they tripped along, laughing and casting sparkling little smiles behind them. Madame Lerat herself put on a certain charm and became quite girlish for the benefit of the button manufacturer, who was still close behind.

'He's very distinguished-looking,' she said as they arrived back in the alley. 'If only his intentions were honourable.'

Then, as they were climbing the stairs, she suddenly seemed to remember something.

'By the way, tell me what they were all whispering to each other— you know, Sophie's dirty joke.'

Nana didn't seem to mind being asked, but she put her arm round Madame Lerat and made her come back down a couple of steps because, really, it wasn't something you could repeat out loud, not even on the stairs. Then she whispered in her ear. It was so obscene that Madame Lerat just shook her head, opening her eyes wide and making a wry face. Anyway, now she knew, and it stopped bothering her.

The flower-makers ate off their knees, so as not to soil the table. They bolted the food down, bored with eating because they'd rather spend the lunch-hour watching the passers-by or exchanging confidences in corners. That particular day they were concerned to find out where the gentleman they'd seen in the morning was hiding, for he had certainly disappeared. Madame Lerat and Nana looked at each other but said nothing. It was already ten past one, and the girls seemed in no hurry to resume their work, when Léonie made a sudden *psst!* sound, of the kind house-painters use to attract each other's attention, to warn them that the boss was coming. They were all instantly on their chairs, bent over their work, when Madame Titreville came in and stalked round the table.

From that day on, Madame Lerat delighted in her niece's first affair. She never left her alone, accompanying her morning and evening, saying it was her duty. Naturally Nana got rather fed up with this, but at the same time it flattered her to be guarded like a treasure, and the conversations they had as they walked along followed by the button manufacturer inflamed her imagination and made her want to take the plunge. Oh, her aunt understood how she felt; she could even sympathize with the button manufacturer, that elderly gentleman who seemed so respectable, because, after all, tender feelings in people of mature years always have deeper roots. But all the same, she remained vigilant. Yes, he'd have to climb over her dead body before he could get to the child. One evening she went up to him and told him bluntly that what he was doing wasn't right. He bowed politely without saying a word, like an old roué used to rebuffs from parents. He was so polite that she couldn't really be angry with him. But she went on giving Nana endless practical advice about love, hinting at the awfulness of men and telling all kinds of stories about silly girls who had given in to them and been very sorry afterwards. All this left Nana yearning for love, her eyes gleaming wickedly in her pale face.

One day, in the Rue du Faubourg-Poissonnière, the button manufacturer dared to thrust himself between Nana and her aunt and whisper something quite unseemly. Madame Lerat took fright, saying she no longer felt safe herself; and she dumped the whole business on her brother. Things now took a different course. There was a tremendous to-do at the Coupeaus'. To start with, the roofer gave Nana a good hiding. What was this he'd been told? The little slut was chasing after old men, was she? Well, just let him catch her fooling about out there and she'd be for it, and no mistake! Did you ever hear of such a thing! A snotty-nosed little brat dragging the family's name through the mud! He gave her a good shaking, saying that, by God!, she'd better watch her step, because he was the one who'd be keeping an eye on her from now on. As soon as she came in from work he looked her over, examining her face carefully to see whether she'd had a little kiss, one of those quick silent ones on the eye, so easy to plant. He'd sniff at her and turn her round. One evening she got another hiding because he'd found a black mark on her neck. The little bitch dared to deny it was a love bite! It was a bruise, she said, just a bruise she'd got larking about with Léonie. He'd give her a few bruises, he'd stop her from larking about, even if it meant breaking a few bones. At other times, when he was in a good mood, he'd tease her and make fun of her. She was perfect for men—as flat as a pancake, with hollows in her shoulders big enough to put your fist in! Nana, beaten repeatedly for the wicked things she hadn't done, accused of all sorts of abominations by her father, displayed the sullen but furious submissiveness of a trapped animal.

'Leave her alone!' Gervaise would say, trying to be more reasonable. 'You'll make her want it in the end, if you carry on about it all the time.'

Oh yes, she was beginning to want it more and more! Her whole body was itching, making her want to run off and take the plunge, as her father said. He kept the idea so constantly before her that even the most modest of girls would have been aroused. And by yelling at her the way he did he even taught her things she hadn't yet known— surprising though that was. So, little by little, she began to behave strangely. One morning Coupeau caught her fumbling in a paper bag and dabbing something on her cheeks. It was rice powder, which her perverted taste made her plaster over her delicate, satiny skin. He took the paper bag and rubbed her face with it, so hard that he broke the skin, telling her she wasn't a miller's daughter. Another time, she brought home some red ribbons to decorate her cap, the old black cap she was so ashamed of. He asked her angrily where the ribbons had come from. Had she earned them lying on her back? Or had she pinched them from somewhere? Tart or thief? Perhaps she was both now! Several times he came upon her with some pretty thing in her hands—a carnelian ring, a pair of cuffs with fine lace trimming, or one of those plated hearts, 'come hithers', that girls wear between their breasts. Coupeau wanted to destroy everything, but she defended her things furiously—they were hers, some lady had given them to her, or else she'd swapped something for them at work. The heart, for example, she'd found in the Rue d'Aboukir. When her father crushed it under her heel she stood there, pale and rigid, seething with a rebellious impulse to fling herself at him and snatch something of his. She'd been dreaming for two years of having a heart like that, and now he'd crushed it to bits! No, it was too much, she couldn't stand it much longer.

To tell the truth, Coupeau's attempts to keep Nana under control were motivated less by a desire to keep her on the straight and narrow than by an urge to tease her. He was often unfair, and this exasperated her. She even started skipping her work, and when Coupeau gave her a walloping she laughed at him and said she didn't want to go back to Titreville's because she had to sit next to Augustine who must have eaten her feet, her breath smelled so foul. Thereupon Coupeau escorted her himself to the Rue du Caire and asked the boss to put her always next to Augustine, by way of punishment. Every morning for two weeks he took the trouble to take her down from the Barrière Poissonnière to the door of the workshop.* And he'd wait for five minutes on the pavement to make sure she'd gone in. But one morning, having stopped off with a friend in a bar in the Rue Saint-Denis, he saw the little devil ten minutes later high-tailing it down the street, wiggling her behind. For the last two weeks she'd been tricking him by going up two floors instead of into Titreville's and sitting on the stairs until he'd gone. When he tried to take Madame Lerat to task for this, she replied in no uncertain terms that she was hardly to blame; she'd told her niece everything she ought to tell her to make her wary of men, it wasn't her fault if the kid still hankered after the dirty brutes. Now she was washing her hands of the whole thing and swore not to be involved in any of it any more, because she knew what she knew, all the nasty things being said about her in the family, yes, certain persons who had the nerve to accuse her of going off the rails along with Nana and taking a wicked pleasure in watching her niece being debauched before her very eyes. In the meantime, Coupeau learnt from the proprietress that Nana had been led astray by one of the other girls, that little bitch Léonie, who had given up flower-making to be a real good-time girl. The kid was obviously tempted by the lure of adventure on the streets, but she might still be able to get married with a wreath of orange blossom on her head; they'd have to be quick about it, though, if they wanted to give her to a husband clean, undamaged, and in proper condition, in a word intact as a self-respecting young lady should be.

In the Rue de la Goutte-d'Or tenement, they talked about Nana's old gent as if they all knew him. Oh, he was always very polite, even a bit shy, but devilishly persistent and patient. Following ten paces behind her like an obedient little dog. Occasionally he would even come into the courtyard. One evening Madame Gaudron came upon him on the second-floor landing, sneaking along next to the banister, with his head down, looking horny but nervous. The Lorilleux threatened to move if that ragtag niece of theirs brought any more men in after her, because it was disgusting the way the staircase was full of them, you couldn't go downstairs now without seeing them on every step, sniffing around and waiting; really, you'd think there was some kind of bitch on heat in that part of the building. The Boches felt sorry for the poor gentleman, such a respectable man, falling like that for a little tramp. After all, he was a businessman, they'd seen his button factory in the Boulevard de la Villette;* if he'd happened on a decent sort of girl he might have set her up very nicely. Thanks to the details provided by the concierges, the whole neighbourhood, even the Lorilleux, treated the old fellow with the greatest respect when he passed by on Nana's heels, with his hang-dog look, his sallow face, and his neatly trimmed grey beard.

For the first month Nana thought her old gent was a great joke. You should have seen him, hanging round her constantly, and he was a real groper, always touching her skirt from behind in the crowd, while looking all innocent. And his legs! As spindly as anything, real matchsticks! And as bald as a coot, with just four strands of hair straggling down the back of his neck, so that she was often tempted to ask him for the address of the barber who parted his hair for him. What an old fuddy-duddy! Nothing to get excited about!

But then, seeing him always there, she began to find him less of a joke. She felt vaguely afraid of him, and would have screamed if he'd come too close. Often when she stopped in front of a jeweller's window she'd suddenly hear him muttering things behind her. And what he muttered was true: she'd have loved to have a cross on a velvet ribbon round her neck, or some little coral earrings, so tiny you'd have thought they were drops of blood. But even if she hadn't felt any great desire for jewellery, she really couldn't go about forever looking shabby, she was tired of patching her things up with odd scraps from the workshop in the Rue du Caire, and she was especially sick of her hat, that old cap on which the flowers she pinched from Titreville's dangled like dags on a sheep, the way bells dangle from a beggar's backside. So it was that, tramping through the mud, spattered by the passing carriages, dazzled by the splendid window displays, she'd feel cravings that tortured her like hunger pangs, she'd long to be smartly dressed, to eat in restaurants, to go to shows, to have a room of her own with nice furniture. Sometimes she'd stop in her tracks, pale with desire, feeling the warmth of the Paris pavements creeping up her legs, gripped by a fierce urge to experience all the pleasures swarming around her in the crowded streets. And without fail, just when she was feeling like that, her old gentleman would whisper his propositions in her ear. Oh, how gladly she would have taken him on if she hadn't been afraid of him, if she hadn't felt deep down an instinctive aversion that stiffened her resolve, and made her angry and disgusted by what was unknown about men, in spite of all her natural inclinations.

But when winter arrived, life at the Coupeaus' became impossible. Every evening Nana got a thrashing. When her father was tired of beating her, her mother would give her a clout or two to teach her to behave. Often there was a free-for-all; as soon as one of them hit her, the other would come to her defence, so that all three would end up rolling on the floor surrounded by broken crockery. What's more, there was never enough to eat and it was freezing cold. If Nana bought herself something nice, like a bow made of ribbon or some cuff buttons, the parents would confiscate it and sell it for whatever they could get. She had nothing of her own except her ration of blows before creeping under her rag of a sheet, where she lay shivering with her little black skirt spread on top as her only coverlet. No, this hellish existence couldn't go on, she didn't want to end her days like that. It was a long time since her father had meant anything to her; when a father drinks the way hers drank, he's not a father any more but just a disgusting brute you'd like to be rid of. And now her affection for her mother was fading fast, because she too had started to drink. Gervaise now enjoyed going to look for Coupeau in Père Colombe's bar, because she'd be offered a few drinks; these days she was happy to sit down, not turning up her nose the way she did the first time; she'd knock the stuff back in one go, hanging around there for hours and coming away glassy-eyed. When Nana walked past the Assommoir and saw her mother sitting at the back, her nose in her glass, looking pretty far gone amid all those bawling men, she'd see red, because the young, bent on other kinds of pleasure, can't see the point of drink. On evenings like that it all made a pretty picture: a drunken father, a drunken mother, a home that was a dump, bugger-all to eat, and the stink of booze. In short, even a saint wouldn't have stayed there. It'd be too bad if she did a runner one of these days; her parents could just say their *mea culpa* and admit they'd driven her out themselves.

One Saturday Nana came home to find her parents in a dreadful state. Coupeau was sprawled across the bed, snoring. Gervaise was slumped in a chair, staring vacantly into space, her head lolling sideways. She'd forgotten to warm up the dinner, a bit of leftover stew. A flickering candle lit up the poverty-stricken squalor of the place.

'Is that you, sweetie?' Gervaise managed to say. 'Your Papa will be after you!'

Nana said nothing. She just stood there, very pale, looking at the unlit stove, the table not set, the dismal room to which this pair of soaks added the awfulness of their drunken stupor. She kept her hat on; she walked round the room, then, gritting her teeth, she opened the door and went out.

'You goin' back down?' asked her mother, unable to turn her head.

'Yes, I've forgotten something. I'll be back... Goodnight.'

But she never came back. The next day, when the Coupeaus had sobered up, they had a blazing row, each blaming the other for Nana's disappearance. As people say to children about sparrows, her parents might catch her if they put a pinch of salt on her tail! Nana's leaving was a terrible blow to Gervaise, crushing her spirit even further; she realized full well that, in spite of her present sorry state, her girl's going off the rails like that and sleeping around would drag her down too, because without a daughter to think about any more she might let herself sink to any depths. Yes, the ungrateful creature had carried away in her filthy skirts the last shreds of her mother's own decency. For three whole days she drank, seething with rage, her fists clenched, her mouth spewing obscenities about her slut of a daughter. Coupeau, after going along the outer boulevards and having a good look at all the tarts on view, took up his pipe again, calm as you please. Occasionally, however, in the middle of a meal, he'd leap up waving his arms and brandishing a knife, yelling that he'd been dishonoured. Then he'd sit down again and finish his meal.

In the building not a month went by without girls taking off like canaries whose cages had been left open, so no one was surprised by what had happened to the Coupeaus. But the Lorilleux exulted in it. Hadn't they predicted that the kid would fly the coop? It was obvious, all flower-girls go to the bad. The Boches and the Poissons were equally delighted, making a huge song-and-dance about their own virtue. Lantier was the only one who made some sort of excuse for Nana, though in a rather twisted way. Of course, he'd say, with his holier-than-thou air, a girl who runs away from home is breaking all the rules; but then he'd add, with a glint in his eye, that, damn it all, the kid was far too pretty to put up with poverty at her age.

'Do you want to know what happened?' cried Madame Lorilleux one day in the Boches' lodge, where they were having coffee. 'Well,

Gimpy sold her daughter! It's the gospel-truth. Yes, she sold her, and I can prove it! That old man we kept running into all day long on the stairs, he was going up to pay his instalments. It's so obvious. Just yesterday someone saw the two of them together at the Ambigu, the little miss and her big tomcat. Oh yes, they've got together all right!'

They went on chinwagging as they finished their coffee. Yes, Madame Lorilleux's claim was possible; worse things had been known to happen. So after a while even the most level-headed people in the neighbourhood were going round saying that Gervaise had sold her daughter.

Gervaise, now, had become a real slattern. She didn't give a damn what people thought. If someone had shouted 'Thief!' after her in the street, she wouldn't even have turned round. It was a month since she'd stopped working for Madame Fauconnier, who'd had to sack her for causing arguments. In just a few weeks she'd started at eight different laundries, lasting two or three days in each place before being sacked because her work was so badly done; she was so careless and sloppy, her mind so befuddled by drink that she was even forgetting the skills of her trade. Eventually, realizing she wasn't up to it, she'd given up ironing and started working by the day in the Rue Neuve wash-house; splashing in the water, wrestling with the dirty clothes, returning to the roughest and simplest job in the laundry trade—she could still manage that, though it dragged her one step further down the slope to degradation. And the wash-house hardly improved her looks. At the end of the day she was like a bedraggled dog, dripping wet, her skin blue. What's more, she was putting on even more weight, despite the days without food, and her limp was now so bad that she couldn't walk next to someone without almost knocking them over.

Naturally, when a woman lets herself go to that extent she loses all her feminine self-respect. Gervaise had cast aside all the things in which she used to take pride, her care over her appearance, her need for affection, decency, and respect. You could have kicked her anywhere, front or back, and she wouldn't have felt it, she was becoming so flabby and indifferent. Lantier had dropped her completely, not even giving her the odd pinch on the bottom for old time's sake; and she seemed not to have noticed the end of their long relationship, which had dragged along to its close in mutual weariness. For her it was one chore less. Even the relationship between Lantier and

Virginie left her totally unmoved, such was her indifference to all that nonsense she used to get so agitated about. She would have held a candle to light them to bed, if they'd wanted. By now everybody knew that the hatter and the shopkeeper were carrying on like nobody's business. It was so easy for them, as well, because the cuckold Poisson was on duty every night, shivering on some deserted pavement while at home his wife and their lodger were keeping each other warm. They could afford to take their time, too, because they could hear the sound of his boots as he paced slowly past the shop in the dark, empty street, without ever needing to poke their noses out from under the blanket. A policeman must put his duty first, mustn't he? So they'd stay there until daybreak, calmly violating his property rights while he watched solemnly over the property of others. Everyone in the Goutte-d'Or neighbourhood thought it a great joke. The idea of authority wearing the horns, that was a scream. In any case, Lantier had earned his right to his special position: the shop and its owner went together. He'd gobbled up a laundress, now he was chomping on a sweetshop owner, and he had drapers, stationers, and dressmakers all lined up ready. His jaws were big enough to scoff the lot.

No, there was never a man like Lantier for wallowing in sugar. He couldn't have made a better choice when he advised Virginie to go in for confectionery. He was too much of a Provençal not to have a sweet tooth; he could have lived on pastilles, gum drops, dragées, and chocolate—especially dragées, which he called 'sugared almonds': they made his mouth water, they tickled his palate so. For a whole year now he'd been living on sweets. When Virginie asked him to mind the shop he'd open the drawers and simply gorge himself. Often, in the middle of chatting, with five or six people around, he'd take the top off one of the jars on the counter, dip his hand in, and munch whatever he found; the jar would stay open and end up empty. After a while no one took any notice; it was just a habit of his, he explained. Also, he'd hit on the idea of a perpetual cold, a throat irritation, which he said needed soothing. He was still not working, but kept talking about business schemes that were grander than ever. Just then, he was working on a marvellous invention, the umbrella hat, a hat that became an umbrella on its wearer's head at the first drop of rain; he'd promised Poisson half of the profits, borrowing from him the odd twenty francs for the experiments. Meanwhile the shop was melting away in his mouth; that was where all the stock ended up, even the chocolate cigars and red caramel pipes. When he was gorged with sweets and, in a fit of amorousness, was treating himself to a taste of Virginie's lips, in a corner of the shop, she found him all sugary, his own lips just like pralines. He was such a lovely man to kiss! Honestly, he seemed actually to be turning into honey! The Boches would say that all he had to do to sweeten his coffee was dip his finger in it.

Mellowed by this diet of endless desserts, Lantier had become quite fatherly towards Gervaise. He'd give her advice and scolded her for being work-shy. Hell! A woman of her age should be up to it! And he accused her of having always been greedy. But, as you have to give people a helping hand even if they don't really deserve it, he tried to find her little jobs. So he'd persuaded Virginie to get Gervaise to come in once a week and scrub the floors in the shop and the other rooms; she knew how to use caustic soda, and she earned a franc and a half each time. So Gervaise turned up on Saturday mornings with her bucket and scrubbing brush, not seeming to mind coming back like this to the very place where she had once presided like a queen, as the pretty blonde proprietress. It was the final comedown, the end of all her pride.

One Saturday she had a terrible time with her work. It had rained for three days, and the customers seemed to have brought all the mud in the neighbourhood in with their feet. Virginie stood behind the counter, playing the great lady, her hair beautifully done, and wearing a little lace collar and lace cuffs. Beside her on the narrow bench of red imitation leather, Lantier was taking his ease, looking perfectly at home, as if he was the real owner of the place. As usual, he was dipping his hand absent-mindedly into a jar of mint pastilles, just to have something sweet to nibble on.

'I say, Madame Coupeau!' cried Virginie, who was beadily watching Gervaise as she went about her work, 'you've left some dirt over there, in the corner. You can do better than that!'

Gervaise went back into the corner and began scrubbing again. She knelt on the floor in the dirty water, bent double, her shoulder blades sticking out and her arms purple and stiff. Her old skirt, soaked through, was sticking to her buttocks. There on the floor she looked like a bundle of dirty clothes, her hair hanging down, the holes in her blouse revealing her flabby flesh, the rolls of fat quivering and shaking with the jerky movements she was making; and she was sweating so much that it was pouring off her face in big drops.

'The more elbow grease you put into it, the more it shines,' said Lantier sententiously, his mouth full of pastilles.

Virginie, lolling back like a princess, her eyes half closed, was watching the scrubbing and making occasional comments:

'A bit more to the right. Now, pay special attention to the woodwork. You know, I wasn't very pleased last Saturday. You left some of the dirt marks.'

And they both assumed an ever more regal air, as if they were sitting together on a throne, as Gervaise dragged herself about at their feet in the black mud. Virginie must have been enjoying it, because tawny glints showed for a moment in her cat's eyes, and she gave Lantier a little smile. Now, at last, she had her revenge for that drubbing long ago in the wash-house, which she'd never been able to forget!

Meanwhile, whenever Gervaise stopped scrubbing, a little sawing noise could be heard in the back room. Through the open door Poisson's profile could be seen, outlined against the pale light of the courtyard. He was off duty that day and was using his free time to indulge his passion for making little boxes. He was sitting at a table and cutting arabesques, with extraordinary care, in the mahogany of a cigar box.

'Listen, Badingue!' cried Lantier (who, as a gesture of friendship, had gone back to using that nickname again), 'I'll take that box, I'd like to give it to a young lady I know as a present.'

Virginie gave him a pinch, but the hatter, gallantly, still smiling, returned good for evil by running his fingers up her leg under the counter, like a mouse, and then took his hand away quite nonchalantly when the husband glanced up, his tuft of a beard and red moustache bristling on his ashen face.

'Well, as it happens, Auguste, I was making it for you,' said the policeman. 'As a token of our friendship.'

'I'll be damned. Then I'll hang on to the little whatsit!' replied Lantier, laughing. 'You know what, I'll wear it on a ribbon round my neck.'

Then suddenly, as though this idea had sparked another one, he exclaimed:

'By the way, I bumped into Nana last night.'

The shock of this news made Gervaise slump down in the puddle of dirty water spreading across the shop floor. She sat there, sweating and breathless, brush in hand.

'Oh!' was all she could say.

'Yes, I was going down the Rue des Martyrs, watching a girl sway-ing her hips on the arm of some old guy in front of me, and I thought to meself: "Funny, I know that backside..." So I put on a spurt and found meself lookin' straight at our precious Nana... Well, you needn't feel sorry for her: she looked as 'appy as anythin', with a pretty woollen dress, a gold cross round her neck, and a saucy bloody look on 'er face!'

'Oh!' Gervaise repeated, more faintly.

Lantier, having finished the pastilles, reached into another jar for a piece of barley sugar.

'There are no flies on 'er!' he went on. 'Would you believe it, she signalled to me to follow her, as cool as anything. Then she parked her old boy somewhere, in a café. And what a sight he was! Looked as if he'd been sucked dry! Well, she came and joined me in a doorway. And it was as if butter wouldn't melt in 'er mouth! She was as nice as can be, chattering away, licking me like a little dog. She even gave me a kiss and wanted to know how everybody was. Anyway, I was very pleased I bumped into 'er.'

'Oh!' said Gervaise a third time.

She was still sitting there, in a heap, not saying anything. Hadn't her daughter passed on any kind of message? In the silence, you could hear Poisson's saw again. Lantier, highly entertained by it all, was vigorously sucking his barley sugar and smacking his lips.

'Well, I can tell you that if I ever see 'er I'll cross over to the other side of the street,' said Virginie, giving Lantier another pinch, very hard. 'I'd be very embarrassed to be greeted in public by a girl like that. I'm sorry to say this in front of you, Madame Coupeau, but your daughter's a real bad'un. Poisson runs in girls every day who aren't 'alf as bad as she is.'

Gervaise, staring into space, said nothing and didn't move. Eventually she shook her head slightly, as if in response to thoughts running through her mind, while the hatter remarked with the air of a man who knows what he's talking about:

'Well, she might be bad, but she looks delicious. I wouldn't mind...'

At this point Virginie gave him such a terrible look that he stopped short and had to placate her with a caress. He glanced at the policeman, saw that he was still bent over his little box, and took the opportunity to pop a piece of barley sugar into Virginie's mouth. She smiled with pleasure, and directed her anger at Gervaise:

'Come on, get a move on. You won't get the job done if you just sit there like a block of wood. Jump to it. I don't want to be paddling about in water all day long.'

And, lowering her voice, she added nastily:

'I can't help it if the girl's gone off the rails!'

Gervaise seemed not to hear. She'd begun scrubbing again, her back aching, almost lying on the floor, dragging herself about with slow, frog-like movements. Clutching the brush in both hands, she pushed before her a pool of filthy water, which splashed her with specks of mud right up into her hair. After she'd swept the dirty water out into the gutter, she only had the rinsing to do.

After a short silence Lantier, getting bored, called out:

'I haven't told you, Badingue, I saw your boss yesterday in the Rue de Rivoli.* He looks an absolute wreck. I wouldn't give him more than six months.* But then, with the life he leads!'

He was referring to the Emperor. The policeman replied drily, without looking up:

'If you were running the government, you wouldn't be so fat.'

'If I was running the government, my friend,' replied the hatter, putting on a serious air, 'things would be going a lot better, that's for sure. Look at their foreign policy. It's a worry. I can tell you, if I knew just one journalist I could get fired up with my ideas...'

He was getting worked up, and as he'd finished his barley sugar he'd opened a drawer and taken out five or six pieces of marshmallow which he gobbled down as he gesticulated.

'It's very simple. First of all, I'd restore Poland to how it was, and I'd set up a great Scandinavian state to keep the giants of the North* in order. Then I'd turn all those little German kingdoms into a single republic. As for England, there's no need to be afraid of her; if she made a move, I'd send a hundred thousand men to India. Then, on top of that, I'd send the Grand Turk to Mecca and the Pope to Jerusalem. You see? That would sort Europe out all right. Watch this, Badingue...'

He broke off to grab another handful of marshmallows.

'There! It wouldn't take any longer than swallowing these.'

He popped them into his mouth one after the other.

'The Emperor has got a different plan,' said the policeman after two full minutes of thought.

'Give over!' scoffed the hatter. 'We know all about 'is plan! The rest of Europe treats us as a joke. Every day the Tuileries flunkeys have to drag your boss out from under the table between two high-class tarts.'

But Poisson had got to his feet. He took a step forward and said, with his hand on his heart:

'You're upsetting me, Auguste. You should discuss things without making it personal.'

Virginie intervened at this point, asking them to stop getting on her nerves. She didn't give a stuff about Europe. How could two men who were so at one on everything else be so at odds over politics? For a moment or two they both growled at each other. Then, to show he had no hard feelings, Poisson fetched the lid of the little box he'd just finished. Written on it, in inlay, were the words: 'To Auguste, in friendship.' Very flattered, Lantier leaned back in such a way that he was almost on top of Virginie. The husband looked on, his bleary eyes expressionless in his pasty face; but the red bristles of his moustache had a funny way of twitching all by themselves, which might have perturbed a man less sure of himself than Lantier.

That devil Lantier had the sort of cool nerve that women find attractive. Since Poisson had his back to them, he thought it would be a hoot if he planted a kiss on Madame Poisson's left eyelid. Usually he was very artful and prudent, but when he'd been arguing with the policeman about politics he'd take any risk to show he could do whatever he wanted with his wife. Those greedy caresses, shamelessly stolen behind the policeman's back, were his revenge against the Empire, which was turning France into a huge brothel. Only this time he forgot that Gervaise was there. She'd just finished rinsing and wiping over the floor and was standing at the counter, waiting for her thirty sous. The kiss left her quite unmoved, as if it were something quite natural that didn't concern her. Virginie, however, seemed quite annoyed as she tossed the coins on to the counter in front of Gervaise. But Gervaise didn't move. She still seemed to be waiting, exhausted by her efforts, soaking wet and as unsightly as a dog who'd just been pulled out of a drain.

'So that's all she said?' she finally asked the hatter.

'Who?' he exclaimed. 'Oh, you mean Nana. Yes, that was all. But what a mouth she's got, the little bitch! Just like a pot of strawberries!'

Gervaise went off clutching her thirty sous. Her worn slippers squelched out water like pumps; musical slippers they were, playing a tune as they left a trail of big wet footprints on the pavement.

In the neighbourhood, all the women tipplers like Gervaise said she drank to forget her daughter's disgrace. She herself, when she took hold of her glass of liquor at the counter, would strike a dramatic pose and, as she knocked it back, say she wished it would make her drop dead on the spot. And on the days when she came home stinking drunk, she'd mumble that it was all because of her troubles. But respectable folk just shrugged; they'd heard that one before, people blaming Père Colombe's poison on their troubles. All their troubles came out of a bottle! Of course, she'd found it hard at first to come to terms with Nana's flight. What was left of her sense of decency was appalled; in any case, generally speaking, no mother likes having to admit that her daughter, at that very moment, may be going off with the first man who comes along. But she was already too numbed, too weary and sick at heart, to feel this shame for long. It would come and go. She'd be fine for a week, never thinking of her tart of a daughter, and then suddenly, whether drunk or sober, she'd be overcome with feelings of tenderness or anger, with a furious desire to get Nana in a corner and take her in her arms or else beat her senseless, according to her whim of the moment. In the end, she no longer had any clear idea of what was decent or not. But, when it came down to it, Nana was hers, wasn't she? Well, when something is yours, you don't want to see it just vanish into thin air, do you?

When such thoughts assailed her, Gervaise would search the streets with the eyes of a policeman. Oh, if she'd caught sight of that little slut, she'd have marched her straight home! That year the whole neighbourhood was being turned upside down. The Boulevard Magenta and the Boulevard Ornano* were being built, which meant clearing away the old Barrière Poissonnière and cutting through the outer boulevard. You hardly knew where you were any more. All of one side of the Rue des Poissonniers was pulled down. Now, from the Rue de la Goutte-d'Or, you could see a huge open space, full of sunshine and fresh air; and in place of the slums that had blocked the view on that side, there arose on the Boulevard Ornano a most imposing building, a six-storey residence with carved stonework like a church, whose gleaming windows, hung with embroidered curtains, suggested great wealth. This dazzling white building, standing right opposite, seemed to light up the whole street. Every day Lantier and Poisson would argue about the place. The hatter never stopped talking about the demolitions taking place in Paris, accusing the Emperor of putting up palaces everywhere, so as to drive the workers back to the provinces; and the policeman, white with anger, would reply that, on the contrary, the Emperor was thinking first and foremost of the workers, saying that he'd pull down the whole of Paris if necessary, simply to provide jobs for them. Gervaise wasn't keen on these beautifications either, they were messing up the dingy little corner of Paris she'd grown used to. Her irritation came from the fact that the neighbourhood was looking up just as she was on the way down. When you're lying in the gutter you don't like having the sun shine straight on you. When she was walking round, looking for Nana, she'd get mad when she had to step over piles of building materials, paddle through the mud of unfinished pavements, or find her way blocked by a makeshift fence. The fancy new building on the Boulevard Ornano was a special bugbear. Places like that were for tarts like Nana.

But she did have news of the girl on several occasions. There are always some good souls only too pleased to pass on bad news. They'd told her Nana had dumped her old gent—not the wisest thing for an inexperienced young girl to do. She'd been well off with him, pampered, adored, free to do what she wanted, even, if she'd gone about it the right way. But young people are silly, it seemed she'd gone off with some dandified young fellow, no one quite knew who. What was certain was that, one afternoon on the Place de la Bastille, she'd asked her old boy for three sous so she could go and have a pee, and that was the last he'd seen of her. In the best circles this is called taking the piss. Some people swore they'd seen her since, dancing the *chahut** at the Grand Salon de la Folie* in the Rue de la Chapelle. That was when Gervaise got the idea of going round the local dance halls. Now she never went past one without going in. Coupeau would go with her. At first they simply walked round and had a good look at the floozies kicking up their heels. Then, one evening when they had a bit of cash, they sat down and had a large bowl of mulled wine by way of refreshment while waiting to see if Nana would turn up. After a month of this they'd forgotten about Nana, and went to the dance halls for their own entertainment; they liked watching the dancing. They'd sit there for hours, not saying a word, their elbows on the table, in a kind of trance as the floor shook beneath them; they seemed to enjoy gazing with their lacklustre eyes at the local tarts as they swung past in the stifling heat and red glare of the hall.

One evening in November they went into the Grand Salon de la Folie to get warm. Outside, a nasty cold wind was cutting into the faces of the passers-by. But the hall was packed. There was one hell of a crowd, a swarming mass, people at every table, people in the middle, people up in the air, a great mountain of meat; yes, anyone fond of tripe would have had a field day. After going round twice without finding a table, they decided to stay and wait for a few people to leave. Coupeau, in a dirty smock and an old peakless cloth cap squashed down on his head, was swaying about on his feet. He was standing in people's way. Suddenly he noticed that a slim young man who'd pushed past him was brushing the sleeve of his overcoat.

'Hey!' he yelled furiously, taking his clay pipe out of his mouth, 'Can't you say excuse me? And there's no need to turn your nose up because somebody's wearin' a smock!'

The young man turned round and looked at the roofer, who went on:

'Let me tell you, you little creep, the smock's the best thing you can wear, 'cos it's the workin' man's uniform. I'll give you a couple of good clips round the ear, if you want, to 'elp you remember! Fancy a pansy like you insultin' a workin' man!'

Gervaise tried in vain to calm him down as he showed off his ragged clothes and banged his fist on his smock, bawling:

'Inside this there's a real man!'

The young man vanished into the crowd, muttering:

'Silly bugger!'

Coupeau tried to go after him. He wasn't going to stand for being talked to like that by some stuck-up little bourgeois in a posh overcoat. Probably not even paid for, either! Just something second-hand he'd picked up to impress a woman without paying a centime. If he ran into him again he'd make him get down on his knees and pay homage to the smock. But there was such a crush that they could hardly move. He and Gervaise made their way slowly round the dance floor; the spectators were squashed together three deep, their faces lighting up each time a man showed off his steps or a woman gave such a high kick that she showed everything she'd got. As they were both quite short, they had to stand on tiptoes to see anything at all, even the women's hairdos or the men's hats as they bobbed up and down. The band was madly playing a quadrille on its cracked brass instruments, making a tremendous racket that made the hall shake, while the dancers, as they stomped their feet, kicked up so much dust that it dimmed the gaslight. The heat was overpowering.

'Look!' Gervaise said suddenly.

'What is it?'

'That velvet hat over there.'

They stood on tiptoe. Over to the left they could see an old black velvet hat, with two tattered feathers like hearse plumes dangling from it. But all they could see was the hat, dancing the devil's own jig, capering, whirling, diving down, and springing up. They'd lose sight of it for a second in the mad confusion of heads, and then catch sight of it as it bobbed about above the other hats, in such a funny, cheeky way that the people around them couldn't help laughing, just to see it dancing away, without knowing who was wearing it.

'Well?' said Coupeau.

'Don't you recognize the hair?' Gervaise whispered, hardly able to speak. 'I bet my life it's her!'

The roofer immediately pushed his way through the crowd. Shit, yes, it was Nana! And what a get-up! All she had on was an old silk dress, very dirty from having rubbed up against bar tables, with tattered flounces hanging loose in all directions. What's more, she was almost naked above the waist, without so much as a scrap of shawl round her shoulders, so you could see her bodice with its torn button-holes. To think the little bitch had had an old gent pampering her to death, and she'd fallen this low just to be with some ponce who probably beat her! All the same, she still looked wonderfully young and appealing, with her hair frizzed up like a poodle's and her rosebud mouth under that fantastic hat.

'Just wait! I'll make 'er dance!' cried Coupeau.

Nana, of course, had no idea they were there. The way she was writhing about was a sight to behold! Sticking her bum out this way, then that way, curtseying so low you'd think she'd break in two, then high-kicking right up to her partner's face as if she was about to do the splits! People had gathered round in a circle and were applauding; and now, quite carried away, she pulled her skirts up to her knees and, fired up by the rhythm of the dance, whirled round like a top, went down on the floor in the splits, then carried on with a little jig, rolling her hips and bouncing her breasts in a manner that took your breath away. It made you want to carry her off into a corner and smother her with kisses.

Meanwhile, Coupeau had got right into the middle of the dancers and was getting in their way. They kept knocking into him.

'That's me daughter!' he shouted. 'Let me through!'

Just at that moment Nana was moving backwards, sweeping the floor with her feathers, sticking out her posterior and giving it a little shake for effect. She received a whacking great kick right on the spot. She straightened up and went as white as a sheet on seeing her father and mother. Not exactly her lucky day!

'Chuck 'im out!' yelled the dancers.

But Coupeau, who'd just realized that his daughter's partner was the slim young man in the overcoat, couldn't care less about anyone else.

'Yes, it's us!' he bellowed. 'You weren't expectin' us, were you? So this is what you get up to, and with that little ponce who insulted me a minute ago!'

Gervaise gave him a push, muttering between clenched teeth:

'Shut up! There's no need to bring 'im into it.'

She stepped forward and gave Nana two well-aimed slaps. The first knocked the hat with the feathers sideways, the second left a red mark on her white cheek. Nana, bewildered, took the blows without crying or trying to resist. The band carried on playing and the crowd, growing restive, kept shouting:

'Chuck 'em out! Chuck 'em out!'

'Come on, let's go!' Gervaise said to Nana. 'You go first, and don't even think of running off, or I'll 'ave you put behind bars!'

The slim young man had prudently disappeared. So Nana walked out, very stiffly, still stunned by her bad luck. When she looked like resisting, a clout from behind kept her heading for the door. The three of them duly left, amid the jeers and hooting of the crowd, while the band finished playing the quadrille at such a thunderous pitch that you'd have thought the trombones were spitting out cannonballs.

Life resumed. Nana slept for twelve hours in her old bed and was all sweetness and light for a week. She patched up a plain little dress and wore a simple bonnet with the ribbons tied under her chignon. In a burst of enthusiasm, she even said she'd like to work at home: you could earn what you liked at home, and you didn't have to listen to all that dirty talk in the workshop. So she found some work and installed herself at a table with her tools, getting up at five on the first few days to roll her sprigs of violet. But after she'd delivered a few gross of them, she started stretching her arms instead of getting on with the job, her hands knotted with cramp because she'd lost the knack of making the stems; and she felt she was suffocating, cooped up indoors after her six months of freedom and fresh air. So the glue pot dried up, the petals and green paper got spots of grease on them, and her employer himself came three times and kicked up a fuss, demanding the return of his materials. Nana just lolled about, getting the usual clouts from her father, and squabbling with her mother all day long, both of them hurling the vilest insults at each other. It couldn't go on this way, and on the twelfth day the little bitch made off, taking nothing with her as luggage except the plain dress on her back and the little bonnet on her head. The Lorilleux, who'd been quite cheesed off by the youngster's return and repentance, fell about laughing. Second act, disappearance number two, off to Saint-Lazare,* take your seats! No, really, it was too funny. Nana could certainly do a great vanishing act! Well, if the Coupeaus still wanted to keep her, all they could do now was sew up her you-know-what and stick her in a cage.

In public the Coupeaus pretended they were glad to be rid of her. Privately they were fuming. But fury doesn't last for ever. Soon they learned, without batting an eyelid, that Nana was walking the streets in the neighbourhood. Gervaise declared she was doing this to bring disgrace on them, and claimed she was above all the gossip; if she bumped into her girl in the street she wouldn't even soil her hand by slapping her; yes, it was all over—even if she found Nana lying naked in the street and dying, she'd pass by on the other side without saying that the little slut was her own child. Nana was the major attraction at all the dance halls round about. She was well known from the Reine-Blanche* to the Grand Salon de la Folie. When she went into the Élysée-Montmartre, people would stand on the tables to watch her do the backwards shimmy during the quadrille. As they'd twice thrown her out at the Château-Rouge,* she just hung about near the door until she saw someone she knew. The Boule-Noire on the boulevard and the Grand-Turc in the Rue des Poissonniers were more upmarket dance halls where she went when she had clean underwear. But of all the dance halls in the neighbourhood, the ones she liked best were the Bal de l'Ermitage,* in a damp courtyard, and the Bal Robert,* in the Impasse du Cadran, two sleazy little hangouts lit by just half a dozen oil lamps, free and easy, happy-go-lucky places, where no one minded if the blokes and the girls went into the dark corners at the back to do their snogging. And Nana certainly had her ups and downs. As if transformed by magic, she was sometimes all dolled up like a society lady, at other times trailing in the gutter like a slattern. Oh yes, it was quite a life!

Several times the Coupeaus thought they saw their daughter in very unsavoury places. They would turn their backs and cross over the road so as not to meet her face to face. They no longer felt like having an entire dance hall jeering at them, just so they could drag a creature like that back home. But one evening at about ten, as they were getting ready for bed, there was a banging on the door. It was Nana, who asked, as cool as you like, if she could sleep there. And my God, she looked a sight! Bareheaded, dress in tatters, down-at-heel boots—just like someone the police would pick up. She got a thrashing, of course, then fell ravenously on a piece of dry bread, and fell asleep, exhausted, still chewing the last mouthful. Then it was back to the familiar routine: as soon as she perked up again, off she went. Without warning, the bird had flown. Weeks and months would go by, so that it seemed she was gone for good, when she suddenly reappeared, without ever saying where she'd been, sometimes so dirty that you wouldn't want to touch her with a bargepole, covered in scratches from head to toe, at other times smartly dressed but so weak, so drained by her excesses that she could hardly stand up. Her parents just had to get used to it. Beatings were no use. They would give her tongue-lashings, but that didn't stop her from using their place like an inn where you can stay by the week. She knew that the price of her bed was a beating, and she came ready to take her punishment whenever it suited her to do so. Besides, you can't go on beating somebody for ever. Eventually the Coupeaus accepted Nana's escapades. She'd come or go as she pleased; as long as she didn't leave the door open it was okay. God knows, habit can wear down decent behaviour just like anything else.

There was one thing, however, that made Gervaise see red. It was when her daughter turned up wearing a dress with a train or a hat with feathers. No, that kind of extravagance was too much. Let her have a good time, if she wanted; but when she came home, she should at least dress the way a working-class girl should dress. The dresses with trains caused a great stir in the building: the Lorilleux laughed their heads off; Lantier got quite excited and hovered round Nana, sniffing her nice smell; the Boches had forbidden Pauline to have anything to do with that tart with her cheap finery. Another thing that made Gervaise angry was the way Nana would sleep until noon after one of her escapades, dead to the world, her breasts exposed, her hair hanging loose and still full of pins, her face so white, and breathing so lightly that you'd think she was dead. She'd shake her five or six times during the morning, and threaten to pour a jug of cold water over her belly. It exasperated her to see this lovely, lazy, half-naked girl, so voluptuous and sexy, sleeping off her carnal excesses, quite unable to wake up. Sometimes Nana would open one eye, close it at once, and stretch out again to sleep some more.

One day, as Gervaise was having a good go at her for the life she was leading, asking her if she came back so exhausted because she was going with soldiers now, she finally carried out her threat and shook her wet hand over her body. Nana, furious, rolled herself up in the sheet and shouted:

'That's enough, Maman! It's better not to talk about men. You did as you liked, I'm doing as I like.'

'What? What?' her mother stammered.

'Yes, I've never said anything because it wasn't my business, and you never seemed to care much. I saw you often enough, when we lived downstairs, creeping off in your nightie while Papa was snoring. I suppose you're not interested in that kind of thing any more, but other people are. So leave me alone. You shouldn't have set such a bad example.'

Gervaise went quite white and her hands began to tremble. She hardly knew what to do with herself. Nana turned over on to her stomach and, hugging her pillow, dozed off again into a deep slumber.

Coupeau still growled at her, but it no longer entered his head to beat her. In fact he was now going completely off his rocker. It made no sense to accuse him of lacking principles as a father, because the drink was robbing him of any conception of right and wrong.

His life now followed a fixed pattern: he'd be drunk for six months straight, then he'd collapse and go into Saint-Anne's. It was like a little outing to the country for him. The Lorilleux would say that the Duke of Rotgut was going to his country estate. After a few weeks, he'd come out of the asylum, patched up and tacked together, and then he'd get down to wrecking himself again, until another collapse and another patching-up. In this way he went into Saint-Anne's seven times in three years. It was said in the neighbourhood that there was a cell specially reserved for him. But the awful thing was that this determined drunkard made a worse wreck of himself each time, so that, as he went from one relapse to the next, you could anticipate the final collapse, the final crack of this worn-out barrel as its hoops snapped apart one after the other.

And he wasn't getting any handsomer, either. He looked like a ghost. The poison was having a terrible effect on him. His alcohol-saturated body was shrivelling up like those foetuses in jars you see in chemists' windows. He was so thin that when he stood in front of a window you could see the daylight through his ribs. His cheeks were hollow and his ghastly eyes ran with enough wax to supply a cathedral; the only part of him that was flourishing was his great red conk, like a lovely carnation in the middle of his ravaged face. Those who knew his age, just forty, would give a slight shudder when he went past, bent and unsteady and looking like an old man. And the shaking of his hands was getting worse, especially his right hand, which shook so much that some days he had to take his glass in both hands to raise it to his lips. Oh, those bloody shakes! It was the only thing that could stir him out of his general apathy. Sometimes he could be heard muttering terrible curses at his hands. At other times you'd see him staring at them for hours, watching them jump about like frogs, saying nothing, no longer angry but simply trying to work out what internal mechanism could make them play about like that. One evening Gervaise came upon him like this, with two big tears running down his drink-inflamed cheeks.

That last summer, during which Nana trailed home on the odd nights she wasn't out on the town, was particularly bad for Coupeau. His voice changed completely, as if the rotgut had retuned his vocal cords. He went deaf in one ear. Then, within a few days, his sight became so bad that he had to hold on to the banisters to avoid falling down the stairs. As for his general health, it was taking time off, as they say. He had dreadful headaches, and dizzy spells that made him see stars. Suddenly he'd get sharp stabbing pains in his arms and legs; he'd turn pale and have to sit down on a chair, staying there in a daze for hours at a time. After one such attack, his arm had remained paralysed for a whole day. Several times he'd take to his bed, curling up under the sheets, panting like an animal in pain. Then, the Sainte-Anne madness would begin again. Distrustful, anxious, racked by a high fever, he'd roll around in mad fits of rage, tearing his clothes and biting the furniture convulsively; or he'd fall into a state of deep self-pity, sighing like a young girl, sobbing and saying nobody loved him. One evening Gervaise and Nana came in together and found he was no longer in bed; he'd put the bolster in his place. And when they discovered him hiding between the bed and the wall, his teeth chattering, he told them some men were coming to murder him. The two women had to put him back to bed and comfort him like a child.

For Coupeau there was only one way to cure his troubles: to pour his glass of rotgut down his throat. It was like a kick in the belly and would get him back on his feet. This was how he got rid of his phlegm every morning. His memory had gone long ago, his mind was a blank. No sooner was he back on his feet than he'd laugh at the idea that he was ill. He'd never been ill. Yes, he'd reached the point where you kick the bucket just as you're declaring you're as fit as a fiddle. And he'd lost his marbles in every other respect too. When Nana came home after six weeks on the tiles, he seemed to think she'd just been running an errand down the street. She'd often bump into him as she was walking along on the arm of some man and start giggling because he didn't recognize her. In short, he no longer meant anything to her. She'd have used him as a chair if she hadn't had anything else to sit on.

When the first frosts came Nana disappeared once more, pretending as she left that she was just going to the fruit shop to see if they had any stewed pears. The truth was that she felt winter coming on, and had no desire to sit shivering in front of an empty stove. The Coupeaus cursed her, because they were waiting for their pears. They were sure she'd come back, though; the previous winter she'd gone down for two sous' worth of tobacco and stayed away for three weeks. But months went by and the girl didn't reappear. This time she must have gone off on quite a trip. June came round, bringing the sun with it, but not Nana. She must have found a cosy spot somewhere. One day when the Coupeaus were broke they sold her iron bedstead for six francs, which they drank up in Saint-Ouen. It had been in their way, in any case.

One morning in July Virginie called to Gervaise as she was passing and asked her to lend a hand with the dishes. Lantier had brought back two friends the evening before for a bit of a blowout. While Gervaise was doing the washing-up—and very greasy the dishes were too, after Lantier's little feast—the hatter, still digesting his meal, called to her from the shop:

'Hey, guess what, I saw Nana the other day.'

Virginie, sitting at the counter and looking rather worried on seeing how empty the jars and drawers were getting, shook her head angrily. She was keeping her tongue in check for fear of saying too much, but things were beginning to look fishy. Lantier seemed to be seeing Nana quite often. Oh, she wouldn't swear to it, but she wouldn't put anything past him where a bit of skirt was concerned. Madame Lerat had just walked in (she was very thick now with Virginie, who confided in her), and she put on her most suggestive expression as she asked:

'In what sense did you see her?'

'Oh, in a good sense,' replied the hatter, very flattered, laughing and twirling his moustache. 'She was in a carriage, I was on the pavement. Really! There's no reason to deny it, 'cos those rich young men she's got to know so well are bloody lucky!'

His eyes gleamed as he turned towards Gervaise, who was standing at the back of the shop wiping a plate.

'Yes, she was in a carriage, and looking ever so smart! I didn't recognize her, she looked so much like a society lady, with her pearly whites shining in her lovely fresh face. But she gave me a little wave with her glove. I reckon she must have got herself a viscount. Oh, she's really made it! She can thumb her nose at the lot of us now, she's got everything she ever dreamed of, the little tramp! What a sweet darling she is! There never was such a sweet darling!'

Gervaise was still wiping her plate, even though it had long since been sparkling clean. Virginie was thinking hard about two bills due the next day that she didn't know how she'd be able to pay, while Lantier, grown round and fat and seeming to exude the sugar he now lived on, waxed lyrical about well-turned-out little darlings, filling the shop with her praises—the shop already three-quarters consumed and giving off a smell of doom. Yes, he had only a few more pralines to munch and a few more sticks of barley sugar to suck, and the Poissons' business would be cleaned out. Suddenly he caught sight of the policeman himself walking along on the opposite side of the street; he was doing his rounds, his uniform buttoned up to his chin and his sword banging against his thigh. This added to Lantier's hilarity. He made Virginie look at her husband.

'Well, well,' he murmured, 'our Badingue looks very impressive this morning! Just look! He's holding his buttocks in too much, he must have stuck a glass eye up himself to spy on people behind him!'

When Gervaise went upstairs she found Coupeau sitting in a stupor on the edge of the bed. He was having one of his attacks. He was just staring vacantly at the floor. She slumped on to a chair, her limbs aching, her hands hanging loose beside her filthy skirt. For a quarter of an hour she sat there opposite him, without saying a word.

'I've had some news,' she mumbled in the end. 'Your daughter's been seen. Yes, she's very posh now, and doesn't need you any more. She's bloody lucky, that girl! My God, yes, I'd give anything to be in her shoes.'

Coupeau was still staring at the floor. Then he raised his ravaged face, gave a mad laugh, and said:

'Well, dearie, I won't hold you back. You're still not bad when you clean yourself up. Y'know what they say, there's no pot too old you can't find a lid for. Bloody hell, why not, if it'd help us along a bit!'

CHAPTER XII

IT must have been the Saturday after rent day, something like the twelfth or the thirteenth of January, Gervaise wasn't really sure. She couldn't think properly because it was ages since she'd had anything warm in her belly. It'd been a hell of a week! They were totally cleaned out: two four-pound loaves on Tuesday that had lasted until Thursday, then a dry crust she'd come across the day before, and nothing more for the last thirty-six hours—bugger-all! But what she was sure of, because she could feel it on her back, was that the weather was foul, bitterly cold, with a sky as black as coal, and full of snow that wouldn't come down. When you've got winter as well as hunger in your guts, you can tighten your belt all you like, it's not going to help to fill your belly.

Perhaps Coupeau would bring home some money that evening. He said he was working. Anything's possible, isn't it? Although she'd been disappointed so often, Gervaise was counting on the money this time. As for herself, after all sorts of kerfuffles, she could no longer find any kind of washing to do in the neighbourhood; even an old lady she'd been doing some cleaning for had given her the sack, saying she'd been drinking her liqueurs. Nobody wanted her anywhere, she was done for; and, when it came down to it, she was half glad, because she'd reached that stage of degradation when you'd rather die than lift a finger. Anyway, if Coupeau brought home his pay, they'd have something hot to eat. In the meantime, since she had to wait, and it wasn't yet noon, she stretched out on the mattress, because you don't feel so cold and hungry when you're lying down.

Gervaise called it the mattress, though in reality it was just a pile of straw in a corner. Bit by bit their bed and bedding had found their way to the second-hand dealers round about. To start with, when they were skint, she'd unpicked the mattress and taken out handfuls of wool which she'd carried off in her apron and sold for ten sous a pound in the Rue Belhomme. Then, when the mattress was empty, she'd got thirty sous for the cover one morning and bought herself some coffee. The pillows had followed, then the bolster. That left the wooden frame, which she couldn't carry out under her arm because of the Boches, who would've roused the whole building if they'd seen the landlord's surety disappearing. One evening, though, with Coupeau's help, she waited until the Boches were stuffing their faces and calmly moved the bed out piece by piece: the sides, the head-board, the frame. The ten francs they got from this operation enabled them to eat well for three days. Wasn't the palliasse, the under-mattress, enough for them? Even the cloth cover of the palliasse had gone the same way as the one for the top mattress, so that in the end they'd eaten up the entire bed, giving themselves indigestion on bread after fasting for twenty-four hours. The straw could be swept together with a broom, so you could easily say the mattress had been turned, and it was no dirtier than anything else.

Gervaise lay curled up on the pile of straw, fully dressed, with her feet tucked under her tattered skirt for warmth. Huddled up like that, her eyes wide open, on this particular day she was thinking some very dark thoughts. No, bugger it! They couldn't go on living like this, with nothing to eat! She no longer felt her hunger, but she had a lead weight in her stomach, and her head seemed empty. And there cer-tainly wasn't anything to cheer her up when she looked round their wretched little room! It was a real dog kennel now, but one where even those back-alley bitches out there, wearing coats, wouldn't stay for a second. With dull eyes she stared at the bare walls. Everything had long since gone to the pawnbroker. The only things left were the chest of drawers, the table, and one chair, but the chest's marble top and its drawers had gone the same way as the bed. A fire couldn't have done a better job of cleaning the place out, all the little knick-knacks had melted away, beginning with the ticker, a twelve-franc watch, and ending with the family photos, which a dealer had taken for the frames—a very obliging woman to whom she'd taken a saucepan, an iron, a comb, and who'd doled out five sous, three sous, two sous, according to the item, enough to bring back a bit of bread. All that was left now was a broken old pair of candle-snuffers, which the dealer wouldn't take, not even for one sou. If she'd known of anyone inter-ested in buying rubbish, dust, and grime, she'd have set up shop straight away, for the room was incredibly filthy! She could see noth-ing but spiders' webs in the corners, and spiders' webs may be good for healing cuts but no tradesman yet had ever bought any. So, turn-ing her head away and giving up hope of finding anything else to sell, she curled up even more tightly on her straw, preferring to look out of the window at the murky, snow-laden sky, feeling chilled to the very marrow of her bones.

They were in such a mess! What was the use, though, of getting all worked up and worrying yourself sick? If only she could take a nap! But the thought of her pigsty of a home kept bouncing around in her head. The day before, Monsieur Marescot, the landlord, had come in person to say he'd turn them out if they hadn't paid the two overdue quarters' rent within a week. All right, he could turn them out, they wouldn't be any worse off in the street! The very idea! That hulking great brute in his overcoat and his woollen gloves coming to talk to them about paying the rent, as if they had a nest-egg stashed away somewhere! Bloody hell! If they had, the first thing she'd have done would have been to get stuck into some nosh, instead of tightening her belt! That fat bastard was so nasty! She'd stick him right up her arse, if she could! And that daft bugger Coupeau wasn't much better. He never came home, now, without clobbering her. She'd give him the same treatment as the landlord. The way she felt now, that arse of hers must have been pretty big, because she shoved everybody up there, so keen was she to be shot of the lot of 'em, and of life itself. She was becoming a regular punching bag. Coupeau had a stick he called his arse-fan, and he fanned his old woman with it something terrible, leaving her drenched in sweat. She was none too gentle herself, she'd bite and scratch. They'd go at it hammer and tongs round the empty room, fighting so ferociously that they almost forgot they were hungry. But after a while she got so that she didn't care about being beaten, just as she didn't care about anything else. Coupeau could stay away from work for weeks at a time, or go on the booze for months, come home mad drunk and itching to clobber her, she'd got used to it all, it was just routine, that was all. And it was on days like that that she shoved him up her arse. Yes, up her arse with her swine of a husband, up her arse with the Lorilleux, the Boches, the Poissons! Up her arse with all the bloody neighbours who looked down on her. The whole of Paris went up there, helped along by a good wallop, a gesture of complete indifference, though it did give her a nice feeling of revenge to shove them all up there.

Unfortunately, although people can get used to anything, nobody has yet been able to get used to not eating. That was the one thing that really got to Gervaise. She couldn't care less about being the lowest of the low, right down in the gutter, and seeing people brush themselves

down when she passed close to them. Bad manners no longer bothered her, but hunger never stopped twisting her guts. Oh, she'd long
since said goodbye to tasty little titbits, and now she gobbled up anything she could lay her hands on. A feast day, now, was when she
could pay the butcher four sous a pound for leftover scraps of meat
that had gone grey on the tray; she'd put them in a casserole with
some potatoes and mix it all up. Or she might fricassee an ox heart,
a dish she really liked. Or again, when she had some wine, she'd give
herself a treat and get some bread to dunk in it. A couple of sous'
worth of liver sausage, a kilo of potatoes, a quarter of dried beans
cooked in their own liquid—these were treats she couldn't often
afford these days. She was reduced to buying the leftovers from dubi-
ous eating houses, where for a sou she'd get a heap of fish bones mixed
up with little offcuts of burnt meat. She stooped even lower, and
begged a kind-hearted restaurant owner for the crusts left by his customers, which she turned into a sort of bread soup, letting it simmer
as long as possible on a neighbour's stove. And on the mornings when
she was starving she even went on the prowl with the dogs outside
shop doors, before the dustmen came round; that was how she came
to eat posh folk's food, overripe melons, mackerel that had gone bad,
chops she had to inspect closely in case they had maggots in them.
Yes, she'd sunk that low! Delicate souls might find it all quite revolt-
ing, but if they went without food for three days we'd soon see if
they'd ignore what their bellies were telling them! They'd be down on
all fours eating garbage like the rest. Oh, the starving poor, their
empty bellies crying out for food, with an animal need to get their
chattering teeth into any rotten stuff and gulp it down, in this great
golden city of Paris, this city of light! And to think she'd once gorged
herself on a lovely fat goose! The very thought almost made her cry.
She was so desperately hungry that one day, when Coupeau had
pinched two bread tokens from her and sold them so he could buy
booze, she got so angry that she hit him with a shovel and nearly
killed him.

After a while, through staring at the dull sky, she drifted off into an
uneasy sleep. The cold was biting into her, and she dreamt that the
sky was emptying all its snow on to her. Suddenly she leapt to her
feet, woken with a start by a rush of anxiety. My God! Was she about
to die? Shivering and haggard, she saw it was still light. Would night
never come? How slowly time passes when you've got nothing in your

belly! Her stomach was waking up as well, and torturing her. She sat slumped on the chair, her head drooping, holding her hands between her thighs for warmth, and was already thinking about what she'd get for dinner as soon as Coupeau came home with the money: bread, wine, and two portions of tripe fried with onions. Three o'clock struck on Père Bazouge's cuckoo clock. Only three? She wept. She'd never have the strength to wait until seven. She started to rock backwards and forwards, like a little girl in pain. She sat doubled up, squeezing her stomach so as not to feel it any more. Oh, hunger like this is more painful than childbirth! Unable to find any relief, she stood up and stomped in a fury round the room, hoping to soothe her hunger like a baby being rocked to sleep by its mother. For half an hour she stumbled about. Then, suddenly, she stopped, a determined look in her eyes. Too bad! They could say what they liked, she'd lick their boots if they wanted, but she was going to borrow ten sous from the Lorilleux.

In winter, on this staircase, the poverty-stricken one, people were constantly borrowing ten sous, or twenty—little favours these starving folk did for each other. But they'd all rather die than ask the Lorilleux, because they knew how tight-fisted they were. In going to knock on their door, Gervaise was showing real courage. She felt so frightened in the corridor that when she did knock she experienced that sudden sense of relief when you finally ring the dentist's bell.

'Come in!' called the chain-maker in his rasping voice.

How nice and warm it was in there! The forge was blazing away, lighting up the cramped workshop with its white flame. Madame Lorilleux was heating a coil of gold wire, while her husband, seated at his bench, was sweating from the heat as he soldered the lengths of a chain with his blowpipe. There was a nice smell in the room, too, for some cabbage soup was simmering on the stove, giving off steam that turned Gervaise's stomach and made her feel faint.

'Oh, it's you,' growled Madame Lorilleux, not even asking her to sit down. 'What do you want?'

Gervaise didn't reply. That week she'd been on reasonable terms with the Lorilleux. But the request for ten sous stuck in her throat, because she'd just noticed Boche sitting by the stove, nicely settled for a good gossip. He looked as if he didn't have a care in the world, the bastard! What an arsehole! That's exactly what he looked like when he laughed, with his round little mouth and his cheeks so puffed out that you couldn't see his nose. Yes, the spitting image of an arsehole!

'What d'you want?' repeated Lorilleux.

'Have you seen Coupeau?' Gervaise managed to say at last. 'I thought he was here.'

The chain-makers and the concierge laughed. No, of course they hadn't seen Coupeau. They weren't generous enough with the grog to see much of Coupeau. Gervaise made an effort and carried on, haltingly:

'He promised he'd come home. He's supposed to be bringing some money. And I really need a few things...'

There was a pregnant silence. Madame Lorilleux fanned the forge, Lorilleux bent lower over the ever-lengthening bit of chain he was holding, while Boche carried on grinning like a full moon, his mouth so round that you wanted to stick your finger in it, just to see what was there.

'If I only had ten sous,' Gervaise said almost inaudibly.

The silence continued.

'You couldn't lend me ten sous, could you? I'd let you have them back tonight.'

Madame Lorilleux turned round and gave her a hard stare. So she was trying to wheedle money out of them now! Today she was touching them for ten sous, tomorrow it would be twenty, and who knows where it would stop. No thank you, there'd be none of that. Maybe later, if the moon turns blue!

'But my dear,' she cried, 'you know full well we haven't got any money! Have a look in my pocket. You can search us if you want. Of course, we'd be only too glad to help if we could.'

'The spirit's willing,' grunted Lorilleux, 'but we just can't.'

Gervaise nodded meekly. However, she showed no inclination to leave, but kept casting sidelong glances at the gold, at the coils of gold hanging on the walls, at the gold wire the wife was pulling through the draw-plate with all the strength of her little arms, the gold links piled up under the husband's gnarled fingers. And she thought that just one little scrap of this ugly, blackish metal would have been enough to buy her a good dinner. That day it didn't matter that the workshop was filthy, with its old iron tools, its coal dust, and its carelessly wiped oil stains, in her eyes it gleamed with riches like a money changer's shop. So she ventured to ask again, very softly:

'I'd pay you back, I'd pay you back, really I would... Ten sous, that wouldn't put you out.'

Her heart was bursting, but she didn't want to say she'd had nothing to eat since the day before. Then, feeling her legs giving way and afraid she'd burst into tears, she continued haltingly:

'It would be so good of you!... You can't imagine... My God, I don't know what's happening to me. I really don't.'

The Lorilleux pursed their lips and exchanged a quick glance. Gimpy was actually begging now! Well, she couldn't sink any lower. Begging was something they couldn't abide! If they'd known they would have bolted the door, because you've always got to watch out for beggars—they wheedle their way into your home and then make off with your valuables. And in their case there really was stuff to steal; you could let your fingers stray anywhere and go away with thirty or forty francs' worth of gold just by closing your hand. Several times already they'd had their doubts about Gervaise on noticing the funny look on her face when she stood looking at the gold. This time they'd have to keep a close eye on her. And so, as she moved closer, stepping on to the wooden slats, Lorilleux shouted at her quite crudely, completely ignoring her plea:

'Hey, watch what you're doing! You'll be carrying off scraps of gold on the soles of your shoes again. Anybody might think you put grease on them to make things stick.'

Gervaise slowly retreated. For a moment she had to lean against a shelf and, seeing Madame Lorilleux looking at her hands, opened them wide and showed them to her, saying softly, not getting angry, like someone who'd fallen so low that she'd submit to anything:

'I haven't taken anything. Look.'

And she left, because the strong smell of the cabbage soup and the lovely warmth of the workshop were making her feel ill.

The Lorilleux naturally made no attempt to hold her back! Good riddance! They'd be damned if they'd ever open their door to her again! They'd seen enough of her mug, and they had no desire to let down-and-outs like that come into their home, especially when their troubles were all their own fault. And they positively wallowed in their own selfishness—how clever they were, how nice and warm it was in their place, with their lovely soup to look forward to. Boche too was in an expansive mood, puffing out his cheeks even more, so that his laugh began to sound quite obscene. They all felt they'd got their own back on Gimpy for her fancy ways, her blue shop, her grand meals, and all the rest. It was such an excellent lesson for everybody, it just showed where a love of food can get you. To hell with women who were greedy and lazy and had no shame!

'What cheek! Coming here to beg for ten sous!' cried Madame Lorilleux as soon as Gervaise had gone. 'Oh yes, of course, I'll lend her ten sous so she can go and spend it on drink!'

Gervaise shuffled wearily along the corridor, her shoulders hunched. When she reached her door she didn't go in, she was afraid to look at her bare room. She might as well carry on walking, to keep warm and pass the time.

She peered into Père Bru's hole under the stairs as she went past—now there was someone who must have worked up a good appetite, for he'd been lunching and dining on air for the last three days; but he wasn't there, there was just his hole, and she felt a pang of jealousy, imagining that perhaps he'd been invited somewhere. Then, as she came to the Bijards', she heard moaning, and went in, finding the key still in the lock.

'What's the matter?' she asked.

The room was very clean. It was obvious that Lalie had swept the floor and tidied up that morning. Even though the wind of poverty would blow through, carrying off clothes and leaving its load of dirt and mess, Lalie would come along and clean up and make the place look nice. The room was hardly luxurious, but you could see it was well looked after. That day the two children, Henriette and Jules, were in a corner, quietly cutting out some old pictures they'd found. But Gervaise was astonished to find Lalie in her narrow trestle bed, very pale, with the sheet pulled up to her chin. Lalie in bed! She must be really ill!

'What's the matter?' Gervaise asked again, very worried.

Lalie had stopped moaning. She slowly raised her paper-white eyelids and tried to form her contorted mouth into a smile.

'It's nothing,' she said very softly. 'Really. Nothing at all.'

Then, closing her eyes again, she said with an effort:

'These last few days I've been getting so tired, so, as you can see, I'm being lazy and coddling myself.'

But her little face, covered in livid blotches, had taken on an expression of such extreme pain that Gervaise, forgetting her own suffering, clasped her hands together and fell on her knees beside her. For a month now she'd been seeing Lalie holding on to the walls as she walked, bent double with a cough that sounded like death. Now she couldn't even cough. She gave a kind of hiccup, and trickles of blood ran down from the corners of her mouth.

'I can't help it, I'm not feeling very strong,' she murmured. The admission seemed to give her relief. 'I've dragged myself round and tidied up a bit. It's clean enough, isn't it? I wanted to clean the windows, but my legs gave way. Isn't it silly! Anyway, when you can't carry on, you go to bed.'

She broke off to say:

'Please watch to see those little ones don't cut themselves with their scissors.'

Then she fell silent and began to tremble, for she could hear a heavy step coming up the stair. Bijard flung open the door. As usual, he'd been at the bottle, and his eyes were blazing with the raging madness of alcohol. When he saw Lalie lying in bed he slapped his thigh, sniggered, and took his big whip from its hook.

'Bloody hell!' he snarled. 'This is the limit! We're gonna have some fun now!... So we're lying down in the middle of the day, are we! Is this your idea of a game, you little bitch! C'mon, get up!'

He was already cracking the whip over the bed. And the child kept imploring him:

'No, Papa, please don't hit me. You'd be sorry, I know you would. Don't hit me.'

'C'mon, get up!' he yelled, 'or I'll tickle your ribs. C'mon, get up, you little bitch!'

Then she said softly:

'I can't, I just can't. I'm going to die.'

Gervaise threw herself at Bijard and wrenched the whip out of his hands. He stood there, next to the bed, looking bewildered. What was the kid talking about? You don't die when you're as young as that, and haven't been ill! It was some trick, so that he'd give her something nice. Well, he'd soon find out, and he'd teach her, if she was lying!

'It's true, you'll see,' she went on. 'I didn't want to give you any trouble, as long as I could... Please, Papa, be nice to me now, and say goodbye.'

Bijard tapped his nose, afraid of being had. It was true, though, that her face looked funny—long and serious, like a grown-up's. The presence of death in the room was sobering him up. He looked all round, like someone waking from a long sleep, and saw how tidy the place was, and the children nice and clean, playing and laughing. He slumped on to a chair, and mumbled:

'Our little mother, our little mother...'

That was all he could find to say, but it was affectionate enough for Lalie, who'd never heard him speak to her so nicely. She comforted her father. What distressed her most was to be going like this, before she could finish bringing up her children. He'd take care of them, wouldn't he? And with her dying breath she gave him instructions about how to dress them and keep them clean. But the effects of the alcohol had overcome him once more; stupefied, he rolled his head as he watched Lalie dying. It was stirring up all sorts of things in his mind, but he could find nothing more to say, and his skin was too thick for him to cry.

'There's another thing,' Lalie resumed after a silence, 'we owe the baker four francs seven sous, that's got to be paid... Madame Gaudron borrowed one of our irons, you'll need to get it back... I couldn't make any soup for tonight, but there's some bread left and you can heat up the potatoes...'

Right up to her last breath the poor sweet thing never stopped being the family's little mother. She could never be replaced, that was certain! She was dying because, though only a child, she had the heart and mind of a true mother in a frame too delicate and small to contain such a huge maternal spirit. And if he was now losing this treasure, it was indeed the fault of her brute of a father. After kicking the mother to death, he'd now murdered the daughter! Those two angels would be in their graves, and he'd be left to die like a dog in a ditch.

Gervaise, meanwhile, was straining to hold back her tears. She stretched out her hands, wanting to relieve Lalie's suffering, and as the torn sheet was slipping off, she tried to fold it down and rearrange the bed. The poor little body of the dying child was thus exposed. Dear God! What a wretched, pitiable sight! The very stones would have wept. Lalie was quite naked, with only the remnants of a chemise round her shoulders by way of a nightdress; yes, quite naked, the bleeding, agonizing nakedness of a martyr. There was no longer any flesh on her, her bones seemed to be poking through her skin. Thin purple weals extended from her ribs to her thighs—the terrible marks left by the most recent lashes of the whip. A livid bruise ran round her left arm, as if the jaws of a vice had crushed this delicate limb, no thicker than a matchstick. On her right leg was a gash that hadn't healed, a nasty wound reopened every morning as she ran around doing the housework. She was just a bruise from head to toe. Oh, what a massacre of childhood—those big paws crushing this adorable young thing; what an abomination—such a fragile creature having to bear such a cross! People in churches worship martyred saints whose naked flesh is not so pure. Once again, Gervaise knelt down by the bed, forgetting to pull up the sheet, overcome by the sight of this pitiful, tiny creature lying there, spread out on the bed. With trembling lips, she tried to say some prayers.

'Madame Coupeau,' whispered the child, 'please...'

With her little arms, she tried to pull up the sheet out of modesty, and ashamed for her father. Bijard stood there, staring stupidly at the corpse he was responsible for, rolling his head about slowly like a bewildered animal.

Gervaise covered Lalie up, but could stay there no longer. The dying child was growing weaker, not speaking now, with nothing left but her gaze, that familiar dark gaze, pensive and resigned, fixed on her two children as they cut out pictures. As the room became darker, Bijard sank further into an uncomprehending stupor. No, no, life was too dreadful! How horrible! Horrible! Gervaise walked out and went down the stairs without knowing what she was doing, her head reeling, so overwhelmed by the misery of life that she'd gladly have thrown herself under an omnibus to end it all.

As she hurried along, cursing the awfulness of fate, she found herself at the gates of the place where Coupeau had said he was working. Her legs had taken her there, and her stomach was starting to intone its old song, its lament for hunger in ninety verses, a lament she knew by heart. This way, if she grabbed Coupeau as he came out, she'd be able to get her hands on the money and buy food. Just an hour to wait at most, she could easily manage that after sucking her thumbs since the day before.

She was at the corner of the Rue de la Charbonnière and the Rue de Chartres, a bleak crossroads where the wind blew from all directions. Christ! It wasn't exactly warm work, walking up and down that street. And it wouldn't have been much warmer with a fur coat. The sky was still an awful leaden colour, and the snow collecting up there seemed to have spread a canopy of ice over the whole neighbourhood. No snow was actually falling, but there was a heavy silence in the air, preparing a fancy-dress costume for Paris, a pretty ballgown, white and new. Gervaise looked up and prayed to the Lord that He wouldn't let that muslin come down just yet. Stamping her feet, she fixed her eyes on a grocer's shop across the street, then turned round because it was silly to make herself get too hungry in advance. There was precious little else to look at round about. The few passers-by, wrapped up in scarves, hurried by, because you don't hang about when the cold's biting your bum. However, Gervaise did notice four or five other women mounting guard outside the gates of the roofing works—poor creatures like herself, no doubt, wives waiting to pounce on their husbands' pay packet so as to stop it disappearing into the boozer. One of them was a tall, gawky woman with a face like a gendarme's, who'd flattened herself against the wall, ready to jump out and grab her man. A small, dark woman, who looked quite frail and timid, was walking up and down on the other side of the street. Then there was another woman, a dumpy-looking creature, who'd brought her two little kids, and was dragging them along, shivering and crying, on either side of her. And all of them, Gervaise and her sister sentries, kept passing each other, exchanging sidelong glances but never speaking. A most pleasant social occasion, yes indeed! They didn't need to introduce themselves to each other, for they knew each other already. They all put up at the same hotel run by Poverty & Co. It made you feel even colder, watching them tramping up and down and passing each other in silence, in this terrible January weather.

So far, not even a cat had come through the gate. At last, however, one workman appeared, followed by a second, and then a third; but these were no doubt good blokes who faithfully took home their wages, for they shook their heads when they saw the shadowy figures lurking near the gate. The tall, gawky woman flattened herself even more against the wall and, all of a sudden, pounced on a pasty-faced little man who was cautiously sticking his head out. It was all over in a flash! She frisked him and grabbed the money. Nabbed, lolly gone, nothing left even for one drop! Greatly put out, the little man went off behind his gendarme, blubbering like a child. Workmen continued to appear, and as the dumpy woman with the two kids moved closer, a tall, dark, sly-looking man darted back inside on seeing her, to warn her husband, so that when the husband came strutting out, he'd stashed away two lovely new five-franc pieces—rear coach-wheels, as they call them—one in each shoe. He took one of the kids on his arm and walked off telling some nonsense tale to his nagging wife. Some high-spirited blokes came bounding into the street, in a hurry to blow their pay on a nosh-up with their mates. But others, as they came out, looked sad and dejected, clenching the pay they'd got for the three or four days' work they'd done that fortnight, cursing themselves for being lazy buggers, and making drunkards' promises. But the saddest sight was the distress of the small, dark woman, the frail, timid-looking one: her bloke, a good-looking lad, had just marched right past her, and so roughly that he'd nearly knocked her over. All alone, she tottered off past the shops, crying her heart out.

The procession finally came to an end. Gervaise, standing in the middle of the street, was still watching the gate. Things weren't looking too good. Two stragglers came out, but still no Coupeau. When she asked the men if he was coming they jokingly replied—for they knew what was up—that he'd just popped out the back with What's'isname to do something or other. Gervaise understood. Coupeau had been lying, he'd played her for a fool again. Dragging herself along in her worn-out shoes, she went slowly down the Rue de la Charbonnière. Her dinner was running away in front of her, and as she watched it go, in the yellow half-light, she gave a little shudder. This was it! Not a bean, no hope left, nothing but night and hunger. And what a perfect night it was to die, this dreadful night that was closing in around her!

She was heaving herself up the Rue des Poissonniers when she heard Coupeau's voice. Yes, there he was, in the Petite-Civette, being stood a drink by Mes-Bottes. That joker Mes-Bottes, towards the end of the summer, had managed to get himself married—yes, straight up!—to a lady who, though well past her prime, wasn't at all bad to look at; what's more, she worked in the Rue des Martyrs, she wasn't one of your ordinary tarts from the outer boulevards. You should've seen the lucky devil, living like a gentleman, with his hands in his pockets, well dressed and well fed. He'd put on so much weight you could hardly recognize him. According to his mates, his wife got as much work as she wanted from her regular gentleman friends. A wife like that and a house in the country, what more could a man wish for to make life pleasant! It wasn't surprising that Coupeau kept gazing at him in admiration. The old rascal even had a gold ring on his little finger!

Gervaise put her hand on Coupeau's shoulder just as he was coming out of the Petite-Civette.

'Hey, I've been waiting... I'm hungry. All you ever give me is an empty stomach.'

He snapped straight back:

'Hungry, are you? Well eat your fist! And keep the other one for tomorrow!'

What a bloody cheek, making a scene in front of people. What was all the fuss about! He hadn't been working, but the bakers had still baked bread, hadn't they! What sort of man did she take him for, trying to frighten him with her sob stories?

'Do you want to make me steal?' she said in a dull voice.

Mes-Bottes was stroking his chin in a conciliatory sort of way.

'No, that's not allowed,' he said. 'But when a woman knows how to use her assets...'

Coupeau interrupted him to express his approval. Yes, a woman should know how to use her assets. But his own wife had always been an old hag, a complete wreck. Then he started singing Mes-Bottes's praises again. Didn't the bugger look smart! Just like a landlord, with his white shirt and fancy shoes! Nothing but the best for him. At least there was one bloke whose missus knew how to manage things!

The two men were walking down towards the outer boulevard, with Gervaise following. After a silence, she said again, from behind Coupeau:

'I'm hungry, y'know... I was counting on you. You've got to find me something to keep me goin'.'

He didn't answer, and she repeated in a heart-rending voice:

'So you won't give me any money?'

'For God's sake, I 'aven't got any!' he yelled, swinging round angrily. 'Leave me alone, won't you! Or I'll clock you one!'

He was already raising his fist. She shrank back, then seemed to come to a decision.

'Right, I'll leave you alone, I'll find a man somewhere.'

The roofer burst out laughing. He pretended to take it all as a joke, but in reality he was egging her on. What a bloody good idea! At night, by lamplight, she might still get off with someone. If she did, he recommended the Capucin restaurant: they had little private rooms where you could get an excellent dinner. As she set off along the boulevard, he shouted after her:

'You can save me some dessert, you know I like cake... And if your gent's well turned out, ask 'im for an old overcoat—that'd do as my commission.'

Pursued by this infernal jabber, Gervaise walked quickly away. Then, when she found herself alone in the crowd, she slowed down. Her mind was made up. Between stealing and doing that, she preferred doing that, because at least she wouldn't be doing anybody any harm. She was only going to dispose of what belonged to her. Of course, it wasn't very nice, but by now what was nice and what wasn't nice had got all mixed up in her head; when you're dying of hunger you don't start talking philosophy, you just eat whatever food comes your way. She'd reached the Chaussée de Clignancourt. It seemed night would never fall. So, while she waited, she strolled along the boulevards, like a lady taking the air before going home to have dinner.

This part of Paris, which was becoming so splendid that it made her feel out of place, was now being opened up in all directions. The Boulevard Magenta, coming up from the heart of the city, and the Boulevard Ornano, leading off into the country, had made a great gap where the boundary wall used to be; a huge number of houses had been demolished to make way for these two great avenues, still white with plaster dust, which had running out of them the Rue du Faubourg-Poissonnière and the Rue des Poissonniers, the ends of which, jagged and scarred, twisted away in dark, winding laneways. The demolition of the barrier had long since widened the outer boulevards, with footpaths along the sides and a central strip for pedestrians planted with four rows of little plane trees. It was now a huge crossroads leading to the far horizon along endless streets that swarmed with people, going on and on in a confused mass of building operations. But, amid the tall new buildings, many rickety shacks were still standing; between the sculptured façades were gaping black hollows where ramshackle hovels exposed their dingy, broken windows. Beneath the growing luxury of Paris the poverty of the slums was still plain for all to see, befouling the new city being thrown up so quickly.

Lost in the bustle of the wide pavement, beside the little plane trees, Gervaise felt alone and abandoned. Glimpses of the distant avenues made her stomach feel even emptier. It was strange to think that in this surging crowd, which surely included people who were comfortably off, there wasn't one Christian soul who would guess her plight and slip ten sous into her hand! Yes, it was all too grand and too fine, her head was spinning and her legs giving way, beneath the enormous expanse of grey sky stretched out above this immense space.

The twilight was that dirty yellow colour typical of Parisian twilights, a colour that makes you want to die on the spot, so hideous is the life of the streets. It was that in-between time of day when distances become hazy and unclear. Worn out already, Gervaise was getting caught up in the crush of workers going home. This was the point in the evening when the ladies wearing hats and the gentlemen who lived in the new buildings were swallowed up by the crowds of workers, an endless procession of men and women still pasty-faced from the foul air of the factories. Droves of them kept emerging from the Boulevard Magenta and the Rue du Faubourg-Poissonnière, panting for breath after the uphill climb. Amid the dull rumbling of omnibuses and cabs, and the rattle of empty drays, wagons, and carts speeding home, an ever-growing stream of smocks and overalls spread across the roadway. Street porters were coming back from work, their luggage hooks over their shoulders. Two workmen were taking great strides as they walked side by side, talking loudly and gesticulating but not looking at each other; others, in caps and cloth coats, walked alone along the edge of the pavement, keeping their heads down; still others came in groups of five or six, in single file, not saying a word, bleary-eyed, their hands in their pockets. A few had an unlit pipe clenched between their teeth. Four bricklayers had clubbed together and hired a cab, their hods bouncing along on top, and as the cab went past you could see their white faces peering out of the windows. House-painters were swinging their paint pots, a roofer was carrying a long ladder and nearly poking people's eyes out with it, while a fountain-keeper, coming home late with his tool-box on his back, was playing 'Good King Dagobert'* on his little trumpet, which added a note of melancholy to the gathering darkness. What a sad tune it was, seeming to keep time with the trampling of the herd, the beasts of burden dragging themselves along, exhausted! Another day over! In truth, the days were too long and began again too soon! Hardly time to fill your belly and digest your meal before it was daylight again and you had to take up the yoke of poverty once more. And yet, these blokes were whistling as they marched on, eager for their supper.

Gervaise, borne along by the tide, hardly aware of being bumped into and jostled from left and right, let the mob flow past. Men have no time to be polite when they're dead tired and ravenously hungry.

Suddenly, looking up, the laundress saw before her what had once been the Hôtel Boncœur. The little building had become a shady café and been closed by the police; it now stood empty, its shutters covered with posters and its lantern broken. It was crumbling and rotting away from top to bottom, its tawdry purple paint all mouldy. But nothing in the area seemed to have changed. The newsagent's and the tobacconist's were still there, and looming up behind them you could still see the peeling façades and tattered outlines of the five-storey tenement blocks. The only thing that had disappeared was the Grand-Balcon dance hall, whose ten windows used to be ablaze with light; it had been turned into a sugar mill, from which came a constant whirring noise. Yet it was there, in that filthy dump the Hôtel Boncœur, that her miserable existence had begun. She stood there staring at the first-floor window where a broken shutter hung down, remembering her early days with Lantier, their first rows, and the disgusting way he'd walked out on her. No matter, she'd been young then, and, looking back, it seemed like fun. My God, only twenty years ago! And here she was now, on the streets. The sight of the building upset her, and she walked back along the boulevard in the direction of Montmartre.

In the gathering darkness kids were still playing on the piles of sand between the benches. The procession was still going on, with shopgirls trotting past, hurrying to make up for the time they'd lost looking in windows; one tall girl had stopped and was still holding hands with a young man who'd come with her to within three doors of her home; others, as they parted, were making arrangements to meet later that evening at the Grand Salon de la Folie or the Boule-Noire. In the groups there would be the odd jobbing tailor with his delivery bag folded under his arm. A stove-setter, strapped up and pulling a barrow full of rubble, was nearly run over by an omnibus. Meanwhile, as the crowd thinned, there were hatless women who'd come back out after lighting a fire, and were rushing to get something for dinner; they pushed through the crowd, dashed into the baker's and the butcher's, and hurried home clutching their provisions. There were little eight-year-old girls, sent out on errands, wandering along past the shops, hugging to their chests huge four-pound loaves as tall as themselves; looking like lovely yellow dolls, they'd stop for five minutes at a time to stare at a picture in a window, one cheek resting on the big loaf of bread. Then the tide receded, the groups less frequent, as they all reached home; and in the glare of the gaslight, now the working day was over, relaxation and pleasure were stirring.

Yes, Gervaise's day was over too! She was more weary than all those
workers who'd pushed past her. She might as well lie down and die,
because work had no further use for her, and she'd toiled enough in
her life to say: 'Somebody else can have a go! I've had enough!'
Everybody was eating at this hour. It really was the end, the sun had
snuffed out its candle and the night would be long. Oh, if only you
could stretch out and never get up again, know you'd laid down your
tools for good and could laze about for the rest of eternity! That'd be
the ticket, after slaving away for twenty years! And in spite of the
hunger cramps twisting her stomach, Gervaise couldn't help thinking of the great feeds and all the good times she'd had in her life.
There was one day in particular, a bitterly cold Thursday during
Lent, when she'd had the most marvellous fun. In those days she'd
been really pretty and young-looking. The wash-house in the Rue
Neuve had chosen her as carnival queen, in spite of her leg. So they'd
paraded along the boulevards in carts decorated with greenery, past
all those toffs who couldn't take their eyes off her. Gentlemen had
raised their eyeglasses as if she was a real queen. A queen, yes, a queen,
with a crown and a sash, for twenty-four hours, twice round the clock!
Now, with her mind and senses dulled by the pangs of hunger, she
stood staring at the ground, as if looking for the gutter into which her
lost majesty had fallen.

She raised her eyes again. Now she was in front of the slaughterhouses which were being demolished. The façade had been torn away,
revealing dark, stinking courtyards still damp with blood. And when
she reached the bottom of the boulevard she could also see the
Lariboisière hospital, with its high grey wall, above which the building's gloomy wings fanned out, with their evenly spaced windows;
there was a door in the wall that terrified the whole neighbourhood,
the door of the dead, a great piece of solid oak, as forbidding and
silent as a tombstone. To get away from it, she went further still, as far
as the railway bridge. The track was hidden by the high parapets of
riveted sheet metal; all she could see was the wide angle formed by the
station's huge roof,* black with coal dust, against the brilliant Paris
skyline; and in this vast empty space she could hear the whistles of the
locomotives and the rhythmic jolting of turntables, a whole vast, hidden world of activity. Then a train went by on its way out of Paris,
with its puffing and rumbling getting louder. And all she saw was
a plume of smoke that rose above the parapet and was gone. But the

bridge had shaken, and she could still feel the vibration of this departure at full speed. She turned round, as if to follow the invisible engine as its rumble died away in the distance. In that direction she imagined she could see the countryside and open sky through a gap between tall, isolated houses scattered higgledy-piggledy on both sides of the track, their walls unplastered or with huge advertisements painted on them, and all turned a dirty yellow by the soot from the trains. If only she could go away like that, far away, away from these dwelling places of poverty and suffering! She might start to live again. Then she turned round and gazed at the posters stuck on the parapet. They were in every colour. A small, pretty blue one offered a fifty-franc reward for a lost dog. There was an animal that must have been loved!

Gervaise went slowly on her way. In the smoky haze of the gathering darkness, the gas lamps were coming on; and the long avenues, which had gradually disappeared in shadow, re-emerged in a blaze of light, stretching out and cutting through the night as far as the dim horizon. It seemed that a great breath of life had swept through the neighbourhood, which had broadened out with cordons of little flames, under the huge moonless sky. This was the hour when, from one end of the boulevards to the other, the bars, dance halls, and sleazy taverns flared up gaily as people enjoyed their first drink or their first dance. The fortnightly payday filled the pavements with noisy louts looking for a good time. There was a mood of revelry in the air; people were getting ready to let loose, but so far it was all quite good-natured, they were a bit excited, that was all. They were stuffing themselves in the eating houses; through the lighted windows you could see them munching away, their mouths full, laughing without even bothering to swallow. In the bars the usual pisspots were already settling in, shouting and gesticulating. The noise was deafening, a cacophony of voices—some shrill, some booming—mingling with the constant tramping of feet along the pavements. 'Hey! You comin' to 'ave a bite? Get a move on, slowcoach!... Hey, there's Pauline! Now we're gonna 'ave some fun!' The doors kept swinging open, letting out the smell of wine and snatches of music played on the cornet. There was a queue outside Père Colombe's Assommoir, which was lit up like a cathedral for High Mass; and, by God, you'd have thought there really was a Mass going on, because the blokes were singing away in there looking just like choristers at their stalls, with puffed-out cheeks and rounded bellies. They were celebrating Saint Payday, a lovely saint who must be in charge of the till in Paradise. But respectable citizens out for a stroll with their wives shook their heads and remarked that, judging by the way things were hotting up, there'd be an awful lot of drunks in Paris that night. And, above all the din, the night was black, still, and icy-cold, broken only by the blazing lines of the boulevards stretching out to the four corners of the sky.

Gervaise stood there in front of Père Colombe's Assommoir, lost in thought. If she'd had a couple of sous, she'd have gone in and had a quick one. It might have taken the edge off her hunger. Ah, she'd knocked a few back in her time! And enjoyed it, too. From where she stood she stared at the booze machine, thinking that that was where all her troubles came from, but dreaming too of finishing herself off with some of that stuff when she had the wherewithal. But a cool breeze ruffled her hair and she saw how very dark the night was. Well, the time had come. This was the moment to be bold and make herself nice unless she wanted to die right there in the midst of all that revelry. Especially as watching other people stuffing themselves didn't exactly help to fill her own belly. She walked more slowly and looked round. Under the trees the shadows were darker. Few people were about, just people walking briskly, hurrying down the boulevard. And on this wide, dark, empty strip of pavement, where the sounds of revelry from round about could hardly be heard, women stood and waited. They'd stay there for quite a while, hardly moving, as patient and stiff as the little plane trees; then they'd move off slowly, dragging their worn shoes over the frozen ground, walking ten paces and then stopping again, as if rooted to the spot. There was one, wearing an enormous scarf round her head, who had an enormous upper body but the arms and legs of an insect; she was rolling along, bursting out of her tattered black silk dress. Another was tall, angular, and bareheaded, and wearing a housemaid's apron. And there were still others, old and tarted up, or young and dirty, so dirty and slovenly that not even a ragpicker would have given them a second glance. Gervaise, however, not knowing what to do, tried to learn by doing what they did. Her throat dry, she felt like a little girl; she no longer knew whether she felt ashamed, it all felt like a horrible dream. For a quarter of an hour she stood there, not moving.

Men walked past without turning round. So then she took the initiative and found the courage to accost a man who was passing by with his hands in his pockets, whistling.

''Ello, love...' she said in a strangled voice.

The man gave her a sideways glance and carried on walking, whistling louder.

Gervaise grew bolder, impelled by the desperation of the chase, her empty stomach driving her on to find that ever-elusive supper. She tramped up and down for what seemed like ages, oblivious of time and place. All around the silent, dark figures of the other women moved this way and that beneath the trees, with the regularity of animals pacing to and fro in a cage. They'd emerge slowly from the shadows, like ghosts; they'd walk into the light of a gas lamp, which showed up their pale, mask-like features; and they'd fade away again, the white edge of a petticoat swinging as they slipped back into the tantalizing shadows of the pavement. Some men let themselves be stopped, stood talking just for the fun of it, then went on their way, laughing. Others would walk discreetly after a particular woman, keeping ten paces behind. Then there'd be murmured exchanges, arguments in low voices, and fierce haggling followed by sudden, complete silence. No matter how far she walked, Gervaise saw these female sentries spaced out through the night as if the outer boulevards had been planted with women from end to end. Twenty paces away from one she always found another. The line seemed to go on forever, guarding the whole of Paris. Angry at being ignored, she kept changing her position, and moved on from the Chaussée de Clignancourt to the Grande Rue de la Chapelle.

''Ello, love...'

But the men walked past. She moved away from the slaughterhouses, with their broken-down walls reeking of blood. She glanced at the old Hôtel Boncœur, shut up and shabby-looking. She walked past the front of the Lariboisière hospital, automatically counting the lighted windows along the façades, windows that glowed pale and still like so many night-lights for the dying. She crossed the railway bridge as the trains rumbled past, rending the air with the desperate screech of their whistles. How sad the night made it all seem! Then she turned on her heels and let her eyes wander over those same buildings, the same unchanging vista along this part of the avenue; and she did this ten times, twenty times, without pause, without taking a moment's rest on a bench. No, nobody wanted her. The men's disdain seemed to intensify her feeling of shame. Once again she walked down towards the hospital and the abattoirs. This was her last walk, from the bloody yards where the slaughtering had taken place to the dimly lit wards where death laid the stiffened corpses in communal shrouds. This space had bounded her entire life.

'Ello, love...'

Suddenly, she noticed her shadow on the ground. When she approached a lamp-post the vague shadow took shape and became clearer, becoming a huge, squat mass, so round that it looked grotesque. It seemed to spread out, the belly, breasts, and rump merging into each other. She was limping so badly that the shadow tumbled over at every step, like a clown. Then, when she moved away, the clown grew bigger, gigantic, filling the whole boulevard, giving bows that made it knock its head against the trees and houses. My God! What an odd, frightening sight! She'd never realized how far she'd sunk. She couldn't help looking at herself, waiting for each gas lamp and watching the capering of her shadow. What a lovely creature she'd got walking beside her! What a doll! The men were bound to come running. She lowered her voice, not daring to do more than mumble after the men who passed by:

'Ello, love...'

It must be getting very late by now. The neighbourhood was shutting down. The eating houses were closed and in the bars, where drink-slurred voices could still be heard, the gaslight had grown dim and red. The fun was turning into arguments and fights. One scruffy great brute was yelling: 'I'm gonna beat the shit out of you, so get ready!' Some tart was pitching into a bloke in the doorway of a dance hall, calling him a rotten bastard and a dirty swine, while he could only repeat 'Fuck off!' over and over again. The drinking had created an atmosphere of violence in the streets, a savage mood that made the few remaining passers-by look white-faced and terrified. There was one fight in which a drunk fell flat on his face, and lay sprawling, while his mate, thinking he'd done him in, ran off with a clatter of boots. There were a few groups bawling dirty songs, followed by heavy silences broken by hiccupping or an occasional dull thud as a drunk hit the ground. The fortnightly payday binge always ended like this, with the wine that had been flowing for six hours now leaving its marks all over the pavements. There were bright puddles of vomit, trickling across the road, so that anyone fussy who was still out had to take great strides to avoid stepping in them. Oh yes, the neighbourhood was very clean! A stranger seeing it before the road sweepers had done their job in the early morning would have gone away with a lovely impression. But, for now, the drunks were running the show, and they didn't give a damn what anybody thought. God, no! Knives were being pulled out and the jollifications were threatening to end in bloodshed. Women quickened their pace, men prowled about like wolves, and the night seemed to fill with lurking horrors.

Gervaise walked on, up and down, with no thought in her head except to keep going. From time to time she was overcome with tiredness, and would almost fall asleep, rocked by the clippety-clop of her gait; then she'd give a start and look around her, and realize she'd walked a hundred metres without being aware of it, as if she were dead. Her aching feet were becoming more and more swollen in her worn-out shoes. She could no longer feel anything, she was so exhausted and empty. The last clear thought she'd had was that her bitch of a daughter might at that very moment be eating oysters somewhere. Then she fell into a daze, her eyes were still open but she found it too much of an effort to think. The only sensation she was still aware of, in this collapse of her whole being, was of bitter cold, an intense, deathly cold the like of which she had never known. Surely the dead lying in the ground were not as cold as this. She raised her head and felt an icy stinging on her face. It was the snow which had finally made up its mind to come down from the hazy sky, a fine, dense snow that swirled about in the light wind. It had been expected for three days. It had chosen the right moment to fall!

This first squall woke Gervaise up, and she started to walk faster. Men were now running, in a hurry to get home, their shoulders already white. Seeing a man coming along under the trees, Gervaise went up to him and said once more:

''Ello, love...'

The man stopped, but didn't react. He held out his hand and said in a mumble:

'Can you spare a few coins?'

They looked at each other. My God! This was what they'd come to: Père Bru begging, Madame Coupeau streetwalking! They stood there open-mouthed, staring at one another. They'd hit rock-bottom at the same time. All evening the old workman had been wandering about, not daring to go up to anyone; and the first person he'd stopped was someone who was also starving, like himself. Lord, wasn't it pitiful? To have worked for fifty years, and now be begging! To have been one of the best laundresses in the Rue de la Goutte-d'Or, and end up in the gutter! They went on staring at each other. Then, without a word, they went their separate ways, lashed by the snow.

It was a real blizzard. Up on this high ground, with wide open spaces all around, the fine snow swirled about as if being blown from all four corners of the sky at once. You couldn't see ten metres in front of you, everything was disappearing under this flying dust. The neighbourhood had vanished, the boulevard seemed dead, as if the snowstorm had silenced the hiccups of the last remaining drunkards under its white shroud. Gervaise struggled painfully on, blinded, lost, feeling her way from tree to tree. As she advanced, the gas lamps emerged from the white pall, glowing feebly like torches that had recently been extinguished. Then, all of a sudden, as she was at an intersection, even these lights were gone; she was caught up and rolled along in a great swirl of snow, unable to make out anything that might guide her. The ground beneath her feet was disappearing in a white haze. Grey walls had closed around her. When she stopped and looked round, unsure which way to go, she could sense, beyond that icy veil, the great expanse of the avenues, the endless lines of lamp-posts—the dark, deserted, infinite vastness of the sleeping city.

She was at the point where the outer boulevard meets the Boulevard Magenta and the Boulevard Ornano, and was beginning to think she might lie down there on the ground, when she heard footsteps. She started running, but the snow got in her eyes and the footsteps receded before she could tell whether they were going to the left or the right. Finally she made out the broad shoulders of a man, a dark blur swaying this way and that as it faded into the mist. This one she must have, she wouldn't let this one go! She ran faster, caught up with the man, and grabbed hold of his smock.

'Monsieur, Monsieur...'

The man turned round. It was Goujet.

So now she'd tried to pick up Gueule-d'Or! What had she done to offend the Lord, that she was being tormented like this, to the very end? It was the final straw, to be throwing herself at the blacksmith's feet, so that he'd see her as just another common streetwalker, pathetic and desperate. They were standing under a gas lamp, and she could see her misshapen shadow on the snow, seeming to caper about making fun of her. It was like the shadow of some drunk and disorderly woman. God! Not to have a morsel of bread or a drop of wine in your body and to be taken for a drunk! It was her own fault. Why did she drink? Goujet must certainly think she'd been drinking and was out on a mad spree.

But Goujet just looked at her, while the snow sprinkled his handsome golden beard with white daisy petals. Then, as she turned away, hanging her head, he stopped her and said:

'Come with me.'

He led the way and she followed. They went through the silent streets, keeping close to the walls. Poor Madame Goujet had died in October of rheumatic fever, but Goujet was still living in the little house in the Rue Neuve, lonely and depressed. That day he'd stayed out late looking after an injured workmate. He opened the door and lit a lamp, then turned to Gervaise who was waiting meekly on the landing. Very softly, as if his mother could still hear him, he said:

'Come in.'

The first room, Madame Goujet's, had been piously preserved just as she'd left it. Her embroidery frame stood on a chair by the window, next to the big armchair that seemed to be waiting for the old lacemaker. The bed was made up and she could have slept in it if she'd left the cemetery to come home to spend the evening with her son. The room still had its atmosphere of calm, decency, and kindness.

'Come in,' the blacksmith repeated, more loudly.

She went in nervously, like a streetwalker going into somewhere respectable. He too was quite pale and apprehensive at the idea of bringing a woman into his dead mother's room in this way. They tiptoed across the floor as if ashamed to be heard. He ushered Gervaise into his own room and shut the door. There he felt more at home. It was the same little room she remembered, with the little iron bedstead with white curtains. But now there were more cut-out pictures on the walls, reaching right up to the ceiling. In this atmosphere of innocence, Gervaise felt self-conscious. She hung back, out of the light. Then, without a word, in a rush of passion, he tried to seize her and hold her tightly in his arms. But, almost fainting, she murmured:

'My God! Oh my God!'

The stove, damped down with coke dust, was still going, and the remains of a stew, which the blacksmith had left to keep warm for when he came back, was simmering in front of the ash-pan. Gervaise, beginning to thaw out in the warmth of the room, could have gone down on all fours to eat straight out of the saucepan. It was more than she could bear, her stomach was being torn apart, she sank down with a sigh. But Goujet had understood. He put the stew on the table, cut some bread, and poured her some wine.

'Thank you! Thank you!' she said. 'That's very good of you! Thank you!'

She was hardly able to get the words out. She picked up the fork, but was trembling so much that she dropped it again. The hunger that was almost causing her to choke made her head shake like a senile old woman's. She had to eat with her fingers. As she stuffed the first potato into her mouth she started to sob. Great tears ran down her cheeks and fell on her bread. She went on eating, greedily devouring the tear-soaked bread, breathing hard, her chin twitching. Goujet made her drink so that she wouldn't choke, and her glass rattled against her teeth.

'D'you want more bread?' he asked softly.

Weeping, she said no, then yes—she didn't know. Lord, how good and sad it is to eat when you're dying of hunger!

He was standing in front of her and looking at her. He could see her properly now, in the bright light from the lamp. How old and worn-out she looked! The warmth was melting the snow on her hair and clothes and it was running off her. Her poor nodding head was quite grey now, and clumps of her hair had become all tangled because of the wind. She sat hunched up, hardly able to raise her head, looking so fat and ugly that it made you want to cry. And he remembered the time when they'd been in love, when she used to be all rosy as she ironed away, with her little baby crease round her neck, like a pretty necklace. In those days he'd go and gaze at her for hours, happy just to see her. Later on, she'd come to the forge, and there they'd known even greater happiness, when he beat his iron and she stood enthralled by the rhythm of his hammer on the anvil. And afterwards, how often he'd bitten his pillow at night, longing to have her like this in his room! He would have broken her bones if he'd ever had her, he wanted her so much! And now she was his, he could have her. She was finishing her bread, wiping her tears from the bottom of the saucepan, the big, silent tears that were still falling into the food.

She stood up. She'd finished. For a moment she stood there with her head bent, embarrassed, not sure whether he wanted her. Then, thinking she could see a spark in his eyes, she put her hand up to her bodice and undid the first button. But Goujet had dropped to his knees and, taking her hands in his, he said very softly:

'I love you, Madame Gervaise, I still love you in spite of everything, I swear I do!'

'Don't say that, Monsieur Goujet!' she cried, horrified at seeing him kneeling before her like this. 'No, don't say that, I can't bear it!'

He then said he could never love anyone else, and this distressed her even more.

'No, no, it's all too late, I'm too ashamed. Get up, please! I'm the one who should be on my knees.'

He got up, shaking all over, and stammered:

'Can I kiss you?'

Overcome with surprise and emotion, she could find nothing to say, but nodded her consent. She was his to do with as he wished. But he simply leaned forward to kiss her.

'This is all we need, Madame Gervaise,' he whispered. 'It sums up our feelings, doesn't it?'

He kissed her on the forehead, on a lock of her grey hair. He hadn't kissed anyone since his mother's death. His dear friend Gervaise was all he had left in life. So after kissing her so reverently he stepped back and fell across his bed, choking back his sobs. Gervaise couldn't stay there any longer: it was too sad, too awful, to be together again in circumstances like these, when they loved each other.

'I love you, Monsieur Goujet,' she cried. 'I love you too... But it's impossible, I know it's impossible. Goodbye, goodbye, it would be more than we could bear.'

She ran through Madame Goujet's room and found herself in the street. The next thing she knew was that she was ringing at the main door in the Rue de la Goutte d'Or. Boche let her in. The building was in complete darkness. Going in was like going into mourning for herself. At this time of the night the gaping, dirty archway seemed like a pair of open jaws. To think that at one time she'd dreamed of living in this dismal barracks of a place! Her ears must have been blocked in those days, for her not to hear the terrible wail of despair rising up within its walls! From the day she'd first set foot in the place she'd been going downhill. Yes, it must bring you bad luck to be piled one on top of the other like this, in these hideous great working-class tenements; poverty was infectious, like the cholera. That night you'd have thought they were all dead. All she could hear was the Boches snoring to her right, while to her left Lantier and Virginie were making a kind of purring sound, like cats who aren't asleep but are lying cosily somewhere with their eyes closed. The courtyard looked just like a cemetery. The snow made a pale square on the ground, while the lofty walls rose up, livid grey, without a single light, like the walls of some ruin; and not so much as a sigh could be heard, as if a whole village had died of cold and hunger, and lay buried there. She had to step over a black stream, the overflow from the dye-works, steaming as it melted a muddy bed for itself in the whiteness of the snow. It was the colour of her thoughts. The lovely streams of pale blue and pale pink had long since run their course!

As she climbed the six flights of stairs in the darkness, she couldn't help laughing—an unpleasant, ironic laugh that hurt. She remembered what had once been her ideal: to be able to get on with her work in peace, always have something to eat and somewhere decent to sleep, bring up her kids properly, not be knocked about, and die in her own bed. No, really, it was quite funny how it was all turning out! She wasn't working any more, she wasn't eating any more, she slept in filth, her daughter was on the game, her husband beat her black and blue; the only thing that could happen to her now was that she'd peg out in the street, and that could be right now, if she had the guts to throw herself out of the window as soon as she got back to her room. Anyone would've thought she'd prayed to have thirty thousand a year and be fussed over. No, the thing is, in this life, even if you don't ask for much you still end up with bugger-all! Not even a crust and a bed, that's the common lot. And what made her laugh even more was remembering her dream of retiring to the country, after twenty years of ironing. Well, she was on her way there now. She wanted her green little spot in Père-Lachaise.

By the time she turned into her corridor she was beside herself. Her poor head was spinning. Her enormous distress came, more than anything else, from having said goodbye for the last time to the blacksmith. It was all over between them, they would never see each other again. And on top of that all the other reasons for being so unhappy were piling up and driving her crazy. As she went past the Bijards' she poked her nose in and saw Lalie lying there dead, looking as if she was pleased to be laid out, free to take things easy for evermore. Children were luckier than grown-ups! As there was a beam of light under Père

Bazouge's door, she walked straight into his room, gripped by a mad desire to go on the same journey as the child.

That old joker Bazouge had come home that evening in an amazingly jolly state. He was so sozzled that, in spite of the cold, he was lying snoring on the floor; but that obviously didn't prevent him from having a lovely dream, for he was shaking with laughter as he slept. The lamp was still burning and lit up his black hat, lying flat in a corner, and his black coat, which he'd pulled over his knees as a blanket.

On seeing him Gervaise began to wail so loudly that he woke up.

'Shut that door, for God's sake! It's bloody freezin'!... Oh, it's you. What's goin' on? What d'ya want?'

Gervaise held out her arms and, hardly knowing any more what she was saying, launched into a passionate entreaty.

'Take me! I've had enough, I want to go. Don't be hard on me. I didn't know! You don't know, not until you're ready. Oh yes, the day comes when you're glad to go. Take me, take me, I'll bless you for it!'

She fell to her knees, trembling all over, stirred by a feeling that made her face go deathly white. Never had she grovelled like this before any man. Père Bazouge's red, bloated face, with his twisted mouth and leathery skin encrusted with graveyard dust, seemed to her beautiful and resplendent as the sun. But the old man, only half awake, thought she must be trying to get off with him.

'Now then!' he muttered. 'Don't try any funny games with me.'

'Take me,' Gervaise repeated more urgently. 'You remember when I knocked on the wall one night and then said I hadn't, because I was still too stupid... Well, now it's different, you can gimme your hands, I'm not scared any more! Take me to bye-byes, I'll keep still, you'll see... That's all I want now, and I'll love you for it!'

Bazouge, ever gallant, thought he shouldn't be unpleasant to a lady who seemed to have taken such a fancy to him. She was going off her head, but she still didn't look bad when she got all worked up.

'You're right!' he said with conviction. 'I packed up another three today who would've given me a bloody great tip if they'd been able to put their 'ands in their pockets. The trouble is, duckie, it can't be done just like that...'

'Take me!' Gervaise continued to wail. 'I want to get out of it...'

'But, damn it, there's one little thing that's got to 'appen first... You know—*aargh!*'

He made a noise in his throat as though swallowing his tongue; and, finding this very funny, started to snigger.

Gervaise rose slowly to her feet. So he couldn't do anything for her either? She went back to her room in a daze and threw herself on the straw, regretting that she'd eaten. No, poverty didn't finish you off fast enough.

CHAPTER XIII

THAT night Coupeau went off on a bender. The next day Gervaise got ten francs from her son Étienne, who was now a fireman on the railway; knowing they didn't have much money at home, the boy sent her a few francs from time to time. She made a stew, but ate it by herself because Coupeau, the bastard, didn't come back at all that day. Monday came and no Coupeau; Tuesday, still no sign of him. The whole week went by. Well, damn it! If he'd gone off with some woman, that'd be a stroke of luck! But, on the Sunday, Gervaise received a printed note, which gave her a scare at first, because it looked like something from the police. But she was relieved to see it was just to inform her that the swine was at Saint-Anne's, dying. The bit of paper put it more politely, but that was what it amounted to. Yes, he'd gone off with a woman, and her name was Susie Snuffit, the last girlfriend of all drunkards.

To tell the truth, Gervaise wasn't much put out. He knew the way home, he could come back from the asylum on his own; they'd put him right there so often that they'd surely do the dirty on him again and get him back on his feet. That very morning she'd heard that throughout the week Coupeau had been seen, completely rat-arsed, doing the rounds of the Belleville bars with Mes-Bottes. Of course, it was Mes-Bottes who had the money; he must have got his hands on his old woman's nest-egg, the savings she'd built up by lying down so often. Oh yes, it was nice clean money they were drinking, money that could give you all sorts of vile diseases! So much the better if Coupeau had buggered himself up with it. What really made Gervaise mad was that those two selfish sods hadn't even thought of coming to fetch her, to ask her to come and have a drop too. Imagine! A week-long booze-up, and not a thought for the ladies! If you drink by yourself you can croak by yourself—so how's that!

However, on the Monday, as Gervaise had a nice little meal ready for the evening, some leftover beans and half a bottle of wine, she told herself that a walk would give her an appetite. The note from the asylum, lying on the chest of drawers, was beginning to worry her. The snow had melted, and the weather was lovely and mild, overcast but still, and with an invigorating nip in the air. She set out at noon because it was a long way, all the way across Paris, and her leg always slowed her down. What's more, the streets were packed; but she liked watching the crowds as she went along and she arrived in good spirits. When she gave them her name, they told her the strangest story: it seemed Coupeau had been fished out of the river at the Pont-Neuf.* He'd jumped over the parapet, imagining a man with a beard was trying to block his way. Quite a jump! And as for what Coupeau was doing on the Pont-Neuf, that was something he himself was unable to explain.

An attendant took Gervaise upstairs. On the way up she could hear shrieking, the sound of which made her blood run cold.

'Just listen to the racket he's making!' the attendant said.

'Who?' she asked.

'Your husband! He's been yelling like that since the day before yesterday. And dancing too—you'll see!'

My God, what a sight! She stood rooted to the spot. The cell was padded from top to bottom; on the floor there were two mats, one on top of the other; in a corner lay a mattress and a bolster, that was all. And there was Coupeau, leaping about screaming, like a carnival figure from La Courtille,* with his smock in tatters and his limbs going in all directions; but not a comic carnival figure, not at all—a figure, rather, whose ghastly capering made your hair stand on end. He was disguised as a man who's going to die. Jesus! Talk about a one-man show! He kept crashing against the window, bouncing back with his arms beating time, and shaking his hands as if he wanted to make them fly off and hit somebody in the face. In dance halls you can sometimes see comics trying to put on a similar performance; but they don't do it very well, you've got to see a drunk doing the dance for real, if you want to appreciate the style of the thing when it's done properly. The song that goes with it is quite something too, a carnival cry that goes on and on, with a wide open mouth emitting the same off-key trombone notes for hours on end. Coupeau was making a kind of howling noise, like an animal with a crushed paw. Strike up the band! Take your partners!

'Oh, Lord, what's the matter with 'im?' she said several times, feeling scared.

A young doctor, a big, fair-haired, rosy-cheeked man in a white apron, was sitting there calmly taking notes. Coupeau's case was apparently an unusual one, and the young man was spending all his time there.

'You can stay for a while if you want,' he said to the laundress, 'but keep still... He won't recognize you, but you can try to talk to him.'

Indeed, Coupeau didn't even seem to notice his wife was there. She hadn't had a good look at him when she came in, he'd been leaping about so much. Now that she could see him properly, she could hardly believe her eyes. God, was that really him, with those bloodshot eyes and scabby lips? She wouldn't have recognized him. To start with, he was grimacing so much for no reason—his jaw jerking sideways, his nose all wrinkled up, his cheeks sucked in—that he looked like some sort of animal. His skin was so hot that it was giving off steam, and it was so leathery that it shone, while great drops of sweat poured off him constantly. But you could see, as he danced this insane, clownish dance, that he was in distress, that his head ached and his arms and legs hurt.

Gervaise went up to the young doctor, who was drumming with his fingers on the back of his chair.

'So this time it's serious, is it, Monsieur?'

The doctor nodded without answering.

'Tell me, he's talking to himself under his breath, isn't he? Can you hear what he's saying?'

'He's talking about things he can see,' whispered the young man. 'Stay quiet, let me listen.'

Coupeau was talking in a staccato voice. But there was a spark of mischief in his eyes. He was looking down, and to right and left, and then walking around, as if out for a walk in the Bois de Vincennes, talking to himself:

'Oh, that's nice, that's really great... All those booths, it's quite a fair. And nice music, too! They're really goin' at it! What a racket! Really great! Oh look, it's all lightin' up, an' there are red balloons in the air, bouncin' about an' flyin' up... Oh! Oh! All those lanterns in the trees! It's bloody marvellous. An' water everywhere, fountains, waterfalls, water singin' like a load of choirboys... Those waterfalls are bloody fantastic!'

He straightened up as if trying to hear the melodious sound of the water better, and he took deep breaths of air, believing he was drinking in the fresh spray from the fountains. But then his face gradually resumed its anguished expression. Bending forward, he started walking faster and faster round the walls of the cell, muttering vague threats.

'Tryin' to fool me again with all that stuff! I thought as much... Shut up, you load of cunts! You don't give a damn about me. All that drinkin' an' singin' with your tarts, it's just to get me goin'. Well, I'll beat the hell out of you, I will, in your bloody booth! You can just fuck off!'

Clenching his fists, he gave a hoarse scream. Then he began to run, but tripped and fell flat on his face. His teeth chattering with terror, he blathered on:

'You want me to kill meself. No, I won't jump! So much water, that means I haven't got the guts. No, I won't jump.'

The waterfalls receded as he approached and advanced when he stepped back. Then he suddenly stopped and looked round in bewilderment, muttering almost inaudibly:

'It's not possible. They've got all the doctors to gang up on me!'

'I'm going, Monsieur. Goodnight,' Gervaise said to the doctor. 'This is all too much. I'll come back later.'

She was as white as a sheet. Coupeau continued to beat a path from the window to the mattress, and from the mattress to the window, sweating, wearing himself out, always marking the same time. She made her escape. But even though she raced down the stairs, the dreadful noise he was making followed her all the way to the bottom. My God, how good it was to be outside, and to be able to breathe properly again!

That evening the whole building in the Rue de la Goutte-d'Or was talking about Coupeau's strange sickness. The Boches, who treated Gervaise like dirt these days, actually invited her into their lodge for a cassis, so they could get the full story. Madame Lorilleux then turned up, as did Madame Poisson. The subject was inexhaustible. Boche had known a carpenter who'd stripped stark naked in the Rue Saint-Martin* and had died dancing the polka—he was an absinthe-drinker. The ladies rolled about laughing, because although it was sad, they also found it very funny. Then, as they didn't quite understand, Gervaise pushed them all back, asking for a bit of space; and there, in the middle of the lodge, while they all watched, she imitated Coupeau, bawling, leaping, thrashing about, and pulling horrible faces. Yes, honestly, that's exactly how he was. The others couldn't believe it: it wasn't possible! A man wouldn't last three hours, acting like that. But she swore by everything she held most sacred that Coupeau had been keeping it up since the day before, thirty-six hours already. If they didn't believe her, they could go and see for themselves. But Madame Lorilleux declared that she didn't want anything to do with Sainte-Anne, thank you very much; and she'd make sure Lorilleux would never even set foot in the place. As for Virginie, whose shop was going to the dogs and who went about these days with a funereal look on her face, she just muttered that life wasn't always a bed of roses—far from it! They finished the cassis and Gervaise bade them all goodnight. As soon as she stopped talking her face assumed the expression of one of the Chaillot* loonies, with staring eyes. No doubt she could still see her man leaping about. When she got up the next morning she told herself she'd never go back there. What'd be the point? She didn't want to go off her rocker as well. But every ten minutes she'd fall to thinking about it again; she'd be somewhere else, as they say. It'd be funny if he was still capering about. When midday struck, she couldn't stand it any longer; she didn't even notice how far she had to walk, so gripped was she by curiosity and so fearful of what awaited her.

There was no need to ask for news. From the bottom of the stairs she could hear his song. Exactly the same tune, exactly the same dance. It was as if she'd only just gone downstairs and was now going up again. The attendant she'd seen the day before was carrying jugs of herbal tea along the corridor and he gave her a friendly wink as he went past.

'Still the same?' she asked.

'Yes, still the same,' he replied without stopping.

She went in but stayed in the corner by the door, because there were some people with Coupeau. The fair-haired, rosy-cheeked young doctor was standing, having given his chair to a bald, elderly, weasel-faced gentleman with a ribbon in his lapel. He must be the head doctor, for he had narrow, piercing, gimlet eyes. All specialists in sudden death have eyes like that.

But he wasn't the one Gervaise had come to see; she peered over his bald head and stared hard at Coupeau. The loon was dancing and yelling even louder than the day before. In the past, she'd seen dances at Mardi Gras* when strapping lads from the wash-house had kept going all night; but never in her whole life would she have imagined that a man could go on enjoying himself for such a long time; when she said enjoying himself, that was just a manner of speaking, because there's no enjoyment to be had from leaping about uncontrollably,

like a fish out of water or as if you've swallowed a powder magazine.
Coupeau was drenched in sweat and steaming even more than before,
that was all. His mouth seemed bigger, from all the yelling. Pregnant
women would be well advised to stay clear! He'd walked so much
between the mattress and the window that you could see the traces on
the floor: the mat had got worn down by his slippers.

No, it definitely wasn't a pretty sight, and Gervaise, trembling,
began to wonder why she'd come back. To think that the night before,
at the Boches', they'd accused her of overdoing her imitation.
Whereas she hadn't shown them the half of it! Now she could see
better exactly what Coupeau was doing, and she'd never forget the
way he looked, with his eyes staring into the void. Meanwhile, she was
able to catch the odd remark exchanged between the young doctor
and the older one. The former was describing what had happened
during the night, using words she didn't understand. All night long,
Coupeau had jabbered away and whirled about, that's what it came
down to. Then the elderly bald gentleman, who incidentally wasn't
very pleasant, seemed suddenly to notice she was there. When the
young doctor told him she was the patient's wife, he started to ask her
questions, rather brusquely, like a policeman.

'Did this man's father drink?'

'Yes, Monsieur, a little, like everybody else… He was killed falling
off a roof when he was drunk.'

'Did his mother drink?'

'Gracious me, Monsieur! Like anyone else. You know: a drop now
and again… Oh, it was a very good family! There was a brother who
died very young, from convulsions.'

The doctor looked at her with his piercing eyes, then asked in his
gruff way:

'Do you drink too?'

Falteringly, Gervaise denied she did, putting her hand on her heart
to pledge her sacred word.

'Yes, you drink! Be careful, you can see where drink leads. Sooner
or later you'll go the same way!'

She cowered against the wall. The doctor turned his back on her
and squatted down, apparently unconcerned whether he'd get dust
from the mat on his frock coat. For a long time he studied Coupeau's
tremors, waiting for him to go past, following him with his eyes. That
day it was the legs' turn to jerk and twitch, for the tremors had gone

down from his hands to his feet; a regular Punch, he was, as if worked with strings, his limbs going in all directions and his trunk as stiff as a board. The disease was slowly spreading. It was like a musical beat under the skin; it would start up every three or four seconds, pulsate for a moment or two, then stop and start again, like the little shudder a stray dog gives when it shelters in a doorway in the dead heart of winter. The belly and the shoulders were already quivering, like water just coming to the boil. But it was a funny way to peg out, to go off wriggling, like a girl who can't stand being tickled!

By this stage Coupeau was moaning softly and seemed to be suffering more than the day before. His spasmodic groans suggested all kinds of torments. Thousands of pins were sticking into him. There was something heavy pressing down all over his skin; a cold, wet creature was crawling up his legs and sinking its fangs into his flesh. And there were other creatures, clinging to his shoulders, tearing the flesh from his back with their claws.

'I'm thirsty! I'm thirsty!' he kept moaning.

The young doctor took a jug of lemonade from a shelf and gave it to him. He grabbed the jug with both hands and greedily sucked in a mouthful, spilling half the liquid on himself, but then he spat it out in disgust, shouting:

'For Christ's sake! It's brandy!'

Then, at a sign from the senior doctor, the young one tried to make him drink some water, keeping hold of the carafe. This time Coupeau swallowed a mouthful, but screamed as if he'd swallowed fire.

'It's brandy, for Christ's sake! It's brandy!'

Everything he'd drunk since the day before had been brandy. This made his thirst even worse, and he could no longer drink, because everything burnt his throat. They'd brought him some soup, but they were obviously trying to poison him, because the soup tasted of rotgut. The bread was sour and nasty. Everything around him had been poisoned. The cell stank of sulphur. He even accused people of striking matches under his nose to make him ill.

The senior doctor stood up and listened to Coupeau's ranting. He was now seeing ghosts again in broad daylight. He was sure he could see spiders' webs on the walls, as big as ships' sails! Then the spiders' webs turned into nets with mesh that got smaller or bigger, like some strange toy! There were black balls bouncing about in the mesh, jugglers' balls, sometimes no bigger than marbles, sometimes the size of cannonballs; and they swelled and shrank, it was all done on purpose, just to annoy him. Suddenly he shrieked:

'Rats! Now there are rats!'

The balls were turning into rats. The filthy things were swelling up and coming through the net; then they jumped on to the mattress, where they vanished. There was a monkey too, which came out of the wall and went back into it, coming so close to him each time that he jumped back for fear of having his nose bitten off. Then, suddenly, everything changed again: the walls must have been jumping around, because he kept saying, choking with terror and rage:

'Ouch! All right, throw me about, I don't care! Ouch! The place is fallin' down! Yes, ring them bells, you bloody black crows, play the organ so I can't call for help! And the sods 'ave put a bomb behind the wall! I can hear the taper burnin', they're gonna blow us all up. Fire, fire! For God's sake, there's a fire! Everything's on fire! Oh, it's so bright! The whole sky's on fire, red flames, green flames, yellow flames... Help me, somebody! Fire!'

The senior doctor pursed his lips. He stood there for another couple of minutes, gazing at Coupeau. Then he said, with a shrug:

'The same treatment: broth, milk, lemonade, weak extract of quinine in liquid form. Don't leave him on his own. Send for me if necessary.'

He went out, and Gervaise followed him, to ask if there was any hope left. But he was striding so quickly down the corridor that she didn't dare try to stop him. She stood there for a moment, not moving, reluctant to go back in and have another look at her husband. The visit had already been very distressing as it was. Hearing Coupeau shouting again that the lemonade tasted like brandy, she took to her heels; she'd had quite enough for one performance. In the street, the galloping of horses and the noise of carriages made her think that the whole of Sainte-Anne's was chasing after her. And the warning that doctor had given her! She felt she was going the same way as Coupeau, she really did!

Needless to say, the Boches and the others were waiting for her in the Rue de la Goutte-d'Or. As soon as she appeared under the archway they called her into the lodge. Well, was old Coupeau still hanging on? Oh yes, still hanging on. Boche looked astonished and dismayed: he'd bet a bottle that Coupeau wouldn't last through the day. What! Still hanging on! They all slapped their thighs in amazement. He was a tough old bugger! Madame Lorilleux worked out how many hours it had been: thirty-six and twenty-four made sixty. Bloody hell! He'd been leaping about and shouting his head off for sixty hours! Nobody had ever heard of anything like it. But Boche, who was trying not to show his disappointment at losing his bet, questioned Gervaise suspiciously, asking if she was quite sure he hadn't snuffed it when her back was turned. Oh no, he was jumping about so much, he didn't want to stop. So then Boche became quite insistent and asked her to imitate Coupeau again, so they could see. Yes, yes, just a bit more! By popular request! They all said it would be really good of her, because there were two neighbours there who hadn't seen her performance the night before, and they'd just come down especially. Madame Boche ordered everybody to stand back, and they cleared the middle of the room, elbowing each other in their excitement. But Gervaise hesitated, afraid it might really upset her. However, to prove she wasn't just being coy, she began with two or three little jumps, but then she came over all strange, and stopped short: no, honestly, she couldn't! A murmur of disappointment ran round the room: what a shame, she imitated Coupeau to perfection. But if she really couldn't! And, since Virginie was already on her way back to her shop, they forgot about Coupeau in favour of a full-on gossip about the Poisson household, which was in a complete mess now: the bailiffs had come the day before; the policeman was on the point of losing his job; and Lantier was sniffing round the girl from the eating house down the street, a splendid creature who was talking about setting up a tripe shop. Ha! It made them all laugh to imagine a tripe seller taking over Virginie's shop: after fancy confectionery, something plain and simple. The cuckold Poisson looked a real mug in all this: how on earth could a man who needs to be sharp and alert in his job be such a duffer in his own home? But they fell silent when they suddenly noticed Gervaise, whom they'd forgotten, trying out her act all by herself at the back of the room, shaking her hands and feet, imitating Coupeau. Bravo! That was the way, that was just what they wanted. She stopped, looking bewildered, as if she'd just woken up from a dream. Then she rushed off. Goodnight all! She was going upstairs to try to get some sleep.

The next day the Boches saw her leaving the building at noon, as on the two previous days. They wished her joy of it. This time, at Sainte-Anne's, Coupeau's yelling and stomping were making the whole corridor shake. She was still holding the banisters on the stairs when she heard him screaming:

'Now it's bugs! Just come a bit closer an' I'll see to you! So, they want to do me in, do they! No, I'm too smart for you lot! You can just fuck off!'

She stood for a moment outside the door to catch her breath. He seemed to be fighting a whole army! When she went in, the sight that met her was more amazing than ever. Coupeau had become a raving lunatic, a runaway from Charenton!* He was throwing himself about in the middle of the cell, lashing out in every direction with his fists, hitting himself, the walls, the floor, falling over, and lunging at empty space; he tried to open the window, then he tried to hide, then he called out and answered himself, making an incredible racket all by himself, with the anguished expression of a man being pursued by a whole crowd of people. Then Gervaise realized that he thought he was on a roof, laying sheets of zinc. He was doing the bellows with his mouth, stirring his irons in a brazier, and kneeling down to run his thumb along the edges of the mat, thinking he was soldering it. Yes, his trade was coming back to him, just as he was about to depart this life; and if he was yelling like this and flailing about on his roof, it was because some bastards were trying to stop him from doing his work properly. On all the neighbouring roofs there were rotten sods trying to annoy him; what's more, the devils were sending hordes of rats to run around his legs. The filthy creatures were everywhere! No matter how many he killed by stamping on them with his foot, fresh hordes kept coming; the roof was black with 'em. And there were spiders as well! He pulled his trousers tightly round his thighs to squash huge spiders that had crawled up his legs. Bloody hell, he'd never get his day's work done, they were trying to lose him his job, his boss would send him to Mazas.* So he started to hurry and, believing he had a steam engine in his belly, he puffed steam out of his wide open mouth, thick steam that filled the cell and went out of the window; bending down, still puffing, he watched the ribbon of steam as it floated away, up into the sky, where it obscured the sun.

'Hey, look!' he shouted, 'It's that lot from the Chaussée de Clignancourt, dressed up as bears, putting on quite a show...'

He stayed crouched in front of the window, as if watching a procession in the street from a rooftop.

'Here comes the procession, with lions an' panthers makin' faces, and little kids dressed as dogs an' cats. And there's that great Clémence, with her hair full of feathers. Ha! Look at that! She's gone arse over tip, showin' everything she's got! Get up, sweetheart, you'd better scarper. Hey, you fuckin' cops, leave 'er alone! Don't shoot, for God's sake, don't shoot!'

His voice rose to a terrified scream as he ducked down, repeating that the cops and some soldiers were down there aiming at him with their rifles. He could see the barrel of a pistol coming through the wall, pointing at his chest. They were coming to take the girl away from him again.

'Don't shoot, for God's sake, don't shoot!'

Then all the houses were caving in, and he was making great crashing noises as if a whole neighbourhood was collapsing. Everything was vanishing, everything was being swept away. But he scarcely had time to breathe before new visions arose before him, with extraordinary speed. Words came bubbling out of him, all jumbled, so desperate was his urge to speak. His voice grew louder and louder.

'Oh, it's you! Hello! Now don't be silly! I don't want to get your hair in me mouth!'

He wiped his face with his hand and blew the hair away. The young doctor asked:

'Who can you see?'

'Me wife, of course!'

He was staring at the wall, with his back to Gervaise.

This made her feel very scared, and she looked at the wall, too, wondering if she could see herself. He gabbled on.

'Don't try to get round me! I don't like to be tied down. Blimey, you're lookin' nice, that's a smart get-up. How'd you pay for that? You've been out on the streets, you bitch! Just you wait, I'll deal with you! Ah, so you're hidin' your fancy man behind your skirts, are you? Who is it, then? Bend over, so I can see... Christ! It's 'im again!'

With a huge leap he tried to bash his head against the wall, but the padding deadened the blow. The only sound was the thud of his body landing heavily on the mat.

'Who can you see this time?' asked the doctor.

'The hatter! The hatter!' yelled Coupeau.

The doctor asked Gervaise if she could explain, but she could only stutter, unable to answer; the scene had stirred up some of the most distressful times in her life. The roofer raised his fists:

'C'mon, let's 'ave it out, mate! You've 'ad it this time! You turn up 'ere, just like that, with that bag on your arm, and make a fool of me in front of everybody. So, I'm gonna bloody well throttle you, that's what I'm gonna do! No messin'! I've 'ad enough of your showin' off... Take that! And that! And that!'

He was hitting out into space. Then a terrible rage took hold of him. He'd bumped into a wall as he backed away and thought he was being attacked from behind. So he turned round and threw himself at the padding. He leapt about, jumping from one corner to another, hitting out with his belly, his buttocks, his shoulder, rolling over, jumping up again. His bones seemed to be going soft, for his body, as it hit the walls, sounded like wet wadding. And this remarkable performance was accompanied by terrible threats and savage, guttural cries. But the battle must have been going badly for him, because he was gasping for breath and his eyes were bulging in their sockets. He seemed to be slowly succumbing to childish feelings of terror.

'Murder! Murder! Fuck off, both of you! The bastards are laughing at me! Look at that bitch, with her legs in the air! She's in for it, that's for sure. Oh, the brute! He's killin' her, he's cuttin' one of her legs off with his knife. The other one's lyin' on the ground and her belly's split open. There's blood everywhere... Oh, my God! Oh, my God!'

Bathed in sweat, his hair standing on end, he was a ghastly sight. As he backed away, he flailed about with his arms as if to fend off his frightful vision. He let out two heart-rending groans and, his heels catching in the mattress, fell backwards on to it.

'Monsieur, Monsieur, he's dead!' said Gervaise, clasping her hands together.

The doctor stepped forward and pulled Coupeau into the middle of the mattress. No, he wasn't dead. They took off his shoes and his bare feet stuck out over the end of the mattress, jigging about all on their own, side by side, doing a little quickstep.

Just then the senior doctor came in. He had with him two colleagues, one thin, the other fat, and both wearing decorations, just like him. All three bent down, not saying a word, examined Coupeau all over, and then conferred briefly in undertones. They'd stripped the roofer from his shoulders to his thighs, and by standing on tiptoe Gervaise could see his naked torso. The process was complete! The trembling had run down from the arms and up from the legs, and now the trunk too was joining in the fun! The puppet was having a real belly-laugh. Ripples of mirth were running all down the ribs, and the tummy was heaving as if it was about to burst. All parts of him were playing their part, and no mistake! The muscles took up their positions opposite their partners, the skin vibrated like a drum, the hairs nodded to each other as they waltzed about. Surely this was the grand finale, like the final gallop at a ball when all the dancers join hands and stamp their feet.

'He's asleep,' murmured the head doctor.

He drew the others' attention to Coupeau's face. His eyes were shut, but the whole face was twitching. Lying flat out in this way, he looked even more frightful, with his jaw jutting out and his features all contorted, like those of a man who had died having nightmares. But then the doctors' eyes fell on his feet, which they began to scrutinize with great interest. They were still dancing. Coupeau might have fallen asleep, his feet were still dancing! The boss could snore as much as he liked, they didn't care, they just kept going, neither speeding up nor slowing down. Proper mechanical feet they were, having fun while they could.

Seeing the doctors putting their hands on her husband's chest, Gervaise wanted to touch him too. She went up to him quietly and put her hand on his shoulder. She kept it there for a minute. My God! Whatever was going on in there? She could feel dancing, deep down in his flesh; his actual bones must be jigging about. From some remote source came tremors and ripples that flowed like a river under the skin. When she pressed a bit, she could sense, so to speak, cries of pain coming from the marrow of his bones. All you could see with the naked eye were little wavelets making dimples on the skin, as on the surface of a whirlpool; but imagine the commotion inside! What a frightful business! An army of moles must be at work! The Assommoir's poison was hard at it with a pickaxe. Coupeau's entire body was saturated with it; so what the hell, the job had to be finished, he'd crumble to bits, he'd be carried off by this complete, continuous shaking of his whole carcass.

The senior doctors left, but Gervaise stayed behind with the junior doctor. After an hour, she said again in a low voice:

'Monsieur, Monsieur, he's dead.'

But the young man, looking at Coupeau's feet, shook his head. The bare feet, sticking out over the end of the mattress, were still dancing. They were none too clean and the nails needed cutting. Several hours went by. Suddenly, the feet stiffened and became still. Then the doctor turned to Gervaise and said:

'That's it.'

Death alone had stopped the feet.

When Gervaise got back to the Rue de la Goutte-d'Or, she found a whole gaggle of women at the Boches', jabbering away excitedly. She thought they were waiting for her to hear the news, as on the other days.

'He's pegged out,' she said quietly as she went in, looking dazed and haggard.

But nobody was interested. The whole building was in quite a commotion. Oh, a priceless story! Poisson had caught his wife with Lantier. They didn't know the exact details, and everybody told the story in a slightly different way. Anyway, he'd come upon them just when they were least expecting it. There were even some details which the ladies could hardly bring themselves to repeat. Naturally, a sight like that had made him behave quite uncharacteristically. A real tiger, he was! That man, usually so quiet, who walked about as if he had a broom stuck up his arse, had jumped about and roared with rage. Then it had all gone quiet. Lantier must have explained things to the husband. Anyway, it couldn't have gone on like that any longer. And Boche told them that the girl from the eating house down the street was definitely going to take over the shop to sell tripe. The hatter, sly dog, loved tripe.

Meanwhile, Madame Lorilleux arrived with Madame Lerat, and Gervaise again said quietly:

'He's pegged out... My God, four whole days of yelling and leaping about.'

At that the two sisters felt obliged to take out their handkerchiefs. Their brother had certainly had his faults, but he was still their brother. Boche shrugged, and said loudly enough for everybody to hear:

'Well, that's one drunkard less!'

From that day on, Gervaise often seemed to have gone round the bend, and people in the building would amuse themselves by getting her to do her imitation of Coupeau. In fact she no longer needed to be asked, she did it for nothing—the shaking of the hands and feet, the little involuntary squeals. She'd picked it all up at Sainte-Anne, of course, from spending so much time watching her husband. But she wasn't in luck: she didn't die of it like him. With her it became limited to pulling faces like a monkey that had escaped from its cage somewhere, and all she got for it was cabbage stumps tossed in her direction by kids in the street.

Gervaise lasted like this for several months. She sank lower and lower, suffering the vilest humiliations, dying a little of starvation each day. As soon as she had a few sous, she'd spend them on drink and be off her head for hours. She was given the filthiest jobs in the neighbourhood. One evening somebody bet she wouldn't eat something disgusting, but she did, to earn ten sous. Monsieur Marescot decided to turn her out of her room on the sixth floor, but as Père Bru had just been found dead in his hole under the stairs up there, the landlord let her have that. So now she lived in Père Bru's little niche. And it was there, on some old straw, her belly empty, and frozen to the bone, that she starved slowly to death. The earth, it seemed, was in no hurry to take her. Her brain had gone dead, she never even thought of throwing herself from the sixth floor on to the yard below, to have done with it all. Death had to take her little by little, bit by bit, dragging her along to the bitter end of the miserable existence she'd made for herself. They never even knew exactly what she did die of. Some said she caught a chill. But the truth was that she died of poverty, of the filth and weariness of her wretched life. She just rotted away, as the Lorilleux put it. One morning there was a bad smell in the corridor and the neighbours realized they hadn't seen her for two days; they found her in her hole, already turning green.

It was of course Père Bazouge who came, with a pauper's coffin under his arm, to pack her up. He was quite pickled as usual, but as genial and chirpy as could be. When he saw who his client was, he delivered himself of some philosophical reflections as he went about his business:

'We all go the same way... No need to push an' shove, there's room for everybody... It's silly to be in a hurry, 'cos it only slows you down... All I want is to make people 'appy. Some want to go, others don't. Let's see about this one... She didn't want to go to begin with, but then she changed 'er mind. So she 'ad to wait a bit... Anyway, it's over now, she's got what she wanted! Off we go, luv!'

As he took hold of her with his huge dirty hands he had a moment of tenderness, gently lifting this woman who'd been keen on him for so long. He laid her in the coffin like a loving father, mumbling between hiccups:

'Listen: it's me, Bibi-la-Gaieté, 'im they call the ladies' comforter... There, you're all right now. Time to go bye-byes, my beauty!'

EXPLANATORY NOTES

5 *Veau à Deux Têtes*: literally the Two-Headed Calf; but, in working-class slang, a *veau* was a young woman predisposed to prostitution. In retrospect (when Gervaise is driven to try to sell herself on the streets), the name ironically deflates her aspirations to live a respectable life.

Grand-Balcon: situated on the northern side of the Boulevard de la Chapelle; in working-class slang, 'faire le balcon' meant a young woman was accessible to visitors, a state of readiness signalled by an item of clothing left on her balcony.

outer boulevards: the Boulevard de Rochechouart and the Boulevard de la Chapelle, immediately adjacent to the city limits formed by the octroi wall (see note to p. 6).

Claude . . . Étienne: Claude (b. 1842) appears as a young artist in Zola's *Le Ventre de Paris* (1873) and is the hero of *L'Œuvre* (1886); Étienne (b. 1846) becomes the leader of the striking miners in *Germinal* (1885) (see Introduction, p. ix).

6 *Barrière Poissonnière*: one of sixty toll-houses which controlled access to the city through gateways in the octroi wall (see note below). The Barrière Poissonnière was sited at the present-day intersection of the Boulevard Barbès (formerly Ornano) and the Boulevard de Rochechouart, a development referred to at the end of the novel (p. 365).

Boncœur: the Good Heart; the name also reflects Gervaise's character.

Lariboisière hospital: major Parisian hospital, very near the Gare du Nord, founded in 1846 by the widow of the Napoleonic general Jean-Antoine Lariboisière (1759–1812); it was completed in 1854.

boundary wall: the original French is 'le mur de l'octroi' from the verb *octroyer* (to grant); this eighteenth-century wall of the Fermiers-Généraux (Farmers-General, an organization responsible for raising royal taxes until 1791) allowed Paris to enforce its right to levy customs duties on goods brought into the city (see note above).

Montmartre and La Chapelle: when the novel begins, in 1850, these were still independent communes beyond the northern edge of the octroi wall and thus outside the administrative boundary of Paris. This was extended in 1859 (the legislation came into effect on 1 January 1860) to the military fortifications (see note to p. 65), and the number of *arrondissements* was increased from twelve to the present twenty.

7 *Eugène Sue*: (1804–57), popular serial-novelist, elected as an opposition deputy on 28 April 1850 (see note to p. 218).

Bonaparte: Charles-Louis-Napoleon-Bonaparte (1808–73), nephew of Napoleon I, president of the Republic between 1848 and 1851; after his *coup d'état* on 2 December 1851, he became Napoleon III (see note to p. 98).

7 *Faubourg-Poissonnière*: the Rue du Faubourg-Poissonnière (as it is more correctly referred to on p. 59) leads due south towards the centre of Paris, continuing the Boulevard Barbès across the line of the octroi wall (see note to p. 6).

9 *Provençal accent*: the most recognizable feature of this is the accentuation of terminal vowels and consonants which remain silent in standard French.

10 *La Glacière*: district on the southern outskirts of the city, in the 13th *arrondissement*, a distance of at least 6 kilometres. We are later told that Lantier goes to live there with Adèle after abandoning Gervaise (p. 165).

13 *sous*: the expression has outlived the actual coin, worth 5 centimes. Monetary denominations are notoriously difficult to translate into modern values. They make more sense in relative terms. In 1860, for example, the average male wage in Paris was about 5 francs per day, while female workers were paid less than half that amount, even when doing the same job. A laundress could expect to earn well under 2 francs at a time when a 2-kilo loaf of bread cost 50 centimes. All the figures in *L'Assommoir* are authentic, the result of Zola's careful documentation in this area.

14 *bluing ball*: cake of detergent for whitening laundry.

16 *Plassans*: Zola's fictionalized version of Aix-en-Provence is the setting for the provincial novels of the Rougon-Macquart series, most obviously in *La Conquête de Plassans* (*The Conquest of Plassans*, 1874).

17 *Rue Montmartre*: running through the 1st and 2nd *arrondissements*, distinctly more up-market than the area in which Gervaise now finds herself.

24 *Belhomme*: this plays with the meaning of the Rue Belhomme as Handsome Gent. It refers back to Lantier being described as 'a bit of a ladies' man'; but the notion of Gervaise doing her 'shift' on the Rue Belhomme has insulting connotations of streetwalking.

27 *Viorne*: Zola's invented name for the Arc, the river which flows to the south of Aix-en-Provence (see note to p. 16).

31 *the Assommoir*: see Introduction, p. xi.

34 *Bibi-la-Grillade*: nickname which defies translation; *griller* is slang for 'to down' (drink or food); *bibi* is a term of affection, but the dictionary used by Zola also refers us to *bibine* (a mediocre drink), *biberonner* (to tipple), *biberonneur* (a drunk), as well as *bibi* meaning the tool of a thief or a small hat.

35 *beating half to death*: refers to Gervaise's birth recounted in the opening novel of the Rougon-Macquart series, *La Fortune des Rougon* (*The Fortune of the Rougons*, 1871). We are told in its fourth chapter that she is conceived during one of the drunken nights when her parents hit each other, or as the French has it, *s'assommaient*, which is picked up in the title of *L'Assommoir* (see Introduction, p. xi). While reading a treatise on heredity in the

course of preliminary planning for his novel-cycle, Zola had noted a possible link between the violence endured by a woman impregnated during sexual intercourse and the physical consequences for her child. The principal function of this reference to 'old Macquart' is to reinforce the link between separate volumes of the family saga. It hardly seems by chance that Gervaise's 'poor mother', Fine Gavaudan, should be an intermittent alcoholic and ultimately die of pneumonia as a result of carrying wet *laundry* on her back outside and in winter (in January 1850, i.e. six months before the wedding described in Chapter III of *L'Assommoir*).

36 *charcutier*: this has a more general sense than a 'pork-butcher', given the variety of food being served at the counter.

Mes-Bottes: another nickname which Zola found in one of his principal sources about working-class idioms; it is probably derived from the Italian (*botte*) and Provençal (*bota*) for bottle or cask, and could be translated as 'in my cups'; but Delvau's *Dictionnaire de la langue verte* also notes that *botter* is slang for 'to please' and that *proposer la botte à quelqu'un* means to 'propose sexual intercourse'.

Cadet-Cassis: Coupeau's nickname is explained on p. 40: 'he was the youngest' (*cadet*) and drinks cassis, the blackcurrant liqueur.

37 *absinthe*: a green anise-flavoured spirit, popular in the nineteenth century, with such a high concentration of alcohol that conservative commentators blamed it for violent crimes and social disorder; it was banned in France in 1915, a prohibition only repealed in 2011.

Rue Coquenard: now the Rue Lamartine, in the 9th *arrondissement*.

39 *Petit Bonhomme qui Tousse*: the Little Coughing Fellow. This anticipates Coupeau's disintegrating medical condition, but also the coughing of other characters as a result of their insalubrious working conditions (see p. 161).

Barrière Saint-Denis: located in what is now the Place de la Chapelle.

Rue des Moines, in Batignolles: the latter was also an independent commune until 1859 (see note to p. 6), north-west of the Place de Clichy; the Rue des Moines runs from the Avenue de Clichy to the Rue de la Jonquière, in the present-day 17th *arrondissement*.

50 *water globe*: spherical glass intensifying light on object in focus.

52 *Paris to Versailles*: a distance of 23 kilometres.

58 *Moulin d'Argent*: the Money Mill, or the Silver Mill, equally ironic in view of the poverty of its clientele.

59 *bolivar hat*: *le bolivar* was a top hat with an extended brim, so called because Simon Bolivar (1783–1830), the Venezuelan military and political leader, had made it fashionable during his time in Paris at the beginning of the century.

60 *Saint-Denis*: the Saint-Denis plain now forms part of the industrial suburbs north of Paris.

61 *Code*: the relevant section of French law which was systematized into five 'codes' during the Napoleonic regime.

from the town hall to the church: French weddings have separate civil and religious components.

65 *fortifications*: built 1840–4, creating a new fortified boundary just outside the line of the present-day *boulevard périphérique*; beyond it was a (military) zone on which no building was officially allowed; but between the octroi wall (see note to p. 6) and the fortifications there also existed rural spaces which have long since disappeared.

66 *Père-Lachaise*: the main Parisian cemetery, named after, and built within the gardens of, the Jesuit confessor of Louis XIV; also known as the Cimetière de l'Est, which the characters could reach by going east along the Boulevard de la Chapelle. While this remains a tourist destination, more telling is that (for Zola's contemporary readers) the cemetery had entered left-wing mythology as the notorious site of the summary execution of hundreds of revolutionaries in May 1871 during the suppression of the Commune.

Héloïse and Abélard: legendary victims of the power of love; Héloïse's (1101–64) secret marriage to Abélard (1079–1142), her spiritual mentor, led to the latter being castrated as punishment for their transgression of monastic vows of chastity; the authenticity of their joint tomb in the Père-Lachaise cemetery is doubtful.

the familiar tu: as distinct from the more formal *vous*.

museum: the Louvre.

67 *Gimpy*: the original French 'Banban' was slang for someone with a limp.

boulevard: the present-day Boulevard Bonne-Nouvelle.

68 *Louis XIV*: king of France from 1643 to 1715. The statue (1822) has him on a rearing charger and dressed as a Roman emperor.

Assyrian Gallery: opened in 1847.

69 *Raft of the Medusa*: painted by Théodore Géricault (1791–1824) in 1819.

Apollo Gallery: only reopened in July 1851 (after substantial restoration); the wedding party's visit supposedly takes place a year earlier.

Salon Carré: it was in this room, otherwise known as the Grand Salon, that an annual art exhibition (thus called the Salon) was held between 1725 and 1848. Only in 1852 was the Salon Carré reorganized, on the model of the Tribune in the Uffizi, in order to accommodate the most prestigious works in the Louvre's collections. Here again, Zola's fictional chronology is not strictly accurate.

Charles IX: king of France between 1560 and 1574; the most notorious event of his reign was the St Bartholomew's Day Massacre (24 August 1572) of Huguenots (French Protestants). The balcony pointed out by Monsieur Madinier was in fact designed during the reign of Henri IV, from 1589 to 1610.

70 *Wedding at Cana*: painted in 1562–3 by Paolo Veronese (1528–88); this huge painting (660 × 990 centimetres) remained in the Salon Carré until 1951.

Antiope's thighs: more likely those of the *Pardo Venus* by Titian (1489–1576).

Murillo's Virgin: there are a number of such paintings in the Louvre by the Spanish artist Bartolé Esteban Murillo (1618–82); the one Zola had in mind is the *Immaculate Conception of the Virgin*, purchased from the Soult collection in 1852 for so scandalous a sum that, for a generation, guides to the Louvre named the price—right up to the last of the 615,300 francs it had cost the nation.

Titian's mistress: also known as *Young Woman at her Toilet*, with Venetian auburn rather than yellow hair.

La Belle Ferronnière: a painting in fact by Leonardo da Vinci (1452–1519); and the lady in question was reputed to be the mistress not of Henri IV but, at best, of François I (King of France, 1515–47) and, more probably, of Ludovico Sforza (1452–1508).

play at the Ambigu: Monsieur Madinier's general incompetence makes it unsurprising that no trace of any such play can be found. It was at the Théâtre de l'Ambigu, on the Boulevard Saint-Martin, that a very successful adaptation of *L'Assommoir* was staged in 1879

71 *Kermesse*: this scene of rural debauchery and ribaldry was composed in 1635 by the Flemish painter Peter-Paul Rubens (1577–1640).

72 *Pont-Royal*: bridge across the Seine, between the Rue du Bac and the western end of the Tuileries Palace.

73 *Marne*: major river, rising north of Dijon and flowing through the Champagne region before joining the Seine at Charenton-le-Pont in the south-eastern suburbs of Paris.

column: the Vendôme column is 44 metres high. It was made from 1,200 bronze cannon captured from the Austrians and Russians, erected in 1810, and dedicated to the veterans of the battle of Austerlitz (1805). As an emblem of Napoleonic glory (it originally had a statue of Napoleon on the top), it was a target for the revolution of the Commune; it was pulled down in May 1871 and rebuilt in 1874.

74 *Invalides . . . Tour Saint-Jacques*: moving anticlockwise, this sweeping panorama takes in the most visible markers of the Parisian skyline: the Hôtel des Invalides (see note to p. 196); the Panthéon, with its 80-metre-high cupola rising above the Latin Quarter, used once again as a church during the Second Empire but housing the remains of the great men of France after 1871; the cathedral of Notre-Dame; and the Tour Saint-Jacques on the Rue de Rivoli, all that now remains of the church of Saint-Jacques-la Boucherie.

77 *Bernard Palissy*: (1510–89), famous ceramist credited with the discovery of how to make enamel, and also well known because of having had to resort to burning the floor and contents of his house in order to keep his wood-stove burning to conduct his experiments.

79 *law of the thirty-first of May*: an attack on radicalism, the electoral law of 31 May 1850 required three years' residence (not two, as Madinier states) in one place in order to be eligible to vote, to be attested by a tax receipt or employer's affidavit. This effectively disenfranchised a very large number of workers regularly forced to move in order to find a job.

loves the people: Louis-Napoleon (see note to p. 7) had gained this reputation through his early writing: his *Rêveries politiques* (1832) and *Les Idées Napoléonniennes* (1839) both stressed the sovereignty of the people; his pamphlet *L'Extinction du paupérisme* (1844) was repeatedly cited in his campaign for the presidential elections of 10 December 1848. Together with his promise to restore France to her former (Napoleonic) glory, this assured him of massive popular support. He would again pose as the friend of the people—betrayed by the legislature—in staging his *coup d'état* of 1851 (see note to p. 98), immediately followed by the proclamation of universal suffrage.

Élysée: the Élysée Palace is the official residence of the French head of state, in the Rue du Faubourg-Saint-Honoré. Louis-Napoléon was the first president of the Republic to occupy it, the Tuileries Palace having been damaged in the 1848 Revolution (see note to p. 98).

Lyons: Louis-Napoleon made a highly publicized trip to eastern France in July 1850, including Lyons and Strasbourg, in an effort to persuade the provincial electorate of his republican credentials.

Comte de Chambord: (1820–83), grandson of Charles X, who had abdicated in 1830, and last surviving member of the senior branch of the Bourbons. The Legitimist party (supporters of the 'legitimate' Bourbon line and its pretender to the throne as Henri V) came closest to achieving the restoration of the monarchy in the period 1871–3.

83 *'Le Marchand de moutarde'*: Zola's work-notes make it clear that he was perfectly familiar with the obscene connotations of this title which translates as 'shit merchant'.

84 *The Pearl Fishers*: opera in three acts by Georges Bizet (1838–75), premiered at the Théâtre Lyrique on 30 September 1863; set on the island of Ceylon (now Sri Lanka), it is a tale of friendship tested by love. As the polka from it is mentioned in a chapter explicitly set in 1850 (see Introduction, p. xi), this is another example of Zola's anachronisms.

85 *Cow Brush*: the French here is 'Queue-de-Vache', meaning a cow's tail, an idiomatic expression used of unpleasantly brownish, or mousy, hair.

87 *Saint-Ouen*: small rural town on the Seine just north of Paris, long since swallowed up by the metropolis.

89 *Pascal*: Blaise Pascal (1623–62), celebrated philosopher and writer, best known as the author of *Les Pensées*—not a text which the Coupeau couple would have actually read!

Béranger: Pierre-Jean de Béranger (1780–1857), popular poet and writer of patriotic songs. As well as being the cultural counterpoint to Pascal, a further irony undermining the heroic status accorded to him by Gervaise and her husband lies in the fact that, having established a reputation as an anti-Establishment figure, he had resigned almost immediately after being elected to the Constituent Assembly in 1848, following the February revolution (see note to p. 98) which had succeeded in overthrowing the regime he had long opposed.

96 *the Nord*: the *département* of which Lille is the administrative centre.

Gueule-d'Or: in colloquial French, *gueule* means face, mouth, or gob.

97 *savings account*: the original French here is the *Caisse d'épargne*, a state-controlled and non-profit-making savings institution set up in 1835 with the deliberate aim of encouraging thrift in the less well-off.

Vincennes: area to the east of Paris, beyond the line of the fortifications (see note to p. 6).

98 *second of December*: on 2 December 1851, Louis-Napoleon—who was nearing the end of a four-year presidency under a constitution which did not permit two consecutive terms of office—staged a *coup d'état*. The date in question was no accident: it was the anniversary of Napoleon I's victory at Austerlitz. During the next few days, a group of Republican deputies tried to organize popular opposition, in the shape of barricades which went up in the Faubourg Saint-Antoine between the Bastille and the Place de la Nation. Such limited resistance was brutally suppressed. The *coup d'état* itself was massively endorsed by a plebiscite, thus confirming Louis-Napoleon's skilful manipulation of the electorate (see note to p. 79).

February and June: the two revolutions of 1848. Rioting in Paris between 22 and 24 February led to the abdication of Louis Philippe, king of France since 1830, and the proclamation of the Second Republic. In the following months, newly won liberalization was checked by conservative forces. A further insurrection between 23 and 26 June witnessed the bloodiest street-fighting Europe had seen and the definitive triumph of the so-called moderate Republicans. Historians are agreed that both revolutions increased the power of the bourgeoisie at the expense of the workers who had manned the barricades.

twenty-five francs: reworking of the famous response made by Alphonse Baudin (1811–51) to criticism of parliamentary allowances. Baudin, who had been elected as a left-wing deputy in 1849, was killed on the barricades in the Faubourg Saint-Antoine on the morning of 3 December 1851, after an abortive attempt to organize resistance to the *coup d'état*. His 'You'll see, citizens, how one dies for 25 francs' became a rallying cry for the Republic.

102 *Grenelle*: to the south-west, in the 15th *arrondissement*, where the Avenue Émile-Zola is to be found today.

Moulin Rouge: *not* the one notoriously associated with 'gay Paree' which only opened in 1889. There existed a dance hall, the Bal du Petit-Moulin-Rouge, in the Place Constantin-Pecqueur, also in the 18th *arrondissement*.

103 '*Oh, I do love pickin' strawberries!*': while it may seem to be about the joys of picking strawberries, this song, 'Ah! qu'il fait bon cueillir la fraise!', is cited in Alfred Delvau's *Dictionnaire érotique moderne* (1864) in the context of the phrase *cueillir la fraise* which refers to the act of sexual intercourse (as does the equally vulgar English expression involving cherries; cf. the translation of 'elle n'en verra pas moins la lune par le même trou que les autres': 'she'll still lose 'er cherry the same way they all do', p. 237). This erotic dimension is later underlined by the mention that 'Clémence couldn't swallow a spoonful of strawberries without saying she was touching them up' (p. 198).

114 *Rue de la Paix*: one of the roads which leads to the Place de l'Opéra, in the wealthy 2nd *arrondissement*.

118 *Pompadour*: furnishing and decor from the reign of Louis XV associated with his influential favourite at court, Madame de Pompadour (1721–64).

120 *Zouave*: Berber name for the indigenous troops of the French army of North Africa. By 1852 there were three regiments of these native recruits who were to gain a reputation for their fierceness and bravery during the military campaigns of the Second Empire.

123 *Capucin*: the Restaurant des Capucins, named after the monastic order and the cowl worn by its members, was located on the right-hand side of the Rue de la Chapelle.

127 *Pied-de-Céleri*: Celery-Stalk.

136 *Petite-Civette*: famous tobacconist's, deriving its name from the even more famous La Civette, in the Rue Saint-Honoré. The latter sold tobacco perfumed *à la civette*, i.e. like the scent of a civet.

145 *Rue des Portes-Blanches*: that Zola should have Gervaise walk along this little street, at the time located between the Rue des Poissonniers and the Rue du Ruisseau (and apparently so named because of its dust-encrusted doors), is thematically consistent with the juxtaposition of filth and cleanliness throughout her fictional life (see Introduction, p. xxvi).

149 *Bec-Salé*: meaning literally 'salty mouth', i.e. (and as his alias suggests) someone who drinks without ever slaking his thirst.

Fifine and Dédèle: affectionate versions of Joséphine and Adèle.

151 *Élysée-Montmartre*: popular dance hall located, since 1807, on the corner of the Boulevard de Rochechouart and the Rue des Martyrs.

153 *Bois de Vincennes*: a park was developed there after 1857, consciously designed to complement the Bois de Boulogne in the west and to ensure that the working-class inhabitants of the east end of Paris would therefore not need to 'trespass' on the playground of the rich.

158 *Gros-Caillou*: area on the Left Bank, in the 7th *arrondissement*.

168 *Crimea*: reference to the Crimean War, with its high number of French and British casualties in the winter of 1854–5, ended by the Treaty of Paris in

1856 which thereby confirmed what Napoleon III presented as a major foreign-policy success.

175 *blanquette de veau*: veal stew with a white sauce.

épinée de cochon: pork stew with potatoes.

176 *petits pois au lard*: peas with bacon.

185 *Papillon*: Au Papillon was a wine merchant on the corner of the Rue Doudeauville and the Rue des Poissonniers; as well as referring to a butter-fly, *papillon* was slang for a laundry, and for 'laundering' (in the criminal sense).

186 *veau à l'oseille*: pieces of veal fried in butter, sorrel (*oseille*), garlic, cream, and white wine.

191 *Cossack*: famed for their military prowess and therefore recruited as mer-cenaries in northern Europe, the Cossacks were an autonomous people of the south Russian steppes before being finally incorporated into the Tsar's army in 1764.

Bedouins: nomadic tribe of North Africa and the Arabian peninsula.

196 *Henri IV's boots*: i.e. at least 250 years ago (see note to p. 69).

the Invalides: the Hôtel des Invalides, in the 7th *arrondissement*, was built by Louis XIV in 1670 to house wounded soldiers. It subsequently became a museum celebrating French military exploits. Napoleon I's remains were transferred there in 1840.

198 *'The Baroness of Follebiche'*: this song had met with official disapproval on a number of counts: its allusion to a notorious term (*biche* meaning high-class prostitute) invented in 1857 by Nestor Roqueplan (1804–70), a jour-nalist, theatre administrator, and editor of *Le Figaro*; its reference to an army (*patrouille* at the end of the refrain in the original French) of lovers; and its Germanic echoes and accents made it one of those songs, pro-scribed as late as the 1880s, deemed to offend the susceptibilities of the Prussians. The sexual innuendoes are reinforced in the chorus: *goutte* (translated here as 'grog') also means sperm in slang; and given the context, it is worth noting that *la goutte militaire* also meant the secretion associated with gonorrhoea.

200 *Riquiqui*: with its sexual connotations, this translates as someone 'poorly endowed'.

vivandière: woman authorized to supply provisions to troops engaged in warfare.

'The Mouse': this is explained immediately below and later in the novel when Zola uses the term *souris*: 'a little kiss—one of those quick silent ones on the eye, so easy to plant' (p. 326).

'Abd-el-Kader's Farewell': the Emir of Mascara (1807–83) finally surrendered to the French on 23 December 1847, having been the main obstacle to their conquest of Algeria. Contrary to promises made to him, Abd-el-Kader was sent to prison in France but later released by Napoleon III.

The grandiose spectacle of his formal surrender inspired a number of paintings too.

205 *"Disgusting Little Beast!"*: the French title is 'Qué cochon d'enfant!' while *être cochon*, in contemporary slang, meant to be sexually unrestrained or 'to make copious use of the virile member' (see Delvau, *Dictionnaire érotique moderne*). Such obscene connotations are reinforced by the wordplay in the song itself (see notes to the song-text below). A more literal, albeit clumsier, translation of the title (e.g. 'What a Pig of a Boy!') echoes Gervaise's disgust when she finds Coupeau sprawled across her bed, lying in his own vomit: 'Oh! Le cochon! Le cochon!' ('The dirty pig! The dirty pig!' (p. 241)).

206 *Grève*: the water's edge, but also the Place de la Grève—the site of the guillotine and the place where workers congregated in the hope of getting a job for the day.

Four sous' worth of beer: the original French here is *poisson*, meaning both a drink and a pimp.

not to take all day | 'E's an hour at the very least: the French is 'en r'montant', playing with the erotic sense of 'mounting' or 'getting back up', following on from 'I stagger up' in the opening line of the song.

half of me booze: the original French is 'la moitié d' ma goutte' (see note to p. 198).

Tinette: slang for a lavatory or a foul-smelling orifice (not always a mouth).

207 *cherries, fresh*: in the coprophagous sense.

209 *Boule-Noire*: well-known dance hall at No. 120 Boulevard de Rochechouart, founded in 1822 by a legendary courtesan who gave it her own nickname of 'Belle-en-Cuisses' (beautiful thighs). The sign outside this establishment figured a large ball, originally white but gradually blackened by dirt. This too is consistent with one of the novel's major themes (see Introduction, p. xxvi, and note to p. 145).

212 *Montrouge*: a district outside the city limits, south-west of Paris.

213 *Rue Notre-Dame-de-Lorette*: leads from the Rue du Faubourg-Montmartre, through the 9th *arrondissement*, up towards the Boulevard de Clichy.

Rue de la Rochefoucauld: cuts into the Rue Notre-Dame-de-Lorette at the intersection with the Rue Pigalle.

217 *Badingue*: abbreviated version of Badinguet, the nickname given to Napoleon III by his political opponents as a result of his having disguised himself in the clothes of a workman of that name when he escaped from the fortress of Ham (50 kilometres south-east of Amiens) on 26 May 1846, where he had been imprisoned since 1840 after an abortive attempt to seize power.

London: although the anecdote is apocryphal, it is true that Napoleon III had spent many of his years of exile in London, both before (May–August 1831, November 1832–May 1833, 25 October 1838–4 August 1840,

27 May 1846–23 September 1848) and after (1870–3) being in power; he died in England on 9 January 1873.

Ledru-Rollin: Alexandre Ledru-Rollin (1807–74) was elected to the Assembly in May 1849 as a Reformist Radical, having been minister of the interior immediately after February 1848 (see note to p. 98). On 13 June 1849 he tried in vain to organize a left-wing revolution and fled to England. As he had also previously been a failed candidate for the presidency in 1848, the fact that the bust has its 'nose broken' seems appropriate.

218 *Brussels*: there was a long nineteenth-century tradition of having published in Belgium books and articles that the French authorities would have censored.

Les Amours de Napoléon III: though the particular book is not identifiable, the subject of the loves of Napoleon III would fill many volumes.

Histoire de dix ans: violent attack on the first ten years of the July Monarchy (1830–48) published in 1841 by the journalist and radical politician Louis Blanc (1811–82), a member of the provisional government of February 1848 who went into exile during the Second Empire, returning to serve as a left-wing deputy between 1871 and 1876.

Girondins: the *Histoire des Girondins* (1847) exalts the ideals of the First Republic while reconstructing the struggle between the Montagnards and the Girondins (the right-wing party briefly in power in 1792–3) at the time of the crisis of Thermidor (27 July 1794). As well as being a famous poet, Alphonse de Lamartine (1790–1869) was a deputy after 1834 and foreign minister in the provisional government of February 1848, but after June 1848 as marginalized a figure as Lantier's other liberal heroes.

Les Mystères de Paris and Le Juif errant: *The Mysteries of Paris* and *The Wandering Jew*, published in 1843 and 1844 5 respectively. Partly because these novels evoked a world far from middle-class respectability, but mainly as a result of his *Le Berger de Kravan ou Entretiens socialistes et démocratiques* (1848–9), Eugène Sue (see note to p. 7) had a reputation as a socialist. His election in 1850 terrified conservative politicians. After the *coup d'état* of 1851, he went into exile.

219 *divorce*: although allowed by the Revolution, renewed Catholic influence under the Restoration meant that divorce remained illegal during the whole of the period between 1816 and 1884.

Cayenne: notorious penal colony on the coast of French Guyana.

221 *galettes*: type of flat crusty cake.

229 *La Chapelle*: see note to p. 6.

230 *Belleville*: working-class district in the eastern outskirts of Paris, now in the 20th *arrondissement*.

tripe à la mode de Caen: still available in French restaurants; to be prepared at home: simply add ox feet, cider, Calvados, carrots, onions, and herbs; and cook in the oven for at least twelve hours!

230 *Ville de Bar-le-Duc*: less a restaurant in the modern sense than a cheap eating-house, the A la Ville de Bar-le-Duc (named after the city 230 kilometres to the east of Paris) was located in the Rue de l'Empereur, subsequently renamed the Rue Lepic.

Moulin de la Galette: in the Rue des Abbesses, at the corner of the Rue Lepic and the Rue Tholozé, and captured for posterity in Renoir's *Le Moulin de la Galette* (1876).

Lilas: La Maison des Lilas was virtually opposite the Boule-Noire (see note to p. 209).

tête de veau: calf's head (see note to p. 5).

Lion d'Or: the Golden Lion.

Deux Marronniers: the Two Chestnuts.

Vendanges de Bourgogne: the Burgundy Wine-Harvest; in 1880 a big restaurant called Aux Nouvelles Vendanges de Bourgogne opened at the same address in the Rue Jessaint.

Cadran Bleu: the Blue Dial (as in sundial, or the face of a clock); located on the corner of the Rue Charlot, at No. 27 Boulevard du Temple.

232 *Bourguignon*: native of Burgundy.

233 *Borgia*: sixteenth-century Italian family notorious for their criminal violence for political ends.

Malle des Indes: an expression first recorded in France only in 1867, referring to the English mail-steamer to and from India; but there is also a pun here on *mâle* (male) and *mal* (disease).

Chaillot: formerly a village north-west of Paris, now part of the 16th *arrondissement* (see note to p. 385).

235 *La Puce qui Renifle*: the Sniffing Flea.

Auvergne: region in the middle of the Massif Central.

236 *piquet*: game of cards in which the aim is to collect the most of the same colour as well as certain face-cards or sequences.

237 *Gaillon*: small town in the Seine valley west of Paris and 24 kilometres south-east of Rouen, in fact in the *département* of the Eure.

Boulevard des Invalides: in the 7th *arrondissement*, running up past the Hôtel des Invalides (see note to p. 196).

Comtesse de Brétigny . . . Baron de Valençay: names invented by Zola.

238 *Year One of the Republic, ninety-three*: at the end of the phase known as the Terror, the surviving leaders of the French Revolution had recast the calendar, starting with 1793 as Year One. These are all slang expressions for the game of piquet.

Montpernasse . . . Bagnolet: more or less garbled allusions to Montparnasse, in the 14th *arrondissement*; Menilmontant, on the eastern edge of Paris; La Courtille, part of Belleville (see notes to pp. 230 and 382); and the eastern suburb of Bagnolet, lying beyond the fortifications.

239 *café-concert*: place of entertainment where spectators could drink, smoke, and walk around during the performance of singers, acrobats, and other kinds of popular artists. The one mentioned here may well have been the Théâtre de la Gaîté-Rochechouart, at No. 15 Boulevard de Rochechouart.

240 *Madame Amanda, popular singer*: invented pseudonym, on the model of the stage name 'Thérésa' adopted by Emma Valladon, one of the most famous café-concert singers of the period (represented in Degas's *La Chanson du chien*, a painting exactly contemporary to *L'Assommoir*); but the name Amanda has connotations of the love which Gervaise so desperately seeks.

'My nose is where it tickles me': this song ('C'est dans l'nez qu'ça me cha-touille') was banned in 1874, a decision on the part of the Censor astonish-ing only to those naïve enough not to confuse one orifice with another in a manner popularized by Charles Colmance's *Le Nez CULotté*.

244 *Saint Anthony's Day*: 17 January.

247 *two children by him*: see note to p. 5. Gervaise being seduced by Lantier at the age of 14 is a cross-reference to this part of her early life described in *The Fortune of the Rougons*.

258 *Gaîté*: the Théâtre de la Gaîté, on the Boulevard du Temple, was famous in the nineteenth century for its staging of popular melodramas. In 1862, the original building was destroyed to allow the creation of the Place du Château d'Eau and replaced by the Théâtre de la Gaîté-Lyrique on the Rue Réaumur.

275 *cemetery*: the Marcadet Cemetery, behind the church of Saint-Denis de la Chapelle.

276 *À la Descente du Cimetière*: On the Way Down from the Cemetery.

281 *Étampes*: town 49 kilometres south of Paris.

289 *Rue du Caire*: just off the Boulevard de Sébastopol in what is known as the *quartier des fringues*, traditionally an area with a large concentration of workshops devoted to clothes.

298 *Hardi*: daring or audacious.

302 *Sainte-Anne asylum*: this was, and remains, a psychiatric hospital set in huge grounds in the 14th *arrondissement*. The distance to La Glacière (see note to p. 10) explains why, for Gervaise, 'it was quite a long way', or, as the French has it, 'c'était un vrai voyage' (a real expedition).

303 *Rue de la Santé*: this divides the 13th and 14th *arrondissements* and borders one side of the Sainte-Anne asylum; the name of this road suggests, with tragic irony, the notion of health.

305 *Bicêtre*: vast hospice in Sceaux, south of Paris, for the old and the mentally ill. The French expression *un echappé de Bicêtre* means a lunatic, and Zola's 'finir à Bicêtre' here ('ending up in Bicêtre') retains that added figurative dimension.

316 *virgins*: a comparison which only makes sense in the context of the pictor-ial tradition alluded to here, namely the depiction of nymphs bathing in bucolic surroundings.

319 *Rue du Petit-Carreau*: now the Rue des Petits-Carreaux (in the plural), near the Rue du Caire (see note to p. 289).

328 *from the Barrière Poissonnière to the door of the workshop*: a good 2 kilometres.

329 *Boulevard de la Villette*: this divides the 10th and 19th *arrondissements*.

337 *Rue de Rivoli*: adjacent to the Tuileries Palace.

six months: Napoleon III's health deteriorated throughout the 1860s. He was often in visible pain caused by bladder problems. By 1868, medical writers were called in by opposition papers to regale their readers with intimate details of how he would die.

First of all . . . giants of the North: this paragraph reads as a not altogether parodic version of Napoleon III's *politique des nationalités*, a foreign policy consisting of the reorganization of Europe roughly in accord with the principle of nationalities. This did indeed include a union of the Scandinavian countries (Sweden was 'the giant of the North'), and in both 1856 and 1863 France was actively involved in the internal affairs of Poland. There is the added irony, in retrospect, that the Second Empire would be a victim of moves towards German unification, with Napoleon III himself having to abdicate in 1870 after defeat in the Franco-Prussian War. Turkey had no place in his design for a Christian Europe, and in this respect he was at odds with the British who wanted to preserve the integrity of the Ottoman Empire.

339 *Boulevard Magenta and the Boulevard Ornano*: see note to *Barrière Poissonnière* on p. 6; the Boulevard Ornano was opened in 1863 though only named as such in 1867. The section of it in question here, between the Rue Marcadet and the Boulevard Rochechouart, was renamed the Boulevard Barbès in 1882; it continues south-east across the line of the octroi wall as the Boulevard de Magenta, commemorating the French victory over the Austrians in the battle of that name on 4 June 1859.

340 *chahut*: rumbustious dance fashionable in music-hall performances at the time.

Grand Salon de la Folie: many music halls and the like included the term *folie* in their names, as is testified by the Folies-Bergère. It derives from the seventeenth-century folly, with its connotations of extravagance and a house built solely for pleasure. But a *folie* is also a sort of comic vaudeville, which explains why so many theatres catering for light entertainment were given such a title. *Faire une folie* and related expressions catch these multiple associations of behaviour freed from the constraints of judgement and common sense.

344 *Saint-Lazare*: originally for lepers in medieval times, this remained a women's prison from the Revolution until 1935, a large section of which was reserved for prostitutes and with a hospital annex for the treatment of venereal diseases. Located in the Faubourg Saint-Denis, it was destroyed in 1942.

Reine-Blanche: the Bal de la Reine-Blanche, famous since the Romantic period, was situated at No. 82 Boulevard de Clichy.

Château-Rouge: otherwise known as the Bal du Nouveau-Tivoli because of its gardens, the Bal du Château-Rouge was extremely fashionable between 1848 and 1864; it was located on the Chaussée de Clignancourt.

Bal de l'Ermitage: at No. 6 Boulevard de Clichy.

Bal Robert: otherwise known as the Folies-Robert; the Impasse du Cadran was just off the Boulevard de Rochechouart. Zola visited it during the preparation of *L'Assommoir* and noted that it was 'very disgusting'.

366 *'Good King Dagobert'*: last Frankish king of the Merovingian dynasty, king of all France, 628–38. The burlesque song about him, which probably dates from before the Revolution, came into vogue in 1814 and was given new impetus by the return of the Bourbons. The habit of inserting satirical couplets into the original song led to it being banned by the police.

368 *station's huge roof*: formerly the *embarcadère du Nord*, built in 1845, the Gare du Nord acquired its present monumental dimensions in 1863.

382 *Pont-Neuf*: built between 1578 and 1606 at the western end of the Île de la Cité. It was lined with buildings, the last of which disappeared in 1854, which made it the very heart of the capital. Its appearance at the time of Zola's novel is celebrated in Renoir's painting (1872) of the same name.

La Courtille: see note to p. 238. What was known as *la descente de la Courtille* was the most celebrated and picturesque Mardi Gras procession at the end of Carnival, so called because of the vast crowds wending their way down from the heights of Belleville wearing masks, etc. Although it never regained the status it enjoyed between 1830 and 1838, the event remained in the collective memory throughout the nineteenth century.

384 *Rue Saint-Martin*: this now runs from the Pompidou Centre to the Boulevard Saint-Denis.

385 *Chaillot*: for reasons which remain unclear, this was so generally considered to be a place populated by fools that the common expressions *un ahuri de Chaillot* (a madman from Chaillot) and *envoyer à Chaillot* (to send to Chaillot) are used by Zola himself in their figurative sense elsewhere in the novel (see note to p. 233).

Mardi Gras: literally Fat Tuesday (more suggestive than Shrove Tuesday), this is the last day of Carnival and the occasion for a final outburst of festivities prior to Lent.

390 *Charenton*: major psychiatric hospital near the Bois de Vincennes (see note to p. 153).

send him to Mazas: this has the colloquial sense of 'send him to jug'. Located on the Boulevard Mazas (now the Boulevard Diderot), the Mazas was the first French prison with a cellular system. Not a single prisoner escaped from it during its existence (1850–98).

*The
Oxford
World's
Classics
Website*

www.worldsclassics.co.uk

- Browse the full range of Oxford World's Classics online

- Sign up for our monthly e-alert to receive information on new titles

- Read extracts from the Introductions

- Listen to our editors and translators talk about the world's greatest literature with our Oxford World's Classics audio guides

- Join the conversation, follow us on Twitter at OWC_Oxford

- Teachers and lecturers can order inspection copies quickly and simply via our website

www.worldsclassics.co.uk

American Literature

British and Irish Literature

Children's Literature

Classics and Ancient Literature

Colonial Literature

Eastern Literature

European Literature

Gothic Literature

History

Medieval Literature

Oxford English Drama

Philosophy

Poetry

Politics

Religion

The Oxford Shakespeare

A complete list of Oxford World's Classics, including Authors in Context, Oxford English Drama, and the Oxford Shakespeare, is available in the UK from the Marketing Services Department, Oxford University Press, Great Clarendon Street, Oxford OX2 6DP, or visit the website at www.oup.com/uk/worldsclassics.

In the USA, visit www.oup.com/us/owc for a complete title list.

Oxford World's Classics are available from all good bookshops. In case of difficulty, customers in the UK should contact Oxford University Press Bookshop, 116 High Street, Oxford OX1 4BR.

CHARLES DICKENS	The Old Curiosity Shop
	Our Mutual Friend
	The Pickwick Papers
GEORGE DU MAURIER	Trilby
MARIA EDGEWORTH	Castle Rackrent
GEORGE ELIOT	Daniel Deronda
	The Lifted Veil and Brother Jacob
	Middlemarch
	The Mill on the Floss
	Silas Marner
EDWARD FITZGERALD	The Rubáiyát of Omar Khayyám
ELIZABETH GASKELL	Cranford
	The Life of Charlotte Brontë
	Mary Barton
	North and South
	Wives and Daughters
GEORGE GISSING	New Grub Street
	The Nether World
	The Odd Women
EDMUND GOSSE	Father and Son
THOMAS HARDY	Far from the Madding Crowd
	Jude the Obscure
	The Mayor of Casterbridge
	The Return of the Native
	Tess of the d'Urbervilles
	The Woodlanders
JAMES HOGG	The Private Memoirs and Confessions of a Justified Sinner
JOHN KEATS	The Major Works
	Selected Letters
CHARLES MATURIN	Melmoth the Wanderer
HENRY MAYHEW	London Labour and the London Poor

ANTHONY TROLLOPE   **The American Senator**
An Autobiography
Barchester Towers
Can You Forgive Her?
Cousin Henry
Doctor Thorne
The Duke's Children
The Eustace Diamonds
Framley Parsonage
He Knew He Was Right
Lady Anna
The Last Chronicle of Barset
Orley Farm
Phineas Finn
Phineas Redux
The Prime Minister
Rachel Ray
The Small House at Allington
The Warden
The Way We Live Now